OF LOVE AND LUST

FROM THE WORKS OF THEODOR REIK

Of Love and Lust

On the Psychoanalysis of Romantic

and Sexual Emotions

by THEODOR REIK

GROVE PRESS, INC.   NEW YORK

Grove Press Books and Evergreen Books
are published by Barney Rosset at Grove Press, Inc.
795 Broadway   New York 3, N. Y.

MANUFACTURED IN THE UNITED STATES OF AMERICA

Contents

	Publisher's Preface	ix
	Author's Note: Theme and Variations	xi
Part One	A Psychologist Looks at Love	1
Part Two	Masochism in Modern Man	195
Part Three	The Unmarried	367
Part Four	The Emotional Differences of the Sexes	405

Publisher's Preface

Of Love and Lust is the second of a series of volumes of selections from Theodor Reik's works, of which *The Search Within; The Inner Experiences of a Psychoanalyst,* was the first. *The Search Within* was a synthesis of his personal life, his training, practice and the development of his philosophy. In this new volume he is concerned with the love life and the sexual life of men and women. It is not only a discussion of the differences in attitude toward love and sex but toward many aspects of the cultural pattern of today. "Only the brave can struggle to love," he writes. This particular volume contains only material written since 1943; not more than a third of it has ever been published in book form; much of it was written within the last year and is appearing here for the first time.

Our publishing relation has been close since Dr. Reik arrived in the United States as a refugee in 1938. He did not wish to edit these books himself and has asked me to do so and to explain them briefly.

Part One of this volume is taken from one of his most successful books, *A Psychologist Looks at Love,* out of print now for some years. It shows his departure from his master, Freud's, theories and from those of most of his contemporaries in psychology and psychoanalysis. "The sex urge," he maintains, "hunts for lustful pleasure; love is in search of joy and happiness."

Part Two is from Reik's great contribution to psychological literature, *Masochism in Modern Man.* In using less than half the book, I have attempted to keep those parts which have a direct bearing on the subject of this particular book and also the core of Reik's new contributions to his subject. Much of his comparison with Freud's theories has been eliminated as have his chapters on social, religious and cultural aspects of masochism. However, the phenomena and dynamics of masochism are here as well as their relation to femininity. The summing up of Reik's theory is contained in the chapter Victory Through Defeat.

Part Three, "The Unmarried," consists of two essays, written for the symposium *Why Are You Single,* edited by Hilda Holland. Reik speaks plainly, as always, of the marriage shyness of the male and the psychological fears and resistances of both men and women to an acceptance of the marriage bond.

Part Four, "The Emotional Differences of the Sexes," is the new and unpublished material. There are some forty-nine sections, some of them are long essays, some trenchant, short, almost anecdotal ones. He asks, "Why shouldn't we know how the other half of the world feels?" and he adds, "In our civilization, men are afraid that they will not be men enough and women are afraid that they might be considered only women." He tries to probe into the secret ways in which men and women search for happiness. The material is clear, brisk, often startling. It is filled with examples from shrewdly observed case histories. His material varies from frank comments on the emotional mechanisms of the sexual act to studies of the differences between men and women in manifold situations and in their fancied and real characteristics. He is often profound, but often satirical and witty as well. There are essays on Guilt Feelings, on Impotence, Jealousy, The Sexualization of Clothes, Homosexuality, Man and Money, Wit, Children. He writes of all this with sympathy and understanding, not hesitating to agree or disagree with other authorities. It is Reik in his mellowest mood, but uncompromising as always.

JOHN FARRAR

Author's Note: Theme and Variations

MEPHISTO, IN Faust's scholar's costume, tells the student that all theory is gray while life's golden tree is green. There is satanic truth in that color-contrast between theory and experience—a seductive half-truth. Only theory that does not grow from the soil of living experience is gray; only theory that originates in speculation is a hot-house plant. Wherever theory does not grow from this soil, it is not able to survive; it shrinks up and withers. Psychoanalytic theory has its deep roots in the mould of clinical practice and retains its earthy color. Freud's psychoanalytic theories are the result of a supreme achievement of synthetic intelligence combining the insights obtained through many years of analytic practice. They are, furthermore, in their best parts works of art. Yet there is nothing artificial in them. On the few occasions when he left the firm ground of the empirical, he soon became aware of his mistake and corrected it. He had learned to control an initial inclination to speculate and theorize. He tested again and again budding theories in his experience in daily analytic practice.

It is unforgettable that he admonished us, who were his students in Vienna, not to trust our theoretical knowledge, not to follow preconceived ideas, but always to approach the material of our practice with a mind open to new impressions and insights. He repeated: "You have to look again and again at things until they themselves begin to speak." Observation, tested over a long period of time self-critically, was for him—and became for us who are his followers—the most important premise of research. He could then dismiss arguments against the validity of analytic theories because he knew how they were built on the firm ground of thousands of individual experiences. I still remember a meeting of the Viennese Psychoanalytic Society during which he made some remarks about a paper which doubted the scientific character of psychoanalysis because it cannot be verified by experiment as can other parts of psychology: "If the nature of a science were dependent on such proof through experiments, astronomy would not deserve the name of science. We are told that it is rather difficult to make experiments with the planets."

The following contributions present continuations of Freud's research and they follow the methods of his investigation which I learned from him, from his example and his words. The model of his way of working was especially important to me in building the theories on masochism to be found in this book. Material observed in many years of analytic practice, patiently passed through the sieve of new experiences, was the foundation on which that theory was built.

The three parts in which the following selections appear are independent of each other and were conceived and written at different times. Yet they are connected by an invisible thread. They try to probe into secret ways in which men and women search for happiness.

American colloquialism has the expression "Number One" for "I." Superficially seen, the pursuit of happiness is contained in reaching the goals of "Number One"—the satisfaction of our instinctual drives, the obtaining of power, sexual gratification, riches and so forth. Yet we all know that happiness is not to be found on this road. We all know that what we call happiness is nothing permanent and is restricted to hours or even minutes. The best that can be reached of that evanescent state is tied to one condition: the forgetting of oneself, the necessity for a transformation by which "Number One" not only loses this numerical value, but does not count any longer. The small share of happiness attainable by man exists only insofar as he is able to cease to think of himself. This happens in love, in enthusiasm, in states of drunkenness, in deep sleep. The self in those states is psychologically almost nonexistent, has vanished or has been absorbed into something else.

The way most passionately sought in reaching for happiness is love—or, more accurately expressed, romantic love. (I regret that I did not add this important adjective frequently enough in the discussion of the psychology of love in this book.) In romantic love, the subject is certainly lost. The self scarcely exists. It is absorbed in the loved object. Yet that feeling of utter emotional surrender has its roots in the dark subsoil of unconscious tendencies which we shy away from. The psychological analysis of romantic love confirms Freud's sentence that what we idealize is intimately connected with trends we abhor. I did not probe here into the emotional secrecy of another feeling that, akin to love, makes the individual forget himself: enthusiasm, giving oneself to an idea, giving oneself—or the self—up.

The self disappears, or at least seems to disappear, in moments of extreme satisfaction of the senses, for instance at the climax of sexual gratification. The mountain cock during the mating season does not see the hunter. Not love but the sexual urge proves to be stronger than the fear of death. The strangest and most significant sexual perversion in which the deepest pleasure is derived from disgrace and pain is certainly an object of research that, by its paradoxical character alone, deserves the interest of the psychologist. It aroused my scientific interest at the very start of my analytic practice, and many cases of sexual and social masochism were carefully observed and studied before I dared to publish a new theory of this deviation. Since *Masochism in Modern Man* was published in 1941 many psychiatrists and psychologists have referred to the book, added to and modified its essential results that had been founded on many years of analytic experience. It gives me satisfaction that the core of my own theory has been recognized as valid by sharp criticism.

A suggestion from outside is responsible for the fact that I followed a side track, branching off from the theme of romantic love and masochism. Hilda Holland invited me to contribute two articles to a symposium, *"Why Are You Single?"** which she com-

* Farrar, Straus & Co., 1949.

piled. In studying that vital problem, I tried to determine why men and women do not marry and dealt with the various factors which make women and men bypass marriage and family life.

This special subject heralded a more general theme of research that had preoccupied my thoughts for many years: the emotional diversity of men and women. While all the world knows and acknowledges basic differences in the emotional attitudes of the sexes, few observers have concentrated their interest on the less visible and inconspicuous causes responsible for these different attitudes. Avoiding beaten paths, I tried to find little-known spots commanding a wide view. The observations and experiences presented here will, I hope, contribute to the recognition of the great divergence between men and women and lead us a little farther in its understanding.

It is a small world, they say. We ought to have at least a notion of how the other half of it lives.

New York, April 1957

THEODOR REIK

PART ONE

A Psychologist Looks at Love

I

Love or Whatever It Is

IN 1927 a new and surprising insight into the origin and nature of love occurred to me—an insight at once adventurous and daring. Some of its implications, in their character and consequences, were even breath-taking. I myself am a cautious and anxious person, and these implications, of the very opposite nature to my own, alarmed me by their boldness. I foresaw the difficulties I would encounter in following them and I had a premonition that I would be incapable of overcoming them. After having made some notes on the subject I felt discouraged and slipped them into one of the folders where I hide my frustrated intellectual attempts. (I have many such folders, handsome covers to my imperfections.)

There are odd coincidences which are not accidental. I was twice admonished to continue and finish the paper. One summer afternoon in 1933, six years later, I visited the Augarten in Vienna. I like this quiet park, perhaps because I played there as a child. I sat down on a shady bank under the chestnut trees and tried to read. (Had I already a presentiment that I would not see the park again? The Nazis were threatening to enter Austria and I was already planning to go to Holland.) But I was absent-minded and could not concentrate on what the philosophical author said.

It was then that two old gentlemen approached my bench. One of them had the white side-whiskers of the old Austrian emperor Franz Joseph and reminded me a little of my father who had died when I was in my teens. The other was clean-shaven and seemed to be the younger, though he too was obviously over seventy years old. Both had fine foreheads marked by intellectual work and grief. Their way of expressing themselves showed that they were cultured persons of the upper middle class. The gentleman with the emperor whiskers was talking about the difficulties his grandson was having in his relationship with a girl. It seemed that the boy was in serious conflict with his own and the girl's parents. The clean-shaven one did not seem to be impressed. He said, "Well, it's the usual frenzy of spermatozoa." His friend with the whiskers did not reply immediately, as if weighing this explanation. Then he said in a somewhat resigned voice, "No, it's not that. Or rather, it's not only that. . . . It's love or whatever it is."

A few minutes later I left the bench and walked through the alleys to the exit of the park. The words "love or whatever it is" echoed in my mind. I wondered about the phrase. Suddenly I remembered the paper I had started six years before. As soon as I got home I searched for the draft but could not find it. So I decided to start again, and I wrote some pages trying to shape the thoughts that had occurred to me in the long interim. But I was not yet ready to overcome the obstacles I had originally foreseen and, disgusted with myself, I thrust this new draft too into a folder. And in the confusion and distress of the next few years the voice that demanded the continuation of that paper became mute.

It was after I had been in New York for some time that I went one evening to hear Mozart's *Marriage of Figaro* at the Metropolitan Opera House. As I surrendered myself to the magic of those melodies, all the problems of my life and of the terrible war in Europe disappeared. The words of the opera scarcely penetrated the conscious mind. All those improbable actions and playful intrigues, those light-hearted mistakes, confusions, and griefs portrayed on the stage—they are merely the exterior of what this music sings and sobs. Now Cherubino was singing his great aria:

> You who do know
> All the heart's turns,
> Say, is it love now
> That in me burns?

On my way home I found myself singing the aria under my breath in the winter night, and suddenly the words seemed to have a significance they did not have before. Cherubino's question no longer seemed merely a rhetorical one but a real one. "You who do know all the heart's turns . . ." The words and the tune sounded no longer playful, but teasing, challenging: Now, you psychologists and analysts who are in the know, is that love? And what is love? Do you really know?

I tried in vain to shake these questions off, to put the tune out of my head. Back in my study I decided to answer a certain letter before going to bed, but I couldn't find it on my desk. Impatiently I started searching through my drawers for the letter and in my haste knocked several folders to the floor. I gathered the sheets and mechanically read what was written on them. On the one I had just picked up I read, "Love or whatever it is." It was the draft I had written seven years ago and which I thought I had lost. There are odd coincidences which are not accidental.

Forgetting entirely about the letter I had set out to find, I went on reading this original draft. Of course it had to be corrected and many passages had to be changed, much to be added . . . I wrote until dawn. The aria of Cherubino did not haunt me any more. I had accepted its challenge. Whenever I hear the tune now, I can again enjoy its sweet compulsion. More than four years have passed since that evening. Here is the book now, not finished, but rather brought to an end.

I once heard a diplomat say that a political statement should fulfill three demands: it should be pleasant, necessary and truthful. If all three of these requirements are not available, then two at least must be present. One of the three qualities might be dropped in an emergency, asserted the diplomatist, but in no case two of them. A psychological concept ought to have analogous qualities: it should be new, verifiable and correct. So far as I know, the thesis here presented is new. I have not met any theory resembling it. I believe that it is also verifiable. Any psychological observer who approaches the material with an unprejudiced mind and applies to it modern research methods will be able to examine and verify it. It is not for me to express a judgment as to whether the third quality is present. Like the diplomat I shall be satisfied if at least two of the necessary qualities are attributed to this concept. A strange idea asks for hospitality in the following pages.

2

The following concept is the result of many observations and experiences in the practice of psychoanalysis and in life, followed through many years and verified again and again. The new start is made independently of the theories of other research workers. It is not taken from speculations, but dragged out of the dark and silent waters of the deep sea. This is not the book of a learned man, but of a seeker after truth. I do not pretend to have solved the whole problem, but I believe my concept is more satisfactory than preceding ones. I do not know all the answers, I do not even know all the questions. Certain dark spots, uncertainties, remain. Some links are missing. I have called attention to them, hoping that other investigators, cleverer or more fortunate than myself, will be able to find them. The blueprint is here. It will be changed, no doubt. Here is a new answer to one of the oldest questions. If it should be proved correct it cannot be considered an indifferent contribution to the subject but a concept which reaches to the core of the problem.

In Plato's *Symposium* the guests agree that research into the nature of Eros is necessary. They assert his character could be defined if they could determine the identity of his parents. Translated into modern thought this means that we would know the essential thing about love if we knew all about its origin. Where does love spring from? We set aside the metaphysical ideas of philosophers as well as the lofty dreams of poets and ask science for an answer. Modern psychology, especially psychoanalysis, considers love to be an attenuated and goal-inhibited form of the sex drive. I shall try to prove that this view is incorrect and that the origin and character of love cannot be explained this way. After rejecting its derivation from sex, our task is to present a better thesis which will take the place of the unsatisfactory concept of psychoanalysis. But if love does not originate in sex is not the whole weight of mystery left hanging over it? When you remove the sexual character from its genesis it seems no longer to be earthbound. Of course we cannot accept the fancy notion of poets who see an indefinable and intangible power in love, nor the speculations of philosophers who conceive of it as something other-worldly, transcendental. The situation is one of those which tempts us to escape into vague generalities. But generalities are no answer. Would not love speak like one of those cherubim who, Montaigne reports, once visited a prelate? The courteous archbishop asked his guests to be seated. *"Asseyez-vous, mes enfants."* But the fluttering cherubs answered, *"Monseigneur, nous n'avons pas de quoi."* Do not be afraid! You may rest assured, loving is nothing so ethereal or seraphic. It is of this earth. And it has plenty *"de quoi."*

Before starting the discussion I must make two remarks in order to avoid other misapprehensions. The first is this: I presuppose love to be possible only as an emotion of one person for another person. I do not mean the same thing when I say, "I love pork chops," as when I say, "I love Jane." That is clear to both you and me. If I say, "I love ice cream," I extend the significance of the word unjustifiably. I mean I like ice cream, am fond of it. A remark like this sounds pedantic, punctilious. Yet confusion of a verbal kind can lead to far-reaching results.

There are other misapplications of the word, unimportant in themselves, but provocative of misunderstandings. Strictly speaking, it is also an extension of the significance of the word when I say, "I love beauty," or, "I love virtue." I do not love beauty or virtue in its abstract form, as a platonic idea, a vision without images. I love it as far as it appears in men and women, and that means that I love these human beings who are virtuous or beautiful. There is, of course, no objection to the use of an expression like, "I love the good, the beautiful, the noble"—but what I have in mind, although not always in my conscious thoughts, is that the idea of beauty and so on is the result of my experiences with beautiful, good, and noble-minded people. Love of mankind means love of many, or if you like, of all men. Even love for one's own country and nation is an abstraction, resulting from many conscious and unconscious experiences and memories. Uncle Sam, John Bull, Marianne are personifications of nations, but they are really the representatives of the American, Englishman, French as we know them. Unconsciously we think of a particular person in spite of the abstract idea.

We experience the development of a similar abstract idea in our own times. We celebrate Mothers' Day, send greetings and gifts to our respective mothers. Yet the personal relationship with one's own mother is obvious enough behind the idea.

The second presupposition which can be taken for granted is that love is only possible when a certain phase of individual development has been reached. Love is not inborn and primal. It is an experience which is acquired in later, individual life. You cannot call love an instinct like hunger or sex. It is the fruit of a late psychical development. Love is decidedly a product of culture. It is impossible before a certain stage of differentiation has been reached among the members of a group, whatever phase that stage may take. The deciding factor is the emergence of the individual from the social group, as a person; that is, when people are not only socially conscious but have become conscious of differences within the same group. It is necessary for people not only to notice the differences between one person and another, but to evaluate these differences. Ethnologists assure us that many half-civilized people realize such personal diversities very acutely, but without attributing any value to them.

It is not enough to be aware of personal differences. A distinction of values is called for. As long as one person meets another and does not see him as a different individual with a different make-up, love is psychologically not possible. The difference has to be felt, although it need not become conscious. If the object is exactly like me, where is the necessity to love him? If the other person is precisely as I am, where is the possibility of loving him or her—except in a psychoanalytical theory that we love only ourselves in the other? Is it necessary to emphasize that the differentiation as such has nothing to do with the fact that the person belongs to the other sex? When in love, a man does not consider the adored girl as only a particular sample of the female species. He sees in her a unique representative of her sex, incomparable with others.

I would like to present my concept in the form of a clinical description, in the cool and dispassionate spirit of psychological research. In studying this passion, passion is out of place. I should like to set forth the premises, the genesis and development of love as a botanist describes the soil on which a plant grows, the way it puts forth buds, and blossoms, and fades. I know, of course, that such a treatment will not always be possible, but it is the aim toward which I strive.

3

Love is one of the most overworked words in our vocabulary. There is hardly a field of human activity in which the word is not worked to death. It is not restricted to expressing an emotion between the sexes, but also expresses the emotion between members of a family. It signifies the feeling for your neighbor, for your friend, and even for your foe, for the whole of mankind, for the home, social or racial group, nation, for all that is beautiful and good, and for God Himself. It is almost incredible that it can be equal to its many tasks. *"L'amour"* in French comedies is obviously not the same as "love" in the Holy Scripture.

Its diversity of meaning, its adaptability and its capability of quick change are astonishing. It is used to describe the infatuation of a boy and girl, and at the same time the noblest and most spiritualized aims of men. The word is used in psychology and philosophy, in religion, ethics and education, in social fields of all kinds. It is indispensable wherever men live together. But time tells on it and it shows all the signs of the wear and tear to which it has been subjected.

The subject which is most talked and written about remains a mystery. It is experienced every hour everywhere on this globe and it is still unknown. That everybody has experienced it does not make its understanding easier. What happens every day often stays unknown, while rare events and extraordinary experiences disclose their nature more quickly. My contention at the outset of this book is that love is an unknown psychical power, its origin not yet discovered and its character not yet understood. If it is true that science is the topography of ignorance, as Oliver Wendell Holmes once said, then the region of love is a vast white spot on the map.

There is no doubt as to which science is qualified to give us the desired information and insight, but psychology seems to be extremely reticent on the subject. Why is that? Are the psychologists unwilling or unable to give the necessary knowledge? Can psychologists not tell us of what kind this emotion is, what is its nature and what determines its power? Is the subject too vague, too elusive and beyond the reach of description? Love is perhaps intangible, but the incessant search and research of intangibles is one of the essential tasks of the new psychology. Where facts and figures are not available there lie the most important problems which psychology has to face.

Has psychology to quit the field and hand it back to philosophers and poets and prophets, to Christ and St. Paul, to Plato and Schopenhauer, to Shakespeare and Goethe? Or do psychologists think that the subject is not worthy of their attention? That is impossible. We certainly know that we cannot understand the hidden impulses of human existence until we have solved this problem. Even if we consider love as an illusion, is it not our task to examine illusions, to find out what they are and what are their origins and their dynamics? Psychologists discuss sex very fully nowadays, but there is a conspiracy of silence about love. They avoid the subject, they seem to be embarrassed whenever it is mentioned. Nevertheless I do not believe that there is a taboo on this particular theme among psychologists. If they keep us in the dark about the genesis and character of love it must be because they are in the dark themselves.

What is this thing called love? Bizet's Carmen declares that it's "a gypsy's child." *"L'amour est l'enfant de Bohème, il n'a jamais connu de loi."* If there were no rhyme nor reason in love it could not be the object of scientific research. But is it so? There must be a method even in this madness. Love can as little escape the laws of psychology as a table can break away from the law of gravitation and float up to the ceiling. Many phenomena of a seemingly mysterious nature have become understandable when once their concealed laws have been discovered. We have come to understand the character of the strangest ideas of the insane, the secrets of hysterical and obsessional thoughts and actions, the mysteries of religions long dead, the habits and customs of primitive Australian tribes. And yet psychology is unable to discover the origin and nature of an experience which you and I and all men know. Must love remain a problem child of science and a stranger within the gates of psychology?

I assert that the last serious book which penetrated this secret domain was *De l'amour* by Stendhal. It was written one hundred and thirty-five years ago—which is a long time when you consider the psychological import of the subject. Since then nothing of real value, revealing the origin and nature of love, has been brought home from the numerous voyages of discovery undertaken.

But Freud? Did not psychoanalysis deal fully and penetratingly with love? It did not. It dealt with sex, but that is something quite different. Freud's great contribution to our knowledge is the discovery of the laws determining psychical processes, the dynamics of unconscious thoughts and impulses and the psychological method which enables us to discover what happens in the depth of the human mind.

4

Before discussing Freud's view about love I must correct a mistake that is quite common in analytical circles. It should be remembered that his opinion about the subject did not remain the same during forty years of psychoanalysis. There was a remarkable change in his view. At the beginning it was simple and consistent. At that time it was presupposed, although never explicitly formulated, that love was identical with sex. Freud then spoke of the love object when he meant sexual object, and of love choice when he meant choice of the sexual partner. He came from the study of medicine and he used the expression libido in the original sense of the energy of the sex urge. He assumed, so to speak, that this urge includes affection as well as attraction. I cannot state when and under what influences he passed on to an intentional enlargement of these two terms. Later on he explained and defended his new use of the words frequently; most clearly in his *Group Psychology and the Analysis of the Ego*. He states there that libido is the quantitative expression for the energy of all those tendencies which we sum up as love. Thus the pith of what is called love is love between the sexes. Freud does not distinguish between this love and that of parents and children, of friends.

The justification for this is that all of these tendencies are the expression of the same instincts whose aim is sexual union between the sexes. They have merely been diverted from their sexual goal, or inhibited in reaching it, but have kept enough of their original substance to make their identity easily recognizable. Psychoanalysis aroused a storm of indignation by its enlarged concept of love, although it did not create anything new thereby. The Eros of Plato is exactly the same as the libido, says Freud, and so is the power of love which Paul the Apostle praised in his famous epistle to the Corinthians. These love tendencies are in psychoanalysis called sexual instincts, *"a potiori* and on account of their origin." Freud then adds pointedly:* "The majority of cultured people felt this terminology an insult and found revenge by hurling the epithet of 'pansexualism' at, and blaming it on, psychoanalysis. The person who considers sex to be a shameful and humiliating aspect of human nature is always free to make use of the more distinguished expressions of eros or erotics. I could have done so myself from the start and spared myself much opposition. But I don't like to make concessions which seem to me to show a lack of courage. You don't know where such a road may lead. At first it is only in words, but in the end you have made concessions in the subject matter itself."

In another passage of the same work Freud repeats that the tender feelings which we call love are turned aside from their original sexual aims but keep some of them even then. Even the person who is affectionate, the friend, the admirer, wants the physical nearness and sight of the object loved, only in the sense in which Paul the Apostle uses the term. What we generally call love is a synthesis of those aim-inhibited tendencies and the sexual ones, a coexistence of direct and indirect sexual tendencies. Aim-inhibited love, Freud never tires of emphasizing, was originally utterly sensual love and is the same still in the unconscious life of men.** Even when those love tendencies are in contrast to the purely sexual ones it remains clear that their descent can be traced back to sex.

Later on Freud built the great hypothesis of Eros which really has the same meaning as Plato's idea but is expressed in biological terms: Eros is the great power that creates life, keeps united that which is separated and secures its renewal against the powers of destruction. At about the same time that Freud developed this concept he wrote in answer to a French magazine asking for his view on love beyond the realm of sex the following: "Up to the present I have not found the courage to make any broad

* *Civilization and Its Discontents.*
** Compare many passages in *Introductory Lectures on Psychoanalysis; Contributions to the Psychology of Love-Life* and so on.

statements on the essence of love and I think that our knowledge is not sufficient to do so."* He never found the courage, and at the end of his life confessed, "We really know very little about love."

Freud did not deny, indeed he emphasized, the fact that he extended the meaning of the word sex. He considered this the first great step in the foundation of his theory of instincts. In a paper on *Wild Psychoanalysis* Freud reproaches a physician who in treating a neurotic widow recommended a lover to her as a cure. This colleague was especially criticized by Freud for misunderstanding the teachings of psychoanalysis and for thinking that sex meant merely sex in the usual sense. "The idea of sex," says Freud in this connection, "contains in psychoanalysis much more. It surpasses the current meaning on both sides. This extension is justified genetically. We include in 'sex life' all activities and tender feelings which originated in the primitive sexual drives, also those impulses when they were subjected to an inhibition from their original sexual aim, or when they have exchanged this aim for another one, no longer sexual. Thus we prefer to speak of psychosexuality, emphasizing the fact that the psychical factor of sex life should not be neglected nor misunderstood. We use the word in the same extended sense as the German language uses the word *'liebe'* (love)."**

The physician stands corrected and justifiably so, but is Freud innocent? Is not he too responsible for the mistake or misjudgment? The young physician was wrong, but only because the word sex means one thing to Freud and something else to the man in the street or to the average physician in his consulting room. It is my conviction, although I cannot prove it, that at first Freud used the word sex unpretentiously and without premeditation. There was of course the idea that a primitive, sexual urge is the origin of love, but this was a biological prejudice rather than a psychological insight.

* Published in Reik's *From Thirty Years with Freud,* Rinehart, 1940.
** *Beyond the Pleasure Principle.*

He repeatedly stresses the fact that he extends the meaning of the word sex to include affection, friendship, love. Is he justified in using the word this way? I think this use of the word is neither just nor justifiable. The word sex has always meant the urges and activities that spring from the biological need to release a particular tension in the organism, an instinct common to men and beast. The word libido was applied long before Freud, but only to express the energy of this instinctual need. Freud stretched the significance of both words so that they are over-extended.

Is it really due to a general hypocrisy that people reject the term sex in its meaning of friendship, love, affection, or is it that they sense the fact that sex and love are different? Is it really only prudishness that leads them to reject the theory of the identity of these two needs? Or is it not rather the vague but profound feeling that the assumption of such an essential identity is wrong? I surmise that they feel somewhere that the thought is not conformable to the facts. I do not shrink from calling a spade a spade, but I am reluctant to call a rake a spade, even if they stand side by side in the same barn. Freud does just that. It sounds like one of those eccentrics whom Alice encounters on the other side of the looking glass. "When I use a word," says Humpty Dumpty, in rather a scornful tone, "it means just what I choose it to mean, neither more nor less." But Alice is somewhat skeptical. She replies, "The question is, whether you can make words mean so many different things." Exactly! That is the question here.

Freud has said that he uses the word sex with the same meaning that Plato used the word Eros. If sex were used in this sense it would not have been necessary to conceive the idea of Eros as Freud did later on, and to differentiate it from sex. In a paper written about a year before his death (the summer of 1938) Freud said: "The best we know about Eros, thus also about its component the libido, is obtained by the study of the sex function which coincides in the current conception, although not in our theory, with the Eros."* Thus Eros is not identical with sex, even in Freud's later view. It dawned upon him late in his life, although he never clearly acknowledged it, that love is a psychical power in its own right.

But even if Freud had used the word sex with the same meaning as Plato, would it therefore be more justifiable? Plato was a philosopher. Freud was a scientist. We make allowances for Plato who lived twenty-three hundred years ago which we are not willing to make for a psychologist of our own day. The one wanted to solve the riddles of the universe in a broad, metaphysical speculation, while the other wanted to solve very definite, psychological problems in a scientific manner. When an ancient Greek philosopher speculates about the nature of a substance, it is very different from the inquiry made by a modern chemist about the same substance. In Plato's grandiose and beautiful speculations Eros is in its place; but it cannot have the same place when identified with the sex urge in a modern analysis of psychical processes endeavoring to give a scientific picture of what goes on in the deepest region of the human mind. What Plato thought and said is different in its meaning from that which a modern psychologist thinks and says. The one sees in visions and describes images. The other sees analytically and in detail and describes psychical facts.

I believe that sex and love are different in origin and nature and I shall endeavor to prove it in this book as far as psychological statements of this kind can be proved—which is very far.

What Freud called sex in the enlarged sense is an alloy of metals of very differing natures and values. Let me here make the provisional statement that it is a mixture of the biological sexual need, of certain ego-drives and of the yet unknown substance, love. In another book which I have prepared I have tried to demonstrate the nature of the crude sex drive and how love entered its realm; and which psychological and social conditions have to be fulfilled in order that sex, the ego-drives and

* "Abriss der Psychoanalyse" in *Schriften aus dem Nachlass*, London, 1941.

the youngest need, of loving, can meet and melt. I shall restrict myself here to one region, but first the lines of demarcation must be drawn.

But is not the view of both ancient and modern psychologists that love is somehow a changed form of sex—sex in disguise, say —justified? Does not every passion of a young couple, every infatuation, bear witness to the fact? No. The most convincing cases only prove that sex and love are frequently united and directed to the same object. We are accustomed to associate love and sex in our thoughts, but that does not demonstrate their identity. It proves only that they are often found together, that they exist together, that they often coincide; but coincidence is not evidence of identity. Two emotions can be commingled so intimately that they are felt as one, but that does not make them one nor does it bring about the disappearance of their specific qualities.

Whisky is usually taken with soda, but the mixture of the two does not change whisky into soda nor soda into whisky. Some people are incapable of imagining soda without whisky, but even they will not deny that both substances have an independent existence, different characters and tastes. Whisky can be enjoyed without soda and soda can be poured into quite a number of different liquids. All kinds of mixtures of both are possible. It is the same with love and sex. There exist different kinds of proportions of both in their fusion. (It is a pity that we are never asked to "say when.") A confusion between whisky and soda is unlikely, except of course when you have already had too much of them. Likewise it is possible to confuse love and sex in a state of intense infatuation. What astonishes me is that such a mistake is possible in the sober spirit of scientific research.

It seems that there is no doubt among psychoanalysts that there is sex without love, sex "straight." What they vehemently deny is that there can be love without sex. Their view has never been disproved. It is the same as assuming that a delinquent is guilty until he is proved innocent. No doubt there

is a communication between love and sex, a connecting link, as
everyday experience shows. The gulf between them is spanned
by an arch or bridge, but I believe that there are two separate
domains, which must be distinguished.

5

We return to Freud's assumption that sex includes love, tenderness, charity and sympathy. What superficially appears to be of
the same kind shows profound differences upon finer analysis.
The situation can be compared with that of chemists who for a
long time thought a certain substance to be homogeneous until a
new examination showed this not to be so. The substance turned
out to be a mixture of two different substances, a fusion of very
dissimilar components.

I choose a very simple instance: our common table salt. The
example is not at all inappropriate.

Was not salt considered a precious and sacred substance
through the ages? It was the symbol of friendship, loyalty and
affection. The Arabs say, "There is salt between us," when they
mean an affectionate and loyal friendship. The "covenant of
salt" which you find in the Bible was recognized as full of
sacredness and deep meaning. For almost two thousand years salt
was considered a coherent and homogeneous substance. We
know now that it is chemically a compound of sodium and chlorine. Any high-school pupil today knows that these two elements
are different, and he would be able to demonstrate to you that
salt is a fusion of both. He also knows that these two substances
can be isolated and can be used for various purposes separately.

What are the facts? We first want to get hold of them. We can
put them together later on. We want to discriminate between
sex and love as the chemist would isolate the sodium element
from chlorine in the combination, salt. To make the differences

clear and clean-cut it is best to contrast love and sex in their extreme manifestations, where they do not yet appear fused.

Sex is an instinct, a biological need, originating in the organism, bound to the body. It is one of the great drives, like hunger and thirst, conditioned by chemical changes within the organism. The time is not far distant when we shall think of libido in chemical terms, and in chemical terms only. The sex urge is dependent on inner secretions. It can be localized in the genitals and in other erogenic zones. Its aim is the disappearance of a physical tension. It is originally objectless. Later on the sexual object is simply the means by which the tension is eased.

None of these characteristics can be found in love. If we do not accept the opinion of the ordinary man and woman that love lives in the heart we are unable to place it. It certainly is not a biological need, because there are millions of people who do not feel it and many centuries and cultural patterns in which it is unknown. We cannot name any inner secretions or specific glands which are responsible for it. Sex is originally objectless. Love certainly is not. It is a very definite, emotional relationship between a Me and a You.

What is the aim of sex? We have already stated it: the disappearance of a *physical* tension, a discharge and a *release*. What is the aim of the desire we call love? Disappearance of a *psychical* tension, *relief*. In this contrast between release and relief lies one of the most decisive differences. Sex wants satisfaction; love wants happiness.

Sex appears as a phenomenon of nature, common to men and beasts. Love is the result of a cultural development and is not even found among all men. We know that the sex urge is subject to periodic fluctuations of increase and decrease. This is of course quite obvious among the beasts, but survivals of its original nature are easily recognized in men. Nothing of this kind is known about love. Sex can be casual about its object. Love cannot. Love is always a personal relationship. This is not necessarily so with sex.

The object of sex may become of no account, boring or even hateful immediately after satisfaction is reached and the tension reduced. Not so the love-object. Referring to the extreme and crudest cases, the sexual partner can appear as a kind of appendage to the other's sexual parts, as a sexual object only. The object of love is always seen as a person and a personality. The sexual object has to have certain physical qualities which excite or arouse one. If they are lacking one remains indifferent. Not so the love object. It has to have certain psychical qualities which are highly valued, the existence of which is not demanded from a mere sexual object. Even when your object is both loved and sexually desired you can often discriminate between the sex appeal and the appeal of personality, and you know that they are different things. The sex urge hunts for lustful pleasure; love is in search of joy and happiness.

Again considering only extreme types, sex is utterly selfish, using the object only in order to get satisfaction. Love is not unselfish, but it is very difficult to name its selfish aims, other than that of being happy in the happiness of the beloved person. In no case can love be only selfish, or as selfish as sex. Then it would not be love. It is always concerned with the welfare or happiness of the other person, regrets the other's absence, wants to be together with the object, feels lonely without it, fears calamity or danger for it. There is nothing of this kind in crude sex. If the individual is not aroused by sexual wishes the presence of the sex object is not desired and its absence not regretted. The same is true after sexual satisfaction is reached. I have heard men say that the only wish they felt after a satisfactory intercourse was to be left alone—alone meaning that the sexual object should leave them. One man said, "Women should be like stars—rise late in the evening and disappear early in the morning." No such wish is imaginable toward a loved object.

Sex (always considering the crudest types) is undiscriminating. It wants "a woman." It is modest in its demands. But love always makes a choice. It is highly discriminating. It insists on "this woman" and no other. There is no such thing as an impersonal love. The sensually desired person and the adored one, the sex object and the love object, can be two different persons. The sex object can become the center of all one's wishes under the pressure of sexual needs. It can, for moments, be idolized. It cannot be idealized. Only love can work that. The other day an American girl, disgusted with the rumor that Australian girls exercised a strong fascination upon the American soldiers stationed overseas, wrote to her boy friend, "What have they got that we haven't?" He answered, "Nothing, except one thing. They are here." This answer you certainly would not expect from love, but you would very readily expect it from sex. Absence makes the heart grow fonder. There is—in normal cases, at least —no similar effect of absence on the sexual partner. Sex gives satisfaction. Love gives comfort.

The sex aim is not identical with the love aim. Recently a patient said of her partner, "He is not the person I love, but the person who gives me sexual gratification." Sex is a passionate interest in another body; love a passionate interest in another personality, or in his life. Sex does not feel pain if its object is injured, nor joy when it is happy. It is possible to possess another person in sex, but not in love. In love you cannot possess another person, you can only belong to another person. You can force another person to sexual activity, but not to love.

Could you speak of sex partners as "two hearts that beat as one"? Would you not rather be concerned with other parts of the body? Could you, without being ridiculous, say that aim-inhibited sex never ends? Could you swear eternal sex attraction? Jupiter laughs at the oaths of lovers, but at such sex-inspired oaths all gods and mortals would laugh. Would it not sound funny for the young Cherubino in Mozart's opera to ask us, "Say, is it sex now which in me burns?" You might think there would be certain signs that would help a young man to decide the question very easily so that there could be no doubt about it in his mind. The only doubt there could be—and which there is—is whether it is merely sex desire that he feels or love.

Sex is bound up with the time element, with the rhythm of the

ebb and flow of the urge. After the orgasm sexual desire sharply
or slowly vanishes. There is nothing comparable to that in love.
There is need of variety in sex, but not in love. The sex object
can be easily replaced, but not the love-object. There are many
possible sexual objects, but only one who is loved. "The world
is full of folks, it's true, but there was only one of you."

Its relation to time reveals the nature of sex as a drive, because
in it we realize the cyclical character of the tissue needs as for
hunger and thirst. We here see the results of the activity of internal stimuli which are activated by chemical changes within
the body. Hunger is connected with contraction of the muscles
of the walls of the stomach. Thirst springs from the dryness of
the mucous membrane of the mouth; sex from organic pressures.
Where are the organic stimuli for love, where the needs within
the organism, the physical tension that drives the organism to
remove the painful and unpleasant stimuli? Where is the analogy
with hunger? When you are hungry the sight and smell of food
rouses strong desire. After satiation your appetite disappears for
the time being. The sight and smell of the dish you enjoyed a few
minutes ago now leaves you cold. In this respect sex is distinctly
comparable to hunger. The urge disappears after being satisfied.
There is a tension, a spasm, a discharge and an anticlimax,
sharply defined in time. Time does not play the same role in love.
Lovers become aware of it only in the hour of parting. "It is the
nightingale and not the lark."

Sex and love are so different that they belong to distinct
realms of research fields; sex to the domain of biochemistry and
physiology, love to the domain of the psychology of emotions.
Sex is an urge, love is a desire.

But is not love a passion? Yes, of course it is, but do passions
originate only in sex? Are there not other passions in us mortals
as ardent and powerful as the sex urge? Is it not possible that
they can blend with the sexual desires? The fact that all philosophers from Plato to Schopenhauer, all psychologists from Spencer
to Havelock Ellis and Freud, have asserted that love is sexual in
its origin and nature does not make the statement true. All their

views have to face a set of facts and undergo the test for truth or falsity.

That love is aim-inhibited sex is more an escape from than an insight into the problem. Love is not a blurred carbon of sex, unconsciously sexual in its essence, derived from the same organic drive. Love can exist before sexual desire is felt for a person. It can outwear and outlive sex. There are old couples in whom the sex desire has vanished and who still love each other dearly. There are other cases in which sexual satisfaction with a particular partner is no longer desired, but where love continues. There are instances in which the sexual desire remains very vivid, while love has long since died. If love were only aim-inhibited sex its existence would not be imaginable with men and women who have no such inhibitions, who gratify their sexual wishes to the point of orgies. Nor would it be possible if all sex urge had vanished. And why should there be an intense desire for love in addition to the desire for a full and satisfactory sex life? If love is just a kind of arrested development of sex, how could the wish to love co-exist beside sexual exhaustion or the fulfillment of every normal and perverted impulse? The peak of sex gratification is ecstasy; the peak of love is beatitude.

Let us not be deceived by the logical fallacy that love and sex are so often united. Even where they overlap and are fused, even where sensual urge and tenderness melt into each other, a finer observation will recognize their qualities as discernible and differentiable. Are we not capable of thinking of love without sex and of sex without love? Even if it were true that there is an element of sex in every affection, it might be so infinitesimal as to be of no importance.

There are basic differences between a person who is sex-starved and one who is love-starved. Love is not a washed-out version of sex, not an anemic remnant, but something entirely different.

I know that sex meant something other to Freud than it means to most of his students, to whom it signifies sex and nothing more; but the word has proved stronger than his will to change its meaning. The result of the confusion has been disastrous.

What is hidden behind the emotions of love is not the sublimated or arrested sexual drive. When the cat is out of the bag it
will be recognized as a different animal altogether.

6

An old Austrian poet asks, "Tell me, where does love come
from?" And he answers, "It does not come; it is there." That may
sound poetical, but soberly judged it is nonsense. Psychologists
cannot be content with such an answer; they have to find out
how love comes into existence. Freud answers the question in the
following manner: originally there is but one love object, oneself. Love of other persons is a later development and self-love
remains the reservoir of love, out of which parts are given to
other persons just as you draw certain amounts from the available
funds in your bank. The result is a contrast between ego-love and
object-love. The more is spent on one side, the less remains on
the other.

Freud calls this primary form of self-love, which is self-sufficient,
narcissism. The term is taken from the Greek myth of Narcissus,
the handsome son of a river god, who fell in love with his own
image seen in a pool. The oddest version of the myth seems to be
that the boy, when he fell in love with the image, did not know
it was himself.

The term originated with the German psychiatrist P. Naecke
who first applied it in 1898 to a sexual perversion in which a person treats his own body in a way similar to that in which he
would ordinarily treat the body of a sexual object. He looks at
himself with sexual pleasure, fondles and caresses himself, and
so on.

Freud gave a new significance to the presumptuous expression,
but unfortunately the new meaning did not fit the word any
more. Naecke and Havelock Ellis applied it to the sexual perversion I have just described. With Freud it does not mean this per-

verted attitude nor does it mean sexual activity in regard to one's own body. He already had an expression for that: autoerotism. Narcissism was used by Freud to describe a primary and normal state of self-love, a common phase of love development. We are all born as Narcissi and the baby is "absolutely narcissistic," he says.

Even with Freud the meaning of the word oscillates at first in its pathological significance between that of a transitional phase in childhood and that of a normal attitude with grownups. His pupils and followers speak of narcissistic sensitiveness, narcissistic vulnerability (but Narcissus, deep in his admiration of himself, was not vulnerable to snubs), of a hurt or wounded narcissism, and so on. They speak of narcissism when they wish to describe a person so full of self-admiration that he does not care in the least what people think of him. But they also call a person narcissistic who needs the approval and praise of his surroundings far more than anything else. It is as if they were out to collect self-contradictory terms. The word narcissistic means first one thing, then another, and then a third, until at last it means not a thing.

By the way, there are several versions of the Narcissus myth. According to the oldest the youth looking into the pool falls in love with himself, but he does not know that what he sees is himself. In another version Narcissus has a twin sister resembling him whom he dearly loves. When she dies he finds consolation for his loss by looking at his own image in a fountain. In the third version the youth rejects his many male admirers. The god Eros is so offended by such an outrageous attitude that he punishes the youth by making him both lover and beloved in his own person. Narcissus is thus doomed to feel the unrequited desire he has inspired in other boys.

You wonder what is in these three versions of the myth which implies a normal, primary, genuine self-love. Is the self-admiring attitude of the boy independent of his experiences of the outside world? Is it of a primitive character, springing from within himself? In the oldest version he is in love with himself without knowing that he is himself. He sees a handsome boy in the mirror

of the pool. Is that primary self-love? He does not see himself in
the pool, but a dream of himself, an ideal, which is a stranger.
And is it entirely insignificant that he, the son of the river god,
sees himself reflected in the water? Such small details are considered full of meaning in other analytical interpretations of
myths. Why not here? Is it irrelevant that in another version the
youth adores his sister and admires himself only as her very picture? Is it of no importance that he is in the third story at first
admired and loved by other boys? It seems that Narcissus himself
is not primarily narcissistic. His falling in love with himself is
not the expression of a primitive need, but the result and continuation of the love and admiration of others. His self-love is
only the reflex of the love felt for him by his father or by other
boys. In this case we would have *an essentially homosexual* myth
quite in character with this preference in ancient Greece. The
somewhat melancholy story seems to point more to the consequences of being too much loved and admired than to self-love.
It is odd to find that Narcissus is neither originally in love with
himself nor absolutely and primarily "narcissistic." Why is the
myth qualified to become the name-giver to a concept of a general, primitive phase of love in everybody's development?

But let us turn from the mythological figures to the facts of
the human soul. Is it true that there is a genuine and elementary
phase in early childhood when the baby loves himself only? The
word narcissism would then be a misnomer, but one that covers
real facts. Freud himself admits that a direct study and observation of genuine narcissism is impossible. His thesis is thus a reconstruction formulated on later observations. These are interpreted
in accordance with the preconceived idea of a primitive and
original self-love of the baby. The infant does not love himself
because he does not exist originally as a separate individual. He
is an egoist without an ego. He is selfish without a self. The child
is psychologically not aware of himself. He will discover himself
by and by. Where there is no self there can be no self-love. To
say that the baby after his birth is "absolutely narcissistic," loves
only himself, has as much sense as saying that he loves the whole

world. If by a miracle a baby could talk and think and still psychically remain a baby, he could never use the expression "number one" in referring to himself. That would mean that there are other numbers, two or three. The baby might be many things, but he is certainly not "genuinely narcissistic." Here is a fairy tale not for children but about them.

What phenomena can be observed in children which might be interpreted as a manifestation of self-love? Perhaps the self-sufficiency and self-confidence which the small child shows? But we meet the same attitude in a kitten or a puppy, and they are not aware of a self. Sometimes one asks oneself if the term does not describe the impression of the observer, instead of interpreting the psychical attitude of the observed object.

Of course in the later life of the child there are enough phenomena which can be interpreted this way, but only if one is satisfied with superficialities. There are many children who at a certain age seem to admire and love themselves and treat their own body as if it were a loved object. Such an attitude is far from being a general phase. It is occasional and is even then the result of certain experiences. We deny neither the existence nor the significance of those phenomena. We do deny the significance which psychoanalysis gives to them as expressions of an elementary and genuine self-love. I assert that such seeming self-love is a late and secondary formation, in origin and nature entirely dependent on experiences with other persons, especially the parents and nurses.

The small child is the object of his mother's love and tenderness. He will later love himself as his mother loved him. He will be the mother's substitute in loving himself. The essence of so-called narcissism lies in seeing oneself with the loving eyes of another. The phenomenon does not mean the expression of self-love but the desire of the self to be loved. This "self-love" is only the reflex of the love and admiration of mother, father or nurse toward the self. You cannot love yourself except as a substitute for another loving person, in remembering and longing for his or her affection. This "self-love" which is really the love of someone else for oneself is thus a late, secondary formation like self-pity, which also unconsciously presupposes the pity of one's mother or another dear person for oneself.

The child who loves himself takes over the role of mother or father. He admires and caresses himself as they did. The indispensable premise of self-love is thus the memory trace of the mother's love. There need not be conscious memories, but there is the continual working over of impressions of the previous, repeated experience. The origin and dependence of self-love upon maternal affection is so obvious that we can dismiss the concept of narcissism as a very unsatisfactory sketch which does not give the correct view of the subject.

The formation of the child's self-love can almost be observed. Look at a small girl whose mother has said to her, "Oh, what a nice dress my little girl has on today!" or a boy whose father has praised him for his efficiency. The little girl when she becomes a grown-up girl will look admiringly at herself in the looking glass when she wears a new dress. And the little boy later on will say to himself, "What a big boy am I!" More than that, our self-love will remain dependent on the reaction of others, and will always be the unconscious anticipation of this admiration or appreciation. It will often be the substitute for the love which is missed, the expression of the desire for it. It is founded on the experience of having been loved, and it anticipates this experience in phantasy in an emergency situation, when the loving person is absent. The ego then takes the place of this missing and missed person as an actor can act two characters in a play.

There is no such thing as a genuine elementary self-love, because this feeling itself is a substitute. It is not the thing itself, but its image in a mirror, a reflected phenomenon. There are two persons present, if not in reality, at least in phantasy: the I who is loved, and the he or she who is loving, and who is replaced by the person who admires himself. In the formula, I love myself, or the I loves the Me, the I is substituted for another, unknown, or sometimes even known person. In the analysis of a young girl I once met unexpectedly intense resistance when she tried to describe her feelings during a conversation with a man with whom she was in love. She had great difficulty in expressing what she felt at a particular moment when, having said something, the man glanced at her. At length she said, "I felt sweet." She meant that at that moment she became aware of the fact that the man thought her sweet and she liked this feeling. Does that mean that it is the expression of a genuine, elementary self-love? Certainly not. The girl became conscious of the particular impression which the man had of her at that moment. She realized how he looked at her, and she then looked at herself through his eyes. The feeling-tone would have been the same if the girl had been alone and had imagined the scene, in a rehearsal situation. The man would then have been absent materially but not psychologically. No person loving or admiring himself is alone. Another person may not be visible but he is the object of the vision. Thus behind self-love is the unconscious knowledge that the person is or will be loved.

This happy phantasy has in most cases the character of a consolation or compensation. The substitute nature of self-love can turn to defiance, namely: if you do not love me I shall love myself. Psychoanalysts speak of a wounded narcissism, but narcissism can only develop as a substitute. The primal narcissism does not exist. The analysts who discuss it as an original, genuine phase confuse the adhesive on a wound with the healthy skin because both have a similar color.

A final view of the situation will result from understanding that self-love is a psychic formation which does not belong to the realm of love. The phenomena described as such belong to the problem-circle of being loved. They can be reduced to unconscious phantasies and vivid anticipations of being loved. It need not be emphasized that the two processes are psychologically very different.

I shall mention only one analytical attempt to solve the problem, because it follows a different line of reasoning. Dr. T. D. Suttie (*The Origins of Love and Hate,* London, 1935) proposes

that the infant brings the will and power to love with him into
the world and shows from the beginning an instinctual need for
companionship. I admit Dr. Suttie saw there something which
none of us observed before. The only trouble is that we could
not observe it after she had turned our attention to it. We
searched for such a primal need of companionship in the infant
and did not find it. It is highly improbable that the baby has such
an inborn love, but if he has he refuses to reveal it to the psychologists.

Arrived at the end of this road, I feel a strong need to salute
the genius of Freud. My uncompromising opposition to some of
his theories on sex has not in the least diminished my admiration
for his work and my love for his person. His greatness is not
based on a theory but on the incomparable profundity of his
psychological insights. People praise and blame him for the wrong
thing. As a psychologist, searching in the human emotions and
throwing light into their darkest corners he is matchless. No one
can replace him.

For more than thirty years I espoused psychoanalysis and did
my best to continue the work of Freud. You can die for the ideas
of another, but you can live only for your own ideas. I understood
rather late that a direct continuation is not possible. What he
created belongs to all times, but our time demands new creation.
Such is the law of change. A Schubert symphony is not a continuation of Beethoven's symphonic work, which marks the end
of a development, but something new and filled with new content.

There are psychoanalysts who proclaim that there is no new
and fundamental psychological insight possible after Freud, that
his was the last word. Here is a little story which amounts to an
answer: Johannes Brahms and Gustav Mahler once took a walk
together in Ischl near Salzburg. The old master contended that
there were no great composers any more and that the end of
creative music had occurred. The two had just arrived at the
bridge of the Ischl River. Mahler pointed down to the stream and
said: "Look, here comes the last wave!"

II

Origin and Nature of Love

A<small>T FIRST I WANT</small> to describe the nature of the soil on which the precious plant of love grows. I shall emphasize these conditions—the psychical preparedness—much more strongly than the authors who have dealt with this subject before because I value its importance so highly. The psychologists seem to think, just as the lovers themselves, that love comes over people as something inevitable and impersonal like a bolt from the blue. The lovers seem to assume that the experience represents the solution of all problems. What they forget to mention is that there were problems before.

I shall start this analysis not with the character of love but with the investigation of what preceded its appearance, just as a good biographer does not begin with the birth of his subject, but first gives us an idea of who his ancestors were and what his descent was. Thus the first question to be answered is: who falls in love? And the second: why does he fall in love? The answer to the first seems easy. Everybody. Which makes the first question no question any longer. The second question is apparently just as easily answered. Because there is a lovable person. It seems to be merely a question of opportunity following the popular scheme: boy meets girl.

But our curiosity is not so easily satisfied. We want to know what kind of boy. We want to determine his psychical attitude before he met the girl. One can no more say that any man and woman however different falls in love at a certain time than that every child is bound to get the measles. It must be a very personal experience, determined by different factors within the individual and an outcome of his emotional history. How a person loves, at

31

what time and under what particular conditions, depends on the kind of person he is, on the psychical situation he is in, on the strength or weakness of conflicting tendencies within him. There is no such thing as a love story. Love is a story within a story.

But how about love at first sight? Does not the expression "falling in love" itself imply the suddenness and violence of the passion? We are inclined to think that it strikes a person like a blow, or that a person falls into love as into a trap. The first comparison is wrong, as is also the second. There is no blow, no *coup de foudre,* even in love at first sight. All has been prepared. Nobody falls in love. He or she rather jumps into it. You hear a girl say to a friend, "I could let myself fall in love with him, if I chose." What kind of falling is that? Really, the most you can say is that a person lets himself fall. I am speaking here about various kinds of love, from a passing infatuation to a lasting affection, from a fleeting inclination to a Romeo's passion for Juliet. In fact I even include the instances in which people "fall" in and out of love as if it were a kind of indoor sport or gymnastic exercise.

The normal rhythm of life oscillates in general between a mild satisfaction with oneself and a slight discomfort, originating in the knowledge of one's personal shortcomings. We should like to be as handsome, young, strong or clever as other people of our acquaintance. We wish we could achieve as much as they do, long for similar advantages, positions, the same or greater success. To be delighted with oneself is the exception and, often enough, a smoke screen which we produce for ourselves and of course for others. Somewhere in it is a lingering feeling of discomfort with ourselves and a slight self-dislike. I assert that an increase of this spirit of discontent renders a person especially susceptible to "falling in love." We cannot measure the degree of the aggravation. It differs in individual cases. Such changes are not sudden, but frequently so gradual that one's friends, and often even oneself, fail to perceive the alteration.

Thus a man "falls in love" to avoid a deeper pit. Everything is all right with the person who is in love, but all is not well with the person who is about to fall in love. It is not accidental that Faust is in despair, realizing the vanity of all his efforts to penetrate to the core of the world's secrets, before he meets Gretchen, whose love promises youth and happiness.

These moods may run the gamut of dissatisfaction from twilight to darkness, from a wish to escape it all (often oneself too) to a real disgust of life. Sometimes it is only a wish to change one's surroundings, because, as Schubert's song puts it, there where you are not, there is happiness. A shadow has fallen upon the ego even in very inconspicuous cases. In them too is present a psychical discord, but the uneasiness is more concealed, even hidden from oneself. "I do not like being Joe," said a patient just before he fell in love. There is an internal disquiet, a displeasure in oneself, a sense of personal inadequacy which characterize the situation.

You will now ask: why is it, if love springs from such a state of dissatisfaction within oneself, that so many people, whom we know to be in this state, do not fall in love? My reply is that love is only one of the means of stopping or arresting this discomfort. The dissatisfied person can also "fall in hate." That is to say, he can nourish in himself hostile feelings against others who are more satisfied with themselves. He can turn his self-dislike into dislike of others. Other possibilities are even more promising. The person can achieve something which removes or eases the psychical distress and fills him with renewed self-confidence and self-esteem. Then, too, he can moderate his demands on himself. It is due to these demands in the first place that the discontent within the ego is aggravated. You may wonder why this last way is not oftener chosen. It seems that men and women prefer the other solutions. We may guess that it is pride which prevents them from reducing the demands that they make on themselves.

All these methods of removing or easing the discords within oneself can be compared to the different therapeutic measures applied to relieve a specific disease. We may carry the comparison farther. Love has all the characteristics of a recovery from the unconscious discomfiture under which the ego suffers. Or better, it is an attempt at recovery. Restoration is the end aimed at, but not always attained. A happy love signifies that the attempted cure has succeeded. The danger which threatens and which stamps the measure as a failure is the increase of internal dissatisfaction.

What pushes us to love is thus an effort to escape from internal discontent. It takes the place of an original striving for self-perfection and is related to ambition. To be in love fulfills this aspiration and is felt as an achievement. That may not sound very romantic but we promised to view the character of passion coldly. We did not want emotions about facts, but facts about emotions.

2

I have tried to describe in a general way the emotional situation of the person who will become a lover before he actually is one. We have seen that there is a mood of dissatisfaction, of incompleteness in him, a kind of nostalgia or loneliness, a feeling of want. In most cases this attitude of disquiet is unconscious, but in some it reaches the threshold of awareness in the form of a slight uneasiness, or a stagnant dissatisfaction, or a realization of being upset without knowing why. You have to dig only a few inches deeper in order to find the roots of this disturbance. So far as I have been able to judge there is only one source from which it comes, only one cause that covers all the different cases: it is the failure to come up to the demands that we make on ourselves. Whatever reasons we may give to ourselves or to others, it is this sense of our personal inadequacy or inefficiency which prepares the ground for the situation.

If we are honest with ourselves we must admit that we are rarely satisfied with ourselves, with our physical and mental qualities, with our achievements and our position in life. Beside the person that we really are is a picture in our minds of the person we should like to be. When we look more closely we even see with pitiless clarity how far short of this picture we fall. We call this image the ego-ideal. This expression may perhaps be found more appropriate than the term superego that Freud used. Ego-ideal is a less abstract description than superego, although both words have, if not the same, at least similar connotations. I am also of the opinion that the term ego-ideal cannot be misused in the same way as the other.

We treat this picture of our idealized selves differently at various times. Sometimes we even revolt against it; but most of the time, especially in our youth, we spend many hours looking at it admiringly, fondly, but keeping it as a most precious, secret treasure. On the other hand the image itself seems to look at us with cold and often disapproving eyes. Only rarely do we observe anything like satisfaction and recognition in its attitude toward us. We try to discover in it a similarity in ourselves, but almost always we are disappointed. We pretend sometimes to ourselves that we resemble the image, but we know at the same time that our personality does not correspond to the figure we created. This fictional self is not the man or woman we are, but the one we would like to be.

Every one of us has painted such a picture. It was meant to be a self-portrait but it was not done in a realistic manner. Looking into a mirror while we worked on it, we painted not so much what we saw as what we would like to have seen in ourselves. As a matter of fact we disliked what we really saw, and so we executed a flattering picture. It is not only homemade, but is also meant only for home use. We do not like to show it to our friends; we keep it secret; we are ashamed because it bears so little resemblance to our real looks.

Actually, the ego-image is a psychical acquisition of our late childhood, a result of our growing awareness that we are not what we would like to be. Of course this attitude toward ourselves is conditioned by the attitude toward us shown by others. We early learn to look at ourselves through the critical eyes with which grownups regard us. Children feel early enough the contrast between what they do and what they should do. The child wants to conform, to fulfill the demands of his mother, but his will to do so is at desperate odds with his powerful impulses and wishes.

There are times later on, of course, when we lose sight of our ego-ideal, even times when we rebel against it and endeavor to throw it overboard. But we seldom succeed. It accompanies us through most of our life and admonishes us to fulfill its aims—aims that are reduced only as old age approaches. We realize then, at last, that its demands were perhaps too high, that there is not time enough left to pay all debts, and we become resigned. The personality of every individual is determined by his actual qualities, his ego-ideal and his attitude toward the gulf between the two. If you could collect all the different ego-ideals of human beings you would know what humanity wants to be. You would have a complete "ideology" of men. If you could see in one broad view all the efforts of the human race to reach the ego-ideal, so near and yet so far away, you could survey the eternal struggle for recognition and fulfillment, the victories and defeats of mortals.

No phantasy is merely fantastic; no imagination can bring forth images from a void. A child of fancy has parents in reality. A fantastic being like the Sphinx consists of the body of a lioness or lion and the head of a man. The most fanciful pictures of Greek and Indian mythology are composites of different pieces of real life. This image-self, the ego-ideal, also has its patterns in reality. There are the examples of our parents and teachers, the representative men and women whom we admire later on. But more important than they, in those decisive years when the ego-ideal is formed, are the patterns held up before us: patterns of virtue in other children, in brothers and sisters, playmates and strangers, heroes in books or pictures. We looked at them with grudging admiration and envy, because we could never attain these high standards. Faced with them we become painfully aware of our shortcomings. Later on other figures are substituted and become examples of achievement that we would like to attain, of virtues that we wish to possess.

I call these patterns, taken from reality, ego-models, because they have a strong influence on the make-up of the youthful personality. The imprints and impressions that they unconsciously leave on the ego, which is too weak to resist such powerful influences, furnish the material for building the status of the ego-ideal which we erect in ourselves. All these pictures are immortalized in this one gigantic figure which we revere. Some of the ego-models are unconsciously kept intact despite later development, like ancient buildings that excavators dig out of the identical ground upon which modern houses have been erected. They really have an indelible character. What we admired and aspired to in late childhood and in our teens, in our boyhood and girlhood, remains important throughout our whole life.

The figures that are the center of these ego-models are alive, while the ego-model itself is a strange product of reality and phantasy, fact and fancy. In it the qualities of living persons appear very exaggerated, the negative side being removed or neglected and the achievements overestimated. It is like the beginning of the idealization with which we later invest a love-object. The ego-models, these in-between forms of truth and daydream, may be compared to the heroes and heroines of the stories and plays, in whom the realities and potentialities of living models are merged. The adolescent girl imagines that she will be very beautiful, gracious, and kind; the boy, that he will be strong, valiant and heroic, like their chosen models. The figures in these daydreams are certainly not identical with real persons, but neither are they identical with the daydreamer as he or she is. They are his or her wished for ego.

The theory of narcissism, generally accepted by the psychoanalysts, proclaims everybody originally to be in love with himself. The creation of an ego-model would thus be a psychological impossibility. It does not reflect the person as he is but as he would like to be. This phantasy does not spring from an overflowing self-love but from a discontent with oneself, and marks an attempt to assuage this unpleasant feeling by means which the imagination can provide.

The ego-model is an extension of the daydreamer. It is his desired shape, the forerunner of the ego-ideal. The frontiers between the two representations are at first fluid. The ego-model of a boy may be a baseball champion; that of a girl may be a film star. The boy becomes a baseball fan; the girl has a crush on the movie actress. Instead of a film star it may be her teacher or an older girl. Here are the roots of childish love before calf love. The continuation of the ego-models, the stuff of which is shaped from living persons, is the ego-ideal, heightened beyond the realm of reality and more or less deviating from real life. Later there are numerous transitions from the one type to the other.

Here is a representative instance of the genesis of an ego-model in early childhood. In analysis a man remembered that from the time he was six years old he had as model a somewhat older cousin who attended a military preparatory school. His mother and aunt praised the absent cousin, Louis, as the embodiment of all the virtues and good behavior. He was pictured as a quiet youth, always obedient to his parents and superiors who gave him their full approval. The younger boy listened to these glowing reports and began to daydream about the admired cousin. Smaller than Louis, the lad was shy and delicate, while his ego-model was vigorous and poised. He was often reproached, while Louis' praises were eloquently sung.

This glorification of Louis made him appear as a being whose high qualities and achievements both inside and outside school were unattainable. The daydreams developed in a strange direction. The younger lad spent much time in imagining what Louis did, what acts he was performing every hour of the day. Wishing he might witness the occupations of the unknown friend, the little boy began to imagine another boy, whom he called William. He made William a friend of Louis, younger, not comparable and yet not unworthy of Louis' friendship. William was imagined as attending a similar military institution and sometimes visiting Louis, accompanying him on duty, to his classes and games. By and by William seemed to emulate Louis, although he did it in a modest manner and was always defeated in the end. This special daydream was only slightly changed with the years. Later William's visits to Louis lasted longer, he became better equipped and gained in importance. He drew nearer to Louis, so to speak. Slowly he began to hold his own with the older boy.

You can observe in this account how the ego-model becomes an ego-ideal, how an example held up before the admiring boy becomes a love-object adored from the distance. Louis, a boy of flesh and blood, becomes almost a super-boy. The creation of the figure of William, who is a heightened double of the daydreamer, marks the desire to be near the worshiped object. The diffident boy does not yet imagine that he himself could visit this superior being; he is too shy to try that out, even in phantasy. His fancy creates a better substitute of himself, so to speak, an improved ego. In this remodeled form he dares imagine himself the pal of the revered Louis. William becomes more important, is even accorded a place near the hero of the daydreamer. It is clear that the love for Louis has passed its peak.

We have followed here the development from the admiration of a living object to its role of ego-model. Louis remained a love-object for a long time, adored from a distance like a star, and just as unattainable. The trend back to life is already signified by the creation of the figure of William, who is much nearer to an average boy than the blameless Louis. This changed, in-between character also reveals some of the hidden tendencies behind the devotion to the ideal—a competitive ambition, a drift toward emulation. William, the "double," becomes more and more a rival of Louis in the later phases of the phantasies. If the development here sketched is reversed, some important gaps can be filled in. There must have been some rancor in the original admiration, some envy or jealous feeling before Louis became idealized.

Some years later the daydreamer made the actual acquaintance of his cousin. The two boys played together, and Louis, who was not only older but also cleverer than the other, lost no opportunity to outwit his admirer. A certain chilliness became apparent in their relationship. There were scraps. Affection had waned.

Louis even became an object of hostility. Instances like this are psychologically instructive in more than one direction. They give us an insight not only into the genesis of the ego-model and ego-ideal but also into the creation of love.

Why do I discuss at such length the creation of the ego-ideal? Because two separate lines lead from this phantom directly to the heart of our problem. The first gives the cause for the discord or the displeasure which, as I said before, runs unconsciously ahead of love. In all cases this discontent is in the nature of a disaffection with oneself. We are now able to say that it is founded on the awareness that we fall far short of our ego-ideal, far below our unfulfilled wishes.

The mood that results from this disappointment—if it is not too desperate—disposes one, more than anything else, to fall in love. Love is a substitute for another desire, for the struggle toward self-fulfillment, for the vain urge to reach one's ego-ideal. The nonrealization of this drive makes love possible, but it also makes love necessary, because the tension within the ego increases. The fulfillment of the ego-ideal would make one self-satisfied and self-sufficient, and would remove the internal distress. If we could silence forever this persistent voice within us we would perhaps lead a loveless but happy life. But that is hardly possible for cultured people. Thus love is really a second-best, a compensatory way for not obtaining the ego-ideal state. Yet it is not self-love, as the theory of narcissism makes out. As a matter of fact it is nearer to self-hate. It is love for one's own ego-ideal, which will never be reached in oneself.

The second line leads to the transition from the ego-ideal to the loved person. The ego-ideal disappears from the stage of phantasy when the love-object makes its appearance there, like a sentry relieving the guard on duty. As we now know, this phantom-ego was not entirely fantastic. Pieces of the pattern were taken from living persons who became ego-models. Under certain psychological circumstances the development can be reversed. The phantom-ego, this second self, can become alive again. The love-object then takes the place that was filled by the ego-ideal in our soul.

In other words, loving means exchanging the ego-ideal for an external object, for a person in whom are joined all the qualities that we once desired for ourselves. The unconscious process by which that is done is in the nature of a projection. As you can cast a picture onto a screen or a reflecting surface, so you can project this ideal image of yourself onto another person. The process relieves the psychical pressure felt by shifting the burden from one's own shoulders. Projection in general means an alleviation of psychical distress, as we can observe in many cases of a different kind. The ascetic in the desert does not feel responsible any longer for the sexual temptations which torment him. It is an outside power, the devil, the evil one, who visits him with lascivious visions. No more is it a conflict within himself. He is fighting Satan. Such is the beneficent effect of projection.

But it is astonishing how seldom people are willing to moderate their inner demands, how insistent they are on achievement. It seems that we have an imperative need to fulfill the secret claims of achievement which have been in us from childhood.

The other day in New York's Central Park I saw a little boy climb up onto a rock. From the modest height which he had reached he shouted triumphantly, "Mother, just look where I am!" On the same walk half an hour later I saw a little girl show her mother how pretty she looked with flowers in her hair. As I walked along it occurred to me that the two children's behavior was a true reflection of all mankind. As the twig is bent, so the tree inclines. We behave like the little boy when we become men. The desire for recognition never dies in us. We all want to be appreciated and admired in these daydreams, in which we secretly polish and shine our ego-ideals. It does not make much difference whether we want to impress our circle of friends, or dream of making the old home town proud of us, or of being praised by posterity. Do we not all think, in grown-up terms of course, "Look where I am!"

It is this very need which is responsible for much, perhaps for most, of our achievements in whatever field we perform them. By achieving something, or even by doing some job well, this inner tension eases up for a time, though not for long. *"L'appétit vient en mangeant,"* and we want to achieve more. Our failure to fulfill the inner claims produces then an increased tension, aggravates the lingering discord in us. We do not know why one person is more inclined to strive for achievement in his work than another who tends to find it in love—which is a psychical achievement too. It is likely that our pursuit of happiness goes in both directions.

The first love-object thus is a glorified ego, the phantom-self as we imagined it in our daydreams. The second is the embodiment of this desired image in a real person. The ego-ideal was built up by outside influences, stimulated by living figures. It is a return, by a detour, to the old pattern, if now the original of the ego-ideal is sought and found in the external world, in the love-object. The new ideal, strictly speaking, is only a renewal of an old one in a different form.

At this point we find ourselves faced with a new difficulty. Suppose we tentatively agree to this concept, then that leaves us no place for the most powerful form of love, that between the sexes. You call your sweetheart your better self, it is true, but can it be that in this kind of love also—the most important one for society and civilization—the emotion is a substitute for the desire to fulfill the ideal ego? Is this love, too, a second best? Yes, I think that the concept here sketched also holds good for this case. It is of course modified and complicated by the mighty factor of sex.

Another question must be asked here: Why do we not choose the most natural way when caught in this internal discomfort set up by the nonfulfillment of our concealed ego-ideal? Why do we not become more modest or more tolerant toward ourselves? I shall present an answer to this question later on.

I have stressed the fact that the beloved person is a substitute for the ideal ego. Two people who love each other are interchanging their ego-ideals. That they love each other means they love the ideal of themselves in the other one. There would be no love on earth if this phantom were not there. We fall in love because we cannot attain the image that is our better self and the best of our self. From this concept it is obvious that love itself is only possible on a certain cultural level or after a certain phase in the development of the personality has been reached. The creation of an ego-ideal itself marks human progress. When people are entirely satisfied with their actual selves, love is impossible.

The transfer of the ego-ideal to a person is the most characteristic trait of love. The development thus starts as a striving after self-perfection, which is frustrated. It ends in finding the perfection which we could not reach within ourselves in this second self. The object now becomes the holder of all values. The image becomes flesh in the beloved person. While before we slaved in the strenuous service of an ideal, now we are in bondage to an actual person.

Is there not another change when we substitute a person for the unattainable ego-ideal? This ideal was a phantom, and the love object is a real, existing person. But is that so? No. The love-object is also a phantom to a great extent, a peg on which we hang all the illusions of ourselves which we longed to fulfill. The living person is, so to speak, only the material from which we create a fantastic figure, just as a sculptor shapes a statue out of stone.

While I write these words someone has turned on the radio in the adjoining room. I hear a not unpleasant tenor voice sing a new song: "I shall never know why I love you so." If the singer would be content with a provisional answer we could offer it. He loves her so because she fulfills his secret ego-ideal.

3

We have discovered some strange things concerning the origin of love: the preliminary state of discontent or dissatisfaction with oneself, the inner tension resulting therefrom, the attempts to remove it or to ease it. Before he fell in love the person is not in an enviable psychical condition but in emotional distress. The man lost his soul to a girl to save it. We have found that the sufferer sometimes tries to overcome the inner discord by achievements or the accomplishment of something important to himself and others. Another way for him to satisfy the inner claims is to enlarge and enrich the ego by means of love. If both ways are blocked he is bound to become psychically ill, because to remain healthy you must be able to work and to love.

It was strange to find that love does not spring from abundance and richness of the ego, but is a way out of inner distress and poverty. We were surprised to discover that our first love is not directed either to another person or to ourselves, but to an imaginary ideal ego, to an image of ourselves as we would like to be. There are stranger discoveries awaiting us the more deeply we grope in the dark and the farther we intrude into the secret places of the human heart.

We finally reached the point where the person meets his future love-object. In order to love someone we have to admire him or her. We need not always know what we admire in the object; we need not even know that we do admire, but only that we feel attracted or fascinated. It seems, however, that admiration is a necessary feeling of incipient love. I do not assert, of course, that admiration must lead to love, but only that it is a preliminary condition which is absolutely essential. But is that not obvious? No doubt. Why then is it mentioned if it is apparent? Because the things that are declared to be self-evident are seldom carefully examined. The obvious is an excellent hiding place for items that wish to conceal themselves. What kind of admiration is this, anyhow? Certainly not a cool, dispassionate, impersonal kind of appreciation. It is of a decidedly different character; much nearer the core of one's own personality. It strikes a chord in one, stirs something, makes one restless or desirous. It arouses certain dark wishes, makes mysterious claims. There is something in it of the nature of a challenge.

It is the kind of admiration that makes one feel small, inferior, unworthy by comparison with the object. At the same time it stimulates wishes to be like the object or to take possession of her; either to be endowed with similar qualities or to own such a personality. It is not a high respect or regard or like other kinds of appreciation. It has a provoking, even an alarming nature. It is not only exciting but also inspiring; not only inspiring but also irritating. In other words, we only admire in this manner someone whom we either wish to be like or to own. These are not incidental, secondary traits of this admiration but its essential characteristics.

This description expresses the positive side of the sort of admiration I mean. Where is the negative side? This becomes visible when you consider that we would like to be the admired person or to possess her qualities or personal excellencies, when you consider that we feel inferior compared with the object. There is a covetous characteristic in it somewhere. The admiration has in it something possessive or greedy, and at the same time something dissenting, recalcitrant, even begrudging. When you follow this thread to the realms of the unconscious processes you will find there a feeling which is otherwise termed envy or jealousy. *In other words, the reverse or wrong side of this admiration for the love-object is envy.*

I want to discuss at length this item, which is the first important piece of my new concept, in order to avoid all possible misunderstandings and misinterpretations. Is envy necessarily connected with admiration? Certainly not. Only with this particular form of it, which makes one feel the desire to be like the object or to own it. But only this kind leads later on to the development of loving. What does that mean, and why must it be like that? Did we not say that the person is dissatisfied with himself, feels his shortcomings acutely, cannot be what he wishes to be or accomplish what he would like to achieve? In this state he meets a personality who is the embodiment of all he wishes to be and to achieve. She has so much; often it seems she has all. Should not his admiration have in it a begrudging, involuntarily unconsenting note? Could it be entirely free from envy? He would not be human if he felt otherwise unconsciously. Rather he would be a fit specimen for a natural history museum as a remarkable exception within the human species. Such is our nature in its depths.

This is the only kind of admiration which is invisibly, inseparably accompanied by envy. Other kinds are at least relatively free from that powerful subterranean component. Respect and high appreciation of this or that quality or endowment in another person need not be coupled with envy. Admiration in part often lacks this quality. It is quite possible to admire this or that virtue in someone without a passionate wish to be that person. I can admire, for instance, the skill of a tennis champion without the urgent desire to be one myself. On the other hand I can desire to play tennis well without wishing to change into him. I admire him, but my admiration is restricted to a particular field. I do not wish to be the tennis champion and I do not feel envious or jealous of him as a human personality. Even ardent admiration need not have as a result unconscious envy. I can be enthusiastic about the symphonies of Beethoven and in my daydreams passionately wish to be an artist like him, to have composed the Fifth and Seventh symphonies. Nevertheless, I would not wish to be Beethoven, or to have his violent temper and obnoxious disposition. I would not wish to exchange my life for his tragic destiny. I only wish to have his divine genius, not his personality. In this case my admiration is restricted, as would be my unconscious envy or jealousy if it were aroused.

The admiration or envy which is a psychological premise of love, an unconscious *conditio sine qua non* of love's development, has two significant qualities. It is directed to the whole personality, to all the combined endowments of the object, and it results in the wish either to be like this person or to be he. Only this wholehearted admiration without restrictions produces the particular envy upon which rests, in my opinion, the solid, unconscious basis of loving. This sort of admiration does not see the negative side of a person, his or her human weaknesses and faults. These minor qualities do not bother us because we are so fascinated by the superiority of the object. Adolescent boys and girls are often inclined to feel such a fascination for some outstanding achievement or some excellent feature of their hero. They are nobly blind to the negative side of the object's character. It needs more than that to inspire a mature personality with the kind of envy which I have described.

Of course even this form of unconscious envy need not develop further nor result in loving. I shall discuss soon other psychological circumstances which are necessary to determine this particular development. It not only need not develop into love, it can even result in hate and intense hostility. It can also become conscious envy and jealousy, can be felt as such and can be conquered. It is possible that it may diminish and disappear in time, especially if one finds consolation in other qualities or achievements of one's own. A mechanism of consolation can thus help to conquer the unpleasant feeling of being helplessly defeated. One gets to know these psychical dynamics by listening to the remarks that women make, in their more sincere moments, about the superior qualities of their friends or rivals. Their words unconsciously coincide with this mechanism. "Yes, she has beautiful eyes, it is true, but she hasn't got my figure." In this way the eternal feminine question, "What has she got that I have not?" is answered in the emergency situation in which the pre-eminence of another woman has to be acknowledged. By means of such a consolation the ego—and not only of women— can overcome the feelings of envy that threaten to cross the threshold of conscious feelings. The other way to conquer this envy, the one with which we are dealing here, is love.

But is not envy a malicious emotion and love a very sweet one? Indeed, this is so. But I did not assert that envy is a conscious element of love; only that it is one of the most important factors which necessarily precede the formation of love. A rose springs from a soil which is fertilized with evil-smelling manure. Has it, on that account, a less sweet fragrance? Indeed it is most astonishing and startling and to many it may even sound incredible that our first emotional approach to an object which we shall love should be a kind of envy or jealousy. But let us not forget that this feeling is entirely unconscious. And let us not forget that love, once called into existence, overcomes these fleeting emotions of envy. Yes, their very absence is the most significant characteristic of love. The tendency to grasp no longer exists. There is no place in love for discriminating between mine and thine. Envy is the very emotion which is entirely foreign to and the most remote from the spirit of love. But that is already the achievement of affection and we have not come so far yet. We are dealing here with the unconscious motives underlying the psychical development leading to this aim.

But why choose the word envy at all, rather than the word emulation? If it were only a choice of words I would not object to the expression emulation instead of envy. But it is more than that. The connotation of emulation is different from envy. It does not signify the awareness of one's own inferiority to the other person, nor does it imply that the other possesses something which one misses and covets. It does not mean that this person has an advantage over one which causes irritation. It has a much friendlier note than envy, it is true, but it is not true that this friendlier note is in place here. Even if we could admit that the emotion in the initial psychical tension starts as a kind of emulation, we would have to add that it quickly deteriorates into envy provided there is no possibility of competing with a person considered very superior. The love-object unconsciously invites competition and discourages it at the same time.

There is a contrast between the future love and the object which has not yet been mentioned and which is of a most disturbing and provoking character. While the admirer is dissatisfied with himself, full of dissonances, split and stirred up, the object seems to remain cool, self-possessed and self-contained. The attraction of such a person with his center of gravity in himself is strongly felt by the other with a weakened self-confidence. The impression of self-sufficiency is not the least of the factors which determine envy. The poise and smooth composure, the apparent imperturbability of the object, have an irritating effect. They appear as antithesis to one's own attitude. A woman's indifference and aloofness, her self-possession and self-sufficiency, her calm and security work on a man like a challenge. Something in her very existence and indifference seems to make us more aware of the discord in ourselves. That she is so unperturbed and imperturbable seems to excite and bewilder us, makes us slightly resentful, almost offended, and this is an excellent mixture for the preparation of love. Between attraction and flight, between desire to get her and to get rid of her, the feeling of one's own incompleteness and restlessness grows. The challenge works unconsciously. There is something that seems inscrutable in her, that arouses a wish to find out about her. She seems so cool and casual, so detached and oblivious of the impression she makes upon us. Her remoteness becomes unbearably annoying and alluring at the same time. She is tantalizing because she seems not to be disturbed by the same nostalgia which we feel. We want to have the same tranquillity and peace. We covet them and their owner. There is a desire to grasp the person, a greediness, a kind of voracity in our envy. These tendencies work unconsciously in the preparation of love, like the enzymes, those catalysts without which life would be impossible. Their existence is a necessary condition for falling in love.

We are now able to see more clearly the connecting threads of the argument that the concealed dissatisfaction with ourselves makes us especially sensitive and inclined to feel envious or jealous when we meet a person who has the qualities which we lack and who seems to be satisfied and self-contained. This object is not a substitute of the ego-ideal but can become one later on if loves takes the place of envy and grudging admiration. The relationship to the envied object can rather be compared to the one which we had for those persons whom we considered ego-models in our youth. We remember that these ego-models sometimes really became our love-objects if they did not become objects of our hate. We realize here that our psychical approach to the future love-object amounts to a return, a regression, to the feelings that we had as children for our ego-models. Even then the nature of those feelings was not as simple as it appeared to be. Even then envy preceded our affection. Now we recognize that we are walking here on a prepared path. We do not forget that even our dissatisfaction at that time started from the comparison of ourselves with others. Why are we not as beautiful, clever, poised and popular? Or, to put it in the form of a wish, if we could only be as gifted, handsome, brave and favored.

We are not astonished to find that envy and jealousy are powerful emotions. What amazes us is that they appear as secret forerunners of love. We are surprised that envy and a certain kind of admiration should only be two sides of the same psychical phenomenon, envy being the reverse side. We are astonished because we were not aware of its existence and effect in this connection. But if envy is one of the necessary preparatory elements of love, would it not be correct to conclude that persons who are incapable of envying others cannot love? Exactly. We shall discuss these strange cases later on.

And so we have added to the unconscious dissatisfaction within ourselves another premise of love which emerges now at the meeting of the future love-object, namely the existence and effect of repressed envy. Put more clearly in other words, the initial admiration for the object included the wish to be or to have this object; to change places with it. Not only the excellent qualities of the person—whether they are there actually or only in our imagination is a matter of indifference—are responsible for this wish, but also our awareness that we lack these qualities or miss these achievements. In this wish to change one's personality into the other's there appears, although in a dim light and scarcely recognizable, an essential feature that will be felt as fulfilled later on, when love has taken the place of envy: the wish to be one with the beloved person, to be united with her, to melt and merge into one being.

The consequences of this new concept of love spread far. When I say that I love my wife, there must have been a combination of qualities in her which I envied or was jealous of; her prettiness, determined conduct, social grace, charm, friendly manners, all of them qualities that I sadly lack. On the other hand, the fact that my wife loves me means that there must have been gifts or qualities in me which she was once envious of, however mysterious and puzzling it seems to me that I have such enviable qualities. If this concept is correct, unconscious envy is an inevitable predecessor of any love. It is easy to understand that the beast was envious of the beauty. It is less understandable, but must have been true, that the beauty was also envious of the beast.

Love appears now, in its first phases, to be more and more comparable to an iceberg of which only a small piece is above the water, while its greater and balancing part is not visible.

There is a long way from unconscious feelings of envy, from repressed tendencies of jealousy to love and tenderness. Everything is wrapped up in fog and we do not know where we shall proceed. The discovery that there must be subterranean feelings of envy before love can develop is so startling that we are entitled to a short respite to recover our breath.

4

Surprised by the findings we have just discussed, which were re-examined and verified in careful observations, I searched in vain for similar views expressed by psychologists and psychoanalysts. My search was, I have to confess, somewhat restricted and I do not doubt that there are psychological authors who anticipated this part of my thesis, but I have not found either their books or their papers.

It seems that one must leave the realm of scientific psychology and psychiatry to find, if not similar ideas, at least views expressed in an aphoristic sentence or in a few verses which touch upon our concept. You will find similar ideas in the speeches or writings of great religious or philosophical personalities, rather in the form of allusions than of statements. You are in doubt as to whether they are meant in the way here characterized or whether they reveal an unconscious insight of the authors rather than a psychological knowledge. Should we for instance assume that the sentence which Paul the Apostle wrote to the

Corinthians belongs to our thesis? "Love envieth not," says Paul, "seeketh not its own." That concerns rather love itself than its preparatory phases. It shows, however, a train of thought in the direction of our own. As a matter of psychological fact love is characterized by a complete overcoming of the initial tendencies of envy. In true love, Paul is right here; envy is only conspicuous by its absence. There are no visible traces left of its one-time presence. The passage from the Epistle to the Corinthians does not touch the essentials of my thesis, but we may well note and welcome it. It contributes a confirmation in an indirect and negative form.

I am sure that poets, who always push forward in advance of psychological research, come nearer to this concept in those flashes which illuminate the darkness of the psychical scenery for a moment and are so soon past. Of course they do not appear in a general, scientifically usable form. They are precious because they reveal, for the few seconds of their duration, what is in the unconscious depths of human nature. The element of unconscious envy in attraction and affection was not unknown to the poet who wrote *Othello*. The Moor himself reports how he won the love of Desdemona by telling her the story of his adventures and experiences:

> She wish'd she had not heard it; yet she
> Wish'd that heaven had made her such a man.

Here is a surprising sentence from *Wilhelm Meister* by Goethe. "There are no means of safety against superior qualities of another person but to love him." Is not "means of safety" a strange expression? Why should we need a refuge when we meet a personality whose superiority we acknowledge? What Goethe here alludes to is clear: if we do not want to yield to the temptation of envious and jealous feelings against such a person, we had better love him. Love is here characterized by way of a suggestion as an escape from the danger of the otherwise unavoidable envy which superiority arouses in us. The noble nature of Goethe could not tolerate such feelings of envy and jealousy in himself. Therefore his "means of safety." The sentence rather implies without stating a piece of psychological insight, but it gives us a hint which we appreciate.

There is, however, at least one great philosopher who has to be considered the predecessor in the creation of this essential part of a love concept. You have to go back almost twenty-four hundred years to meet him: Plato.

In the *Symposium,* the poet Agathon has just made a speech in which he has extravagantly praised the god Love, whom he calls the fairest and best of all things. Socrates half ironically says that Agathon has made a marvelous speech, but he, Socrates, cannot be a eulogist, he can only tell the truth. He wants to ask Agathon some questions before starting his own speech. What follows is a kind of mental exercise, a quiz in ancient Athens. The two men are not so much discussing as arguing. The old philosopher and sophist tries to argue Agathon out of his glorification of Love, to win the admission that a person loves "what he lacks and has not." Agathon admits that. "Then Love wants and has no beauty?" asks Socrates. "Certainly," replies the poet. "And would you call that beautiful which wants beauty and does not possess beauty?" "Certainly not," answers the unsuspecting playwright. But now he is already trapped. "Then would you still say that Love is beautiful?" asks the catcher of souls. The poet, led to this point, has to confess that he did not understand what he was talking about before. He also has to grant that Love wants the good and is not good itself. Socrates does not wish more than these admissions. What Socrates means is simple enough: I love someone not because I am beautiful and good, but because this other person possesses these qualities and I do not. Else, if I considered myself as beautiful and good as he is, I would not love him.

As if not satisfied with saying it only once, Socrates makes the same point in the course of the great dialogue which he had had a long time before with the wise priestess Diotima, who was his teacher. At that time Socrates praised Love in nearly the same words that Agathon had just used, as a mighty god and fair. Diotima proved to him that Eros, or Love, is neither fair nor a god. We follow her syllogism in the report of her pupil: Would he not acknowledge that the gods are happy and fair? He would not dare to say that any god was not? "Certainly not," I replied. "And you mean by happy those who are the possessors of good and beautiful things?" "Certainly I do." "But you have admitted that Love from lack of good and beautiful things desires these very things that he lacks." "Yes, I have." "How then can he be a god, if he is devoid of things beautiful and good?" "By no means, it appears." "So you see," she said, "you are a person who does not consider Love to be a god."

Socrates now asks the essential question, touches the cardinal problem. What is the origin of Love? How does it come into existence? After being told that Love is not a god but a great demon, he wants to know, "And who was his father and his mother?"

"That is rather a long story," replies the priestess, and being a woman adds, "but still I will tell you." It is not a fairy tale, but a story of the gods on Olympus. It sounds fantastic enough to our modern ears. But when you remove the dressings, the mythological camouflage, you find here a theory of the origin of love the profundity of which has never been equaled by the philosophers and psychologists since.

The myth tells us that on the birthday of Aphrodite the gods made a great feast. The god Plenty (in Greek, Poros), the son of Cunning (Metys), was among the guests. When they had banqueted, there came Poverty (Penia) abegging as was her custom on such occasions. She hung about the door. Now Plenty had become tipsy with nectar, so he went into the garden of Zeus, where he fell into a heavy sleep. Poverty, who was without resources, plotted to have a child by him. She lay down by his side and conceived Love. Diotima enlarges then upon the quality and fortunes of Love, which are the result of this, his parentage. "As the son of Plenty and Poverty he is in a peculiar case. First he is ever poor and far from tender or beautiful as most suppose him. He is hard-featured and squalid and has no shoes nor a home to dwell in. He lies under the open sky on the bare ground and takes his rest on doorsteps or in the streets. Like his mother he is always in want. But he takes after his father too. He is always scheming against the beautiful and good. He is bold, enterprising, strong, a hunter of men, always up to some intrigue or other, keen in the pursuit of wisdom and never wanting resources, a philosopher at all times, terrible as an enchanter, sorcerer, sophist. For as he is neither mortal nor immortal, he is alive and flourishing at one moment when he is in plenty and dead at another moment, but revives again by force of his father's nature."

Love seems to be an odd or droll creature in Diotima's description, something like the shepherd Strephon, Iolanthe's son in the Gilbert and Sullivan operetta—half a fairy and half an ordinary mortal. But the idea is rather that love changes its nature from one moment to the other.

No doubt Diotima here describes in her picturesque manner the changes in the moods and attributes of the desperate, the hopeful and the satisfied lover. She contrasts the dissatisfaction with the happiness, the poverty with the riches which characterize those states.

As Poverty goes abegging in her distress, just as the poor one asks something from Plenty, so searches the lover for his object. The emotional relationship between them is at first that of a starving person to the one who has plenty. Or, translated into the language of today: that of the Have-nots to the Haves.

5

To my knowledge no philosopher or psychoanalyst since Plato has acknowledged that love is Janus-headed, that its one face shows the features of a passionate admiration while the other is that of the green-eyed monster. We have to rely upon our own experiences and to verify them with the living material offered by unconscious processes of men and women.

Before penetrating deeper into these regions, the particular qualities of envy have to be examined. This emotion was long neglected by psychologists and did not receive the attention which its importance in human nature merited. It is one of the most powerful passions in childhood. If later on in life it does not come as freely to the surface it does not mean that it has disappeared, but only that it has been submerged.

As a matter of sober, psychological fact no one likes to admit that envy is a feature of his character. You would more willingly disclose that you have hostile, aggressive, mean or perverted feelings, that you are driven by this or that passion, than that you are full of envy. You are more ashamed of it than of any other "vice" which might be considered socially much more harmful. There must be one or more reasons for this reluctance to admit a human weakness, of which we all have a share. You can immediately guess at least one reason. When we confess other emotions or passions it does not necessarily expose our complete diffidence in ourselves, our smallness and insignificance, our feeling of inferiority to other persons. Other admissions or confessions we make shamefacedly, but they need not be felt as shameful. They do not include the acknowledgment that we feel less than the next man or woman. But whoever says that he is consumed with envy is also saying that he lacks strength and courage, that he has a low opinion of himself, that he feels incompetent compared with others or so it appears at least. Whoever admits cruel or mean thoughts can keep his self-respect to a certain extent, even when he condemns these impulses. But the person who confesses his envy admits (or seems to admit) the complete absence of self-esteem. When you confess that you wanted to kill, you confess a failing of yours. When you reveal how envious you are, you apparently admit that you are in your own opinion a failure. The one confession is humiliating, the other dwarfs you.

There are other qualities equally present in envy when it is repressed and when we are not aware of its existence. Envy is sharp-sighted, not blind like love. No advantage and no achievement of the object escapes its observation. Not the slightest accomplishment, not a single expression of endowment, no insignificant improvement of a position remains unnoticed. And every one of them is magnified in imagination. We are now in a position to reverse our previous statement: admiration of a certain kind is the other side of envy. The sort of ardent admiration which we discussed before is just the same: it is all-observant and exaggerates the smallest gift, the inconsiderable endowments, the limited achievements of its object.

Whoever envies, intensely acknowledges that he admires the other person very much. Whoever curses the envied object praises it along with his abuse. And here is another quality: envy of this violent kind cannot remain stationary for a long time. Only two developments for conscious envy are possible. Either it is withdrawn from the person, who then becomes an object of indifference, or it is bound to result in hate and hostility. When envy is repressed only the second case is possible because our unconscious life does not know the category of indifference. We associate envy with hatred in our thoughts. There is no friendly envy.

Is it then possible that the forerunner of any love is unconscious hatred or hostility? Yes, that is so. It sounds paradoxical until you take into account that there is a dissatisfied ego in want of an envied object, and that the hostility is bred from this envy which wishes to take possession of the object. Need makes greed. It is a kind of greediness, a covetousness, a grasping or possessive tendency which unconsciously precedes love and dies in it. This is the nature of the bacteria that cause this disease, these the microorganisms that can be seen only under the psychologist's microscope. They were not visible before and I have to magnify them here for the purpose of investigation. The unconscious hostility is already a symptom produced by these invisible bacilli which are always moving and working, as do the material ones.

Envy of the kind described—this emotional possessiveness—presents itself here as the microorganism that causes the infection, and unconscious hostility is the first symptom. Feelings of aggressiveness or hatred demonstrate that the bacillus is virulent and has begun its work in the emotional system into which it has been introduced. It depends on many factors, just as in the development of an infectious disease, what the outcome will be of the fight between the intruder and the organism. We follow this development in the particular case in which the bacteria, having been at work, are emotionally conquered and absorbed. We thus see love as the splendid result of a recovery process, not as a disease.

The comparison extends farther. The infected person is usually not aware that bacteria have entered his body, is not aware of their initial effects. We know that there is an incubation time that varies in different diseases, from a few days in the case of diphtheria to months and even years in that of sleeping sickness and leprosy. Within this general divergency in diseases there are also individual differences in the determination of which the physical and sometimes even the emotional state of a person plays a considerable role. One child contracts measles after eight days; its playmate, after a fortnight.

If love is thus likened to a recovery from an infectious disease caused by envy or jealousy we have to assume that there must be a kind of incubation period preceding it. Love at first sight seems to contradict this supposition, but perhaps that is only because the infection worked rapidly there. Such cases catch the disease. The incubation time appears to be very short between the exposure and the first symptoms. As long as we do not know more about the pace of emotional processes of this kind we cannot venture to say why it takes a long time in one case and occurs so quickly in another. The emotional state of the individual before he falls in love is one of the decisive factors. So much is certain.

We compared hatred or hostility to the first symptoms of an infectious disease. Such symptoms are sometimes quite apparent, but not always recognizable as such during the incubation time (like being tired, in a bad mood, feverish). In most cases the initial symptoms are hardly observed. They are usually passed over as unimportant. Often they are not even noticeable. The hostility against the object may be compared to those imperceptible first symptoms because this emotion is in general unconscious. But just as in these infectious diseases, so there are many cases of love in which the initial symptoms appear on the surface and cannot be overlooked. Some may argue that such signs of resentment or hostility are just an expression of an especially passionate character and not a regular forerunner of love. But it is rather so that this emotion, which is so often unnoticeable in most persons, is conspicuous in the case of violent characters. The fact that folk tales and proverbs of most nations acknowledge that hostile or aggressive feelings often herald the coming of love speaks in favor of this assumption.

The resulting hostility is the predecessor of any love, but of course is not always succeeded by it. Emotional tension as a necessary condition without which love cannot develop remained unknown to most psychologists, but not to the poets. I can prove that it was discovered hundreds of years ago, but it was not rediscovered by modern psychology.*

In the early nineteen hundreds there appeared a number of popular stories in which the hero and oftener the heroine fell first in hate and then in love with the same person. That is a pattern which exaggerates, simplifies and cheapens the emotional process. It does not consider its complexity and many-sidedness. These stories disguise rather than reveal the fact that unconscious envy and competitiveness are the seeds from which the antagonism sprouts; that it appears when the hero, or heroine,

---

* Here are two representative instances: La Rochefoucauld understood this emotional condition better than modern psychology as is shown in his *Maximes* (1665): "If love is judged by its effects, it resembles hate more than friendship." In the *Table-Talks* by S. T. Coleridge, written more than a hundred years ago, is the profound sentence: "Sympathy constitutes friendship, but in love there is a sort of antipathy or opposing passion. Each strives to be the other."

fails to take possession of or dominate the other reluctant figure. They deserve our attention, however, because they show that their writers felt vaguely that dislike or even hatred is nearer to love than a mild liking or sympathy. Often you will even find in these unpretentious love stories a description of the emotion that I characterized as the challenge of the object. However false and sentimental they sound, however melodramatically presented they may be, they contain scenes that prove that what becomes love did not always start on friendly terms; that romance often starts as distinct antipathy and that it frequently takes the form of a contest, of a clash of wills.

Does this subterranean hate cease to exist when love governs the hour? No, it only disappears as some rivers do which reappear again at another and distant place. In lovers' quarrels it is really love that has the character of an interlude, while hostility remains the principal action of the play. And is not love often changed again into hatred as it perishes? If earth has no rage like love to hatred turned, it is only the reinforced power of the original emotion which was swept away by affection.

Of course love need not develop from envy and hostility. There are other fields of action for these repressed emotions, but they are the unconscious perquisites for deep affection. In other words, if you cannot hate you cannot love. If you cannot bite you cannot kiss. If you cannot curse you cannot bless. Who cannot be a good hater will be a poor lover.

The balance between these powers remains very delicate, the transition from one to the other an easy one. Love excludes hostility only on the surface; in reality it includes it. The opposite of it is not hostility but indifference, and the transition from it to love is more difficult than from a grudge and a resentment. The danger of falling in love is not past when you think you hate a person. It can be there when you see a vamp or a vixen in a woman, or when you call a man a scoundrel or a swine in your thoughts. The danger is past when you see permanently a man or a woman as other people see her or him. He may remain attractive as a devil, it is true, but not as a mediocrity. I once heard a woman say, "Whenever I do not hate him, I love him dearly."

Our old wrong concept of love brings us unnecessary unhappiness and causes much misery as long as we are young. We are then very intolerant of feelings of resentment and hatred that sometimes rise in us against beloved persons. We feel that such an emotion has no right to exist beside our strong affection, even for a few minutes. We are afraid that the appearance of so unwelcome a guest seriously endangers our feelings of affection. But to feel angry or hostile sometimes toward a person does not mean that you do not love her or him any more.

This mistaken impression is only due to our wrong idea of affection and to our secret conceit, as if we were more than weak human beings. We have no right to imagine ourselves patterns of virtue, so noble that there cannot be hostility and resentment in us besides affection. We have to make allowances not only for the human frailties of others, but also for our own. No one of us is meant to be or to become Jesus Christ or the Holy Virgin. To be so intolerant toward one's own hostilities and resentments reveals a secret arrogance. Men are no angels and least of all are they angels of peace. Hostility remains the sleeping but active partner of love. When you come down to the very heart of the problem you realize that it is rather difficult to like those whom you love.

6

Before we proceed a few words of caution and consideration are in place. They seem appropriate as we approach the turning point of this thesis, but they apply as well to its preceding part. Whenever we talk about unconscious processes we run the risk of transferring qualities and peculiarities of our conscious thinking and feeling to a field that is very different. We cannot help using expressions and words taken from our conscious life in de-

scribing what happens in this underground realm because we
have no other words at our disposal. It remains, however, an unsatisfactory attempt to grasp something that almost eludes our
efforts. The meaning we give to the words is only approximately
correct, as a translation from a foreign language cannot give all
connotations that words had in the original.

The profound difference between the conscious and unconscious processes that makes the translation so inadequate has always to be considered. When I say that there is at first a grudge
and a hostility against the love-object I should really add: if we
could translate what takes place in the region of repressed impulses into the language of conscious emotions these words come
nearest to the meaning of the process. This "almost" characteristic of the interpretation does not justify wrong or absurd trans-
lations. There is no such thing as a full mastery of the idioms, of
the unconscious, and those who boast of their command of these
prehistoric dialects are like persons "who can speak nonsense in
different languages."

But even the admission that the description has necessarily
an "almost" characteristic does not cover all our failings. We
should have to add every time that the existence and activity of
a certain thought or impulse includes at the same time the presence and activity of the opposite in the unconscious process. Opposites do not exclude each other on this level of primitive thinking. It is as if when you say "without" the word could mean
simultaneously "with" and "without," or when you say "I hate
you" it could also mean "I love you." The unconscious hostility
we have just discussed in the prephases of love also means attraction and beginning affection. There are other peculiarities of unconscious processes which we should bear in mind; for instance,
the facility with which transitions from one idea to another are
made, the transferring of whole trends of thoughts to another
field that seems remote. Consider the easy transition from the
wish to be like a person to the wish to possess that person, to in-
corporate his qualities and accomplishments.

When we thus translate unconscious or, better said, repressed thoughts or impulses into the language of our everyday life, we exaggerate their intensity because only in this way can they become visible. I do not mean here that we exaggerate their emotional efficiency, but we make them larger, we magnify them. In the same way the most virulent bacilli with which we compared the emotion of envy and jealousy in the initial phases of affection are invisible and can only be observed through a microscope. In our description of what takes place unconsciously before love we have to use such magnifying glasses in order to view these developments on an enlarged scale, otherwise they would remain imperceptible. When we remove the powerful glass of analysis unconscious emotions of envy, jealousy and possessiveness pale into insignificance; but as we know very well in the case of the bacilli they are efficient and important enough.

What happens to the tension within the person, to the waves of hostility he unconsciously feels toward his object? Of course there is the almost instinctive reaction to get rid of the emotional pressure. The ego tries to expel the image of the beloved-hated person which is such a welcome-unwelcome intruder and disturbs, annoys, stirs us up and irritates us. The ego attacks this image, wants to expel the new usurper who threatens to govern every thought, to direct every emotion and to change the whole inner household. We vaguely foresee that if this idea or ideal is not driven out it will take possession of everything we are and have. It will govern our soul in a totalitarian manner.

An attempt is made to eliminate the beloved person whose aloofness has increased her attraction. The wrestling with the object is like a fight with a demon in the darkness. What takes place there in the depths is a regular attack undertaken with much vigor and bravery and supported by all the weapons of wounded pride. The emotional independence of the ego is threatened and it is ready to defend its freedom with all energy, to drive the invader out. The assault is made to deprive the object of its superiority, to besmirch its image, to bring all its ugly aspect to the fore and to tear it down. The battle rages within the person, who is in most cases not aware of it.

The intruder cannot easily be expelled. The image stubbornly defends the ground that it has won in us. The notion of its excellent qualities and endowments, which aroused our admiration and envy, remains unshaken. The aim of the psychical battle is the elimination or destruction of the object inside ourselves. It has to be ejected or to be incorporated, otherwise we are afraid that we may be unable to call our soul our own any more. The furious attack on the object within ourselves may have the character of a sudden revolt or that of a bitter struggle which can continue for a long time. It may take the form of complete annihilation of or a lingering doubt about the value of the object.

If the usurping image has not consolidated its position within the ego the assault may be successful. The charge overwhelms the image and love will not develop. For the moment the ego feels some relief as if it had been freed from a dark menace. Then the old dissatisfaction returns, the previous discomfort within oneself is there again. The ego has saved its independence in the life-and-death struggle, but now the individual feels again alone and out in the cold. The emotional situation is similar to the one that a little girl imagined when she saw a single sparrow hopping about in the snow. The little girl shouted, "Look, Mother, at the poor little bird! It hasn't got a cage!"

But what happens in those other cases, in the majority of instances in which the process does not result in indifference or dislike but develops into love and tenderness? It is very simple to describe. The attack has failed, the revolt is defeated and the powers of the aggressor have been considerably weakened. The invader has been hurled back with great losses. This is the turning point of the underground events. The repulsed attack does not leave the ego in the same situation as before. It has exhausted the ego's offensive power. But the short, violent, or long, bitterly contested struggle has also weakened the ego's capability of defending itself. It is just at this moment that the counterattack starts.

It is a critical hour in the history of a soul, and one which makes history for the individual and his emotional development.

The great counterwave makes rapid headway. The receding powers of the ego are pursued and decidedly beaten by this counterthrust. Speaking without figures: the failure of the hostile and aggressive tendencies to reach their aim is followed by a reaction and overreaction of tenderness and longing for the object. The pendulum now swings very far the other way. The revolt against the intruder, the attempt to get rid of the subtle chains which held the individual prisoner, has failed and love has won. The image of the object, more glamorous than before, now governs the emotional life. The dark and delightful picture, which before was at the back of the person's heart and mind, is now in full light. It becomes an obsession, and the lover's thoughts are occupied with it not only when the object is present but also and even more so when it is absent. Nothing can stop him any longer, there is no fear nor hesitation now. A power stronger than his conscious will drives him forward and lets him seek out the nearness of the loved person. Her shyness makes him bold, and her reticence cannot prevent him from conquering. The wave of rebellion that welled up from hidden sources is engulfed in the overpowering undertow. The reaction against the uprising of unconscious hostility becomes victorious. All resistance is swept aside. A complete reversal takes place with all signs of a purification, an upheaval with the character of a catalysis. The affection born from so powerful a reaction will increase on the rebound.

The idea that love results from a counterreaction to the activity of repressed envy and hostility is so remote to all current concepts of psychology that it is difficult to formulate it in the precise terms of psychological language. It is not doubt or lack of courage that makes us hesitate but the very character of the concept never before formulated. Here are the two conclusions at which we have arrived, and which in my opinion are inescapable.

Love is not originated in the sexual urge but belongs to the realm of the ego-drives.

Love is in its essential nature an emotional reaction-formation to envy, possessiveness and hostility.

This characterization covers all kinds of love, infatuation and passion, tenderness for one's wife, friendship and love of one's neighbor. All these are founded on the overcoming of envy and the will to dominate, of hostility and jealousy. We understand that the accent has to be laid on the triumph over these unconscious emotions, on the intensity of the counterreaction to them or on the decisiveness of the victory of the opposite feelings.

Looking back we wonder how we could have failed to see this for so long. What else could love be? Only consider love's character and its most strongly marked features, those which signify its very nature. They are all expressions of the opposite traits that belong to the realm of envy, hostility and destructiveness. Real love does not know envy. It rejoices in the happiness, achievements and fine qualities of the object. Love is not hostile but the supreme expression of tenderness. The characteristics of the reaction are so marked and so much in the foreground that we cannot even imagine how it could have been different. Victory was so triumphant that it seems as if there had never been a fight. The regime of love is so uncontested and incontestable that no one thinks it was wrested from an enemy.

We know many similar reaction-formations in psychology and psychopathology. Frequently an intense emotion is not replaced by a balanced state but swings over into an even stronger opposite feeling. It seems that new reinforcements, gathered during the action, strengthen the coming reaction, that the counterblow becomes more powerful than the original one. Thus an unconscious impulse of cruel satisfaction often turns into pity and compassion. A depression is overcome by a manic mood. Love itself in the realm of normal psychology shows all the signs of such a manic attitude. It is the most important reaction-formation in human emotions that we know.

Thus, "I love you" does not mean, "I do not hate you" but, "I have reversed all my hostile emotions and domineering feelings and have turned them into tenderness for you." The Arabs and the Palestinian Jews greet each other with the word *"Schalom"* which means "Peace" or, "May peace be with you." It is an expression of friendship and good will, but it was originally an assurance that there were no aggressive and hostile intentions on the part of the speaker.

It is not unlikely that what is now only an unconscious process once took place in the conscious mind in those prehistoric times in which during thousands of years the birth and growth of love in society was taking shape. What happens now to human emotions was perhaps once a succession of events, a clash of wills, a contest that was followed by affection. There are traces of such a development left. Many deep and lifelong friendships in the old sagas were cemented between two knights only after they had first been engaged in bitter single combat. The beginning of friendship among adolescent men of our own time strikes us sometimes as an echo of such early developments. And is it not sometimes a clash of wills which precedes love between the sexes? Did not Isolde want to kill Tristan? The scene in which she draws the sword and has to drop it, overwhelmed by the dark counterwave, works upon us like an illustration of those conflicts which are in all of us but do not break through to the conscious surface. Before they yield to tenderness and affection there are aggressive and murderous wishes and impulses against the loved and hated object. We have arrived here at the most secret place in the realm of the underground region. There is a skeleton in the cupboard of the vault and it is the mate's body. The unparalleled miracle that romantic love performs is that of bringing this body not only back to life but to a transfigured and radiant life such as it never had before.

7

To describe how it feels to be in love cannot be our task. We have to leave that subject to the lovers and poets. We cannot describe the miraculous change that the entrance of love works in a person, we can only try to understand why it came about and put it in psychological terms. Our curiosity wants to know what happened there and what became of the emotional tendencies that we met before. How did the new state change the ego? What was the destiny of the initial dissatisfaction with oneself, the discomfort or discord? Where is now the phantom of an ideal ego? What became of all that envy and jealousy, those strong drives within the ego? Do possessiveness and hostility still exist under the new regime? Did love really conquer all or is there an underground movement left? We know that a great reaction has swept all these emotions away, a flood has submerged them. They have disappeared. But does that mean that they are not there any more, or only that they do not appear?

As far as the realm of conscious feelings and emotions reaches the overpowering reaction has been complete, but part of the old impulses has remained indestructible in the unconscious. The Flying Dutchman of the old saga will be redeemed if loved by a woman. The miracle of elation blots everything else out. It is like a revelation to find yourself in love, as if you had turned a corner in a dark maze and find the exit staring you in the face. The feeling that results from it has very few analogies in emotional life. The certainty of salvation in religious feelings is comparable to it. It gives a similar internal peace, sureness and self-confidence to the true believer. As with God in religion, so the figure of the beloved person grows to gigantic proportions while the ego dwindles and diminishes. Or rather the ego is almost absorbed in this larger ego, grows in it and with it. There are only small survivals of the previous lack of faith, of the old defeatism left. They are restricted to occasional fears that one will not be worthy of the object. They are like a faint echo of the original diffidence. This faintheartedness has not the character of inferiority but of modesty before the object. "If I were you and you were I, how could I love you, say?" By a play of fancy the lover changes places here with his sweetheart and for the life of him he cannot see what she loves in him or what could be lovable about him. If the situation were reversed he could not love a person like himself. With this exception, the lover feels self-confident and filled with courage. He wants to be cleverer, nobler, more gifted than he is only for the sake of the object. He has not the feeling that he is loved because he deserves it but despite the fact that he has no merit. He wants to grow and become a better man to please the love-object.

There can be a remnant of a feeling of inferiority but only with regard to the beloved. Portia says:

> You see me, Lord Bassanio, where I stand,
> Such as I am: though for myself alone
> I would not be ambitious in my wish,
> To wish myself much better; yet, for you
> I would be trebled twenty times myself:
> A thousand times more fair, ten thousand times
> More rich;
> That only to stand high in your account,
> I might in virtues, beauties, livings, friends,
> Exceed account, but the full sum of me,
> Is sum of something, which, to term in gross
> Is an unlessoned girl, unschool'd, unpractised.

There is this sense of a new humbleness in the lover, while at the same time he is self-confident. Sometimes a woman even daydreams that she becomes more beautiful, much more glamorous for her love-object. There are occasional renewals of those old fantasies of a better and more attractive ego; images of how one would like to look, clear embodiments of oneself which the lover would look at with enchanted eyes. This humility does not exclude a new feeling of self-confidence while the center of gravity is in the person of the beloved. It excludes it as little as religious submissiveness to God shuts out a certainty of resting in His grace and of being sure of His kindness. A new freedom is in the person who loves. I once heard a lady say, "When I drink wine it does not make me say things I should not. It makes me, on the con-

trary, say things which I ought to have said but did not dare to."
That is exactly the spirit of the new courage that waives all other
claims and erases all debts. Every state of love is accompanied by
such a tonic change within the ego. It is not a glandular factor
that has transformed the person but an emotional change that
makes the glands work differently.

It is not true that the miracle happens only in imagination.
Look at a woman before and after she falls in love. She is a
changed person and the effect is such that no beauty salon could
have produced it. Or look at a man who is not even in love but
merely infatuated. He stands straighter, looks younger, feels
surer. There is a vibrant vivacity of well-being about him. When
in love one feels on top of the world and it seems that nothing
ill can happen to one. A hidden light seems to burn in one which
is not only the fire of passion. It is as if the lover feels invulnerable against the slings and arrows of outrageous fortune. There
is a springing motion about him, an evidence of full life. He
feels not only alive but newborn; he feels a new life so exultant
and full of power that he does not walk but floats on air. In the
state of dissatisfaction and discord preceding love the person
struggled for a philosophy of life that could console him and
strengthen his confidence. But now he has no need of that. Young
Romeo, whom the Friar comforts with "adversity's sweet milk,
philosophy," shouts, "Hang up, philosophy! Unless philosophy
make a Juliet."

Nothing is newborn in love. It cannot alter one's inherent
nature, but it can develop latent gifts and bring out into the
open what is best in a person. Dante is thus psychologically
justified when he records his first sight of Beatrice with the
words, "*Incipit Vita Nuova.*" For him it was an emotional rebirth, it worked a regeneration.

But how is that possible? The dissatisfaction that was the
psychological preparation for the whole development often made
the person wish to change his being, to get rid of his personality
and to turn into another. Love has fulfilled this desire and not
only by means of the change in himself. Love has taken away

the heavy burden of self from him. It has unselfed him, freed him from the pressure of carrying himself around with him. By its magic transformation redemption is worked, for which only the idea of salvation gives us an equivalent. The deep inner satisfaction of a troubled person who has found peace in God, who can trust his conflicts and destiny to God's care, corresponds to the emotional situation of the lover. "Restless is our heart until it reposes in Thee," says St. Augustine, who proclaimed the immediate efficacy of grace. The lover can thus speak to the beloved. The emotional upsurge in him is in great part due to his being able to rid himself of the conflict with which he has been loaded since childhood.

God is the supreme and universal ego-ideal of a tribe, of a nation and of a great part of mankind. Likewise the beloved becomes the embodiment of the ego-ideal of a single person. It took the place of this phantom. The conflict that haunted us so long even when we were not aware of it—and especially when we were not aware of it—has ceased to exist for the time being. There is bliss in self-forgetfulness, as there is in giving oneself entirely to religion and into the hands of God without reservation. A new stream of emotional life results from the ending of the inner tension. Romantic love is a faith in which we relax and repose, and its appearance is a revelation as overwhelming in its effect as a miracle vouchsafed to us from above. The person feels chosen as the true believer, as if something had borne him away from his griefs and troubles. When asked how he is, he need not even answer "excellent" or "very fine" but "it does not concern me," because his I, his ego, is somewhere else, it has melted and become merged in another person. It is not an identification with this other; it is rather a disappearance of the most troublesome part of the ego and a substitution by the beloved who becomes the center of him. She is a superlative ego which fills the person with a new sense of personal value, expands his personality, gives him self-confidence. No one can say "I love you" who feels as a nobody. You have to regain yourself before you can give yourself away. In this sense to love means to become what one wants to be.

Every deep change in ourselves changes also the outside world for us. It changes with us. After a religious conversion all things become meaningful and the grace and beauty of God's creation is in them. Likewise, all things and all persons appear in a new light and acquire a new dignity when you are in love, all seem friendly and to have a hidden meaning. There is no place in you for indifference toward them any more. I have described how the essence of happiness in love is conditioned by liberation from the troublesome and sometimes even quarrelsome ideal ego, the suspension of the tyranny of the self through finding the ideal embodied again in the mate. It is a loss in the sense of getting rid of a burden and a gain in finding the fulfillment of hopes almost relinquished. The second ego is not a substitute and continuation of one's actual self, it is its extension, enlargement and enrichment. The ego-ideal disappears when you are in love. It disappears in its fulfillment. All rays are collected into the one focus of the beloved person. The ego has broken its shell. There are still some faint echoes reminding one of a previous state in which not a living person but an image governed the hour. The lover sometimes feels that it is a dream, that it cannot be true. It is not a dream; it is true, but it *was* a dream. You do not compare dream figures later on with living persons, but sometimes living persons remind you of a dream which you had. It is like that here because the fantasy was there before the object appeared. There is also no comparison with other objects because the standard for such a comparison is lacking. I do not see why love is sometimes called an "egoism *en deux*." It is rather an "idealism *en deux*," the fulfillment of the ideals of two persons.

This feeling of oneness in two persons, of an emotional unity, is a strange phenomenon when you consider that it sprang from a situation of discord. A house divided against itself became a unit by the very process of being joined with another house. Originally there was an insistence on the frontiers of the ego, an unwillingness to give oneself up, a deadly terror of the loss of one's individuality and precious singularity. Now it seems as if it is this very surrender that promises salvation and that keeping one's person anxiously for oneself means spiritual danger. St. Luke's paradox is in place here. "Whosoever will save his life shall lose it; but whosoever will lose his life for my sake, the same shall save it." Persons in passionate love do not insist on their rights and mights any more. They assure us that they are not two but one. This fusion of two personalities, this fading away of the boundary lines between the individuals has been celebrated by thousands of poets. Here is a beautiful instance from the far Orient. Kuan Tao-Sheng, the wife of the great Chinese painter Chao Mang-Fu, felt that her husband had withdrawn his affection from her and bestowed it upon a mistress. She wrote this poem:

> Take a lump of clay,
> Wet it, pat it,
> Make a statue of you
> And a statue of me
> Then shatter them, clatter them,
> Add some water,
> And break them and mold them
> Into a statue of you
> And a statue of me.
> Then in mine, there are bits of you
> And in you there are bits of me.
> Nothing ever shall keep us apart.

How well this poem describes the interchange of the images or statues into a fusion of two persons! Chao Mang-Fu was so touched by the poem that he turned his affection again to his wife.

We do not forget that this merging is the most tender form of taking possession of the other person, even though it accompanies the surrender of oneself. In this roundabout way the individual has fulfilled his original desire to own the other person or to be the other person. He has thus also reached the other aim: to be released from the prison cell of his own individuality, to be dismissed from his solitary confinement as long as his passion lasts. He has found ego-fulfillment and ego-completion in the form of a *"pénétration pacifique"* in which the I and You are becoming fused. It is possessiveness on its highest plane that here performs the miracle of making one individual out of two. Marie de France felt it: *"Ni moi sans vous, ni vous sans moi."*

This sense of the indivisibility of love has even the power to change the connotation of everyday words. "You" and "I" become interchangeable and "we" may turn into the singular pronoun. There is a peculiar change in the attitude to one's name, which is the result of the metamorphosis of the person. A name is unconsciously considered as an essential part of us, which we appreciate highly. We are sensitive to its distortion in pronunciation and spelling and we do not like having it confused with another name, as if a piece of our individuality were contained in it. We observe then with astonishment that passionate love is willing to renounce this privilege of a name as if the expression of a separated personality is of no value any more. "Isolde is no more, Tristan no more, and no name can any longer part us." This declaration reveals the tendency to break down the wall of separation that is signified by the different names of the lovers. It is not accidental that the same desire to remove the name as a symbolical frontier of individuality appears again in Shakespeare's play. Juliet speaks:

> Tis but thy name that is mine enemy;
> Thou art thyself, though not a Montague.
>> O, be some other name!

Romeo would be himself were he not Romeo call'd.

> Retain thy dear perfection which owes
> Without that title. Romeo, doff thy name
> And for that name which is no part of thee
> Take all myself.

Romeo is immediately ready. He wants to be new baptized, henceforth he never will be Romeo.

> My name, dear saint, is hateful to myself,
> Because it is an enemy to thee;
> Had I it written, I would tear the word.

In those two love tragedies, which show how hatred is turned into passion, appears the same eagerness to lose one's name as if it were the symbol of separation. But the name of the other is also a dear and endearing sound and will be repeated in thoughts a thousand times. It will be called, it will be invoked, as a god by his name is implored. It is a "silver-sweet sound" pronounced by the other. The name is thus the bridge between the lovers that brings them nearer to each other. But it is also the abyss that separates them. The name not only signifies the other. It is also a symbol that he remains the other in spite of all efforts to unite, to become one. It symbolizes the impossibility and the agony that they are powerless to surmount the barriers of individuality. They wish so much to be one but remain two. They remain separate even in the most intimate union. They tremble at the thought of separation, but are they together, has love achieved the miracles of oneness?

Not only are the lovers remodeled, but all things are, by passion. All become charming because he or she is under a charm. Not only he who loves, but the whole world loves a lover. His sensitiveness has been sharpened and he feels as if a new world is open to him which he had never seen nor heard of. Nothing is trivial and stale. Everything is new to him and nature itself has the unique imprint of his passion. He felt for so long like a stranger in this world and now he feels at home again. He rediscovers it. Sounds and sights gain a new significance or regain an old one that was long lost. Everyone seems to nod in a friendly way to him and to recognize him. All appear lovable because he loves. The world is unfolding itself to him. He feels an insider of it with an overflowing affection for all that lives.

There is again the analogy to the reverential and adoring attitude
of the worshiper who admires the beauty and profound sense of
God's creation in all things, the greatest and smallest. It would
be possible to compare the all-love in which St. Francis of Assisi
includes all things, even lice, with Romeo's view of the world.
As God sanctifies all of His creation for the one, so Juliet's presence transfigures everything "and every cat and dog and little
mouse, every unworthy thing, live here in heaven and may look
on her." In this intoxication of souls and senses people and
things appear as if they become known anew. Everything is
touched with the new life that corresponds to the one in the
lover and ennobles all objects.

Time and place gain a new significance as if they borrow their
significance from the love-object and from it alone. It seems as
if our ideas of time and place change with the new ego-attitude.
The sense of time is controlled by the presence or the absence
of the object.

We have already said that the ego-ideal is fulfilled in the person
who is loved. The drive to achieve it oneself is not dead, it is
only dulled. The discontent, the timidity and the displeasure with
oneself have disappeared. A new dignity has taken place in the
lover. Possessiveness and greed have been renounced, but a part
of these emotions has reached its aim, by a detour. Love itself
is a blend of tenderness and domination, of surrender to and
taking possession of the object.

What happens to envy and jealousy? When the emotional
reaction-movement reached flood tide it swept those impulses
away in a mounting, encircling wave of tenderness. They are as
conspicuous by their absence as the contrary tendencies by their
presence and prominence. The last remnant of the sense of
property expresses itself sometimes in an unwillingness to share
the company of the object with others. The deep and hard compulsion of envy gave way to the desire to give and to enjoy the
gifts and achievements of the mate, the second and better self.
You cannot be envious of yourself. Where before you begrudged
the other her privileges, now you feel pleasure in her pleasure,

joy in her enjoyment. The object stirred you up before, now it cheers you up. You were tongue-tied before, you are eloquent now. Now you are not only interested in her being but in her well-being. Instead of feeling jealous of her superior qualities you are proud of them, as if they were your own now. They are felt as your own.

You often hear that the perfection of love lies in the fact that it is so "exquisitely unselfish." That is very debatable. It should not be discussed in a dialectic manner but by psychological research. The touchstone of love is not the absolute absence of hostility or cruelty but of envy and greediness. It is not a decisive criterion when you feel grief at the suffering of a person who is near to you. There is grief and pain in pity, which is not love. We can feel those emotions for people whom we do not care for. In my opinion love on its highest and most passionate level is entirely selfish as long as you feel the other person as an integral part of yourself. It is not an altruistic feeling in me when I enjoy the enjoyment of a beloved person. It is the same joy that I feel if I imagine giving pleasure to someone dear to me. When I am prevented from giving pleasure to my mate it is as if pleasure were withheld from me. It is not true that we enjoy the pleasure by proxy. We enjoy it ourselves, but this self is changed, it has incorporated the other person.

While our primitive wish is to take away what the other has and what we covet, the desire in passionate love is to give and give. An insatiable thirst for it results in the miracle that it is more blessed to give than to receive. The pursuit of the happiness of the other has become your happiness. Who could ask for anything more? Juliet feels that her bounty is:

> . . . as boundless as the sea
> My love as deep; the more I give thee
> The more I have, for both are infinite.

He who hates is furious because he cannot take away, cannot deprive the other of the things he wishes. He who loves is grateful when he may give. We have arrived here at the very criterion of profound love. It is not whether I allow another person a thing that I love myself but whether I enjoy having the other person have it more than having it myself. The negative proof of it may easily be found. When I enjoy something less without her it is because I and she do not have it simultaneously. My pleasure is diminished by the regret that she is not present to enjoy the same music, the same play. It would be incorrect to say that I want to share the pleasure with the beloved because that would presuppose that each one of us has a share in it or of it. That would mean separating and apportioning it. I do not share the joy with the other one, but I have and I feel her pleasure as my own.

The psychology of love makes even the odd fact possible that I enjoy something which I am ordinarily indifferent to because the beloved enjoys it. The difference in these cases can be clearly felt. You go with your children to a puppet show that is childish or stupid, but you are not aware of it. You enjoy it because they do. You hear them laugh at the jokes and your heart goes out to them. (There are two kinds of immortal music: the tunes of the great masters and the uninhibited laughter of small children.) Compare this situation with an opportunity that comes your way to attend a children's matinee, unwillingly. It is possible that you will be infected by the hearty laughter of the children here, too, and enjoy the performance with them, but here is a clear case of identification. You share the children's feelings, but you don't have their feelings. You feel superior to them even while you enjoy the spectacle, a feeling entirely foreign to love. In the one case you share in their enjoyment, in the other, you enjoy it together. This "together" signifies the particular character of affection. It is one of the most magic English words.

Here is another instance that illustrates the difference in feeling-tone. A hostess enjoys having her guests think that the dinner she prepares for them is excellent. She enjoys the food with them. In love you yourself enjoy in imagination a magnificent dish that the beloved eats. It is not a shared but an entirely selfish pleasure. The food she eats does not make you satisfied, but her enjoyment of it makes you happy. Who asserts that love is altruistic is sadly mistaken. It is as selfish as breathing, but this self has changed, it has incorporated another being.

It seems that conscious envy is the emotion that is entirely incompatible with love or deep affection, a fact which, I think, is highly significant for their character and origin. Here the countermove or the reaction has reached its peak in a kind of reversal of the original tendencies that were rejected. The lover is grateful that he is able to give. He thanks her for receiving his offerings. Giving means both taking and spending. Therefore the idea of sacrifice is foreign to the spirit of highest love. Making a sacrifice means giving up something to another person although you cherish it. The purest love cherishes a thing only in so far as it can be a possession of the beloved object. The figure of the self-sacrificing or self-effacing lover is thus a contradiction in itself when we apply the highest standard to love. A deed felt as a sacrifice does not mean true love. When the lover sees a sacrifice and a merit in his action in behalf of the object the gold is already debased with less noble metals. But such an alloy is perhaps unavoidable in everyday use, just as it is in such objects of gold as rings and bracelets.

Hostility became merged in tenderness, but a part of it remains intact. Mixed formations like lovers' quarrels, violence interrupting gentleness, belong to this realm. Not the absence of hostility but that of envy within one's affection decides how deeply one is in love.

It is the mixture of pride and humbleness which signifies first love. A young, beautiful girl who was unusually restrained in her shyness tried to describe to me once how love entered her life. Not many sentences had been said between the young people, but afterwards they walked hand in hand through the streets as if drunk. She felt that her heart expanded and was peaceful. Everything seemed resolved, she could suddenly answer the questions which had troubled her. Events and things which had been meaningless became full of significance. There was a world open, common to their relationship. She could not say what she felt, but he said the things she had thought as if he were a mind reader. "I did not consider any more whether it was wrong or right to kiss him good night. It did not matter, nothing matters any more." She had promised to write him first because he had to leave for camp. She could not write. After she had gone to bed and turned off the light she could tell him in the dark what she felt, "I shall change in many ways, but I shall always love you."

Some days later she could not stand it any longer. "Oh, mother!" she cried and told what had happened to her young life. But then she spoke of the doubts she often felt whether she really loved the young man, that she knew that he had many weaknesses, she was not certain any more. The mother listened quietly and said then, "These doubts pass. Have only faith in yourself!" Who revealed to the woman, who was not very clever otherwise, the secret, unknown to our psychologists, that in order to love you have to be self-confident and that doubts of one's affection often means diffidence in oneself?

<h2 style="text-align:center">8</h2>

It has been said that the proof of the pudding is not in the eating, but is evident some hours later. Time will tell whether it was love or a passing infatuation; but time will also tell what real love is. And why should love not change in a world in which everything changes and in which life is impossible without change? The idea of permanence, of sameness of character is also fantastic in the realm of love. In evaluating this emotion as one of the main sources of human happiness the observer should realize its power and its limitations. However, he should not make its value dependent on its duration. The length of time it lasts is not its criterion. Those philosophers who attribute the quality of permanence to it make the same mistake as a Labour leader in the House of Commons who gave an apparently endless speech. The chairman, Lord Snell, afterward remarked, "Speeches to be immortal need not be eternal." You sometimes get the impression that lovers often have to compensate for the unconsciously foreshadowed, insufficient, short space of time given them by the intensity of their passion. Romeo and Juliet's love lasted only a few days, Tristan and Isolde's only some weeks. Who dares to say that theirs was only a passing infatuation and not true love?

Unlike the work of other psychologists I did not start my investigation from the character of love but from what preceded it. I hoped to make its character transparent in describing where it came from. In my description of its prephases I showed the soil in which its seed was planted, the silent life of those roots as they pushed upward, the struggle to break through the resisting dark earth and then the manner in which love put forth buds, unfolded and flowered. The character of its blossoming is to be contrasted to that of its blight. The nature of its fading tells us as much about this precious flower as we learned from our study of its earliest phases. What contradicts love brings about its decay and throws light upon its origin. The way in which it withers and shrivels, its anticlimax, demonstrates in reverse how it started, sprang into existence and reached its bloom. What precedes and succeeds it is more instructive than its blossom. Its end is in its beginnings.

In this concept love appeared as a great emotional reaction-formation. Affection reached its aim after a violent internal struggle from which it emerged triumphant over a powerful adversary. There was a true melee in which it was difficult for a time to decide who was foe and who was friend. The opponent was defeated, but he never really capitulated. It would be trivial to say that love is no static state, but it is important to realize that love gained its supremacy against stubborn resistance and still has to be defended against sudden attacks of the old enemy. When love dies it succumbs to the increasing power of these attacks from within. The lover passes down the same trail that he came up. The end may be a long and dreary process of decline and decay; it may come as a sudden collapse. It may be relatively painless and it may mean torment and agony. It is sometimes just as much of a struggle as the initial fight that saw the victory of love, a struggle in which the whole being is thrown into dislocation, convulsion and uproar. It is cruel toward the object if the process of withdrawal is pitilessly performed and sometimes even more cruel if it is planned with pity. The old bacteria have become virulent, are working on the material of love, which they disintegrate and destroy.

It is the picture of a retrograde development and confirms a psychological law which I formulate thus: all emotional formations tend to run back over the road of their development to their origin. The observer can recognize that the backward movement passes through the same phases which he saw in the opposite direction. It sometimes seems as if the one or the other state were skipped, but this wrong impression results from the unconscious character of the whole process, which has a remarkable speed.

Most people are inclined to think that the lover experiences a disappointment or disillusionment with regard to his object, that he realizes suddenly that he and she are not well mated. He became quickly rich, so to speak, and is now suddenly impoverished. But even if it were true that the object is responsible for the changed feelings, that cannot be the only factor. It oversimplifies the situation. In many cases the love-object did not change considerably. Yet the eyes looking at it see new and unpleasant features or do not see the old ones any more which were charming and fascinating. It can sometimes be proved that the same qualities that were felt as most attractive are now hateful, even repulsive. The object need not really have changed. The image of it has. What has broken the spell?

This image was once so powerful that either we were unaware of the blemishes of the person or considered them almost irrelevant. Besides, there were so many superior qualities that they far outweighed the slight defects and failings. The lover was not critical before. He did not want to reform the object even when he was conscious of defects because love in blossom time does not wish to change anything in the beloved. He ignored the little imperfections or saw them only as trifles. With an ideal image in his mind he adorned his love with a complete array of attributes; and he comes away with a changed image. The development proceeds slowly, almost imperceptibly, or in leaps and bounds. Now he picks on every little thing, frets and fusses about minor mistakes. Is he disappointed in the object, who is human after all and not a deity? Certainly, but that is not all. He is pulled back to reality. But what happens to the image, the ideal and better self? There are two possibilities that must be differentiated. The first is the separation between the image and the actual person of the beloved. The second is the replacement of the one image by another image.

In the earliest phases when love started, the idea of the real object had to fight with the image that was already there before the beloved appeared on the scene. As a result the picture of the actual person was changed by imagination, remodeled in conformance with the preexistent image until the two coincided. Now just the reverse process takes place. The concept of the real object, the realization of what he or she actually is, slowly or suddenly begins to separate itself from the image. It stands now beside the previous idealization and soon will be painfully contrasted with it. The likeness of the woman as you see her now is no longer identical with the image that you had of her before. But that does not necessarily mean that she has really changed very much. As long as this image persists love stays with incredible tenacity. Love does not give up its internal position easily. It defends it stubbornly against the new emotions and often even against reason. The lover then thinks of a person, speaks to a person who is not there any more. But when the separation of the notion of the person from its idealized image is completed love also is gone.

The second case, although similar in its emotional effects, is quite different. It is more intimately connected with a change within the ego of the lover. The sudden or slow end of an affection always marks the failure of a mission. The ego went out to conquer or to fulfill the demands of his ideal self and all its endeavors were directed toward that aim. He found it in the person he loved. He or she personifies the ideal for the time being. This ideal, or rather its picture, is a fragile thing. Psychoanalysts like to emphasize that the ideal is unattainable because it goes beyond the possibilities that a mortal person can achieve. Is it so high that no individual can reach it? That is so; it is no longer human but superhuman. What analysis has failed to see is another side of the ego-ideal, an inner difficulty that makes its full realization impossible. It is this quality which, transferred to the object, brings an inevitable disappointment, partial or complete. The ideal is an unstable mixture of contradictory features. It is this inner contradiction that is brought to light in the fading of love.

Let us say that your ideal object or its image of your sweetheart or your wife was chaste and modest. It happens that she is modest and chaste. But if she were as blameless as Caesar's wife she will not escape your criticism. Why? Because unconsciously you wanted and desired at the same time the great cocotte, the mistress, familiar with all vices. You wanted the license, frivolity or even impudence of the prostitute at the same time, only you did not know it. It might be possible to unite these contradictory traits in the same person but very rarely in the desired proportions. You live on familiar although unconscious terms with these contrary and contradictory qualities which take their turn on the stage of your imagination. It seems that when a person comes near to satisfying the one side of the ideal the desire for another, different from the first and often opposite to it, appears. A girl daydreams of a courageous soldier, a hero, a kind of knight. She finds the fulfillment or embodiment of this image in her real world, but she wants him to be an intellectual, gentle and most considerate man at the same time. Another falls in love with a glamorous lady-killer, a man about town and a charmer, but she discovers in time or too late that the man is not the most loyal husband with eyes for her charms only. No, the ideal is not attainable because no human being can fulfill the exaggerated demands for certain qualities. It is unattainable because it includes so many qualities in their perfect forms that contradict each other and often exclude each other. The situation is complicated by the remarkable psychological fact that only a part of the ideal is known to us, so to speak, only a part of the image is visible, while another is in shadow. There are unconscious traits in this image that we would often not even like if they became discernible.

Is falling out of love really only the result of a disappointment in the beloved person? It is often rather the end of the transference from an image to this person, the withdrawal of it. This process of dissolution of an image of our own fabrication is often concealed behind the claim that the person has changed. There is the other possibility, that the one image is relieved by another and we are unaware of the change that has taken place in us, not in the object. Of course there are cases enough in which the real persons prove to be unsatisfactory objects. There are cases in which change or transformation of character takes place, but there remains the question whether the fading of love is due only to such changes in the chosen object. Perhaps oftener than not alterations in the one who chooses are responsible.

Lovers ask themselves sometimes whether the fault is really theirs and regularly answer, no, the blame is with the other person. Sometimes it is better not to ask yourself this question, for then you will not hear lies about yourself. Are we then justified in supposing that the end of love comes as the certain result of natural laws, that it occurs as inevitably as the sequence of spring, summer and fall, as the ebb and flow of the tide? Or would it be better not to search after this law and to speak as the poet:

> Let this be said between us here;
> One love grows green
> When one turns gray.

This year knows nothing of last year;
Tomorrow has no more to say
To yesterday.

But such a point of view, which belongs to the realm of biological considerations, begs the question which is a purely psychological one. Even if we would admit—which we do not—that
there is such a rhythm similar to that of nature's processes, its
existence would not release us from the obligation to explain
its peculiar psychological manifestations. There is the possibility
that it is not a considerable change in the object that causes the
decay of love, but there must be a change in the subject. It is
an indispensable premise for the emotional development that we
call falling out of love. (Is not this expression just as inappropriate as falling in love? No one falls out of love. One climbs out
of it or jumps out of it, if you like.) We are thus forced to turn
our attention once more to the ego.

Love was a displaced attempt to fulfill the demands of our
ideal ego. This drive took the place of the original striving for
self-perfection. The failure of romantic love, its fading, is to a
great extent due to our being frustrated in the fulfillment of
these demands with the help of another person. If for the moment we exclude that the beloved object was really disappoint-
ing, we are referred back to the emotional situation in the lover.
It was a change in him that made love possible, we remember,
a change almost independent of the character of his object. There
was a discontent in the ego caused by the nonfulfillment of self-
produced ideal claims, by the failure to catch one's own larger
shadow. The beloved person took the place of this ideal ego.
The object has now to meet all the expectations, hopes, and
demands that the ego could not satisfy himself. But this object
is a personality in his or her own right, not merely an instrument for wishful thinking of the lover. We put aside here the
point that the beloved has his or her own hopes, inner demands
and failings. The lover was in deadly need of the object, of this
substitute for his own ego-ideal. All his thoughts and impulses

were directed to get this particular girl. Why is all his desire now concentrated on getting rid of her?

It is difficult to live with her. But was it not difficult to live with himself? He had a hard time with her. But had he an easy time with himself? He needs a heavenly patience to cope with all her shortcomings and failings. But was he so tolerant toward his own? Here appears the psychological doom of high and contradictory ego-claims. They were displaced and transferred to the beloved person, and discontent will follow this transference. For a time it seemed as if love were redemption. It promised and fulfilled suspension of the ego. The emotional conflict stopped, the dissatisfaction with oneself disappeared. But it returns now. It was only shifted to the object and with it one's own imperfections. You are now deeply dissatisfied with her, out of tune with her, as before you were with yourself. The higher the claims on yourself the more difficult it becomes for the object to fulfill them. In cases where no other outlet has been found than that of love, where all hopes have been pinned on this one card, affection is doomed after its promise of redemption for the soul in trouble. If your ideal claims are very high and are concentrated upon your love-object, you cannot find their permanent fulfillment. Those unhappy many who have such high aspirations and put all their hope and emotional energy in love are caught in the web of their own imagination. Those dreams are destined to shrink and fade. Not only is no object capable of realizing them but they cannot be realized by an external object on account of their very nature.

The solution of the emotional problem can be found only in the person himself. No man can forever be concentrated on one person as an ideal. It is a futile chase after a phantom that eludes one. The way necessarily leads from love to renunciation and resignation.

The Midas touch of love turned everything into gold. The withdrawal of love changes the gold to dust again. The criticism of the object is, to the greatest extent, self-criticism displaced to the other person, self-judgment and self-condemnation by proxy. And this judgment will be the harder and more cruel the higher are the unfulfilled demands and claims on oneself. That may seem astonishing, but our daily experience in psychoanalytical practice confirms it.

Thus the falling out of love means really the falling out of a dream, the daydream of a better self. The love object no longer represents the ideal. That means it does not fulfill the ego-ideal whose place it took. The contrast between the image you had of the object and her real personality reflects only the abyss between the ego-ideal and your actual self. In her you now dislike and hate yourself, that part of you which you wanted to get rid of when you fell in love with her. Joseph de Maistre's observation that a battle is lost only because one believes it to be lost may well be applied to the phenomena of love and its results. You must add, however, that battles are won this way too. (Anatole France asserted that Marshal Joffre learned from the newspapers that he had won the Battle of the Marne in the first World War.) Victory, like defeat, in love is of our own making and unmaking.

The change of the ego-ideal plays a decisive role, too, in those cases in which a person turns his affection away from one object to another. This other person now seems to impersonate the unconscious ego-ideal better than the former. After the disappointment the person realizes that love was a fool's paradise. If he followed the good old pattern and searched for salvation in love he perhaps realizes now in his disappointment that he was a damned fool. Deprived of the glory of love, the ego is where it stood before, or almost there. He feels again unworthy. Again he is the prey of discord and depression. He belongs once more to the Have-nots of the earth.

Nature has everywhere a horror of the void, not excluding the emotional sphere. The freedom from want is also desired here. All the person has conquered in love, or almost all, is lost again. The sense of oneness has vanished as if by magic. There are again two separate human beings. Each one of them lives in a private world again from which the other is excluded. The other has become just a man or a woman like any other, nothing more and sometimes even less. They now lead a separate life in which there is no need to share experiences. Life has again become dreary, difficult and joyless. Even during the period of love there would suddenly appear moments of a vague fear, an agony. The lovers felt their powerlessness to surmount the barriers of individuality that divided them, the invisible frontier created by their different natures. The rush and sweep, the passion and power have left their attachment. There were moments before in which they suspected that there is no escape from human solitude. But now they are convinced of it. I am I and you are you, and we shall remain divided. In the end the object appears as a creature about whom you know nothing and in whom you have no interest. There is a wall between you and her. The island self has no permanent connection with the continent.

9

The downgrade movement of love begins with the recurrence of the same phases that comprised the initial one only in reverse order. There is again irritation and resentment against the object, again ill-will that may increase to the degree of unutterable loathing. Love in receding is again nearer to hate than to indifference, and hatred appears as an aftermath as it was the unconscious prelude to love. There is a renewal of the revolt against the emotional dependence on the object. Even within love there were sudden and enigmatic currents of hostility, but they passed quickly like clouds that darken the sun for a few minutes. But now the whole horizon appears gloomy and dark again as before a storm. Again one may observe the attempt to devaluate and depreciate the object, but this attempt is now successful. You repeat in your thoughts the words and actions of the object, feel your pride to be hurt, and the sharp criticism that was swept away by love reappears. Things that charmed you before make you impatient, little habits exasperate you. You want to hurt and sometimes even wish to strike the once loved face. That is the truth and there is no use in trying to gloss over or soften the emotional situation. Cruel and malicious thoughts against the object occur, a longing for revenge and a temptation to sneer.

It is generally remarkable how often and how persistently conscious or unconscious revenge phantasies occur in this phase, as if they had been waiting a long time, as if they had taken all this time to reach the surface. It is as if the person said grimly, "Now it's my turn to make you suffer." Love is again a kind of torment as in the beginning, but not a delightful one any more. An argument or lovers' quarrel is not a passing thing now. It is a link in a chain. It does not merely hurt, it feels like the flaying alive of one's feelings. After having loved and fallen out of love and, after many years of married life, out of sympathy, the picture that Dante paints of the tortures of the damned has no horrors any more. You feel convinced that you could easily put up with hell. There is again the tension in words and in silence. Before, the lovers were wrapped up in each other. They are now chained together. You hear in their conversations the rattling of iron and you realize that the chain is pulled first to one end and then to the other.

If the concept of the origin of love needed further proof it could be found in these end-phases where the old emotions return and the previous tendencies reappear. There is, however, an important difference which is not conditioned by the development and decay of love alone. As in love's first stirrings, when the person tried in vain to escape it, envy, tension and resentment were unconscious. Now, when love fades, the same impulses are present but in most cases reach the conscious level. You feel and know them. Before, you were unwilling to face them, and even now you are reluctant to realize their full impact and import. But you cannot disavow them for long. A certain woman, when asked if she knew another, replied, "Yes, from looking away." You first become aware of those feelings in the same way by looking away from them.

The material of love divides itself into its different ingredients like a compound subjected to certain reagents in a chemical analysis, the antifeelings now becoming consciously contrasted with the original one. In love you were always discovering new and charming qualities and your enthusiasm grew with each new discovery. Now you are always finding new failings and defects and your distaste increases. The striving before was directed toward becoming a unity, one piece; now you want to tear the other to pieces. The heavenly patience in love contrasts with the short temper in its end. Life was colorful, now it is drab again. You felt important and now you feel insignificant. Your personal insecurity has returned. The greater your initial success the more staggering will be your defeat. The great anticlimax shows that love signified a false prosperity of the ego which is now deflated. The liquidation leaves the ego in utter despair and misery.

During the dwindling of love there is increasing tension as in the beginning. When tension is no longer there love is dead. The last feeling you will experience is envy. The lover understands that there is a price to pay for his affection, that the subject seems to exact a sort of tribute. And then into the relationship there comes slowly a kind of greediness. The man grudges his erstwhile love the time, attention and even the money that he spends on her. He compares her pleasures with his own, feels resentful when she enjoys herself, is gloomy when she is popular and resents her leisure while he has to work. Envy is the last phase before indifference. If you compare these last stages with the initial ones you realize that they correspond to each other but everything is turned upside down. What was at the bottom is now on top. But the end of love lies in its beginning.

It would seem therefore that there is an inevitable rhythmical movement that starts from dissatisfaction with oneself, astonishment about the object, admiration and envy, hostility, all of which then lead to the powerful reaction-formation of love, which in turn is followed by the countermovement retracing the same path in the opposite direction. We cannot help submitting ourselves to this cycle. Those who revolt against it and refuse to love think that they thereby shun the evil; but, poor souls, in avoiding the bad they run into the worse. When all is said and done, it is better to have loved and lost than never to have loved at all.

10

The developments here sketched are differently felt and received according to whether you are young or old at the time. How fragile, how vulnerable and defenseless is youth in love! When it ends young people feel as if the skies were falling. An older man often anticipates how it will begin and how it will end. While he deeply feels how sweet the wine is he already knows what bitterness awaits him at the bottom of the cup. As a youngster he could be deeply, transcendently happy. As an older man he no longer experiences this all-consuming happiness in love but the urge and craving remain.

The distinctions are not differences in the essential character of love but in the proportions of the underlying emotions. Admiration and envy, hostility and possessiveness are there in the young as in the old, but they differ in their intensity and correspondingly in the power of their reactions. Old people often reach the depth of love in which even the clearly seen failings and shortcomings of the other are tenderly observed and loved. We all learn how to love the hard way, but perhaps later in life we realize better how difficult it is. Youth, which has so much time, is impatient. When one grows older and matures enough to be patient one no longer has so much time at one's disposal.

What is sketched here is not the inevitable end of love, it is only the end of romance. There are transformations of passionate love that are not considered in this description. Love need not be followed by this aftermath, but by an afterglow. The development need not retrace its entire journey. A new kind of companionship, different from romance but no less valuable, may result in a sense of ease and harmony. Although idealization has ceased and passion is gone yet the atmosphere is clear and calm. The lover has changed into a friend. There is no longer the violence of love but the peacefulness of tender attachment. Indian summers of love are mellow and soft. There is a mutual identification and common experiences, joy and grief that bind two people more intimately together than romance ever did. Yes, even across the abyss of hostility there is sometimes a small bridge to a new relationship. The most serious enemy of love is not the hostility but the indifference that one feels toward the other. When silence and indifference have entered the life of a love-couple and they ask themselves where love has gone to, the situation is similar to that of a man who has put his money away in a safe and forgotten the combination.

Spring with its miracles cannot last forever. Romance is not identical with love. Affection and tenderness can exist and work outside romance. Love can outlast passion. It need not die. It can survive, but only if it changes its character or, rather, if it gains its real character. It is not necessary to idealize the person. It is not necessary to put her on a pedestal. Romance can disappear and will evaporate, but something else can stay. The other day I saw a little picture in a magazine of many love-couples on a crowded beach. Two girls sit alone together apart from the others and the one says thoughtfully to her friend, "It's been my experience that even more important than love is how much do you really care for the fellow." That sounds funny, but it is full of a wisdom which does not come from the brain but from the heart.

III

The Widening Circle

B Y THIS TIME, when you by chance look at one of the pictures
or engravings of Watteau or Boucher who present an amorous shepherd and shepherdess engrossed in adoration, you do
not take the attractiveness of the shepherdess for granted and
you are curious as to why the man chose her instead of another.
What did he see in her? What determined his choice of this
particular girl? Gentle shepherd, tell me why.

The problem seems quite simple. There are two people who
feel that they are made and meant for each other. Are there really
only two people? Certainly in material reality, but not psychologically. The situation reminds one of another which seems
remote and comes to mind through one of those mysterious
channels of thought which connect two separate domains. I believe it was a contemporary of Watteau and Boucher, Voltaire,
who refused to enter a particular discussion with another gentleman because he said that there were too many people involved
in it. The astonished visitor answered that they were alone and
only two. But Voltaire said, "You are mistaken, sir. There are
at least six persons involved. There is the man I think you are,
the man you yourself think you are and then the man you really
are, and the same is true the other way round."

Are there really only two persons in the picture of the loving
couple? The problem of the mutual love choice does not seem
so simple any more if one considers that the factor of the ego-
ideal and of the idealized object is at least as instrumental in
determining the selection as the real personality of the mate.

Is there a problem at all? There are two groups who deny it.
The lovers and the poets feel that psychology is out of place

94

here. If one believes them there was no choice, only necessity. The lovers were predestined for each other. They were pulled to each other by a supernatural power. They recognized their proper complements through many obstructions. If there is a problem at all it cannot be solved by psychology. It belongs to the region of metaphysics, unsolvable by scientific research. The elective affinities which draw the one person to the other seem to be inexplicable. The presence of a problem is also denied by another group which declares that love has only an imaginary existence. Dr. Johnson laughed at the notion of a man in love, which he considered a "mere romantic fancy." He thought that there are "fifty thousand women in the world with any one of whom a man might be as happy as with some one woman in particular." G. B. Shaw thinks likewise that to fall in love with a particular woman means to overappreciate the difference between one woman and another. But this school of thought, which is here represented only by the two realists, and which no doubt numbers many millions of men (and many less women), does not go so far as to deny the existence of a "mere romantic fancy." This element may be elusive and delusive, but it is there. Fancy, overvaluation or whatever it may be, it is the task of the psychologists to explain why just this particular object was selected.

Theories abound as to the general and individual conditions of love choice. Goethe guessed that there are elective affinities between individual man and woman which determine the mutual attractions. He thought there must be undiscovered laws comparable to those of chemistry, and powers like the chemical agencies which attract this person to that other one. Otto Weininger asserted that the selection of a mate follows a mathematical formula according to which the part of masculinity and femininity in two individuals supplement each other to produce a constant. M. Scheler's sympathy-theories, which contain many fine psychological observations, take their start from too idealistic, not to say mystical, assumptions. The views of Schopenhauer and Freud have this in common, that they consider love as a

sublimated extension of the sex drive alone. I have pointed out
that however interdependent the two needs may become, they
are in origin and character different.

The impact of the problem for psychology is obvious. It is
highly significant what kind of mate is chosen, who is your friend.
The choice tells much about the chooser because it originates
in the depth of his nature. Tell me whom you love and I will
tell you who you are and, more especially, who you want to be.
The principles of this selection reveal the most intimate and
secret values that make up your character. A sentence of Montaigne about friendship gives the quintessence of the problem.
Looking back on his lifelong friendship with Etienne de la Boëtie,
Montaigne writes, as an old man, that if he were to be asked
why he loved de la Boëtie, he could only answer, "I loved him
because it was he, because it was I." (*"Je l'aimais parce que
c'etait lui, parce que c'etait moi."*) It is interesting that this formula is not found in the original edition of his works. Montaigne wrote at first only, "because it was he." The second part
of the sentence is a later addition and appeared in 1588. What
was added brings out, of course, the more important side of the
sentence. It turns the attention away from the chosen object to
the chooser.

We cannot content ourselves with the general insight about
love choice which the wisdom of common people provides. This
wisdom, alas, has more than one meaning. It asserts for instance
that extremes meet, but at the same time it indicates that like
will gravitate to like or that birds of a feather flock together. Both
statements can be confirmed by daily experience. The wisdom of
proverbs, sayings and folklore seems to mirror the confusing
complexity of the problem. If you consider the poetic handling
of the problem you will judge that there is plenty of rhyme but
little reason in the choice of the object. It is one of those subjects on which a general agreement is reached about the most
contradictory views. If you assume that the familiar, the similar
or akin is chosen, why is it that so frequently the foreign, the
exotic, the opposite is preferred? Desdemona does not take to

Roderigo or some other Venetian gentleman but to the Moor. On the other side there is a general inclination to choose someone from within one's own national, racial or social circle. Love is certainly not only a sentimentality of the opposites, but it is even less one of the similar types. If there should be no differences love could not come into existence. But if the differences are too great it cannot develop either. There must be differences and similarities of a particular kind, concealed supplements which could not yet be defined.

We consider the problem from a new angle: The starting point is the feeling of ego-deficiency and the need for ego-completion or ego-improvement. There is the unconscious but powerful striving to complete our ego-ideal. The mate is chosen because he or she is needed for this aim, because she fulfills this image of our ideal. But if it were as simple as this no problem would remain. Love choice would become predictable. It could be foreseen in any individual case. It would then be sufficient to ask a woman or a man which particular qualities she or he considered desirable in a mate, to have her describe her ideal fully, in order to say precisely what the mate would be like. But such an experiment would produce many surprises. The man who gives you a description of a kind and gentle, simple girl as his wished-for mate falls in love with a spoiled society lady. Another who feels attracted to the virginal type sells himself in bondage to a siren. The girl who has made a phantom-image of a serious and ambitious man who cares for her deeply finds herself in love with a playboy who does not care for her at all. Now it can be argued that in cases like these the sexual factor is the decisive one, but there can be no doubt that in many of them it is true love. The picture thus offered is really confusing. We sometimes see that the reality of the chosen object agrees to a greater or lesser extent with a preceding phantasy; but we find an astonishing number of discrepancies and frequently we observe that just the opposite of the described image is the chosen object. Sometimes we are taken aback when we see that the reality has not the slightest resemblance to the image. Is love as blind as that? Does the idealization of the object transform and transfigure the person to such an extent that we are blinded to the fact of having chosen the opposite type? No doubt there are such cases, but they do not appear frequently. And they occur rather seldom with women, who are much more realistic than men. Men are the real "idealists" (in the sense of ideal) and the incurable romantics in love. I never doubted that Titania in *A Midsummer Night's Dream* could fall in love with an ass, but I consider it one of the few psychological blunders of Shakespeare that he did not permit her to realize that the chosen object was an ass. Women are not so unwilling to face the facts, even under the magic of love.

If it must be acknowledged that the object so frequently fails to resemble the ideal image, does that not prove that this part of our concept, the theory of the ideal supplement, is wrong? It does not prove it wrong, but it proves it incomplete, or not clearly enough formulated. Those ideal images, after which we search, are only to a certain extent conscious. Some of them and some part of them have never passed the threshold of our thoughts while we were awake. Only fragments of these phantasy-islands in the middle of material reality are above water. The greater parts are covered and invisible. You sometimes hear a woman say, "I never thought I could love anyone like him." To her astonishment she did. We know only a part of what attracts and what repels us. We sometimes feel strangely attracted to someone who, a few moments before, we considered hateful. Many men think that they are devoted to one type of girl while, unknown to themselves, they desire quite a different one. It can happen that these images suddenly change places with their counterpart, with images which we consciously abhor and which we reject. It is not only the Dr. Jekyll but also the Mr. Hyde in us who chooses.

There is enough room in our mind for such opposites. There is also enough space for changes that correspond to the transformations of our own ego-ideal. When we were small boys we passionately wanted to become engine-drivers, later on, knights at King Arthur's Round Table. As we grow into manhood we

do not desire such things any more. The objects which we idealize change also with our own development. It is remarkable,
however, that early and half-forgotten or disowned types of idealized objects can return very late and surprisingly, and can take
their places beside those of today. Our images of the objects
we admire seem to be comparable to the great churches to whose
completion many centuries contributed, and which in the end
show characteristic features of generations with different styles.
We must consider further that we ourselves are not always united
in our egos, and that also our object choice, corresponding to the
splits and conflicting traits of our personality, often become
difficult. We may envy and admire one part of a personality very
much while being indifferent to or even disliking another; and
we may envy and admire another person for these other qualities. We have here the germ of a situation which is characterized by uncertainty and by oscillation between several objects.
The one satisfies a need in us, the other fulfills some other wish
of ours. They make up for different deficiencies of our ego.

It sometimes happens that there are two objects whose qualities supplement each other and you regret that nature has not
made a single person of the two who only together seem to be
the ideal whom you expected to meet.* You often observe that
a man and a woman fall in love with a person quite different
from the preferred type or image after a disappointment in love
or an unhappy relationship. It is as if the one psychological
possibility is exhausted and has to give way to another which is
often the opposite one. Two people meet, that means two pasts
meet and the images of a desired mate are an important part
of their past. Men and women should not only be judged by
the company they keep, but also by the company they wish to
keep.

The concept that a person finds qualities and endowments in
the beloved which he misses in himself can be correct only in a
general sense. Finer observation reveals that these same qualities

* That seems to be the deepest meaning of the mysterious Indian legend of
the "Exchanged Heads" by Thomas Mann (1941).

are also there in the lover but in a different proportion or mixture with others, sometimes only in a latent state. They are suppressed or disowned, their development checked. They belong to
the subterranean part of the personality, and their expressions
are only faintly audible as the knockings of miners who are
buried in a deep shaft. The other person, the love-object, shows
these qualities in a clear, manifest form, or the same tendencies
directed to a different aim. Not certain qualities are envied and
admired in the love-object, rather a certain constellation of unconscious tendencies in their different intensities and aims is unconsciously caught like radio waves by a receiver. You know a
woman, appreciate her excellent qualities, are susceptible to her
charm. Why are you not in love with her? She loses nothing by
your comparison of her with other women. Just here is the catch.
There is no comparison in love. Love forbears comparison. The
object stands alone and apart from others. The lover is a mono-
theist who knows that other people worship different gods but
cannot himself imagine that there could be other gods.

The ego searches for the appropriate emotional complement,
for the particular psychical atmosphere which surrounds a person.
The love-object is thus determined by the impulse-constellations
of two individuals. In other words, it depends on the emotional
potentialities of two persons. Woman has, it seems, a finer sense
of discrimination of character than man. She knows, for instance,
nothing whatsoever about the nature or the value of a man's
work—let us say it is an engineer in whom she becomes interested
—but observing him in his work she realizes what kind of person
he is and often more correctly than the men with whom he
works. But here are deep waters and we are in doubt whether
our ship will bring us safely through.

It is not true that unfathomable forces are operating in our
love choice. We are searching for the counterpoint to our melody,
for the complementary personality, for an old image which takes
on flesh in the person of the beloved. And in the deepest sense
we search for the perfection of ourselves, for the person who
matches the demands we make on ourselves. We want to be loved

by this person as we would be loved if we were ideal persons. Our love choice is not accidental. It is determined by the attitude we have toward ourselves. There are no small considerations working in our selection. Our whole unfulfilled personality is involved in the choice, whether we know it or not. The object is not only what we desire but what will also pacify the desire to reach peace with ourselves. It is even doubtful whether we choose or whether we are made to choose by unconscious motives.

True, it is by trial and error that we arrive at the right choice, but that is due to the fact that we deceive ourselves so much about our own personality and fool ourselves about our inner demands and the concealed needs of our nature. There is a deep meaning in the words of a wise man that it is not only important "to pick the right mate, but to be the right mate."

What gives the person the strength and courage to love since he feels so inferior compared to his love-object? He who is too humble and considers himself utterly worthless does not dare to love or show his affection. An invisible gulf has to be bridged, a certain self-acceptance has to be gained, before a love choice can be made. Is the difference between two human beings really so deep-reaching that we should feel humble and discouraged if we meet beauty, charm and other endowments? Are not the superior beings whom we worship also born as helpless, crying babies? Are they not later on subjected to the same pains, frailties and restrictions as we, and will they not die as we all must, miserable and alone in the last fight? How small are these seemingly great differences, *sub specie mortis!* Are they really so important in the short time that we spend here passing from one nothingness into another?

I like the story of the courtship of Moses Mendelssohn, the famous German-Jewish philosopher, whom Lessing called "a second Spinoza." It is a story not only of human frailty but also of affection. It proves that love is as great a leveler as death. The young philosopher Mendelssohn was on a visit in Hamburg, almost two hundred years ago. There he made the acquaintance of the noble merchant Guggenheim and his family.

Mendelssohn, who was small and hunchbacked, fell in love with Guggenheim's charming daughter Frumtje.

After a stay of several weeks in the city he visited the banker in his office and asked him what the girl had said about him. Guggenheim hesitated, but the young philosopher insisted on being told the truth. So the father said, "Well, you are a philosopher and a wise man: you will not take it amiss. The child said that she got frightened when she saw you, because—" he hesitated. "Because I am a hunchback?" asked Mendelssohn. Guggenheim nodded. The philosopher said he guessed as much and that he only wanted to say farewell to the girl. He went upstairs and found her busy with some needlework. She avoided looking at him during their conversation. Cleverly he led her around to the subject which was in his mind. She asked him whether he too believed that marriages are made in Heaven. "Certainly," he replied: "and something quite unusual happened to me. As you know, they call out in Heaven at the birth of a child, 'This one and that one will get this and that girl for a wife.' When I was born, my future wife was also thus announced, but it was added: 'She will, alas, have a terrible hump.' I shouted: 'Oh, God, Lord, a girl who is humpbacked will very easily become bitter and hard. A girl should be beautiful. Good Lord, give the hump to me and let her be handsome and well formed.' " The girl, deeply moved, stretched out her hand for Mendelssohn's. She became his faithful and loving wife.

2

It is obvious that the two situations of loving and being loved are psychologically different. Self-observation convinces us that the emotions can even be differentiated in the fortunate case when we feel loving and know that we are loved. It is just as clear that there is an emotional connection between the two situations.

Does not the person who loves desire to be loved? Does not the other person react to this wish? Whatever might be the nature of these between-threads, it will be advantageous to deal with the two situations separately at first to avoid confusion. Such a clear division is also justified by the observation that the two needs are not equally developed in individuals.

You know many people whose desire to be loved is much stronger than the other wish. There are types who spend an extraordinary emotional energy in the effort to become the object of affection while they seem not to appreciate the happiness of giving affection themselves. There are other individuals who find more satisfaction in the feeling of loving and who seem not to be stirred by the passionate wish to arouse the response of the object. "When I love you, what does that concern you?" asks a character of Goethe's.* There are persons who freely admit that the emotional enrichment, the inner change brought about by loving is much more important to them than the feeling of being loved. The Duc de La Rochefoucauld must have been one of them because he remarks in his *Maximes* that "the pleasure of love is in loving, and one is happier in the passion one feels than in the passions one arouses in another."

Are these opposite types only exceptions which prove the rule that love wants response and that it awakens this desired reaction? That would be difficult to decide as long as we did not convince ourselves that there is really such a psychological rule. We know only—or at least experience teaches us—that there seems to exist a functional relation between the two needs, but what kind of function? Is it true that affection awakens affection? It certainly is not always true, because there is unrequited love and there is love without any previous emotional appeal from the other. It sometimes seems even as if the one need diminishes when the other is fulfilled. A person who becomes loved does not any more feel to the same extent the urgent desire to love.

* *Wilhelm Meisters Lehrjahre,* IV.

There is an old epigram which says: "To be loved, love."* That sounds like practical advice. Undoubtedly the recipe is good, but it does not always have the desired effect. This can only be produced if certain other psychological suppositions are present. We know that the demonstration of affection may have no effect or even the contrary effect. It could seem that we are moving here in a field where no rules are valid and in which the laws of emotional cause and effect are incalculable.

The best way to get some psychological information about the subject is, I think, to start from some simple questions. What happens in the case where love awakens the effect wished for, when the other person who is wooed feels attracted and finally affectionate? If we get a satisfactory answer to this question, then it seems to me it can no longer be so difficult to solve the other problem—namely, why the same reaction does not take place in other cases, why the response is absent or different. To my way of thinking it is rather surprising that the fortunate result is produced so frequently.

If my thesis is correct—that is to say, if all love follows the same emotional pattern—then the person who returns another's affection passes through the same processes as the lover. She—let us suppose it is a she—is moved by admiration and envy, wants to be like the wooer and to be him, tries to escape from being preoccupied with him in her thoughts, attempts to reject and to devaluate him and finally submits to the powerful emotional counterwave. So far so good, but there is a decisive difference between the two situations, when she "falls" in love spontaneously and when her affection is the response to his courtship. This difference will be reflected in a divergence of the emotional reactions. To make the difference clear we need not search far for comparable situations. There are quite a few available. Let

* There is no doubt that the psychological prescription was already known to the ancient Greeks. Seneca quotes it as originating with the Stoic philosopher, Hecato, a pupil of Panaetius (second century, B.C.): "I will show you a love potion without drug or herb or any witch's spell; if you wish to be loved, love." (Seneca, *Epistles*, IX, 6.)

us choose the psychology of the composer and an audience. Has the listener of a symphony the same emotions as its creator? Certainly not from the start, not before he entered the concert hall. He had his own moods, feelings and thoughts before going to the concert, perhaps sad ones, perhaps cheerful ones. He may have come from a depressing business conference which still lingers in his thoughts as the musicians tune up their instruments and he settles into his place. He hears the great waltz from *The Bat* by Johann Strauss and in a few minutes he feels inundated by the waves of *joie de vivre* in this tune. Life appears easy and charming. There is a promise of happiness in the atmosphere. He feels as if he had sipped the sweet wine made from the grapes that grow on the hills around Vienna. Or he has come from a cocktail party where he flirted with a girl and enjoyed the company of his friends, and life smiled on him. He hears the adagio of Tchaikovsky's *Pathétique* and is deeply stirred. All is swept away in despair and regret. No happiness seems available any more. Every effort seems futile. Death is near and there is no escape. He feels as if he had drunk bitter tea from a Russian samovar.

It is not the aesthetic but the psychological problem that interests us here. The composer has expressed his emotions, his thoughts and impulses in the music he created. Does the listener feel the same emotions? What is the psychical process in him? We assume that his emotions are the same or similar to those of the artist before and during the creation of his work. These emotions were awakened by the music, but isn't that implying that the listener has had the same or similar experiences as the creator of the music? The two emotional situations of the composer and the listener are basically different in their direction. In the artist the emotional experience translated itself into the musical expression, which reawakens in the listener the emotional experience appropriate to this kind of music. It does not create the experience; it renews it. The work did not cause the emotions. It called them forth, awakened them from their sleep. If the person in the audience is preoccupied with other thoughts, stirred by other emotions, the endeavors of the composer will fail, his call will be futile and his magic will not work. In general the hearing will work like an induction of the hidden impulses and emotions expressed in the music. The feelings of the composer are not only communicated to the listener by means of the tunes, harmonies and disharmonies but they unconsciously communicate themselves to him. In any listener of serious music something of the emotional process unconsciously takes place which Nietzsche described in listening to *Carmen*. "I put my ears to the ground to catch the undercurrents of this music. I hear its causes . . . and. strange, I do not really think of it or I do not know how much I think of it."*

There is in general an emotional similarity between these situations and that of the lover with his object. The lover awakens the emotions which he himself feels in the object by a kind of induction process. As between composer and listener, the direction of the emotional flow is opposite. The conscious or unconscious signs and expressions of affection in the one awaken responsive love in the other. But that explains only the general nature of the interplay. The specific conditions become clearer if we consider the situation before the lover appeared. As the composer did not create the emotions in the listener, so too the lover does not create the emotions of affection in the other person. They were potentially there. The ego had a concealed readiness for them. It expected to be loved and had unconsciously been awaiting love for a long time. But is not the discovery that one is loved a surprise? Does it not strike the person loved sometimes as a miracle, a revelation? Yes, but a miracle can also be unconsciously expected.

If we were very sincere with ourselves we would admit that we walk through life with the concealed expectancy that the world will suddenly discover our hidden excellent qualities, our kind intentions and our good deeds. Deep down in us we believe

* *The Case Wagner,* 1888.

that people will detect these virtues of ours, just as in the Catholic legend the crowd of Alexandria discovered suddenly that the heart of a simple man, walking along the streets, was glowing, and by this miracle realized that here was a saint. The psychological premise for such an expectancy of a miracle is obvious. We all long for appreciation and admiration. Every one of us expects that he will meet recognition sooner or later. Everybody likes to be liked.

There is this fundamental insecurity in us besides the unconscious expectation. We discussed it in speaking about the dissatisfaction with ourselves, the ill content determined by the nonfulfillment of the demands on our ego. This insecurity is removed by the certainty of being loved. The person who feels sure of affection gains a higher degree of self-esteem and self-confidence. This reassurance gives courage to him so that he can dare to love. To be able to love one must have a certain confidence in oneself. Being loved reassures a person that he is worthy, that he is lovable. In this sense you can say the feeling of being loved really amounts to a miracle.

It seems that women need to be loved more than do men. That has nothing to do with a "narcissistic" attitude, as the psychoanalysts think, but with the fact that women in general are more insecure than men, although they can conceal it so much better than men can. Women need to be needed. They want the assurance that they are needed. Much more at the mercy of their well-concealed insecurity than men, women want to hear it and hear it repeatedly, both that and how and why they are loved. It is as if an old doubt has to be dissipated. They know better than men that it is more important what men think of them than what they really are. They model themselves frequently according to the image men make of them. They are secretly afraid that the beloved man will find out how weak and vulnerable they are.

They know well that they are no angels, but know too that it is necessary to appear so for these shortsighted men. Not the lady but the gentleman is so unstable in his affection, because his ego-ideal is so much higher. Women in general have not so strong an urge, therefore, to idealize their mates. They can love men, although realizing the latter's shortcomings and failings. This is much more difficult for men. This is why women are so reluctant to admit their faults and human weaknesses, although they are often aware of them. They sense the psychological necessity in men to make an ideal out of their beloved. Women protect themselves with their pride because their deeper insecurity and vulnerability make such a protection necessary. They need oftener than men the reassurance of being loved before they themselves can love. Sensitive to every slight act of inattentiveness, of neglect and lack of appreciation, they are afraid to yield too easily to the wooing of men. This fear, so often justified, makes them wait and hesitate, rouses their resistance and postpones their response to courtship.

If the reaction to being loved is thus an answer to a call like the listener's response to the emotions expressed in a tune, there must have been experiences before which were reawakened when a person realized he was loved. It is easy to answer that he who is loved, himself responds by loving. He returns what he has received. It would be too simple to say that the feeling of being loved reminds us of the love we received from our mothers as children and thus awakens old emotions. Such a psychological explanation is full of truth, but is not the whole truth. It begs the question. It is true that we could not love if there were not some memory in us—to the greatest extent an unconscious memory—that we were once loved. But neither could we love if this feeling of being loved had not at some time suffered doubt; if we had always been sure of it. In other words, love would not be possible without having been loved and then having missed the certainty of being loved. A person who has never loved would himself be unable to love. But a person who has always been loved and loved by everybody would likewise be unable to love. The first assertion might easily be accepted, but the second is more surprising and its psychological consequences are far-reaching.

The need to be loved is not elementary. This need is certainly acquired by experience in later childhood. It would be better to say: by many experiences or by a repetition of similar ones. I believe that these experiences are of a negative kind. The child becomes aware that he is not loved or that his mother's love is not unconditional. The baby learns that his mother can be dissatisfied with him, that she can withdraw her affection if he does not behave as she wishes, that she can be angry or cross. I believe that this experience arouses feelings of anxiety in the infant. The possibility of losing his mother's love certainly strikes the child with a force which can no more be coped with than an earthquake.

It is certainly a terrible experience when the child first learns that being loved by his mother is not an unconditional situation. I do not think that the experience is comparable with the love disappointment of a grown-up person because the ego of the child is so much weaker and so much more dependent on his mother. Perhaps there is a faint echo of a similar emotional reaction in the feeling of a grown-up person who was certain of being loved and then suddenly deserted by the beloved. The experience that he is not loved any more is for the child such a shock that only many repetitions can make him understand it. Then the child begins to realize that such a terrible situation can happen when he behaves in a manner not conforming to his mother's wishes, when he is naughty and disobedient. He tries to avoid this dreadful consequence after seeing the connection with his own behavior, certainly not realized at first. Every temptation to yield to forbidden impulses is by and by accompanied by the anxiety of losing love. The child would perhaps never feel the need of being loved without having experienced this failure and the anxiety after seeming withdrawal of his mother's love.

This anxiety is originally not identical with the fear of punishment. I know a little girl who, having been naughty, wished to be punished because she was certain that her mother would then love her again. It can easily be guessed what is the core of the child's anxiety—fear of being left alone. This is the fear—an echo of the threat, "If you are naughty I shall go away"—which is often felt later on in life at the thought that a person who is dear to us will desert us. This feeling will accompany us through life. Not only the eighty-year-old Anatole France died with the cry, "*Maman!*" Thousands of soldiers shout thus for help on the battlefields. The fear of being left alone is as strong in old age as in early childhood. It remains at the roots of our desire to be loved.

> If my hair gets grey
> Will you come and say,
> "I love you as I did in May"?

It is this experience and this anxiety which makes us always so eager to be appreciated and wanted. In the deepest sense we wish to be loved as we were once by our mother. This demand is as tenacious as it is unreasonable and unrealizable. We cannot be loved this way any more and mother's love cannot be replaced by another's. A man once asked his mistress whether she would love him if he were suddenly to become poor. "Of course," she answered. Then he asked whether she would love him if he became crippled by an accident. This question, too, was answered in the affirmative. But still the man was not satisfied. He tried again, asking whether her affection would be the same if, in addition to these handicaps, he were to become deaf, blind and insane. The woman finally became impatient and said, "Why in the world should I love an impoverished, crippled, deaf and blind idiot?" Exactly! Why should she? Only a mother could love her child in spite of everything.

We understand that this anxiety will later on gain a social note; that it will be shifted from the mother to other persons whose opinion we appreciate. It will appear in the form of guilt feelings whenever we are in danger of being rejected by society, because we do not behave according to its demands. The core of this social anxiety is the fear of being excluded, of being left alone.

The child's certainty of being loved will often be shaken by the possibility that mother or nurse can withdraw her affection. It seems that a considerable part of our childhood is shadowed by this fear. I shall not easily forget a scene which I witnessed twenty years ago. The little daughter of an acquaintance was left in the belief that she was bought in a department store by her mother instead of being born by her. The girl had been naughty and the mother had threatened to return her to the store in exchange for a better child. The small girl sobbed heartbrokenly and cried: "Not change! Hilda quite good." It seems that the difficulty of becoming a model child will later be an important factor in creating the phantom of an ideal ego which is perfect in the sense of education. Thus we link the creation of the ego-ideal with the desire to be loved. The need for affection has taken the place of the striving for perfection. And now we have come round to meeting again the dissatisfaction with oneself which was the point of departure for this research.

Loving would be impossible without the previous experience of being loved, and the other experience—perhaps even more important—of not being loved any more. The zeal to regain paradise springs from the memory that men once possessed it and lost it. With the foregoing discussion the question is also answered, which need is first? To love or to be loved? Of course the wish to be loved is not only earlier in the development of the child, but it is and will remain the stronger need. If that is correct, then the new question arises, what is the connection between this and the other intensive urge, to love? The question was seemingly answered long ago, but psychological problems of this kind have a remarkably tenacious life.

I have tried to show where love originates, that it represents a counterreaction to impulses of envy, possessiveness and hostility.

How does the new insight that the need to love is acquired after the experience of not being loved fit into this concept? It certainly does not contradict it. It only completes it. This early experience precedes the origin of the need, and it also answers the question why such a yearning for affection appears at all in the human soul. The new insight makes us understand that loving is originally an attempt to regain the happy certainty of being loved. This effort originates in the dissatisfaction with oneself and the failure to change one's troublesome ego for a better, a model-ego.

It seems that the discussion of the relation between the situation of the lover and the beloved can reveal even more and deeper insights. It adds to our understanding of the emotional process itself, especially of the, as yet, unsolved problem of the reaction-formation. The general lines are clear. The person appears at first not so much lovable as enviable. He is at first the object of jealous, possessive and aggressive impulses. Then, it seems, after the failure of these tendencies to reach their goal, there appears the powerful and mysterious counterwave of tenderness, which we call affection. We see the process now in a new light, from the new point of view that its aim is to be loved.

The child who experiences his mother's dissatisfaction and apparent withdrawal of affection reacts to this menace at first with fear. He tries to regain what seems lost by expressing hostility and aggressiveness. He wants to get hold again of this most precious possession, the mother's love, with all the violence which is in the infantile character. The desperate attempt to regain that love has the nature of primitive possessiveness. It has almost reflexlike traits. It wants to hold and clasp the object and cling to it. There is more hostility and possessiveness in this effort than tenderness. The change of its character comes about only after failure; when the child realizes that the effort is a failure. And now something very strange takes place, something which is foreign to our conscious thinking but which is very near to the infantile way. Instead of grasping the object directly and taking possession of it in an aggressive way, the child identifies himself with the object as it was before. The child does the same that the mother did to him in that happy time which has passed. The process is very illuminating because it shapes the pattern of love in general. The little boy thus demonstrates in his own behavior what he wants his mother to do to him, how she should behave to him. He announces this wish by displaying his tenderness and affection toward his mother who gave these before to him. It is an attempt to overcome the despair and sense of loss in taking over the role of the mother. The boy tries to demonstrate what he wishes by doing it himself: look, I would like you to act thus toward me, to be thus tender and loving to me. Of course this attitude is not the result of consideration or reasoned planning but an emotional process by identification, a natural exchange of roles with the unconscious aim of seducing the mother into fulfilling his wish. He demonstrates by his own actions how he wants to be loved. It is a primitive presentation through reversal, an example of how to do the thing which he wishes done by her. In this presentation lives the memory of the attentions, tendernesses and endearments once received from the mother or loving persons. The psychical dynamics of the process is primitive enough, but it is so peculiar to the infantile attitude that it needs an effort to grasp its meaning because we grownups have lost the gift of changing our attitude so easily for that of another. The mechanism is in the nature of a presentation of the attitude desired from another person by acting it out oneself. The boy who now behaves lovingly toward his mother shows her what she should do to him. He wants to be treated tenderly and has no other means of expressing this urgent wish than to act it out, to display it in an active form. His passion corresponds thus not so much to his own desires as to the desires he wants to rouse in the other person.

This acting is preceded by an unconscious fantasy, the wish as to how the object should act. The impatient ego then impersonates the role of this other person, conjuring up the desired behavior of the object and presenting it before her or him. The individual manner of wooing and courting reveals the kind of affectionate treatment a person wants to receive. Love begins as an unconscious fantasy of being loved.

This presentation is an active form, this display through reversal is an anticipation of the desired attitude of the object. Later on it will determine the character of loving in general. We all unconsciously behave like this when in love. In our attentions and tenderness toward the object we show what we ourselves want to receive, what we would like to experience passively. We all play, so to speak, two roles in this delightful game. Our display of loving is the anticipation of the love we desire from the other person. It is as if we were to demonstrate: I would like you to be thus wild about me. It is obvious that we act out a fantasy in this two-role play. We are both the other person whose love we yearn for and the beloved which we want to be. Our love is the unconscious advertisement of how we wish to be loved. It is a demonstration by proxy. We act toward this other person the way we would like that other to act toward us. In this way we unconsciously announce what we miss and what we long for.

We have thus arrived at the point of finding the deepest meaning of love. Its aim is to be loved. This goal is originally pursued in the form of aggressive conquest. It will be reached in the two-role performance which is there at first only in fantasy and is later acted out in the declarations, attentions, tendernesses, gentle words and actions which we show the object.

3

In childhood love is restricted to only a few persons—the parents, the nurse, a playmate. The child wants to be appreciated and admired by this small circle which represents his whole world. A world is not characterized by its spaciousness and expansion in a material sense but by the ability of the individual to imagine its extent. For my grandson, two years old, the discovery that other people have fathers was a revelation. He had thought that there was only one papa existent.

The circle of persons by whom the child wants to be loved, appreciated and approved of increases by and by and includes teachers, friends and acquaintances, the gang at the playground. Later on it extends to even larger groups. A man does not search for social recognition from his family and friends alone, but beyond them, from the community, the nation, the continent, the whole world, corresponding to the extent and character of his ambition. To be loved by a woman is only one form of this same need; it is restricted to a single woman. You could also say that the need for social recognition is the enlargement of an original wish to be admired and appreciated by one person. This need is alive in every one of us in one form or another. We all long for social recognition. The poet or the composer may put his work into a drawer and decide never to publish it, but in its conception and in his labors he consciously or unconsciously imagined an audience, many readers or listeners, or only one—that is enough. He might have felt the bliss of creation in his loneliness, but unconsciously he was not alone. He has an invisible audience. Reality is less important in this instance than the psychological significance. No one creates for himself alone, because achievement as well as love is of a social nature. The wish to be socially recognized is the most general form of the individual need to be loved. It can become strong enough to displace the other need, that of being loved by a particular person or by several persons, as if society had taken the place of these individuals. It is a remarkable development that a group or a great number of people can occasionally substitute for the desired acknowledgment and admiration of a single person, whose appreciation was originally longed for.

I was interested in a certain problem of which there are many in this realm: in the problem of the emotional effects of sudden social recognition. What kind of emotions does a person feel who at a certain moment is taken by surprise and finds himself the object of admiration and social recognition? I was interested in this little psychological problem because I observed that the emotional reactions of different persons are almost the same. The individual divergencies are negligible.

Here are a few instances at random. The first is of recent occurrence. My little daughter Miriam celebrated her fifth birthday the other day. In the small mountain hotel where we spent this summer's vacation the little girl soon became the darling of the guests. Not at all shy and of a very sociable temperament, she conversed in a friendly way with everybody and her easygoing and confidential manner took their hearts by storm. By some accident, some of the women guests in the hotel learned that Miriam had a birthday. She herself contributed to this knowledge as she questioned the manager, the waitress and the guest with, "I bet you don't know what day today is," and then proceeded to inform them that it was her birthday. Nor was she shy when some guests congratulated her at the breakfast table and presented her with small gifts. At lunch a little scene took place in the dining room, in which the guests—not many more than a hundred —had their meal at small family tables. Before the dessert was served the manager of the hotel clapped his hands, asked for everyone's attention and made a speech in which he said it was a special day, on which the youngest guest had her birthday, a guest whom everybody loved and he wanted everyone present to congratulate her. He shook the little girl's hand, she smiled, appeared flattered and courteously thanked him. Then the door opened and a waitress brought in a beautiful birthday cake with five lighted candles. She placed the cake on the table. The guests, taking the cake as one large family, began to sing, "Happy Birthday to you. . . ." Little Miriam, until now happy and flattered at having received many gifts, suddenly reacted strangely. Her eyes filled with tears as she realized that everyone looked at her smilingly and sang to her. She tried to hide her face in her mother's lap, then suddenly crawled under the table where she remained crying but protected from all eyes by the tablecloth.

It was quite clear that the little girl, otherwise so carefree and courageous, was shaken, quite moved and shamed to tears at the same time. When she was asked the same evening by her mother why she had behaved this way, she said, "It was too much. All people looked at me and sang to me."

I would like to compare her emotional attitude with that of a man seventy years older. Anatole France was very modest and did not like to be complimented, yet he was celebrated and worshiped like a god on his trip to North Africa. The journey from Morocco to Tunis, undertaken to visit the antiquities of these countries, was one long ovation. From the little village in which the schoolteacher and the children waited to offer the old man a bunch of wild flowers to the great cities in which the intellectual elite assembled around him to dine him in full dress, it became a continuous enthusiastic demonstration of his many thousand admirers. Each town competed to honor him. His friend Michel Corday, who accompanied him on the trip, reports the reception in Tebessa in the ancient temple of Minerva, a Roman ruin which is excellently preserved. On both sides of the staircase stood young girls in echelon. They were dressed in white, in antique garb, great green palms in their hands. Across their breasts were sashes of mauve satin on which the titles of the books of Anatole France stood out in relief, in letters embroidered with gold. The old writer had to mount the steps between the two charming groups. He wept.*

What is the character of the emotion which the great writer and the child had in common? From that moment on they felt a lump in their throats, and then they had to cry. It is obvious that they were touched by the unexpected honor conferred upon them. But why the tears? You could argue that sudden happiness makes people feel like crying but we want to understand

* Michel Corday, *Anatole France—D'après ses confidences et ses souvenirs,* Flammarion, Editeur, Paris, 1927, p. 67.

more of this psychological process. It must be different from the case where a celebration is anticipated and expected. That it came as a surprise must be an important factor. In a book published many years ago* I ventured the theory that the emotion of surprise is felt when an old expectation which has become unconscious becomes a reality, is suddenly fulfilled. For example, there was once a strong wish which was frustrated, and —as far as conscious thoughts go, long buried—and then its fulfillment dropped from the sky. The feeling is one of surprise with the realization of an unconscious wish (or fear). In our particular case it must have been an old daydream of being loved, generally recognized and appreciated, which was unexpectedly fulfilled. But in both cases the persons were somewhat prepared for it, since they expected some honor to be shown them. During his triumphal trip the famous writer foresaw that he would be celebrated at each new stop. The child also anticipated that some guests would make friendly remarks and give her candies, etc. It seems thus that the condition of unexpectancy mentioned above is not there. This is due to the fact that though both Anatole France and little Miriam expected to be honored, they were not prepared for such an extraordinary celebration. The element of surprise is certainly present in both cases. It was the grandeur of the celebration which overwhelmed them and shocked them with emotion. The preparation was there but the intensity of their emotions can only be explained as resonance from previous daydreams, in which the great old man and the little girl once imagined that they would be very much loved.

Having now dealt with the factor of surprise as intensifying the emotional reaction, we have yet to answer the question why they were touched to tears. Would we not rather expect expressions of happiness such as a laughter of triumph or other facial signs of deep satisfaction? The argument that intensive joy also expresses itself in tears is justified, but let us add that it is not valid for all

* Theodor Reik, *Der Schrecken,* Vienna, 1926.

cases of great happiness. It does not free us from the obligation
of explaining this special kind of emotion.

Several emotional factors are combined here—surprise, pride
and shame. The result is the upsurge of a feeling of overflowing
happiness together with being touched. My psychological analysis of this rather complicated emotional situation is certainly not
sufficient. I present it because it is the only one known to me.
From the psychological literature that I have looked through
I discovered that nobody has tried to elucidate this strange
mixed feeling. It is clear that the factor of surprise is efficient
in the result but it contributes only to its intense character. An
old wish is suddenly fulfilled, a forgotten daydream is realized.
The fact that the realization was once expected and then renounced is certainly important, but the unconscious motivation
of this renunciation is more essential for the psychological evaluation. I suppose that most of us find resignation necessary not
only because of the failure of the external world which refuses
to recognize one's merits or endowments but as a reaction to their
absence. It is as though the people around us do not want to
recognize and appreciate us because we do not deserve it. Their
restraint is only the expression of their negative judgment of us.
We consider their lack of appreciation not only as an expression
of neglect or indifference, while we remain aware of our worth
—that happens only consciously—but as their verdict. They express by their attitude their sentence, that we do not deserve
the general recognition we expected. This unconscious interpretation of the negative reaction, or of the missing or insufficient
reaction of society on our efforts, can be traced back to the concealed feelings of unworthiness we carry around with us.

When a surprising and great social recognition is given to us
our sense of happiness is not only due to the fulfillment of an
old unconscious wish. It is more than that. We are touched
because our feeling of unworthiness and our feeling of guilt is
taken from us. Suddenly we get unmistakable and convincing

signs that the community, small or large, has pardoned our thought crimes, has absolved us. More than that, it is ready and glad to recognize our merits and efforts. We again become justified and are transferred from the shadow into the sun. We are not only welcome to the others but appreciated, admired, recognized, and that means loved by them. It is comparable to the redemption of a sinner by God's grace.

This feeling of sudden forgiveness produces that deep satisfaction, gives the sense of happiness to the person. Such a miracle of redemption can only be performed by love—and what else than generalized love is social recognition? It can be performed by religion—and what else is religion than the awareness that God loves men? The unconscious guilt feelings are carried away by waves of happiness, by the conviction of being loved. Then in the middle of this proud emotion comes an echo, a reminiscence of past feeling, which made us believe that we were unworthy and we do not deserve to be recognized and loved. This reminiscence results in a mixture of emotions. It is as if the person feels like saying, "But I do not deserve so much happiness and love!" The contrast of the present deep satisfaction with the concealed suffering of the past is really what touches the individual. It is to him as though he were granted such a great honor not because he deserves it but even though he does not deserve it. The situation is comparable to the one a sinner might find himself in when God's grace touches him. In the middle of the certainty, to be saved by a miracle, reoccurs the humble reminiscence that he thought himself damned, that he would have deserved his severe punishment. Pride is mixed with humbleness in the blessed feeling of sharing the salvation of the saints, while unworthy of it. It is this mixture of high and low feeling which gives some bittersweet taste to the situation. Something of humbleness in the exultation, a delicate note of doubt whether such joy is deserved is even sometimes felt in the first glorious union of lovers. Here, as there, the increasing triumphal melody drowns the echo of the old tune.

4

In the description of the original phase from which love stems the working of inner discontent and unrest appeared as the decisive element. The more we understand its nature the more apparent becomes its importance, not only in the prephases but also in the emotional formation of love itself. In contrast to other concepts ours emphasized the fact that there is a push away from oneself which is more essential than the pull exercised by the chosen object. Some power in a man compels him to run away from and to get rid of himself. It drives him to wanting to escape from his own presence. There are several ways of eluding one's inner dissatisfaction or self-dislike. One can get drunk and thus feel changed from one's usual self. Another way is to become enthusiastic about a political or religious cause and thus to forget oneself. Or one can get into a creative mood in which one feels that it is not the depressed or discontented Mr. Smith who writes the novel but someone else.

In love this tiresome ego melts away and becomes merged into another person. Most psychologists who occupy themselves with the subject of love neglect or do not even see this essential point of emotional departure. They observe the psychical movement that inclines toward the object, but they overlook the fact that the direction itself is indicated from the start, when one turns away from oneself. It is obvious that two factors determine the result of a person's effort to overcome his inner discord: namely, the intensity of the original dissatisfaction with oneself and the amount of energy which one can raise to get out of the unpleasant situation. If the thesis here presented is correct there are two kinds of people who are unable to love: those who are self-satisfied and self-sufficient and those who are too deeply dissatisfied with themselves.

Are there people who are so self-satisfied and self-sufficient that they cannot love, or better, need not love? No doubt there are, for instance, many men of genius, investigators, composers, writers, philosophers and great religious minds, who are engrossed in their work. They have chosen another way to escape from themselves, because at times they too, like the rest of us, are troubled by their ego. Their capacity for loving is restricted by the fact that this ego is absorbed in their work. But how about the millions who are not creative in this way, who have no such strong interests to consume their psychical energy?

We can approach this question more easily by returning to another point. We said that he who loves must unconsciously have felt jealous or envious of the object at the start. He must have admired the object and by comparison felt inferior to it. At this point we arrive at the following psychological conclusion: he who cannot be envious is unable to love. That is a strange statement, but it seems to me incontestable as far as it concerns unconscious emotions. The creative people mentioned above are not incapable of envy, but they are either so engaged in their work that their envy is short-lived or they quickly subdue their jealousy by dwelling on their own endowments and superior qualities. Here we may enlarge on our previous statement and say that in order to be able to love one must be capable of being envious for some length of time and of continuing to be jealous of the person, not of his accomplishments.

Are there people who are unable to be envious and jealous longer than a fleeting moment? Are there mortal beings who are never envious or jealous? I doubt it. In fact I am inclined to deny it with the possible exceptions of Robinson Crusoe on his island and similar cases. It is very questionable if envy and jealousy can ever be avoided when men live with other men. But there are so many men and women sure of themselves, apparently self-sufficient and satisfied, who are certainly not envious and jealous at this time. Are they then incapable of loving? That need not be so. Their lack of dissatisfaction and their self-confidence may be just the result of their being in love or having been in love. They may have achieved some remarkable thing or given themselves entirely to a religious or political cause. It does not mean that they were never able to be envious or jealous.

However, there are characters who seem to be protected against the onslaught of envy and jealousy. They seem to have been made invulnerable to Cupid's arrows, as poets two hundred years ago would have put it. What is their secret? They seem to be indifferent to the endowments and charms of another. But are they? They enjoy the other while they themselves remain emotionally unreachable beyond a certain point. They are not unfeeling. They are only unloving. You find persons of this kind especially in the group called by psychiatrists hysterical characters and paranoid personalities. But they are numerous also in the group which is not pathological. Most of them are not aware of this shortcoming of theirs. They blame external circumstances or deficiencies of their object for their frustration.

Psychoanalysis can prove that their superiority toward others and their apparent lack of any feeling of envy and jealousy is only make-believe to themselves. It is the expression of an unconscious defense mechanism which provides their life with a charm against strong feelings of affection. Their emotional remoteness, conceit, smugness and self-reliance are only pretenses, substitutes. Theirs is only a substitute self-confidence. They protect themselves because they feel so vulnerable and weak. They bolster up artificially an insecure ego. The self-aggrandizement and better-than-thou attitude cover but poorly the loneliness which their owner feels when his armor of self-sufficiency cracks. The French expression *cache-misère* appropriately denotes the psychological nature of such an attitude. The aloofness of these people in one direction is usually connected with an eagerness to inflate some qualities that they wish to display to their surroundings. They lead a secondhand life, always keen on impressing and pleasing people. To ingratiate themselves with others is often used as a cover for the lack of real affectionate feeling. It is characteristic of these people that they frequently have a kind of self-reproach or a sense of guilt after a conspicuous demonstration of their superiority, as if they knew that it is only a substitute.

They try in vain to drown the voice of an incorruptible observation station inside themselves which complains of a frustrated life. It is as if somewhere deep in themselves they are aware that their arrogance is only a pretense, their self-reliance a sham and their pride a concealment of weakness. A lady whom I once knew in Vienna understood these surrogates when she said, "God should always give me enough self-confidence so that I won't need to become conceited."

The self-possessed spares himself the psychologically necessary emotions of envy and jealousy, but he also deprives himself of happiness and deep satisfaction. His self-sufficiency is grief-saving but condemns him to life under a glass bell with no chance to relax or be off guard emotionally. In the end he feels fed up with himself. It's a sit-down strike against a powerful inner need. This self-possessed rigidity amounts to self-denial; restraint to asceticism. It sometimes makes the impression of egotism and people say really of such persons that they are too selfish to love. But is it selfishness which deprives them of great satisfaction and joy? It is rather fear of losing their independence and of being found wanting which keeps them from love. They won't allow themselves to feel the deep urge to unite their destiny with another. They are reluctant to yield to the hidden need for companionship, preferring self-expansion and—aggrandizement. They want to feel not only independent but important, to be the center of the stage. Loving means making the other person the center.

They succeed, but meanwhile life escapes them. They don't feel consciously any lack of affection, but sometimes they feel like living corpses. Their pride and the little gratifications which they get from their aloofness and emotional self-sufficiency do not pay in the end. Sometimes they half believe this lie, embroidering it with half truths, but they know somewhere it is only play-acting. Sometimes they try to fall in love but succeed only to find out eventually that it was not love at all. Their fear is too deep even while they play hide and seek with themselves. It is only fake love, a cheap sham article, because no one who is so much afraid can love.

In most cases their superiority feelings cover an unconscious sense of guilt or inadequacy. They are afraid to abandon themselves and surrender because they think they are not worthy of being loved. Behind their self-assurance is a terrible lack of self-confidence. Much patience and psychological understanding are needed in psychoanalysis to remove the unconscious protective wall that these persons build around themselves. They will display the same complacency and self-assurance toward the psychoanalyst, showing him the same emotional defense and coolness that they bear toward others. It is necessary to remove their sham self-confidence and apparent conceit, and to penetrate to the deeper level of inner insecurity and inferiority feeling. A Jewish colloquialism well expresses the direction of this therapeutic procedure. It advises a person of this kind, "Do not make yourself so big, you are not so small."

The psychoanalyst not only has to remove the surface conceit but to eliminate the emotional motives which made the seeming superior attitude necessary. He has to replace the self-confidence and even self-righteousness that he has to take away with a real and justified sense of security. Oddly enough those who seem overconfident and full of self-esteem have to be encouraged. It is a hard task, not easily successful, and sometimes not successful at all. They often defend their position with incredible obstinacy, appearing not to appreciate the real value of their personalities which they readily exchange for sham qualities. It is like a woman who keeps locked up an old, precious dinner set while trying to impress her guests with a new, cheap and glittering one. What I should like to stress is the psychological fact that the attitude of most of these characters is self-pretense. Only a few inches below the surface of self-sufficiency and complacency is a deep inferiority feeling and a sense of inadequacy.

The other group of persons who are incapable of giving affection are those who feel unworthy of being loved. Of course such
a feeling is not often conscious. In most cases these persons think
that they are the victim of an inscrutable fate which will not
allow them to find an appropriate love-object. Actually they are
deeply insecure, doubting if anyone can love them. They won't
take a risk because their self-confidence is too weak. They often
have a crushed or crippled ego and are filled with diffidence, as if
they had been shell-shocked by life. In spite of all superficial behavior they feel inadequate and anticipate being rejected. Loving
is impossible without a certain self-esteem and self-respect. He who
is not even a little friendly to himself cannot be a friend to anyone. You have to get along with yourself at least moderately well
if you want to get along with others. These faint hearts not only
accept their rejection in anticipation but they sometimes even
provoke it. Disliking themselves, they are unconsciously prepared
to be disliked by others. They are timid souls suffering from an
intense fear that no one could care for them if he knew how vicious, stupid or shallow they were. They ask little from others because they think they themselves have so little to give. The other
day a well-brought-up girl told me an experience she had in company with a group of college boys and girls who went out to enjoy themselves. As time went on my patient became more and
more insecure. She said, "I wanted to get drunk because I was
afraid that after fifteen more minutes I wouldn't be interesting."
Many of these persons try to escape from their feeling of inner
insecurity by having affairs, but sex is a very inadequate refuge.
The incapability of loving pursues the person and makes his
sexual life also unsatisfactory.

We understand that the primary condition for the formation
of love is dissatisfaction with, even a certain dislike of, oneself.
But that is only the incentive. To love means to overcome this
inner discord. One feels a hindrance, but also the energy to remove it. It is as if, though a river blocked the road, strength
could be found to build a bridge and thus span the stream. The

recapture of a certain amount of courage is an emotional prerequisite for a person who wants to love. A certain self-confidence is
essential. He who feels utterly unworthy will also be despised by
others. He who feels entirely crushed and without any self-respect
cannot be an object of admiration and envy. He is only pitiable.
But not only can he not be loved. He himself cannot really love.
What I mean can best be expressed by means of a comparison.
Two summers ago we were on a farm in Pennsylvania. Nearby
was another farm. From my porch I used to watch the neighbor's
dog run out to greet his master as the latter returned from work.
The animal jumped all over the farmer, licking his face, wagging
his tail and giving every evidence of joy and affection. One day
the dog failed to welcome the farmer upon his return. Instead,
the creature lay in a corner licking a sore. I learned later that the
wound had been caused by some malicious village boys who had
stoned the animal. He who licks his wounds cannot be affectionate.

He who is convinced that nothing in him is lovable cannot
love. The initial self-dislike and depression which precede love
have to be overcome to a certain extent before a person dares to
love another human being. We return at this point to the one
leitmotiv or theme, namely, that it is a person's attitude toward
himself which is decisive, whether he can muster the courage to
conquer his self-discontent enough at least to try to love. Let me
add that the essence of this unconsciously felt insecurity or inferiority is a hidden guilt feeling which not only originates in
repressed hostility and greed toward others but recreates this feeling in an odd vicious circle itself. Not our malicious or mean
thoughts but evil conscience makes evil. He who wants to love
has to become tolerant toward his own hostile and aggressive
thoughts and impulses. He has to pardon himself before he can
be affectionate toward another. Only a grown-up person can pardon himself. But here we enter the realm of the problems of
guilt feelings. Their connection with affection we shall discuss in
another chapter.

An individual's ability to love is fundamentally decided by his courage and fear. Let me contrast two remarks made by two young women in analytical sessions. They were made within a week of each other and both seemed so paradoxical at the time that I made a note of them. The first was made by an intelligent young girl who said, "I cannot love because I am not pretty." That sounds puzzling but can be understood well enough psychologically. This young girl certainly overestimated physical attractiveness, even apparently thinking sometimes that it was the only quality of value in the eyes of young men. What she meant was: I know I am not pretty. When I am tempted to fall in love I feel at the start that the man won't be attracted to me. Thus I shall know only unhappiness and frustration. I can't risk falling in love because I foresee with pain that my feelings will not be reciprocated. The other remark was made by a young married woman some days later as she discussed her relationship with her husband. She said, "I know very well that I am not pretty but I love John nevertheless." Certainly that is as paradoxical as the first remark. What has her supposed lack of looks to do with the fact of her devotion? It is not only feminine reason which speaks like that but also the logic of an unconscious process which means: I dare to love my husband although I am not pretty because I have other good qualities which make me hope that he will someday respond to me. What constitutes the difference between these two cases? Is it really a difference in the amount of attractiveness of the two young women? It can't be that because, speaking objectively, the girl was both much younger and much prettier than the married woman. In the opinion of most of her friends and acquaintances she was even very attractive. But something inside her spread an atmosphere of coolness, making her appear casual, remote and sometimes even conceited. She had very few suitors. Her complaint that young men didn't like her, apparently, was almost justified. Unconsciously she scared them off. When she was freed, through analysis, from her unconscious guilt feelings, her emotional life also became freer and she had many suitors. The difference between the two cases, then, is not one of the abundance or lack of attractiveness but one of courage toward oneself. In one case courage was lacking. In the other it was present and worked. There are many women whose self-confidence is weakened by the knowledge of being less attractive than others or of lacking this or that physical endowment. Then a consolation mechanism begins to operate, as the psychological observer will notice; and the question, "What has Miss X got that I haven't got?" and its answer, "A better figure," or, "Naturally wavy hair," will be followed by the consoling thought, "Yes, but I have nice eyes, they say, and am a better conversationalist." The successful working of the consolation mechanism depends not on the possession or lack of certain qualities—for after all, every woman has some attractions—but on courage. The problem remains whether or not a person can regain his self-respect and conquer fear, especially the social fear which we call unconscious guilt feeling.

I contrast this view with the ideas which Freud's followers present. They contend that an individual's capability of loving is restricted by narcissism, his self-love, that a person who loves himself too much cannot love others. We assert that there is no original and genuine self-love and that one's ability to love is impaired by lack of self-confidence, by self-dislike or self-contempt and by too little "self-love," that most of the emotional difficulties which we have with others are mere reflections and manifestations of the conflicts that we have with ourselves.

5

There is an intimate connection between the problem of not being able to love and that which is often characterized as unhappy love. It is the same relation as between frustration and failure. The term unhappy love applies not only to those cases

where affectionate feelings are not returned but to many others
in which the person fails because of some conflict within himself.
He does not avoid the task but rather fails to accomplish what he
undertook. Unhappy love means that one hears the call but cannot reach the destination. It signifies the failure of a mission.

He who has observed unhappy lovers and unfortunate love
through the course of years will get a strong impression that
much of the failure is caused not by external circumstances but
by one or more unconscious factors in the lovers themselves. Of
course unfortunate, unfavorable external situations often exist.
Sometimes they really do exclude the possibility of reaching the
goal. "Never the time and the place and the loved one together."
But more often such outside hindrances are unconsciously utilized to bring about failure. One gets suspicious after observing
how one pair of lovers easily overcome obstacles which to another
pair appear absolutely unsurmountable. One is forced to believe
that there are unconscious tendencies operating against the accomplishment of the specific aim, and that a person often unconsciously stage-manages the failure when he repeats his experience
again and again, though with different partners.

Such secret countertendencies may begin to work even in the
choice of a partner—the choice being wrong to start with—and
may determine the outcome from the first. These countertendencies may destroy ties which seem to have been made for life. Some
people seem to have an unconscious foreknowledge of which mate
will be the most incompatible, and they choose precisely that one.
I am not speaking here of infatuations and affairs but of that
which is felt to be real affection. I refer not to excursions just
over the borderland of love but to journeys into the country itself. A strong initial attraction can hide irreconcilable differences
of temperament and character. There is no doubt that in the unfortunate choice of a partner tendencies of self-defeat and -destruc-
tion are already at work, frequently behind the scenes. One observes cases which seem to move through cycles of upsurging love
followed by subsequent failure and unhappiness. Each time the

man or woman in quest of happiness feels certain at the start of having finally found the real mate, only to be thrown into a state of despair soon afterward upon discovering that it is only another failure.

Then there are the other cases, the men and women who alternately doubt first themselves and then their partners, who, when in love, get rid of their inner insecurity, only to become again its victim when they fall out of love. They rise from the depths of despondency only to be hurled back into an even darker and deeper despair. There are persons who make the greatest efforts to reach the goal and then let go of all that they have gained. Many of them dash madly about in search of a love-object and just manage to succeed in missing it. Then there are those who do not dare to enter into competition with rivals. They step aside, letting others have the middle of the road, when they should stand their ground. One sees people who wish to be loved but when they get just so far cannot accept, indeed even feel obligated to destroy, the tenderness given them.

Other characters remain in doubt as to which of several objects is the right, the real one. Psychoanalysts can report many cases in which a man is unconsciously forced to oscillate back and forth among three or four girls, as if he felt an emotional need for uncertainty and doubt. It is obvious that he does not want any of the girls. He is not yet capable of loving. There are so many persons who confuse sex and love, sensual attraction and permanent affection, only becoming aware of the difference when it is too late.

There are so many possibilities for failure and frustration that another book could and should be written about the hidden motives which cause them. Very often these abortive forms of love cannot be differentiated from the others at the start. Only the development of the emotional relationship of the couple will determine which form it is. The expression of doubt often concerns not the value of the object as it appears but one's own capacity for loving. He who feels real affection for one object cannot oscillate among several because love means to choose definitely one object—at least for a certain length of time. He who doubts his ability to love someone is like the boy who after playing for Mozart asked the master, "Do you advise me to become a child prodigy?" Mozart told him no, decidedly not. Taken aback the boy said, "But, Mr. Mozart, you yourself became a child prodigy." Whereupon Mozart replied, "But I did not ask anyone." This example well illustrates the contrast between self-confidence or self-conviction and self-doubt. If you doubt a miracle that happens to you, you may be sure it is not a miracle.

Whenever the mission of love fails the psychological observer can see why it had to fail. In its decomposition its component parts may be clearly recognized. Its disintegration reveals the very nature of the pieces which failed to make a compact whole. The unprejudiced will admit that the elements into which it is separated in its dissolution prove the theory here asserted: namely, that love is a reaction against original envy, greediness, hostility, possessive lust and the drive to dominate. By examining the ruins of a building we find what materials have gone into its construction. The psychologist knows that castles in the air are also erected by an emotional effort. From nothing, nothing comes, not even such a phantom or mere shadow.

Here the contrariness of all human affairs becomes apparent. While a structure is being erected its final form cannot be predicted. Will it be a permanent home or only a casual, temporary shelter? Neither can it be foretold whether or not the builders will enrich themselves in the long run. They may only impoverish themselves.

Is there a way to help people avoid these failures, a means for turning frustration into success? There are many of them, I am sure, but none that can guarantee complete accomplishment. Psychoanalysis can undoubtedly help and often does succeed in its task. It is not a universal remedy. It has the shortcomings and insufficiencies of all human endeavor. Freud admitted that readily enough and likened the situation to that in the following anecdote: a man complains about the many faults and shortcomings of women, their vanity, inconsistency, flirtatiousness, and so on. His friend listened patiently and then said, "Yes, you are quite right, but you know they are the best of the kind that's on the market."

6

The person whom love approaches does not welcome it as a guest but tries to chase it away as an intruder. Love appears at first as an emotion which the person is afraid of, however desirable it may appear to the conscious mind. We feel that there are some unknown factors operating here. Perhaps we could best learn about them from pathological cases, which show what takes place otherwise, in a distorted and exaggerated way. During the analysis of a young girl I saw that she repeated a particular experience which puzzled me. She felt attracted to a man, her interest in him became intensified as he wooed her, she felt that she was going to fall in love with him. Then always the same scene followed. She suddenly withdrew from him. She stage-managed a quarrel about some trifle or other, or used a subterfuge not to see him any more or broke up the relationship abruptly without any apparent reason. An analyst who had treated her before explained her strange behavior simply. She was afraid of sex. But nothing in her emotional attitude justified such a view. She was rather afraid of love. That is, she was afraid to love.

Such a case, representative of so many others, deserves the attention of the psychologists because it shows that the emotional development which leads to love can be disturbed and prevented not only by hostility but by other tendencies. It is as if the ego were afraid of a danger, of a threatening loss. A French writer once defined love as "absence of fear." The statement is very surprising. You feel startled and inclined to contradict it. Of course you cannot qualify an idea by a negative. You argue that the absence of fear need not mean love at all. You know many people whom you even dislike, but you are not afraid of them. Then you realize that there is some truth in the remark, nevertheless. As far as such aphoristic contributions go there is something penetrating in the thought. What is it? We cannot be afraid of a person and love him or her at the same time. It seems that the two emotions are incompatible. A feeling of anxiety, an intense shame, a pronounced mistrust, exclude affection. But are we not all, to some slight extent, mistrustful or afraid of others? Yes, we have to admit that, and thus we conclude that love means the overcoming of this general fear. What the French writer means is only that a very essential feature of love, one of its criteria, is that there is no fear toward the beloved person. He did not want to define love but to give one of its characteristics.

It is odd that such an unconscious fear increases in many cases when the individual feels the approach of love, as if this emotion were an enemy. What is the girl in our case afraid of? There is a vague but intense fear in anticipating what love would mean to her. It would mean to surrender herself entirely, to become defenseless and without armor, to be at the mercy of the new feeling. If you give in to it you give yourself up. The girl felt that there could not be love with emotional reservations. But what threatens her? It is as if the ego had a preknowledge that she would be hurt and would suffer in such unconditional surrender. Warned by the unhappy marriage of her parents, the girl anticipates that she would be subjected to the change of passion, to the cruelty and brutality of the man, to the risk of being deserted and left alone. The ego feels vulnerable and knows its weakness.

In many cases this fear to love results in reactions similar to fears of danger from outside. The person who feels endangered from within tries to run away, to escape. The girl whom I mentioned often found a pretext to go on a trip or felt the urgent wish to change her environment. She seemed to hang onto her independence as onto dear life itself, but her reactions showed also that she felt the increasing urge to give herself up to the emotions of affection, that she also longed to lose her independence. She anticipated that she would give herself entirely to the man and that he would not give her as much tenderness as she had to offer. She was afraid of future rejection. Like so many women who feel that they could care for a man but that he would not love them in the long run, she wanted to escape. In none of the cases could she deny that she had begun to care for the man or that he showed the signs of affection and genuine attraction. Nevertheless an increasing anxiety always forced her to break off the relationship.

Here are two points which interest us: what does her flight mean and what is behind her fear? What motives cause her to be so scared of love? Superficially considered she ran away because she was afraid to give her affection to a man. That at least was her conscious explanation for her odd behavior. More deeply seen she suddenly broke off with the man because she became panicky that she would grow too fond of him and that he would then desert her. She protected herself against such a shock, against the future grief, in doing to him what he could do to her. Her behavior showed all the signs of a flight forward, a defense mechanism which I first described in the psychology of masochism.* She got so frightened that she turned the tables suddenly whenever she felt that the danger of falling in love was increasing. She acted similarly to a woman known to me who, whenever her maid seemed to be moody or dissatisfied, fired her. The woman was so afraid that the maid would leave unexpectedly that she preferred not to stand the suspense and thus took the flight forward.

But what is the girl really frightened of? Why does she not take the risk and accept and give love, unafraid of the future? It is a deeper insecurity than the general one. There is a possible danger which lurks around the corner within the girl herself and against which the guard is necessary. Her fear of being crushed by the man, of being rejected and repudiated, has its roots in her own sense of insecurity. She, like so many of her sex (and not a few of

* *Masochism in Modern Man*, Farrar, Straus and Company, New York, 1949.

the other), is afraid that her shortcomings, her weaknesses, yes, even her unworthiness, would be found out by the man when she let go her restraints. They feel not only vulnerable, they feel unsafe and uncertain. They refuse to love because they are afraid that they are not lovable. The man would not approve, yes, would reject them if they should let their emotions go free. The anxiety of many women increases when they find out that a man cares for them because then the question springs up, will he care for me when he really knows me? I once saw a young woman during the first months of her pregnancy obsessed by the thought that she must run away from her husband who loved her. Unconsciously she was terrified that her husband would consider her very ugly with progressing pregnancy and would desert her at the end, and she could not stand the suspense.

Many women feel unconsciously that they have little to give and become scared when they have to come out of the shell which everybody has built around himself. They are distrustful of the men they love; they try to devaluate them, but, more deeply seen, they are distrustful of themselves and doubt their own value.

Shame is not restricted to the region of sex and excretion. The ego also is afraid to be found out in its weaknesses, has to conceal much. The psychoanalysts would be quick to detect here sexual shame, but this fear to love is not motivated by inhibitions and anxieties of a sexual nature. Here are problems of the deep layers of the ego. The psychoanalysts behave as helplessly toward them as babes in the wood, in which they do not see trees but phallic symbols.

We realize that the fear to love which is founded on anticipation of the reaction of the mate is unconsciously there in every case but is usually overcome when the ego is reassured. Perhaps such reassurance is even sometimes a factor in the attempts to run away. An observer will often have the impression that to escape a suitor is a good way to get him, that the aim of running away is to be caught.

Nevertheless there is a genuine fear of love present. Is that all the ego is afraid of, all that frightens it? No, there is something beyond it, something which can hardly be reached with the knowledge we possess at the moment. The problem touches here the mysterious circle of the ego-frontiers, the last dark continent of psychology. We are aware of ourselves as individuals, as definite persons different from others. We are perhaps poor and ready to sell everything we possess but our souls. We are proud of being ourselves and we put up the strongest resistance against the idea of being someone else or someone else's. It dawns upon us that the deepest fear to love is connected with the fear of losing our self-possession.

There are jungles which cannot be penetrated. You have to go around to continue your way which seems to be blocked. As long as we do not know what constitutes the awareness of a personal self we cannot approach the problem directly. It is better not to start from the nature of this impenetrable fear of love but from the point where the danger appears past. Otherwise put, from the point of being in love. We learn from the lovers that they do not feel as two persons any more but as a oneness, as a unity which cannot be separated. They do not only admit that they have lost their individuality but they rejoice in it as if to be an individual self had been a burden which they got rid of. It is as if the magic of love has transcended the frontiers of the self, has leaped over the barriers of singleness and aloneness. To use a comparison: it is as if two healthy children who had led separate lives should awake on a morning and discover with ecstasy that they have become Siamese twins overnight. To us sober onlookers it does not seem to be a state of sheer delight and bliss.

Such is the emotional situation of two persons in love, such is the result of overcoming the mysterious fear to love which we could not understand. But if this is the effect of the victory over this fear, is it not likely that we can guess what the fear was about? According to a universal principle of depth-psychology it must be just this condition of giving up one's individuality which the future lover feared. But what does that mean? There is a better chance to understand it if we do not restrict our search for a clue to the state of amorousness but to others which resemble it in a general manner. You know other emotional states in which the frontiers of individuality seem to be removed and the self is not any more bound to the earth but floats on air as in love. In these states the ego also appears not only beside itself but beyond itself, not loosened up but lost in a wider region. And strangely enough these states also promise and grant happiness to the person.

The drug addict knows the happiness and even the beatitude of the loss of the self, and so do some psychotics and the visionary personality. To a certain extent the artist feels the same in his highest creative moments and the enthusiast who gives himself entirely to a cause with which he identifies himself. In all these conditions whose psychological resemblance to love is obvious the self seems to be lost in an enlargement of its frontiers. In all these conditions the person does not only feel enriched and powerful but also as if the self had broken its limitations and the chains which imprison it.

And strangely enough although we may envy some of those persons who have such profound and overpowering experiences —for instance the artist—we feel also that we would not like to change places with them. We feel something like fear in losing ourselves, this our present, unique self. We would not like to be lost to the world and we are not ready to pay the high price of the loss of our individuality for the happiness of an ecstatic fakir or an opium-eater. We are scared of the radical change to which such experiences would subject us. We do not want to be the victim of the mysterious power of a mania or of an unintelligible passion to which we should give ourselves over. Did I say passion? But that is just the expression we often apply to violent love.

It dawns upon us it must be the same fear here and there which scares us, the fear to give ourselves up and to give ourselves over. At the same time we understand there is a lure in the thought of losing ourselves and getting rid of this tiresome ego. Did we not say that the person who will become a lover is dissatisfied with himself and yearns to escape himself, wants to be someone else, someone who is not burdened with all kinds of shortcomings and imperfections? At the approach of love he is in a situation comparable to that of a sick person who is in mortal fear of a lifesaving operation. He looks forward to it and is afraid of it at the same time. There is the promise of a new life, but there is also the threat of annihilation.

We may be dissatisfied with this ego of ours and we may want to be different, but it is united, firmly established, we are familiar with it and afraid to give it up for something unknown. In the moment we have to surrender it we feel endangered and are full of nostalgia for the despised individuality of ours. The fear to love reaches sometimes the depth of a panic, resembles sometimes the fear to die. There are threads which run from the one to the other form. "I wanted to die and become you," says the heroine of an old play of O'Neill. So many persons feel likewise when in love. They want to feel like the other person, act like him, be him, but at the same time they want to protect themselves. There is the deadly fear of surrender in them.

Let us frankly say we do not know what is at the roots of this mysterious fear. What can be said about it is hardly more than probable conjecture. The problem transcends the reach of our present knowledge. There was a time in our childhood in which we did not possess this precious self, in which we were not aware of ourselves as separate personalities, the I-less time. The knowledge that you are you and no one else is a new acquisition for which one has paid with the loss of some happiness. The transition from the egoless time, in which the boundaries of the individuality are not yet defined or felt, must be a deep experience. We forgot it or we covered it up somewhere, but we are now unconsciously afraid of the possibility to return to this old, egoless state. We feel the change would shake the core of our existence, would mean giving up an essential part of our personality, like becoming crazy or going under an anesthetic. The frontiers of the self would again become uncertain and fluid. However tired we are of the old ego we are afraid of the new one. To be oneself or not to be oneself, that is the question. The alternative here is similar to the doubt of the noble Dane: to bear those ills we have than fly to others that we know not of. It is not the loss of freedom of action which the person fears, or if so it is only a reflex of a deeper fear, but the loss of individuality. He wishes to be free and wishes to be held; the beloved is both friend and foe. Women nearly in love with a man often escape him because they are afraid they could care for him too much for their own peace of mind. They are afraid of the object but they are more afraid of themselves.

While this fear is often conspicuous in violent characters it reflects in general the emotional situation of a person before he falls in love. It mirrors silently the depth of his feelings, the refusal to be rescued and the longing for it. It is as if a horse shied away from its own shadow. But what is this self, what does this sense of identity consist of? What does it mean? We are ourselves and no one else. Do we remember the time in which we were not so certain of who this I is? No one has described the miracle of first feeling oneself an ego, this dawn of a new era for the child who finds himself not as a part but as a distinct whole, who gets a new sense of his existence. We do not know how the child's mind struggles to this clarity, how the dawn breaks out of the darkness at the beginning of a consciousness of a self. Is it really a process of a unification of component parts of the ego as the psychologists assert? Is it not rather a new awareness that the ego is separated from and in contrast with what appeared as his world before?

Here is something which still eludes our analysis, something we cannot fathom in terms of our psychological research. Whenever we reach such points where psychology has to admit failure we are astonished that poets have gone beyond the realm of the tangible. They, not the psychiatrists and the physicians, are the vanguard of depth-psychology. They have divining rods telling them where are the most precious secrets of human nature. No psychologist could have described the loss of the self in love as precisely as the beautiful line of complaint:

Before you were coming,
I was I.

Clearer still and nearer still to the nature of the fear to love
which my unsatisfactory and clumsy words described in this futile
attempt are the verses of Delaleddin Rūmi, one of the greatest
Persian poets and thinkers, who lived about 700 years before our
time (1207-1273):

So shrinks from Love the tender heart
As if from threat of being slain,
For when true Love awakens, dies
The Self, that Despot, dark and vain.
Then let him die in night's black hour
And freely breathe in Dawn again!

Yes, when love awakens, dies the self, that despot dark and
vain. In these lines the core of the present thesis was touched. But
the self celebrates its enhanced and glorified resurrection in the
beloved person.

7

The gist of the discontent in the ego that characterizes the
emotional situation from which love springs is unconscious guilt
feeling. We feel guilty not only when we have committed an
offense or crime in our thoughts but also when we are unable
to fulfill the demands which we make on ourselves. Guilt feeling
is a reaction not only to unconscious impulses of hate and
hostility but also to the awareness of our inadequacy.

Love overcomes this dissatisfaction with ourselves. It sweeps
away the unconscious guilt feelings like the powerful wave that
carries obstacles along with it to bury them in the depths of the
ocean. The irresistible magic of love is beyond good and evil.

It does not permit social anxiety—which is what guilt feeling is essentially—to coexist with it. While sex is compatible with guilt feeling, love does not tolerate it. It silences all pangs of conscience. It works in us as a great atonement, expiating all sins. It makes one fearless and remorseless. It not only dissipates guilt feelings rooted in the past but prevents their development. We are forgiven and made sinless. Love is redemption. That which is done in love and from love cannot be wrong. This motive alone justifies not only all means but its own aims. All is fair in love and war.

Crimes committed in its name appear justified, crimes which otherwise would fill men with a terribly guilty conscience. It is obvious what makes such an extraordinary situation feasible; the love-object has become the personification of the ideal ego. As such it is the redeemer of all sins in the same way that Jesus is to the religious mind. All that is done for the beloved issues from supreme authority, giving it the highest sanction. Only fanaticism, itself of a similar emotional character, works on men in that way. Love has the same nuance of feeling as religious salvation. Those who are saved cannot commit a crime. Love elevates the man beyond others, ennobling him with a new dignity and decisiveness. The king cannot do wrong. This feeling is just the opposite of the pressure and depression produced by guilty conscience. The latter pulls one down to earth. In love one floats on air. He who is conscious of guilt feels alone and lonely, isolated, ostracized from the community of men. Who is in love never feels lonely. He is closely connected with all that breathes. With the disappearance of guilt feelings comes an amazing increase of self-confidence and spirit. Lovers show a grandiose neglect of danger, a carelessness for one's own security, an absence of death fear. The lover will find the way to his sweetheart, come hell or high water.

Guilty conscience makes us feel timid and afraid. Love removes anxiety. While conscience makes cowards of us all, love makes heroes of us all.

We could have reached this insight, that love abolishes guilt feelings, by two other roads. On the first we would start from the fact that the suspicion of being unable to love produces in us a guilt feeling whether we know it or not. In studying cases which convince you that the unconscious recognition of lack of love produces guilt feeling you do not at first understand why this should be so. Then it dawns on you that scarcity of love is unconsciously considered equal to hostility. In its emotional reaction the feeling of not being able to love is the same as that of hating. This corresponds to the Freudian view that the unconscious does not know negation, cannot say no.

When affection and friendship are shown to us which we cannot reciprocate we feel embarrassed and slightly guilty. Why? One would think that too little of a certain emotion needed no excuse. Why should we feel culpable if we cannot return love? We feel nevertheless that we have failed someone who has trusted us and are guilty for our failure in emotional response. It seems as if our lack of affection not only expresses indifference or absence of interest but downright dislike, aversion or even hostility. The same emotion is felt whenever one withdraws his inclination from another who has neither wronged nor offended him but has remained worthy of affection. Why should we feel not only responsible for this withdrawal but also guilty? Are we under an obligation to return affection? Has the other person a claim on us merely because he or she loves us? That cannot be asserted, but nevertheless we behave as if it were so.

A well-brought-up girl receiving a declaration of sincere love which she has to refuse feels embarrassed and tries to sweeten the pill. It rarely happens that she declares plainly and coldly that she does not care for the suitor and then goes on to discuss other subjects. There came under my observation the case of a girl who, when surprised by sudden and indubitable signs of real love on the part of an unloved man, started to sob and ran away crying. Later she said she felt "such a terrible person," although she never had encouraged the man. She felt like a criminal for having deeply hurt and offended an innocent person who cared for her. This feeling remained despite the fact that she realized later she had overestimated the grief which she had inflicted on him. Another young woman, married to an unloved man of whom she is "quite fond," confesses that she feels "like a heel," because she cannot respond to his ardent love-making. The more guilty she feels the less she is able to reciprocate his affection. In the end she feels guilty for having felt guilty. She often complains, "I am so ready to give him what he wants, but I cannot go through with it." In these as in similar cases the demand for response which cannot be met acquires a moral character. One feels fearful, as if threatened by a danger from within.

We feel similarly guilty when a person dear to us dies and we know we did not give proof of our affection for him. Everybody knows this terrible feeling of the irrevocable "too late." In some cases our nostalgia for the dead, increased by this silent guilt feeling, reaches a degree of despair and deep depression. It is said that the main feeling on looking back at the past is one of regret. A recurrent regret is that we have not given enough love to those who are now dead.

And do we not have a cause of guilt when we pretend to love? It is not the same as when we feign pity or gratitude. It has a different emotional quality. Other sham feelings may be venial offenses but to feign love is a sin against the Holy Ghost. It is like cheating, promising something that we cannot fulfill. To feign love is to offer a cheap and inferior substitute for affection, to hand out a shadow for the substance. It is not possible to pretend love for any length of time. Insincerity is quickly sensed. The unconscious of one person understands the unconscious of another as if by wireless telegraphy, in spite of all conscious misunderstandings and mistakes. To love, one must be entirely oneself. It happens sometimes that we ourselves confuse this unconscious sense of guilt with affection. The inner demand to respond becomes so urgent that we yield to it on the surface, although not really returning the affection. Sometimes women find themselves in this strange emotional situation. They feel sorry for a man who suffers from frustrated love for them, yielding to his lovemaking out of pity. Psychical and physical reactions later on prove that they fooled themselves. It was not love which made them capitulate but guilt feelings because they could not return the man's affection. Some are introspective enough to recognize the difference immediately. One woman, feeling that she had hurt a man who had wooed her a long time, went to bed with him, only to find that she was entirely without feeling. Then she realized that her surrender was a kind of atonement for having wronged him. It was not love as she had at first thought. Accepting love without returning it also makes us feel guilty, just like getting heavily into debt without being able to discharge our obligation. To love eases or even removes guilt feeling. To be loved without loving oneself produces guilt feeling or intensifies it.

Perhaps here is the appropriate place to introduce some remarks about shyness. This is an emotion which can be considered from two sides. It may be seen and understood as a kind of fear or anxiety in facing others, or as an expression of insecurity in oneself which appears especially when an opportunity offers to meet other people. A sense of insecurity is apparently the primary feeling. It seems to be founded on the unconscious awareness that one has no free-flowing feelings toward other beings, cannot feel at ease with them, as if one were somehow ashamed or afraid. Shyness cannot develop without anticipation of a critical attitude of others. Such a critical or negative reaction, consciously or unconsciously imagined, now evokes in the owner feelings of hostility or vivid annoyance. Shyness is then the emotional reaction to this unconscious feeling. It is well known that shyness is infectious. A shy person coming into a group sometimes makes others shy as if his concealed antagonism aroused the same emotion in them together with the same reaction. It is also a psychological fact that the feeling of shyness disappears—at least for the moment—when the shy person announces openly, "I am so shy." It is as if this spontaneous confession of one's hidden antagonistic impulses dissipated the emotion of shyness which is the social reaction to one's own hostile feelings.

With the discussion of the psychology of shy people we have entered the realm of other problems, namely that of the guilt feeling which prevents or dwarfs the development of affection. We have already dealt with it in a previous chapter. What has to be added here is the fact that the most essential part of the insecurity feeling, which is such a handicap in love, is guilty conscience. The person who cannot overcome it to a large extent does not reach the inner liberty that is necessary to love. You could also say that he does not dare to love. This statement is not restricted to the relationship between the sexes. It is at least as valid and valuable for social relationships in general. Individuals with too much guilty feeling cannot develop affection for their fellow men. Put differently, we might say that he who feels very culpable on account of his malicious, cruel and hostile tendencies toward others, who makes too exacting moral demands on himself and who cannot be somehow tolerant toward his unfriendly thoughts and impulses is incapable of loving.

8

Zoology teachers in elementary schools like to introduce their subject by determining to which family an animal belongs. You have some notion of what a tiger is like when you hear that it belongs to the species of cats, or of a dog's nature when told that this beast is a descendant of the wolf. Why are psychologists unable to determine to which class of emotions love belongs? Why, for instance, should psychoanalysts blunder so badly as to classify love as a particular, aim-inhibited form of the sex drive? It is as if a zoologist should say that the nightingale belongs to the family of flying fishes. Love is akin to enthusiasm, ecstasy, inspiration, ardent zeal. It is made of such stuff as dreams are made of. It belongs to that family which embraces among its members artistic inspiration and religious zeal. I should like to add that fanaticism must be assigned to the same group of feelings, as a sinister, isolated relative, the black sheep of the family. In all members of the group there is the same singleness of purpose, consuming passion, flame. Inspiration and infatuation are lit essentially by the same spark.

Loving means achieving something, being filled with a spirit which is related to the one that inspires artists and priests. It is creation, like the work of the poet or prophet. Nowadays every little boy and girl thinks they can love just as they think they can write poetry. But in both cases though many are called few are chosen. Loving in the right way comes only to the genius. The love of the Brownings is to the infatuation of a playboy what one of their best poems is to the miserable lines of a poor versifier. There is nothing contemptible in amateurishness. It may even be an honest attempt at creation; but the creative power is lacking, no matter how good the intentions may be. What in one case springs from deep wells comes in the other from shallow waters.

Every rascal is convinced that he is as capable of loving as the next man. He does not know that loving means creating, a high and concentrated activity of phantasy and will power, a combination of free-flowing current and control. He has no idea that love is achievement, that to love means to accomplish something and that the way of loving is deeply rooted in the personality of the lover. Here as in every creative feat the individual character is the determining factor, deciding whether the outcome shall be fruition or failure, bloom or decay. In artistic creation, too, not alone the gifts of the artist but even more his concealed character will destine the value of his work. Goethe recognized this latent factor when he wrote, "To produce something you have to be somebody." To love you have to be a personality.

Loving is a personal achievement, I say, like creating, and its accomplishment, of the same emotional kind, namely, to master the unconscious countertendencies in oneself and to find oneself in something or somebody outside or beyond the self. There is the same search for perfection in both emotional productions. Ibsen once said that to write means to sit in judgment on oneself. He should have added: and to pardon oneself, finding atonement through and in the creation. Consider the unconscious process in the formation of love, the dissatisfaction with oneself, the search for an ideal ego and the self-fulfillment in the beloved person. It is a similar piece of creation with identical values.

These values are not added to it from outside. They are imminent, inherent in the creation itself and in its success. It is not the subject which the lover or the artist chooses that is the decisive factor but rather how he deals with it, what he makes of it. The great German painter Liebermann once said, "Not he who paints a prostitute is immoral, but he who paints her badly." It is the same displacement of moral values from the subject onto the production which characterizes Emile Zola's remark that a sentence well written is a good deed. *("Une phrase bien faite est une bonne action.")* It is not the worth of the chosen love-object but the way of loving her which proves whether the creation spells achievement or failure, from a superior viewpoint. In love as in art the object itself need not be noble. The achievement in creation ennobles it, even transfigures it.

As I said before, the emotion which becomes creative in love is of the same kind as enthusiasm. This word is Greek in origin, meaning the state of a man in whom God dwells. It means the union with God which exalts the one so favored above all earthly concerns. To the Greeks the mystic was enthusiastic; so too was the seer in the frenzy of prophecy and the poet in whom Apollo dwelt. Later on enthusiasm meant direct intuition of the divine, but originally the union with deity which resulted in enthusiasm was represented in a very crude way. It was brought about by drinking, since Dionysos materialized in wine. (Do we not say drunk with love?) It could also be brought about by eating the god. (The lover says he could eat his sweetheart.) At first all expressions of enthusiasm meant to take material possession of the god. The suddenness of the illumination which enthusiasm kindles is considered a guarantee of truth. Is it any different in the case of love at first sight?

The resemblance between these two emotions is not restricted to their general character. The psychology of enthusiasm reveals that a phase of depression with feelings of inadequacy or dissatisfaction—which can even become conscious to some extent—precedes the frenzy. Here too an internal conflict is going on. There is an attempt to reject the idea or the truth which would take possession of the personality. There is an increasing resistance and then the sudden counterblow, ending finally in the complete submission of the ego and its submersion in the overthrowing emotion. The boundless violence and exuberance is the result of the emotional overreaction to the resistance of the first effort to expel the object.

Cases of sudden and violent conversion furnish the best analogy for such infatuation. The enthusiasm of the religious zealot and the rapture of the lover are conditioned by the fact that a flood of reactive feelings have swept away all doubts and resistance. An irresistible power from without seems to govern and to lead the recipient, floating through him and carrying him beyond himself. The prophet, the artist, the lover—they all feel that destiny pulls them. It is not, they feel, a psychological process which is taking place but something independent of their will. A storm swirls them wherever it will. The inspiration of the religious genius and the emotion of the lover are related in origin and character. The one claims that God speaks through him and the other feels himself to be the blessed vessel of a supernatural power beyond his grasp. A miracle has happened to and through them. Thus favored, their self-confidence mounts to astonishing heights. All dissatisfaction has vanished and the frontiers of the ego are so far enlarged that the latter seems boundless. The changed person is so inundated with one overflowing emotion that there is no place for others. The enthusiast and the lover know only one God. Neither one of them can understand how it is possible for others not to worship their ideal.

You can call love an achievement because it means mastery by an unconscious effort of will over the great countertendencies.

Here, as in artistic and religious creation, we are inclined to underestimate the power of imagination and the supremacy of will in love which overcome obstacles in the human soul. The lover, like the artist, takes a bit of reality for his creation, breathes into it and gives it life. This creative power attains its aim in wrestling with an unseen enemy in the dark, with the adversary inside oneself. The lover, like the artist, could say with Jacob, who struggled with the angel of the Lord, "I shall not let ye go until ye bless me." To love and to create fill the soul with delight as does any victory gained by self-mastery. The emotional effect of reaching the sublime state for both the lover and the artist means happiness. Freed from guilt and want, his achievement puts him in tune with himself and all others.

But this elation exists only when the miracle of achievement takes place. It does not exist earlier or in those interludes when the lover, artist or prophet feels dissatisfied and insecure or doubtful of his mission. Enthusiasm can as little be preserved and kept alive as romantic love. It vanishes when it has to wait. Both love and art begin as play, fancy, but the play becomes reality, taking possession of its creator until he is "the world forgetting, by the world forgot." Both art and love are emotional recovery processes, as is every creation. They sometimes appear as a holy madness, but actually they rather prevent a person from becoming mad. As long as one is really loving or enthusiastic he cannot be unhappy. He has good safeguards.

The lover is as "selfish" as the artist in his work, or as the saint in his prayer. They are all devoting themselves to the achievement of their own private salvation. That one subject excludes all others. All three enthusiasts need the response of their object. The lover hopes his affection will be returned; the artist that his work will be appreciated and the saint that his prayer will be answered. At the same time the will to create and to love are independent of external reaction. They exist in their own right. In art, religion and love the drive for self-perfection is unself-seeking.

The idealization of the love-object is related to religious worship. Romeo approaches Juliet at their first meeting as "this holy shrine" which his lips, "two blushing pilgrims," kiss. His love blots out all offense. "Thus from my lips by thine my sin is purged." The salvation which religion promises to the believer is granted likewise to the lover.

9

Poets and writers of the last century often pictured a situation in which love and pity appear to be intimately connected. A woman falls in love with a man because she feels sorry for him or a man becomes infatuated with a girl because she is so unhappy and miserable. Love, sympathy and compassion here seem to flow into each other. Shakespeare knew better than these romanticists. He draws a sharp line between the feeling of love and compassion. Viola in *Twelfth Night* destroys the hope that her sympathy for a suitor means "a degree of love." She argues,

> . . . for 'tis a vulgar proof
> That very oft we pity enemies.

I assert that pity and love are incompatible, which means they cannot coexist. If one of the two emotions is very pronounced the other has to yield. It seems that a deep pity is irreconcilable with love. That appears to contradict all our traditional ideas, but psychological facts are not concerned with conventional views. My statement applies also outside the realm of people's relation to each other. It includes the relation of a person to a social or religious group. It is obvious that you can feel pity for an oppressed racial or religious minority without loving its members. It is equally clear that you can feel very sorry for the poor, can be passionately socialistic or communistic, and at the same time feel no love for the needy and miserable. I know a man who is full of compassion for workers deprived of their

rights. I have seen him fight for them, stirred by his strong feelings, but many observations have proved to me that he really
does not care for them. It need not be proved that affection and
pity are emotions of a different kind which are very distinct in
their nature. It is rather difficult to prove that they are incompatible. Is it because there is no place for two prima donnas
on the same stage? Are both emotions so strong that they do not
tolerate each other beyond a certain degree in the human soul?

I shall try to prove the incompatibility of pity and love from
the points of view presented in my thesis on love. We assumed
that a person is unconsciously envious or jealous of another with
whom he will fall in love. There is, we said, a kind of grudging
admiration for the object, who is considered superior. The object has qualities which the lover lacks; it achieves where he
fails; it is successful, strong and self-confident where he feels
frustrated, weak and doubtful, full of contradictions and dissatisfied.

Compare this emotional situation with the other, that of feeling sorry for someone who is ill or unhappy or indigent. This
person for whom we are sorry we do not consider superior to us.
In general we feel superior to him. You may dispute this point,
contending that you do not, in any way, feel superior to this
pitied person, that pure sympathy is the only emotion you are
aware of. But in this case the feeling of superiority is unconscious. If you are a bit introspective, exerting sharp self-observation (and if you don't take fright at unpleasant facts within
yourself) you will discover that this feeling of superiority exists.
You can then correct my statement, but only to this extent, that
the feeling of superiority remains unconscious. How can it be
otherwise? Unconsciously we feel privileged when comparing
our own circumstances or happier lot with the situation of the
afflicted person. If we were in the same or a worse predicament
we would not feel sorry.

In comparing the lover with the one who feels compassion we
often meet contrasting traits. In pity we unconsciously look
down on the object of our emotion as if we were on a higher or

more advantageous plane. But love has the upward glance. There is no incentive to feel envious or jealous toward the person we pity as we do toward the beloved. The relationship of the charitable person toward his object may be one of tender-heartedness, but this tenderness is not the same as that of the lover. As far as the unconscious attitude goes, the relationship is that of the Have for the Have-not. In other words, it is the reversal of the situation of the lover. We slowly come to realize that love and pity exclude each other psychologically. It is impossible for any length of time to look up and down in quick succession, to feel inferior and superior, change about, permanently. An internal decision becomes necessary.

I am ready to meet the counterevidence which will be brought forward at this point: cases in everyday life where someone falls in love with a person who has aroused extreme sympathy. Like everyone else I have seen instances in which pity for the object seemed coupled with admiration, yes, even with a certain envy of the sufferer because of his superior courage, patience or dignity. But every penetrating psychological analysis proves that such coexistence of pity and love only marks a transition phase and leads to an unconscious conflict in which one emotion eventually conquers the other.

I once observed the case of a man who fell in love with a girl who was suffering from tuberculosis. His pity for her, his attentions and efforts to secure every possible help, his solicitude during the disease, were really touching. There is no possible doubt not only that he took care of her but also that he cared for her. This became increasingly evident as the girl slowly recovered and regained a certain independence in which she did not need his help as urgently as before. She expressed her gratitude and tenderness and frequently assured him that he gave her heart to live again. Isn't such a case a strong argument against my thesis? It is not, because pity did not change into love nor compassion into passion, but affection grew as something new within pity and eventually became so intense as to push the earlier attitude aside. During the disease the man realized the girl's excellent qualities, her endurance and gentleness, her silent dignity. Her endowments filled him with admiration and the continuation of this kind of admiration into the unconscious is known to us as envy. The most essential presupposition for rising love was thus formed. Pity and affection did not stand their ground together. Pity yielded to love.

In all similar cases the same development can be studied. The birth of the new emotion of love is not dependent on the old feeling of pity. Compassion does not beget love, as the phantasy of some psychologists imagines. Love is born in spite of pity and finally displaces it. It is a new plant in the same ground and its growth will soon overrun the plant of pity. The person who was the object of charity does not remain the same but becomes a love-object. In the case just given the pitiable girl became an enviable one. The man then felt really inferior to her. Sometime later the girl had a serious relapse and the affection of the man slowly took on again the form of compassion. He couldn't help it. In spite of himself he felt that his love retreated. Contrary to his conscious wishes his affection gave way to pity. His fixation on the girl continued a long time but the tie was different and with the girl's recovery the relationship slowly dissolved.

In every case of this kind that I have been able to examine psychologically the same thing happened. Whenever love appeared to blossom from pity the development proved in fact to be a new and independent growth, springing up in spite of pity and having its origin not in pity for but in admiration of the object. The suffering of the object had no connection with the new feeling of love. You could say that a man fell in love with a girl not because he first felt sorry for her but in spite of that fact. He was attracted to her not by her sufferings and tribulations but by her fine qualities, her charm and character which he had remarked during her suffering. It is obvious that we have here a distinction of utmost importance for the psychological inquiry of this subject. The cases which have been noted as counterevidence do not invalidate our thesis. They rather prove the assertion that pity and love cannot coexist for long. In these cases the one emotion is the successor of the other. The idea that such cases appear to contradict my statement is founded on psychological fallacy and incorrect observation. To imagine that pity changes into love is fancy reasoning.

You might be tempted to follow up the contrast between love and pity a bit farther and to re-examine the astonishing prospect before us. Expressions of condolence might sometimes be mistaken for manifestations of love, but they are distinct and usually felt as such. We can differentiate very well between a person who feels sorry for us and one who loves us. Our pride makes us dislike to be pitied. Pity seems a kind of subtle insult, and if displayed, touches our human dignity. Does not such a reaction also reveal that the one who feels sorry for us unconsciously assumes a superiority which we are unwilling to allow him? Who is offended by love? Everybody likes to be loved. Nobody likes to be pitied.

Put in now familiar terms, the picture of the two emotions can be confronted and contrasted. The love-object is the fulfillment of our ego-ideal. We are in want of something which the beloved has. In pity the other person is or seems to be in want of something which we have to offer. In love we need the other person. In pity the other person makes a silent claim on us, he needs us. In the one case we feel that we can get so much from the object, in the other that we can give what means much to him. In love we want to become one with the object. In pity we are in one place, the object in another. In the first case the tendency is toward union. In the second, toward differentiation. He who loves feels the same as the love-object. He who pities tries to feel with the other. A mother does not pity her child, she does not suffer with it, she suffers as the child does, as being part of herself. To the lover, giving is unconsciously felt to be a privilege, but to the charitable person it is considered a tribute. Love is a grace, in the religious sense. Pity is a kind of atonement. No one thinks of love as a virtue in the sense that many think of charity, the "sweetness" of which originates in self-righteousness and self-aggrandizement. We do not feel feverish,

violent or frantic when we are compassionate. Only those burn
in their holy zeal whom we would call philanthropic hyenas
and who tempt us to become misanthropists. We know why, and
how much they have to conceal and atone for.

Pity is often interwoven with a kind of sentimentalism, foreign
to love. Sentimentality is not the expression of genuine feeling,
but its substitute, made of cheaper material, proof of and compensation for the lack of real feeling. The identification with another person common to love and pity is not only different in its
extent, but also in its character. The lover feels: if I could be you!
The pitying person feels: there, but for the grace of God, go I.
In the one case the outlook is a promise of happiness, in the other
a menace of impending calamity.

From this psychological insight we understand that pity and
love are incompatible. The increase of the one means the diminishing and often disappearance of the other. We frequently see
that pity gains as much ground as love loses, and sometimes we
see the opposite. There is no bridge from one realm to the other.
The two emotions might live in the same psychological neighborhood, so to speak, but they live in separate houses with different
atmospheres. There is a fence between them. Where compassion
reigns, there is no place for passion.

Perhaps this is the place to add some words about another conflict of emotions. Love is incompatible not only with pity but also
with duty. We owe many things to the travelers who accompany
us on this short trip from the cradle to the grave; we do not owe
them love. Love cannot be exacted. It can only be asked. Duty
contradicts the spontaneity which is a necessary condition of love.
The idea of duty itself arouses all our unconscious powers of resistance and repulsion. There is no love if you lay down conditions.

It is not possible to say, "I am ready to love you, if . . ." The
essence of love is to give voluntarily, not under duress. Dutiful
love is a contradictory expression because affection means ease
and freedom from fear. The spirit of love is at variance with that
of duty and obligation, which spirit tries to dominate a person.

There is no moral obligation for love, nor any enforcement of rule or law. You cannot be devoted to your love and to duty at the same time and to the same extent. The sweet-natured Juliet, ready to obey her parents and fulfill all filial obligations, becomes a scheming, lying and deceitful woman overnight. Duty, that stern daughter of the voice of God, has herself a harsh organ when it calls us. But Juliet's voice is for Romeo, his soul "that calls upon his name":

> How silver-sweet sound lovers' tongues by night,
> Like softest music to attending ears.

10

Nowhere in the course of our discussion until now has appeared the necessity to differentiate between various kinds of love. I have stated the psychological preparations of love, its nature and meaning, and have tried to sketch its unconscious development and dynamics. Love appears here as a unity in the psychological sense with certain well-defined and definite characteristics. There are other emotions akin to and often confused with love, but they do not fulfill the psychological conditions and should not be called love.

To like someone and to love someone are two different things. There are many ties between human beings, but only a special relationship ought to be called love. Other and related emotions should be recognized under different names as individuals of the same family are recognized, like, for instance, James and John Smith. As we shall see, people mistake even those emotions which are irreconcilable with love. We psychologists fight in vain against such confusion. The difficulty is a purely verbal one and due to the wretchedness of our language. Why is it that we freedom-loving people so seldom rebel against the unshakable tenacity and intolerable tyranny of certain words?

The immediate cause for these remarks is the necessity of discussing the most celebrated form of love, that of a mother for her child. Is it possible that mother love also can be brought into harmony with this thesis? Could it be that even here on this high road of love we might meet such suspicious figures as dissatisfaction with oneself, as envy, greed and hostility? It does not fit in with all our previous and present ideas.

Certainly I am not the first nor shall I be the last to express the wish for another word when speaking of the quality of feeling that a mother has for her child. The beggarliness of the language falsifies the picture and deludes us. It makes us believe in a sameness where none exists. I shall deal with the matter briefly, only demonstrating that it is beyond the realm of our subject. In the beginning I made it clear that love can only exist between two human beings who are aware that they are separate persons. Our analysis could add that love is an attempt to bridge the gulf between them, to overcome the separation and to change it into identity.

The "love" or whatever you may call it of the mother for her child is originally not of this kind and does not belong to this psychological category. A mother does not consider her child as an entirely separate human being. The umbilical cord is cut only in material reality, but psychologically the child remains part and parcel of the organic life of the mother. Here are operating powers much more vital than love, upshots of instinctual needs which go beyond the temporary nature of passion.

The tie of the mother to her child, I mean, is largely of a biological nature, founded on the fact that the child grew inside her and on her, was and is a living part of her. This attachment is of course much more solid, intimate and permanent than the thing we call romantic love. It is not as fragile, nor is it in danger of being destroyed by time. It is not doomed to fail as most other human relationships are. It happens very rarely and only in pathological cases, under extraordinary circumstances, that this tie is severed. It also happens that a person cuts off his own foot or hand, but that is certainly an unusual event. I do not know how we should name this almost vegetative feeling, but the word love is certainly a misnomer in the light of our concept, which makes psychological separation a preliminary condition. The relationship of mother and child does not fulfill this condition of an I and a You, of two persons. Love cannot start from the feeling of oneness. It only arrives there.

Is that all there is in the mother's "love"? Oh, certainly not. So much has been woven into this tissue which was worked on so long, so much even of love in our sense of the word. It is only our need to simplify the picture which makes us see it as a single figurehead. For instance there is a trait which we always neglect that is connected with the phantasy life of the mother. I mean the phantasies and daydreams which develop before the baby is born, and during the long interval when the mother takes care of it, when it is growing up and becoming an independent being. But when will these daydreams stop?

Before becoming a mother the woman has the same lingering dissatisfaction with herself which we all have. Then a miracle happens. Something comes into her life that changes it psychologically to an extent beyond anything for which hearsay has prepared her. A new life grows in her which is not only of a material nature, but which from now on becomes the permanent object of her imagination, at certain times the only object. A phantasy life begins which has no analogy except in the conceptions and daydreams of great artists. In these day-dreams, which play around the baby long before it is born, there appear features which are well known to us from our inquiry into the prephases of love.

We meet here the transfer of the ego-ideal to the baby. It will realize that life which was denied to its mother. It will be beautiful, happy and successful, and it will conquer the world. Everything will be fulfilled which was frustrated in the mother's life by external factors and inner conditions. It will represent the perfection of humanity because kind fairies will bend over its cradle and fulfill all the wishes which the mother had as she lay tired and smiling in her bed after her baby's birth. The arrival of the baby assures a second chance to its mother, the possibility for a life which is in great part already spent to live again. The mother is again happy in the anticipation of the future. It is in the day-dreams of pregnant women, better than elsewhere, that the trans-fer of the ego-ideal, so essential for the love-process, can be studied.

The only question is whether we can call the phenomenon a transfer. Will the child now in the mother's womb not be the mother herself again, a better, more beautiful, cleverer second ego? Is that really comparable to the shifting of the ego-phantom to another person? Is not the child rather a continuation, an ex-tension of the ego-ideal, which becomes flesh and figure? The deep gratification in these daydreams and the happiness in the mother's face, which seems transfigured when she looks at her baby, reminds one of the bliss of love's young dream fulfilled. It has, however, other features, which do not fit into the picture.

We have forgotten that the baby, the future son or daughter, is not only a better second ego but is also the love-object. In the formation of the phantasies (of which it is the center) the father also plays a considerable role. The baby will inherit certain traits from him—other, less pleasant traits will not be inherited—and these traits will be improved, his endowment even greater than his father's. I heard a remark by a young mother which strikes me as psychologically very illuminating. Her baby was born while the father was away in the army. After she had greeted the father on his return, she looked at him intently and said, "How big your face is!" This strange remark which puzzled him at first was soon understood. The young mother had looked attentively for so many hours at the baby's face, in which she saw the image of her absent husband, that the latter's face appeared large by compari-son with his likeness in the baby's face.

We understand that in the daydreams of the mother there is not a search for the personified ego-ideal but the finding of it. This ideal became realized, the dream fulfilled. In this extension of the mother all the psychological and physical possibilities which she once desired for herself have become potential realities. So far the resemblance to the unconscious process in finding a love-object is striking enough. Here, as there, is the finding, the realization of the ego-ideal in an object. But is the child psychologically an independent object for the young mother?

In reality it is the fulfillment of the demands of an ideal ego in oneself, and that is very different from the process in love where you find the ideal ego in another person. There now dawns upon us a new insight. The mother does not look at her child with the eyes of a lover at his sweetheart but with the eyes of an artist at his masterpiece, the perfect fulfillment of his creative dream. Only observe a mother as, labor pains over, she gazes for the first time at the child which the nurse holds up to her. It is a real and perfect baby, she sees, and her own. Here is the pride and modesty of an artist who has created something beyond his conscious powers of imagination. It must be like the feelings of God as He looked out on His finished creation that last day and saw that it was good. No, not like God because He is almighty and all-knowing, while a mother can only hope and guess. In her look there is much more proud surprise. A miracle has happened to her and miracles happen only to mortals, not to God.

The child is her creation, something which she has produced, which grew inside her for many months, nourished on her body and is now outside to be contemplated. The thing is unbelievable to her. How could she, an insignificant, poor, weak mortal, have created this wonder? Yes, here is the artist, looking at his best work in the moment of his proudest triumph and self-fulfillment. He regards it as a materialized part of that which is best and richest in and of himself, and at the same time, of something which is beyond himself. "I could not have made it. It was not I who produced it," cried Haydn as he heard, with the tears streaming down his cheeks, his "Creation." The mother feels her child to be her achievement, the realization of a proud dream, and she is filled with the emotions of a man who looks at his best accomplishment. She has created something in her own image, and unlike God she does not know how she could have done it. There now becomes clear to us not only the analogy between the mother's feeling for her child and the unconscious phases of love but also the differences between the two emotions. We have two ways of fulfilling the demands of the ego-ideal. Its materialization may be reached by our choice of a love-object or its claims satisfied by our achievements. What the mother feels for her child is certainly a combination of these two processes, but the larger part of the feeling is that of the person who has accomplished his best dreams.

Of course I do not mean to deny that there is also love in the relationship of mother and child in the sense that we mean love, but this emotion develops later and beside the first, which is much more permanent. "The soul is a wide country," wrote Arthur Schnitzler, who time and again showed how much space there is in us for different, related and contradictory emotions. Later on the mother reluctantly becomes aware that her child has grown to be an independent human being, separated from her in spite of everything. Then and only then love develops, and along the same lines as we have sketched.

A mother is also unconsciously envious and jealous of her child, of its better opportunities, future chances in life and greater endowments. Indeed it is even a sort of unconscious jealousy of the child's present happy and carefree condition; a feeling which is expressed in the Brahms song: "Oh, if I knew the road back, the dear road back to childhood's country!" ("*O, wüsst ich doch den Weg surück, den lieben Weg ins Kinderland!*") This unconscious envy also leads to a kind of resentment or hostility which contrasts strongly with the deep affection for the child. The reaction sets in and the complete rejection of the negative tendencies results in an intensified tenderness as in other cases. But what may be called love in a mother's feelings is an addition to the one woven much earlier, the biological tie for which I have no name.

In considering the emotional relationship of the father to his child I do not feel on such firm ground as when I deal with the mother's psychology. One guesses that it must be, so to speak, a diluted or weaker solution of the same mixture without its biological factor. There is also a concentration of hopes and expectations, of phantasies, originating in the needs of the ego-ideal, a similar self-fulfillment in the small being, which is felt as a continuation of oneself. There is to some extent the same pride and satisfaction in one's own product—I could almost say, in one's work of art or achievement. Aside from these prefigurations, love develops out of the same desires as elsewhere and in other relationships.

And the children? Should we not talk about their love for their parents? The biological tie, so strong in the mother, does not exist in her child whose only connection is one of dependence and adherence growing out of its infant needs. The baby does not perceive that the mother is a separate and independent being; and love, according to our definition, can only be possible if this condition is fulfilled. Even later on we do not observe any signs of love of the small child for its mother, but only expressions of emotional dependency and gratitude. (You can be grateful to a person without loving him.) You might call it attachment, resulting from the child's helplessness and the mother's care, but not love.

Whatever signs of affection we may observe in later months are, so to speak, imitative in nature. The child reacts to the mother's attentions. It gives back what it received in a kind of primitive identification with the mother. It reflects the manifestations of love shown by the mother. Could you call such a phenomenon an induction of love, similar to the electric process? The possibility remains that the baby learns to love the mother as it is loved by her. That means that the baby makes a shift with the mother as it does in many other ways. It changes places with the mother, in play, so to speak, each one becoming the other. Thus love enters the child's life. In such a reversal the baby in the mother's role loves itself in another person.

If we could accept the possibility of such a thought—namely, a changing of places—then we would have here an exception to the emotional development which we are outlining. But would the whole phenomenon deserve the name of genuine and spontaneous love? If we consider its origin we should rather call it responsive love. The baby would respond to the love received with its own love, just like a grownup who is long wooed and overwhelmed with attentions and compliments. It is then not unlikely that when the baby misses these signs of affection it plays the mother's role toward itself—is her proxy, so to speak, adopts the role corresponding to its wishes of what the mother should play toward it. Like an actor it demonstrates by its behavior a desire to be loved again, and by loving its mother shows the situation in reverse.

There is no doubt that later on the child loves its mother and father with all the characteristics of genuine affection. But this love develops late and alongside the earlier form of response. It passes through the same phases, starting from dissatisfaction with oneself and unconscious envy, and results in a reaction in the form of tenderness. It has the same preparation in fantasies as in all other cases we have seen.

Should all the self-effacing love of the mother, her attention, care, sorrow, have no other emotional effect than that here described? No other consequence than the child's responsive love which reflects what it received? Where is the permanent and deep-reaching effect of the parents' love after the child grows up? It is impossible that the psychical effects of so many years of affection can be merely superficial. The long years of parental affection must influence the personality of the child, the adolescent and the adult. We can guess how deeply affected children are in a silent way by the love received. It comes out in the care and attention which the child, later on, gives itself, the so-called "self-love" which is nothing but a result of an unconscious identification with the parent who took such tender care of it. Unconsciously we love ourselves later on with the affection given us, as if we had incorporated those who loved us and who thus continue their existence in us.

Is that all? Are there no deeper effects, ones intimately connected with our life, invisible repercussions of the affection that our parents gave us? I shall not answer this question myself. I shall let another who lived three hundred years ago say what is to be said on the subject. An old manuscript written in Jewish was found in Germany and edited about thirty years ago.* It is the life story which an old Jewish widow of a merchant, the mother of fourteen children, has written. She wanted her children to know what her life had been like with all its troubles and joys. It was not destined for publication, of course, but only for the use and profit of the next generation. The woman's name was Glueckel van Hameln. She was born in Germany, where she spent her whole life, in 1646—a contemporary of Pepys. Her memories are often interrupted by pious thoughts, advice to her children, God-fearing and moralistic meditations. Sometimes they are illustrated by simple fables taken from the treasurehouse of Jewish tradition. Here is one of them in a brief form. It answers our question fully. A bird once set out to cross a windy sea with its three fledglings. The sea was so wide and the wind so strong that the father bird was forced to carry his young in his strong claws, one by one. When he was halfway across the sea with the first fledgling the wind turned to a gale. Then he said, "My child, look how I am struggling and risking my life on your behalf. When you are grown up will you do as much for me and provide for my old age?" The fledgling replied, "Only carry me to safety and when you are old I shall do everything you ask of me." At this the father bird dropped his child into the sea where it drowned, as he exclaimed, "That is the fate of such a liar as you." Then the father returned to the shore and set out with his second fledgling. Again when over the sea he asked the same question and received the same reply. So he drowned the second child with the words, "You too are a liar." Finally he set out with the third fledgling to whom he put the same question. And the third and last fledgling replied, "My dear father, it is true that you struggle hard and risk your life for me and it would be wrong of me not to repay you when you are old, but I cannot

---

* An English translation *The Memoirs of Glueckel van Hameln* was published in New York in 1932.

make any binding promises. But I can promise this, that I, when I am grown up and have children of my own, will do as much for them as you have done for me." Whereupon the father said, "Well spoken, my child, and wisely. I will spare your life and carry you to the far shore in safety."

In this little fable of the old, uneducated woman lies the wisdom of her people, the psychological insight shown in their proverb: "The love of the parents goes to their children; the love of these children goes to their children." Here is the answer to the deep-reaching effect of our parents' love upon our life. Thus mothers and fathers, long dead, and perhaps never great pedagogues, become educators. Like light which reaches us from stars that have perished many decades ago, affection once given shines forth in our own lives and in that of future generations. Romance fails us and so do friendships, but the relationship of parent and child, less noisy than all others, remains indelible and indestructible, the strongest relationship on earth. There is no call coming from those living as insistent, permanent and penetrating as the silent voice of our parents from the country of the dead.

11

The human language, otherwise so discriminating and differentiating, often proves that it has remained a poor medium of expression. Do you love your friend? You feel tempted to answer, "Yes." At the same time you feel that love is not the word to express your emotion adequately. It is certainly not the same feeling a man has for a woman. No, it is not the same, but it is, nevertheless, something similar. You try to distinguish between the two feelings. You say you love her, but you are very fond of your friend. You like him very much, etc. The fact that the object belongs to the other sex makes, of course, a great difference. But is it the only factor? You discuss other matters with the girl you love than you do with your friend, and even if you discuss the same things you do it in a different way, in another spirit. And why is it more difficult to have a friend who belongs to the other sex? Is it that the sexual element disturbs the development of such a relationship? It is certainly untrue that sexual desire differentiates love from friendship. Did we not draw a sharp line between love and sex and did we not point out that one could be distinct from the other? It seems it is difficult to find the differences between love and friendship even between persons of the same sex. Of course it is possible to love a person of the same sex. For example, a man loves his father, a girl her mother or a teacher, but that does not mean that the object is a friend. And how should we understand a sentence which states that there is more love in friendship than friendship in love? We feel that there are emotional shades and nuances which are hard to grasp.

Whenever you think you understand the differences some similarities or likenesses occur to you. You get confused to such an extent that one moment you think there are sharp distinctions between love and friendship while the next moment you are under the impression that one feeling differs so slightly from the other that they almost appear identical. You assume then, that a great many of the difficulties you meet are rooted in the inadequacy of our language. They are of a verbal kind. Nevertheless, in addition to this factor there are certain delicate points differentiating the two emotions which originate from their psychical nature.

I suggest that we first collect some characteristic features of friendship which seem to be absent or at least not pronounced in love. If we succeed in finding certain traits which were not discovered before we will perhaps have an idea as to the underlying differences and their meaning. Such an indirect pursuit may even lead us to the origin of friendship. I propose that we collect these psychological data quite systematically. In so doing we shall be guided by the impressions gathered by our own experience and that of others.

Should we start with the impression that friendship is not as intense as love? Immediately we shall see many instances in which friendship between men, for example, proved to be stronger than the affection for a woman or in which the friendship outlasted the love-relationship. When we point out that friendship usually does not plunge us into trouble and misery as love does we shall see illustrations in which a friendship was the undoing of many people. Nevertheless it is our definite impression that friendship does not have the same urgency and insistency, the same violence as love. You might miss a friend and long for him but the emotional temperature of this feeling is different from the painful nostalgia with which love sometimes fills us.

Could you speak of "passionate friendship"? It sounds a bit gaunt, exaggerated or ridiculous. It even sounds somewhat odd when we hear a man say he loves a friend. Nowadays we feel that this is an exaggeration. We are aware that the language of friendship has changed during the centuries. Comparing the manifestations of friendship today with the expressions of the past, we cannot fail to recognize that the language of friendship has become less ardent. It has lost the expression of enthusiasm, of gushing. In the time of Shakespeare you could unhesitatingly have declared that you loved a friend passionately. Today the adjective does not go well with the noun. Even an essay like Emerson's on friendship speaks about the subject in an exuberant way, which means that it sounds this way to our ears, while it did not sound like that to the contemporaries of Emerson. Reading novels of a hundred years ago we are aware that people talked about their friendship in a way which would fill us with embarrassment today. We do not gush about this emotion any more. We prefer not to discuss it at all. We do not like protestations of friendship which have a passionate character. Listening to the talk of men about the emotions which surround their friendships in the language of Emerson would sound to us as if a musical passage which should be played piano is performed fortissimo. Friendship today is thrifty in its verbal expressions.

Does that mean that there are no longer any intimate friendships as in the past, that relationships like David's and Jonathan's, Orestes' and Pylades', are unthinkable? Certainly not, just as in our day we often hear of proof of true friendships, not only on the battlefield but also under the hardships of civilian life. Nevertheless, our final impression is that friendship also differs from love in degree. It does not have the same passionate atmosphere. It is cooler. There is nothing of the ardent zeal here which so often appears in love. Nothing of the self-forgetfulness, the full surrender, the superabundance of emotions. Friendship is sounder and saner. It can never be compared with being drunk and its moods cannot be called insanity or madness. Friendship does not hit you like a cataclysm or an earthquake. Friends in one another's company might feel very pleased with each other but they are not wildly happy, enchanted or delirious as lovers sometimes are. Friendship is a warming open fireplace while love is a house on fire.

If your impression is correct it would mean that there is a difference of intensity or degree in the two emotions. This finally results in qualitative differences. I have already mentioned the contrast between our feelings when we miss a love-object, or a friend. Friendship does not develop those permanent, strong desires which lovers feel when their loved one is absent. Friends need not stick together to belong together.

It appears further that the feature of idealization so characteristic of those in love is unnecessary for friendship. You appreciate the excellent qualities of your friend but you also know his shortcomings and faults. Friendship need not be blind as love usually is. It can be critical and yet tolerant, which love very seldom is. Your friend does not represent your ego-ideal as the beloved does. At best he is part of your ego-model. We said love begins with the wish, "I would like to be you," or the desire to change one's personality with that of the beloved person. Nothing of such a possessive character can be observed in friendship. Apparently it is not our wish to be like our friend but rather a wish to have some of his qualities which we lack. Do you really want to be your friend, or even be like your friend? Isn't it rather a desire on your part to have some of his traits or endowments? You wish to be him or to be like him only in a certain direction, but you would not care to possess all of his characteristics and are quite satisfied to be yourself. The stoic philosopher Zeno when asked, "What is a friend?" answered, "Another I." The answer is much more appropriate for the love-object whereas a friend is only a certain and definite part of "another I." Our thesis that love can be traced back to unconscious envy, jealousy and greed toward the object concerned the whole person. The object is wanted to the very last morsel. In the case of friendship, only certain intellectual, emotional, mental or physical qualities of the person appear desirable. Our unconscious envy concerns only those and not all of his person and nature.

Here is another and, it seems to me, very important difference. You feel, when in love, that your object is superior to you. For the man the beloved is, so to speak, a higher being, an angel. Such an inferiority feeling, such humbleness toward the object, is certainly lacking in friendship. You might recognize and acknowledge your friend's superiority in one direction or another but you do not think that he is your superior in every way. Not only is such an attitude lacking in friendship—it would make friendship impossible. It seems that friendship can only flourish on the level of equality. A pronounced and conscious superiority or inferiority of one's self or of the object is a serious handicap in the development of true friendship. Goethe called Eckermann his friend but Eckermann would not have dared to call himself a friend of Goethe. He was too aware of the other's superiority. A person who is so much superior to you might be very friendly but he is not your friend. To be so called by him is certainly something to be proud of, but such a distinction cannot be used in treating him as a friend. It is one-sided. It will awaken feelings of pride and will favor love, respect and admiration, but not friendship. You cannot be the friend of a genius when you feel only a bit better than mediocre yourself. The feeling of equal value is a necessary condition to mature friendship. If the superiority of the friend is emphasized, mutual friendship becomes impossible. The human distance is too great to be bridged. Let us now compare love and friendship in another direction. You are in love with a girl. Does that exclude being in love with another girl at the same time? It certainly does, if you are not too neurotic. Romeo's passion for Rosalind vanishes immediately when he sees Juliet. There is no place for another woman as Tristan feels his fateful love for Isolde. Love means singleness of the object. It demands like the God of the Old Testament, "You shall have no other God besides me." Is the same exclusiveness valid for friendship? No. Friendship, it is true, is no mass article. One who is everyone's friend is nobody's friend, but you can have several friends, and good ones too, at the same time. The difference which the two emotions present in this direction is caused by the different claims they make. Love is much more pretentious, its demands are greater. It engulfs the victim like a maelstrom. Friendship carries you like a friendly river. Love takes possession of your whole heart while friendship claims only a part of you. It is not as consuming a passion, does not engross you and does not tax you to the utmost. It does not make excessive demands; it has a more democratic character. It does not want to own you; it merely wants a place in your life.

Are these differences which were for the most part neglected in the psychological analysis of love and friendship clarified sufficiently to attempt a solution of our problem? Is the insight which we gained from these impressions sufficient to venture a guess about the essential difference? Love is a reaction-formation to envy, jealousy and greed. Friendship is a reaction to original feelings of rivalry and competition which were aroused by the unconscious acknowledgment of certain qualities of the object. Some of your friend's traits or characteristics appear to be attractive to the degree that you would like to have them for yourself. He is a supplement of yourself but only in a certain way. Some features of his character or nature are enviable. The original feeling which the observation of his presence or his actions awakens in you is a wish to overcome him, to conquer him in this or that direction. He arouses feelings of competitiveness in you. You want to measure yourself with him and to be the better of the two. The emotional reaction then sets in. These original impulses are rejected, the tendency to fight and to overcome him changes into the wish to help him, to unite your own efforts with his, to join him and to combine your energies. The reaction which follows the initial tendency to fight sweeps the original impulses away and gives in to the opposite strivings. Rivalry and competitiveness disappear from the emotional surface. They retreat into the unconscious where they are kept alive, ready to break through when friendship dissolves. The earlier tendencies lurk around the corner which in some cases is easily turned. The unconscious effect of envy and jealousy in friendship cannot be denied but it is not as concentrated as it is in love.

The ingredients of friendship are slightly different since its unconscious roots reveal merely a stimulus to rivalry and not so much to envy and jealousy, as explained by its less passionate character. The fact that it becomes possible only when two friends are about equal in their achievements and like traits discriminates the relationship from love.

In the realm of friendship the unconscious contest leads also to a point where it threatens to become hostile. If the reaction then proves less intense it is because the tension which preceded the formation of friendship was not as strong as the one which preceded love. Before the forming of friendship there is hostility in the air too, but of a less fateful character, more like that prior to a wrestling match than to a duel. Not who will survive but who will be victorious should be decided. In the case of love the opponents make up their minds, so to speak, at the last moment not to fight to the death but to embrace and kiss. The future friends also raise their arms for the blow but instead of tussling they shake hands and walk off together to have a drink. What unconsciously prepared the ground for friendship does not concern the whole personality. It is not a decision on which life and death depend. The tide never turns as high as it does just before love sets in. If it did, worship or love would be the result of the following reaction, not friendship. In love the end is really a giving up of one's own personality, the melting of two human beings. This does not take place in friendship.

In fully developed friendship the results of the emotional reaction appear on the surface; kindness in the place of hostility, the tendency to spare the friend, to support him instead of the impulse to harm him, a successful effort to help him reach his aims instead of a desire to frustrate him.

Are there no traces left of the old and now unconscious spirit of contest and competition? Of course. You are very ready to praise your friend but you are not so happy when others praise him—quite in contrast to the attitude of a lover. The original contest continues to exist also in the form of peaceful emulation between friends. It even permeates the Christian friendship of brotherhood in which everyone competes with another for the love of Christ, and in which friends incite each other in God's work. The highest form of friendship is reached when competition is replaced by the gentler form of emulation. Even the concealed activity of hostility is somewhere kept alive. You seldom overlook a mistake your friend has made. Is your friend a well-wisher? Certainly, as far as his conscious thoughts reach, but four hundred years before psychoanalysis discovered the existence of the ambivalence of feelings between the most intimate of friends La Rochefoucauld remarked that there is something in the calamity of our friends which does not displease us.

Friendship between women has a shade of its own. In this relationship the survival of petty competitions or jealousy seems to be more marked than it is between men friends. The friendship itself may be as genuine as between men but it sometimes reveals a touch—and sometimes more than a touch—of the original rivalry. It was Rivarol who called friendship between women "a suspension of hostility." It may be true that friendship between women does not generally have the same steady or lasting character as it does among men, but is not the latter also a kind of armistice? Fields once maliciously remarked that in the forming of female friendships beauty seldom recommends one woman to another. Of course we all can report instances which can be argued as counterevidence. There are many cases in which women have become friendly with more beautiful girls than themselves, enjoying their friends' successes and triumphs as if they were their own. In the words "as if" is, however, the clue to the psychological explanation of such surprising generosity. The girl identifies herself with the prettier one and in this way enjoys her friend's successes by proxy.

But to be frank, is it so different with men? The objects which unconsciously awakened the spirit of rivalry may be different but behind the cloak of friendship the spirit of contest is also concealed. The aims may be of a less materialistic or immediate nature, perhaps not dresses, popularity or sex appeal, or anything of a vain nature, but ambitions or aspirations instead. This lends a different color to the reaction-formation of the two sexes but it does not change its nature. With men, also, the way to avoid competition is to enjoy a friend's triumph by proxy, to feel it as one's own. I am reminded of a play of Arthur Schnitzler's, *The Lonely Road,* in which one man says to another, "We give the clues to each other so cleverly—do you not agree? There are pompous people who call a relationship of this kind friendship." Did it not, however, start as a result of overcoming the original rivalry as to the smarter, wittier or more socially successful of the two? Is giving the clue to the other not a reaction to an earlier tendency to steal the other's line? Who now displays his friend proudly and brings him into the spotlight, did he not unconsciously want to outshine him? They are friends now, not friendly enemies, but they were enemies before they became friends, nevertheless. There is no real friendship without such a background, which exists mostly in the unconscious. "Defend me from my friends, I can defend myself from my enemies." Does such a saying not reveal the unconscious existence and efficiency of hostile impulses which are ready to spring unpleasant surprises on the friend?

Insight into the psychology and genesis of friendship can perhaps help us to understand two phenomena which remain puzzling and which cannot be explained when you take friendship as it presents itself only to conscious thinking. By these I mean the strengthening of ties in the face of common enemies and the rarity of friendship between men and women. Of course there are enough explanations for both, but none of them are sufficient. The facts themselves are not debatable.

There is an interesting aspect in the fact that even a lukewarm friendship becomes stronger when an enemy appears on the scene. An adversary who is hated by the two friends seems to intensify the companionship even more than a common interest or a common cause. Why should such an outsider, toward whom we feel hostility, tighten the bonds of our friendship? Is it merely the common danger he presents to our congeniality which makes us act jointly against him? No doubt this factor operates in such instances but there is another reason which is even more powerful, although silent. I said that there is concealed competition and hostility at the bottom of every friendship, a kind of animosity covered by kindly feelings. When an enemy appears the temptation to turn against our friend is awakened by the very feelings the enemy shows toward him. This temptation is followed by the old reaction-formation which the third person has stimulated and is rejected. The hostility, thus aroused, will undergo a deflection. Instead of being turned against our friend it will express itself against the outsider who feels hostile toward our friend. Due to this mechanism of deviation our hostility will use him as an object instead, since he represents a refused psychological possibility of myself. I turn against him because I vigorously reject the temptation he personifies: to assail my friend. By such a mechanism of diversion the concealed antagonism between friends has its outlet against the hostile outsider instead of within the relationship itself. The common foe, a hated political party or a social situation, as the case may be, cements the friendship. Not only does it create an excellent preservative element but it intensifies the affectionate feelings by purification of the hostility which accumulates within every friendship as time goes on. The enemy from outside thus has a preservative effect upon friendship. We should feel grateful to him. Our psychological presentation has revealed how little it takes to change a friend into a foe and a foe into a friend.

The other question, why friendship between men and women is so rare, was quickly and easily solved by the so-called explanation that sexual desire is a disturbing element in the development of friendship. Such a theory can be supported by facts but they are mostly distorted or unfairly selected ones. There are cases where, due to differences in age, etc., the sexual desire toward the other person is absent, or only present to such a very small degree that it can rightly be overlooked. There are also cases in which common interests seem to favor the development of friendship but nevertheless it is not formed. What prevents an affectionate tie in these cases? It must be due to the sex difference which is certainly not identical with the assertion that the unconscious or conscious sexual desire is the only hindrance. If the view I present here is correct the obstacle to such a relationship is rather the absence of strong feelings of rivalry or competition between two persons of the opposite sex. Just the contrast between the sexes alone disfavors the development of such feelings of competition except in a very general way. Where real rivalry between a man and a woman exists it cannot easily be overcome by the reaction of friendship. It expresses itself in bitter hostility and finally results in indifference or—seldom enough— is absorbed in love.

It seems thus that love between man and woman is within easier reach than friendship, when preceded by a special type of rivalry. The outcome of such a situation depends of course on many psychological factors, but love apparently has a better chance to develop than friendship. In most cases where the rivalry is strong bitter feelings of hostility will remain prevalent and friendship will rarely be the reaction which follows. On the other hand I have observed friendships between men and women which were deeply disturbed and quickly destroyed by emotions of rivalry in one of them. The contrast of the sexes does not help in this instance to overcome this rivalry and to form the reaction of friendship instead. It is much more likely that this contrast intensifies the competitiveness as the rivalry gets a resonance from the difference of sex. It is as if the road runs back into the oldest hostility, the battle of the sexes. One person feels that the other claims certain privileges and assumes too much, is unfair not on account of his personal achievements but because of his or her sex. He or she claims to be superior or refuses to feel inferior in the name of the sex difference. Such an attitude is most unfavorable for the development of a friendship, which, as we have seen, flourishes best on the level of equality. The absence of rivalry between persons of different sexes is, it seems to me, the deepest psychological cause for the infrequency of friendship between man and woman. Of course, unconscious rivalry is only one of the factors which attracts one person to another. There are other attractions between the sexes which result in different relationships.

12

The Christian admonition or ideal to love one's enemies has been called the noblest expression of man's highest aspiration. There is no doubt in my mind that the Lord himself did not intend it to be so considered. It is one of the many paradoxes of Christ misunderstood by Christianity. To understand its contradictory character you have to repeat it loudly to yourself: "Love your enemies, do good to them that hate you, bless them

that curse you and pray for them that despitefully use you."
Suppose an intelligent, unprejudiced man, born and bred in a
remote, foreign culture, were to hear this precept for the first
time, assuming he had had no contact with Christianity. What
would be his immediate impression? I daresay he would be
puzzled and bewildered and that after understanding its full
impact he would declare, "But that is impossible! It contradicts
human nature. Nobody could feel that way." He would be right.
It does contradict human nature: it was meant to contradict it.
It sounds like and is unconscious mockery. That means it is a
masochistic order, turning some painful thing into something
joyful. It is part of an ascetic and self-torturing program, similar
in character to the command that a fakir rest for days on a bed
of needles.

Does it really contradict human nature? No, because human
nature also includes masochistic impulses. In another book* I
tried to find the psychological origin and the concealed aims of
this strange emotional attitude which derives pleasure from pain,
disgrace and self-degradation. I showed there that social masochism does not search for torment and humiliation as its final
goal but that they are only necessary stations on the road to
satisfying the individual guilt feelings. In this situation punishment must be endured preliminarily to the enjoyment of forbidden pleasures so that there could be no self-reproach. Pain is
desired not because of any pleasure in it but because it clears the
way for satisfaction which is otherwise completely blocked. The
satisfaction of our wishes and needs is also the concealed aim of
masochistic tendencies. This satisfaction is paid for by first accepting, indeed by even enjoying, the necessary unpleasantness,
humiliation and disgrace. The aims are the old ones. Now they
are reached after defeat has been suffered. The secret, unconscious
aim of the demand to love our enemy is to humiliate him, to
conquer and destroy him by humiliating and conquering ourselves. The final gratification is anticipated in phantasy. He who

---

* *Masochism in Modern Man*, Farrar, Straus and Company, New York, 1949.

humiliates, degrades and disgraces himself only takes beforehand the punishment for that which he wanted to do to others: to degrade and punish them. The command to love one's enemies thus is really an advice on how to get pleasure out of something highly unpleasant by unconsciously anticipating in phantasy future satisfactions. It follows the emotional pattern of other paradoxical words of Christ, like, "He that humbleth himself shall be exalted," or, "The last shall be first." The secret meaning of the injunction to love one's enemies is to love them to their shame, to their destruction. The attitude here described has this unconscious meaning, "I do not hate you as you deserve, you brute. On the contrary, I love you. By so doing I prove how superior I am to you." But this meaning is expressed by the opposite in a paradox of unconscious irony and mockery not unlike the language of the older prophets of the Holy Scripture. Is it possible to love one's enemies? It is, in this hateful way by shaming them. One can love them by humiliating oneself, by being humble and thus proving how superior one is. In Christ's admonition an ingenious way is found to be proud of one's humility, to take revenge through affection, degrade others by self-abasement and conquer them by complete submission of oneself. All the theological and moralistic sophistry which has been wasted on the discussion of Christ's command cannot change the original unconscious meaning of the sentence, which is: love them to finally conquer them. Here if anywhere it becomes clear how love and hate are separated by only a nuance, how one can simulate the other and how possessiveness and greed can turn into affection in a moment.

There is only one way to love your enemies, namely, after you have hated them deeply and passionately enough. After you have enjoyed the full satisfaction of fulfilled hostility and revenge in phantasy you can feel inclined to forgive them, even to the point of feeling a certain amount of sympathy for them. I had a patient who sincerely complained that after a time he began to like his enemies. He was not capable of carrying around feelings of unchanged and undiminished hatred throughout the years. He said jokingly that God had an unfair advantage over men because He could wreak his vengeance unto the third and fourth generations. Decidedly He is not like ourselves. This man failed to take into account the fact that his hostility and thirst for revenge exhausted themselves in unconscious phantasies; that his available amount of hatred became spent before he detected his strange inclination for his enemies. It is indeed quite possible to love one's enemy after having punished him in phantasy, even by loving him in the Christian sense.

Some weeks ago I listened on the radio to a discussion of college professors about the subject, "Is it necessary to hate our enemies?" Of course it was not a theoretical discussion. It concerned the war, the attitude of the soldiers and sailors who are on the battlefields fighting the enemy on land, sea and in the air. The question was asked seriously enough but I imagine many listeners were as amused as I was. How could you fight without hating? A war is not won by moral sentences. Either you fight —which can only be done in hate—or you do not fight, thereby giving up your liberty, and even that can only be done in hate. But to fight in a reasonable, unemotional way because it is necessary and useful is impossible for men. To kill one's enemies, bomb their cities, destroy their women and children and property in cold blood, emotionally indifferent, would be monstrous. Imagine yourself a soldier attacking Nazis. Is it possible to drive a bayonet through a human body in a mood of benevolent detachment? How abominable it would be to kill because of some well-considered reason! It would be atrocious to wipe out lives without passion, hate or vindictiveness, simply because it is a useful thing to do.

There are philosophers who say that we should hate cruelty and barbarism in the abstract, but not our cruel fellow men; that we should despise evil but not the evildoer. You can no more hate an abstract idea than you can love it. Both emotions concern living persons. Your enemy in battle is not cruelty or barbarism. He is a living Nazi. To persuade yourself that you shoot a doctrine of cruelty or terror when you shoot him, and that you hit the spirit of tyranny and intolerable conceit but not the man himself, is just nonsense. Some of the professors said that if we hate our enemies now we shall poison the future generations' minds with the spirit of hostility. This overrates the stability of our emotions. We cannot hate that long.

The whole question is not very serious, it seems to me. It is impossible to order men to love or not to hate. To command certain emotions and forbid others is beyond our power. Emotions need no excuse. It is possible to issue the command, "Thou shalt not kill," but not to order, "Thou shalt not feel like killing." Emotions are not commandable. The subject is introduced here in connection with our psychological examination of the Christian ideal to love one's enemies only to prove again that love is impossible without preliminary negative feelings. If you have never hated your enemies you will never love them. You will be a cold fish with friend or foe, as incapable of loving as you are of hating. Christ himself was passionate in love and hate.

There is another admonition of Christian morals which seems easier to heed: to love your neighbor as yourself. Likewise this demand has a chance of being realized only after you have overcome the emotions of envy, jealousy and greed which, according to our thesis, are necessary unconscious premises for love. The original, primary feelings toward one's neighbor are hostility and resentment, because he is one's neighbor. At best one feels indifference. But in this case there would be the least chance of fulfilling Christ's command. No road exists from indifference and emotional detachment to love. Love can only be reached by way of unconscious hostility or envy. The Christian requirement is not for consideration or friendliness of one's neighbor but for love. That means that it takes into account the unconscious hatred and resentment and goes into an extreme reaction-formation, like so many of Christ's paradoxes. The subterranean hostility is driven to the other extreme: to love one's neighbor as oneself, as the better part or, as we would say, as one's ego-ideal. In this precept the concealed hostility is not only the sleeping but the active partner. It is not the absence of the emotions of competition and resentment that makes affection for one's neighbor possible but the conquest of these feelings.

From the psychological analysis of these two commands we return to the conclusion that love is not a ready-made article. Its existence is not possible without a complicated emotional, preceding process. The precept to love one's enemies now appears to us in a new light. One could say paradoxically: you can love only your potential enemies, those whom you once unconsciously considered enemies, because love is only the conquest of those hateful tendencies. Without them there would be no love on this earth.

In the gentle and sweet melody of Christ's message we can catch an undertone of hidden irony and masterful mockery which not many in the audience can hear. It sometimes sounds as if the tune of love were played by sounding brass and tinkling cymbals.

13

Affection seems to become thinner, weaker and more anemic as the group which it embraces grows larger. It is easier to love one's friend, girl or father than one's nation or mankind. The spirit of brotherhood is more highly developed for a real brother than for a community. To press a nation or a religious sect to one's heart is rather difficult. It is only in a figurative sense, as an analogy, that we can use the words "love of mankind." We speak of the emotion, of course, as if it had all the content of the real thing, but it has not. We love our families; that means we love certain members who represent the whole to us. We love our nation; that means those men and women who personify the best in it.

We can readily compare these two groups from the point of view of our attitude toward them. The affectionate feelings we have for the members of our family and for our fellow countrymen can be reduced to a common denominator familiar to us. This means that our feelings of affection really amount to our having no fear. We don't feel afraid of our family's or our nation's hostility or maliciousness; or better, we don't feel as much afraid of it as of the evil intentions of those outside these circles. It would seem that being a stranger was originally identical with being an enemy. *Homo homini lupus* is a kind of slander of the honest society of wolves.

This absence of fear and relative sense of security is often mistaken for affection. But also love of one's family and one's nation grows out of conquering one's animosity and hostility against them. Is one not proud of being a member of his own family or nation? Maybe sometimes, but the feeling is a secondary one, not the result of an original and genuine affection. If we are sincere with ourselves we will agree with the observation of Arthur Schnitzler that every race or nation appears originally as antipathetic and that only the individuals can reconcile us with it. That means that any nation or race, including one's own of course, shows its peculiarities and distinctive features, which, if too pronounced, make an unpleasant impression. It seems that even here in the wider field of national and racial groups affectionate feelings appear as emotional reactions to the original hostility.

The comparison between nation and family goes even farther. The observer is puzzled to find that the affection for one's own family and nation increases with the intensification of one's animosity and hostility against other families and nations. Need that be so? Can't we imagine being devoted to our own family and countrymen at the same time that we are attached to others? It is possible of course to a certain extent, but daily observation shows that there is usually an interrelation between affection for the one and hostility toward the other. It is as if positive feelings in one direction were intensified by strong, negative sentiments in the other. The same thing is true of religious groups.The zeal for one's own religion is powerfully increased by hostility against others. Fanatical aggression from outside works as a strengthening element upon the devotion and mutual attachment of the threatened community.

The correctness of this view is proved by the fact that the affectionate feelings within a certain national or religious group diminish in proportion to the absence of outside danger or enemies. Then lukewarm feelings between individuals soon give way to old tendencies of rivalry, envy and the lust for power which create inner conflicts in the group. Hate against outsiders thus has a very useful function. It preserves and increases the attachment between members in a community. A common hatred ties individuals together. The streams of envy and aggressiveness, undercurrents in every group, are drained off toward those outside it. Friendliness and kindness to one another are the exception, not the rule, whatever may be the surface behavior. The members of any group behave like the Irish as Samuel Johnson saw them. He reassured the timid Dr. Barnard, "Sir, you have no cause to be afraid of me. The Irish are not in a conspiracy to cheat the world by false representations of their fellow countrymen. No, sir, the Irish are a fair people. They never speak well of one another."

He who wants to have a good idea of what people's real feelings are toward each other has only to observe little children in a nursery, because any community is like a thin-veiled society of children. Anyone who observes the goings-on in a nursery or on a playground will no more doubt that envy, jealousy and possessiveness are strong and lasting emotions. The "me-too" attitude is common to all children. A Danish proverb says, "If envy were a fever all mankind would be sick." To keep up with Mr. Jones—and especially with Mrs. Jones—is only a specific form of a general tendency. If you ask a little girl who has three toys to give one of them to poor Jane who has none, she will answer, "But Jane will destroy it," or, "Jane's mother should give her one." You will hear similar pretexts and evasions by grownups. Children are possessive, preferring sometimes to destroy a toy rather than give it to another child. A child wants to keep the things it owns, and it wants something the other child has. The origin of the social question is not to be found in highly industrialized society but in the primitive society of children. There at the beginning of civilization are the Mine and the Thine. They remain to accompany us all along our progress. Only in love, not in sex, will the demarcation line between mine and thine disappear. He who knows human nature knows that envy is more irreconcilable than hatred.

The original form of all envy, if we can trust our impressions of the nursery, is food envy. Jealousy of others' possessions comes later. Money envy, which devastates our society, is a later substitute of this oldest manifestation. Food envy in the nursery already shows the character of the emotion which demands more than the child immediately needs. A child's envy can be aroused by merely seeing that another child has different or more food. One may also observe that a child at this age already begrudges his playmate the dish which he himself does not want—just like his parents. His mother, for instance, may not be invited to a party which she hasn't the slightest desire to attend. Even so, when she discovers that Mrs. Brown has been invited she may surprise herself by feeling envious and jealous.

I well know that also in the nursery affection can overcome these original tendencies of greed and jealousy which seem to be our human inheritance. One sometimes sees a child give a piece of his cake or candy to his mother or playmate. Similarly later on the gift of something that one would like to keep oneself is a certain sign of love.

Considering the essential elements in human nature, the ideal of universal brotherhood is a spectacular vision. "With malice toward none; with charity for all" is an ideal, and like all ideals also indicates the emotional situation from which it sprang. The libeled society of wolves may possibly reach the degree of savagery and brutality of men. But wolves don't pretend to be a brotherhood. To love all mankind may become an excellent excuse for those who are unable to love a single soul.

A humanitarian program is often a convenient substitute for real achievement. Building castles in the air can prevent one from securing roofs for the homeless. The savior-spirit is the strongest reaction against man-hatred known to us. It is at the same time the most dangerous temptation to becoming complacent and self-righteous. One has to be egregiously conceited to want to save mankind. Lip service to the ideals of humanity, fellowship and brotherhood is often accompanied by concealed hate and rage. Brotherly love does not keep men from rejoicing at the calamity of their neighbors. We trust each other, yes, but we do not take any chance. Such is life among men.

In the last forty years we have seen that all the high-sounding phrases of human brotherhood were mere words. The whole program collapsed like a house of cards. It does no good to cry over the spilled milk of human kindness, but our thoughtless optimism is partly responsible for the fact that we now must cry over streams of spilled blood. There is no love of mankind which is not first preceded by hatred of it. It even seems very difficult to love mankind without hating at least a part of it. There are odd mixtures of such feelings of love together with intense hostility; and they all present a program for saving mankind.

The fight for God and virtue is only the other side of the hatred for Satan, to whom God gave so much power on earth. Love of mankind would have been considered incomplete without fury against the contrary-minded. Their affection did not prevent the deeply religious princes of the church from burning alive thousands of heretics, infidels, Mohammedans, Jews and Christians, whose eternal blessedness, the zealots hoped, would thus be assured. By burning bodies souls should be saved for heaven. It seems that high ideals do not exclude extreme cruelty and intolerance. Loving one's neighbor has as its complement hating one's neighbor's neighbor. Love of the German fatherland and the high value put on the virtues of virility and warlike qualities were accompanied by hate and contempt of the so-called non-Aryans and of different virtues that appeared as terrible vices.

Having high ideals and a lofty preconceived idea of what men should be is an irresistible temptation to destroy those who do not come up to these specifications. Most of the tyrants, zealots and dictators have been idealists with a high opinion of human nature. Therefore they had to kill, burn and destroy millions of human beings. Wise old Anatole France was right: only if one has a very modest view of human nature can one be kind and tolerant toward one's fellow men and oneself. Whoever has too high an opinion of what human nature is originally is bound to become intolerant and cruel. He who demands too much of men will eventually hate them. Only he who expects little from mankind can love it.

Here is a very interesting contrast. Love of an individual is impossible when we do not start from an overestimation of his endowment. Love of mankind is possible only when we start from moderate ideas of its value. Today many profess a burning love for their fellow men and are full of the highest praise of mankind and of zeal for its cause. But I do not believe it is true love. At best it is an infatuation for mankind such as we might expect from the young generation; sometimes it is only a flirtation, quite harmless.

I do not know why the glib and oily preaching of human love, the high-sounding phrases, the high school pretensions and the idealism of a puerile culture make me depressed, while a realistic concept of human nature makes me feel optimistic and hopeful. Man is not a first-class saint, but neither is he a first-class rascal, because he is not a first-class anything. He who expects less will often be pleasantly surprised by the kindness and friendliness of his fellow men. Sometimes he will even be touched by their attention and affection. By reducing one's high moral standards one has a better chance of getting good results. A little less idealization would make quite a difference in practice.

The spirit of brotherhood, so often called upon in political speeches and religious sermons, is slow in appearing. It will only come, after the mentality of men has radically changed, when kindliness toward our fellow men is not considered any more as a "moral" duty but as a natural and spontaneous reaction. Do you remember the story of the boy who carried a smaller one on his back uphill? A man who passed by remarked: "That is quite a burden." But the boy replied: "It is not a burden, sir. It is my younger brother."

14

At this point we arrive at the fringes of our subject. An attempt to evaluate love does not belong in the realm of scientific research. You cannot have a judgment about it. The best you can do is to have an opinion. And your opinion is as good as mine. With this fair warning in advance, I dare to ask: what is the value of love for men? I say "dare to ask" because someone might say at once, "Listen, brother, there is no Santa Claus." We knew that before. Yet our skeptic (we should rather call him a positivist) has to admit that there is a person who poses as Santa Claus and that children enjoy his performance and his gifts. Just as little can he deny that there is an emotion called love, whatever it may be, and that this emotion plays a part in our lives. The radical realist may call it foolishness or madness, but he cannot deny its existence in this world of ours.

Nobody expects to find general agreement on such a subject. Yet is it not surprising that love has been called God's best gift to men, and the devil's worst curse? As cooperation of the old enemies is beyond question, it is possible that they both have a

share in it. The whole problem would be more easily solved if
we knew the answer to a few simple questions. For instance,
why is love necessary, what would life be like without it or what
want does it satisfy? But neither is an evaluation of love possible
if you do not specify which kind you mean. Obviously the love
between the sexes must be evaluated differently from the love
for one's mother or neighbor. Moreover it is necessary to determine a standard of value. Is it to be considered on the basis of
the happiness to the individual or of the importance to society?
The two may be quite different. The influence that love has
upon the individual while it makes him happy might be opposed
to the interests of the community. Here again is the question:
which kind of love is meant—infatuation, romance, adolescent
or mature love (which need not coincide with age), a passing
attraction or a lasting affection?

Let us only discuss the value of love between the sexes. Some
will say that the question as to whether it is true or not can only
be decided by the results accruing to the individual: by their
fruit shall ye know them. But in reply others will say that that
is merely begging the question. Who will decide what the fruit
is worth? Then the answer will be: the fruit is in the nature
of happiness for the individual. Love almost reaches the illusion of this phantom, which always eludes us, of the perfect ego.
True, it is an inflated ego which is thus reached in the incorporation of the love-object. It is perhaps a false prosperity, but
while it lasts it makes the lover happy. At this point someone
will ask, "Is it really a happiness which endures? Should not
so much zeal, passion and psychical energy rather be spent in a
better cause?" But the lover will impatiently interrupt, "Is there
a better cause?" No admonition to be reasonable and to stop
making a fool of himself will help. Reasonableness is a good
thing, but it does not make young people happy. At best it prevents people from being unhappy. At worst it keeps them from
becoming happy. Reason is often flat, is, as Henry James once
said, "a bed with the mattress removed." To make a fool of
himself is in certain emotional emergency-situations the best

thing a man can make of himself, and he who makes a fool of himself need not necessarily be a fool. A fool's paradise is paradise, nevertheless. Is it not better to make a fool of oneself in love than to make an ass of oneself in politics, science or literature? Certainly there are real fools who are always thinking about "making love" because they have nothing else to think about. They say that all other things can be had for a song, a love song. They are love addicts as other men are cocaine or morphine addicts. No one deserves to be called a man whose life is filled only with romance, but neither does he whose life was never touched by it. The man who has never made a fool of himself in love will never be wise in love.

All love is founded on a dissatisfaction with oneself. It is an attempt to escape from oneself in search of a better, an ideal self. The lover imagines that he has found it in his object. Is love thus an illusion? Of course it is, but that is not the most significant thing about it. Illusions are also psychical realities. Freud called religion an illusion, but he did not deny that it was a great educational factor in the history of mankind. We attend a theatrical performance and give ourselves up voluntarily to an illusion. We don't like to be deprived of the illusion while the performance lasts or to be reminded that Lady Macbeth is really Peggy Smith and King Duncan a certain Harry Brown. We enjoy the illusion and follow the scenes on the stage with an interest as genuine and emotions as strong as if we were here concerned with "real life." Love is an attempt to change a piece of a dream-world into reality. Every study about love faces the task of tracing the relation of phantasy to reality and the compromise between them.

"Romantic love" is not different in its origin from others but in its density and intensity. Its violence—one might almost say its ferocity—reveals that the impatience to get rid of the troublesome self and to change one's personality had reached a high degree. The suddenness of the "falling" in love does not indicate the depth of the emotion but its emergency character, the urgency of the lover's situation. It is as if a swimmer, in danger of being drowned, gained the shore in his last desperate efforts. Romeo thus falls in love to escape from his dire distress. Juliet appeared just at the right moment. The ecstasy, the bliss in romantic love is caused in no small part by the unexpected surprise at being rescued from the mysterious powers which try to push the unhappy person to destroy himself. The feverish heat in mind and blood proves how dangerous was the disease which the counterforces of the psychical organism have to fight and overcome. Romantic love is a desperate attempt at rescue of the menaced ego.

Perhaps the short duration of romance is connected with this characteristic. Of course the "wine, bread and Thou" phase cannot last. Romance lasting for many years is only imaginable in Utopia. After intoxication comes the hangover. The exaggerated character of romance inevitably calls for a reaction. No person can remain in the grip of a strange fascination for a long time. No psychical economy can endure the inflation of the ego without damage. Romance is a nine-day wonder. Love which would last undiminished through many years would be a miracle greater than those recorded in the Holy Scripture.

In romance the idealization of the loved person becomes idol worship, an apotheosis. This vehement character shows how intense are the counterstrivings of hostility and envy which must be overcome. It is as if the lover became a worshiper, increasing his affection to a frenzy in order to keep it up. He who worships his god with such fanatical zeal has had to conquer unconscious tendencies of doubt and rebellion in himself. He is more in danger of becoming a heretic or an atheist than other pious souls. In this exaggeration one senses a nongenuine element, of the nature of unconscious play-acting. This trait is comparable to the hysterical character which exaggerates the intensity of an emotion because it is contradicted from within. I certainly shall not assert that there is no genuine affection in romance—forms of youthful romance in life are not as disgustingly sweetish as in Hollywood—but this element of exaggeration is seldom missing. Romance is thus an alloy, composed of precious metal and some less pure. It is half love, half lie, half belief, half make-oneself-believe. If the sincerity of affection is indicated by a certain restraint then it is true that insincerity is revealed by gushingness. But who can measure the quality of genuine feelings? We have no instrument which can indicate the amount, no "sincerometer." Romance can be evaluated as a kind of preparation for true love, as child-talk is for the speaking of adults. And how charming child-talk can be! There is a factor of shallowness and sham behind the glamor of romance, but how glamorous it is!

What romance is worth will be decided when it mellows, changing its character of frenzy into one of love. Juliet asserts that her bounty and love are boundless as the sea. "The more I give to thee the more I have, for both are infinite." Juliet, after being married a few years, would have had to admit—at least to herself—that her love had limitations. Romeo would then, perhaps, be the dearest companion, but certainly not "Thy gracious self, the god of my idolatry." Mature love does not need such emotional extravagance. It lacks the characteristic of despair in the escape from oneself. The ego felt defeated before it loved, but it was not on the verge of a rout. Love makes one feel happy, but romance means moments of bliss, not elation but rapture. As in the recovery process in cases of hysteria the change from romance to love is characterized by the transformation of idealization into a more realistic appreciation of the good qualities of the love-object and by the deepening of affection which loses its noisiness and exuberance. The lie becomes slowly truth. Excess yields to measure and moderation. "They live happily ever afterward" is a fairy tale, but it is sometimes a fact that a couple can retain a precious part of their mutual illusions despite the unavoidable demands of reality.

Perhaps love is as a Frenchman said, *"l'ombre d'une ombre,"* the shadow of a shadow. But this shadow which our ego-phantom casts gains substance and reality in time. Romance appears sometimes as a kind of rehearsal. The real performance comes much later. Age knows love without too much possessiveness, with more care for the real welfare of the beloved. Youth is cruel and quickly sobered by the faults and shortcomings of the love-object. Maturity can see these imperfections clearly and still feel tender —indeed, sometimes even love the defects. (Perhaps the rarest form of love.) There may not be ecstasy or intoxication but there is an emotional companionship which cements the tie between two people, forming an intimacy which grows as they live together through the same joys and griefs.

The social value of love is uncontestable. It overcomes the differences between classes, races and creeds. It serves as a great equalizer and uniter. While it remains a fact that love cannot banish all envy and hostility, it is indisputable that only love is able to do it insofar as it can be done at all. It is one of the greatest educators of mankind. "Love and the gentle heart are one, same thing," sang Dante. Its function in taming men, in mitigating and pacifying the brutal forces, the lust for power and destruction in us, will continue, no doubt, in the days to come.

The value of love for the individual can be disputed but not denied entirely. Imagine a world without this most persuasive of all emotions, without the reassurance that it gives and which we so badly need, without the ego-gratification it grants. Earth would be a lonely place: "Bright reason will mock thee like the sun from a wintry sky . . . leave thee naked to laughter when . . . cold winds come." Life without love would merely be something to be endured, not lived, something to plod through without great hopes and gratifications. Happiness and loneliness cannot coexist. When we enjoy a deep satisfaction alone we do so for only a short time. Very soon we want to share it with another, whom we at least imagine as present in our unconscious daydreams.

To live only for oneself would mean only to half live. He who lives for others shares many lives. But are we not all of us most unwilling to cast aside this precious self of ours? To surrender it to others? To think more of others than of ourselves? Do we not in slang speak of ourselves as "Number One"? We do, but happiness exists, perhaps, only when number one becomes number two or three. The older one grows the more convinced one is that to be only selfish means to be unhappy and unfulfilled. "It seems to me that to put oneself in the second place is the whole significance of life," wrote Turgenev once. There are only two roads that lead to something like human happiness. They are marked by the words: love and achievement. They are both of a social nature, including others in the pursuit of one's own happiness. There comes to mind a sentence made by an old, uneducated woman which contains the same basic wisdom as Turgenev's remark. A neurotic patient who tried to live only selfishly, unloving and unloved, complained to his mother of his feeling of permanent loneliness. After some moments of silence the old lady said, "Whom did you make happy in your life, Howard? Not even yourself." In order to be happy oneself it is necessary to make at least one other person happy. If that is a condition is it then true that men are quite selfish? The secret of human happiness is not in self-seeking but in self-forgetting.

Love is, I think, the most successful attempt to escape our loneliness and isolation. It is an illusion like every search for human perfection, but it is a necessary illusion. It comes nearest to the ego-gratification we all need in pushing the ego aside. To connect one's life in thoughts and deeds with others is the only way to make it worth living.

Wise men warn us again and again not to expect permanent and serene happiness from love, to remember that it brings misery, makes one dependent on an object, has downs as well as ups, like any human creation. It is not love's fault that we demand too much of it, putting all our eggs into one basket. We should know that there is no heaven on earth. It is even doubtful if there is heaven in heaven.

PART TWO

Masochism in Modern Man

Introduction

How did philosophers ever come to think that man is an animal which seeks pleasure and avoids pain?" This is not the introduction to an abstract philosophical essay but a question which was addressed by a gentleman to his companion on a ski trip in Switzerland. Under the conditions the skier describes in a letter to the *New Statesman* (London, January 15, 1936), one can easily understand how such a question could come up. The remark was made as "side by side we toiled with a contorted crablike motion up a frozen mountain in a biting wind, only to slide down again in a helpless tangle, to the accompaniment of the caustic comments of an attendant demon." In such circumstances one is inclined to doubt that the search for pleasure and the avoidance of pain are universal characteristics of mankind. The skier asked whether there can be any pleasure so laboriously won and so dangerously indistinguishable from pain as skiing. "If you do not sprain your ankle," he continued, "you break your leg, and if you do chance to keep your limbs whole, you still pass hours of humiliating and painful effort in very uncomfortable circumstances, when you might be spending your week's holiday at much less cost reading or sleeping by a warm fire, with a cat curled up on the mat . . ." This humorous account closed with the epigrammatic remark, "Man is a masochistic animal!"

This writer, certainly a well-educated man, probably had in mind that English philosophers from Herbert Spencer to Bertrand Russell have held that man, like other animals, strived to obtain pleasure and to escape pain. No matter how much they might disagree on details, they were all convinced that man tried to avoid discomfort. In his *Analysis of Mind* Russell stresses the fact that the primitive urge is in the direction of being freed from actual pain rather than of seeking pleasure, the urge thus being "a push and not a pull." But how does an instinctive phenomenon such as masochism fit into this scheme? Pain, ordinarily avoided, is the very aim of masochism. Not only is masochism not "escape from pain and discomfort" but it is the exact opposite, a desire for them, an actual "pull" toward them.

Of course, the skier was only joking when he pretended to wonder about the philosophers. Everyday experience confirms the theory that man always seeks pleasure and avoids pain. To say that "Man is a masochistic animal" sounds like a reversal of reality, hardly to be taken seriously. Or did the writer really mean what he said? His joking does not preclude his being serious. Perhaps man, through thousands of years of environmental changes, of transformations in his psychic structure, has finally become a masochistic animal. I shall discuss this point later.

It is noteworthy that we do not object to the word "masochistic" in the letter. No one would have understood it in this context forty years ago. At that time masochism meant a sexual perversion, a meaning obviously not intended by the skier. The word has extended its significance. The original restrictive meaning of sexual aberration which derives satisfaction from a passive relation to the partner has been retained. Masochism, however, has come to mean also a particular attitude toward life or a definite type of social behavior: of enjoying one's own suffering or one's own helplessness. The word has outgrown its narrower, sexual meaning and has become desexualized.

Increasing psychological insight certainly has contributed to this shift in meaning. In Krafft-Ebing's works and in the early writings of Freud masochism unequivocally signifies that peculiarity of love life in which satisfaction is bound up with physical and mental pain. But Krafft-Ebing already used the expression *ideeller Masochismus* (mental masochism) designating not a somatic relation but the idea of submission and dependence as the essential element in the pleasure experience.

Subsequent psychological and psychopathological research made it clear that such pleasure-toned ideas have little relation to primitive sexuality. Probing farther into the problem, psychoanalysis showed that ideas of this kind were not necessarily conscious. Many people consciously avoid pain and at the same time strive for it unconsciously. It is due to psychoanalysis that today we speak of masochism as a form of behavior peculiar to many people without thinking of a sexual perversion.

In this book I use the word "masochism" in that general sense as a peculiar attitude toward life. Why men unconsciously strive for physical and psychic pain, voluntarily submitting to privations, deliberately accepting sacrifices, shame, humiliation and disgrace is a problem that has interested me for many years. My first attempt to solve the paradox of voluntary suffering and the pleasure connected with it was in *Flaubert and His Temptations of Saint Anthony*. This book concerned the ascetic writer and his work picturing the psychic crisis of a saint. During the twenty-nine years which have passed since the publication of this book my interest in the problem has not flagged. Whenever I observed neurotics and masochistic personalities analytically the problem gripped me anew and I kept myself informed on the pertinent literature. Some aspects of the question were dealt with in later publications, but there was no attempt to present the whole problem of masochism as such and to bring it closer to a solution. In this book I have tried to set down the results and conclusions which have crystallized during three decades.

There is no doubt that despite the efforts of sexologists, psychologists and sociologists the problem of masochism has remained unsolved until today. Freud's works do not give a solution. We are indebted to him not only for the most significant insight so far attained into the nature of masochism but also for the method by which alone a deeper understanding of the aims and motives of this instinctual tendency can be gained. His own contributions—of a psychological profundity heretofore unattained and fruitful even in their errors—have really put us in a position to attempt a new method of approach to the problem.

He has shown us the way, although he himself has not taken it. Various of his pupils have offered new points of view without, however, throwing light on the core of the problem. The psychological question of masochism has remained unanswered.

Although dissatisfied with former attempts to find a solution, for a long time I did not succeed in formulating the insight which I had acquired from my analytic cases. This insight, repeatedly verified, was what might be called the distillate of many experiences which had but slowly acquired the cast of final conclusions. In addition, I had to find a new approach to these results, for it proved impossible to connect them with former research which had led to a dead end. Only after having found a new way of presenting characteristics of masochism, which had been overlooked so far, was I in a position to tackle the problem anew. Many theories had to be abandoned as inadequate. If new facts contradict accepted theories the facts must be retained and the theories molded to fit them.

What others have said about masochism I shall not repeat; not because I consider their work unimportant but because it is already known. My aim is to bring new insight into the basic problem of masochism. Rather than add new material to the abundance already available I have attempted to use new material to solve the problem itself. This is not a matter of stating simple facts but of grasping the facts behind the facts, of ferreting out what lies behind these interesting phenomena, what conditions their occurrence and governs their aims.

The implications of this problem reach far beyond the sexual peculiarities of single individuals and lead into the realm of culture development. How can a man find pleasure in suffering disgrace and humiliation? is the original problem presented to the psychologist by the sexual perversion. There is no doubt that the instinctive masochistic inclination is widespread. Thousands of persons have confessed that they are acquainted with such sexual enjoyment. Most of them have revealed further that this is the only sexual pleasure they know. How many more there must be who could say the same thing but who keep silent! Freud labeled masochism "the most frequent and most significant of all perversions." Only ignorance and the hypocrisy of society have prevented us from estimating the increasing cultural significance of this peculiarity of love life—from its most primitive physical forms to its most refined spiritual aspects.

Beyond the sexual sphere, however, emerges a social type of masochism which is apt to dominate the entire life of individuals and social groups. Separated from the sexual aberration by an abyss, there exists a plethora of tragic phenomena ranging from the failure, bad luck or mysterious vicissitudes of the individual to the overwhelming castastrophes affecting whole peoples, phenomena governed by a dark desire for suffering.

I am concerned more with the problem of a typical rather than a tragically abnormal attitude toward life. Here is a problem which increasingly endangers our whole culture. I want to point out this aspect of the human situation today.

Only now that psychoanalysis has supplied imperativeness of such a drive can it be understood and defined. Insight into the depth and width of the problem of masochism leads us to agree in all seriousness with the joking statement of the skier: Man is a masochistic animal!

To solve a problem means for the scientist to move a question mark one step farther away. In this sense, and in this sense alone, can I say that this book solves some of the problems of masochism.

I

Phenomena

THE INVESTIGATOR's first task is to answer the question: what happens? His second is to answer the question: how does it happen? To fulfill the first we have to start in our case from the phenomenological world of masochism. We shall have to seek for definite features and characteristics of this instinctual disposition, what its forms of expression have in common and what distinguishes it from other instinctual phenomena. Before undertaking such a task of sifting and sorting it is advisable to pause and state the first general impression masochistic phenomena make on the observer. One should certainly not surrender to such first impressions; yet they should not be underrated. They may be deceptive and true at the same time. These fleeting impressions, so obscure and yet so distinct, are the very ones which deserve to be retained. They keep to the surface, but the surface —correctly seen—is the extroverted inside. Every secret that man would hide will betray itself on the surface, will manifest itself on the outside.

The unprejudiced observer's first general impression of masochistic phenomena is paradoxical. The literal meaning of the word paradoxical is: contradictory, incredible, running counter to general opinion. Applied to phenomena it can only mean: something that rationally could not exist and yet is there. It is a strange phenomenon that a river should disappear and reappear on the surface of the earth many miles away. But such examples are known and are explainable. It would produce a paradoxical impression, however, if a river suddenly changed its direction and began running backward toward its source. Inconsistency, of course, is not to be confounded with absurdity. The element of antagonism, of apparently intentional contradiction, proves rather that there is a meaning in this inconsistency. The inconsistent is not nonsensical; it is merely contradictory. It does not stand outside of general belief. It takes a stand against it. It is easy to recognize that this first general impression is common to all forms of masochism. It is equally incredible and contradictory that the ego's own abasement and defeat, degradation and rejection, are aimed at in social masochism.

The impression of a paradox is due not only to the factors of aberration and queerness of the instinctual gratification. Such factors are indeed common to all perversions and yet the picture of masochism acts differently upon us. This impression must result from features which are not clear to us at first, items additional to the general character of the aberration. The impression discriminating this instinctual expression from others is best seen by a comparison. Other perversions are comparable to single participants of a hiking group who have strayed from the highway and have erroneously taken a wrong route. The masochist is comparable to a person who "intentionally" goes astray in order to reach his secret aim by a detour.

This is the first general impression gathered before scrutinizing details of the phenomena. Such an impression can be ignored —it has been ignored up till now—but it cannot be denied.

This impression of paradox must also have its psychological justification.

Are there any characteristic elements invariably common to all different forms of masochism? The sexological and psychological literature surely offers sufficient observational material to make characterization of masochistic phenomena easy. Although there might be even too much of such material I dare state that up till now not even the phenomenology of masochism has been adequately investigated. A description of the essential single features, of what is common to all masochistic forms, is still lacking.

It will be worth while to quote some examples as illustrative material. In selecting examples the primary consideration will be the fact that there can be no doubt as to their masochistic character. Neither differences of sex nor the question of whether we deal with an actual masochistic scene or with a fancied perversion are considered in this selection. From this point of view the three following examples may claim to be representative of the essentials.

A young girl has the following phantasy to which she clung through the years with but trifling variations. It is late evening or night. In her daydream she goes through the streets to the butcher shop which has closed its shutters a long time ago. She knocks and when the butcher opens she says, "Please, I would like to be butchered." He grants her request without any fuss as though it were something quite usual and lets her in. She undresses in the rear of the big shop and lies down naked on one of the butcher's stalls. She has to lie there and wait a long time. The butcher is cutting up some calves. Once in a while one of his employees comes by, touches her body and tests her flesh like an expert testing an animal to be slaughtered. Finally the butcher himself comes. He also tests the different parts of her body, hauling her about as if she were a dead calf. Finally he grabs the butcher knife, but before he makes a cut he puts his finger into her vagina. At this moment she has an orgasm.

Let us follow up this unquestionable masochistic phantasy with another one, a man's. A man of thirty-seven, father of three children, is fully potent sexually only with the aid of varied and different phantasies. I select one at random: to an ancient barbaric idol, somewhat like the Phoenician Moloch, a number of vigorous young men are to be sacrificed at certain not too frequent intervals. They are undressed and laid on the altar one by one. The rumble of drums is joined by the songs of the approaching temple choirs. The high priest followed by his suite approaches the altar and scrutinizes each of the victims with a critical eye. They must satisfy certain requirements as to physical beauty and athletic appearance. The high priest takes the genital of each prospective victim in his hand and carefully tests its weight and form. If he does not approve of the genital, the young man will be rejected as obnoxious to the god and unworthy of being sacrificed. The high priest gives the order for the execution and the ceremony continues. With a sharp cut the young men's genitals and the surrounding parts are cut away.

The patient, who is of a decidedly visualizing type, imagines the progress of the scene very vividly. He himself is not a participant but only a spectator. Here the question might be raised whether such a phantasy is masochistic or sadistic. The phantasy first was used in masturbation and only later was invoked in intercourse with his wife. The decision as to whether the phantasy is primarily masochistic or more sadistic in character must rest on information as to the person with whom the patient identifies. In our case it is certain that the daydreamer identifies with one of the victims, usually not the one who is just being castrated but with the next, who is compelled to look on at the execution of his companion. The patient shares every intensive affect of this victim, feels his terror and anxiety with all the physical sensations since he imagines that he himself will experience the same fate in a few moments.

Rather than take the third example from the field of phantasy again I shall select an actual instance of masochistic perverse practice. A married middle-aged man visits a prostitute from time to time and enacts the following scene: on entering he asks her whether she gives "Russian lessons." The phrase is used in certain newspapers of his country to advertise masochistic practices. In the patient's imagination the term connotes the terrors of pogroms and scenes in Russian prisons which he has read about. If the girl says "yes," he gives her explicit directions as to what she must do. She must scold him in a certain manner as if he were a little boy who has been naughty. She must say that he deserves a good hiding and so on. He obediently pulls off his trousers and receives a blow on the buttocks. Sometimes the blow is superfluous since the ejaculation has already occurred. In coitus the patient is impotent.

It is not to be doubted that these three examples are representative of masochism as a perversion. It is perhaps accidental that in none of them the sensation of pain is emphasized or the perception of pain is of any importance. Even in the phantasy of the execution of the young men there is no stress on the pleasure of suffering pain; rather is the stress on the pleasure in the idea of anxiety and terror. We recall that the pleasurable excitement lay in the next victim's fright at the sight of his predecessor's castration. The castration itself appeared in the phantasy merely as a surgical operation. No stress was laid on the sensation of pain.

If we thus have excluded the pleasure in pain as an indispensable element, what remains as a common denominator? Surely everything else that hitherto was known and acknowledged as characteristic of masochism: the passive nature, the feeling of impotence and the submission to another person, the cruel, humiliating and shameful treatment by this person and the consequent sexual excitement. There is nothing new yet disclosed as characteristic or at least not yet sufficiently valued. These newly emphasized characteristics not only have to be essential. They have to claim acknowledgment as indispensable elements of masochism. Naturally they do not always appear in the same form or with the same intensity, yet they are always present. Where they are lacking we cannot speak of masochism.

2

In what follows I describe three such constituent elements which can be demonstrated in masochism as a perversion as well as in its desexualized forms. They are: the *special significance of phantasy,* the *suspense factor* (that is, the necessity of a certain course of excitement) and the *demonstrative feature*. It will be shown later that these three factors are intimately associated, that they are only expressions of a more deep-seated essential.

Of these three factors *phantasy* is the most important. The neglect of this factor in analytic investigation of masochism is responsible for the fact that the essence and origin of this aberration has not been understood heretofore. Without psychological appreciation of these phantasies masochism is not to be explained. Phantasy is its source, and at the beginning there is nothing but masochistic phantasy. The importance of this factor is proved by the fact that individuals with weakly developed imagination show no inclination to become masochists. So we are justified in starting from this feature when characterizing masochism.

The importance of phantasy as a preliminary for sexual excitement appears clearly in every single feature of the three above examples. The girl in the butcher shop has to wait for a long time until the butcher is through with his other business. When he turns to her, he begins with testing, fingering and examining the flesh and hauling the body about. The prisoner in the man's phantasy has first to participate in all religious ceremonials, to witness the slow approach of the priest, the preparations for the execution and the castration of his comrade. He must listen to the victim's cries of anguish, share in his moaning and writhing. The prelude to the scene which the masochist enacts with the prostitute is more important than the blow on the buttocks. His entering, the conversation, question and answer, the scolding, the forced and yet desired exposure, the waiting for the blow, are designated by the patient himself as the essentially exciting factors.

The special importance of phantasy for the masochistic excitement is demonstrable not only in the well-established forms of masochism. It can be observed already in the original scenes which gave rise to the perversion. For example, take the basic scene in the case of the young girl. As a child she had lived in the neighborhood of a butcher shop; as a matter of fact the butcher was her uncle. Because of his trade, however, the parents cut him dead. This may have contributed to the fact that the activities of this uncle gained a mysterious and shady significance for the child and her slightly older brother. Both children had ample opportunity to watch the butcher-uncle and his men working and had attended closely the cutting up of animals. Afterward they played in their own garden a game of *slagertje* (Dutch for "little butcher"). The little girl lay down on a bench in the garden and the brother imitated the butcher. First he was busy elsewhere, then he came up to his expectant little sister and played a "cutting up" as he had seen his uncle do. With light, flat strokes of the extended hand he cut her body—which by the way, was clothed—in pieces. The preliminaries to the procedure as well as the procedure itself were at this time already in some dim way pleasure-toned for the little girl. The waiting and the light blows on the body produced sensations in the clitoris. The example shows the importance of the phantasy for sexual excitation even in one of the early situations that was decisive for the genesis of masochism.

When, while waiting to be touched and slaughtered, the girl becomes sexually excited, imagination fulfills the same task as in my other patient's Moloch scene when he anticipates terrible future possibilities. The material for this latter phantasy is also easily recognizable as a recasting of infantile ideas. The religious disguise originated later and shows the result of varied reading. When the patient was a little boy his older brother was operated on for phimosis and showed the little one the recently healed wound. The boy's later phantasies were based on this impression. They were directed at his kindhearted but stern father whom he both admired and feared. He must have assumed at that time, that he, like his brother, would have his penis operated on by his father or by a doctor, the representative of his father. In this idea homosexual stirrings are joined to others springing from the need for punishment, which resulted from early masturbation. In

the Moloch phantasy the young men before the altar represent his
brothers, among whom he too had his place. It is significant that
he identifies with the one who watches the operation and experiences the entire anxiety of the next sufferer.

The childhood scene, too, from which the third patient's practices with the prostitute can be derived, gains significance through
the medium of phantasy. The boy, who was pampered at home,
had been naughty and unmanageable. In his presence an aunt
had expressed her disapproval of the educational methods used.
If he had been her boy, she said, she would have drawn off his
trousers and given him "clap, clap." This onomatopoeic threat
was the start of his visualizing such a scene.

But is the significance of imaginative preparation for sexual
stimulation so surpassing just in masochism? Its importance is
certainly not to be denied in normal, sexual life either. Does
masochism show a departure here from other perversions? With
those as well the desired situation will be frequently anticipated.
It is indeed the essence of perversion that the phantasies linger on
the preparatory activities instead of progressing to genital satisfaction. We may compare, then, the significance which phantasy
has for sexual stimulation in sadism or in peeping. Certainly also
the voyeur and the sadist anticipate in phantasy the situation
desired and thus get excited. It might seem, then, that the difference is reducible to a plus or minus of excitability.

However, this is not the case. This is not a question of quantity. The difference is rather, that the masochist cannot miss the
phantasy, that it represents a preliminary which is indispensable,
a *conditio sine qua non*. The sadist or the voyeur is also capable
of satisfaction without such preparation. If a voyeur out walking
in the woods has opportunity to see a woman exposed, no preliminary phantasy is necessary to produce strong sexual excitement in him. Compare with this the situation in the case of the
masochist. Let us assume that the specific conditions for excitement are that he receive a box on the ear from a Junonian woman and is abused by her. Let us assume further that such a

situation happens incidentally, that is, without the usual pre-liminary phantasies. The man in question walks peaceably out on the street, a huge woman comes up to him, showers him with words of abuse and gives him a mighty box on the ear. To give the scene some verisimilitude it is only necessary to assume that the poor man is the victim of a mistaken identity. The woman so prone to strike believes she has recognized in him a man who wronged her. Will the masochist be sexually stimulated by this sudden attack? That is well-nigh impossible. Of course it is quite possible that the scene will subsequently be used in a phantasy to produce sexual stimulation, but its immediate effect will not be of this kind even though it exactly reproduces a desired situation. Nothing but the preparatory phantasy is lacking. This assumed situation is designed to make clear the indispensability of phantasy for the masochistic gratification. Here the assertion is not that phantasy is unessential or unimportant as a preparation in the other perversions but that for masochism it is absolutely indispensable.

Yet there are two objections to such opinion. The first would remind us that preparatory phantasy is of especial importance in exhibitionism. Analytic experience shows that this is really the case. We thus would be compelled to make a correction, saying: in the perversions with a passive instinctual goal there is a need for a preliminary phantasy in order that sexual excitement may be attained. Psychologically this is quite intelligible and what is conspicuous is only the fact that this has not been recognized hitherto. These perversions do not depend alone on the will of the pervert. It is also contingent on the independent reaction of the partner. If his reaction is not the desired one then no sexual effect is produced, or only a diminished one.

This reaction is more important for the masochist or exhibitionist than for the sadist and the voyeur, who are less dependent on the behavior of their partners. It has been reported that one winter evening an exhibitionist suddenly appeared before an English lady at a lonely spot in the Parisian Bois and exposed his genitals. The woman with great presence of mind went up to him and said: "My good man, won't you catch cold?" One may assume that this thoughtfulness had a very moderating effect. But for all that, phantasy is not as important for the exhibitionist as it is for the masochist. A group of young girls who have just come along can instantly decide the exhibitionist to expose himself.

Another objection has it that in certain cases the sudden appearance of a detail suffices to generate a masochistic excitement. Thus a colleague referred me to a case treated by him in which the killing of a chicken had become the focal point of a masochistic phantasy. Later the mere sight of a chicken leg was enough to produce sexual excitement in the patient. But can such an example really convince us that there is no need for preliminary imaginative preparation? I do not think so. Rather should this be counted as confirmation of my opinion. Actually the preparation is very extensive and of ancient date in such cases. The material has been gone over so often that everything is in readiness. The glimpse of the chicken leg is simply the factor which releases this prepared psychic material. It is exactly like hearing, faintly touched on the piano, the first notes of an old familiar melody.

In one of my cases in which the patient had a pleasure-toned memory of a beating scene in school it was sufficient for him to see tightly stretched breeches to get sexually excited. In another case words like "strike" recalled the masochistic situation with all its sensations. The patient with the Moloch phantasy felt some kind of excitement when he saw young, strong men in certain postures, sometimes even when he looked at photographs where the postures were of a sort that resembled the posture of the victims in the Moloch phantasy. Thus the sight of a young man lying on a couch with extended arms brought back to him, with the corresponding sexual excitement, the image of the victims on the altar of the cruel idol.

The objection, then, is not so strong as it would seem. In these cases there is not a smaller but a higher degree of preparatory phantasy. The psychic mechanism which is effective here is the well-known displacement onto a detail, a singular feature which becomes a substitute for and a representative of the whole. The hoarse voice of a man can set into motion the whole masochistic phantasy of a woman. The sound of clinking iron awakened the pleasurable phantasy of being chained in one person. In this there is nothing peculiar to the excitability in any perversion. The same effects of such substitutive details can be observed also in the field of normal sexuality. A trifling sketch in a magazine recently pictured a woman stopping on a remote street corner to fix her garter. She had to raise her skirt. One of two men happening to pass by remarks at this sight: "It's not much, but it gives you a kick."

The objections we have considered then do not make us revise our opinion. It still stands that the preliminary phantasy has a special importance for masochism. The phantasy is also the primary factor in a historic sense. Masochistic practices are but an acting out of preceding phantasies, daydreams that are transferred into reality. Every thorough analysis shows that the masochistic perversion is a reproduction of previously imagined situations long familiar to the individual. In the beginning there is no action, as far as masochism is concerned, but the phantasy.

The actual scene corresponds thus to the staging of a drama and is related to the phantasies as is the performance to the dramatist's conception. They are exposed to the same accidents, incidents and necessary adaptations to the means at hand and are just as dependent on the mood and the cooperation of the actors. Only rarely does the performance surpass the ideas of the author. More often, even as with the masochistic scene, it falls short of the conception. There are cases when the person in the actual scene is unsatisfied or only faintly excited while the recollection leads to an orgasm. The rules, given in such a scene, are comparable to directions to the stage manager. It is in accordance with the theatrical element in masochism that it seldom becomes a matter of "deadly earnest" as with the sadistic perversion.

It is perhaps wrong to emphasize the theatrical aspect in masochism. The analysis of the traits in the ritual of perverted scenes proves that there is a full meaning in every one of them. I am using the expression "ritual" purposely, since the peculiarly rigid rule and order which govern the masochistic scene are to be compared with the conscientiousness in the performance of religious and magical rituals. A change or a disturbance of this masochistic ritual diminishes its lust value. It can even destroy it. A kind of tradition will develop which has to be kept as in ceremonies of the church. First this has to be done, then that; words have to be pronounced in a certain manner, and so on. All these traits may seem to be haphazard and unpremeditated, but the psychologist who studies the history of the ritual recognizes that there are meaning and connection. In no other perversion does ritual play a role similar in importance. As in other aspects, the phenomena of masochism approach here those of obsession neurosis.

What is the relationship of the masochistic ritual to the phantasy? I shall clarify this point by giving a representative instance. A young man performs a kind of uniform-ritual in his masochistic sexuality for many years. He puts a very tight jacket on, girds it with a belt which he tightens to the utmost, and then adds a high leather collar which scarcely allows him to move his head. The trousers are put on backwards, so that the backside is in front. Thus dressed he walks to the looking glass, makes certain turns and movements, as far as such are possible in the extreme tightness of his suit, and admires his image—or, more accurately, imagines how others would admire him. During this ritual, which he repeats almost every night, he becomes sexually excited, finally throws himself on his bed and masturbates in spite of the handicaps which make it difficult for him to reach the genitals.

What is the meaning of these activities which appear to be insane? There seems to be neither rhyme nor reason in them. I shall discuss this question later on, but here I wish only to point out its historical premises. The mother of the patient, whose father died very early, had difficulties in managing the unruly boy in the prepuberty years. She often threatened to put him into a military school and described the severe discipline in these institutions. The scene before the looking glass is thus to be explained historically. The boy had phantasies dealing with the discipline in the military college and imagined how tight the uniform would be, how unpleasant the exercises, and how severe the punishments. At the same time he imagined that he would appear very virile in the uniform. The scene before the looking glass, starting in puberty, shows the stage-managing of these phantasies. It has the character of a rehearsal. He himself calls them a "mental preview" of what the situation would be like. It is easily to be guessed what place masturbation has in this picture. At this point I should like to emphasize the point that the phantasy precedes the masochistic scene, that sex excitement already starts as he plans to play the scene and makes his preparations for it, laying out the single pieces of his suit in advance, and so on.

The masochistic ritual thus appears as the performance of the phantasies, which often are sufficient to excite the person without being put on the stage. The performance on the thought stage proves unsatisfactory in the long run. What the person at first imagined has to be put into action in mirror scenes and often in perverted scenes with a partner later on.

Some unrelated remarks about the peculiarities of masochistic phantasies may here be added. One particular feature is the tendency to "synchronization," an admirable expression I obtained from the patient with the Moloch phantasies. The phenomenon he frequently had observed in himself was that the sexual excitement runs a temporal course corresponding exactly to the course of events on the stage of phantasy. The daydreamer experiences the same feelings as the victim of his phantasy in the course of events. The same movements are made as the victim would have made, the same sounds uttered. Thus the ejaculation always occurred at the same time, that is, at the moment the high priest applied his knife.

The conservatism or tenacity of phantasy is striking and certainly in keeping with the essence of masochism. Masochistic situations are frequently maintained for years with little or no change, and yet remain exciting. Alterations are usually restricted to trifling displacements and substitutions of persons, times and places, while the main theme, if it may be called so, is adhered to. After long intervals, however, great and extensive alterations are introduced bringing about a completely new theme, a process comparable perhaps to a reform in an institution of old standing. The masochistic situation now appears to be wholly altered. The new content in turn will be maintained again for a long time, almost unchanged. Now and then the old, "worn-out" phantasies obtrude again, regain their old power for a short time but disappear.

It is thus possible to distinguish phases during which the individual is dominated by this or that sharply circumscribed phantasy content. The patient referred to above spoke of these phantasy groups as "cycles." During analysis a sort of slang was uncovered as among persons who understand each other by intimations. I knew what he meant when he spoke of the period of the "Aztec cycle." That was a phase during which he was sexually excited by the idea of sacrifice of prisoners in the Aztec kingdom. The "Queen cycle" was a group of phantasies in which a queen of the Amazons had her lovers subjected to horrible torments. The "Laocoön cycle" clustered around various phantasies that had their origin in this sculpture. The "Marsyas cycle" centered round the well-known myth of Marsyas' quarrel with Apollo, but was not limited to those two figures.

One gets the impression that after a long while the masochistic phantasy loses its exciting quality and is therefore superseded by a new one. My analytic experience indicates that only countless repetitions weaken the tenacity of a phantasy if it has once proved satisfying. It is noteworthy that these phantasies and actions are by no means restricted to the visual field. According to my impression, speech also plays its part. There are verbal masochists who get sexually excited when they imagine themselves abused or insulted. In the enactment of these phantasies the masochist expects to hear insulting or humiliating words and a certain selection, succession or emphasis seems important for the sexual excitement. In a certain masochistic scene the woman was expected to say *"Du!"* (familiar form of address in German) to the patient because this gave him the feeling of happy intimacy. When imagining the scene he pronounced the word himself. Here, too, certain small deficiencies of the dialogue are corrected in repeating the phantasy, a more plastic diction is strived for but the essential remains unchanged.

Dialogues during the masochistic phantasy are pretty frequent. Certain accents or expressions are then deemed very important, the cadence of a certain sentence is tasted voluptuously. The significance of such details is due to the shifting of mental accents. In one case a sentence used by the patient's father—"Be careful you don't do it again"—became the content of such a phantasy scene and had to be repeated again and again with a definite melody. The son, who had to be on his knees, would ask with a certain fearful expression, "May I get up?"

The imaginative material is, more frequently than in other perversions, capable of extension and elaboration. It can assume the form of a story and bring many people on its phantasy stage to act and suffer. It frequently finds support in the patient's reading or in his daily experience; or the distilled memories of films or plays or of some talk or other may be recognizable. In the last-mentioned case the imagination of the schoolboy was aroused in a masochistic scene by the tale of Marsyas who was flayed by Apollo. This nucleus proved so strong and persistent that twenty years later, in altered form, it still exercised the same excitement when the patient saw the picture of the flaying of the judge, by David, in Brussels.

The fact that the masochistic phantasy clings to details, selects them carefully and tests them lovingly has a bearing on another characteristic of masochism, the suspense factor, which we shall discuss later. The different pictures are selected according to their capacity for producing sexual excitation and they are discarded if they prove inadequate.

Mental objections against one or another of the details may result in a dispersion or dimming of the phantasy. It appears underexposed. According to a patient's pithy expression, it sometimes proves difficult to "focus" it. She used the expression when describing a raping phantasy which failed because the disturbing idea of a tramp's disgusting smell intervened. Masochistic phantasies sometimes are interrupted. A young woman used to imagine that she would die in childbed. She was amazed at the satisfaction this idea gave her. This sentiment was maintained as long as she imagined her husband's mourning and even his marrying another woman. She was even able to think in this connection of this or that girl she knew. But she had to interrupt the phantasy when she thought of her successor taking care of the baby. The idea was too painful to be borne any longer. Another patient frequently referred to a "martyr cycle," the core of which was the agonizing death of Christian martyrs. At this time he had found a medieval picture in a book presenting St. Laurentius on the grate. An attempt to reproduce the picture in his imagination and to utilize it for masochistic excitement proved to be short-lived. The saint's face in the picture had been quiet and unmoved in spite of his unspeakable agonies. It was unfit for phantasy, being—according to the patient's pertinent expression—"not convincing."

As a rule single pictures come up as in a kaleidoscope and persist for a shorter or longer period. It happens, of course, that certain features of the phantasy which have been effective for a long time are later rejected on indications of their diminishing value as a sexual stimulant. Thus a need for variety prevails over the conservatism of masochistic phantasy, unveiling psychic changes in the daydreaming person.

Whether or not a phantasy "succeeds" depends, of course, on various factors which can occasionally be determined in advance. A successful phantasy naturally is accompanied by a satisfactory orgasm. Otherwise there is none, or at best a flat orgasm. It is not always obvious with whom the phantasying person identifies. Certainly with the victim, the passive person of the scene, but also with the active cruel figure. Frequently he identifies with a nonparticipating spectator who nevertheless is mysteriously familiar with the thoughts and sentiments of the active and the passive person of the scene. The oft-quoted stanza of the masochistic poet Charles Baudelaire:

> *Je suis la plaie et le couteau!*
> *Je suis le soufflet et la joue!*
> *Je suis les membres et la roue,*
> *Et la victime et le bourreau!*

is incomplete in this sense. The masochist in his phantasies is also the spectator at the execution enjoying the pleasure of watching, a pleasure which seems to be a moderated, attenuated sadistic gratification.

The most important factor for the selection of the images and scenes referred to above is their propensity for evoking sexual excitement; but this is not the sole determining factor. Other factors such as conformity with the reality situation are influential. Frequently the imagination dwells on details until they seem to conform to reality. Imagination arranges and alters the situation until it shows no serious contradictions with other details. This is all the more striking as the masochist at other times completely disregards such considerations and reflections. The patient with the Moloch phantasy, for instance, while dwelling frequently on the idea of a red-hot grate on which the victims of an antique idolatry were laid, was striving to have all technical details correct. That was not too simple as the grate had to open automatically in order to throw the men into the flames beneath at the exact moment when the victims were sufficiently singed.*

---

* For the interpretation of this phantasy a reference to I Cor. 7:9 will be sufficient. "But if they cannot contain, let them marry: for it is better to marry than to burn."

On the other hand he did not hesitate to introduce gross anachronisms into his phantasy. He was well aware of impossibilities as to temporal or local circumstances but he did not mind. This attitude can be compared to that of a poet who at one point adjusts his creation to minute historical verities only to indulge in the greatest poetic licenses at other points. This patient had studied the ancient history of Mexico and Peru thoroughly and intensively. He was familiar not only with the principal works on the history of these countries but with special investigations on their ancient sacrificial rites as well. He himself had frequently visited the relics of these dead cultures, examining buildings, altars and so on. He therefore knew perfectly well that castration was no ritual sacrifice with the Aztecs, yet this was just what his phantasy insisted upon. I choose the following example as one of these phantasies contradictory to history because it illustrates the psychical conditions in many striking particulars.

An English officer has been captured by an ancient tribe of Aztecs who periodically sacrifice their prisoners to their gods by solemnly castrating them. Until the execution the prisoner is a guest in the house of his captor who also is supposed to carry out the sacrificial operation. One day he takes the officer—who otherwise is treated very kindly—into a room in order to show him the genitals of previously castrated men. At this point in the phantasy there is a characteristic hesitation and reflection. The question arose: just where and how are the genitals preserved? Originally the patient imagined them deposited in a beautifully carved chest, but this idea was rejected in the course of the phantasy because thus the flesh would decay and shrink. The possibility of their being stuffed and displayed like dead birds was rejected as well. Finally the daydreamer decided on having them preserved in bottles filled with alcohol. Here is found the unconscious connection with a childhood experience, with a segment of reality from which the phantasy sprang. As mentioned above, when the patient was four years old his older brother had been operated on because of a phimosis. The little boy seems to have identified this operation with a complete castration, though he was able to make sure later by examination that his brother's penis, though wounded, had been retained. Yet this assurance was less potent than the former impression, which assumed the character of reality in his imagination and to which he clung obstinately. This impression seems to have been revived some years later when the same brother underwent an appendectomy, especially since the patient was shown the excised appendix in a bottle of alcohol. Here then is a bit of historical reality transplanted to a later phantasy incognito and by way of a detour.

Part of the material of which the whole phantasy consists is clearly recognizable. The doubt concerning the detail about the means of preservation represents the boy's as well as the adult's unconscious doubt: do fathers castrate sons? Shall I be castrated? The patient's attitude toward his phantasies was ambiguous. On the one hand he devoted a great deal of mental energy and sagacity to their elaboration. On the other hand he found them crazy and ridiculous, was ashamed of them and could not understand how such childish and grotesque stuff could so intensively occupy and excite him.

It has been stressed that the scenes which masochists enact are, so to speak, staged phantasies, that they add new features and change old ones in order to attain a maximum of pleasure. Judging from numerous impressions gained from analytical observation the exciting phantasy originally turns up spontaneously and is produced intentionally for the sake of excitement only later. Occasionally it can be forced to turn up. Goethe was able to "order about" poetry. Thus it seems that from the genetic viewpoint masochism also starts with phantasies. Their importance is not lessened in later masochistic configurations but may even increase. If sexual excitement is originally accompanied by a phantasy it may happen later that the former is itself sufficient to invoke the phantasy which had theretofore been dormant.

The part which phantasy plays in the desexualized forms of masochism, in masochism as an attitude toward life, is peculiar and has not yet been acknowledged. At first view it would seem to be either completely lacking or without any importance. That is correct only in that it is rare to discover the production of persistent individual phantasies which dominate the subject's life and which contribute patently to masochistic gratification. Production of individual ideas is superfluous here because any single person can fall back on socialized mass phantasies accessible to him in religion and tradition. Phantasy as an individual configuration has vanished and is hardly discernible as such. However, it has spread over the whole life and fate of the person concerned, assigning him a certain role. His whole conception of life is ruled by an unconscious masochistic phantasy, the offshoots of which are rarely apt to become conscious. The place of the sexual partner has been occupied by higher forces; erotically tinged torment has been replaced by blows of destiny, which yet grant secret satisfaction. I shall discuss all that more explicitly later.

I only wish to stress here that the importance of the phantasy as the very essence of masochism has not yet been appreciated in analytical theories, that its indispensability has not yet been recognized. Imagination, thus neglected, has taken its revenge nevertheless. It penetrated the theories of some analysts and made them so fanciful.

3

The second characteristic of masochism involves a peculiar process of gaining sexual gratification which so far has never been considered in all its implications. The process to which

reference is made is a specific development of tension. Two qualities of this peculiar element of tension are demonstrably different
from anything in normal sexuality: the preponderance of the
anxiety factor and the tendency to prolong the suspense. Masochistic tension vacillates more strongly than any other sexual
tension between the pleasurable and the anxious, and it tends to
perpetuate this state. This is at variance with the natural impulse
toward discharge. Apparently there is an intrinsic connection
between these two features, a connection we are obliged to
explore.

To begin with we are tempted to assume this vacillation to be
the signal of general mental uncertainty. But as this uncertainty
is limited to the sexual sphere we have to reject this assumption.

The sexual pleasure of the masochist is always tainted with
this anxiety which is either completely lacking, or nearly so, in
the normal sexual experience. The course of tension is entirely
different here.

For the normal sexual tension curve the word "tension" is perfectly adequate. The masochistic tension curve is best characterized by the word "suspense." In contrasting these two words we
find that tension denotes a simple state of excitation with an
inherent tendency to reach a climax and a discharge. Suspense,
on the contrary, includes the element of the uncertain, of "being
suspended," of dilatoriness; and at the same time the idea that
there is no definite termination to this state. You can speak of
an agony of suspense, thus designating the painful, even unbearable element in it. But the same word can be used for the joyful anticipation of children at Christmas who are waiting with
fevered excitement for Santa Claus. The criminal waiting for the
verdict of the jury is in "suspense," just as is the reader of a
detective story. Goethe's *"Hangen und Bangen in schwebender
Pein"* depicts both the pleasurable and the anxious element in
such a suspense situation. Being hung, or suspended, from some
contraption happens to be among the favorite masochistic practices. Presumably it gives a functional objectivity to the sensation
of suspense.

The second characteristic of the masochistic tension curve is the tendency to prolong the tension, while we meet with the opposite intention, of resolving the tension, in normal sexual life. We will put it cautiously: there *seems* to be such a tendency in masochism. Viewed superficially this would mean only that the masochist wants to perpetuate the pleasure in the sense of the phrase of Nietzsche: "For all joys want—eternity."* But this is only the appearance; any critical investigation shows that his striving is to prolong the forepleasure or, what is more important, to avoid the end-pleasure. Here masochism can be distinguished from all other perversions which also cling to the forepleasure: in masochism the end-pleasure is shunned because it involves anxiety.

The postponement and ultimate renunciation of the end-pleasure can easily be elucidated by an analogy: we all know children who leave their favorite bite of food to the last. Such a tendency might seem an advantageous habit to the tutor, a grounding for later self-control. But he ought to notice also the danger involved from the hypertrophy of this practice: that the child eventually learns to renounce the precious last bite entirely. The reservation has become a renunciation, the training in self-control has taken on an ascetic feature. I know of a youngster who put a Swiss pastry, of which he was very fond, into a drawer, and kept struggling against his desire to eat it. When he opened the drawer after several days he found that the cake had become moldy.

The corresponding sexual behavior is not uncommon to puberty: a typical form of masturbation consists in avoiding discharge by interrupting the manual activity and diverting the thoughts. After a while the masturbation is resumed and again interrupted just before ejaculation. Those given to this sort of masturbation often claim that they do this in order to protract the sexual pleasure. But the result is that not unfrequently the ejaculation occurs prematurely, or without pleasure, or not at

* F. Nietzsche, *Thus Spake Zarathustra*, p. 321, Modern Library edition.

all: all tantamount to a renunciation of the end-pleasure of orgasm.

Apparently this putting off, or rather shunning of the end-pleasure conforms with the nature of the suspense feeling. The end-pleasure is desired and longed for on the one hand; on the other it is shunned for reasons as yet dark to us. The conflict between these two strivings produces, in every case of masochistic fixation, a psychic situation which gives to the tension curve its characteristic vacillation between the pleasurable and the unpleasurable, a pleasurable displeasure, to put it paradoxically. It looks as though the masochist wanted both to get rid of and to cling to the tension, to "eat his cake and have it." The result is that he gets rid of it, or rather that it leaves him in the lurch. The striving for pleasure tapers off into displeasure, into a pleasureless ejaculation or a dissipation of tension without ejaculation.

In the suspense factor the stamp that masochism places on sexuality can be recognized. It represents an alloy composed of the contradictory striving both for pleasure and for self-torment. In masochism the typical course of sexual excitement tends to restrict tension so as not to let it overflow into a satisfactory orgasm but rather to keep it in "suspense."

The suspense factor finds expression either in the phantasies or in the course of excitement during the masochistic scene. One of the Moloch scenes to which I referred previously contains an example of its effects. The phantasy has the following content: a line of young men are to be sacrificed to Moloch by being burned to death. They are put one by one on a grate which is movable and under which the great fire of the Moloch mouth is gleaming. The victims are suspended above this grill; the parts of their bodies which come in contact with it are singed. The pivotal question of the phantasy, however, is this: will the youths remain suspended and be burnt bit by bit, or will they throw themselves into the flames, seeking a quick and merciful death? Or rather: how long will they stand the torture before they "let go" and voluntarily fall into the enormous fire? Considering that the patient usually identifies with the next victim, thus experiencing his predecessor's *"Hangen in schwebender Pein"* and at the same time anticipating his own fate, the extension of the suspense element becomes obvious. Sometimes the phantasy was started with a depiction of the details of the fire being prepared by two stokers who, being prisoners themselves, know that they too will finally have to suffer death by fire. If the "synchronization" is successful the ejaculation occurs at the moment when, in the phantasy, the victim finally "lets go."

Another phantasy of the same patient was built up around a feature taken from the book of Diaz del Castillo: A Portuguese prisoner of the Aztecs is forced to watch the executions of his comrades during an eighteen-day period, only to suffer ultimate death by torture as the last of the condemned. The suspense factor in this phantasy was frequently provided by speculations as to which part of the living human body would first be skinned, which part would be next, what reactions the victim would show and how long he would stand the agony before fainting. This cycle of phantasies had been suggested by the myth of Marsyas. The technical details of the grate above the Moloch fire were pondered over during phantasying, turned this way and that, while the sexual excitement calmed down or ebbed away.

To report on a feminine counterpart I submit a phantasy concerned with the wearing of a tight cast or of a very constricting corset. The pressure of the apparatus, which the patient would like to wear always, produces in her an intensive sexual excitement which she is able to prolong at a certain level for an extended period. The phantasy usually begins with the idea of buying the apparatus, the doubt about what the saleswoman thinks about it and the postponement of the purchase. The origin of the phantasy is found in an historic event. The little girl, having a bad posture, had actually been ordered by her mother to wear for some time an orthopedic cast. The erotic meaning of the pressure against her shoulders was increased in the next historic stratum. Some years later the half-grown girl used to wrestle with her brother. According to the sporting rules the shoulders of the vanquished had to be forced to the floor and held in this position for a certain time. The girl would defend herself desperately but finally always had to "succumb" both in the figurative and in the literal sense of the word. The suspense sensation here was tied up with the phantasied uncertainty in the course of the wrestling match and with the duration of the lying there. There always was the chance that her brother after all would not force her down or else that she, while lying on the floor, would still be able to raise her shoulders.

It is erroneous to conceive masochism as an unchangeable unity. Mistaken interpretations and notions come from this erroneous conception which does not acknowledge any phases, progressions and transformations. Assuming that a peculiarity which is the result of a prolonged psychic development is constant and consistent from the very beginning means that one has come to a dead end. It means an unsurmountable barrier to the solution of the problem if some analysts, as for instance Wilhelm Reich, declare that masochism is incapable of increase of excitation. I have stated that the masochist wishes to avoid letting the tension increase to the point of orgasm. The obvious explanation lies not in the incapacity of the masochist but in the avoidance of end-pleasure because of its association with anxiety.

In the further course of development and also by displacement of the anxiety the increase of tension, which eventually would lead to orgasm, is avoided. Impotence which we so frequently find in masochists represents only the final result of this process. W. Reich's assumption, that any more intensive pleasure is inhibited immediately and transformed into displeasure so that end-displeasure takes the place of end-pleasure, is not correct. This may be, but is not necessarily, the result of masochistic development. Originally the increase of excitement was very much desired so long as it did not lead to orgasm. Only when fear of the end-pleasure—or to put it exactly, the fear of the *consequences* of the end-pleasure—has become overwhelming is the increase of excitement avoided. Insight into the significance of the suspense factor admits of no further doubt as to this. The increase of sexual excitement, however, produces increase of anxiety as well, so that every indication of increased tension, is reacted to with a more urgent "danger signal."

The extension and displacement of anxiety finally makes every increase of excitement appear to be undesired until eventually impotence results. This result, however, resembles the one attained by the ascetics of early Christianity who did not permit their moral will power to stand the test of temptation but carefully avoided any such occasion. Orgasm and sexual gratification are not shunned as such but because they lead to mysterious punishment.

We now understand better the nature of the suspense factor. It represents, so to speak, a tension within the tension. Its divided nature—between pleasure and anxiety—is attributable to the doubt or the hesitation as to whether or not an orgasm should be attained. The desire to trespass the forbidden threshold is urgent enough, but the fear of the consequences is just as strong, and finally stronger. Therefore the suspense feeling is not identical with the sexual tension but with the sexual tension transformed by anxiety. Originally it is not at all pleasurable and only becomes so because in some degree it is next best—a substitute for the orgasm.

Again I have to stress the importance of different stages of development and various possibilities in masochism. The position of the suspense factor can be compared to a compass revealing the direction of these manifold paths. One of these developments can be described in the following manner: in the place of pleasure—accompanied by anxiety—there steps anxiety producing pleasure, resulting in an osmosis of pleasure and anxiety. When masochism is established, it may happen that—by a shift of psychic stress—this very anxiety is desired and enjoyed. The suspense feeling can be displaced so far as to produce a voluptuous.expectation of anxiety. Such a peculiar mixture is altogether compatible with developed masochism. "It torments so charmingly," is the phrase of a patient designating the masochistic sensation.

Comparing the course of excitement of other perversions we come to recognize in suspense a prominent characteristic of mas-

ochism. However, it has to be noted here that the importance of
the suspense factor is not restricted to the field of masochism. It is
a peculiar nuance of feeling tone which—hardly recognized till
now—encompasses a wider range of psychic situations and plays a
role in many different psychic phenomena.

We stated that the disturbance in the tension curve either does
not permit end-pleasure by causing it to become insipid or even
transforms its character into the opposite, into end-displeasure.
If pleasure penetrates anxiety the suspense positively intensifies
the pleasure, thus being utilized for the increasing pressure of the
striving for pleasure. It gives way to the stronger adversary—
reluctantly yet gladly. No expression seems to characterize the
nature of this reluctant-voluntary yielding so well as the words
in which Milton describes the power of music:

> Such sweet compulsion doth in music lie,
> To lull the daughters of Necessity
> And keep unsteady Nature to her law.

Up to this point we have examined the suspense factor as to
its effectiveness in masochistic phantasies, without considering its
relationship to concomitant masochistic practices. The situation
changes with the institution of masochistic procedures. The intervention of the suspense feeling will prevent the masochist from
attaining the end-pleasure until he has experienced punishment,
humiliation or discomfort. There is a distinctly marked alternative to be noticed: punishment, humiliation, discomfort—orgasm,
or: no discomfort and no punishment—suspense and no satisfactory
orgasm, eventually end-discomfort. To put it another way: if the
masochist has experienced pain or discomfort (even if it is only
in his imagination) he is quite capable of attaining the orgasm
and of feeling intense pleasure. In this case the increase of tension is about normal. However, if there has been no intensive
discomfort beforehand the suspense takes the place of the increase of tension, producing a disturbance of potency later and
finally impotence. There are certain transitions between these

possibilities but the picture of the alternatives as a whole is correct beyond a doubt. It can be demonstrated in any single case
of masochistic attitude.

A correction is necessary only in so far as the suspense moment can also be demonstrated in those cases where masochistic
practices have preceded sexual satisfaction—at an unexpected
place, though, in a displacement. Let us pursue the description
of a masochistic scene: a patient, mentioned above, periodically
goes to a prostitute, has her abuse him, is told to undress and
receives a blow on the buttocks. Thereafter the ejaculation occurs. That is the scene, crudely described by its externals. A
closer and more careful observation of details must convince us
that the scene is separable into two distinct parts: the expectation of the blow and the carrying out of the masochistic act. The
whole prelude goes within the first part: the phantasied anticipation of the scene, the expectation while climbing the stairs,
the bandying of words. The abuse, the verbal threats accompanied by expressive gestures and finally the minutes of waiting
expectantly for the blow are more important libidinously than
the blow itself. In some cases the tension attained by being
scolded or threatened is sufficient to produce the end-pleasure.

The psychic character of this expectation corresponds absolutely to the suspense. It wavers between pleasurable and apprehensive sentiments. To put it more accurately, we might say that
it enjoys the fear of punishment and humiliation. We can therefore correct our previous assertion by stating that in this perverse
practice, too, the suspense feeling is experienced and noticeable.
Its role has only been diminished and shifted to the pleasurable-
anxious expectation of discomfort.*

We can see now that the preliminary phantasy and the suspense factor belong together psychologically. The phantasying

* S. Nacht, observing a sentiment of this kind, speaks of an *attente anxieuse
de la douleur* (fearful expectation of pain). The twofold nature of the suspense
is missed in this description just as is the shift of stress from anxiety to
pleasure. It would be much more to the point to speak of an *attente volup-
tueuse de la douleur* (voluptuous expectation of pain).

of details, of delays and impediments, of doubts and uncertainties, is serving the same purpose as does the suspense moment. They are indeed nothing but intellectualized offshoots of the tendencies that also create the suspense.

By comparing the suspense allotment in the masochistic scene with the phantasy we come to the following aspect: in the first case the tension, vacillating between pleasure and anxiety, is directed toward the expected punishment, humiliation and disgrace. In the second case it is directed toward end-pleasure. There is but a single step from here to the surmise that the end-pleasure is avoided for fear of humiliation and punishment. It can be considered the result of this anxiety that end-pleasure in sexual intercourse either is not attained or is transformed into end-discomfort.

The tension in the phantasy is originally pleasurable and its character changed by the influence of the anxiety accompanying the idea. To put it in a different way: the suspense factor is now revealed as being the old, well-known sexual tension transformed by the influence of unconscious anxiety. In the masochistic scene —a new phase of development—the anxiety has become pleasurable. An anxiety-ridden pleasure slowly has developed into pleasurable anxiety, determining the character of the suspense feeling. The psychological insight into this development, the completion of which alone constitutes real masochism, must lead to a changed conception of this perversion. Here it is: masochism is not, as has been surmised up till now, characterized by the pleasure in discomfort but by pleasure in the *expectation* of discomfort. The stress, which originally lay on the pleasure in end-climax and orgasm, was shifted to anxious expectation. This displacement deprived anxiety of its specific character. Anxiety itself became an element of pleasure. As to the relationship between suspense feeling and forepleasure, the forepleasure anticipates the end-pleasure in small doses. It is a kind of sample of orgasm. The suspense feeling is of the same kind but simultaneously it is an anticipation of the discomfort to be expected from punishment —comparable to a sample of a forbidden but desired dish. Thus

it is forepleasure plus forediscomfort and is ultimately transformed more and more into the latter.*

But how is it that this forediscomfort finally is sought after
in masochism? All of us, when we expect some discomfort or
pain, will try to repel and not invite the feared sensation. We
certainly do not wish to take an advance on a coming pain. Surely
no one who faces a severe operation would cut his finger in order
to get a presentiment of the future pain. Yet under certain circumstances everybody has done something comparable.

For example, I notice a toothache, one of those twinges which
come up suddenly and then stop, and I make a resolution to
go to the dentist as soon as I have the time. Half an hour later
the toothache has ceased. I know it will reoccur and that I should
see the dentist very soon. I move my tongue and cautiously approach the sensitive tooth. The contact hurts. Some minutes later
I repeat it although I know that it will hurt. In doing this my
purpose certainly is not only to convince myself that the tooth
still hurts. There must be another motive too. I am afraid that
the pain will start anew, of its own accord. I touch it with my
tongue to prepare or to harden myself against this eventuality.
Or, to put it the other way round, to avoid anxiety or to prevent
its becoming too intensive. Thus I seek out something I am afraid
of—because of my anxiety. I voluntarily endure a bit of pain in
order not to be exposed to it suddenly and without preparation.
This is an intentional seeking of foredispleasure, a masochistic
activity in miniature.

Here is another and more plausible example: a patient with
distinct masochistic features, neurotically elaborated, reported
that she had noticed some kind of masochism in herself when still
a little girl. When the little one was put into the bathtub and the
nurse left her—perhaps to get a towel—the girl turned the cold

* Such transformation naturally is not restricted to the masochistic practices
of perverts. The suspense feeling can assume this character elsewhere. This
insight makes doubtful the general applicability of Josh Billings' funny understatement: "Waiting to be whipped is the most uninteresting period in
boyhood life." Memories of the boyhood of masochists prove that such expectation filled with suspense can also be enjoyed.

water tap a little bit and let some drops fall on her arm—thus experiencing a disagreeable-pleasurable feeling.

It is hardly necessary to stress the fact that the little girl hated the cold shower and was very much afraid of it. She knew that the sponging off with cold water was coming and she anticipated it by letting a few drops fall on her arm. We do not hesitate to assume that the little girl acted thus because she was very much afraid. She sought the forediscomfort in order to be better fortified against the greater discomfort, or not to be obliged to experience too great anxiety.

The forediscomfort, which is anticipated here as in masochism, is thus supposed to protect against a shock or to work against the increase of anxiety. In order to avoid anxiety the unpleasant is brought about voluntarily. By producing the frightening or alarming event in miniature, by having some drops fall on her skin, the little girl has allayed fear. It is important that what she is afraid of is not done to her. She herself does it. She did it, she is active, the mistress of her own fate. Besides this anticipation, which includes a transformation from the passive into the active, another temporal factor is important: the tension is spread out over a longer period and thus prepared for. When the nurse turned the cold water tap a shock was to be expected. When the child turned the water on she diminished the tension by division into several time units. She has prepared herself mentally and has escaped a sudden increase of tension. By having at her disposal a longer period for mastering her impressions, she has transformed a strong tension into a moderate one.

The factors mentioned here can be demonstrated in every case of masochism. The forediscomfort does not come as a surprise to the masochist but actually by his deliberate instructions. He induces or even orders what shall be done to him in the way of unpleasantness. It is not inflicted upon him against his will. What happens to him or what punishment or humiliation he suffers happens at the moment, in the rhythm and in the sequence chosen by himself. The tension is diffused over a certain period and thus anxiety is appeased or eliminated. Surveying these factors we begin to guess why—as has often been stated—the masochist does not show any symptoms of anxiety. Anxiety cannot develop, for the masochist has achieved his aim of avoiding anxiety. Instead of suffering anxiety he has exposed himself to suffering. Instead of being afraid of humiliation, disgrace or punishment he has brought it about himself, thus mastering a hard destiny. By anticipating all these sensations he deprives them of their terrors. The masochistic mechanism is—with regard to its direction—a flight toward the future.

The suspense sensation has revealed itself to be the last residue of an anxiety. It is the study of just this factor that enables us to understand how it is that the masochist, by his perversion, succeeds in avoiding the development of anxiety. In order to escape the fear of punishment and humiliation he arranges them himself. Yet the appreciation of the suspense factor leads us still farther—to the disclosure of mental preparedness for discomfort as an important factor in masochism. It can be asserted that masochistic pleasure is more dependent on this expectation of discomfort than on discomfort itself.

The insight into the function of the suspense factor, on the other hand, elucidates the second possibility of masochistic development. If avoidance of anxiety is one of its most essential features it becomes plain how it is that later pleasure develops into discomfort, how eventually end-pleasure is postponed and finally renounced. A comparison may prove helpful here: let us assume that somebody at one time or other has hurt himself badly when making a high jump. A long time later an occasion to jump reoccurs. He takes a run, reaches the jump-off spot, even starts the movement of jumping—and, at the last moment, is mysteriously prevented from actually jumping. Surely an unconscious anxiety at the memory of the previous experience is the obstacle. Later on he again reaches the jump-off spot, but the anxiety occurs earlier, before he even starts to jump. Still later he just takes the run, and finally he gives up jumping entirely, being sure of his failure in advance.

But are we entitled to use such a comparison? Numerous

analytic experiences with perverts and masochistic characters, constructions forced upon us by memories and symptoms of patients, support it. These constructions, however, are in a way indirectly confirmed if in the course of analytical treatment we succeed in traversing the path in the opposite direction. Thus we find an impotent man with masochistic phantasies passing all the above sketched stations on his way back to recovery. In certain cases of a typical nature it can be demonstrated that avoidance not of the development of anxiety but of the outburst of an intense fright-affect was aimed at.

Should the little girl who protects herself from the intrusion of intense anxiety by turning the water tap be called a masochist? Certainly not. The distinctive factor of pleasure which she would have to gain from her procedure is missing. It only complies with one prerequisite of masochism: protection from anxiety. Its other function is the satisfaction of urges and this is the more primitive and more important one. Anxiety springs up later, disturbing the drive for pleasure just as a policeman unexpectedly turning a corner would disturb a high-spirited, merry celebration. The intruder must either be hushed or removed before resuming the previous unrestrained merrymaking. Thus it becomes the task in hand to get the better of or get rid of anxiety. Yet the attainment of the instinctual aims remains the essential idea.

Masochism as a perversion succeeds better with the subjugation and the avoidance of anxiety than does phantasy with masochistic ideas which accompanies normal sexual intercourse. The perversion meets punishment or discomfort in order to send the intruder about his business at once and—being freed from its threat—turns toward pleasure. Such anticipated discomfort may even, eventually, lead reactively to intensified pleasure, bringing increased satisfaction, as does every fear we are able to master.

The suspense feeling vacillating between pleasurable and anxious sensations is disclosed as the expression of the attempt to attain pleasure and yet avoid pain. Thus masochism is a peculiar attempt resulting from two antagonistic tasks. The suspense factor is a sign and evidence of its development and essence. It turns up in the situations which determine the genesis of the perversion. It escorts the masochistic phantasies and remains as a survival when masochism has developed into an actual perversion. Though its forms of expression are altered in the stages of nonsexual, social masochism its character is not.

4

I promised to describe the characteristic features which are never missing in any case of masochism. The surpassing importance of the phantasy appeared to us to be the primary and the suspense factor the secondary of these characteristics. The third distinctive feature will be called the demonstrative, a designation which will be justified later. It is meant to stress that in no case of masochism can the fact be overlooked that the suffering, discomfort, humiliation and disgrace are being shown and, so to speak, put on display. Considering the conspicuousness of this feature in some cases one may well wonder why it has been underestimated for so long. Though some analytical observers such as K. Horney, J. Lampl, and K. Menninger have come near it, they still have passed it by, merely pointing out the narcissistic or exhibitionistic character of masochism. I shall show later that these designations are misleading. Though I am of the opinion myself that designations generally are of small importance— what's in a name?—this one actually conveys a mistaken conception.

In the practices of masochists denudation and parading with all their psychic concomitant phenomena play such a major part that one feels induced to assume a constant connection between masochism and exhibitionism. If I prefer to designate this feature as demonstrative rather than exhibitionistic I do it for two reasons. First of all that misconstruction is avoided which associates exhibitionism solely with the showing off of what is believed to be beautiful or attractive. Moreover, by the word "demonstra-

tive." I want to hint at a hidden meaning of such displays, which
later on will become more evident. It is sufficient to cite here
the example of Jean Jacques Rousseau, who felt compelled, in
spite of all his sense of shame, to show his naked buttocks to
passing ladies, thus not only demonstrating the exhibitionistic
nature of masochism but a very important additional trait as
well, which I will characterize as "provocative." The showing or
wanting-to-be-seen is actually a means to invite the sexually grati-
fying punishment.

Occasionally the demonstration in phantasy or, less frequently,
in reality is sufficient to attain masochistic satisfaction. I refer
to the girl with the phantasy about the butcher. Her lying there
naked, which she felt was most humiliating and disgraceful, was
one of the most pleasurable moments especially when she imagined that all the butchers ignored her. In the second example
quoted, of the man who used to go to a prostitute and have himself beaten because of having been "bad," the undressing and
baring of his backside was almost as important as the subsequent
blow. Here we have to note what distinguishes such demonstration from narcissism. At first glance it seems to be immaterial
whether what the others get to see is considered beautiful or
ugly. In one case the masochist's own body might be thought of
by him as attractive and the excrements as sexually stimulating,
while in another they appear to be merely disgusting and repulsive. Closer investigation, however, reveals a more complicated situation. In cases of conscious pride in one's own body, or
of special pleasure in it, the following punishment or discomfort
becomes more intensive and the humiliation deeper. When the
body is consciously felt as ugly and the phantasy or the display
as disgusting this feeling itself becomes a characteristic of the
masochistic pleasure and contributes essentially to sexual excitement.

We recall the example of the extensive sacrificial phantasies
of the man who found his satisfaction in imagining that young
men were being offered to Moloch or to an Aztec deity. For this
horrible death by fire only the most beautiful youths of the tribe

were chosen. They were shown to the whole people. Here we can actually assume narcissistic pride in the idea that these youths— all of them "doubles" of the daydreamer—are standing in front of the idol "with nothing on but a smile." Their beautiful bodies rouse the admiration of all. They themselves, however, consider it a distinction, being called to suffer terrible death in the flames. The proudly borne agony of this phantasy can be contrasted with the deep feeling of helpless humiliation and disgrace in a young girl's phantasy of being watched while urinating or defecating— a phantasy which, nevertheless, brought her distinct masochistic pleasure. The place of psychical discomfort or pain is frequently taken by a humiliating or degrading display of psychical or mental deficiencies, which in the phantasy have an exciting effect. The "embarrassing situation" is enjoyed with the same anxious-pleasant feeling as the physical punishment.

Here we are at the threshold leading to the desexualized forms of masochism. Even in cases where there is no question of a perversion in the grosser meaning of the word, where masochism signifies an attitude toward life, this demonstrative feature is distinctly recognizable. When W. Reich found a close connection between masochism and "inhibited exhibitionism" he allowed himself to be duped by the external aspects of the phenomena. A conscious inhibition of exhibitionism does not contradict a hidden and yet victorious tendency in the opposite direction. The resultant of such contradictory forces is usually a demonstrative concealment or an exhibitionism with reversed sign. A young woman who as a girl had extensive masochistic phantasies no longer gave any indication of these. But she did not miss any opportunity whatever to draw attention to the fact that she could not accomplish anything, had no distinct character, and was inferior to other women as to charm and amiability. It seemed as if she wanted to demonstrate to all the world her complete insignificance. Yet it was striking that she repeatedly pointed out her unattractiveness as if she took pride in it. Here to the spectator or listener is a *conditio sine qua non,* as in other cases of masochism. Such display or glorification of one's own deficiencies is hardly compatible with an inhibition of exhibitionism. It is not to be understood why these "inferior" persons do not endeavor to be as reticent or modest as might be expected of them.* There is no doubt as to the self-humiliation and self-depreciation which Reich feels is so striking, but it is the *showiness* of these symptoms that is their essential feature. They are there, but what is more important, they are so conspicuously there.

The young woman for instance, of whom I just spoke, was asked one day whether she could typewrite. "Not very well," she said, "really not at all." Next day she mentioned as it were casually that she possessed a diploma in typewriting. There is thus seen to be frequently a divided or ambiguous attitude. One is induced to say: "Pride cometh *after* the fall." The universality of the demonstrative feature among addicts to suffering can be proved even if antagonistic psychic tendencies have forced a disguised hybrid, or reactive formation. As mentioned above the most frequent result is a compromise between display and concealment. That sounds more paradoxical than it is. Such peculiar ambivalence is to be found in all walks of life. Take a commonplace example: a gentleman enters a room where a lady sits with legs crossed in a very free and easy manner. She is sure to alter her position at once and adjust her disarranged skirt. Now, there are cases in which the person will do this in a manner which stresses or demonstrates her modesty. The lady's movement may betray a mixture of wanting both to show and at the same time to hide.** In masochism we encounter such compromises from the most delicate to the crudest forms. The following example made

* To what an extent my views deviate from those of contemporary psychoanalysts may be judged by a comparison with those of K. Horney for whom masochism is an attempt "to gain safety and satisfaction in life through inconspicuousness and dependency." (*New Ways of Psychoanalysis*.) The author seems to have been misled by the impressions of superficial ego-gains in masochism.

** The essence of so striking a concealment had been discovered—sixteen centuries before psychoanalysis—by St. Jerome in his letters to Roman women: "The cloak accidentally slides from the white shoulders exposing them and is quickly pulled up again as if one hastened to hide what one would gladly have be seen."

quite an impression on me: a patient was supposed to attend a
gala concert of a famous conductor. She would have liked to
wear her new evening frock and the pearls she had recently received as a present. Yet she was reluctant to do so for fear of
attracting attention in this small city by such a gorgeous attire.
So after some hesitation she wore for this concert—*pour épater
les bourgeois*—her simple everyday dress. The result, naturally,
was that she was the only woman there not in evening dress and
was critically inspected by all. Now indeed was she conspicuous
—which was just what she had wanted to avoid. She felt ashamed
and yet superior. By this display, the attainment of which might
be called almost cunning, a *coincidentia oppositorum* was
reached. The aim had remained—to attract attention; the result
was—she was looked at. The original desire, struggling with the
antagonistic tendency, had brought about a masochistic compromise, a kind of negative demonstration or an exhibitionism
with reversed sign.

A lawyer had for years been attending the sessions of a professional club without ever contributing a single word to the discussions. Yet he sincerely wished to participate in the discussions,
knowing that he had important things to say. Nevertheless he was
prevented from speaking because he asked himself how his silence was taken. He actually attracted attention by saying nothing. A distinct tendency to become the center of attention shows
up here behind the appearance of modesty. Comparatively speaking: a violet lets it be generally known that it blooms in concealment. Any closer investigation of masochistic psychology shows
that there can be no question of a predominant inhibition of
exhibitionism. At best there is an exhibition with reversed sign.
Even in cases of self-deprecation and self-humiliation, of pseudo-
debility and ostensible stupidity the very same desire to display
and to boast of one's own defects and shortcomings is plainly
recognizable. It is striking indeed that so many masochists are
not ashamed of their weaknesses and bad qualities but boast of
them. Those masochistic characters who rejoice in minimizing
their own qualities, in displaying their shortcomings and vices,

are inverted hypocrites. In reality they are proud of themselves and proud even of their self-degradation and self-abasement. Their good qualities and gifts will appear the more brilliantly later on. Their modesty is make-believe. They want glory and glamour perhaps more keenly than we do. The tendency to be overshadowed is a reaction derived from the desire to shine. It is at the same time an expression of this continuing desire.

Everybody knows examples of people who make a parade of their sufferings. Suffering in masochism has such an external aspect distinctly destined to confront the environment, a façade designed for the outer world. Without the attention of this environment suffering loses much of its pleasurable character. Anyone who has attentively followed the reports of masochists will approve that the words, "It is half-pleasure, half-complaint," may aptly be quoted from the *Moerike* song. The flagging of attention directed at the suffering can produce exasperation and temper. A woman patient, whose family was usually very worried about her frequent attacks, one day lay a long while moaning on her sofa. As her lamenting did not find any responsive sympathy she got up and dressed without taking any further notice of her own pains. A member of her generally oversolicitous family, who for once had not been concerned over the invalid, heard her mutter to herself, "Well, nothing doing!"

Frequently we find the mixture of the desire to hide and to show manifested in the masochist's demonstrating that he suffers in silence. In certain characteristic cases when the person actually has been wronged it is like a demonstration signifying: "I bear no malice even if my heart breaks." Such conspicuously silent suffering is meant to be seen. The equanimity with which it is borne is meant to be admired. Here an objection could arise: is there no suffering without demonstrative intention? Certainly, but then it is not masochistic suffering. The demonstrative feature is essential to and not separable from masochism. When this demonstrative feature is accented it frequently sounds somehow false or hypocritical. The masochist in the social sense then appears as the actor of his own misery, praising and proclaiming his suffering. I feel this feature is effective even in the demonstrative manner in which the suffering Job shows his misfortune to his friends.

Nor is this demonstrative feature restricted to the physical field. Take for instance the figures of the Russian epic writers Dostoevski and Tolstoi who show a real voluptuousness in exposing themselves in weaknesses to all the world. The same feature can be rediscovered there. The demonstrative feature is there in cases of masochistic perversions as well as in masochistic characters. Rousseau's *Confessions* and *Correspondence,* Baudelaire's indulgence in masochistic phantasies and his compulsion to confess (*coeur mis à nu*) are easily available examples. The history of religion furnishes the same combination of characteristics. The martyrs of early Christianity attached strikingly great importance to the fact that their suffering *ad majorem Christi gloriam* was seen. These witnesses to the faith desired to have witnesses of their martyrdom. They loved to show their wounds and their disgrace. They wanted all the world to know about their passionate zeal. There were the pillarists, like Simeon Stylites—impressively described by Anatole France—who displayed his asceticism, his privations and penitences high above the market place for all eyes to see.

A French passional of the 15th century contains a naïve confession of masochistic enjoyment and the demonstrative character that goes with it. It is reported that in Perugia a saint among others was imprisoned to wait for his execution. His companions were depressed; he was cheerful. He said, "You shall know that I am glad because I shall be honored as a saint by all the world!" A direct line leads from such behavior to the performances of the Hindu fakirs and the Mohammedan dervishes with their self-tortures. One's own suffering and one's own excruciating death should be watched by a great number of illustrious spectators. Counterexamples of lonely ascetics or martyrs turn out to be only apparent contradictions. Even for the solitary monks, the holy Jerome in the desert, Saint Anthony in the Thebais and for all the hermits who subjected themselves to the most terrible flagellations, there was the one and all-important witness: God. To Him they wanted to show how they suffered for Him, to prove to Him how they punished themselves for their sins.

However genuine the penitence, however voluntary the suffering, it can't do without a public. In most cases it has the character of a performance and frequently it does not dispense with a certain theatrical flavor. This demonstrative note is not restricted to masochistic individuals. It can be rediscovered in the attitude of groups or peoples to whom fate has ordained an afflicted past and present. In the lives of these peoples the connection between the ideas of being loved and of being punished reappears on a higher, frequently on a religious, level. The suffering of the people is conceived as a sign of a definite mission, as a token that a very important part in the history of mankind has been assigned to them. God has distinguished this people by imposing on them special suffering and severe afflictions. The sexualization of punishment is demonstrable in the psychic life of groups as of individuals. "God loves him whom He chastens."

Thus a tribe with a particularly tragic destiny regards itself as a chosen people, whom God loves best. This is the ethno-psychological analogy to the infantile idea: father beats me and loves me. The secret pride in suffering is revealed here. It is displayed as a distinction or as a higher diploma. The hope for an ultimate triumph can lead to an ecstasy, to an orgy of suffering. The increase of privations and suffering betokened the close proximity of the day of redemption and of victory over the enemy. So the increase of pain in the practices of perverts can become a signal of imminent orgasm. It is welcomed as pleasure-pain only fictitiously. In reality pain is saluted as a phase preceding pleasure. The difference consists in the fact that the sexual factor prevails in the psychic life of perverts and the social one with peoples and masses. Masochism or rather masochistic attitudes of religious or ethnical masses as well show this demonstrative behavior.

To return to the individual psychic life we have to add that here, too, the same feature is present in the transition from perverted to desexualized masochism. It reappears in self-deprecation and self-derision in front of others. Even if they are alone some of these masochists show a behavior quite opposite to that of the queen in the fairy tale: "Mirror, mirror, on the wall, who is the stupidest, ugliest, etc., of us all?" The attention of others has to be drawn to the ego by clumsiness, bad behavior, even crime. I was in a position to observe closely such a case of transition: a middle-aged man, who for many years had known masochistic sexual gratification, had during analysis dropped his perversion and attained a normal sexual life. His character, however, had slowly undergone a peculiar development. He frequently went into society and amused his friends and acquaintances greatly by telling numerous anecdotes in which he figured as an unlucky fellow or dupe. He produced a constant stream of witticisms—by the way, mostly very pertinent ones—which made unmerciful fun of his own stupidity, tactlessness or egotism. In other words he simply played the clown in order to make others laugh at him.

His sexual perversion had, so to speak, been transformed into a social one. His masochism had survived by his assuming the role of a Debureau, a self-deriding punster. His self-humiliation had put on a social mask. In displaying his own ignominy, in his cynicism directed against his own ego, he had clearly shown at the same time the self-demonstration. Just as he previously had exposed his buttocks in the beating scenes he now exposed his psychic nudity.

I want to emphasize here that investigation of such a psychic development leads to valuable insights into the psychology of witty persons—especially of the type who turn the shaft against the ego—as well as into the genesis of the intentionally comic. It is a kind of masochistic demonstration to confess one's shortcomings before the world so as to make others laugh. It certainly is no contradiction that such intentional demonstration of one's own weakness and foolishness occasionally discloses its masochistic character as in the comical figures of Falstaff or Don Quixote. Even clowns sometimes produce this peculiar mixture of wanting both to show and to hide. "Laugh, Pagliacci, make foolish faces

. . ." sings Leoncavallo's hero. But the purpose of such laughter is not only to conceal suffering. It should also betray it. The production of laughter is a special means of masochistic gratification for the comical person. That he makes a fool of himself does not mean that he is a fool.

An objection based on the performance of solitary masochistic practices by certain perverts is easily disposed of. Frequently young men—rarely women—practice self-flagellation before a mirror. In one case a patient, who thus attained orgasm, first had to see in the mirror the bloody weals he had produced on his buttocks by beating. Such solitude is materially, but not psychologically, real. The masochist imagines a spectator whom he sometimes plays himself. This phantasied witness partakes in observing and enjoying the exposure and the beating. This second person cannot be eliminated in the phantasy because he is the carrier of the pleasure-bringing action. In solitary masochistic practices the second person is as essential as in self-pity when unconsciously another person (father, mother) is phantasied as present and sympathizing with us in our trouble.

It can easily be guessed how such beating scenes in front of a mirror come about. They are attempts to realize phantasies in which one person has taken two parts by himself. Such attempts signify a step from phantasy to real masochistic scenes with a partner who eventually will be sought out in real life. This is the point at which to recall what previously has been said about the importance and the primary role of the phantasy in masochism.

Perhaps this is also the moment to justify the designation "demonstrative" for the described feature and to differentiate it from similar designations. It has been stated before that the word "exhibitionistic" is not adequate because it would presume that the demonstrator is proud of what he displays or considers it to be beautiful or commendable. This, however, is the case neither with the pervert nor with the moral masochist. Many of them consciously experience their own exposure or degradation as humiliating and shameful. Ultimately one could only speak of an exhibitionism with reversed sign, as with the Gueux, those Dutch nobility who *subsequently* seized on a designation meant to be abusive ("*gueux*—beggars") and made it a term of honor, wearing small silver or copper beggars' buttons on their hats or belts as fraternity badges. They converted the ignominious sign into a kind of lurid triumph as Hester Prynne in Hawthorne's novel wore the Scarlet Letter and prided herself on what the magistrates meant for a punishment. Even if, with these important restrictions, one could designate this typical feature as exhibitionistic it would be quite wrong to align it with narcissism as some observers did (Lampl, Menninger). I have depicted the attitude of masochism toward exposure as being a means to attract attention. For the moment we will set aside the question whether it is intended to get punishment or evidences of love from others or whether another instinctual aim is desired. It seems strange to me whence comes the idea of calling this behavior narcissistic.

We restrict this designation to an attitude of self-amorousness. The characteristic of self-satisfaction is its most definite evidence and its most visible expression. The beautiful youth of the Greek myth who fell in love with his own image reflected in the pool's surface surely did not give a thought to the attention of others. He was absorbed by the sight of his own beauty and did not care about his environment. How different is the impression the masochist makes on us! His displaying and showing himself have all the characteristics of wooing, of making himself noticeable. His behavior is just the counterpart to narcissistic behavior. It would be more correct to state that evidently the narcissism of these masochistic persons had been deeply disturbed as they make such frantic efforts to attract the attention of others. Therefore masochism is never a sign of narcissism but an expression of its being damaged and of an attempt to restore it. The designation "narcissistic" for the typical attitude of masochism as described above is as justifiable as a comparison of a gourmet who enjoys exquisite food in solitude with a man who marches at the head of a hunger parade carrying inflammatory posters. The misuse and abuse of analytical terminology show up in such designations and misleading characterizations.*

The designation "demonstrative" for the characterized feature has been selected because among all those possible it is most apt to convey the idea of the typical behavior described above. Furthermore it seems to me the most neutral term since it does not convey anything as to the purpose aimed at by the masochistic display. For this reason alone I would prefer it to the unambiguous "exhibitionistic."

In surveying the characteristics of masochism I have pointed out the close connection between the predominance of phantasy and the suspense factor. Psychologically they form a pair. The demonstrative feature of masochism stands isolated and aside. If there are any connections with the two others we are not yet in a position to recognize them.

The purpose of the demonstration cannot be guessed in advance. One could rather state negatively that it is not what many analysts ascribe to it: narcissistic or exhibitionistic. Something is gained anyhow if such assertions can be rejected or excluded. Perhaps the secret tendency of the demonstrative feature could be approached by observing what it tries to show or present. The answer seems simple enough. The spectator or witness is intended to see the discomfort, the pain, the humiliation or disgrace of the masochist. In the field of social masochism he is presented with the person's own failure, his shortcomings, his stupidity or inferiority. Does this answer furnish a satisfactory explanation of the secret purpose of the demonstration? As far as I can see it does not. It answers the question of what is shown first. It does

---

* K. Horney for instance asserts (*New Ways in Psychoanalysis*) that "a person with pronounced narcissistic trends, though incapable of love, nevertheless needs people as a source of admiration and support." The solution of the enigma is not hard to find. It consists in the incorrectness of the assertion. A pronounced narcissist who urgently needs the admiration of others is surely no narcissist.

not clarify the point as to what is being concealed and hidden in such a display. If a man sitting in a room incessantly and conspicuously stares at the right-hand corner of the room this could very well signify that he sees something conspicuous there. On the other hand it can just as well be a means to distract the attention of the persons present from the left-hand corner. Maybe he has concealed something there. Anyhow it is conspicuous that one's own disgrace and one's own punishment are demonstrated so openly.

All psychic phenomena have a tendency toward self-betrayal, even masochism. The demonstrative feature is designed to show or prove something. There is no doubt about it. It is its very essence. But in conspicuously showing something it hides something else. The existence of the demonstrative feature, in itself a puzzle, strengthens the impression of a hidden paradox in masochism.

5

I have tried to provide an objective description of features not previously appreciated that are common to all forms of masochism. No attempt was made to explain the meaning of these characteristics in regard to the essence and the genesis of this instinctual tendency. The three characteristics stressed above may be observed by any analyst and are lacking in no case of developed masochistic inclination.

Naturally there are other features as well that do not appear regularly but stand in a definite relation to masochism and demand the attention of the psychologist. They are clearly visible in some cases and are hardly noticeable in others. The temptation is great to accredit a frequently attendant phenomenon as essential to masochism. Careful investigation must decide whether such features belong to "pure" masochism or whether they represent associated symptoms springing from other instinctual sources.

At the beginning I too was tempted to list one such feature, frequently associated with masochistic phenomena, with the three characteristics. I called it the *provocative factor* and I shall first outline its nature and only later comment on its relation to masochism. It is best to describe it as follows: the masochist uses all possible means at his disposal to induce his partner to create for him that discomfort which he needs for attaining his pleasure. He forces another person to force him. Such a formulation sounds bizarre, but that is due less to my stylistic shortcomings than to the nature of masochism.

In its grossest form the provocative factor is easily recognized in the actual scene. The man who explains to a prostitute in what highly uncomfortable and shameful manner he wishes to be treated offers the simplest and crudest example. There is something grotesque in the fact that he asks another person to bring pain or shame on him, a thing most men would abhor. I do not know whether in the literature pertaining to this topic the invitations or instructions are considered to be part of the masochistic forepleasure. I doubt it. With prostitutes surely one need not mind giving orders. With other partners it becomes necessary to use more refined methods, hidden ways of finding the approach to the instinctual aim, and of making known the personal prerequisites for excitement and satisfaction. The masochist frequently strives most actively for this passive goal. In many instances he shows in this striving an expenditure of psychic energy, of cleverness and of intellectual accomplishment which can be compared only to that invested in compulsion neuroses. The effort it takes to arrive at the desired displeasure that is pleasure is in itself a part of masochistic forepleasure sensations. The expression of this tendency extends from a kind of gentle invitation ("Bully me again, dear!") to impudent provocations.

But if the goal is not attained then the efforts take on a direction and character very similar to expressions of the sadistic instinct. It is as if obstacles which turn up on the way to achieving the masochistic aim made the person impatient and aroused his sadistic tendencies. Where the direct and immediate satisfaction of the impulse is not immediately in view the masochist becomes provocative, seeking to elicit the appropriate action from the partner. There are a great many "exasperated" masochists who torture their objects until they retaliate with the desired punishment or revenge. Till then the pressure will be increased. A peculiar spying on and watching of the object goes with this maneuver without the masochist being aware of it. In this behavior the masochist strongly resembles a naughty child who plagues his mother or nurse until he gets punished. Such a child too gets naughtier and naughtier all the while, nor is the watching and spying lacking. He seems to ask himself in the presence of the patient mother, "Will she now get angry? Not yet? Can she remain patient even now?" I once heard a little girl who was reprimanded by her mother in such a scene ask curiously, "But if I keep doing it, what will you do then?"

In the behavior described above the boundaries between masochistic and sadistic conduct are effaced for a short time. Aggressive and forceful means are used in order to attain punishment, scolding, humiliation. The pain addict becomes a tormentor. Roles appear to be reversed for this period. The masochist behaves like a sadist and his object, from whom he expects pain, suffering and degradation, behaves like the victim of a sadist. This challenge, enticement, provocation to give the desired masochistic satisfaction goes on in a sadistic form. As far as I can see, this provocative feature scarcely has received any psychological appreciation. When Freud said the real masochist offers his cheek where he has the prospect of receiving a slap he surely had in mind the same factor which, as he put it, has assumed the milder form of an invitation. The infantile prototype of this masochistic behavior is also shining through—though the child in most cases offers another part of the body for the slap. This infantile prototype conditions the provocative expression. It extends, however, to the most sublime and sublimated forms of masochistic feeling that are to be found in moral and religious development. From the sexual pleasure of being beaten to Christ's doctrine of offering the right cheek when one has been struck on the left, and thence to Gandhi's Non-Violence Program there is a long but a direct line.

Moreover it is remarkable that the masochistic provocation is of less importance in phantasy than in reality. That may be due to the fact that the way to masochistic satisfaction offers less resistance in phantasy. Especially in the life of masochistic characters the provocation easily assumes the form of teasing, of jeering, of quarreling or tormenting, according to whether the instinctual aim includes a lighter or a more severe way of punishment. This behavior can progress from slight irony to impudent challenge of the object, from apparently harmless teasing to rude abuse if the satisfaction is not forthcoming. The malicious bawler and reviler Thersites, as described by Homer, was a scandalmonger who kept irritating and ridiculing the Greek heroes until he got a sound thrashing. He may serve the reader as a model of such a tormenting masochist.

In considering the obduracy and the relentlessness of the provocation one is inclined to ascribe to the masochist who behaves in this way a tyrannical and despotic character. A strong will is to be sensed in this instigation which refuses to be repulsed and does not take a "Yes" for an answer. It is strange and worthy of meditation that the masochist whose character is one of complete submission to his object, of utter obedience, insists in his approach that his will alone be carried out—disregarding his object's wishes. Could this despotic character be only the reverse aspect of the masochist's humility and submissiveness? In psychoanalytic treatment of masochists the provocative feature becomes perceptible either as exasperated resistance or defiant obedience; as direct animosity, or other comparable expressions. The scale extends from obstinate silence to insolent remarks and behavior. The aim of such behavior generally can be called *masochistic sabotage.*

It is as if the patient could not rest content until he had been treated coolly or had been rejected; as if he could not do without blame and humiliation. In the pungency of the aggression the masochistic character is in no way inferior to the sadistic. Sometimes the typical provocation will manifest itself in immoderate insults aimed at exhausting the analyst's courteousness and patience. One such masochist started an analytic session with the jeering words, "Do you do anything at all? No, you just sit there. Do something with me!" His unconscious aim was to be scolded or insulted.

This form of provocation shows up more strikingly in desexualized masochism than in the perverted form. Nevertheless it can easily be observed in such cases too. Let me quote a splendid example from the life of a patient who found his only sexual satisfaction in being beaten on the buttocks by a woman. In a later phase of his analysis, during which the man successfully fought against his compulsory perversion, he nevertheless obtained his former gratification by a strange detour. He used to take his evening walk in one of Vienna's crowded streets, where he found opportunities unobtrusively to approach women walking in front of him and give them a light slap on that part of the body which was so pleasure-toned for him. This was usually done so stealthily that the women did not take any notice of the touch. But once it happened that one of the strolling beauties did not care to accept as homage this caress, which perhaps had proved a little robust. She turned around quickly and vigorously boxed her unknown admirer's ears. Whereupon the patient yelled in sincere indignation, "Hey, what's the great idea, you bitch? I'm a sadist myself!"

Here is an example of a provocation in the social field taken from the case of a patient who was a lawyer and occasionally had to defend thieves or swindlers in court. In doing this his behavior toward the judge was peculiar. At the beginning he was most respectful, even humble, as long as he had to fear severe punishment for his client. As soon, however, as it began to look as if his defendant would get away with a light sentence or even be acquitted, the lawyer changed his conduct in a striking way. He

would become insulting toward the judge, would brawl and behave insolently. His unconscious intention seemed to be to provoke the exasperation of the judge and a sharp reprimand. It was
easy for analysis to discover that the lawyer had identified with
the criminal and wanted to provoke a severe punishment. It may
not be superfluous to stress that numerous, even innocent, de-
fendants exhibit in court a similar provocative behavior of a
masochistic sort.

If a masochist thus has succeeded in inducing his victim to
injure him it not seldom occurs that he actually feels offended
and hurt. This reaction, of course, is restricted to consciousness.
But it does not exclude an unconscious satisfaction. A certain
type of person who constantly feels slighted and offended is to be
counted among the unconscious masochists who provoke their
associates until at last they produce an insult or a humiliation. I
believe that the score of those neglected by destiny includes a
great number of such disguised masochists who claim to have
been unjustly treated. The pertinacity and single-mindedness of
the masochist nearly always succeeds in attaining his secret aim.
As a reversed Shylock he insists on being injured although he
consciously resists it with all his power. Of course his incessant
and indefatigable efforts arouse all aggressive and vengeful tendencies of the partner who is tempted to give free rein to his own
cruelty. In his unconscious search the masochist unfailingly finds
his sadistic counterpart.

The provocative factor is not always easily detected in the
character structure. Sometimes it hides behind a psychic attitude
of martyrdom. Many people who are numbered among the host
of the humiliated and the offended entice their environment to
victimize them. The provocation has the function of getting them
badly treated, of insuring their being exploited and sacrificed.
This psychic martyrdom, eager to sacrifice itself, is aimed at a
cherished and hated victim, the wife, the parents, the children, a
friend. An adverse destiny has been personified. It has saddled the
masochist with a grumbling boss, with an eternally sick and

nagging wife, ungrateful children, exacting relatives and faithless friends. Yet his reaction, tantamount to enjoyment of suffering, is characteristic. Furthermore, the "gentle art of making enemies" must be considered as an excellent form of provocation. The secret urge to arouse envy and jealousy, hatred and wrath in others, to create a host of enemies for oneself, is part of the provocative technique of social masochism.

If it is the instinctual aim of the pain addict to be scolded, chastised and punished and if this instinctual aim is of an unconsciously sexual nature then it was obvious to assess the provocation as a masochistic wooing. Many analysts like W. Reich have preferred an obvious explanation of the masochistic challenges. An early infantile disappointment in love was easily assumed. An increased need for love of the masochistic character is not hard to verify. Growing, without resistance, the theory drifted in the wake of the equation: to be punished = to be loved. There remained the single though not unimportant question as to whether being chastised really was the masochist's primary instinctual aim. We are not concerned here with a psychological interpretation of the provocative feature but with its description and classification only.

What place may be claimed for it in the totality of masochistic phenomena? I believe that there is no doubt about it. It belongs to the technique of masochism. Its aim is to produce a certain conduct, a certain action of the object. It is peculiar that this technique of masochism is of an active, even aggressive character. Yet we hope to be able to perceive and describe the principle of this peculiar technique. It has a definite importance not only in love life but beyond this sphere as well and can be conceived as a variation of a German proverb: what you want should be done to you, do it to the other.*

What is the relation between the provocative factor, to which we have now ascribed the character of a masochistic technique, and the previously described demonstrative characteristic of mas-

* *Was du willst, dass man dir tu, das füge einem Andern zu.*

ochism? Provocation is a means of attaining the obscure masochistic instinctual aim. The demonstration, however, is inherent in
the very structure of masochism. The two features lie on different
levels. The manifold techniques for producing a certain state
certainly stand in a definite relation to the nature of this state
but they do not belong to the inalienable characteristics of this
condition. I do not contribute anything concerning the nature of
heat by merely saying that striking a match on a box is a means
of producing heat. The demonstrative feature is characterized by
the masochistic need to have a witness to his state of pleasant suffering. The provocative factor strives to bring about this condition.

Added to this consideration there are two reasons which make
it inadvisable to count the contribution of the provocation among
the characteristics of masochism. It does not appear regularly in
the picture of this instinctual inclination and becomes conspicuous only when satisfaction is withheld or put off for a long time.
It can be replaced or covered by other features. The second reason for excluding it from the characteristic features is that its very
nature is somewhat alien to masochism. The description of this
tendency shows its active and aggressive character. Put differently:
it originates from the sadistic instinctual source. It represents in a
way sadism as the sleeping partner of masochism, the sadistic contribution to the antagonistic instinctual tendency. It does not belong to the essence of pure masochism. The contrapuntal melody
to the given voice becomes audible therein. The provocative feature is no essential point of the masochistic entity but a representative of the counterpoint.

We therefore notice the existence and effectiveness of this contribution as psychologically remarkable but postpone its appreciation until the time when we have a better understanding of
the relations between sadism and masochism. Now we turn to new
problems in the hope that the conception and description of the
characteristics of masochism may bring us closer to the solution
of the enigma which challenged our psychological curiosity.

II

Dynamics

W E BELIEVE we have found a new approach to the problem of masochism. The description of several as yet unappreciated characteristics which are never missing in any case of masochism has crystallized out of long-continued observations which have been tested time and again in new situations. The psychological comprehension and description of these three characteristic features is a fruit of empiricism and a result of unprejudiced investigation. This achievement was independent of previous analytical views as to the nature of masochism. Any psychological observer —the nonpsychoanalytical as well—can convince himself of their existence by carefully studying and critically testing the details of the phenomena.

The three characteristics we have found in masochism do not at first appear to have any psychological connection. They stand in a line, isolated and unrelated to one another. We have reasons to suppose that the peculiar significance of phantasy is connected by a bridge with the suspense factor. But as yet there is no discernible connection between the demonstrative feature and the two others. Whoever prefers an elegant and smart solution to an honest one will find fault with the fact that the three characteristics of masochism at first resist a homogeneous conception. Even the significance of any single factor for this instinctual peculiarity as yet defies our judgment. It might be guessed that the significance of phantasy is a basic factor, that the suspense factor is decisive for the deviation from the normal and the demonstrative feature is designed to reveal or betray something hidden. Any definite assertion would be premature and we distrust all specu-

lations in a field that is accessible to psychological experience—
including our own speculations.

The discovery and appreciation of the three characteristics
of masochism may be of theoretical interest. A new conception of
the perversion and of the attitude, however, could only be derived
from understanding their significance in regard to its nature and
genesis. One should be able to prove why they have to be present
in every case of masochism and in what way their presence determines the genesis and development of sexual and social masochism. Our task is comparable to that of a chemist who has to analyze a new substance and has hit upon three of its essential
properties. He has to determine the significance of these features
for the synthesis and the nature of this substance in order to
classify it among those we know. What follows now is an attempt
to solve this problem. This cannot be done without uncertainties
and repetitions.

We choose the suspense factor as a starting point. It commands itself to us by its striking deviation from the usual psychic
process. Two apparently antagonistic tendencies are recognizable
in its manifestation. The one, aiming at an increase of tension up
to discharge; the other, which opposes the increase of tension and
avoids the relaxation. The suspense is the result of the mutual
interplay of these tendencies, the resultant of their conflict. We
discover it to be an effort toward maintaining the stimulating
tension on a certain medium level and toward postponing the
discharge. The tension of suspense gets its particular note from
the combination of pleasurable and anxious elements. It is evident that both feelings are meant for the increase of tension, or,
to express it more accurately, the increase of tension up to a point
which leads to discharge, to end-pleasure. Thus end-pleasure is
the object of pleasurable and anxious expectation. The deviation
from the normal course of tension consists in the deliberate postponement of this increase and in the presence of anxiety. There is
a single step from here to the assumption that the increase is
avoided out of anxiety. It is a single step but such a precarious

one and psychologically so important that it should be taken only with the utmost precaution.

We usually assume tension to be unpleasant and discharge to be pleasant. The tension which we call hunger is experienced as unpleasant by all of us and we seek to avoid the increase of this tension. There certainly do exist pleasurable tensions too. The sexual excitement is an example of them. But even such a pleasurable tension has its natural limits. If it lasts for too long a time it changes its character, becomes unpleasant, and its termination, the discharge, is desired and aimed at. The masochist apparently wants to provide a counterexample for this normal course of things. He wants to maintain the tension as long as possible and to avoid the discharge or postpone it as long as possible.

Does it really seem to be the correct conclusion from such behavior that—as some analysts have it—a long tension is pleasant for masochism at the outset and the discharge is unpleasant? There seems to be a lack of logical thinking in such an assumption, even a lack of psychological thinking in it. If a dog, every time he approaches a sausage, is threatened with a whip so that he finally avoids the sausage, does it mean that he has no more appetite for the sausage? The avoidance of the neighborhood of the sausage is far from being a symptom of the dog's idiosyncrasy against the sausage. It is but the sign of his fear of the whip.

The anxiety factor in the suspense indicates that the increase of excitement and the discharge—comparable to approaching and eating the sausage, in our example—is avoided because one is afraid of it. The masochist like any other mortal wants the orgasm, the pleasurable discharge, but he is afraid of it, or rather of something associated with it. He avoids the increase of excitement not as such but because it brings him into immediate proximity of discharge and thus of the things he dreads. He meets the approach of the orgasm as a signal of danger and he reacts to it as if to an urgent warning. In the same way a man who nears a railroad track and hears the sound of the bells signaling the approaching express will be careful not to cross the tracks.

The next question of course is: of what is the masochist afraid?

The simplest way to find out apparently would be to ask him. But his answer surely would be that he knows nothing about any such fear, that he fears nothing, and he puts off the sexual discharge because the postponement gives him pleasure. He would be right. He actually does not fear anything consciously—only the anxious note in the suspense betrays the influence of an unconscious anxiety. Nor can we doubt his assertion that the postponement is pleasurable for him. We believe that it became pleasurable only later, secondarily. Our opinion still is valid. The postponement originally was a precautionary measure. It was designed to put off the discharge because the masochist was afraid of it—or of something connected with it.

Of what is the masochist afraid? There is no direct way of answering this most essential question. So we make a detour and attempt a side approach. From the nature of the suspense we have deduced the surprising presence of anxiety in the masochistic character. The suspense itself appeared to us—viewed from one angle—as an attempt to diminish or exclude the anxiety. We know—the anxious note betrays it—that the attempt was not completely successful. Is this the only possible outcome? There is a more successful one in the masochistic field and we approach the heart of the question by investigating it psychologically. Though the tension of suspense is demonstrable in all cases of masochistic inclination it does not exist in the same degree in all its manifestations. It is most outspoken in sexual intercourse accompanied by masochistic phantasies. It is mildest in the perverse act. In the very scenes of punishment and humiliation the feeling of suspense is restricted. That is to say, the factor of anxiety which we discovered is less perceptible here. The man who has himself beaten by his wife in order to attain orgasm will still feel something of the anxious pleasure of suspense in the preparations and the ceremonial. The duration and intensity of this feeling, however, is not to be compared with that which would be experienced in the sexual act with the same partner accompanied by protracted masochistic phantasies. This same anxiety unquestionably is extant in the scene but, so to say, attenuated.

That cannot be a mere coincidence. We have hit on a clue. Why is the attenuation of the anxiety brought about in the realized perversion? The answer is because the punishment, humiliation or degradation actually are carried out. Let us assume for a moment that the anxiety in the suspense is concerned with a punishment such as being beaten. That certainly is the crudest, certainly an insufficient assumption, but it simplifies the facts for the purpose of the present examination. This being granted, it would, of course, be easy to understand how the execution of the perversion diminishes anxiety. The masochist is being beaten. He can stop fearing the future threat. It is present. The punishment no longer is imminent; he is through with it. May I recall what I mentioned above? The punishment is not the essential thing in masochism but the fear of punishment. And that is increased if the punishment has to be waited for or fails to occur.

Let us for a moment go back to the comparison with the hungry dog. We could easily understand that the dog—under pressure of increasing hunger—might snatch the sausage in spite of being very much afraid of the whip. But no dog would invite a cut of the whip, half ask for a thrashing. He might accept the cut of the whip in the bargain if he can thus get the sausage, but he certainly would not make the painful blow the object of his pleasure. Here we recognize the inadequacy of the comparison. It limps like a dog who has received a blow on his hind legs. Anyhow the comparison suffices to reaffirm the opinion that only man is a masochistic animal.

In the suspense factor we have seen at work a tendency to exclude the anxiety attendant on the orgasm by avoiding an increase of tension beyond a certain level. The cause of anxiety is circumvented. In the practices of perverts the object of anxiety, the punishment, is not only not avoided but on the contrary sought for, brought about. Yet, we believe, both antagonistic ways of behavior aim at the same or a similar effect: to diminish or exclude the anxiety. Is there a contradiction and how is it to be solved?

I go back to the previous example of the little girl who sat

in the bathtub dreading the moment when the nurse would let
the cold water run over her body. She is afraid and yet she turns
the tap herself and lets the cold drops fall on her bare arm. I mentioned already that one could not very well call the little girl a
masochist. The essential element of pleasure in displeasure is lacking, although in a way it does timidly show up as a kind of satisfaction, as if the child had outwitted the nurse. Perhaps it is also
an indication of an agreeable sensation mingling with the really
disagreeable one of cold. Nevertheless, the little girl is no masochist. Nor would there be any reason for chaste souls to shrink back
in alarm from such early moral depravity. But the little one is
well on the way to developing masochistic inclinations later on.
What is it that connects her apparently foolish conduct with that
of the masochist, the adult pervert? Just this: something one is
afraid of is brought about intentionally and this procedure
diminishes the anxiety.

Is this assertion correct? One dares not miss an occasion of
testing one's own assumptions. In the case of the little girl it is
not the dreaded event itself that is brought about. She did not
suddenly let a cold shower fall on her body but cautiously let
only a few drops run down her arm. Thus she lets happen only
a fraction of what she is afraid of, just an indication, a very small
dose. The child, no doubt, feared the cold water and yet herself
produced what she was afraid of; but not as a whole, just a small
part, a sample, so to speak. Although it may sound paradoxical,
she has produced it herself, *because* she was so much afraid of it.

It becomes inevitable here to refer back to the peculiar significance of phantasy for the essence of masochism. We shall encounter this phenomenon always. The child was so much afraid
because she anticipated the approaching, threatening event in
vivid phantasy. The fear of the cold shower may appear to us as
being exaggerated. But who can ascertain beyond doubt that the
intensity of this infantile fear is inferior to the horrors of dooms-
day? As the anxiety of the little girl rose while she waited she
could no longer stand its increase, and therefore preferred to
realize at least partly the inevitable phantasied trouble. By this

action, however, she has diminished and almost overcome her anxiety. Out of extreme anxiety she has become a sort of heroine. It may sound ridiculous but the turning of the tap is no less heroic than Beethoven's determination ". . . to thrust his hands into destiny's jaws."

The anxiety was allayed and mastered in a twofold way, first by the transformation of passive bearing into active doing; and then by anticipation, thus changing a future threat into something extant. Anticipation in phantasy increased the anxiety infinitely. Anticipation by action permitted it to die away. A test-event—for that is what phantasy is—turned into a test-action. Two coinciding alterations have cooperated in diminishing the anxiety. The first is concerned with the situation of the ego in respect to activity and passivity. The other with the relation of the ego to time.

By the first alteration the ego changes from a passive role to an active one. By the second one a future event becomes a present one. By the first, the ego has made himself master of the world's events, and by the second, master of the time at which they have to occur. A third alteration is coordinated to these two. The test-action is concerned only with a part of the events anticipated in phantasy. The dreaded danger situation is not brought about in its entirety but only partially and playfully. I will summarize the result: the three alterations, by which the small person in the bathtub has mastered her anxiety: concern the ego's passive or active attitude, the temporal course of an event and the extent of this dreaded event. I anticipate some future insights by asserting that these three alterations cause the anxiety to diminish or even vanish in cases of perverse masochism.

Of these three alterations the one that relates to time seems to me the most interesting one and promises the most extensive psychological clarification. It also has the most intimate relation to the problem from which we started, the question of the increase of tension in the masochistic pleasure experience. Let us recall that, generally speaking, every increase of psychic tension means discomfort, every diminution means pleasure. The example of sexual excitement, however, cautions us against taking this proposition as universally valid. For in this latter case increase of tension, at least for a certain period, produces pleasure. Referring to this very example Freud emphasized that pleasure and displeasure cannot simply be proportional to increase and decrease of tension "although they undoubtedly have much to do with this factor." He thinks that they do not depend on a factor of quantity but upon one we would have to designate as qualitative. "We were much farther along in psychology," he continues, "if we had discovered which this factor is." He suggests that it could be the rhythm, "the timely process within the changes, increases, and ceases of the enticing quantities. But we do not know."

We enter here, as Freud has put it, "the darkest and most inaccessible sphere of psychic life." Not only is the increase and decrease important for the result (pleasure or discomfort) but the time schedule of these alterations as well. Freud himself believed that increase or decrease in relation to time probably was "the decisive factor for the decision." He presumed this to be a field open to experimental investigation. As long as we have no exact observations and experiences in this matter we had better share Freud's caution.

Nevertheless we venture to take one step beyond what he has stated, one only. But for our purposes it is a decisive step into the darkness of the mysterious border-sphere. I believe that a certain increase or decrease of tension in relation to the time factor is decidedly unpleasurable. To put it more simply: a sudden alteration of tension is associated with intensive discomfort irrespective of whether it is a sudden increase or decrease of tension. The relation to the time factor is decisive here. The quality of displeasure is conditioned by the alteration in the quantity of the tension requiring psychic reversal which cannot be performed at a moment's notice. We feel a disagreeable sensation, if a sudden flash of light changes the darkness surrounding us, although we wished it would not be dark. In other fields good news for which we are fully unprepared calls forth a violent resistance.

The constitution of the psychic apparatus which has been

subjected to such sudden change of tension has here to be taken into account. It is obvious that the infantile organism and the infantile psychic life are less capable of absorbing sudden increases or decreases of tension than are those of adults. Children react to sudden alteration of tension with far more violent defense actions. This is the point at which to refer to the primary fright affect, the attenuated repetition and continuation of which we conceive to be anxiety.*

On the other hand the adult can easily bear an amount of increase and decrease of tension in the time fraction which would tax the child's psychic apparatus to the utmost.

Pleasure and discomfort therefore not only depend on the increase or decrease of tension but on the temporal condition of the alterations of tension as well. Only when this alteration occurs at certain intervals, permitting regular transitions, can it be pleasurable. Whenever it happens to the unprepared, and by fits and starts, it will generally be experienced as unpleasant. It would surely be better to say that it is unpleasant whenever it does not follow a definite, though for us not yet discernible, rhythm. The relation to the rhythm should be emphasized; for there are sudden alterations of tension which we experience as pleasant. I shall only refer to the example of the pleasure in wit, the greatest part of which is based on a sudden decrease of psychic tension.**

We have apparently strayed far from the problems of masochistic pleasure. Actually we have only taken a detour and have returned to them. Was it not the example of the little girl in the bathtub which led us to these psychological meditations? She was

---

* The relations of fright and anxiety to the time element are dealt with from many points of view in my books, *Der Schrecken* and *Surprise and the Psychoanalyst,* and in a review on Anna Freud's book, *The Ego and the Defense Mechanisms.*

** Of course it must be noted that this sudden alteration of tension does not take place in relation to material forces but rather in an esthetic medium. Therefore the danger element is attenuated. The decrease of tension was described by Freud in his work on *Wit.* The factor of suddenness which he had overlooked was introduced and appreciated for the first time in my books on wit.

so much afraid of the sudden alteration of temperature that she
sought to protect herself against it by turning the tap just a tiny
little bit. She could not stand the increase of tension in the phantasied anticipation of what she feared. That would correspond to
a particular intolerance of the sudden influx of tension.

In similar fashion the ego of the masochist protects him at
first against a psychic shock, against being subjected to an assault
of tension, by depriving the coming event of its overwhelming
quality. The preparation consists in altering the distribution of
tension. The little girl in the bathtub did not evade the unpleasantness, which was unavoidable anyhow, but went to meet it.
The preparation furthermore consisted in an alteration of the
events as to their sequence. The little girl by turning the tap altered not so much the event itself but the rhythm of the event.
She created a transition which otherwise would not have been
there. She cannot perhaps protect herself against being surprised
but she can against being overwhelmed. By letting happen in an
attenuated form what she dreads she has reduced or even eliminated the tension of anxiety.

But how then explain the prolonging of the tension, which we
observe in the suspense and which is so contrary to the above-
described behavior? The two ways of reacting are typical for
different phases of development of the masochist attitude. The
postponement, the suspense, the avoidance of decision is the older
way of reaction which will be maintained for a long time. The
precipitation of the dreaded event is striven for when the person
has become more impatient and is no longer able to withstand
the instinctual urge. The older form of behavior reduces to a
typical childhood situation in which the influence of educational
forces had to battle against the compelling force of natural needs.

We assume that the little girl in the bathtub had under other
circumstances often experienced such situations when she was
some years younger. At that time perhaps, alone in the nursery,
she had suddenly felt an urgent need to relieve her bowels. The
first impulse naturally was to give in to the urge. But memory
told her that such giving in to the urge would make her mother

or nurse angry. The idea that her mother would be angry was apt to inhibit the natural impulse to let go or to let it happen. The result of this vivid prohibition then expressed itself in resistance against the impulse physiologically in a contraction of the sphincter muscle. The child now was between two forces: she wanted, indeed, she had to give in to the need, but she was afraid at the same time. She had anticipated her mother's anger, the loss of love. She will ultimately give in to the impulse to defecate and soil herself but with the anxiety previously expressed in the postponement. The interval between influx of tension and surrender will stand under the sign of suspense and show all its characteristics: the postponement of a discharge and the pleasurable-anxious feature. Will she succeed in mastering the imperious impulse? The surrender to the instinctual urge, the discharge under apprehensive anticipation of the threatening consequences, is the basic situation out of which the suspense feeling later fully develops. Thus the apprehensive idea of the scolding mother can produce a prolonged delay. The delay will be extended, the check will receive a different psychic tone. The final result of this vacillation between anxiety and pleasure is a mixture of both.

The two modes of conduct, the suspense and the precipitation of the dreaded event, are two different reactions to a similar, not to the same, situation. The situation later has been altered by the increasing impatience on the part of the pleasure urge. A survey will make things clearer: a tension which was roused by instinctual need is deflected from its natural course by the interference of a fearful idea. A stoppage results from the conflict of the two tendencies. The tension acquires a tinge of anxiety which is associated with its concomitant pleasurable tone. There are two ways of attenuating or eliminating this anxiety. The first is the postponement of the end-pleasure which is feared on account of its consequences; in other words an effort to prevent the tension rising beyond a certain degree, to maintain it on a certain level. That would be equivalent to an escape from the feared event: punishment, reproof, or whatever it may be.

The word "escape," of course, can only be used here with reservation since the conduct were better described as a vacillation between escape and approach. Moreover it is evident that the delay determined by anxiety is taken advantage of by the pleasure tendency. The masochist transforms the compulsion into a pleasure as if "to make the best of it." The other way of dealing with anxiety is to anticipate the dreaded event by bringing it about. I designate this procedure—to distinguish it from the other—as the flight forward. Also this reaction is not designed solely to keep away anxiety. Its task is also to assist the impatient desire to attain victory—even at the cost of pain or discomfort. The series of interesting psychological questions which become visible here must be put aside for later discussion.

For the moment we return to our original question. Starting from the discussion of the suspense factor we arrived at the investigation of several conditions of pleasure and discomfort. We discovered that the masochist, vacillating between his anxiety and his striving for pleasure, attempts to keep the tension "in suspense." This attempt has been preceded by several others to gain pleasure in spite of anxiety. However, this aim receded farther and farther under the influence of unconscious anxiety. The psychic situation is comparable to that of the mythical Tantalus who, formerly a companion of the gods, was banished to the underworld for punishment. There he had to stand in water up to his chin, the most beautiful fruits within his reach. Yet he had to suffer eternal thirst and hunger, because fruits and water receded the moment he reached out for them. This impressive picture becomes still more comparable to the suspense situation in another version of the myth: a rock constantly threatens to fall on the unfortunate king and crush him.

The course of this investigation hitherto has convinced us that the masochist has an unusual intolerance against the tension of anxiety. The result is the same whether we take the suspense or the production of the feared event as decisive for our conclusions. Whether he avoids allowing the tension of anxiety to increase by holding the excitement in suspense or whether he himself brings about what he is afraid of, he cannot stand the increase of anxiety. In contrast to current opinion it is our impression that the masochist—compared with the great majority of his fellow men—is uncommonly impatient. He is a poor waiter and his patience is a psychic reaction-formation.

2

The natural tendency of every human being to strive for pleasure and to avoid discomfort seems to be set aside in the phenomenon of masochism. Does it form the exception which confirms the rule formulated by Freud as the pleasure principle? For the masochist on the contrary seems to avoid pleasure and to seek pain, or better, to gain pleasure from pain. Our previous meditations, however, arouse doubt as to the correctness of this formulation and as to whether the masochist is not simply seeking, in a peculiar way, to diminish pain and to attain pleasure like all the rest of us. It is always possible to approach a goal by a detour.

Perhaps it would further our progress if we did not start from the dominance of the pleasure urge but from its counterpart. Education has the important task of enabling us to postpone the pleasure which results from instinctual satisfaction until such time as it can be enjoyed in safety. The child must be taught to wait, to put off the satisfaction of his wants. The postponement of instinctual needs is a requirement of culture. This not only enhances the child's safety but is necessary for his adjustment to the outer world and to the conditions of social life. Ultimately it might be necessary in certain cases to exchange the instinctual gratification for another sort of gain.

We are trained and we train ourselves to forgo easily attained instinctual satisfactions in favor of other interests. We all learn to avoid the path of least resistance and to travel that of greatest advantage. Freud has called the claim of culture the reality principle. It does not mean the abolition of the elementary striving for pleasure but its restriction through the necessities of life and the adjustment to the environment. It does not invalidate the pleasure principle, but it restricts its totalitarian claims. All of us learn to a greater or lesser degree to postpone the satisfaction of our wants. But this means that we learn to bear the unpleasant tension associated with such delay.

But if tolerating a tension is one of the conditions interposed by the reality principle then what about the suspense factor? Is not the tension borne willingly, even gladly, in masochism? It is extended, prolonged; even more than that—it becomes pleasure. At first sight it does seem as if the masochist were especially fitted to bear unpleasant tension, as if he were especially patient toward it. But that he searches it out instead of just accepting it, that he goes to meet it and makes it the object of his enjoyment, indicates how impatient he is in reality. He seems to acknowledge the demands of reality.

Does he really accept them? No, he exaggerates them. The result of this exaggeration is on the one hand a great deal of un-necessary anxiety and discomfort which is not provided for in the reality tension. On the other hand he gains from this pro-longation a bit of pleasure that sidesteps the dominance of the reality principle. Actually the masochistic suspense means an effort—an effort that failed, by the way—to follow the demand of reality. At the same time it is a sabotage of this claim through exaggeration. The masochist exaggerates the delay and transforms it into pleasure. Moreover he does not put up with the necessary tension but distributes it, putting it in here, doing away with it there, just as he likes. He submits to the demand but with such a defiant obedience that he turns its meaning into the opposite. The comparison of his conduct with that of certain railroad men who went on strike in old Austria is obvious. When these workers were discontented with their wages or their working hours they did not stop their work. On the contrary they carried it out with increased conscientiousness and accuracy, with the most careful consideration of the board's most trifling regulations. By observ-ing these regulations to the letter and all following every given instruction in every detail—with no regard to the practical consequences—they paralyzed traffic. Trains could neither arrive nor leave. Such sabotage through exaggerated obedience was called passive resistance. With reference to the claims of reality the masochist is in a state of passive resistance.

It seems, we said, as if the masochist would reject pleasant tensions and enjoy the unpleasant ones. We know that this is a pretense and we know how it originated: through not considering the phantasied anticipation of what is coming. Here we meet again with a topic dealt with previously, with the significance of the predominance of phantasy for masochism. The myth of Tantalus has rendered us good service in elucidating the suspense situation. The relation of phantasy to the compliance with the reality principle in masochism can well be illustrated by another mythical figure of less importance. German folklore tells many tales of the peculiar behavior of the foolish yet clever lad Till Eulenspiegel. This rogue used to feel dejected on his wanderings whenever he walked downhill striding easily, but he seemed very cheerful when he had to climb uphill laboriously. His explanation of his behavior was that in going down hill he could not help thinking of the effort and toil involved in climbing the next hill. While engaged in the toil of climbing he anticipated and enjoyed in his imagination the approach of his downhill stroll. One feels tempted to see in such strange behavior a paradox reminiscent of masochism, an expression of worldly wisdom. It sounds like a reminder to keep one's chin up in hardships and worries and not to become presumptuous in times of ease and comfort.

Does not the merry-gloomy fellow look like a relative and neighbor of the masochist? He stands pleasure badly, he is depressed when things go well with him, cheerful when he has to meet difficulties. In a way he has reversed the natural order of feelings as they would be appropriate to the occasion. He feels at ease when others are displeased and becomes doleful where others enjoy life. These moods are not determined by his present situation but by anticipation of the future. The phantasied anticipation destroys the enjoyment when an unpleasurable event is ahead and makes toil seem pleasant when pleasure is the ultimate expectation. The second process especially makes for the resemblance between the mythical rogue and the masochist. Were he to get out of his grave in Moellen he could furnish excellent information on the psychology of masochism. The comedian could instruct not only a preacher but also a psychoanalyst who has not recognized the significance of anticipation in phantasy for the masochistic experience.

We made the notion of impending disaster responsible for the character of anxiety in the suspense factor. The approach to orgasm is dreaded and avoided. The masochist cannot stand the increase of anxiety connected with this approach. He therefore has to stay in suspense. Yet when the pleasure tendency predominates, gets impatient, pushes forward, then it can happen that the masochist is unable to wait for the future danger, that he rushes to meet it and precipitates it. He is impatient not only with regard to the tension of anxiety but also with regard to the tension of pleasure. His imagination, more vivid and more excitable than other people's, anticipates not only danger but also enjoyment and satisfaction. Not only does the anxiety increase but the urge for pleasure as well. Having become discontented and ruthless it overthrows the anxiety and crosses the borderline respected so carefully theretofore.

The question arises whether this special impatience, this intolerance against increase of tension, can be traced back to earlier experience in childhood. Has the masochist once upon a time in childhood experienced some scene in which he felt pain, disgrace and humiliation and which would justify the extent of the anxiety? Analytical experience does not exclude this assumption but it does not confirm it either. Naturally there are many instances to be found in the histories of masochists when the child had been reproved and humiliated. It is just as certain that there are many life histories of masochists telling of no special ill-treatment, no rough or frightening treatment on the part of the educators. Rather we get the opposite impression that the child met with an especially affectionate and kind treatment. Any memories of severe reproofs and chastisement in childhood are exceptions; and the extent of these reproofs rarely exceeds the limit of what is psychically easily bearable by children as a rule. The exaggerated impression caused by such punishments in certain cases does not depend on the extent or severity of the punishment but on an as yet unknown factor and an increased sensitivity in the child's structure, both of which seem to play a leading part.

We can much rather assume in the majority of cases that education was too mild and indulgent and thus spoiled the child. If such children are occasionally scolded or chastised the contrast to the usual treatment will be of greater psychic value. A similar reaction is promoted if the education is irregular and vacillating, if it is indulgent and granting freedom of impulses on the one hand and on the other hand severe and suddenly forbidding. The factor of suddenness has been stressed already. In some cases it is of a certain significance that threats in childhood take the place of punishment and humiliation. Such a prospective punishment or humiliation sometimes occupies the child's mind for a long while, being anticipated in phantasy and depicted with likely details.

The importance of threats for the genesis of masochistic phantasies and of the sexual sensations accompanying them has not been acknowledged till now. Phantasies of this kind originated directly from such threats in the case of a little girl. Mother threatened, whenever she was naughty or disobedient, that father would flog her after his return home in the evening. The girl had to spend many hours of anxious suspense waiting for the punishment, which she imagined. To her surprise she felt sexually excited in anticipating the ordeal. The case is similar to that of a child, a boy, who was threatened by his mother that he would be put under the strict discipline of military school. Sexual sensations started as the boy imagined the details of the exercises and punishments awaiting him in military college. It is clear that the content of the threat becomes later on the condition of sexual excitation.

It is striking that many masochists recall no exceptional punishments inflicted on themselves but on brothers or sisters or play-mates which then become the core of their phantasies. Still stranger is another aspect which was derived from many analytical cases. It is concerned with just those exceptional recollections of a punishment or humiliation which have been retained and still arouse vivid feelings. I have well-founded reasons for surmising that in these exceptional cases the punishment was already unconsciously wanted and striven for and intentionally provoked by naughtiness. In other words, the punishment was not the cause of the masochistic instinctual development but its effect, invited by the child. It did not make the child masochistic but was already a product of one of the child's instinctual aims. The reverse of this assumption is based on a mistaken psychological perspective and the fact that we relate the different phases of the child's psychic development to belated periods of growth.

If, then, it is not correct that the masochistic inclination originates from too hard training, could there be a tendency discernible in the child's disposition that makes him less able than others to stand tensions? Some analysts (Sadger, W. Reich) presuppose an intensified muscle- and mucous-membrane eroticism as such a constitutional factor. This assumption does not seem to me more necessary than any other and it could not be soundly established in any case. Naturally it has occurred to every observer that certain zones of the body have become preferred regions for masochistic sensations. However, that is not equivalent to a constitutional hypersensitiveness. The nurse or the mother has given special attention to these regions. The tensions of the anal muscles are the first which the child must learn to bear. This should have been the first success of education. Instead it became its first defeat.

No unequivocal solution can be found as to the problem of constitutional "Anlage" of masochistic inclinations. It may be that a decisive anal-sadistic tendency constitutes the most probable promoting factor. The masochist would then be the psychological resultant of the later vicissitudes of this instinctive disposition.

The first tensions the child must learn to bear are concerned with his needs, with the alterations the child has to undergo in the training for cleanliness and punctuality. He is required to bear discomfort temporarily in connection with the control of defecation, the changes of body temperature, etc. Education has often spoiled the child by satisfying his instinctual desires too quickly or too willingly—and certainly not without falling occasionally into the opposite mistake of unreasonable and surprising denials.

We are able to trace the path which leads from the first elementary tensions to those of later periods and to greater psychic tasks. The control of the muscles was required by early childhood education.

The child's anxiety at this time was concerned with the loss of love, with punishment and humiliation if he indulged in his inclinations. This anxiety later is replaced by the one relating to the consequences of masturbation or even of sexual excitement. Instead of the parents the conscience is feared, the superego. Instead of outward requests there appear moral or esthetic claims on the part of the ego. The aggression roused by the frustration of instinctual needs has no adequate means of expression both on account of weakness of the ego and also on account of the education toward kindness. It therefore has to be repressed. Yet this aggression fettered in its expression deepens the guilty feelings of the individual, that is, his social anxiety.

This social anxiety is going to replace the earlier fear of the big people around him, of the parents' anger and the loss of their love. The danger which once threatened from the outside world has now been introverted. The analysis of masochists makes it plain that this anxiety originally pertained to the scolding or punishment by persons in the child's closest environment. It is probable that perverse masochism has retained many more intimate personal relations to the object while in social masochism these object relations have been loosened extensively.

The attitude of masochism toward the two principles of reality and pleasure was our starting point. In coming back to them we now observe that the two principles follow a different rhythm. In hunger and satiation, in taking nourishment and giving it, in sleeping and waking, the little creature obeys the rhythm, natural to all creatures, which I will designate as instinctual rhythm. This behavior has to undergo changes when the child learns to protect himself against dangers which threaten his existence and to adapt himself to the demands of social life. He now has to sleep and eat at definite times and he must learn to restrict the gratification of his instinctual needs according to time and place. Formerly he obeyed only the rhythm dictated by his impulses. But now he is supposed to pay heed to the one forced on him from the outside and to change the original one.

It becomes every child's task to adapt all his doings and not-doings to this new rhythm of culture. The child has to live not only according to the laws which are inherent but also to those which beset him from without. The adjustment to the new rhythm is carried through with the aid of education and under the pressure of social necessity. The outer influence which alters the former instinctual rhythm, slowing it down or attenuating it, is later to become an inner possession. The child has to appropriate it until he feels it to be his own impulse in order to be prepared for an independent life in the group. This retardation of the rhythm bringing about intervals and delays enables one to stand tensions both from within and from without.

It seems that the masochists succeeded only too well in substituting the cultural rhythm for the instinctual rhythm. The suspense appears as a special arrangement for postponing the instinctual gratification for a long time and for being able to bear discomfort. Yet what succeeds too well is a failure. The masochist behaves so obligingly because he is afraid of the greater amount of tension and because he is particularly intolerant of discomfort. He has not adjusted himself to the cultural rhythm, he exaggerated and thereby falsified it. The aim of education has not been attained. What has been attained is a distortion or caricature of this aim.

Willfully and obstinately the masochist opposes his own

rhythm to that which rules all our lives. He is one measure (or several) ahead or behind in the suspense as well as in the perverse act. By this detour we again have met that rogue Till Eulenspiegel and his peculiar conduct during his wanderings. When he is leisurely walking downhill he is downcast. When he toils up the hill he is happy. He gladly submits to discomfort, enjoys it, even transforms it into pleasure. This, however, constitutes the very essence of masochism. The masochist and Till Eulenspiegel obey another rhythm, their own. They do not march in step with us. Perhaps that is because they hear another drummer.

3

Freud has claimed as a condition for every theory undertaking to explain the phenomena of masochism that it must give satisfactory information on the relation of this instinctual tendency to its counterpart, sadism. The behavior of analytical psychologists toward this demand is remarkable. One group does not take any notice at all of this postulate. Its members single out from the psychological context one factor, such as narcissism, mucous membrane eroticism or the need for love, and scarcely touch on the relationship, sadism-masochism. The other group bases its theories on this relationship. Its advocates start with it but they go no farther. They keep the point sharply in focus but cannot turn their eyes away.

Naturally the only correct procedure is to base the investigation on the phenomena of masochism itself and on nothing else and to scrutinize them without any preconceived notions. The explanation of that invariable relation to sadism cannot be made the aim of investigation of the masochistic tendency. But it must be the result. This prospect never can be the starting point. But it must be the conclusion. Wherever this is not the case we are entitled to reject the theory as unsatisfactory.

In our discussion so far we have met with the interplay of

sadism at one point only, at the moment when the provocative factor turned up. At this point we recognized that we had overstepped the boundaries of pure masochism, had unexpectedly come upon a foreign field, and we therefore immediately returned to our own problems.

While dealing with this factor, however, we hit upon the very important moment of anxiety. We were in no way prepared for this. Analytical literature attaches no importance to the connection between masochism and anxiety.* Even Freud did not ascribe to anxiety any special significance for masochism.

I am amazed that this factor of anxiety in masochism has hitherto escaped notice. I can only explain this oversight by the fact that it lies in the background, in the shadows. Anxiety plays no role in the picture of masochism as it presents itself at first glance. The expectation of pain and humiliation not only does not produce any anxiety but on the contrary it awakens pleasure. The absence of anxiety might explain the fact that it has not been considered in the analytical theory of masochism, yet it does not explain the lack of inquisitiveness about it. This very absence should suggest the question to the psychologist: what about the anxiety one ought to expect in these phenomena? Is it invisible? That can mean that it is not there. It can just as well mean that it is hidden.

It actually is hidden, but it betrays itself in small trivial signs, as for instance in the suspense. And there is a time when it steps forth from its hiding place to express itself freely. I cannot understand how it is that it has not been seized upon and attention focused on it at this point by psychoanalysts.

I allude to the time when masochism retreats and yields to the normal attitude as the phase of recovery, if one should wish to call it so. At this point the perversion or masochistic phantasies are replaced by anxiety. Such signs of anxiety may be in-

---

* The above assertion was justified up to the publication of S. Nacht's book (*Le Masochism*, 1938). This author acknowledges the role of anxiety from a different point of view, but he was mistaken in deriving masochism from anxiety exclusively.

terpreted as proofs that the masochistic inclination is slowly forfeiting its power and the phantasies are losing their pleasure value. But if anxiety hardly ever appears in the perversion or in the phantasies and now is set free and develops in full, what is the inevitable conclusion? Only this: that the phantasies had tied up the anxiety. As soon as the perversion loses its influence the hitherto hidden anxiety becomes visible.

We meet with the same mechanism frequently in the psychopathology of neuroses. They too frequently involve endurance of suffering and pain in order to avoid an outbreak of anxiety. I would remind the reader of the extremely precise and most exacting observance of compulsory neurotic defensive measures, of the many acts of penitence and the extensive ceremonials necessitating such a waste of psychic energy. In difficult cases of compulsion neurosis these morbid prohibitions and orders are observed with an amount of severity leading to exhaustion. The patients submit to a tremendous burden of suffering and privation. Any negligence in this severe service is marked by the appearance of anxiety exactly as is every weakening of the masochistic tendency. The isolated effect of anxiety here is of a different kind; often it is a symptom of defense, directed against sadistic temptations, sometimes it manifests itself as compulsory apprehensions. In one case of perversion the anxiety, now emerging free, appeared as a peculiar terror of hidden psychic potentialities in the ego. The patient—one of those spoken about—had renounced his masochistic perversion under the impression of certain experiences. Some strong impulse seemed to drive him into doing something against which strong forces of the ego resisted. Only when the idea of a lustful murderer occurred to him, when he compared himself with Jack the Ripper, did he begin to realize what it was all about. Phantasies of violence and murder—which excited him sexually—had taken the place of the former masochistic love scenes in which women used to beat him.

Also in cases we see so frequently in analysis, in which the perverse tendency is alloyed with neurotic symptoms, the anxiety is intensified as soon as masochism decreases. If this impulse has manifested itself, let us say, in provoking accidents, in self-injuring and self-punishing actions, then it is replaced by social anxiety, that is, by guilty feelings. If analysis succeeds in attenuating the self-deprecatory tendencies the patient feels the pressure of conscious guilty feelings which were lacking previously. It never happens in such cases that unconscious self-punishment and unconscious guilty feelings exist simultaneously in the same degree. We consider it a decisive therapeutic progress in analysis when grievous self-punishment has been replaced by social anxiety. It is much easier to get the better of this symptom than of the intentions directed at self-punishment, which are as hard to attack as were those suddenly appearing and disappearing groups of Cossacks who harried Napoleon's army in its retreat from Russia.

Certainly anxiety is present in masochism but it has hidden behind discomfort and humiliation and so is covered up. The psychologist has to rediscover it just as the puzzle fan has to find houses, trees and animals hidden in the lines of a picture puzzle. We first discovered the secret existence of anxiety in the suspense experience. When we investigated the peculiarities of masochistic pleasure its presence betrayed itself as unmistakably as would a certain element in a chemist's test tube. This anxiety is related to the maximum increase of pleasure because this is connected with the expectation of trouble (punishment, reproof, humiliation). The suspense is introduced to avoid or at least to postpone that dreaded event. The only paradoxical feature in this context is that there is at the same time a temptation to approach this dreaded event, and a rejection of this temptation out of anxiety. Thus it represents simultaneously an approach and an escape. That sounds more confusing than it is. In reality it is a vacillation between the attempt to approach the pleasurable and the rejection of this temptation out of fear. A vacillation between the urge to approach and the urge to run away. The masochist cannot renounce his aim because his urge for pleasure is too intensive. But neither is he able to attain it since his anxiety is too great. That is the situation in suspense.

The residue of anxiety in this situation, its decrease if the masochistic perversion is acted out and its increase simultaneously with the diminution of perverse activity permit of only one explanation: masochism ties up anxiety. To express it more carefully and yet peremptorily: masochism represents an attempt to bind anxiety. Yet if this is the result of perverse tendencies the assumption becomes imperative that mastery of anxiety is one of the purposes of masochism.

The suspense is an attempt to parry anxiety by avoiding a too close approach to what is feared. It is the expression of a flight and then again of an approach—a peculiar in-between thing, but for all that more of a sort of escape. When the urge for pleasure becomes more pressing and is followed by an increase of anxiety then another outlet is found which I have designated as *the flight forward.*

The tendency to experience pleasure has become so intensive that it breaks through in spite of the danger. In such a situation we would expect a person to pursue his pleasure with no regard for the risk. What we observe with the masochist is something quite different. He conjures up what he fears, staging scenes of pain, of scolding and humiliation. What had been previously dreaded is now sought for and met. The ego was unable to stand the increasing anxiety any longer. It has to go forward and meet the dreaded event. However, the increase of the pleasure tendency remains decisive. The ego not only is willing to pay the high price of discomfort and humiliation but even claims them, longs for pain and humiliation, makes them the center of its desires in order to attain the pleasure more quickly.

Formerly, during the suspense period, the approach to the instinctual aim was avoided because the anxiety increased simultaneously. Now the otherwise avoided event is sought for in order to attain the instinctual aim and to have pleasure increase sooner. The tension of anxiety formerly withheld the pleasure. Now this same tension attracts the pleasure and gradually becomes its prerequisite. The suspense and the meeting of the dreaded event are not a matter of two contradictory psychic situations, but we are confronted here with the same situation on two different levels of development. In the suspense the urge for pleasure and the fight against anxiety are counterbalanced. In the masochistic perversion the urge for pleasure has become so powerful that it transforms the feared into the pleasurable. The situation has, so to speak, turned on its axis.

The increasing anxiety, which formerly inhibited any greater pleasure, has now become a precondition for pleasure and brings it closer. In one case the sight of a skeleton aroused sexual excitement. The patient had as a little girl struggled against her sexual excitement by evoking phantasies of Death, whom she pictured as a skeleton. At this time she had been kept from masturbation by the threatening skeleton phantasy. Now this very same idea excited her sexually.

There is no doubt that the closer approach to the pleasure goal accelerates the increase of anxiety. Yet it is not the increased anxiety but the intensified pleasure tendency which determines the flight forward. There is a tale of a Serbian peasant girl who was told that her future husband would be sure to beat her, as is the custom in that country when the husband comes home late at night drunk with raki. The girl said, "I wish he'd already beaten me!"—Was the girl impatient to be beaten? Certainly not. She was impatient to be married. Impatient enough to be longing for the blows which went with being married.

If it is the increasing impatience of the urge for pleasure that prescribes the direction of the movement then it is the hidden anxiety which confers on it the character of a flight forward. Without anxiety there would be no masochism but merely a striving for the pleasure aim which would become more ruthless and impatient because of external obstacles.

The flight forward is itself an indication of impatience. The punishment lying as a threat behind the pleasure is met intentionally out of inability to bear the tension of anxiety any longer. The cart is, so to say, put before the horse. The driving factor, however, remains the impatience of the urge for pleasure. To be sure, the cart has been put before the horse, but the horse pushes the cart ahead. The impatience is an indication how hard it was originally for the masochist to stand such procrastination, even if it was a matter of a few minutes. In his annoyance he behaves like Louis XIV, who once gave orders to a courtier to accompany him to a festivity. His majesty was ready to start and the appointed moment had just come when the courtier appeared. The king said with icy arrogance, *"J'ai failli attendre!"* The masochist too feels it an insult if he almost might have been compelled to wait.

In studying the relevant literature one is kept wondering at the mistaken conception of masochism as an unchangeable psychological unity. Actually everything depends on the phase of development the individual masochist has reached. The foregoing description enables us to survey the masochistic experience from the genesis of the suspense to the sensation of the developed masochistic perversion. The experience in the first place is determined by the relations of the ego to pleasure and anxiety and by its reactions to their influences. Any attempt at any explanation which does not enable us to elucidate these relations must be considered a failure.

The initial situation may be supposed to look somewhat like this: in an individual gifted with phantasy an impulse for instinctual gratification is aroused. This urge has to sustain a delay, an *arrêt,* through the interference of anxiety, since the idea of enjoyment becomes associated with a notion of trouble (loss of the parents' love, punishment). The ego makes an attempt to master the anxiety. A vacillation arises as to whether the instinctual aim is attainable despite the increasing anxiety or whether it should be renounced. It is clung to in spite of the anxiety. The suspense feeling now is a pleasurable tension with a tinge of anxiety. The increase of anxiety at the approach of the instinctual gratification is comprehensible as the threat of trouble becomes imminent. The suspense begins as an expression of the endeavor to separate the idea of pleasure from the accompanying and disturbing idea of anxiety. It emerges as an expression of the tendency to assimilate the anxiety, to utilize it for the prolongation or the deepening of pleasure.

The suspense indicates primarily that the ego wished to avoid the anxiety and to gain pleasure by a detour. At a later stage it becomes evidence of the inextricable combination of the pleasure urge with the idea of anxiety which have been welded together. It is in consequence of this development that the ego also experiences the anxiety as pleasant. In the primal masochistic situation the anxiety constitutes a severe disturbance of the pleasure urge. It is presented as an alternative: either the one or the other. The attempt at a solution goes in the direction of mastering the anxiety by anticipating it. At first it could mean: now the one and then the other. The final result is the reception of anxiety among the preconditions of pleasure: the one and the other have become one and the same.

The flight forward does not indicate the antithesis of this development but its continuation in reality, in developed masochism. It repeats the process of the suspense on another turn of the spiral. It, too, begins with an attempt to isolate anxiety, to meet the dreaded event halfway in order to attain pleasure freely. As this proves a failure the dreaded event itself becomes a precondition of pleasure and ultimately becomes pleasurable itself. The transition from suspense to flight forward first of all is a result of the increasingly urgent pleasure drive and the correspondingly increased anxiety tension. For this result the inner experience expressed in the words, "Suspense is worse than reality," is codetermining. This, however, means not only the risk of a decisive step toward anxiety but just as well the transition from phantasy to reality, to the perverse scene. What then appears to us as a deviation of instincts is only a detour, though a very expensive one, to attain the normal instinctual goal.

The calamity, once sensed as a threat, now increases the pleasure. The threat of anxiety has been transformed into a promise. When pain and discomfort have reached their climax pleasure and satisfaction are bound to be near. The original feeling was: where pleasure is increased to such a point, punishment is bound to be near. It was a threat, a terrifying prospect. The flight forward signifies the reversal of this prospect: where the punishment is so severe, the pain so sharp, the pleasure must be near.

Ultimately the conscious boundaries become indistinct: the discomfort, the pain and the humiliation themselves become pleasure.

The flight forward as a defense mechanism is not restricted to masochism. It is independent of masochism and can be observed in situations which have no relation to this perversion and in which there is only an overwhelming drive to get rid of an unbearable anxiety tension. It does not need to be only anxiety that is overcome in that way but just as well the expectation of severe suffering or inescapable blows of destiny. This way will often be chosen when an end with terror is preferred to a terror without end.

If the flight forward serves the purpose of gaining an instinctual satisfaction we can conclude that its nature is masochistic. Naturally there are cases in which it is not easy to decide whether the issue is determined more by anxiety than by the pleasure urge. Yet the basic distinction remains valid. I have observed a little girl clumsily overthrowing a glass of water on the table and thus wetting the tablecloth. The mother was expected to enter the room any moment. It was obvious that the little girl's fear of reproof and punishment was increasing. And before the mother entered the child went and stood in a corner with her face to the wall. This certainly is a definite case of flight forward. But just as certainly it did not contain any element of masochism, that is to say, of pleasure in suffering. The attempt to check anxiety is obvious, but the pleasure element is restricted to a minimum.

The flight forward does not primarily go in search of discomfort or pain. It rather constitutes the removal of an obstacle which obstructs satisfaction. By anticipating the dreaded punishment the way to instinctual enjoyment has been opened. The masochist is not keen on blows and humiliation. He longs for them only in order to prevent the thought of them from disturbing him while he strives for his aim. Secondarily only, by displacement of psychic accent, the discomfort which is the sign of approaching climax becomes pleasure.

Therefore the masochistic scene or phantasy falls into two parts which must be sharply discriminated psychologically and which only in the end phase grow into a unity. First discomfort, humiliation, punishment: then pleasure and instinctual gratification. To put it theologically: first the atonement, then the sin. The discomfort is not desired as such, but it constitutes the price of pleasure. Finally pleasure edges into discomfort itself. The atonement itself is transformed into a sin. The flagellation which originally served the purpose of self-castigation with early Christian monks and ascetics later became a means of sexual excitement. The increase of pain produced ecstasies. Ultimately the Church was forced to forbid too severe expiatory practices because they frequently led to sexual gratification.

The psychic course as described can be traced from the everyday masochistic scene to the most sublimated and most sublime phantasy. It covers every stage from the orgasm, resulting from being beaten by a woman, to the blissful feeling of the martyr, who breathes out his soul while being torn by lions. What in the one case furthers sexual gratifications in the other brings closer the approach to heaven and to the infinite richness of God's kingdom. The masochist welcomes the whipping he receives from a prostitute as eagerly as does the martyr the final and liberating ill-treatment from his persecutors. The succession of pleasure and discomfort is welded into simultaneity. What once was inimical overflows into each other, becomes identical. "She is condemned," said Mephisto of the poor Gretchen. But a voice from above answered: "Is saved." In masochism too the severest punishment becomes the switching point to bliss and to salvation.

4

At this point, however, the question we previously put aside becomes imperative: of what is the masochist actually afraid? Let us recall the little girl in the bathtub. She does not permit the full force of the water to fall on her body but a few drops only, a representative, a symbolic or token substitution. What is the adult masochist afraid of? The answer closest to hand naturally runs: he is afraid of what is indicated by his flight forward, of what he stages himself.

This answer cannot be correct. A grown-up man surely is not afraid of a light blow on the buttocks, nor of being scolded severely by a woman. The little acts which masochists often perform frequently show bizarre features. For instance, a man has to crawl on all fours through the room while his woman partner rides on his back setting the pace and direction. Then again the woman has the task of abusing the masochist and of ordering him to do his homework or else get a good hiding. Another man is laced with straps and whipped. Still another is put in a corner, scolded as naughty, and so forth. It is impossible that any of these punishments can justify as intense an anxiety as we have inferred. It is also hard to deduce from the contents of these staged perverse scenes with whom the anxiety is concerned. They represent, of course, restagings of preceding phantasies.

But if we go back to these phantasies themselves—for instance, the Moloch ideas or the cycle of the homicidal queen—then we are more than ever faced with an enigma. What can we say of the phantasy of a prisoner who lies bound and is sexually incited by beautiful virgins until he has an orgasm? What of that other phantasy, so exciting for a patient, of Laocoön, who is held in the deathly grip of snakes, or of Marsyas, who was so cruelly flayed by Apollo? Can we hope to discover the nature of the thing the masochist fears behind all these distortions? Do these phantasies, different as they are individually, reduce to a common denominator? There is actually a way of disentangling all these disfigurements and of penetrating to the nucleus of these conceptions. The analytic technique of interpretation offers a method as precise as anatomical dissection by carefully peeling off the wraps and thus reaching the innermost hidden parts.

Generally it can be stated that the punishments and humiliations which the masochist submits to, indeed, prays for, are not what he really fears and that he is unconscious of this fearful something and of its nature. What he seems to fear is a sort of substitute or commutation of what is hidden. It could best be compared to an indulgence. As is well known an indulgence was an ecclesiastical fine or tax to which the believer submitted voluntarily in order to evade the terrible punishments which his sins would bring down upon him on the day of judgment. Against the terror which threatened him any indulgence, even a grievous one, was a mere trifle.

Analysis has discovered that the calamity, for the indulgence of which the pervert submits to so much discomfort and humiliation, is in many cases the mutilation of the masculine member —in other words, castration.

The blow which the masochist receives from the active person is in most cases unconsciously interpreted as a symbolic displacement of this terrible punishment. In a case I observed a long time the exciting phantasy was to be hit by a woman on the backside. The scene from which the phantasy originated could be reproduced in analysis by putting together small pieces of recollections and filling up some important gaps. When the patient was a small boy his mother threatened that some punishment for small misdeeds would overtake him unexpectedly. The words she used facetiously at the time were said by her representative in the phantasies later on and were felt as exciting: "I'll catch you bending!" (The patient is an Englishman.) Behind this incident I could uncover another which contained the real essence of the masochistic daydream.

The incident took place some years before the other one. In his memory it was not sexually exciting, but on the other hand it was impressive. The father of the patient, then an officer on active service in the World War, had been home on leave. He often played with the youngster and his brother. Sometimes they made believe that the father was King Arthur and the sons were shield-bearers in the circle of the king's Round Table. On one occasion the boys were to be knighted. The youngest, later the patient, had to kneel before King Arthur, who sat on his throne in his anachronistic uniform. He made a speech, touched his son's shoulder softly with his saber, and spoke solemnly, "This is the last blow you shall receive unrevenged." Very soon after this scene the father returned to the front and was killed. This early scene of the knighting was displaced later by the incident of his mother threatening the boy and was transformed into a masochistic phantasy with her.

Remembered in a wholly different context the original was later discerned in this scene. As it will be recalled, the ceremony of being knighted by a stroke is a medieval transformation of older rites such as were celebrated in ancient times and among primitive tribes up to our time as initiation of youth into puberty. The central point of these ceremonies, though not castration, is yet its attenuated substitute, circumcision or subincision. This is a piece of archaic psychic life projecting into present time from prehistoric times and inaccessible to human recollection.

While castration may be an important unconscious idea of punishment in masculine masochism it is in no way the only one as was many times presupposed by analysts. Separately or in association with the castration idea there occur other and more grotesque ideas, such as that of being used as a woman by a man, of being violated or impregnated. It is certainly noteworthy that the novices in the puberty rites of the natives of Australia are actually used for such passive-homosexual purposes by men after the circumcision. It is furthermore noteworthy that the circumcision and the manifold tortures to which the youths are subjected and which can well be compared to masochistic practices result in the license to have free sexual intercourse, marking as it were the entrance to manhood. It is certainly worth noticing that here, too, the punishment precedes the otherwise forbidden pleasure, that it represents a license to instinctual gratification exactly as in masochism. One is almost tempted to designate these young native Australians who voluntarily submit to the cruel puberty rites as masochists. After closer consideration, however, we had better compare them with the masochists in our cultural areas. What was approximate reality within the religious or social system of the tribe becomes the subject of individual phantasies or disfigured and playful representation.

Behind the castration and in addition to it appear other vague terrors which are not restricted to the masculine member. That is not surprising. The castration anxiety is appropriate to an age which knows the dominance of the genital in sexual life. The castration plainly stands for a punishment for forbidden incestuous wishes—exactly like the circumcision among primitive tribes. It is the anticipated punishment for the incestuous lust according to the old Talion law. Masochism, however, is older, can develop in an infantile phase which as yet does not know of such wishes. The often grotesque phantasies and scenes, in which being soiled with fecal matter has a sexually exciting effect, or in which being eaten is a pleasant idea, can only be derived from the conceptions of a much earlier infantile period.

I have previously designated discomfort or pain as a sort of indulgence, an anticipated atonement, which ought to substitute for or do away with the more severe or terrible one. The masochist, I stated, gives up a part, sacrifices a piece, in order to obtain the whole. In this *pars-pro-toto* conception, I closely approach the sagacious arguments of S. Nacht and other analysts. W. Reich also has a somewhat similar conception of substitute punishment.

Yet deeper insight will not overrate the importance of such an economic conception according to which the masochist sacrifices a part to save the whole. It is definitely of secondary standing. The substitute punishment has taken upon itself the strong affects from the original one. All anxiety is now transferred to it. Its affective value is exactly the same as, for instance, that in an insignificant breach of compulsive prohibition for the compulsion neurotic. Though the economic mode of consideration is justified in such a case its significance is by far inferior to the dynamic one. In reality it is not so much a matter of giving up a part for the whole but of sacrificing the whole in a part. I therefore withdraw the comparison with the indulgence. It was not incorrect. It was just insufficient. It would be more appropri-

ate to express the relation to the dreaded event in masochism
by designating pain or discomfort as a symbolic substitute for
the actual punishment.

Starting from his theory, according to which the masochist
sacrifices a part to save the whole, S. Nacht arrives at an interesting consideration of the question of value. He designates this
account—which seems to be rather a settling of accounts, as we
shall see later—with an elegant turn, a *calcul à dupe*, a fool's
reckoning. He justifies this designation by the statement that the
sufferings and sacrifices to which the masochist submits are real
while the danger which he flees—we, by the way, now can add:
into which he flees—is nothing but a fiction of the unconscious.
Certainly such valuation is logically justified in many cases. Its
psychological value is poor. In most cases it is reasonable, but
it is too rationalistic. Moreover the calculation—if as a calculation it has been conceived—cannot concern itself one-sidedly with
the stakes risked. The gain too must be taken into account.

To paraphrase it: does the suffering and sacrifice in masochism
counterbalance the pleasure? Nacht seems to assume that the
game is not worth the candle. This judgment may be correct
from the spectator's point of view, but no doubt it is the player's
point of view that counts. The masochist seems to find the pleasure well worth the suffering. He shows a tenacity, an obstinacy,
an adhesion, which is characteristic of no other perversion. The
question of value cannot be answered solely from the standpoint
of cool objectivity. The writing desk on which Napoleon planned
his battles may for this reason represent a higher value for some,
while to others it would still be simply a piece of Empire furniture. Certainly perverse pleasure too has its value for the connoisseur. I am of the opinion that there are pleasure values in
the masochistic action and phantasy which have not yet been
discovered. We might say that the game is not only for the stakes
on the board but also for concealed ones. That is why I believe
Nacht to be mistaken when he considers the masochistic balance
of suffering and instinctual gratification to be a *calcul à dupe*.
I believe that he himself did his own calculation without con-

sidering the pleasure factor. I moreover question his conclusion that the axis, around which the phenomenon of masochism revolves, is founded only on anxiety.

As to the nature of this danger I am fully in accord with him in considering these dangers to be fictitious; but are they, for all that, less real for the masochist? The anxiety is not that of an adult but corresponds to the fixated infantile one. When Gulliver in the land of the Lilliputs jokingly made a threatening gesture with his hand he caused a panic among the crowd surrounding him, although to his own countrymen the gesture would have appeared as a harmless swinging of his arm. It must repeatedly be emphasized that the masochist knows neither that he is afraid nor what he is afraid of. Thus he does not know anything about the fact that by acting out his perversion he undertakes a flight forward. What he is able to state in the course of an analysis about the dangers he shuns is of such a trivial and absurd nature that it cannot be responsible for that deep-rooted anxiety. These statements, however, are representatives, substitutes, for what was dreaded primarily and which, originating in childhood, is immortal like everything unconscious.

What appears to be grotesque or bizarre in practices and phantasies of masochists has a meaning which actually can only be elucidated by analytical interpretation. The point of observation one chooses becomes decisive for the psychological judgment. The peculiarities or ceremonials of masochism considered as such often seem silly or futile. But if one makes the effort to view them as indications of a hidden sense they gain meaning and significance. Whoever sits in the first row of a theater and soberly observes the scenery can see only painted canvas and movable boards and recognizes the sham and artificial side of the illusion. The spectator in the gallery, however, receives the impression of the dark depth of a forest he is looking into, or of a spacious hall leading to many rooms. From a view restricted to the foreground one must assume that masochism pays with great sacrifices and great discomfort for a tiny bit of evanescent pleasure. Whoever is able to look at things from a more distant point will find in it an attempt to master the old, oppressing infantile anxieties and will know that "to be or not to be" is here the question.

Any psychological explanation of masochism would have to answer two questions: what is feared? What is longed for? These questions inevitably force themselves on whoever recognizes the characteristic vacillation between anxiety and pleasure in the masochistic suspense. What danger is feared, what pleasure is sought? What is the punishment and what the reward justifying so much suffering, so many sacrifices? What constitutes the threat which is instrumental in the flight forward and what is the promise, what is the price, beckoning to those who embrace discomfort and humiliation? Whoever offers a theory of masochism which leaves these two main questions unanswered has failed to satisfy our psychological curiosity.

We have now heard enough of the nature of the anxiety in masochism. But what about the pleasure? We stated that the anxiety was unconscious, that it was concerned with a danger that overshadowed the infantile years with an uncanny and inexpressible threat. The pleasure cannot be too far from consciousness: it is indeed freely admitted in perverse masochism. It is actually the decisive motive for the perversion. Though it is harder to discover in social masochism it nevertheless must be extant. Some immense satisfaction is bound to justify such severe and lasting sacrifices and discomfort.

Actually, the pleasure in masochism is still more puzzling than the anxiety not only with regard to its origin and to the not-yet-explained fact that it arises from discomfort, pain and humiliation but also with regard to its intensity as well. It is an argument against the psychologists who hitherto have dealt with the problem of masochism that they did not wish to believe the assertion that the masochistic pleasure is of varied nature and intensity. We frequently hear in analyses of perverts that this pleasure is deeper, more colorful and more satisfactory than that of normal sexual intercourse. Such assertions were acknowledged but psychologists and doctors would reply that every perversion rates its own specific pleasure higher than the customary form of gratification.

The case of masochism is somewhat different. There is something added which intensifies the pleasure experience and confers a special nuance to it. I believe I have found in the analysis of perverse and masochistic characters that this unknown something is somehow connected with the fear which otherwise inhibits the development of pleasure. Did we not say that mastery of anxiety and pleasure flow into one channel? Have we not traced out how anxiety originally disturbed the development of pleasure but then was mastered through the flight forward and ultimately contributed to the intensification of the pleasure? The fact that the pleasure originating from pain and shame is more profoundly sensed is bound to have some significance. The intensity of pleasure is not ultimately diminished but increased by pain or discomfort. We now have a suspicion that it is the mastery of anxiety and not anxiety itself which produces so peculiar an effect.

The psychic situation must be similar to that which is manifest in mania. The ego which has overcome a deep depression gains a feeling not of reassurance and courage but of extreme unconquerable self-confidence and arrogance. The background of the depressive mood, which continues to exist on a higher level, bestows upon the manic phase the tinge of the violent, the overdone and the exaggerated. In masochism, too, the amount of pain or discomfort which precedes the gratification must be responsible for the intensification of pleasure. Who has suffered so much can experience a deeper pleasure. What has been for so long dammed up knows a more powerful release. The in-spite nature of the masochistic pleasure contributes a particular tone to it which we shall have to discuss. On the background of pain there appears a more intense and more voluptuously experienced sensation than that of the normal and of the bourgeois. There are hidden pleasure values here which do not appear in sexual experience otherwise. We divine that besides the instinctual gratification of sexuality other, not purely sexual, factors here come into their own.

The peculiar nature of the masochistic pleasure experience and its intimate relation to discomfort, pain and humiliation are not to be understood, however, if the dominant significance of the anticipatory phantasy is not fully appreciated. I have pointed it out as the foremost and most important characteristic of masochism and I have shown its relation to the suspense. We encountered it again when we examined the role of anxiety and found out that the masochist is intolerant of an increase of anxiety. In his thoughts the approaching danger becomes so imminent that he can only master the anxiety by hurrying to meet it. Out of paramount anxiety he becomes daring, he can no longer wait for the punishment but must challenge it. The flight forward is only possible on the basis of such anticipatory phantasies.

Masochism shows a Janus face one half of which is distorted by anxiety the other entranced with pleasure. It is certain that the curve of pleasure, too, is influenced by the power of anticipatory phantasy. Here I come back to a topic which I have lightly touched in a previously published book* the psychological significance of which has not yet been fully appreciated: the topic of anticipation. This mechanism of anticipation determines the nature of the masochistic pleasure experience in its most developed forms. It is this same factor which maintains the tension of suspense. The mechanism of suspense does not permit the tension to rise above a certain level, but neither does it allow it to sink.

If under the increasing pressure of the pleasure urge this barrier is broken through the phantasied anticipation will increase the tension and drive it to the climax. While pain and discomfort still are felt the pleasure aim is anticipated in phantasy. Certainly the phantasied anticipation helps to bear the suffering and the humiliation. Does it merely help to bear them? No, the

---

* *Surprise and the Psychoanalyst,* Dutton, 1937.

phantasy welcomes the discomfort and its increase, for the acme of the discomfort is the signal for the approaching pleasure. When the blow is felt most distinctly, when the disgrace is sensed most keenly, the climactic point of orgasm is reached. Thus in growing stronger pain becomes a signal, a token, of the coming climax of pleasure, a *promesse du bonheur*.

This seems to be the place to point out a phenomenon which I should like to call "masochistic tests." These are trials to which the person subjects himself in order to prove to himself that he can endure a great deal of discomfort, pain or humiliation. We know now that the increase of discomfort in these self-imposed tests goes together with increased sexual excitement. The reader will think of the patient who tightened his belt and collar more and more while he pictured himself in a military college. With the discomfort sexual excitement was increasing proportionately. The man with the Moloch phantasies subjected the victims of his imagination, with whom he identified, to numerous masochistic tests which showed their capability of standing increasing pains. He continued these tests until he reached the orgasm.

The meaning of the test seems at first to be: shall I be able to stand this trial and that one? On more precise observation another meaning becomes clear: if I endure this discomfort or that increased pain may I then permit the sexual satisfaction?

The anticipatory function of the phantasy surely has certain relations to the character of the instinctual life itself. For the impulse there exists subjectively only one time: the future. That means that the subjective relation of the impulse to the past and the present is purely negative. The memory of an instinctual impulse brings it back to a certain extent, reanimates it and makes it actual again in the form of a need. There is no impulse which has its aim in the present for thus it would lose its nature as a drive. The instinctual aim lies in the future. The impulse has one positive relation to time only, a relation to the future, which promises gratification and thus temporary cessation.

This reference to the future, common to all instinctual life, is intensified in masochism because it first met with dams and obstacles in its progress. The suspense constitutes one such dam, the preoccupation with phantasy another. As soon as the way to satisfaction is found in reality these dams are violently ruptured. The masochist, accustomed to postpone satisfaction for a long time, gains it even now only by anticipating it for one measure. Just when the pain is at its peak pleasure, having become impatient with waiting, occurs. Unconcerned with pain and humiliation, indeed even stimulated and incited by them, the sexual urge now hastens to its goal.

From the standpoint of our psychological presuppositions it is easy to understand that the mechanism of anticipation develops its full effect in this situation. The flight forward grants the masochist the most dreaded punishment and liberates him from unconscious anxiety. The pleasure tendency can unfold in the midst of discomfort, indeed it does so in spite of it and to spite it. While the pervert still feels the painful effect of the blows his phantasy has hastened forward to the goal he has so dearly purchased. Increase of pain or discomfort, more severe punishment, are not longed for as such but as forerunners of the prospective pleasure. Only superficial psychological observation can assume that the masochist desires pain as such, that it is the original instinctual aim. It is only the herald announcing the approach of the master, pleasure.

The neglect of the mechanism of anticipation in phantasy is particularly responsible for the fact that social masochism has remained almost incomprehensible. How should one understand the working of secret psychic tendencies which strive to injure the ego as much as possible, to wrong it and lead it into disgrace and defeat? It has struck home that the attempt to explain a phenomenon so hard to understand did not start from what is secretly feared, what is desired, what punishment is avoided, what pleasure striven for. At this point I only want to state that there, as in perverse masochism, the mechanism of anticipation determines the psychic course. There, too, phantasy is ahead of reality by one or even several measures.

5

In looking for the specific meaning of masochistic anxiety and pleasure the suspense factor has become our guide. Since we want to continue our march from the point reached we have to seek for a new guide.

The other characteristic, designated by us as the demonstrative feature, shows the direction. We remember its revelation that the masochist needs witnesses to his pain and degradation. The instinctual inclination cannot exist without it. The comparison with such inclinations as sadism or voyeurism shows that these perversions can be satisfied without witnesses. Why does the masochist differ in his behavior? Why does he insist on persons seeing his humiliation and knowing about his misery? Why should he not be content to have his pleasure and pain alone? Where this seems to me the case he calls in an onlooker at least in his imagination; an onlooker who really looks at his suffering and, be it only the image in the mirror, to whom he shows his disgrace.

This demonstrative feature is designed to indicate a special contribution to the pleasure experience. Something important must be betrayed in what is shown to the onlooker, in what is displayed while it is conspicuously hidden.

At the entrance of a previous section of this investigation we placed a legendary figure, Till Eulenspiegel, who, so to speak, welcomes us at the door and prepares us for what is to follow. Similar figures of myth and folklore aided us in embodying essential features: Thersites seemed to us the personification of that provocation which invites a chastisement. The situation of Tantalus offered itself for comparison with the suspense situation. Till Eulenspiegel's buffooneries oscillating between tomfoolery and wisdom promoted our understanding of the specific impatience of the patient sufferer.

Here another notable figure shall furnish an illustration: Job, the figure out of the postexile conception of the Old Testament.

The relation of this man from Uz, perfect and upright, to the characteristic feature of masochism now to be dealt with may not be clear at first sight. If we recall, however, that chapter of the Bible, the picture of a lamenting and accusing, of a doubting and desperate sufferer rises before our eyes. We can see him sitting on an ash heap with shaven head, with torn clothes, covered with sores, scratching his psora with a potsherd and surrounded by his three friends to whom he complains. This figure of the lamenting Job could certainly impersonate the demonstrative feature. He not only displays his life and his misery but says in his desperation: "Therefore I will not refrain my mouth; I will speak in the anguish of my spirit; I will complain in the bitterness of my soul." (Job 7, 11.) At the end it is not his friends who are his auditors; he complains to God and describes to Him his grief, asserts to Him his innocence. This resembles the characteristic attitude in moral masochism when the masochist accuses a destiny that persecutes him, an innocent victim.

The demonstrative feature could be called the representative of the external side of masochism while the two other characteristics, preparatory phantasy and suspense, represent the inner side. Does it make any sense to display one's suffering, shame and punishment to the surrounding world? Like so many others in masochism this feature too is paradoxical. Most of us certainly prefer to hide shame or punishment. It must have a meaning or even a number of meanings if the masochist directs the attention of his environment to his misery unconsciously, if he exposes the punishment or the degradation inflicted on him with such obtrusiveness. Does he want to show something? Or does he wish to hide something by doing so?

I shall repeat here a comparison, previously used: if a man sitting in a hall among many other people constantly stares at the left-hand corner of the room, one would assume that he sees something very conspicuous there and wishes to draw the attention of the others to it. But it would also be possible that he deliberately looks at the left-hand corner because he wants to divert the attention of those sitting around him from the right-hand corner. The conspicuous glance in the one direction could mean that there is something to be hidden in the other. Finally both "points of view" can be united if there is actually something noteworthy in the one corner and in the opposite corner something still more important to hide.

Judging from appearances—and what could be a better start in dealing with the demonstrative feature?—one arrives at the same opinion that was presented by most analysts starting from other theories. Without considering the demonstrative feature they have come to the conclusion that the masochist wants to arouse sympathy. He woos love. He wants to be loved because of his suffering. This would agree with a reminiscence of childhood experiences: the sick or injured child is sure to receive more attention or tenderness. Actually the masochist meets with sympathy only when those around him see his sufferings and privations. But this is sympathy, not love. Contrary to the general belief analysis proves that if you invite pity you do not increase love but diminish it. In many cases sympathy takes the place of love. The opposite procedure is improbable. Moreover, pity is aroused only by social, never by sexual masochism. We sympathize with those who like Job have become victims of destiny undeservedly, with unhappy, unlucky fellows, who are driven by a bad wind in the wrong direction again and again. In such cases it may be one of the masochistic purposes to arouse sympathy.

But what about the claim for sympathy in the sexual perversion? The partner is witness to the displeasure or the shame. But the sight of this disgrace is not meant to arouse sympathy. The accounts given by the masochists themselves contradict such an assumption. On the contrary, the sight serves to increase the appetite of the active partner to further beating or chastising. In some cases the masochist insists on the continuance of the chastisement in spite of a compassionate impulse in the partner.

The unconscious purpose to arouse sympathy and love, however, cannot, even in the field of social masochism, be considered a strong, still less the sole, motive as some analysts believe. The actual psychic achievement of such a hidden purpose, granting its existence, contradicts such an opinion. Even if one sympathizes with the man who is so conspicuously persecuted by destiny and who continuously complains, this does not last long. The reaction is profoundly changed when the masochist insists that destiny has chosen him for its victim, when the exposure of his misery obviously contains ungenuine and playful elements. The stubbornness and plethora of the complaints turns pity into impatience.

From this, however, there is only a single step to defense against obtrusiveness and then to aggression. The demonstration thus finally leads to such a point that the masochist is ill-treated, abused, blamed. Not even Job finds overpatient listeners in his friends, although they have come to deplore his misfortune and to show him their sympathy. At the end he incurs their severe censure. It is as if they had discovered a breath of rebellion, a shade of haughtiness in his insistence that God wronged him. Actually, his complaints in the main sound like accusations, like reproaches and attacks. They become more urgent as though they were meant to provoke a counteraction.

Analytic investigators hitherto always pointed to the need for love in masochism, interpreting the provocative behavior of the masochist as an unconscious wooing of love. K. Horney, W. Reich and others stress this point of view untiringly. But it is by no means the need for love that manifests itself. Rather is it the need for condonation which is easily mistaken for the previous one.

The "need for love" in its enhanced form is a sign that the security of the ego is lessened by unconscious feeling of guilt. He who needs so much love doubts whether he deserves to be loved. He yearns for the proof that he is loved in spite of everything. The insecurity of the ego is conditioned by the inner perception which has recognized repressed hostile and aggressive impulses. During analysis one often witnesses such a growing need for love.

One of my patients, for instance, was tormented by impatience because she had not received a letter from her fiancé for some time and showed all the indications of being hurt and feeling neglected. Her increased need for love, however, soon betrayed its origin in a torturing anxiety lest she might have offended her lover in her letters without knowledge or intention. The tender substance of her writings wholly contradicted such an assumption, but the self-reproach was psychologically justified: her unconscious hostile impulses made her anxiety rise. She wanted consolation and appeasement for her unconscious guilt feelings. This appeared in the guise of a wish to receive proofs of love as a kind of insurance that he did not harbor any grudge or wishes for punishment against her hostile impulses. Her increased need for love corresponded to her need for being sure of his pardon.

The provocative behavior is to be understood as an unconscious confession: "Look how bad I am!" which, however, is continued thus: "But for all that you must forgive me!" This enacted confession, to be sure, results in a mishandling of the masochist that satisfies his need for punishment. Thus the "vicious circle" is developed which we meet so often among the phenomena of masochism.

We postpone the discussion of the meaning of this circular course and at present investigate only the purposes of the demonstration. There is no doubt that the tendency to provoke a new punishment is existent as well as the opposite one that tends to seek forgiveness. They penetrate each other in such a manner that finally the appearance prevails: being punished is the same as being loved. This, however, is valid not to the starting phase of masochism but for its full and completed development. For the starting phase we assume another, more neutral and vague purpose of such demonstration, saying: the masochist wishes to draw attention to his suffering, his punishment, his degradation. To put it into the language of consciousness: "Look at me, at my sufferings, at my shame! Look, how they ill-treat and punish me!"

To this two meanings can be inferred. One is: "I am punished justly"—that would mean a lamentation or sorrowing. The other is: "I am punished unjustly," which equals an accusation. It can also mean something entirely different in which the question of being right or wrong plays no part at first. It can mean: "I have been punished; I have atoned; now gratification of my instincts will be permitted." The punishment thus would precede the misdeed and, so to speak, legalize it. Such reversal and anticipation would certainly fit into the mechanism of flight forward.

Some examples of masochistic demonstration will lead us beyond that. They belong to the class of social masochism and represent typical phantasies. A man financially dependent on the generosity of his brother indulges in the fancy that one day he will appear at his brother's house with torn clothes, worn shoes, never to leave the house again. This is quite a distinct presentation of a misery that is coyly enjoyed in imagination. It is easy to recognize the motive: not only shall the indigence be displayed before the brother but also he shall be upbraided. The behavior of the masochist does not so much intend to awaken sympathy and love as to punish the brother. Digging deeper in the psychological context one recognizes the characteristic form of this punishment, the display of one's own misery. It is the form of exaggeration, typical of masochism.

The brother had often blamed the patient for spending too much money on clothes and shoes. The phantasy caricatures the reproaches and, in rejecting them as unjustified, says in a way: "So I am dressed too well, I spend too much money? Well, just look at my torn clothes and shoes. That is what I look like. I have to stay in your house because I cannot walk in the street like this." No doubt this demonstration serves still another purpose than the one aimed at arousing pity and love, the only one the analysts recognized.

In another case a little girl imagines that her father will not return from his journey and will die in a foreign country. The daydreamer decides that she will then work hard, become a teacher and take over the care of her mother and her sisters. With great pleasure she dwells on the phantasy, on the hardships of such living standards, on the sacrifices she will have to make, the privations she will have to suffer. A special feature pictures the appreciation by friends and relatives of her misery and untiring work. The motive of this oft-repeated phantasy is not alone to gain love and sympathy. There are more unconscious motives, easy to guess, such as the close union with her mother in which the father is excluded; her ambition; her superiority to her sisters.

Another instance: a man depending on his relatives has during analysis so far recovered from his inability to work that he succeeds in finding an occupation in which to earn some money. He opens up a shop but queer misfortunes, puzzling bouts of forgetfulness, incomprehensible negligences, seem to persecute him. He intended to send a prospectus describing his goods to several thousand persons. He wrote the addresses on the envelopes but frequently interrupted his work in order to turn to more urgent matters. When he was about to mail these letters he left them at home and remembered them only on his way to the post office. He went back to get them, took the letters in question but went to the post office without taking the envelopes. He lost orders, was late for important appointments, forgot phone calls, and so on. He complained about his misfortunes movingly as if he had had no part in manufacturing them but rather as if hostile powers had conspired against him. He complained to his family that adverse incidents hindered the delivery of goods ordered. Added to the different single determinants of his skillful ineptitude and forgetfulness there was one constant unconscious aim: to prove to his relatives that it did not work that way.

This masochistic sabotage was meant to say: "If you do not arrange for an office and help me to write and mail my letters, to take note of orders, I cannot go on with my shop. As long as I have no car for delivering the merchandise such wearisome and damaging misfortunes are bound to occur." I did not see in this case a single detail whose aim was to arouse love or pity. The whole display barely hidden by many lamentations had only one meaning: "I told you so!" It had to prove that business could not be done in the way his relatives wanted him to do it.

I shall not argue that the wish to arouse love and pity is lacking among the motives of masochistic demonstration, but I deny that it constitutes an important aspect of the problem, or one hard to discover. On the contrary it is that element that offers itself immediately and to the most unpracticed observer. The masochist offers it conspicuously. He behaves like our oft-mentioned subject who constantly looks into one corner of the hall so that everybody present follows his glance. Several of the examples described above foreshadow many noteworthy and important things to be found in the other neglected corner.

The demonstrative feature, as I said before, represents the surface aspect of the masochistic characteristics and transmits this instinctual inclination to the outer world. What does it want to show and what does it want to hide, exposing even this latter effort by the very attempt to keep it secret? It shows the punishment, the shame, the degradation. This is certainly because a prohibition was violated, a forbidden impulse was satisfied—but this forbidden satisfaction of an instinct follows at once. If the display of discomfort and pain proves the guilty feelings of the masochist, what then is the gratification of the impulse immediately after meant to show? Does not such a sequence resemble the ambiguous and double-dealing ceremonies of compulsory neurotics, those procedures in which first the atonement is performed and then the forbidden action?

Observation and analytic investigation of many masochistic phenomena induced me to surmise a historic development. In the beginning there is really the display of an executed punishment, of shame, of atonement as testimonial of a belated obedience, of guilt feelings and of the impression that the punishment is deserved. We have not forgotten what insight in the effects of the flight forward has taught us: that the execution of the punishment has become an indispensable condition, the *conditio sine qua non*, of instinctual gratification. This execution of punish-

ment is now displayed humbly and dolefully. Thus the weak
who are afraid offer tribute. They do not simply deliver it, they
present it as a proof of their submission and their submissiveness. Thus rebels show that they feel guilty and deserve the
punishment for their deeds.

The demonstration, however, changes its character while the
development is in progress. The punishment is drawn more and
more into the sphere of the urge for pleasure. If at first it had
been the punishment which was displayed meekly it is now the
transmutation of punishment into pleasure that is definitely
exposed to the onlooker. If the first emotion is to be interpreted
by the word: "Look how I am punished and how I suffer," so
the latter must be translated into the words: "Look how I enjoy
even this suffering." The first is a concession submitting to the
powers of education and of the prohibitory outer world. The
latter is a declaration of war against the same. The demonstration in its beginnings proves the efficiency of educational and
moral regulations. It finishes up with the exposure of their
bankruptcy. During the first phase of masochistic development
the success of those forces is demonstrated. During the second it
is demonstrated how its success is turned into failure.

I obtained insight into this change of aim through long analytic observation of many masochistic characters. As a witness to
a strange scene I believe I saw the embodiment of the end-form
of this development. A boy of six years, who had early shown
himself to be backward and unruly, was chastised by his young
and irascible father. My intervention had been rejected. And
while the boy was severely beaten he kept screaming: "I am
laughing, I am laughing!" He wished to prove to his father, as
well as to me, that he did not care about hard blows, that on the
contrary he enjoyed them. This example is not to be taken for
infantile masochism. Obviously the child was in no mood for
laughing. I simply mean that such a demonstration in the end-
phase of masochistic development unconsciously determines the
surface of the event. I frequently remembered this scene when
I listened to the lamentations and complaints of masochists when

they opened, as an American patient expressed it, their "complaint department." The penetration of pleasure into discomfort, conspicuous in the perversion, well hidden in social masochism, betrays the tendency that the boy expressed so accurately when he cried: "I am laughing."

The demonstration of the punishment for a forbidden satisfaction of instincts has turned into a demonstration of the forbidden instinctual satisfaction in the punishment. The exposure of discomfort as expiation turns into a display of pleasure at the bankruptcy of the proceedings of atonement.

What has been described as development here appears to the retrospective glance of the psychologist as an unfolding of those features that determined and accompanied masochism from the beginning. The masochist requires a witness to his discomfort, to his pain, to his degradation; somebody to whom he may show his punishment and his fault. He needs this same witness, however, to demonstrate that this punishment was senseless, in vain and even turned into pleasure. He exhibits the punishment but also its failure. He shows his submission, certainly, but he also shows his invincible rebellion, demonstrating that he gains pleasure despite the discomfort. He proves that he gains pleasure from resisting the discomfort. The purpose to obtain satisfaction *in spite* of all threats develops into the tendency to gain satisfaction *to spite* all threats.

In perverted masochism this development of display is evident. In the social configuration the punishment, the failure, the shame is demonstrated and complained about more pointedly than ever. If our conception of masochism as a psychological unit in all its forms is right the same development must be recognizable there as well. The demonstration must have the same meaning even when only one side is discernible. This will be proved later. But here already a side glance at the fate of the sufferer Job reveals the fact that the friends who look at his misery as a proof of his guilt are proved wrong and finally become witnesses to his rehabilitation and triumph. It is beginning to dawn on us that a similar psychic process happens in so many masochistic characters. They make themselves a public disgrace or nuisance. They minimize themselves, but that is a self-advertisement with a minus sign.

The demonstrative feature really shows something: but it shows one thing to the superficial glance and another to the deeply penetrating glance. To the one it shows utterances of striving for love, of guilt feelings, of weakness and submissiveness. To the other it shows expressions of revenge, of rebellion and of triumph. The two halves of the lamenting face express two different feelings. And what is shown so plainly is aimed at hiding the other half. That is part of the paradox of masochism: if something which otherwise would be concealed is put on the surface it is a good guess that something else is meant to be hidden at the same time. The conspicuousness of the one side is meant to effect a concealment on the other side.

In the course of development, however, this hidden thing squeezes through more and more and penetrates the darkness. What was audible previously only to the third ear is plainly audible now. As yet the discomfort, the degradation, the shame is shifted to the foreground, but the psychologists will recognize why it is pushed there. Thus the demonstrative feature will at once show something and hide something. The result, pleasure in spite of discomfort, is meant to prove something. Its secret meaning, now manifest to the psychologist, is: "Even if you beat me, punish me, I persevere until I attain the instinctual satisfaction." The designation "demonstrative" for this significant feature of masochism was chosen by me because it indicates the tendency to display without saying too much about the motives of such exposure. We know what was meant to be pointed at openly and what kept under cover. We know that the purpose was not only to be seen. Something had to be proved. The unconscious aim was: *quod erat demonstrandum.* We recognize that the choice of the term "demonstrative feature" gains a significance that it did not own before and we become aware of its full significance.

6

Some analytic investigations emphasize the fact that the aim of the masochistic perversion is to gain sexual gratification without taking responsibility. The formula, "pleasure without responsibility," is set up by W. Stekel and W. Reich as shedding light on masochism. Masochists seem to like this characterization. Sometimes they put it forth themselves. It appears to corroborate what they frequently say themselves: that they are lazy and inferior people. One could put it like this: such a formula is flattering to their negative vanity. In addition, such a characterization has the advantage of shutting the door to the secret pigeonhole.

Pleasure without responsibility? It sounds plausible enough and it certainly contains a sparkle of truth. Nevertheless one is bound to ask why such exoneration from responsibility should take the form of being beaten and being tied. Perhaps the representatives who hold the opinion mentioned will think questions of that kind indiscreet. We shall take their delicacy into consideration and select as an example what seems to confirm their opinion: the masochistic daydream of a man.

The substance is: his boss steps into the room and orders the daydreamer at the point of his gun to copulate with his, the boss's, wife. This seems to me a perfect example of the classification of pleasure without responsibility, especially since the phantasy is very exciting whenever it shows up—and it shows up frequently. Maybe it would not disturb those theorists that the whole procedure is not very likely to occur. But there are other features in this dream that do not fit into the formula. And that is an understatement because we might more truthfully say: features that definitely contradict the formula. Thus, for instance, one could doubt whether sexual intercourse under such conditions would be very pleasurable. The presence of the husband in the bedroom with a gun in his hand would almost certainly impair the mood of the lover.

But on the other hand does not the phantasy excite the day-dreamer? True enough, but this does not prove the correctness of the formula. Other psychological conditions may be decisive for the exciting effect of the phantasy. With a little imagination another possibility can be conceived. The sexual stimulus of this situation—sexual intercourse with a beautiful woman under compulsion by her husband—need not be derived from the formula "pleasure without responsibility." Many a man has imagined a situation that brings pleasure without responsibility differently, with less imaginative expenditure. He might, for instance, imagine an undisturbed enjoyment accompanied neither by a prohibition nor by an order at the point of a gun. In this sense pleasure is derived from being permitted to do what one likes. There is certainly little satisfaction in having to take one's pleasure under threat of compulsion. May we add the question: is this indeed pleasure without responsibility? Actually it is pleasure with responsibility, pleasure forced upon him by another who threatens: "If you do not enjoy this I'll shoot you like a dog." The reader will begin to wonder whether life in fool's paradise really looks like that.

You may guess how this phantasy came into existence. It can be explained from the masochistic reversal of the following situation. The daydreamer wishes to possess the beautiful woman but is afraid of the gun of the husband. He fears the revenge. The desire for this sexual relationship stands under the threat of death. In the phantasy the prohibition is turned into a command: the dreamer is even forced to do what he desired. Now the threat of death is directed at the omission. There is a further alteration of this original situation, which does not refer to the content but to its time schedule. In the scene originally phantasied the sequence was: sexual intercourse—threat of death. Here it is: threat of death—sexual intercourse.

The temporal reversal points at a reversal of the contents. That agrees perfectly with the essence of the flight forward. We could guess further that there is a presentation through the opposite. One could assume that the daydreamer says to himself: "Wouldn't it suit me to perfection if the husband would force me to have intercourse with his wife!" It would then be an ironical phantasy. Actually the daydream reaches far beyond this frame and says: "I want to possess this woman, even if her husband shoots me for it." It is a defiant, savage emotion expressed in the language of masochism. No trace of "pleasure without responsibility." Rather pleasure with heightened responsibility.

The previous, "You must not do that," has been transmuted into, "You have to do that!"; the prohibition has been changed into the command. Examples of this sort are fairly frequent in masochistic phantasies. The discomfort is emphasized in imagination. Sexual excitation accompanies this phantasy and shows that the discomfort is not always truly felt. One patient phantasies that he is caught by Amazons and laid down in a garden with chains on hands and feet. The beautiful virgins undress him and stroke his genitals tenderly until excitement and orgasm is reached. This serious play is repeated until the prisoner is exhausted. The daydreamer, educated in the puritan way, offers resistance. He tries to prevent the excitation, sets his teeth, grimaces grimly, but with the prisoner as well as with the daydreamer orgasm is reached several times. One could apply the formula, "Pleasure without responsibility," here as well, but it would not give the nucleus of the psychic situation. The formula sounds attractive. But if we aim at intellectual honesty we must not be bribed by attractiveness.

The same patient developed a phantasy the analytic investigation of which shall lead us farther. His substitute in this phantasy is a prisoner of an Aztec tribe who, as representative of God, is to be immolated ceremonially at an appointed day. During the preparations for these festivities he is highly honored and treated with every consideration according to his assigned role. Every night one of the most beautiful virgins of the country is led to him for sexual intercourse. Here a good deal of the substance of the original phantasy is preserved. The sequence is: sexual intercourse—threat of death. Already, however, the situation is altered inasmuch as the expectation of death allows unrestricted gratification.

We remember that the same patient had become sexually excited at the vision of Laocoön strangled by the serpents and with the phantasy of Marsyas excoriated by Apollo. But he connects the cruel punishment with the exceptional offense. The gratification is derived primarily from the offense and only later transferred to the punishment. We recollect the girl who became ecstatic at the sight of a skeleton. There too the reversal was undeniably apparent. At first the skeleton was a recollection of death as a threatening punishment for a forbidden gratification. Later on it became the exciting reminder of this gratification itself. Must not this pleasure be more profound and more desirable if it is savored under threat of death? The reversal in the sequence pleasure-punishment, however, is not the only one that is characteristic of masochism. Another reversal, hardly ever recognized, is even more important, since it appears as a deformation that hides the essence of the instinctual inclination.

At first sight one gains the impression that masochistic scenes are repetitions of small occurrences in childhood. It looks as if the masochist wanted to be treated like a naughty child. Where else but in childhood are there any models of scenes in which an adult man is abused, chastised, tied? An adult must stand in the corner, get the rod with which he will be beaten, and so on. Other features, however, resist the conjecture that true repetitions of childhood scenes are enacted here. The impression remains confusing because many features that recall such childhood scenes are mixed up with others that do not permit such a derivation. One is ready to assume enormous exaggerations and enrichments of originally harmless childhood scenes and phantastic extensions. The examination of this surmise, however, does not produce an unambiguous result. Even where it is confirmed the question remains: why does a banal scene, like scolding or punishing a boy, become in one case the center of masochistic phantasies while in the majority of cases it has an indifferent result?

We search, for instance, for the primary scene which gave rise to the following: a man crawls on his legs and hands in a brothel while the woman riding on his back orders, "Slow trot!" "Easy trot!" "Gallop!" "Halt!" and beats him with a small horsewhip. The latent meaning of such a scene becomes evident if one considers the mechanism of reversal. The reversal is often used in dreams and in nervous symptoms in order to deform the original meaning of a phantasy group and to withhold it from consciousness. If in such cases we try to reverse the phantasy content a definite meaning is discovered. The man who lets the woman ride on his back certainly refers to a childhood phantasy: he wished to ride on his mother or his nurse and beat them. This is a sensual wish sadistically expressed. Probably at this time dim sexual feelings arose when he rode on the back of his father or mother. But why the reversal of the situation?

Even the scene in which a man has a woman urinate into his mouth obtains a meaning through revocation of the reversal of the phantasy. We know that babies wet only people they love, as if the wetting with urine were a gift of love. Here too the return into early childhood would be combined with the reversal in phantasy. Certainly many masochistic scenes will lose some of their strangeness if one remembers the effect of the reversal and accepts childhood as their source. Naturally these childhood scenes or phantasies are revitalized much later.

Frequently the masochist himself does not understand why such grotesque or disgusting matters excite him sexually. He is under the compulsion to do certain things or to have them done, but he wonders about it. In other cases, to be sure, he gives a score of reasons for their power to excite him sexually. These explanations, however, impress us as later rationalizations. The grotesque or strained element of such scenes carries a nuance that contradicts an alleged yearning for the paradise of childhood. Nobody who ever listened to a detailed description of masochistic ceremonials will get the unadulterated impression of a yearning, as it is expressed in the song of Brahms: *O wüsst ich noch den Weg zurück, den lieben Weg zur Kinderzeit . . .* (If only I knew the way back, the dear way back to childhood . . .) How can these contradictory features be explained? The contradiction is not unsolvable. A return to childhood phantasies is not to be doubted in some of the features, but this is not the cause of masochism, but its consequence. That is to say: Masochism likes to regress to such childhood images, likes to use material of that period in order to achieve its instinctual aims, aims which are still dark to us. In some details this return will be tied to recollections or memory traces. Mainly, however, it is a work of phantasy that deforms the material by reversals.

Now what is the secret meaning of the reversal? We were able to guess something about it in the example of the man who was threatened by the husband with the gun. There it signified: "If only things were the other way round! If only I were not prevented from intercourse with the young woman by fear but were actually forced to have it!" This need not be the only motive for the reversed presentation but it certainly is an important factor. A desire of this kind frequently turns up when instinctual urges meet with external or internal resistances that are impossible to overcome. If the resistances are represented by forbidding or punishing persons the reversal readily turns into an expression of revenge or defiance. This element will hardly ever be missed in cases of masochistic perversions.

The other form of reversal which does not deal with the contents but with persons is of a similar nature. I cite an example from the psychology of dreams in order to elucidate the mechanism. A grown-up man sees himself in a dream standing next to his mother, who is sitting on a chair. He soaks a sponge with water, soaps it thoroughly and washes the face of his mother, who struggles against it. She cries pitiably and kicks with her legs. It is plain that, in addition to other factors, the dreamer takes a belated revenge on his mother because of her merciless insistence on cleanliness. In the masochistic scene a wish is expressed in passive reversal: "That's how I would like to treat you!" We understand now the proceedings of the man who has a woman riding on him. What ought to happen to the other is represented in such a manner that it is done to the ego through the other.

The other form of representation of masochism is easier to describe: it is a configuration the nucleus of which can be termed a grotesque distortion or exaggeration. If grotesque or absurd elements turn up in a dream the meaning as relating to the subject-matter is: this is absurd, nonsensical. By it, a judgment of the dreamer is expressed and also his scorn and contempt. It is the same with caricatures: if the artist wants to draw a person with a big nose he will not limit himself to the natural proportions but will distort the nose into giant size. He will exaggerate a characteristic into the bizarre. In the same way the distortion and exaggeration in masochism are meant to be expressions of scorn. Instead of saying: "This is grotesque or nonsensical," a grotesque or absurd scene is enacted. Some of these overdone and intentionally distorted scenes frequently give the impression of a parody or travesty, of a sarcastic demonstration of the defeat of educational methods or of later discipline.

Here is an example of such a grotesque masochistic phantasy: a man imagines that he is put on the weighing scales by his father in punishment for having kissed several girls. To explain this phantasy I must add that as a boy of thirteen he actually had kissed a girl and had been reprimanded by his father. The father had threatened to punish him if this misdemeanor should occur again. The thought or the phantasy connected with this possible punishment already had a slight touch of masochism at this time and had brought about sexual excitement. In the phantasy of the adult the punishment is executed in such a way that his father takes him in his arms and puts him, who is absolutely helpless, on the scales. The exciting factor in this procedure is mainly the conception of helplessness of the man who appears as a boy and of the humiliation of such a treatment. There are certainly good reasons for assuming a strong homosexual impulse as a component of pleasure in this case. A strange detail of the phantasied punishment is noteworthy: when the boy lies on the scales the father pushes the penis and the testicles which project beyond it onto the scales to have them weighed too. Let me mention that there were scales in the bathroom of the parental apartment and that at the time when the daydreamer was a boy his father frequently had shown himself worried whether the boy's weight was all right and had urged him to weigh himself.

What is the meaning of this grotesque detail? My patient could not contribute any association except the popular line: "Weighed in the balance and found wanting." The hidden meaning of the detail can be found only by filling in the gaps in the course of his thoughts and by guessing at the concealed factor through the indications given. Then the detail can be translated approximately in the following way: "If I masturbate and discharge you would make as much fuss about it as you did when my weight was insufficient. You would go so far as to weigh even my testicles in order to test whether I had had a pollution." This then is a bitter derision of his father and a demonstration of the absurdity of his educational methods by exaggeration and distortion.

We begin to guess that the paradoxical—the first impression masochistic phenomena have on us—is not merely a superficial feature but deep-rooted in the core of the instinctual urge. In order to grasp the nature of that hidden mockery one has to realize that the prohibition or demand is carried out to extremes in phantasy. By this literal acceptance and this very obedience, by this defiant submissiveness, its foolishness is recognized and exposed. By this slavish fulfillment the demand seems to prove its own futility and absurdity. Thus the way to the forbidden instinctual satisfaction is opened. This sarcastic acceptance of commands and prohibitions as well as of threats of punishment in masochistic phantasies and ceremonials leads us into the vicinity of expressions of compulsion neurosis.

It would appear at first that the mockery is of later standing and was added only afterward to the masochistic structure. Deeper experience, however, shows that it was typified much earlier, in childhood. A patient with distinct masochistic tendencies remembered a walk with his father during which the adolescent ran up the steps in front of houses and jumped down again.

His father rebuked him: "What are you doing there?" The youth answered: "I play the games that fit my age." Here indeed the mockery at paternal authority came into its own.

For the interpretation of the whole or of details of masochistic phantasies or ceremonials the analyst has to make use of a technique which does away with the disguises and distortions. These formations have frequently grown incomprehensible because of gaps or of an elliptical presentation. Let me give for an example another phantasy of a previously mentioned patient which also produced sexual excitement: a very poor fisherman's family consists of his wife and his three sons. The father needs a new boat and decides to sell the oldest son in order to buy the vessel. Since the amount received was not sufficient, the second and finally the youngest son, who believed himself safe, are sold and auctioned. The sons are ordained by the priests as victims for the approaching festival in honor of the tribe's deity. The sexual climax of the phantasy is reached with the idea of the sacrifice, when the anxiety of the youngest at the sight of the tortures of the elder brothers is pictured. The daydreamer himself is the youngest of three brothers.

I want to give here the analytical conception of the outline of the masochistic phantasy. The picture of the poor fisherman's family is a reproduction of the patient's family transferred to another social class. That means to say: "If my father, who is a very wealthy man, were a poor fisherman. . . ." The secret meaning of the phantasy is easily guessed now: "In such a situation my father would not hesitate to sell me and my brothers if he thought it profitable for his material interests." No doubt we are confronted here with a grotesquely exaggerated and distorted thought formation.

Distortion, exaggeration and reversal here appear as a means to express defiance and vindictiveness, irony and disdain. We guess that children and adolescents frequently make use of such means in their phantasies in order to parry the superiority of adults. We ourselves, the adults, make use of the same means to express our bitterness or our contempt when we speak sarcastically or ironically. Let me illustrate with an example the effectiveness of reversal as a weapon of aggression. During the period when in Germany every misdeed and defect in the world was attributed to the Jews while the Germans appeared as the innocent victims of Jewish wickedness the following anecdote was told. A German anti-Semitic paper printed a paragraph intended to illustrate the wickedness and cunning of the Jews. The headline ran: "Jewish Peddler Bites German Shepherd Dog." That surely has never happened. But just as surely the opposite has, namely, that a German shepherd dog—mind, the adjective designates a certain breed!—has bitten a Jewish peddler. The wickedness of the Jews is described so exaggeratedly in the anti-Semitic propaganda that a devilish Jew is portrayed assaulting and biting a peaceable shepherd dog of German blood. Here the motive of the reversed presentation is obvious: the stupidity of anti-Semitic propaganda is thereby derided.

If analysis did not enable us to peep behind the silhouettes of conscious proceedings who would be able to recognize defiance, vengeance, sarcasm and derision, altogether a murderous satire, in masochism? And who, even with the help of analysis, has discovered all these? Were not the masochist's utmost gentleness and submissiveness, his complete devotion and dependence, always stressed as prominent characteristics?

The masochistic behavior certainly justifies such a judgment if observed only superficially. Many analysts were deceived by these superficial features. According to Dr. Horney the essential purpose of the masochist is to give up his whole personality completely and to be submerged in others. All his striving is said to be directed toward redemption of his self, toward losing his ego. Obviously the opinion as represented here is the opposite one: by a peculiar detour the masochist attempts to maintain his ego, to enforce his will. The masochist is a revolutionist of self-surrender. The lambskin he wears hides a wolf. His yielding includes defiance, his submissiveness opposition. Beneath his softness there is hardness; behind his obsequiousness rebellion is concealed.

Although the boundaries between defiance and rebellion are

vague, and silent rebellion can change imperceptibly into open derision and jeering, yet we can guess at its development. The progress from sullen endurance to derision is bound to become manifest in the forms of expression of masochism. The reversal probably is better qualified to express vindictiveness and resistance, the exaggeration to express derision and sullying. For instance, let us take the reversal in a picture book for children where adults pull a car, on the driver's seat of which sit the horses with crossed legs, and compare it with a perverse phantasy of the oft-mentioned patient: several naked young men are exhibited in the slave market and sold to women, chiefly elderly widows. When these slaves are brought to the homes of their mistresses and refuse to satisfy them sexually they are castrated.

These many examples of exaggeration which we assumed to be of a derisive tendency may be contrasted with a similar detail in the behavior of a little boy, whom I also mentioned above. He was often rebuked by his father because of his bad table manners. "Do not eat like a pig," his father kept nagging when the boy sipped his soup noisily. When the father again expressed his disapproval the sipping stopped but the boy instead grunted audibly after each gulp. Called to account he declared: "Well, I am a pig!" and he repeated triumphantly: "Sure, I'm a pig and must grunt!" The purpose of such self-irony certainly was meant as a blow against the father. No great sagacity is necessary to discover the similarity of the self-humiliation and disgrace in masochistic thought, expressed not in words but in actions.

The masochist's irony, however, is more perfidious and more cunning. In the analytical literature this defiance appears as an additional trait, a tendency to be right like a vignette added to the picture. It is belittled. But in spite of appearances it is no narrow-minded effort to be right in the end. Though the masochist wants to be right in apparently unimportant matters and details this is, as in compulsory neurosis, only the result of a psychic displacement. The foremost interests of the individual hide behind it. Masochistic defiance pervades the individual's whole life. The point is not that of being right in the end but of aiding the inborn right to victory over traditional rights. Thus it becomes a battle for right in the sense of Rudolf von Ihering, but fought stubbornly in one's own direction. No mythological figure can better impersonate this masochistic defiance than the Titan Prometheus who is chained to the rock by the highest of the gods. The wrath of the fettered hero equals the character of the hidden defiance in masochism.

But how is this defiance, this sullen derision, expressed? It is only in this way that the masochist succeeds by preserving his personality even in surrender, by remaining stubborn while yielding, by staying haughty in humility. By giving in on petty details he maintains his claim to his existence and to his particular kind of pleasure. The derision represents a step beyond defiance. Having become prouder through humiliation, more courageous through pressure, the masochist becomes a spiteful scoffer. His sabotage assumes the form of complete docility. His resistance consists in not-resisting. His blind obedience becomes rebellion. There are nations who in such a masochistic manner produce the most malicious and most biting jokes against their own national peculiarities and weaknesses, jokes that in their accuracy of aim expose their own community. I have dealt with these peculiarities of Jewish jokes in another book. However, such self-humiliation and self-derision do not exclude a hidden pride in national merits that are unknown and inaccessible to strangers. The jokes, while deriding the shortcomings of one's own people, yet secretly praise the virtues of these defects. But this touches a topic that is not to be dealt with here: the feeling of self-dignity concealed in self-disgrace.

Analytical literature scarcely has recognized the effects of derisive and sneering impulses in masochism and has hardly appreciated those of defiance and rebellion. The presence of defiance, however, was so conspicuous that it could not be totally overlooked. Yet it has been noticed by analysts only to the extent that such impulses actually showed up, say, in transference. W. Reich describes this as a childish effort to be right in the end. That is correct only insofar as defiance also shows up naturally in analysis and insofar as the childish element can be reduced to its origin in childhood. Thus defiance was misunderstood more than understood, even where it was noticed. Nothing could be more mistaken than to imagine this defiance to be a feature that appears now and then during analysis.* Rather does it belong to the constitutional factors of masochism which never would develop without its secret participation.

Masochism, however, slowly passes on not only to thwarting another will through complete submission but to exhibiting and proving this failure in a peculiar way. Here is one phantasy as an example: a young man had been refused a new car by his father, in place of his old damaged one. One of the son's daydreams dealt with the possibility that, while driving this broken-down car, he would be involved in an accident in front of his father's shop. The car would run right into the show windows and he, covered with blood, would be carried into his father's office. Don't say that this only shows that in masochism the tendency prevails to "cut off one's nose to spite one's face." It is not only one's own face that is damaged in such phantasies; it is the other one's too. He "loses face" as the Chinese would say. He loses prestige. The father in this phantasy was to be convinced that his refusal was nonsensical and his behavior absurd. There is the concealed hope: it will hurt him more than me. By pursuing the course prescribed to him to the very end the masochist demonstrates that it is the wrong course. It is like the hara-kiri of the Japanese. It is incorrect to assume that masochism is introverted sadism, a violent instinctual inclination that later became directed against the ego. In spite of all and at the bottom, its object remains the other person. We could rather term it sadism put on its head, violence upside down.

---

* As mentioned above, W. Reich has recognized the participation of defiance in masochism, at least during psychoanalysis. My opinion comes close to his on this point as well as on a few others. Such an approach, however, helps sometimes the realization of how far apart we still are. On some points no abyss separates my opinion from W. Reich's, but what is more: a nuance.

The description of the masochistic character as weak, dependent, easily influenced, helpless, continues to amaze us. All these
features serve the purpose of concealing the utmost determination and stubbornness. What the masochist has to say to the existent ruling forces sounds like slavish submissiveness. It is, however, a scornful "No" to the world of appearances that became
dominant. He submits—in order never to yield. He remains in
opposition, especially where he is servilely devoted. When Dr.
Horney keeps emphasizing the dependence of masochistic characters, their tendency to cling to the loved person, she overlooks
the fact that one can draw somebody down by clinging to him.

The masochist is guided by the pride and the defiance of
Prometheus even if he wishes to appear as a Ganymede to the
world. Under the mask of the constant "yes man" he remains the
spirit of eternal negation. By fully submitting he remains independent. Humiliated a thousand times, he is inflexible and invincible. Defeated again and again, he stands to his rights. Quot-
ing the English poet he could say: "My head is bloody but un-
bowed."

Strong and everlasting impulses of rebellion and defiance can
also be recognized as profoundly effective in the general forms of
expression and the development of masochism. It begins with
doubts concerning the justification of the pleasure urge, expressed
in suspense, with vacillation between pleasure and anxiety. The
masochist then runs to meet the dreaded event, undertakes that
flight forward by anticipating instead of expecting the punishment. The end-phase of its development, however, is marked by
the fact that the masochist finds his pleasure in punishment and
disgrace themselves, preferring the most painful pleasure to any
other.

That looks like increasing surrender to the authority, a deeper
submission. Actually, however—and this is proved by the pleasure
extant in the punishment—it is nothing but the intensification of
the scornful rebellion, the factual evidence that any influence
from without failed. What else but a demonstration of absurdity

is aimed at when the punishment for forbidden pleasure brings about this very same pleasure? Pain and humiliation are sought for in order to enjoy the forbidden. Slowly pleasure sneaks into punishment. The punishment itself becomes pleasure; what was meant to disturb satisfaction turns into satisfaction. The derision is not less effective because it is hidden.

The fully developed masochism shows us how much the quality of "in spite of all" dominates all its appearances, if one only can see and interpret them analytically. The reversal of punishment into pleasure may be considered as the inner sign of that procedure, the significant reversal of the sequence, punishment—forbidden instinctual gratification, as its external mark. Here the hidden meaning of the masochistic instinctual inclination reveals itself plainly. The reversal is meant to say: "I will bear everything, pain, suffering, humiliation and disgrace, but I will not renounce my satisfaction!" The anticipation of punishment with subsequent sexual pleasure permits of only one interpretation: "Even if you beat, tie and humiliate me—I will yet attain my pleasure!" By ordering his own punishment the masochist has made himself the master of his destiny.

This sovereign anticipation of punishment is in itself a symptom of rebellion. The pleasure springing from punishment moreover becomes evidence that the masochist insists on his satisfaction. The unconscious thought that is realized in developed masochism can be expressed in a conditional sentence: "I shall attain my gratification even if I shall be punished, abused and beaten for it!" Expressed negatively: "I will not renounce my satisfaction even if you chastise me!" This conditional sentence appears dissolved in the masochistic scene and is expressed in the sequence of the two parts: punishment—sexual pleasure. This sequence itself should have pointed at the in-spite character of masochism.

May I again point to an oft-mentioned case, whose psychological meaning is not yet disclosed? You remember the patient who put on his trousers backward, who pulled them over his feet, compressed his body in a tight jacket and pulled his belt and collar so tight? Thus squeezed in he became sexually excited, threw himself on his bed and masturbated. What is the meaning of such extraordinary doings? We already know that his mother threatened that she would put the disobedient and unruly boy into military college. She, and later on other persons, depicted the terrors of severe discipline to the boy, among them the neatness and orderliness of dress, the necessity for buttoning the jacket, and so on. The boy imagined the uniform tighter than it actually was and thought that it would probably be even more cruelly tightened if a boy was to be punished. He thought that the uniform had to be worn even during the night sometimes by way of punishment. His vanity connected the uniform with the idea that he would be admired in it. It appeared to him as something especially virile, and his suit, which exaggerated the slimness of the uniform, proved to him that he was a perfect he-man.

But what does it mean, that the sexual excitement is roused by the discomfort of the tightly buttoned suit and trousers, the pressing belt and the high collar—all a kind of caricature of military uniform? What is the meaning of the scene in which, thus hindered and pressed in, he masturbates? The meaning becomes clear if we remember that masturbation was one of the naughty actions for which his mother admonished him. It is as if the scene anticipating the realization of all threats would demonstrate: "If I am put in the military college, even if I am forced into the tightest costume so that I can scarcely breathe and cannot reach my genitals at all, if my trousers are sewn up and my body almost inaccessible to my hands—even then I will get the sexual gratification you forbade."

Consider the sequence of putting on all those tight things, which condemn the man almost to immobility, and of the subsequent masturbating—does that not mean that he will get his satisfaction in spite of all, and to spite all? Many analysts hold that such a ritual is an expression of the servility and of the weak, dependent and guilty mind of the masochist. But did no one see the expression of wild revolution in a ritual of this kind? Does it not reveal a rebellious, independent mind?

It surprises me that there are psychoanalysts who still think that masochists are in search of pain and discomfort from the start. Every case of masochistic behavior contradicts such an assumption. All cases show that the masochist has originally, like every one of us, felt discomfort and pain as unpleasant and unwelcome. Of course you have to take the trouble to search in the history of the person to find this result.

Let us consider one single trait of the masochistic ritual of our patient: the fact, for instance, that he sewed the ends of his trousers up in such a manner that they covered his feet completely. The origin of this detail proved to be that when he was a boy his mother bought him pajamas into which he had to slip at night and she closed the feet ends to protect him against catching cold. The boy did not want to wear them, kicked and screamed every evening. Of course, in the end, he had to give in. In his present ritual he put the specially prepared trousers on spontaneously.

Does this mean that he does not feel the discomfort? Ask him and he will say: "Of course I feel it, and acutely too, but it increases my sexual excitement." We realize that what was most unpleasant remained unpleasant but became a condition necessary for the reaching of the satisfaction. Pain appears as a stimulant of lust, humiliation as a premise for elation.

The sequence of manifest submission and latent rebellion is certainly not restricted to the sexual forms of the masochistic attitude but is expressed for the same purpose in its social forms. Here again the secret meaning of the masochistic inclination is: "If you oust, humiliate or kill me—yet I will do what I want." I have pointed out already that the proof or the exhibition of this instinctual feature determines the essence of the masochistic demonstration. Prometheus, fettered, banished into Tartarus, still refuses to bow to the gods. I wonder how anybody, in the face of such inflexible though passively expressed will power, can speak of weakness, helplessness and the effort to renounce one's own personality. That seems to be like denying courage and decision to a martyr, who would rather burn than abjure his creed.*

The masochist is flexible. He cannot be broken from outside. He has an inexhaustible capacity for taking a beating and yet knows unconsciously he is not licked.

Why did we not sense that there is a blending of firmness with flexibility in the masochistic character? He is convinced against his will which means that he is of the same opinion still. This hidden combative energy of his character makes him as unmanageable and immalleable as a ton of iron ore.

There is a principle never to admit defeat. The masochist follows the opposite rule. He always admits defeat, but in reality he is undefeatable. His complete surrender has more power than

---

* Dr. Horney believes the common denominator of masochism is a feeling of one's own weakness expressing itself in a certain attitude toward oneself, others and destiny. The masochist thinks himself deprived of all will and all power, completely at the mercy of another. Dependence is for him a "life condition." He feels like a reed easily moved by every gust of wind. But many a reed that bows to the wind may resist the storm that uproots oaks. Certainly the trend toward weakness and dependence is there, but valid only for the conscious. Dr. Horney has permitted herself to be deceived by the external aspect of masochistic lamenations. The weakness is but an appearance and the dependence serves the purpose eventually to humiliate the protector and to rule the person on whom one depends. It is also true only as far as consciousness is concerned that the masochist "feels a helpless toy in the hands of fate, or that he feels doomed and cannot visualize any chance to take his fate into his own hand." Even while he complains about the power of destiny and recognizes *la forza del destino* as hostile to him, he unconsciously knows that he will remain victorious. Did Dr. Horney never hear the oriental adage, old as the hills, that the softest on earth will conquer the hardest on earth? We hear an echo of this wisdom in the sayings of Lao-tse, who lived 2500 years before our days:

> What is in the end to be shrunk,
> Must first be stretched,
> Whatever is to be weakened,
> Must begin by being made strong.
> What is to be overthrown,
> Must begin by being set up.
>
> .   .   .
>
> It is thus, that the soft overcomes the hard
> And the weak the strong.

wild rebellion. Because he does not resist he can endure a lot. His obedience kills the commands of his aggressors. His shameful and ridiculous acceptance of the authorities makes them impotent and his uncompromising acknowledgment of their power prepares for their overthrow.

It is obvious that the forbidden sexual satisfaction is the aim of such defiance in perverse masochism. The driving power, however, that leads to masochism is not solely of a sexual nature. It receives mighty support from the efforts of the ego to maintain itself against superior forces, to save its internal independence when it has to give up the external one.

This tendency toward rehabilitation springing from injured self-esteem will receive a still greater significance in social masochism. There it is concerned with the unconscious aim to enforce one's own will even at the risk of disgrace, failure, poverty. And it does not make any difference psychically whether the person of the opponent is still alive or has been dead for a long time. As in compulsory neurosis, the strong unconscious affects of defiance and rebellion remain attached even to persons who have left this world a long time ago. The late attainment of the instinctual aim must give such profound satisfaction—just as it does in the sexual sphere—that the masochist gladly submits to all sufferings and pain.

There is a Christian legend about the monk Basilius whom the Pope had excommunicated. After his death he was committed to the care of an angel who was to discover the place for the most terrible tortures for him. The monk, however, found something to praise even in hell, thus turning it into a kind of heaven. Discouraged, the angel returned, together with the prisoner, reporting that no fire could burn Basilius and that he had remained himself even in the most dreadful abyss of hell. The legend has it that the excommunication was withdrawn and Basilius admitted to heaven. The masochist resembles in his behavior this pious monk, stubborn in his mildness, who submitted to the punishment inflicted, thus proving its futility and reaching his secret goal by the detour of humility.

III

Sexes

FREUD SAYS OF masochism that it has an intimate relationship to femininity. The behavior of the male masochist certainly shows many features that justify this statement. The passivity within the sexual behavior is but the most conspicuous factor. There are others that are more important. The phantasies of the masochist circle around the topic of being sexually overpowered, of becoming impregnated. That may sound grotesque but analysis shows that anatomical inadequacy becomes an event in the phantasy of the masochist.

Other features, however, resist the assumption that the relation of masochism to femininity is as intensive as Freud believes. This relation is by no means as plain as with the passive homosexual. Passivity may not be easily separable from feminine sexuality, but the suffering of pain, being beaten or tied up, disgrace and humiliations, do not belong to the sexual aims of the normal woman. When such ideas appear conspicuously on the psychical surface and become conditions of sexual gratification we should call the woman concerned a masochist.

Even if one is inclined to presume that features of this kind are somehow included in the picture of feminine sexuality they do not dominate the scene as they do with the masochist. Nor does the preference for the anal zone as an erogenous center agree with the female conduct generally. Expressed in a different way: masochism, looked upon from a certain angle, may be the expression of a feminine inclination in a man, but the feminine conduct in itself is certainly not the expression of masochistic feelings.

Here again, as so often in the observation of masochistic phenomena, we are confronted with the impression of the para-doxical. The masochist who plays the female part in his phantasies and scenes seems at the same time to make fun of it by his distorted presentation. What he shows is less a picture of femininity than its parody or caricature. Such mockery is frequent with adolescents, where it may be used consciously. A patient remembered a similar attitude from his boyhood. He especially enjoyed pronouncing four words and accompanying them with particular gestures and movements of the body. It was the romantic sentence, "The dear, wild man!" He recognized the origin of this exclamation himself later on. It came from one of the books of his teen-age sister. In this book the words were spoken by a young girl who thinks tenderly of an absent man. While exclaiming them she turns away shyly with a blush. The boy had read this passage of the book; later he pantomimed the scene in front of the mirror, reiterating the sentence aloud and accompanying it with expressive corresponding gestures. He imagined the girl's skirt swinging when she turned.

So here is another mirror scene! Could we assert that the boy who later developed into a masochist betrayed femininity by his playful behavior? Surely not. We venture to guess at the original motive of his play. He must have wished that an attractive young girl would have behaved like that while thinking of him. We thus recognize a phantasy acted out in a two-role play. Later, only after something has been changed in his relations to girls, does the scene acquire the tinge of mockery. The phantasy that had originally betrayed something of the boy's desires later on became the expression of mocking impulses against girls of his sister's generation. His timidity in associating with the other sex makes it easily understandable that he ultimately assumed the attitude of the fox in the fable who refused the grapes he could not reach, saying they were too sour.

The behavior of the masochist shows a feminine character, but it does not reflect this character untarnished. Femininity is not so much represented as disfigured, not so much characterized as distorted.

Insight into the hidden primary significance of the mirror scene has brought us closer to the female element in masochism. But not yet close enough. Perhaps a comparison will serve us better: I once witnessed a rather plump, vivacious, bald-headed dancing master giving a lesson to a number of young ladies and gentlemen. After having taught the paces and figures of the new dance to his girl pupils he tried to perform the dance with each one of them. Of course, he led them. Occasionally, however, when one of the girls proved to be unusually awkward, he had to take over the female part in order to demonstrate the lady's carriage while dancing. He therefore intentionally copied the bearing, pace and behavior of his lady partner.

It was a peculiar sight indeed when the corpulent little dancing master stepped back, daintily seized the tails of his dress coat as if they were the train of an evening frock and began tripping gracefully forward. The man was deadly serious. He was obviously tired, yet he forced the stereotyped smile of the role to his face and he did his work literally in the sweat of his brow. How did it happen that his performance, against his will and certainly against his intention, made such an overwhelmingly funny impression on most of his spectators? To a great extent this effect was certainly due to the contrast of his appearance with that of a dancing girl. But after some repetitions of his performance you became serious, even sad. You guessed that necessity forced the man into his tragicomical role.

The process in masochistic phantasy must be approximately the reverse: the scene is primarily serious, springs from sexual need, carries all signs of frustration and privation and only later on assumes the note of mockery or parody. The boy's mirror scene and the dancing master's imitation of the dancing girls have one factor in common which makes them apt for comparison with masochistic phantasies and scenes: the original aim of their action. The nature of the performance is determined by the unequivocal wish to have the female object imitate the demonstrated actions. The youth longs for a girl who will bashfully confess her affection for him and the dancing master would like the girls to copy the paces and bearing he shows them.

To put it more directly: the masochist indicates to the woman by his feminine behavior in what position he wants to see her. Whatever he does represents a performance, a kind of enacted scene. The scene certainly seems to have the flavor of parody for us outsiders. I say "seems to have," because no psychoanalyst or psychologist has felt this element of parody so far. The actual situation is that a man portrays the sexual behavior of a woman. The essential point, however, as well in phantasy as in the perverse situation, is the fact that he plays for her. For it is in general a woman who witnesses his performance. The parts are exchanged. If the situation has a hidden meaning in relation to the woman at all then it can only lie in the intention of a performance or production, that is to say, in the reversal: what you do to me I want to do to you, or: I want to see you in this passive or suffering role.

As far as I know this sense of the masochistic scene and phantasy has not been realized so far. It agrees fully with the above-described process of reversal and demonstration. It has, however, a meaning that reaches far beyond that. The masochistic phantasy and practice is a sadistic one, expressed by reversal, represented by the contrary. I have described and proved this sufficiently as far as sexual masochism is concerned. Yet even where masochism is no longer a definitely sexual phenomenon but assumes a social character its nature remains essentially unchanged.

The assertion that masochism only shows its façade, that it is only an appearance, would be erroneous. One rather could state that it is the reflection of what goes on in the opposite direction on the inside. We arrive at an understanding of masochism only by applying a psychological method that corresponds to the repeated reversals within the psychic process. Borrowing an expression from Goethe,* I have termed this procedure in another book a "recurrent reflection." Contemplating the phenomena of social masochism from this angle, one recognizes there also the presentation of the effects of primary tendencies through reversals. Unrestricted submission expresses unconscious rebellion, yielding expresses obstinacy. Servility stands for defiance and self-humiliation for arrogance.

But how does this unconscious mocking or parodying character, which the masochistic phantasy or practice secretly but distinctly assumes, come about? This character springs from different sources. Here I just want to point out the historical side which is revealed to the analytic observer if only he observes long and attentively enough. This aspect does not explain everything but clarifies a good deal of the grotesque and burlesque features of some masochistic practices and ideas.

The masochistic scenes and phantasies are not only reversals of sadistic ideas but reanimations and reproductions of what children had imagined to be the sexual activities of adults. Unconsciously people regress to those infantile ideas of sexuality which once upon a time as boys they nourished with regard to the course of sexual relation. The grotesque mixture of truth and error springing from these infantile sexual theories reappears here in practice and theory. The infantile character, to which the grown-up man unconsciously clings, frequently betrays itself in details of such phantasies and actions. The important part played therein by the excrements, urine and feces, as well as the lack of reserve or disgust that has been built up as an educational barrier at a later date only, points in the same direction. Thus the element of parody originates from long-forgotten infantile

---

* Compare Reik, *Surprise and the Psychoanalyst,* Leiden, 1935. (English and American edition, 1937.) Goethe has taken the designation from the sphere of entoptics. The poet wrote with regard to some cryptic passages in his *Faust:* "Since we have many experiences that cannot be plainly expressed and communicated, I have long adopted the method of revealing the secret meaning to attentive readers by images that confront one another and are, so to speak, reflected in one another." It is obvious that this method of reciprocal elucidation has to undergo a far-reaching transformation in the field of psychology.

ideas, as, for instance, that the woman is treated cruelly by the man, that he urinates or defecates on her, and so forth.

In all these ideas, reversed as they appear in masochistic practice, there is a covibration of an aggressive and violent note. The woman appears as a subdued, suffering being, dependent on the man's will.

I want to test this conception by just one significant example. It concerns a patient whose sexual satisfaction consisted in being beaten on the buttocks in a certain position and wearing black trousers. The little boy had broken into his mother's bathing cabin in a health resort where she took mud-baths. He saw her in a moment when she, with her legs covered with mud, had bent forward to pick something from the floor. At the sight of his mother's back the child had felt the impulse to strike the part of her body turned toward him. That would amount to a sadistic action expressing an early aggressive and sensual impulse. In this idea he had identified with his father, who used to bestow the same little caress playfully upon the mother or the maid.

We are confronted with a definitely masculine attitude of the boy which later in the masochistic scene is completely reversed into a passive and feminine one. He now is going to play the feminine part and get himself beaten on the same part of the body. But does this express the meaning of the perverted scene plainly enough? No. It goes beyond that. He is going to play the role that, according to his wishes and ideas, the woman ought to play. He is going to enact it for her. Here then is the connection with femininity; the reversal becomes lucid. The primary character of the performance is an invitation to dance. The origin of the masochistic idea from childhood cannot be doubted any longer.

Is that the role the woman longs for herself? The answer is a definite "No"—yet, strange as this may sound, followed by a timid "Yes." That is to say: according to the reactions that the boy was able to observe with the women at home he was allowed to presume that the women were not totally averse to such rough handling. Or were they? The resistance they put up was often not too serious and accompanied by laughter and giggling. Even if we admit that this kind of caress was not too disagreeable to the women we must concede that the boy's imagination was by far exaggerated. He mistook an introduction for the whole thing. In his imagination the blow was the essential and really pleasurable element of the mysterious sexual procedure between the adults. After he had become masochistic later on the blow itself, applied under circumscribed conditions, sufficed to produce orgasm.

The erroneous supposition consists in the idea that the woman enjoys such a blow, that it is even sufficient for full gratification. This opinion, however, springs from the sadistic infantile conceptions and agrees with the child's own violent desires rather than with that of the woman. The female form of sexual satisfaction is not identical with being beaten, though there might exist several points of contact. The circular descent of this masochistic scene from the sadistic phantasy was proved during analysis when it was replaced later on by a crude sadistic one. The reversal was undone. When he now took his evening strolls through the streets he nourished the phantasy that he was a lust-murderer on the lookout for his female victims. When he now went for a walk with a girl he sometimes felt the impulse to change a tender movement into a brutal injuring one. He doubted, as he put his arms around her neck, whether he did not want to strangle her in reality.

The masochist has the hidden and unconscious idea that the woman would appreciate as pleasurable the treatment he submits to, that she would even long for it. The little bit of justification at the bottom of this idea is tremendously and grotesquely exaggerated. A woman does not want to be punished, abused, tormented or flagellated but wants to be loved. She may appreciate a certain amount of recklessness at the proper moment and of disregard for her scarcely serious resistance as evidence of masculine energy and as proof of the masculine will to possess her. The acceptable amount is limited however.

The psychological miscalculation of the masochist, if we are permitted so to call it, is the fact that he holds that the sexual gratification of woman is essentially enjoyment of suffering and disgrace. Here I refer to the patient who felt excited sexually at the sight of medieval pictures of martyrs and identified with them in his phantasies. He thought a picture of St. Laurentius on the grate was "not convincing" because the saint's face bore a calm, gentle expression instead of an ecstatic one in which pain mingled with most intense pleasure. If masochism is the expression of femininity, as Freud believes, it certainly is a distorted and caricatured one. As such, however, it has the meaning of a performance: "That's what I would like to do to a woman and she then would behave in such and such a manner." It is a plastic representation of a wish reversed. Which is the original wish? The same which is expressed in the sentence: treat them rough and make them like it.

I just want to hint here that the intermediate phase of development during which the individual plays the two-role play in this unconscious way is continued in developed masochism. The unconscious phantasy is so important for this instinctual satisfaction that reality as such is insufficient if not supported by phantasy. I should therefore like to state that the masochist clings in his phantasy to his masculine character in spite of his seemingly feminine behavior.

Another feature that is frequently played or represented—wherein the masochist is an animal, submissive to his mistress's will—favors this opinion. Frequently a thoroughbred horse is imagined on which the woman rides.

Goethe admirers will remember the poem "Lilly's Park," wherein the poet compares himself to a bear who is beaten by his lady love and who lies at her feet, "up to a certain point, of course." The poem concludes with the prayer to the gods to liberate him from his slavery and with the words: "Yet should you not send any help to me—not altogether in vain do I still stretch my limbs! I feel, I swear, I still have strength myself!" I believe that the contrast, emphasized in phantasy, between the masculine strength and fervor of which the masochist remains conscious, and his manifest submission and weakness, contributes considerably to his pleasure.

The unconscious relation to the man, that is covered up by the figure of the woman on the stage, must be denoted as another expression of femininity. In a previously cited case a patient found sexual satisfaction in being beaten on the behind by a woman. After some years in which the scene enacted was fully satisfactory, a disturbance arose which inhibited sexual excitement. For some reason he had turned around before the blow and had seen the woman, who had just raised her hand to strike him. Suddenly the magic of the scene had vanished. The woman wore a fur scarf around her shoulders. The sight of the fur around her cheeks and her chin had unconsciously reminded the patient of his father's beard. With the resurgence of this repressed image the course of sexual excitement was interrupted. It was the idea of the man which threatened to become conscious at the sight of the woman's fur scarf which put an end to the perversion. As long as it remains repressed the phantasy is important among the conditions of the masochistic gratification. Fur, known as an attribute of the perverted scene since Sacher-Masoch, the high boots, the whip or birch are revealing attributes. They are only lent to the woman, but belong to the outfit of the sadistic man, who remains backstage during the perverse scene. From this point of view it appears as a transmutation of the passive-homosexual phantasy: "I am used and beaten by my father." This transfer, comparable to a transposition from major to minor scale, is excluded from consciousness.

The entry of this idea is permitted if it is sufficiently disfigured, loosened from one's own person and made unrecognizable as to its meaning. A masochist, for instance, thinks that pictures representing female pupils of a boarding school who are beaten by their lady teacher on the naked buttocks are exceedingly exciting. This is a transfer to the other sex. The primary phantasy was turned about face, a revolution at an angle of one hundred and eighty degrees. He himself clings to the woman as the active person in his perversion and would refuse a phantasy of chastisement by a man.

But why and how does the man come into the masochistic scene at all? What does his appearance mean even though he remains in the darkness of the backstage? Let us assume the analytical view for the moment. The content of the original phantasy was: "I am loved and punished by my father." Then we go on to wonder why it is that neither the tenderness nor the love of the father or his female substitute shows up in the beating scene but only his severity and cruelty. The reply is: in the scene as well as in the phantasy the homosexual erotics coincide with the gratification of the unconscious guilt feelings.

To what do these guilt feelings refer? To the child's incestuous desires which we acknowledged as forbidden and to the hostile impulses which sprang from the rivalry with the other man, originally the father. The masochistic scene consequently would be the reaction against punishment and atonement for the instinctual impulses of the Oedipus situation. Thus the formulation, "I am loved and punished by my father," would add one more quasi reversal. It would be a late transformed substitute of a still older phantasy: "I want to possess the woman and to slay the rival." The sequence of the changes is a historical one, corresponding to different psychological strata.

This derivation of the feminine behavior of the masochist that corresponds to a tender-passive attitude toward the father is backed by Freud and his pupils. Its psychological foundation is unquestionable. Another problem, however, is that of the psychic evaluation of the different motivations. It is at this point that the other analysts and I part company.

The factor of the hidden homosexual inclination appears to me of less importance than the guilt feeling that demands satisfaction. To put it in another way: punishment achieved by the flight forward and relieving the masochist of his anxiety is more important for him than being loved. It is not so much tenderness but anxiety that makes him unconsciously offer himself as a homosexual object to the man. The grotesque idea, "I want to be loved by my father as a woman," is not only the expression of a feminine disposition but of its scornful parrying as well. If this is love for a man then it mocks itself and does not know how deeply it is mocking itself. "Was ever a man wooed in such a mould?" you would like to ask with Richard III. This strong resistance consequently corresponds to a struggle against the idea of being loved and chastised by the father.

The resistance turns up immediately when the idea concerned approaches consciousness, for instance, if, instead of phantasy figures, one's own person in distinct relation to another man steps into the foreground. At a certain point of the analysis the patient, whose sacrificial Aztec phantasies have been mentioned here so frequently, resisted with all his might the necessity of reporting certain ideas he had just associated in analysis. Urged repeatedly he said he would prefer being tortured or even killed by me to betraying what his phantasy just now had been. But he had to admit immediately that by this very attitude he had exposed the contents of his thoughts. In his phantasy he had compared the couch, on which he was lying during analysis, with the sacrificial altar, had seen himself as the prisoner put there as a victim and finally had compared me with the old bald-headed high priest who was to carry out the execution. What luxurious and superfluous delicacy of feeling to hide a phantasy which was so close!

There cannot be any doubt as to the existence and efficaciousness of the passive-homosexual idea in masochism—but much doubt as to its prevalent importance. It does not show up regularly nor is its importance always the same. One of the ideas produced by the patient just mentioned was this: strong young men are auctioned publicly in the market place in order to be sold to elderly women whom they have to serve sexually. These ladies, in need of love, pay considerable sums for the slaves to the state, a small amount of which is credited to the men themselves. These are the preconditions for the phantasy.

The phantasy itself sets in when in the house of a purchaser the new slave does not prove willing. If the erection is not sufficient for sexual intercourse the young man is whipped by the woman until the result conforms with her wishes. In such an example the reversals and disfigurements of the basic thought are obvious: the elderly ladies as mother substitutes, the ordering of sexual intercourse as reversal of the prohibition. It is quite as obvious that the punishment primarily threatened the erection and not its failure. No doubt it is the generation of fathers in the background who react with threats of punishment to incestuous impulses. So far our conception agrees with the one prevailing among analysts in this and similar examples; the homosexual-feminine attitude toward the fathers may hide behind the façade, but it is of no decisive importance.

With this we are back at the question of the psychic evaluation of this factor. The erotic attitude toward the man is of less importance than is the punishment threatening from his side. That means that the threatening vision of the father or his substitute interferes with the desire for the woman, disturbing this desire. Ultimately it is partly admitted, partly rejected in that peculiarly mixed figure of the woman with masculine attributes. Consequently, however, this father figure, though invisible, steps into the sphere of the masochistic scene, becomes a part of the puzzle picture, which therefore also conceals the question: Where is the man? The father who is expected to love is less important than the one who is expected to punish—to punish for the forbidden wish and, in anticipation, for the realization of this forbidden wish which became possible through this very punishment. For that is the masochist's worry: he wants to have the punishment "behind himself" (done with)—as a pervert who enjoyed being beaten on his behind expressed it. The punishment has to be executed so that one can attain the forbidden pleasure. With this I assigned a secondary, or a historically more recent, place to the satisfaction of unconscious guilt feeling. The main thing is not the punishment but the achievement of the instinctual aim. The punishment happens to be the only road leading there.

The psychological situation is a very complicated one and to simplify it would mean to cheat intellectually. In the confusion that threatens to get hold of us in this entangled situation, rendered hardly intelligible by displacements and reversals, there is a glimpse of light as if from a faraway lighthouse showing us the path. It is the essential contents of the masochistic phantasy and scene in which a woman beats or mortifies a man. Hence a kind of translation of the unconscious thought into the language of the conscious could start: "If I have to be beaten, humiliated, chastised, then at least by a woman." The idea of punishment is admitted, even welcomed, under the condition that the woman executes it, not the man. He remains excluded from the surface of conscious thought at least. Whenever he appears the sexual excitement vanishes.

The oft-mentioned patient had a cycle of phantasies in which beautiful virgins caressed a chained prisoner's genitals until the ejaculation reluctantly occurred. This "despite"-satisfaction was attained in the "synchronized" phantasy of masturbation. Once in the midst of the phantasy the idea turned up: "What if the caressing hand were a man's . . . !" The thought proved so disturbing that all excitement vanished. The relation to the woman is clung to, the old object is maintained. We could even discover the old desired aim appearing in reversal in the background. Certainly the beating woman substitutes for the father. She has taken charge of the executive power yet she remains the object of the desires for the sake of which so much suffering and humiliation are borne gladly and even enjoyed. Not suffering is the cherished thing but the subsequent sexual gratification. Punishment in the end not only brings about anticipated reaction to a forbidden action but brings back the pleasure too.

A similar attitude toward women is held by the masochistic character who does not practice the perversion. He is—and no one, it seems, has realized this so far—a hyperidealist or even a romanticist. Suffering is sweet for him not in itself but in anticipation of a premium. He enjoys suffering as Don Quixote enjoyed his defeats—for his lady's sake. In the most sublimated forms of masochistic character an abstract ideal takes the place of the desired woman. Thus Saint Francis gladly suffered for the sake of his beloved Lady Poverty.

A witty Viennese once said: "A man is young as long as a woman can make him either happy or unhappy. He is middle-aged if a woman can make him only happy. He becomes old if a woman can make him neither happy nor unhappy." Now apart from the question of age, into which category does the masochist fit? He is a man whom a woman can make happy only if she makes him unhappy.

After having considered, tested, and put all this in the balance, there yet remains a doubt. It could be suppressed for the sake of simplification and comprehensibility as well as of a more pleasant and elegant presentation. However, mental honesty is the analytical investigator's duty and glory. It forces us to resist the temptation of such intellectual chicanery. The doubt has the following content: viewed genetically, does not the oldest stratum of masochism as phantasy and action regress after all to the mother-child relationship as to a historical reality? That would correspond to an age that has not yet reached the Oedipus situation and in which education had still other tasks than to master incestuous impulses. In this time of infancy the mother actually was the unrestricted ruler who had to instill cleanliness, punctuality and obedience in the child and certainly sometimes threatened the child with punishment. Thus masochism would represent a late memorial of difficulties of adjustment to a reality that proved unpleasant to the child. The sequence of yielding and defiance, punishment and instinctual satisfaction then would be the echo of long-forgotten difficulties of the education by the mother. At that time she must certainly have been feared as the object from whom punishment and loss of love threatened.

Before our mind's eye appears a procession of cruel mother-goddesses of ancient cultures: the Hindu Kali with her many weapons; the Babylonian Ishtar, goddess of war, hunting and prostitution; the destructive Astarte of the Syrians; the Minoan mistress of the snakes, and many others, personifications of the

Beautiful and the Terrible. The female tormenter has the same irresistible charm of these idols for the masochist. She is the Lady Astarte of modern times.

This is perhaps the place for the long line of cruel, mythical figures of women, such as Salome, Brunhild, Turandot, who threatened to kill or behead the man and who are substitutes of the primal mother as seen in masochistic phantasy. The individual development could thus be a reflection of human prehistory. The discipline and severity of the father ruling the background of the masochistic scene is but a continuation of the mother's pedagogical power—just as the rulership of the father generation replaced the primary matriarchy. The Sphinx, which we have classified as the plastic representation of historic strata, would consequently be an originally female figure, the masculine parts having been added later on. Is Heine right with his assertion: "The figure of the real Sphinx is identical with that of the woman—and the addition of the clawed lion's body tomfoolery"?

Such an hypothesis would not be contradicted by the fact that the masochistic scene is of later origin and has suffered manifold disfigurements. It is always possible that the later formations regress to old patterns. To use a comparison: the domineering position of women in American social and cultural life can certainly be traced back to historical conditions. For instance, it was conditioned by the aftereffects of the pioneer period, when the energetic women frequently had to take care of the duties and the work of the men. That does not exclude the possibility that it may be as well a partial return to the social organization of primitive society.

If this hypothesis were right, there would certainly be some hostility and defiance against the woman expressed in masochism, a residue and echo of similar feelings of the child toward the woman that played such an overpowering role in his first years of life. But also, setting aside the question as to whether or not that hypothesis is right, we recognize features of resentment and mockery directed toward the woman in masochism. Still, the decisive impression is that the secret defiance, the unconscious sabotage, is directed mainly toward the man as the prohibiting authority.

This impression is even confirmed in the very cases in which aggressive and mocking impulses toward the woman become noticeable: by the different manner that is assumed toward the woman and toward the man. It is as if somebody threatened one person with his forefinger, the other with his fist.

2

The term feminine masochism was avoided in the preceding section and in its place we talked of masochism of the man. The feminine feature is, to be sure, one of the characters of masculine masochism, but only one of them. We came to know other and more essential ones. Freud himself has chosen the term "feminine masochism," as he says *"a potiori."* The designation would be irreproachable if one could distinguish also a masculine and a feminine masochism of the woman. Feminine masochism of the woman? Sounds like a pleonasm. It is comparable to an expression like, "the Negro has a dark skin." But the color of the skin is defined simply by the term Negro; a white Negro is no Negro. The comparison does not fit after all. Surely one can imagine a white Negro only as a freak of nature (but anthropology knows of such a group). We do indeed talk of the masculine character of many women.

The difficulty apparently lies only in the language, not in the matter. The psychical sex difference does not coincide with the anatomical. The fact of bisexuality of both sexes, now generally acknowledged by biology as well as by psychology, supplies explanations for many previously misunderstood phenomena. Therefore we had better avoid the term feminine masochism. If it should be used, it would have to be reserved for the perverted inclination of the man and to distinguish it from masochism of the woman.

Part of this "linguistic" scruple seems to be justified after all. Something in us resists the conception of masculine masochism as contrary to feminine masochism. The adjective does not fit the content of the phenomenon which is designated by the noun. Masochism as an instinctual aberration and as character seems to disagree with the idea of masculinity and to be more in harmony with the idea of the woman. Freud expressed the same opinion by saying masochism sustained an intimate relationship to femininity. There are of course in such situations various kinds of relationships, even one-sided ones. So there is the possibility that masochism contains a quality of femininity but women need not show any trace of masochism. In Freud's cautious but laconic remark nothing points to the fact that women as such feel masochistic.

His opinion had a peculiar consequence. Some analysts, and still more female analysts, came to the conclusion that masochism was a feature immanent in female sexuality and female psychic life. The patristic writer Tertullian first promulgated at the turn of the second century that the human soul has a natural inclination toward Christianity. Similarly in some analytic publications the woman is said to have an *anima naturaliter masochistica*. I am afraid this opinion is not better founded than that of the great Carthaginian religious champion. It is for instance expressed by S. Rado with a logic that wavers between sagacity and subtleness. Among the publications of female analysts, too, the opinion seems to prevail that the role attributed to woman by nature urges her to masochism. One gets almost the impression that a woman who does not incline to masochism is perverse, and must appear unwomanly. In the discussion it looks as if it were a prerogative of the woman to be masochistic; rather like a privilege than an aberration. The more subtle ear hears something like a challenge in this claim. It sounds less feminine than feministic.

S. Nacht has raised many good arguments against this conception. In addition, as it were, some weak ones are offered such as: if the woman is masochistic by nature, then she is not masochistic. That is to say: in this case it would not be a pathological reaction but a common natural phenomenon, a sort of a secondary sex characteristic. This argument would stand the test if masochism were only a pathological phenomenon. But this is the old and too narrow conception. Masochism is an instinctual inclination the possibility and reality of which is common to all human beings and does not become pathological before surpassing certain limits and assuming a nature that almost excludes all other instinctual directions.

In this argument about the nature of feminine masochism I should be inclined and convinced enough to attribute some right and some wrong to both parties. The relation between masochism and femininity, which Freud discusses, is not to be rejected. The question is: what is the nature of this relationship? The problem must be touched with the tips of the fingers, with the tips of the fingers of a psychologist and not those of a psychiatrist or sexologist.

Nacht states that the character of a masochistic woman does not differ clinically from that of a masochistic man. That is possible, although not very probable. What is not to be distinguished by a physician may still show differences for the psychologist. The microscope accomplishes a good deal in the laboratory. It would not be wise to demand that it should accomplish everything.

Nacht goes beyond the border of intellectual self-defense when he classifies masochism simply as a sexual perversion. Also he does not seem to realize that tradition and education in our cultural media favors a vague and mild masochism of the woman. We are unable to decide how far sociological factors influenced the psychological development. It is striking, however, that the social development in the United States favors a mild—and not even always mild—psychic sadism of the woman.

On the other hand one must admit that the biological conditioning of the feminine life (menstruation, defloration, childbirth) seems to promote the development of a masochistic inclination. These factors make it probable but they do not make it necessary. The woman can bear the passive and painful occasions of her life patiently. She need not enjoy them. Masochism is effective with the enjoyment of the passive situation. Passivity in regard to sexuality professes a condition of masochism but does not make up the whole of it. The typical masochist looks for discomfort, shame or disgrace. The woman will as a rule come to terms with these agonizing situations, or when they arise will even try to gain some pleasure from them. That does not mean that she feels masochistic: she does not strive for discomfort. It is extremely important that masochism as a perversion is rare among women while it certainly is the prevailing perversion among men. In this respect Nacht is right when he asserts that the woman is less masochistic than the man. The question remains whether the appearance of the manifest perversion is to be the sole measure for this judgment.

Nacht declines to mark something as normal with the woman that is considered perverse with the man. His discerning refusal of the assumption of a natural or biological inclination of the woman toward masochism is justified, but he puts himself in the wrong by neglecting sociological factors. A kiss among women is an utterance of love as among men, but nobody will take such a kiss as evidence of a prevalent homosexual inclination. It is the same action as performed by men, but it does not mean the same for the woman. If two persons do the same thing it need not have the same meaning psychologically.

Something that would be evaluated as masochistic when it occurs with men would not be considered as such with regard to women by society, although it belongs to the same category. The difference in evaluating instinct expressions of a subtle form calls our attention to the fact that labels like normal or perverse are valid only for the coarsest and most obvious utterances of instinctual life but are simply conventional on the whole. In a strictly puritanic milieu, for instance, I heard the desire of a girl to go to a dance called perverse in all seriousness.

If we look at masochism as a crude instinctual perversion then the question whether the woman is more or less masochistic than the man is quickly decided. In this sense the woman certainly is less masochistic. The aspect is changed when we approach the question starting from masochism as an instinctual inclination. In this case it will be more difficult to answer.

There is no doubt that the biological circumstances may favor an inclination to masochism with women. They need not, however, lead to this result. They could contribute to the fact that the woman utilizes certain psychic situations that might occur in a masochistic way. But there would still be a difference between this and looking for situations that are enjoyed as painful. Thus, one could say, the woman puts up less inner resistance against the masochistic emotion as a function in the role that nature has allotted to her.

There is further to be considered the fact that the education of the girl promotes a sort of mild masochism in two directions while the education of boys opposes it. The girl is called upon to accept the passive role and to suffer pain and wrong patiently. Her aggressive and violent impulses are more decidedly suppressed. The education of the girl is fashioned after a womanly tradition many thousand years old. There is a chance that even the judgment of many women analysts who accept masochism as the natural expression of womanly feeling stands under the shadow of this still effective tradition. Female masochism thus would be much more the product of education than is that of the man. The external and internal changes of puberty, the preparation for passivity and for other conditions of the female role, must be counted as psychical conditioning factors. The masochistic inclination of a girl is easier built into the life of a woman than that of a boy where it would be out of harmony with his adult behavior. In the texture of a woman's social attitude such a quiet inclination will not be conspicuous in any way, whereas it shows up like a flaw in the cloth of a man.

Are there differences between the masochistic behavior of men and women? We have heard that "clinically" none could be established. That of course does not mean that there are none. Compared with the masculine masochism that of women shows a somewhat attenuated, one could almost say anemic, character. It is more of a trespassing of the bourgeois border, of which one nevertheless remains aware, than an invasion into enemy terrain. The woman's masochistic phantasy very seldom reaches the pitch of savage lust, of ecstasy, as does that of the man. Even the orgy in the phantasy does not ascend in so steep a curve. There is nothing in it of the wildness of the chained Prometheus, rather something of Ganymede's submission. One does not feel anything of the cyclonelike character that is so often associated with masculine masochism, that blind unrestricted lust of self-destruction. The masochistic phantasy of woman has the character of yielding and surrender rather than that of the rush ahead, of the orgiastic cumulation, of the self-abandonment of man.

The explanation of this difference can be derived from two assumptions: from the difference in the libido apportionment of man and woman and from the difference in intensity of the sadistic impulse of both sexes. The libido, the sexual desire, is of masculine nature, even if inherent in a woman. As a rule it is distributed differently to both sexes: just as sexuality envelops and determines the whole life of the woman, although it is not of the active and tumultuous character of the man's, so the masochism of the woman is of a different kind. Its significance may be greater with regard to the space occupied, but it is less distinct and more vague than that of the man. It may be even farther extended in the psychical life of the woman, but for that reason has become less intense. The diffuse character of the female erotism in general determines also her masochistic inclination.

Our derivation of masochism has demonstrated that it has developed from the sadistic phantasy. Where there is no distinct and strong sadism no masochistic inclination can or will develop. As pointed out before, the education of the girl suppresses sadistic impulses earlier and more energetically than does the education of the boy. We meet here with a factor favoring masochism.

But how does it happen that in female masochism the ferocity and resoluteness, the aggressiveness and the vigor of the male masochism is missing? I believe personally that the anatomical situation does not permit the cultivation of a strong sadism within the woman. The prerequisite of the penis as the carrier of aggression is missing. We do not deny that there are sufficient sadistic impulses effective in the woman, but they do not attain the intensity and consistency of the male impulses. What we are saying seems to lead to the conclusion that physical conditions are coresponsible for the difference in masochism in both sexes. If sadism as an instinctual expression of aggression does not carry the same degree of strength with the woman as with the man, there is a chance that the reaction to it will also be markedly different.

I consider it as another sex differentiation that female masochism in its development does not deviate so far from its motherly soil as the masculine one. Even in its diffuse state it remains more intimately connected with sexuality than the man's. Women rarely prove so madly intent on lust, nor are they so prone to fanatic, absurd and useless self-sacrifice as men. If we have previously recognized masochism as demonstrating the absurdity of the principle of reality by exaggeration, we must admit that such a revolutionary urge—outrage in reverse—is more alien to women than to men who consequently often become stubborn, queer, peevish and querulous.

Female masochism in its sexual and social form seldom equals the masculine type. Women even here present the practical realism which often amazes us and which we sometimes admire. Yet even in the form of social masochism the woman will remain more intimately tied to erotic life than the man. Her capacity for self-sacrifice will less frequently aim at abstract, ideal, ego-alien goals than his. The history of religion has brought forward fewer female martyrs than male. This too proves the minor share of oppositional stubbornness and defiance in the nature of female masochism. The detachment from reality is hardly ever carried through with so much consistence or with such a trend into the wild-phantastic. In general men are much more idealistic and romantic than women. They feel a necessity to be heroes, active or passive. This is because they are ambitious while women in general are vain.

The contrast between urge of pleasure and prohibition hardly ever reaches such acuteness. The woman rarely feels such embittered, actually implacable antagonism to her environment and therefore will not develop as much scorn and defiance in her phantasies as does the male masochist. The Beethoven-like rebellion of the male masochistic phantasy is lacking in the female. The Promethean defiance is replaced by a milder, softer longing for suffering. The male urge for torture in its distinct forms reveals titanic traits; that of the woman is more inclined to endurance. She does not hold with that secret revolt against all earthly and heavenly powers which governs man's masochism.

We believe furthermore that the guilt feeling springing from aggression and the corresponding unconscious urge for punishment do not as a rule reach the same intensity with women as with men. The different development of the male and female superego, the representative of moral demands, pertinently described by H. Sachs, are likely to become decisive here. The flight forward, the escape from the conflict between pleasure and anxiety, is also demonstrable with the woman. It has not, however, the nature of a panic as with the man. It is more of a bending forward than a rush ahead. It is not to be denied that masochism in the form of enjoyment of passivity, of submission and suffering agrees better with the sexuality of the normal woman than with that of the man. Something in her abandonment and her devotion, in her enjoyment of the partner's strength and power combined with her own passivity, is closely related to masochistic feeling if not part of it. But it surely does not total up with the whole of masochism.

Disagreeing with former psychological observers we discovered that female masochism differs in intensity as well as in distribution and character from that of men. The common features are so conspicuous as to have made the differences escape attention hitherto. They exist nevertheless. The expression of the aggression against the ego can well differ and yet the result be the same. Is it not noteworthy and psychologically important that women prefer poison or drowning as a means to suicide whereas men choose the gun or the rope? From the point of view of Freud's hypothesis, too, it would be comprehensible if the struggle between death instinct and Eros were expressed differently with women and men, if their interplay were subject to another and different ratio of combination. The woman, being supposed to wrest a new life from the death instinct, also proves in masochism to be less exposed than her companion to its cruel destructive lust.

There are certainly other differences than those we have mentioned in the development of masochistic instinctual inclination with men and women. Up till now sufficient attention has not been bestowed upon them because they show up chiefly in the phantasies of both sexes. We get a closer approach to comprehension by comparing a female phantasy with the corresponding male one. Here is an example of such a female phantasy: an oriental commander in chief has conquered the daydreamer's home town. He is sitting in his sumptuous tent playing chess with his vizier. During the play the most beautiful women of the town, stark naked, are presented to him in a long row. Each time one of the naked women is brought to him, he raises his eyes from the board for a moment and nods silently if he wishes this or that woman to be reserved for him. In the next moment he concentrates his attention again on the game either by moving a figure or by contemplating his vizier's countermove.

It is unnecessary to stress the fact that the daydreamer is among the beauties who pass the sultan in order to be examined for a moment. The phantasy is exciting sexually. Its masochistic quality is not to be doubted, since the women appear naked by the sultan's order and he hardly wastes a glance on them. He considers the game of chess more important than the beauty of the women who are at the disposal of his pleasure. His behavior is still more insulting than that of Napoleon, who had Viennese girls brought into his bedroom in the castle of Schönbrunn, interrupted his state affairs for a minute, stepped into the room where the lady was waiting, shouted, *"Déshabillez-vous!"* and rushed back to his important files. The sultan's behavior in the phantasy is like an exaggeration of the Corsican general's behavior. In producing this phantasy the daydreamer used elements of the history of her native country, which repeatedly had been invaded by Turkish armies, as well as her personal memory of her father's passion for chess.

We attempt to imagine the same phantasy *mutatis mutandis* as originating from a man, as for instance: a queen of the Amazons has conquered a town and has the strongest young men presented to her in her tent, and so on. We do not change any of the essential features, except the sex of the daydreamer. The masochistic character of the daydreamer remains unchanged. The phantasy will be exciting for a masochistic man as well. I only have to recall the previously mentioned phantasy in which young slaves are sold in open markets to elderly ladies in need of sexual satisfaction in order to prove the probability of similar masochistic phantasies with men. But let us stick to the same phantasy. Are we able to prove differences in the sources of pleasure of men and women in the face of this phantasy?

Obviously both derive definite pleasure from the same ideas, the compulsory presentation, their own passivity, the contemptuous treatment. And yet, the quality of pleasure differs. That becomes evident if we examine details alternately with the eyes of the male and then the female daydreamer. The compulsory nudity of the men who are to appear before the queen of the Amazons and that of the women before the sultan is of different psychic significance and emotional value.

We mean that the phantasying woman will deduce a more intensive masochistic pleasure than the man due to the fact that this idea does injury to her chastity. The single feature that the Amazonian queen examines the men only superficially and becomes immediately absorbed in her game again is less pleasurable to the masochistic man than to the woman in the corresponding scene, when the sultan hardly pays any attention to her beauty. The trifling impression she makes by her exhibition, the humiliating treatment by the sultan, the fact that she as one among many, appears in the scene only as an object of sexual desire and not of personal affection, all those features that would be of minor psychic importance for the man become special sources of masochistic pleasure for the woman. Such a comparison clearly reflects the differences of sensitivity of both sexes. It seems that such subtle or fine differences elude the gifts of clinical observation. At least they did so till now.

It will certainly be humiliating also for a man to be used only as a sexual being, to be chosen, so to say, without appreciation of his personality. But for the woman it is an incomparably deeper insult. It may even occur that this single idea, isolated from others, will become the subject of masochistic phantasies for a woman. Whereas in the case of a male daydreamer it will not be without importance if the Amazonian queen pays but little attention to his appearance, yet this idea alone would not be enough to excite him sexually. The corresponding feature in the phantasy of the woman can carry the main stress of masochistic excitement.

In the imagination of that sophisticated patient humiliation as a sexual object played a definitely masochistic role even when the relation to her own person was not as distinct as in this case. So for instance she started telling me about peculiar customs of her native country on the day after she had produced the phantasy of the sultan. She reported some details in a way that left no doubt as to her unconscious masochistic pleasure in them. Thus she related that once during war games the general with his staff had come to a small provincial town. After having washed himself in his hotel and prepared for a walk he met a not too young woman at the entrance of the hotel who greeted him with a deep curtsy and said: "If you please, I am the town whore!"—

The patient, who vividly imitated the prostitute's gestures and mode of speaking, had not recognized the connection between this story and the phantasy she had produced the day before. Neither had she realized that her narration had been accompanied by a visible masochistic pleasure in self-humiliation. Proud women, who are hardly accessible to any approach, frequently incline toward this kind of phantasy, full of pleasurable sexual humiliation.

Perhaps it is not superfluous to mention that phantasies of this kind come forth in analysis only after decided resistance has been overcome. The patience of the analyst will have to cooperate with the moral courage of the patient, who has to overcome her own resistance and the obstacles of modesty and pride in the effort to produce such confessions. I remember only two women who were able to talk about such pleasurable humiliating phantasies with comparative ease. With one of them, a physician, this ability was not the result of her professional frankness toward her own sexual needs, as one would have been inclined to hope. It was conditioned by a blocking of affects, a divorcement of the contents and the associated feelings. This alone enabled her to talk about these phantasies as a reporter would about a local event. Since she held herself aloof from all emotions, the contents of her reports had become almost void of meaning and she was able to talk as unconcernedly as if she were talking of a third person.

The other patient had made so much headway in analysis as to be able to report even crude sexual phantasies. Yet whenever she did this an impetuous wrath against me, her listener, showed itself a few hours later. Then she was always bound to ask herself angrily: "Why have I got to talk about such intimate matters to a stranger?" And she felt violent indignation against herself and me. We can easily deduce from this that the analytic situation and the self-imposed psychological compulsion to tell everything are themselves used masochistically, in a secondary fashion, and are apt to become the nucleus of far-reaching phantasies.

It is evident that preparatory actions, displacements, allusions and paraphrases frequently replace actual sexuality in the phantasies of women, although coarsely sensual and cruel ideas are by no means lacking. For the woman more frequently than for the man, a trifling event or a tiny sign is sufficient to give rise to a pain-addict phantasy. In one case the hearing of a man's rough voice was sufficient to instigate such excitement. In another case the daydreamer at first visualized in her phantasy the frightened, wide-open eyes of a young girl, lying on the floor. Later she saw hands clamped into the girl's hair and ultimately quite dimly a female figure tearing the girl's hair. Not before masturbating did the daydreamer realize that she herself was the young girl of her phantasy. I am inclined to consider this hesitating admission of the essentials of the masochistic pictures to be a typical female feature. Corroboration of this peculiarity from another side, however, is lacking so far.

As far as I know only one difference of male and female masochistic phantasy has been pointed out by analysis. It concerns the sex of the object and does not refer to the phantasy life of adults but of masochistic children and adolescents. Freud was able to demonstrate this difference of the ideas of both sexes in the analytical interpretation of a typical phantasy whose subject was that a child is beaten. The phantasy develops in three phases, the last of which consists of the fact that one or several children are beaten, or chastised, in some way or other. This phantasy is accompanied by sexual excitement which as a rule is quieted by masturbation. The beating person in the phantasies of both sexes is always the father or his substitute. The persons who are beaten are always boys, even in the phantasies of girls. It is, however, unequivocal that the person who gets the beating substitutes for the phantasying one in the last phase. Such change of sex may be assisted in the phantasies of little girls by the fact that in reality boys are more often naughty than girls and more often get a hiding from their father.

It is indeed conspicuous that the scapegoat is always a "whipping boy" and never a "whipping girl." This typical infantile phantasy of a child being beaten is apt to be amplified and developed. Its essential features remain the same even if they assume the character of a novelette. By surveying such masochistic phantasies one is reminded of musical pieces of Mozart or

Beethoven with, for instance, the title, "Variations on a motif of . . ." A single musical theme is varied with melodic abundance wherein this motif distinctly stands out in one part, then seems to vanish among the profusion of accessories, then is just hinted at by the accompanying voices and suddenly shows up again in a new transformation.

Here is an example of a phantasy of this nature of a girl of preadolescent age: she sees herself as a cabin boy who has behaved awkwardly in her duties or has faultily executed an order. The captain is angry and orders that she, or rather the cabin boy, be tied to the mast for punishment. There she has to stand for many hours and feel the ropes biting into her flesh. During this phantasy her sexual excitement increases. I may add, for the analytical elucidation of the phantasy, that her father was a shipowner who frequently took along the daydreamer's brothers on his cruises, but never the little girl. The girl's boy-phantasy almost seems to be a parallel to the feminine role of the masochistic man. The differences, however, are obvious: in the girl's phantasy the chastised person is a boy, the sex seems to be changed. Whereas the boy keeps to his masculine role in the masochistic phantasy.

Whenever a woman develops a form of social masochism, the nexus of her erotic life is less likely to be given up than by a man. Female masochism is less apt to be desexualized. The woman as well as the man is capable of harming herself in phantasy and in life with unconscious intention and secret pleasure, but voluntary renunciation of home and husband and motherhood is bound to be the damage felt most intensely. The sexual origin in her social masochism remains marked and the threads connecting it with sexual life do not seem to be severed suddenly. As pointed out above, the woman's conscience rarely attains the overseverity of the man's and rarely drives her into destroying herself and her life to such an extent as the masochistic man.

We said previously that this difference presumably springs from the fact that the woman has no need to fight such violent and overintensive aggression within herself, the defense against which only leads to such far-reaching reactions. The nature of the female development, which is gliding and not abrupt, guards her against falling a prey to such vast antagonistic impulses directed against the ego. The submersion of the Oedipus constellation does not happen in such a cataclysmic way with the little girl as with the boy. Accordingly the superego, which as the internal moral tribunal has entered into the picture of the inherited Oedipus situation, will not assume the same rigor as with boys.

Even the self-destructive form of female masochism is expressed by sexual self-humiliation. I was impressed by a case of this kind: a young woman had had an incredible number of lovers during a few years by all of whom she was invariably treated in the same offensive manner and finally deserted. The superficial impression of a nymphomaniac inclination soon was corrected by insight into a strong mother fixation. Her sexual life was guided by a painful and defiant protest against her mother who once had disappointed her. The mother had time and again without foundation suspected the young girl of intimate relationship with the young men she had met socially. Finally the daughter reacted to these constant insulting suspicions and to the baseless reproaches by putting into effect the slogan: "If I have the name I shall have the game."

Psychically refined women are bound to connect a feeling of degradation with a hurried, unscrupulous surrender which was scarcely preceded by courting and did not spring from personal sympathy. And they are right, for experience shows that men do not appreciate women whom they come to possess easily. Frequently this feeling of being degraded and debased by such a behavior becomes the subject of extended phantasies. Some women are astonished that such ideas, which they experience in their consciousness as very much embarrassing, are apt to arouse intense feelings of pleasure against their will. Like the sexual masochism of men, that of women definitely shows the character of punishment, which, however, lacks an active note.

In one case which I observed a young woman remained frigid if her husband treated her gently. If, however, he behaved brutally during sexual intercourse, and hurt her, for instance by seizing her by her throat, she attained orgasm. Here surely a definite masochistic inclination is to be ascertained, but the passive role of the woman and the aggressive one of the man sometimes mask similar tendencies. Probably a certain, individually varying measure of masochism has inconspicuously entered into the woman's psychic life as punishment for the originally forbidden sexual gratification. It is sometimes difficult to recognize, for it is as indistinguishable from the rest of the sexual life of woman as are tiny flaws in their skillful embroideries.

Refined observation certainly will find other differentiated features in the masochistic inclination of women and men. We stand here at the start of new investigations. I only want to point out one more conspicuous conformity that we would not have expected. The first impression, that a masochistic woman in her phantasies always expects a man to inflict pain and punishment on her, soon disappears. That he generally stands in the foreground does not mean that he was the domineering person from the very beginning. That role was the mother's or her substitute's who later frequently shows up as companion, spectator or in another episodic part.

One of my patients had a phantasy which dealt chiefly with the beheading of some aristocratic ladies during the French Revolution. The phantasy had turned up shortly after she had seen a picture of this kind. The way the women were treated by the brutal executioner excited her intensively, but she could not achieve orgasm by this idea alone. Finally the phantasy inserted in front of the figure of the brutal fellow that of a female spectator of the execution, one of the *tisseuses,* a white-haired witch, who derided and tormented the sentenced women. Only this idea produced gratification.

The same daydreamer once imagined herself sold to a brothel. The woman who solicits the men, forces the girl to surrender to them, torments and abuses her, was discovered to be the mother's substitute. In other cases the tormenting active person was a combined figure of substitute images of father and mother. It can well happen during analysis that this combined figure dissolves into two persons. A woman had for years only known phantasies in which she was subjected to humiliating treatment by men. In the course of analysis this picture changed: she or the passive figure substituting for her was ill-treated simultaneously or successively by a man and by an elderly full-bosomed woman. Ultimately the phantasy retained only the woman, who was equipped with a small penis similar to the one the daydreamer, as a little girl, had seen on a cousin of her own age. In the end only the woman was the sadistic person.

In the transition period she was masked by the figure of a man. For instance, the patient once saw in her phantasy the big hand of a man moving into her genitals and tearing out pieces of flesh. Immediately behind it, however, there appeared the image of her mother whom she, as a little girl, had watched in the kitchen disemboweling poultry. Obviously the earlier and determinating stratum showed up as the later one in phantasy.

The following example, originating from the same patient, can prove how far the masochistic phantasy can go on its way back to infantile ideas: she watched her mother at supper moving the laden fork to her mouth. This reminded her of a book of travels she had recently read containing a description of an Australian cannibalistic tribe who had devoured a white missionary. She wondered which parts of her mother's body the cannibals—provided they could get hold of her—would prefer: the hips, the thighs or the breasts. Actually that represents an extremely sadistic phantasy. However, she continues watching her mother, the old face, the wrinkled features. "Mother really is rather inanimate," she thinks. Later, before falling asleep, she resumes the thread: "Yes, mother is only interested in food. That was obvious today in the manner she greedily moved her fork to her wide-open mouth. All other sentiments are extinguished in her. She does not feel either love or sympathy for her people. She could eat up her own family as cannibals do."

One can watch in this case the originally sadistic phantasy leading up in a gliding transition to the masochistic idea of being devoured by the mother. The fact of this idea turning up in a general and potential form is noteworthy. It does not say: "Mother devours me," but: "Mother would be ready to devour her own family." This generalized form naturally proves the effect of the psychic refusal of the original representation. At this place the chain of thoughts is interrupted. An unequivocal symptom for the masochistic nature of this phantasy is the accompanying sexual excitement.

The phantasy goes back to infantile anxieties, the same that have left their traces in our fairy tales. There children are frequently in danger of being devoured by evil giants, witches, magicians, who are easily recognizable as substitute figures for the parents. The bad mother-figure, such as the witch in *Hänsel und Gretel,* is contrasted with the good one. It may be worth mentioning besides that cannibalistic phantasies that are felt as masochistic sometimes appear more unconcealed with men. One of these, for instance, turned up following a report describing how some shipwrecked sailors and a cabin boy for many days were adrift on the ocean, tormented by hunger. In the phantasy the sailors eventually decided to kill and eat the boy. The daydreamer identifies with the cabin boy, who was informed of this decision, he experiences his anxiety, and so on. The increasing excitement drove him to masturbation.

From which original psychic stratum does the female masochistic phantasy generally spring? The examples given seem to indicate that it cannot be the period of the fully developed Oedipus situation. The man in the phantasy serves as a dummy, behind which the original figure of the mother is concealed. Let me give you an example of such a bipartite phantasy showing this connection: a mature woman imagines herself sitting on the lap of a man who orders her to discharge urine or feces. Then the situation changes. The active person becomes indistinct: is it a man or a woman?—But now this person orders her to hold back urine or excrements. Both ideas are pleasurable.

In the first case one could think of the pleasure of degradation, of the compulsion to overcome the inhibitions of shame. But the second case is different. The contents of this idea are based in an age in which the Oedipus situation was not yet developed and in which the physical and psychic difficulties of the little girl were connected only with her mother. The primary masochistic phantasies of the female child have the mother for an object. The man appears on the scene only later. Referring to the origin of masochism one could say: he was too late. The phantasy dealing with him is a second, totally revised issue of an original edition, the center figure of which was the mother.

Here then is the unexpected common feature in the phantasies of both sexes. It starts from ideas connected with the infant's education, with nursing, cleanliness and mastering of the sphincter, and which gather around the mother as the active figure. The later development is different for both sexes. The boy consciously clings to the sex of the first object. The active person is and remains a woman. Corresponding to the changes that are due to the Oedipus situation the girl later on alters the sex of the active person in her phantasies. Now the man takes the position that previously was the mother's.

The dominating figure, however, from whom in those early times came pleasure, suffering and pleasurable discomfort, keeps in the background and can be visualized as through a transparent curtain. Thus the impulses toward development of masochism, which emanated from her care, nursing and education during the first years, remain operative. The development, manifold though it might present itself later, yet sprang originally from the desire for gratification from her and by her.

IV

Victory Through Defeat

WHAT IS THE secret meaning of the masochistic attitude, what
does it hide and what betray? We have searched for this
meaning and believe we find it everywhere. When we were children we used to play a game: one boy had to leave the room
while the others hid some small object. In his search for it this
boy was guided by certain clues from the other children. When
he moved away from the hiding place they shouted: "Cold, cold!"
When he approached it again they called out: "Smoke!" and then
"Hot!" "Hotter!" and "Fire!" when he was about to touch it.

We proceeded in a similar manner in our search for the hidden meaning of the masochistic inclination. We have set out on
a search confident of our power of observation, of our finder's
luck. We have come close upon what we were looking for. We
can almost hear them calling "Smoke!" We are prepared to see
the flame which burned secretly, hidden by the ashes of masochism. Instead of the many items in the room through which we
hunted as children we were confronted with the manifold appearances of this instinctual inclination. The features common to all
the formations of masochism served us as small treacherous signals guiding the search. Their detection has been most useful
to us.

We started from the impression of the paradoxical conveyed by
the phenomena of masochism. This instinct did not strike us,
as it did so many other observers, as absurd or as nonsensical—
but as contradictory. Our final theory confirms this first vague
impression. The paradox, the defiance, the secret rebellion are
not accessory elements of masochism. They not only crop up on
its surface but they constitute its basis and essence.

We began to sense this when we contrasted our conception of the nature of masochism with the existing theories. An intimate connection between this instinct and its counterpart, sadism, had always been assumed. We took a different view of this connection both as to its nature and its genesis. Sadism is preserved in masochism not only as an identification with the active person. Masochism is not merely sadism turned against the ego. It is still sadism directed against the partner but turned upside down. It has been disguised by presentation through the reversal and it rages at the ego as the second best and the nearest object. Its native soil is not the sadistic action but the phantasy. Thither it returns in its final and its most spiritualized phase.

One of the most striking features of masochism, the reversal of all pleasure values, has proved to be fictitious. The masochist aims at the same pleasure we all do but he arrives at it by another road, by a detour. Intimidated by threatening anxiety, inhibited by the idea of punishment and later by unconscious guilt feeling, he found his particular way of avoiding anxiety and gaining pleasure. He submits voluntarily to punishment, suffering and humiliations and thus has defiantly purchased the right to enjoy the gratification denied before.

Avoidance of castration anxiety cannot have the significance that was ascribed to it up till now. This psychological condition would cause the formation of a passive-feminine character, not of a masochistic one. His tough and stubborn attitude, his insistence on punishment, his latent rebellion do not go very well together with the humility and the passivity with which the masochist is usually identified. Neither can the satisfaction of guilt feelings be considered the most important criterion of masochism; it is merely the indispensable prerequisite for the realization of his instinctual aims.

What we are looking for is the common denominator contained in all the features brought to light. It would have to include the cooperation of lust and anxiety, to single out the place of defiance and rebellion in the entire picture, to connote both the nearer goal of sexual and aggressive gratification and the more distant goal of the enforcement of one's own will, and of the rehabilitation of the ego. There is no doubt that the sexual factor is prevalent in the perversion, nor has it altogether vanished in the social masochistic configuration. Disguised aggression, imperiousness and ambition appear in the limelight, but there still exists in the background the erotic affinity to the man as model and rival. Sexual and egotistical needs are satisfied with varying intensity in all forms of masochism. Dread of external punishment or of the pangs of conscience is mastered in every case by the flight forward.

I am looking for a psychological formula to summarize pertinently all these essential features without neglecting any of them. This formulation ought to indicate the aim of masochism and the road toward this aim. It has to be valid both for the sexual and the social development, it has to include the crudely sensual and the spiritualized manifestations and to characterize the nucleus of the sexual perversion and of the general attitude of the life we call masochistic. This, of course, is a pretty big task, too big, I know, for complete solution. I hope to draw near it by summing up the essence and the aim of masochism by the three words: *Victory Through Defeat.*

In masochism the principle of spite, the character of *quand même,* has found an instinctual expression. The sexual and aggressive impulses have temporarily given in to the prohibitive and punishing forces and by this detour have forced their way to their gratification. Pushed away from their road to the pleasure aim by superior powers, they have arrived at their goal by the road forced on them. Masochism has perpetuated its own pyschological genesis in the sequence of punishment and gratification, by mockingly reversing these essential psychological elements. The masochist does not accept punishment and humiliation, he anticipates them. He not only demonstrates their impotence to withhold the forbidden pleasure but he affirms and demonstrates that it was they which helped him to it.

By taking the place of the authority and chastising himself he suspends it. By punishing and disgracing himself he transforms punishment into an enticement. By clinging to discomfort, by insisting on pain and abasement, he spitefully demonstrates that all inhibitive measures of education and culture are condemned to failure since he only pretends submission but never really submits in spirit. He shows the absurdity of all endeavors to force him to renounce gratification by making punishment the condition of gratification. By attaining satisfaction not only in spite of suffering but through suffering he ingeniously changes the Via Dolorosa into a triumphal road. In the same way the road to Golgotha became the road to eternal salvation.

The masochist, too, loses all battles except the last. He knows —at least in the anticipating phantasy—that the prize beckons after he has experienced all defeats. He lets his opponent, sadism, taste all the pleasure of the hour—he even joins in the feast— but he patiently waits for the moment to bring the great turn. He tells himself in anticipation that one more such victory and the enemy will be defeated. Masochism is sadism in retreat, but with the inner expectancy of the ultimate push forward. It is characterized by unconscious defiance in defeat and by the secret foretaste and foreknowledge of coming conquest.

This secret feeling of superiority draws its power from a phantasy that denies the laws of time and that keeps extending the suspense. If not in his lifetime, the masochistic character will assert himself after his death and gain the rights denied to him on this earth. Posterity will judge him better and will take revenge on his enemies. The sexual masochist is willing to pay for transient pleasure with discomfort and pain, with torture, even with his life. The masochistic character has expanded his sufferings to cover his whole life. He faithfully believes that misery, humiliation, disgrace will be made up for by what is to come afterward. Foreseeing future appreciation and sure of the praise of posterity, he enjoys divine raptures. On a higher level, to be sure, but connected with him in some dark corner of the soul, the martyr feels like the masochistic pervert: a moment spent in paradise is adequately paid for by death. Both are moti-

vated in the last instance by the pleasure aim. All other phenomena, among which is the appeasement of the guilt feeling,
are nothing but an inevitable interim phase. The martyr and
even the saint, anticipating in their tortures and sacrifices the
impending ascent into paradise, look at them as a sort of
imaginary advance on the coming eternal happiness.

Such an anticipation of future success or happiness is not
limited to the individual. The Hebrews had dreamed the mass-
dream of the Messiah, the Savior, of national resurrection, before Christendom took it up and enlarged it. The idea of resurrection and the expectation of salvation made it easy for the
medieval Christian to endure earthly suffering. The Church
gave him the promise of eternal bliss in exchange. Even Adam's
guilt and the original sin were revaluated into a guarantee of
heaven. *Felix culpa* says the hymn. Nations as well as individuals enjoy satisfaction amidst abuses and offense and look
forward to the reward at the end of all suffering: they who
suffer so much now will be among the chosen, are superior to
others and have a mission the world is bound to appreciate
sooner or later. The triumph to come, as conceived by the individual masochist, is turned into the anticipated triumph of a
nation or of a religious national or social group.

The aspect gradually changes with the decline of religion as
a social factor. Instead of the Kingdom of Heaven an improved
earthly future for mankind is the aim of the struggle, and for
its sake all present suffering is willingly endured. The prospect
of being gathered to one's forefathers and of sharing the heavenly
bliss with them is replaced by the hope of a better future for the
coming generation on earth, for our children's country. The suspense factor has altered only its aims and not its nature in mass-
masochism. It has prolonged the delay from a moment to a lifetime, from minutes to eternities. "The traces of mine earthly
being cannot in aeons perish—they are there!"—thus Faust anticipates gratification in the ages to come.

The shift of stress from the energy of sexual and aggressive
will power to the capacity for suffering testifies to the still exist-

ing defiance in masochism. The increase of this defiance becomes manifest in the transformation of suffering into pleasure, the scope of which extends from sexual orgasm to the ecstasy of religion or art.

A young man's daydream assumed an increasingly masochistic character by the accumulation of retarding and obstructing elements which had gradually entered into it. The patient had developed a passion for the theater and wanted to become an actor. His father refused his consent. The young man imagined he would leave his father's house and go abroad without a penny in order to become an actor. Finally he would grow famous under an assumed name. His father would visit a theater many years later, would witness his success. Later on re-presentations (the Dutch language has the more plastic expression, *denkbeelden*) of his misery, hunger and humiliation on his path to imaginary success were emphasized and the road grew longer and longer. The scenes of bitter need and privations in this period were depicted in detail and almost with relish, while the success was postponed. When the daydreamer ultimately arrived at this stage the success had grown into a triumph and the father was all the more mortified.

In a similar way nations, religious or national groups, postpone the victory of the idea they embody; and they rest assured of this final victory in spite of the severity of their present afflictions. Just as in sexual masochism the mounting pain announces the arrival of the pleasurable discharge, in collective suffering the deepest distress and oppression becomes signals of imminent redemption and triumph. The power which, in the sense of Schopenhauer, is effective in "the focus of the will" is replaced here by ardent ambition and longing for the glorification of the ego. Just as in individual masochism the shame of being blamed is deeply felt, in social masochism it is the humiliation and the abasement of a nation or a religion. In both cases the last will be the first according to the anticipating imagination. Ignominy and abuse will be turned into fame and honor. The jeering remark, "How odd of God to choose the Jews," is opposed by the Jews' imperturbable faith in being God's elect, based on the very suffering of two thousand years.

Both in the lives of individuals and of communities masochism represents an unavoidable transitory phase from the development of unmastered sadistic instincts to their conquest and domestication in the service of culture. As a first step to its recognition it appears in defiant and rebellious shape, facing superior forces and enforcing its will by a detour. It undoubtedly constitutes a cultural step ahead when the masochist, faced with the necessity to choose, prefers to be hit rather than to hit. In its pathological distortions and in its exuberance it endangers the progress of civilization because it imposes needless sacrifices and too great psychic burdens on the ego and on communities. From a biological necessity suffering grows into a psychic luxury. Time, to be sure, heals all wounds. Those, however, which we inflict on ourselves are the most difficult to heal. We were able to study the masochistic instinctual inclination in its function of promoting culture as well as of obstructing it.

All the different and frequently discordant tunes we heard in masochism finally united in a full and sonorous accord: to uphold oneself despite all force, and where this is not possible to perish in spite of all force.

That is the grim tragicomedy of the martyr attitude of modern man or at least of its essential characters. Here is a tale of human frailty and sorrow which is at the same time a tale of human force and lust.

My task was to give this side of the phenomena, demonstrating at the same time that some of the theories now considered true are wrong. I do not doubt that future research will find other characteristic features of the complicated nature of the human craving for suffering. Research will perhaps come to even more astonishing psychological conclusions and continue to destroy wrong views taken for granted. Truth is stranger than scientific fiction.

The Unmarried

The Chip on the Shoulder

WHY IS IT THAT the problem of bachelors and spinsters does not exist among primitive and half-civilized peoples? And why is it that we do not read about a surplus of unmarried women in China and Japan? And why did not the question arise in medieval culture; why was it not discussed two hundred, yes, even a hundred years ago?

The change in economic conditions in the Western World is certainly a prime factor, but there is more to it than the industrial evolution. Something in the nature of marriage as an institution and as an expression of human relations must have changed.

Marriage is not what it used to be. To modern man nothing about the whole problem is more obvious than the statement: marriage is a private affair. Every man and every woman who comes of age is free to decide whether to marry or not and whom to marry and whom not. This was not always the situation, which is different even today in other culture patterns.

In no primitive society is marriage a private affair; it is the business of the family or the group. Not only does the clan or the tribe have to agree to the marriage, it makes the decision; it decrees it. That two individuals of opposite sex should enter marriage on their own initiative would be considered very shocking, probably worse.

The Australian aborigines* would call a woman who runs away with a man to marry him little better than a prostitute. The Hidatsa Indians use a bad name to describe marriages made with-

* The material for the following anthropological sketch is taken mainly from Robert Briffault's interesting work, *The Mothers*, 3 vols., Macmillan, 1937.

out an agreement between the families. The Haidas look upon marriages which have not been arranged by the parents while their children were infants as highly irregular. A West African Negro declared in a court of law that, "a man was a bastard because his parents married for love." To the Malays of the Pataui States such a marriage is not legal. Thus in all primitive societies throughout time.

The conviction that marriage is a family matter, not an affair between two individuals or the proper culmination of romantic love, has been shared by many civilized cultures. Roman marriage was in its essence a family contract, and in ancient Athens, according to the classical scholar and archeologist, Karl Otfried Müller, "we have not a single instance of a man having loved a free-born woman, and marrying her from affection." The modern conception that any individual can marry whom and when he will was altogether alien to the Greeks.

In France, until quite recent times, marriages were arranged by parents, often before the girl had met the selected young man. Marriage was an *affaire de famille*. Among the aristocratic families of Italy marriages were considered a matter of pure business and attended to by the two families. Many a bride and bridegroom met for the first time on their wedding day. Similar customs were prevalent in Spain, Portugal, Russia and other European countries, and not only in aristocratic circles but among all classes of people. The same is still common in much of China, Japan and India, where even infants may be betrothed.

In such societies marriage was not, as with us, a problem of sentiment but of economics and expediency. Women were not chosen because they were beautiful, ardent, young or refined but because they could work hard and were healthy, industrious and able to bear children or add to family riches, social standing or political power. Mutual attraction was irrelevant; only practical considerations counted.

Old maids are almost unknown among primitive and half-civilized societies. Sexual relations are separated from the problem of marriage; they belong to another realm. Since very few repressions before marriage are recognized by uncultured peoples, the question of love has nothing to do with the selection of a partner. Love in our sense does not exist even in the married life of primitive tribes. Man and wife often live separately and do not eat together. Women are not competitive with regard to their beauty and charm. They are much less feminine than our women; they are not educated to attract men by their appearance but by their abilities as worker, housekeeper, cook and mother.

Love is a comparatively recent element in the relations of the sexes and was unknown as long as wives were valued only as workers and not as sexual objects. On the lower levels of human evolution women are considered different from one another only in their economically useful skills.

With the entrance of the agricultural and, even more, of the industrial age, woman's value as a worker decreased. With the change in the economic situation the position of women was radically altered and with it the character of marriage. While their relative economic value diminished women's sexual value increased.

Along with this change in women's status men became more discriminating and chose their marriage partners on account of personal attraction. With the improvement in the economic situation time and opportunity were given to cultivate the female arts of fascination.

The progress of civilization manifests itself also in an increasing differentiation among the members of the sex. The one woman is now preferred to the other. Romance brought into modern society all the passions which are children of the imagination, the magic which refines the crude sexual desires of men. This new factor, love, became the most important one in the choice of a mate.

Romantic feeling, personal preference, without which mankind lived reasonably happily for many hundred thousand years, has made men and women now unreasonably happy and unhappy. Among our young girls—and more so among our young men—love is almost the only criterion used to determine the choice of a mate and, of course, often enough it decides whether an individual in our society remains single or marries—and whom he marries, if he does.

We have cast a retrospective glance at the institution of marriage in order to show how radically wedlock has changed its character. Radical changes have, of course, their good as well as their bad sides. A new code of values cannot gain victory without discarding old values. I once heard Freud say (it was in the last years of his life and he was in a resigned mood) that, in his opinion, there are only two values left in our modern civilization—money and the beauty of women. We think that the brave new world of postwar society will prove him wrong, but it is human nature that our view of the future almost invariably goes in the direction of our wishes and hopes.

At last we arrive at our own, the psychological, era, and at one of its most interesting manifestations: the attraction of the sexes.

It need not be stressed that this attraction is in its original nature biological, that men and women follow the dictates of an organic need of the sexual urge. This is so obvious that modern psychology, especially psychoanalysis, did not interpret the new phenomenon of love—which entered human evolution so late—otherwise than as a derivative of older and primary needs. Freud declared that love is sexuality in origin and nature, sexuality which is inhibited in its aim of physical satisfaction. New insight into psychoanalysis proved Freud's view erroneous and evolved a different concept of romantic love.

It took its point of departure not from love in blossomtime but from its prephases. It inquired into the nature of the soil in which this precious and quickly fading flower grows. Here is a hasty sketch of the development of romance, more fully described in Part One of this volume.

Before the individual meets his love object certain psychological moods make him (or her) ready to fall in love. The most important of these is an inner, mostly unconscious dissatisfaction with himself, a concealed self-dislike which is frequently displaced and expresses itself in discontent with his family, job and environment. The roots of these moods reach deeply into the underground of his intimate history.

Each of us has in his childhood and early adolescence painted a picture of himself as he wished to be. We call this wishful image the ego-ideal. Each of us has also a vague, unconscious idea of what he really is and is endowed with a critical sense which measures permanently the distance between this actual self and the ego-ideal. It is obvious that the ideal image takes many traits from models—from parents, teachers, other persons whom we would like to be like. If we had the combined attributes—the attractive appearance, the cleverness, the brilliant endowments —of these admired persons, we would be satisfied. As we realize unconsciously that we are full of shortcomings and failures we nourish a kind of dissatisfaction with ourselves which moves us to search for this ego-ideal outside ourselves. We yearn for a better self.

Thus psychologically prepared, we find a person who seems to have all of the excellent qualities we sadly lack and who is, in contrast to ourselves, apparently self-sufficient and self-satisfied. The sexual urge shows the road when this person is of the other sex. The man sees in her the ego-ideal personified, envies her and even hates her (here is the psychologically important unconscious hate component in romance) and finally yields to her overpowering attraction by falling in love.

Dissatisfaction with oneself has given way to an exultant feeling because the love object has taken the place of the ego-ideal which seems to be fulfilled in the beloved and which is realized in making the other person part of oneself. The deeper this self-dislike was the stronger will be the passion which the love object arouses. It can be quite independent of the beloved's real qualities and charm. Falling in love in a romantic sense has thus the character of a rescue which brings the person endangered by increasing discontent into emotional safety, like the swimmer who, in danger of being drowned, wins the shore by a new effort.

The depression which threatens the individual can have many causes and can reach the depth of melancholy, as in the case of young Romeo, whose self-confidence is badly shattered by his disappointment with Rosalind. He falls in love with Juliet on the rebound. It is the unconscious recurrence of this deep melancholy and self-hate that brings the passion of the couple to its fatal end.

Romance is an attempt to rescue the ego, dissatisfied with itself; but there is no guarantee that the attempt will succeed. It often fails, either because the choice of the mate is unfortunate or because the ego is too weak to become secure in the love of another person.

Envy, hostility, possessiveness and the will to conquer have not disappeared during the period of romance. They are only submerged and reappear sometimes in a surprising manner.

There are many factors in the evolution of romance which determine its outcome. Romance would not be possible if we were entirely self-satisfied. On the other hand romantic love becomes impossible if the ego is too weak, so that it distrusts itself to such an extent that it does not dare to search for happiness.

To regain one's self-esteem and self-respect to some extent is necessary; otherwise one cannot love. He or she who considers himself or herself not worthy of being loved will not be able to love. Only the man who likes himself again in a way or values himself at least to some extent can give love to another person. Long before psychoanalysis Nietzsche wrote: "We must fear him who hates himself because we shall be victims of his revenge. Thus we must see to it that we seduce him toward loving himself."

Everyday experience teaches us that women often succeed in curing these self-haters in such a way that they can love again.

The ability to attract the other sex depends to a great extent on self-confidence because it appeals to the other person who feels discontented with himself. In this sense I cannot but admire the psychological insight of a young girl who during psychoanalysis uttered the following remarkable sentence: "When I am badly dressed I hate everybody."

Another patient said, "A girl who has psoriasis cannot love." It was quite obvious that she meant: when a girl is affected by this skin disease she anticipates that men will not be attracted to her and she does not dare to hope against hope that the unimaginable will happen.

"I am not enough of a person to fall in love," said a third patient. "I am licked before I start."

You have to live with yourself at least reasonably well before you are able to live with a mate. There must be a certain self-esteem before you can expect that other people will value you highly. A woman is often in danger of depending entirely upon the opinion of the man with whom she is in love. I know a girl who in her engagement period had an intense feeling of self-hate whenever her fiancé made a critical remark to her. "I am so tied up with him," she said, "that he is the measure of my security and of my worth. When he is not satisfied with me I utterly dislike myself." Nobody should be dependent to such an extent upon another's opinion of him.

Men take women according to their self-evaluation. A woman who does not consider herself worthwhile is not worth a man's while. You can only accept love when you are sure you have something to give. Women are unconsciously aware of this. They know that they do not appear attractive when they do not like themselves—and it needs courage to be oneself.

On the other hand the feeling of being loved increases a woman's self-esteem. She does not need a man because she wants someone to love but because she needs to be needed, wants to be loved. "She must be secretly engaged," said one girl of another, "because she is so sure of herself."

Girls know that the beloved man represents their own ego-ideal by proxy. "I hate him," I heard one say of her young man, "because I am not important in his life." A young woman who was not very satisfied with her own sex fell in love. "When I

am around him," she said, "I lose every desire to be a man because he is every ounce the man I would have liked to be."
Women want to be proud of their men because they represent
for them an extension of their own personality.

The choice of a mate is thus an expression of unconscious
self-evaluation. Strange to say, overvaluation of oneself leads to
the same mistakes as does a low opinion of oneself because opposite extremes can replace each other in our unconscious thinking. One woman refuses a suitor because she thinks that Prince
Charming on a white horse will come to marry her. She has a
weak ego and needs too much reassurance in the person of a
husband. "If I cannot be anything special I want at least a man
who is something admirable," said one of these women with a
concealed self-seeking character. On the other hand, women
often reject a man because they think they cannot live up to
the man's idea or ideal of them.

That the choice of the mate depends upon evaluation of oneself may even become conscious. The other day a girl had one
of those sudden insights into her own psychical processes which
frequently occur during psychoanalysis. "When I am high,"
she said, "I want to marry the Duke of Windsor or Clark Gable.
When I feel low I would choose an illiterate immigrant from the
East Side or a bum. When I am in the right mood I want a
decent, healthy guy who cares for me and has a good job as well
as a good character."

Not all women are as sincere as this girl. Many play hide-and-
seek with themselves. In two succeeding analytical sessions I
heard quite different women express their dislike of the idea of
marriage itself. The first, a girl of twenty-three, said that every
woman has to lower her demands for worthy qualities in a husband so much that it becomes intolerable. She finished her tirade
against the other sex with the words: "Jingle, jingle, I am glad
that I am single." The second patient, a woman of thirty-seven,
who has had some unhappy love experiences, could not stand the
idea of being dependent on a man's will. She came to the con-

clusion that she was not made to be a doormat for a man and announced her conclusion thus: "No wedding bells for me. I am glad that I am free."

It is not for the psychoanalyst to evaluate the quality of folk-poetry quoted by the two ladies but he may judge whether the sentiment expressed in them is genuine. These verses illustrated the nature of the consolation mechanism which we all use when we are frustrated. The two patients want what every woman wants: a house, a husband, children.

Nature undoes all pretenses. There is no hiding place.

The foregoing declares the themes of our *symphonia romantica.*

There appeared at first a simple and primitive tune, that of marriage among uncultured and ancient societies, with some variations which prepare for the changes to come. This crude theme yielded slowly to a gentler one which became in its development sweet and tender—the theme of romance. For a time they went together until a new tune unfolded, expanded and displayed all its potentialities. Dissonances appeared from another source and fought with the dominant theme, were drowned out and recurred. They are undercurrents and are not easily resolved because they represent discord within the ego, within the person himself or herself. The main theme of our composition has its point of departure here; it is really a motif of frustration.

We said romance was born out of the spirit of self-dissatisfaction and is an emotional attempt to overcome this self-damaging tendency. The rescue effort is made by other forces within the person, the same forces which offer self-preservation and give courage. The ego which cannot find realization of high demands in itself searches for their fullfillment in another person who now becomes the personification of one's ideal.

Only he who is dissatisfied with himself can fall in romantic love which gives him, alas, a fleeting feeling of exuberant security. Only he who dares to fight his self-discontent and self-dislike can fall in love. A modicum of self-confidence must remain to strive, or romance cannot develop. Only the brave can struggle to love.

2

More than thirty-five years of psychoanalytic practice and comparative observation in Europe and America have given me the impression that women in general have a lower opinion of their sex than men have of theirs. This difference cannot have its origin in biological divergences but must reflect the evaluation of social environment. No analyst who has listened with the third ear to women talking sincerely and unconventionally about their own sex will deny that their opinion of females is surprisingly low. It seems rather a prejudice than an opinion, and one attributes it to inferiority feelings taken over from men's conceit or to feelings of inadequacy born out of competition with men.

The French philosopher Chamfort wrote more than two hundred years ago: "However bad the things a man may think about women, there is no woman who does not think worse of them than he." Madame de Staël once said: "I am glad that I am not a man because I should be obliged to marry a woman." Such contempt for one's own sex is very rare among men.

If women themselves feel sorry for men because the poor darlings have to marry women, what do they expect men to feel? Although men may agree wholeheartedly and frequently with Madame de Staël's opinion, fortunately they do so only in a theoretical or general way. Neither an abstract contempt for women nor making fun of their weaknesses has ever prevented a man from marrying a particular member of the sex.

We frequently hear women in psychoanalysis, where they dare to express their real opinions, say: "Why should a man marry? Why should he work hard to support us and tie himself for life? If I were a man I would never marry. I would have many affairs and live a marvelous life."

The warning, "Never underestimate the power of women," is directed to men. But as a matter of psychological fact, it should rather be said—and repeated again and again—to women themselves.

But women have resigned. They are not aware of their power; sighing, "It's a man's world," they forget to add, "ruled by the hand that rocks the cradle."

This deflated opinion of themselves as a sex and as individuals comes often to surprising expression. In an analytical session I heard a girl say about her fiancé, with whom she had visited a technical exhibition the day before: "Charles is so nice to me. He answered my questions as if they were really important and not just silly, woman's questions."

I know, of course, as well as the next man (and sometimes better than the next man on account of my profession) that this feeling of female inadequacy is carefully concealed by most women and often overcompensated by pride. But pride is necessary only when one is very vulnerable and the combination of pride and sensitiveness is itself revealing.

It cannot be denied that the modern woman has a chip on her beautiful shoulder, precisely because she is a woman. I am of the opinion that it is not an adornment but rather a stigma, a badge of insecurity.

It is characteristic enough that the ideals of boys from ten years on are almost always men while the ideals of girls are not women but also men. Eighteen out of a hundred college girls state that they would rather be men than women. More than forty years ago a scholarly educator came to the conclusion that unless there is a change of trend, we shall in time have a female sex without a female character.* The trend has not changed; on the contrary, the identification of women with men has made progress and the turning point is not in sight.

Modern women's deflated idea about their own sex leads not only to their overappreciation of the male as a sex but, some-

* Quoted by G. Stanley Hall, *Adolescence,* Vol. II, p. 619.

times, by a strange detour, to contempt of the particular male
who appears as a suitor.

It is as if he cannot be worth much if he considers a woman
so highly. Such an attitude can be frequently observed in a
type of women which psychoanalysis calls masochistic characters. Their attitude reminds one, to a degree, of an anecdote
which was told in old Vienna. A man used to play chess with
another in a café where the game was sometimes interrupted
by heated arguments. During one of them the man abused his
opponent with the cry, "Look, what kind of a guy can you be
when you sit down and play chess with a guy like me?"

Not to be satisfied with one's own sex—that is the tragedy of
many young women, the more tragic because the situation cannot be changed! "Anatomy is destiny," said Freud in a variation
of a sentence by Napoleon. Paradoxically, a low opinion of their
sex combines in many women with contempt for the male sex
while it does not exclude the conscious wish to be a man. The
paradox exists in spite of the fact that there is no other alternative.

A cultured and mature woman whom I was analyzing never
tired in her efforts to prove to me how worthless men are. She
ended every report of their inferiority with, "Are men people?"
This question, repeated like the refrain of a song, sounded as
if there could not be any possibility of her ever being tied to a
member of so contemptible a sex. Yet the lady had had several
affairs and at last got married. If you cannot get what you want
(in this case it would have to be a superman) you want what
you get (in this case quite a decent man). The patient was, by
the way, often aware of her wish to be a man herself, a wish
she traced back to her rivalry with her brothers in childhood.
"I am fed up with being a neuter," she complained.

The chip on the shoulder is subject to fashion. Often it is
worn in such a way that it is not visible. Hostility against men
is such a concealed chip. The question becomes not whether you
like this man or that man but whether you like "men." A keen

observer published recently an article with the title "American Women Don't Like Men." Much of what the writer, a highly cultured European woman who has lived many years in this country, had to say about her sisters can be confirmed by the psychoanalyst—with reservations, of course. Not only is the dislike of men often enough only a play for the gallery of a male or female audience, it is not a belief but rather a make-believe. Sometimes it seems to be the use of an old trick to attract—to seduce men to act as Petruchio in *The Taming of the Shrew.* But, alas, the bait is often thrown in vain. The supply of women who do like men, and say so, is almost unlimited.

Where hostility against the male appears to be genuine it is the psychological expression of unconscious self-dislike and, even, self-hate.

Hatred of men is an expression of inferiority feeling in women. It is the result of a displacement of self-dislike by dislike of the other sex. The old theme reappears here in a new and defiant variation. "I am tired of waiting until some man comes along who convinces me by his love that I am not an inferior being," one of my patients declared. Such a protest against the "unfairness" of waiting and of women's general role in our culture pattern is often expressed: "Why should I sit and wait until a boy comes around to court me?"

Manifestations of dislike of men do not help, however. Men are vain and the old advice, "When you want to be loved, love," is still good. Take my lady with the refrain, *Are men people?* "You know, it is not important to be a glamour girl," she confided after she became engaged. "There is a secret about men. You get them only when you show them that you like them."

I am not sure whether it can be interpreted as a symptom of her emotional improvement that she added thoughtfully, "With them, it is no good. Without them, it is worse."

Another badge of women's insecurity is the excessive emphasis on appearance, the exaggeration of the value of good looks, of dress, of adornment, in our culture pattern. It would seem as if, in the mind of women, beauty is the only attraction which appeals to men and as if charm, kindness, grace, intuition and delicacy of feeling were of no avail. Women are admired for beauty, it is true, but rarely married for it. How often we see that men prefer girls with other qualities than their conspicuously beautiful sisters. *Cinderella* is more than a fairy tale. Psychoanalysts hear strange expressions of the exaggerated evaluation of beauty and of self-abasement because many women consider themselves not beautiful and are overaware of certain physical shortcomings which appear to them as fatal.

"I cannot go skating because I have fat ankles," said a patient.

Another girl had a nice time with a young man with whom she spent an evening. She became suddenly cool and abrupt with him when she anticipated that she would say good night soon and turn away; then he would see that she had not beautiful legs. "You can afford to wear a swimming suit," said a girl to a friend, "but I cannot go to the beach with my figure." Another girl came to the conclusion that she must break her engagement because when she scrutinized her naked body in the mirror she became convinced that, "if he sees me like that he will have no desire to live with me."

"You know," said a girl who was quite attractive, though not slim, "what happens when you are fat? You do not go out to a dance but stay home and pretend to yourself and to others that you do not care about dancing." The feeling of frustration which such a woman feels is often pathetic and hard for men to understand.

Conspicuous beauty is a curse. The most beautiful women do not arouse on the third day the same admiration as on the first; it seems that their beauty prevents, in some way or other, the process of crystallization which Stendhal considered essential in the development of romantic love. In *De l'Amour,* writing about especially beautiful women, he said: "The more generally one is admired the more fleeting is the admiration." Women who are not beautiful but have the attraction called "charm" make an impression which is not as intense, perhaps, but more profound and longer lasting. It is not enough that a woman cast a strong spell on a man; the spell has also to continue in its effect and to increase in intensity.

Women's task in the field of love is, in reality, twofold: to get men and to keep them. The woman who succeeds only in the first task has failed, whether she admits it to herself or not. The old saying cannot be turned around; it is not true that "only the fair deserve the brave."

Many a woman is ridden by a superstition that it is wrong to show a man she cares for him. There is an unconscious or conscious fear that as soon as men are shown affection they desert. But extreme restraint causes many women to lose their naturalness and spontaneity with men. The fear that the man will not stay with her when she dares to be herself haunts too many mistaken girls. He would, she thinks, wake up as from a dream and find out that she is mediocre, dull, insignificant. He would realize "how stupid and small I really am." He would, she thinks, lose respect for her because he would recognize that she has nothing special to offer—and go off in search of a more attractive girl.

"I can only be perfectly natural with men if there is no danger that I may fall in love with them," said a young woman. As soon as she began to feel romantic about a man she was sure he would lose all interest in her. Another girl used shrewd self-control in order not to give away the secret that she cared for one of her admirers. "To let him know even in a subtle way," she explained, "means to stick my neck out, and he would leave me."

The wise girl knows better. I saw her in a cartoon the other day. Two girls observe another girl meeting a young man. The caption says, "I am sure he's in love with her. She calls him up every day."

The theme, *I have nothing to offer,* returns in all kinds of variations as an expression of emotional inadequacy. In this self-doubt the whole anxiety about the future comes to the surface:

(1) *He deserves a better person to make him happy.*
(2) *I cannot live up to his expectations of me.*

(3) *When I am always around him he will quickly tire of me.*
(4) *What can I mean to a man like him?*
(5) *He will soon find out that I am a phony and there is nothing to me besides this sparkle.*

This fear of being found out later on—or found wanting—is experienced by many women, but an assumed front of over-confidence and self-assurance is a poor cover for a frail ego, a *cache-misère* as the French say. The fear concerns almost all qualities, physical and mental, and prevents women from being themselves in the company of men whom they want to attract. Often such a woman gets panicky when she becomes aware of her real or imaginary shortcomings. She thinks, then, that her social charm is a miserable substitute for real warmth, her conversation shallow, her personality superficial and insignificant. She fears that the man will laugh at her or lose interest when he discovers she is "a failure as a woman."

"I am not pretty and I am not intelligent. I am afraid to talk about serious matters with him because I would expose myself and he would find out that I am an impostor. A false front is the best I can put up." There is the hope that the man will love her not on account of herself but in spite of herself. She feels that she is not good enough for him and she ends her pathetic confession with the words, "I have no redeeming feature to my name." Such self-abasement of course makes a defense necessary.

The will to fail, especially in their relations with men—to destroy their own chances and to become frustrated—is evident in many women in our civilization.

Here is not the place to demonstrate what psychoanalytic research reveals about the origin and the characteristic features of this emotional attitude, how its motives have to be searched for in the life history of the individual, and how the combination and cooperation of many emotional factors lead to the typical result of masochism. It belongs, however, to our theme to describe a few of the masochistic mechanisms some women use when faced with the possibility of marriage.

We have already discussed the leading role which self-doubt, self-criticism and self-dislike play in the development of unconscious self-defeat. All these features are sometimes conscious but they usually (as far as their existence and emotional effects go) remain hidden to the person herself; they operate secretly in the individual. Psychoanalytical experience shows us that we can penetrate to their realm by working backward from their effects to the subterranean emotional motives.

One of the familiar mechanisms of masochistic self-doubt in a woman is its displacement to the man, as before mentioned. Not only are his qualities devaluated. She begins to doubt her love for him. She questions whether she can be happy with the man who wants to marry her. She criticizes his manners and character, finds fault with him in other ways and asks herself whether she really cares for him. Often enough, haunted by uncertainty about the genuine character of her own affection, she begins to test it and subjects the man to subtle mental torture. She withdraws suddenly and seems possessed with all kinds of scruples and hesitations. Of course, there are many cases in which doubt regarding the man is justified, but every experienced psychoanalyst can spot an excessive doubt.

In one of my cases the unconscious projection became especially clear. A young girl began suddenly to question whether the man to whom she was engaged would be too old for her, whether she would be bored, whether she could remain faithful to him, whether he could compete with other men, and so on and on and on. In a short time, while we analyzed the nature of these doubts, they changed their direction: she began now to ask herself whether she was not too immature for the man, whether she had enough interesting things to say to him, whether he would not prefer other girls to her later on. She used to sing to him a popular song, "Don't Fence Me In," and, in conversation, to use that title as a catch phrase. She was afraid he would endanger her independence.

Analysis revealed that this girl was justifiably afraid of her own possessiveness, of tendencies in herself to restrict the free decisions and movements of the man.

It is easy to dismiss doubts that come and go like clouds in the sky on a serene summer day. But they can become so serious that they endanger the relation with the man and lead finally to defeat and frustration. This effect speaks loudly for the power of masochistic trends of unconscious character in women.

A special mechanism in cases of this kind is that of the "flight forward." The person who is very afraid of a danger which she wants to avoid becomes so frantic that she does just what she is most afraid to do. Let me describe a representative case. A young and charming girl described to me how all her relations with young men led to the same unfortunate result: her suitors left her. There were many of them, of different character and various positions in life, but the outcome of her love affairs was always the same. When the man felt attracted to her and wooed her she slowly responded and began to feel inclined to him. The relation became more cordial and the man declared his love. After some hesitation she became engaged to him.

Then, always, some unexpected thing happened; either she got into a furious argument with him about a trifle or she found out that he had had a love relation with a friend of hers some years ago or he neglected her in not calling on her daily or she had to make a trip which seemed to estrange him from her or whatnot. Something or other invariably happened so that she would break her engagement suddenly. It was never the man who wanted to leave her. She herself managed the breakup, but she made the man responsible.

It became clear that what happened was the result of her own unconscious doing and undoing. As soon as marriage "threatened," she made unconsciously every effort to frustrate herself. As long as being married—having a home, a husband and children—remained in the realm of daydreams she enjoyed the prospect. When these aims approached realization dark powers within herself forced her to do something which would make fulfillment impossible.

During the early portion of her psychoanalysis she did not want to acknowledge that she herself was the stage manager who arranged her own destiny behind the conscious scene. The impression psychoanalysts get in cases of this kind, from the reports of past experiences and actual events during psychoanalysis, is that the person acts under compulsion. The fact that the same experiences recur against all wishes of the individual, repeat themselves as if some outside power determined their course, justifies the name which Freud gave to the described phenomenon —*compulsion of repetition.* He asserted that most persons are forced to repeat the same experience when they act under the dictation of unconscious tendencies. It is as if they were under the command of a totalitarian regime.

Another case shows how strong this compulsion can become and that it often determines even the form of the flight forward. The patient lost her mother when she was a child and was brought up in a puritanical way under the supervision of an aunt who, it seems, did not like her ward very much. After reaching puberty the girl became very fat because of an endocrine disturbance. Boys avoided her. She was not invited to dances and on the rare occasions that she went alone she remained a wallflower. Convinced that she was not attractive, she tried to get the attention of young men by being bold, using tough language and by taking the initiative generally. This attitude was, of course, intensified by the absence of a mother who could have taught the girl feminine ways and by her dislike of her severe aunt. The girl learned to keep her secrets and led a double life.

When my Lady Jekyll and Mistress Hyde, now almost twenty-six years old, came into my consultation room the first time I saw a rather attractive woman who seemed very sure of herself. By means of severe diet and certain drugs she had gained a slim figure. But her failure with men repeated itself in a very characteristic manner. Whenever she made the acquaintance of a decent young man she soon tried all means to win him and mostly took the initiative.

The outcome was always the same. The man got tired of her,

after having conquered her easily, and deserted her. She cried often, and for long hours was full of the best intentions, but yielded again to her mysterious stimulus. She had had two abortions and quite understood that she had made herself "cheap" with men.

It became clear that she acted under an unconscious compulsion—the need to convince herself that she was attractive and could be liked and loved by men. Her apparent overconfidence and aggressiveness was too thin a veil to conceal her feelings of inadequacy, her grief that she had not been carefully educated and reared and that she had no social graces. I was often surprised by the excellent qualities which she showed during psychoanalysis—her fine feelings and human kindness. Nevertheless, it was very difficult to overcome her unconscious inferiority feeling, to bring her so far that she no longer made advances to men.

In time she regained, happily, her self-confidence and self-respect and the "diamond in the rough," as her friends called her, became slowly polished in spite of or just by the process of unavoidable suffering, of feelings of remorse and shame.

I could go on with many another case in which the chip· on the shoulder determined failure and frustration in the lives of women whose conscious wishes were directed to happiness in marriage. Feelings of inadequacy, especially of an unconscious nature, play a big role in the frustration of many a woman's desire to find a mate. Similar feelings are of course present in many men, but there they show a different character and their importance is not the same as in the life of woman.

My modest task here was to throw light upon the figure of the "Lady in the Dark." There are more such ladies than we think, even among the women who shine in society and are considered glamour girls. They all wear the invisible badge of this secret society, the chip on the shoulder.

If mankind shall not perish—if the interest of society is to be served—this wasteland of human relations has to be changed into cultivated ground, producing young couples who can face the dawn of a new day.

II

The Marriage Shyness of the Male

MANY YEARS AGO a patient who was considering matrimony showed me a cartoon picturing a small boy with his father at the zoo. The caption gave the dialogue between them. The boy asks: "Daddy, do asses marry?" The father answers: "*Only* asses marry."

In the previous chapter I discussed the unconscious inadequacy feelings of women and their importance to the problem of marriage.

It is not difficult to discover inadequacy feelings in men, but where is their connection with marriage?

There is nothing similar to those doubts which a girl has as to whether she will be able to "hold" her man in later years, whether she has enough to offer him, whether she will appear desirable and attractive to him later on. There are doubts about marriage in men but they are of another kind. Men, too, have their insecurities but they do not concern their own personal shortcomings and feelings. Something else is conspicuous: there is a certain reluctance in the face of the idea of marriage itself, a resistance which every man has to overcome before he says, "I do."

Arrived at this point, I remember the characteristic traits of many cases in which this reluctance appeared clearly enough when men faced the possibility of marrying. I remember the last time when I had heard a patient talk about his engagement to a charming girl and about what marriage might mean to him and contrasted it with what a woman in the same situation had said.

Doubts about the future were expressed in both cases but the difference was obvious. The girl had complained about herself, had said that she had no personality, that she did not know what to say when in company, that she knew so little, and so forth. The man had expressed doubts not about his personal qualities but about his financial situation, about the possibility of supporting a family and finally about his willingness to take over all the obligations a man has to face when he is married. He ended with: "I cannot imagine that Anne will be the last woman I shall sleep with. It is an impossible idea."

The essential part of the question I had missed is the fact that men are by their nature marriage-shy. The problem with them is not so much whether they should marry this girl or that girl but whether they should marry at all. And if the woman were a combination of the Venus of Milo and Helen of Troy—to be or not to be married, that is the question.

It must be significant that women and men have a different attitude toward marriage, and this difference must be based not only on sociological but also on psychological factors. If we could understand this divergence, we could add material to the comparison of the psychology of the sexes. It is obvious that many psychologists and sociologists make a serious mistake when they start their investigations about the problem of marriage with the inquiry into the situation of married couples.

What young men and women hope and fear when they think of marriage will to a great extent decide the destiny of their union. Two persons who vote to stay together until death do them part have formed certain ideas, nursed certain daydreams, pictured the state of matrimony in their thoughts. What becomes of a marriage is not independent of these expectations or of fulfillments and frustrations of these visions of the future.

It cannot be denied that the outlook on this future is different in women and men. Before discussing the other aspects of the problem this one has to be dealt with in the light of the comparative psychology of the sexes. I am well aware that such an approach is one-sided but I do not see that one-sidedness is detrimental so long as one knows that there are other sides to a problem while one observes only one of them.

There is one side of the marriage problem which most psychologists skirt as if it were too dangerous to uncover. This problem has to be faced. More than that, it has to be first stated. The thought of marriage is natural for a woman; she takes to it as a duck to water; but there is something alien in the idea of marriage to men. Men are marriage-shy. Imagine that drakes are at first water-shy; then you have the full analogy.

Logan Clendening gives the male viewpoint in his book, *The Human Body.** Man, says this physician, "is expressly made to roam over the earth impregnating as many females as he possibly can." It is "simply silly" to pretend that this is not the case or to try to control this desire by moral admonitions. The one thing that can control the male is common sense of the female, the sense "to lead him to the altar or to the Justice Court, the sense her old mothers fashioned for her to bind him with hoops of steel."

Man will bow his neck to matrimony only if there is no other way out, and "he wonders all the rest of his life why he did." Clendening emphasizes that the average man lies, coaxes, fawns in order to make woman give in to him, that he promises to love her forever to have his way. After it is accomplished, "he is alertly ready for the next candidate, and to remind him of the means he used to accomplish it or to call him names for using them is as unworldly as to rebuke the flowers for blooming or the bees for visiting them." Here is the biological truth, plainly spoken.

Let's see what Bernard Shaw has to say on the subject. Tanner, in *Man and Superman,* asserts it is "a woman's business to get married as soon as possible and a man's to keep unmarried as long as he can." Marriage is for this bachelor "apostasy, profanation of the sanctuary of my soul, violation of my manhood, sale of my birthright, shameful surrender, ignominious capitulation, acceptance of defeat." A married man is to him a man with a past while a bachelor is a man with a future. When Anne reminds him that he need not marry if he does not want to, he answers, "Does

* Second edition, p. 274, New York, 1931.

any man want to be hanged? Yet men let themselves be hanged without a struggle for life, though they could at least give the chaplain a black eye. We do the world's will, not our own."

Shaw believes that a mysterious Life Force, operating irresistibly, pulls man into this mantrap. Nothing of such a biological necessity can be discovered by science. The sexual drive is certainly not tied to marriage. Marriage is an institution which civilization imposed upon men, a result of the organic evolution of mankind under the influence of certain cultural factors.

Many attempts have been made to trace marriage back to the lowest and most primitive forms of human society and to conceive of it as the result of a monogamous drive in the male. The famous anthropologist, Dr. Edward Westermarck, went so far as to place the origin of marriage in the gorilla, which some travelers described as monogamous. More trustworthy observers report that the monogamous tendencies of gorillas do not exist in the beasts but in the phantasy of men with preconceived ideas.

Westermarck's efforts to construct the history of marriage in primitive society along the line of an imaginary monogamous nature of primitive men were appreciated and admired by the late Victorians but did not stand the examination of scientific research. He tried to define marriage as "a more or less durable connection between male and female lasting beyond the mere act of propagation till after the birth of the offspring."* The characterization of a "more or less durable" connection between the sexes can, of course, be applied to association of a very temporary kind.

Anthropologists have great difficulty in distinguishing between marriage and other sexual relations in most primitive societies. Where sexual chastity is unknown marriage is not associated with sexual possession. Among the old North American Indians women "are purchased by the night, week, month or winter," reports the Rev. D. Jones.** The Cherokee Indians "commonly change wives

---

* *The History of Human Marriage,* 3rd edition, Vol. 1, p. 71, London, 1921.
** D. Jones, *Journal of Two Visits to Some Nations of Indians,* p. 75, New York, 1865.

three or four times a year." One of the early observers, La Houtan, states that "what is spoken of as 'marriage' among the North
American Indians would, in Europe, be spoken of as a criminal
connection."* The marriage tie, "if it can be so called, has no
force" among the Oregon tribes** and of the Seminoles we hear
that marriage "seems to be but the natural mating of the sexes,
to cease at the option of the interested parties."*** Father
Morice**** says about the Athapascan tribes that marriage
is rather a misnomer applied to their associations before the
arrival of the missionaries. "Cohabitation would be better to the
purpose." When you read in those early reports that a man could
easily be married forty or fifty times, you get the impression that
these Indian tribes may have surpassed the Hollywood gentry.

In the same way as the North American Indians, before Christians infiltrated, the aborigines of other continents looked upon
marriage as a transient association. There are all kinds of such
associations and it is difficult to draw a line between sexual relations which have nothing to do with marriage, a kind of trial
marriage and living together as a married couple.*****

Modern students of primitive customs agree that marriage did
not always exist but is an institution introduced by a chief or a
law-giver of the nation or the tribe. All known facts contradict
the Westermarckan view that the institution of marriage is deeply
rooted in human nature. When sociologists discover an original
monogamous drive in primitive men who appear to them but
little lower than the angels they have become victims of wishful
thinking.

The truth is that marriage is originally contrary to the instincts

* Armand L. de la Houtan, *New Voyage to North America,* Vol. I, p. 456,
London, 1735.
** George Gibbs, *Tribes of Western Washington and North Western
Oregon,* p. 199, Washington, 1877.
*** May MacConley, *The Seminole Indians of Florida,* p. 497, Washington,
1877.
**** A. G. Morice, *The Western Denes, Their Manners and Customs,*
proceedings of the Canadian Institute, Series III, Vol. 7, p. 121, Toronto, 1890.
***** Robert Briffault, *The Mothers,* 3 vols., New York, 1937.

of men, that they have to overcome strong resistances within themselves to marry at all and that they have to conquer certain tendencies in themselves, fierce and independent traits of their nature, to accept it.

If this is the case, why do men marry, how did marriage become possible and why was such an institution necessary? These are interesting problems, but this is not the place to discuss them. An inquiry would have to demonstrate which economic and psychological factors brought about the change that made marriage a necessity for men.

There is small doubt that it was the male who introduced marriage into primitive society, that this institution, like most social and legal constructions, is his creation. What I want to emphasize here is the fact that marriage is originally alien to the character of men, that men are marriage-shy. More than that: they are afraid of being married.

As long as men are young and vigorous and filled with the spirit of masculinity marriage goes against the biological grain. There is a bridge from this biological aspect to the psychological side—the side where you find the natural reluctance of the male to be tied down to one place, his resistance against giving up his lust for conquest and adventure.

Man as long as he is young wants to be free, does not want to settle down, does not want a fixed job, does not want to have a family and be a provider. He really wants to roam over the earth, wants to conquer life and women; he is restless and pursuit of happiness means to him to see new things, new countries, new women.

How can he do that with a wife and children? "He travels the fastest who travels alone." The soldier, the sailor, the traveler, all those men who go out on dangerous expeditions have to be alone and under no obligation but to reach their aim or destination, married to naught but the spirit of adventure. Nobody can be adventurous who has to think of wife and children, who has to think that his destiny will determine what will happen to his family.

Marrying means giving up adventure in more than one sense. It is saying farewell to the mentality of adolescence.

Wives sometimes remark patiently, "Boys will be boys," when they look at some difficult traits of behavior in their husbands. They do not know how much of boyhood mentality their men gave up when they married and that what they show now is only a pitiful remnant, a distant echo of their adolescence. Not all married men are mature, it is true, but the pressure of life is great enough to be felt in the long run—boys will be men.

Marriage means for men not only happy union with a beloved woman. It means duty, obligation; it means responsibility, effort and work—yes, sometimes it means only work and no play. The boy in the man wants to play, and even his work is a kind of play for him. The man in the man has more and more to renounce his play. If he is married he has to work not only for himself but also and often in the first place for his wife and children. He has to make good; his whole education (against his nature) is directed to the aim that he take his responsibilities seriously. Here is the point where I have to return to the area of the comparative psychology of the sexes. When girls think of marriage they are not afraid; they see in the state of being married their destination. Men are scared. At first sight such a fear appears mysterious and entirely unreasonable, incomprehensible as the fear women have of a mouse running across the room.

Dread of marriage is not the only fear in men which makes many women wonder about them. Why are their men filled with awe when they have to face an income-tax collector? And why this great respect before the cop around the corner?

Here is a difference in the psychology of the sexes which is significant. A policeman is for men the personification of law and order; he looks at you and his glance awakens in men the idea of the eye of the law. That is true even in the case of the gangster who rebels against the law and for whom the policeman is a hated enemy whom he wants to kill. Even for the criminal the policeman is law personified. In male underworld argot a police officer is "the law."

For women a policeman is nothing of this kind. He is simply a uniformed man, at whom you smile and whose help you ask if it is necessary and, sometimes, if it is not so necessary. He does not fill women with the spirit of rebellion nor with the respect men show to him as representing authority. Here is one avenue on which we can get nearer to the different attitudes of men and women to the evaluation of marriage.

For women marriage is a question of legitimacy; it is a bond acknowledged and approved of by convention and society. For men marriage is connected with associations like the thought of duty, obligation, responsibilities. It is a moral problem. For women duty is something which has to be done because society wants it. For men it is the voice of the daughter of God, whom you could not forget even if you were an atheist. Women act often because they feel affectionate, men oftener because they are under the pressure of duty. Obligation, duty, responsibility— these words have for male ears an undersound which is for women as little audible as are, for male ears, the emotional undercurrents which women feel when they think of kindness, tenderness and affection.

I am, of course, very far from asserting that women do not know or acknowledge duty, but I think that the idea has not this sacrosanct, this highly sacred and inviolable character it has for men. Men follow duty as their supreme authority while women are more often led by the wish to fulfill needs.

I shall not remind you here of the unbelievable sacrifices of men during the war but give a single instance reported by a French flier—the behavior of one of his comrades, a pilot in civil life. You will find it in the beautiful book, *Wind, Sand and Stars,* by Antoine de Saint-Exupéry,* a flier who was killed in the war.

Guillaumet was an airline pilot who had to fly over the Andes regularly. He was once gone a week and every hope that he would be found had been given up. ("The Andes never give up

* New York, 1945.

a man in winter," said the people.) When he was rescued his first intelligible sentence was: "I swear that what I went through, no animal would have gone through." He had had to land on the snow, forced down by a storm.

He lay there helpless for two days and two nights and then walked for five days and four nights. When they found him his hands were numb and useless and his feet frozen.

Without provisions, without tools, the man had crawled on the face of almost vertical ice-walls in a temperature twenty degrees below zero. It would have been paradise to give up, to yield to the beatitude of peace which the snow and the cold promised, and he felt the foretaste of the delight of throwing off this burden of life which seemed to creep out of his frozen extremities.

And then came the thought of his wife. "She would be penniless if she couldn't collect the insurance." When a man vanishes his death is legally acknowledged only after seven years, he thought. It was this awful detail that blotted out the other visions. If he could reach a rock jutting up out of the snow and if he could prop himself up against the rock they would find his body next summer and his wife would get the insurance.

He had to stop frequently to cut his shoes open a bit more and massage his swollen feet. His heart was not going well. He lost his memory. But he dragged himself forward. The thought which pushed him was that they would find his body after half a year and his wife could then collect his estate. His friend, who tells the dark tale of this adventure, concludes with these beautiful sentences: "To be a man is, precisely, to be responsible. There is a tendency to class such men with toreadors and gamblers. People extol their contempt for death. But I would not give a fig for anybody's contempt of death. If its roots are not sunk in an acceptance of responsibility, this contempt for death is the sign either of an impoverished soul or of youthful extravagance."

It is this high sense of responsibility, the unconscious foreknowledge of what marriage might mean to them, which often makes men—and the best of them—afraid of marriage.

Their lust for conquest, their spirit of adventure, their love of freedom, their sexual instability make them shy away from the idea of marriage.

But what really makes them afraid is just this: they know they have to fulfill their obligations, that they must and will take their responsibilities seriously to the end.

They are afraid of the high price they have to pay, not forced by authorities outside but by something within themselves which they have to obey whether they want to or not, even if it means misery, death and self-destruction. Psychoanalysis has a name for this unpitying factor within oneself: it calls it the superego. The superego is more severe, makes higher demands, on men than it does on women, who seldom have this terrible feeling of duty and guilt when obligation is not fulfilled.

It is not true that this sense of responsibility operates only in the good citizen. It is there in every male who founds a family; it is there even in the ne'er-do-well. You remember Liliom, the rough and tough guy in Molnar's play. He does not hesitate to strike his wife when he is impatient or ill-humored, and to strike hard. They are penniless, and Julie, the poor little wife, tells him that she is pregnant.

The brute goes out and attacks a cashier, fails and kills himself. Generally worthless though he is, he feels he has to provide for his wife and the baby who will come, and the sense of responsibility which a male has to fulfill to his last breath surrounds his head, when it falls back, as gloriously as a halo surrounds the head of a saint.

I do not believe that women deeply understand what responsibility means to a man. Otherwise they would understand much better what makes men afraid of marrying.

It is easy to accuse men who do not want to marry of selfishness, egotism and lack of seriousness, to blame them for the avoidance of doing their share within the community. Men themselves often confess this selfishness, and I heard an incorrigible bachelor say: "Why should I support the daughter of a man, with whom I am not in the slightest degree related, all my life?"

I have heard the bravados of men who are proud of the fact that they have maintained their freedom, but I heard, too, in their voices, the concealed fear, the anxiety that they would become slaves of their overconscientiousness, of their severe demands upon themselves if they married.

Women should understand this and comfort men, not emphasize that being married means more duties and responsibilities. It is not necessary to make him take it easy but to make him take it easier, to reassure him that he is quite capable of doing what will be necessary, that married life means not only heightened burdens, increased responsibilities, but also *shared* responsibilities, that there will be a companion at his side able and willing to carry the burden with him and—above all—that the burden will not be as heavy as he anticipates.

A young man came to me shortly after his wife had announced to him that she was pregnant. He saw the future somberly, already saw privation and misery looming on the horizon and worried because his earning power was so limited and the expenses were increasing. He came the next day in a better mood and reported that his wife had convinced him that a baby costs almost nothing during the first two years. She really succeeded in her pious lie because the man half-wanted to be convinced.

What he needed more than the assurance of financial security was the moral support. What he needed was the certainty that his wife believed in his capabilities and had faith in him. He must have known that what his wife had said was well-intentioned fraud, but he now faced the future more courageously. I took off my hat to the young lady who understood her husband so well.

"If I were the marrying kind I would ask you to marry me."

"What is a girl supposed to say in such a situation?" asked a young patient. "I could not tell him that he is the marrying kind. He must know best."

I am not so sure that she is right. The statement, "I am not the marrying kind," need not mean what it says. It is perhaps not a statement at all but rather a confession.

Perhaps it means only: I have this or that peculiarity which makes me think I should not marry. I have often heard men use the words in this sense. One man meant that he would not get along with his wife because he was critical of women, demanded almost perfection. Another thought that his need for variety in sex was too great to be satisfied with one woman only. (The girl to whom he confessed this need answered courageously, "I know all men want variety. I am variety enough for you.") A third man was of the opinion that women are all unfaithful and was afraid that a wife would deceive him. (One girl had double-crossed him and he was under the influence of this disappointment in love.) Another man knew that he was homosexual and did not feel attracted to women at all.

The sentence, "I am not the marrying kind," can thus amount to a basic insight into one's character (as in the case of the homosexual man) but it can also be the expression of a basic self-deception. No man *is* "the marrying kind," but most men *become* the marrying kind.

My experience tells me that the surest victims of this self-deception are those men who think of themselves as woman-haters or as Don Juans.

The incorrigible bachelors are mostly men who assert that they worship women, that they are great idealists who put women on a pedestal, who see in women the pattern of all virtues and pure perfection.

Beware of bachelors who have an idealistic view of noble, chaste womanhood and look upon women as if they were unattainable images. Such men do not subject women to the test of everyday life. They prefer to admire women from a safe distance and have an evasive attitude to marriage. If I were a woman I would avoid the company of these noble souls not only because a pedestal is a very uncomfortable living place but because one cannot believe them.

Their admiration of women as a sex is a concealed attempt to avoid a real relationship with a woman of flesh and blood. They flirt with the idea of marriage all their lives and they are ready to nurse this desire until the end of a comfortable bachelor life.

Young women should prefer the company of declared woman-haters. They always marry. The *hausfrauen* of old Vienna had a proverb which is valid not only in the marketplace: "He who criticizes the wares buys."

A man who has all kinds of criticisms against women in general, who believes he knows all about their shortcomings, will be the victim of the first charming girl who laughs his accusations off and realizes that behind his declared misogyny is a concealed desire for a woman for whom he could care.

The man who is a woman-chaser is certainly not a single type, but a subdivision of this class is the man who searches for a certain woman, who wants to find among all women the one who will fulfill his desires. He thinks that what he wants is excitement, the chase, the adventure. But what he really wants is the realization of his wishes, the end of his restlessness, peace of mind. Not what he says is important but what he leaves unsaid.

The other day I met an old acquaintance who liked to be thought of as a real Don Juan when we both were young men.

"I have failed in my mission," he said. "I was not made for marriage."

"What else were you made for?" I asked.

"For the opposite," he said, "for love."

I had to laugh because the man, now twice a grandfather, is a model husband.

Such men who imagine that they are made to be great adventurers in love regularly marry. Even woman-haters in whom misogyny reaches a pathological pitch do marry. They get divorced and marry again. Thirty years ago a young lady at a party in Vienna was jokingly asked, "You are Swedish? When were you married to Strindberg?" The profound hatred of women in this mentally ill genius did not keep him from marrying, only from remaining married.

Freud once declared that one of the decisive trends of our civilization demands that the mature man loosens his ties to his family in order to found a family himself. In every man lives the wish to take over the place, position and authority of the man whom he admired so much as a small boy—his father. Psychoanalysis reveals how many hindrances there are on the way to this goal, how many unconscious factors operate as forbidding or preventing powers, how dangerous even the approach to the aim appears.

A part of this fear, originating in childhood, is at work in the fear of marriage found in so many men. They are only imaginary dangers, it is true, but they are psychologically not less real.

What could married men do to mitigate this fear among their sons and brothers? They could say they were not immune from it themselves and that marriage is neither so terrific nor so terrible as apprehension threatened. If their bachelor friends call them tamed elephants who help in the capture of wild ones the masculine appeal to moral courage remains. They cannot give any better advice than Emerson's: "Always do what you are afraid to do."

PART FOUR

The Emotional Differences
of the Sexes

Introductory Note

IN THE EXPERIENCE of everyday life, and in almost forty-five
years of psychoanalytic practice, a great number of observations and insights into the emotional differences of men and
women have been gathered. Not all of them deserved to be followed up. Many of the things observed were lost because they
were not written down. Sometimes, however, in pauses between
books, I would take the folders from the drawer of my desk
that contained this material gathered through the years; many
sheets were thrown out, and many others describing new experiences were added. Some of the differences between the sexes
that were less visible and had been less clearly perceived demanded to be analytically explored. Some others were briefly
discussed because they had escaped the attention of psychologists.

Not only the measure and depth of psychological inquiry will
be different in the following chapters and paragraphs, but their
character will also vary. Sometimes I was able to follow threads
to their end. At times other tasks demanded my attention and
I had to be content with jotting down observations and impressions. No systematic and complete comparison of the emotional
differences of the sexes was intended. A fragment cannot be
pretentious. I am uncertain whether the mine we shall dig will
be rich or poor.

There have been frequent opportunities to discuss some of
the subjects dealt with here in lectures and seminars, and I have
always been eager to find out what my colleagues and students
thought of my observations and of the conclusions at which I
had arrived. Observations and experiences contradicting my own
were especially welcome. They still are and they often made corrections or qualifications necessary.

Since old age and restriction of my time might forbid a systematic continuation of the work, what would happen to this

material that was so rich and manifold? Should the shaft I had drilled be deserted even though it might perhaps, if penetrated farther, lead to a hidden source? I decided to collect at least the material prepared for so many years, in the hope that it will awaken the attention of those interested in these problems and stimulate other psychologists to continue the work.

I asked some men and women, friends and acquaintances, to read the first draft of my manuscript and give me their opinion about the impressions, observations and experiences I had reported. I first asked several men if the conclusions I had drawn were similar to theirs with regard to the differences in the emotions of men and women. Their answers were, of course, of various kinds. Some agreed and some disagreed; some agreed only with some of my statements and not with others. Their reactions were, at all events, both informative and useful.

The first lady whom I asked to read the manuscript said smilingly: "Many of your impressions about us (women) are correct. No man should read the book!" A few seconds later, she said: "Or rather, every man should read the book!" She thus used the privilege of her sex—even in omitting to give the reasons for her sudden change of opinion. But, with this episode, we are already in the middle of the subject we are going to discuss.

Here is the harvest of many seasons.

New York, May, 1957.

1. SIMPLE SAMPLES OF COMPARATIVE OBSERVATION

Here is as hors d'oeuvres a little piece of psychological field work, an everyday observation which everyone can repeat and whose correctness can be tested. The point of observation is a crowded street in Manhattan. You want to study the behavior of the next young man who comes along. Here he is: just an average man, enjoying his walk on this delightful day of early spring. A young couple is coming toward him. The pretty young girl and her boy friend are now near him and he notices them. Our young man looks at the girl. Did he, in passing, look at the other young man? It seems not; if he did, his glance lasted no longer than a second and then was directed to the young girl, whom he eyed carefully.

Here comes a well-dressed young woman; she passes the same couple. At whom did she look? If our observation is correct, she merely glanced at the young man; but then she looked attentively at the girl—she inspected her carefully, then for a moment her glance took in the the young man and returned to the girl.

We chose a young man and a young woman at random. There is no doubt that their reactions in meeting the couple were different. But has this difference any psychological significance? We cannot be sure that the result will be the same with another young man and another young woman. Yet we assert that an attentive observer who repeats the little experiment frequently enough will find that, in the majority of cases young men and women will react similarly in meeting a couple. Is the described behavior representative of a sexual pattern?

All beginnings are easy. It was not difficult to observe and to describe what we had seen. The task becomes harder when we are asked to give a psychological interpretation of the facts observed. Why should the young man turn his attention to the girl only, while the interest of the woman is not restricted only to the man? Since we are not mind readers we can only guess what each one thinks in meeting the couple. The thought associations our patients report in their analytic sessions might help us in surmising the directions in which the thoughts of the young man and woman will move.

Those thoughts are, of course, individually different; but let us assume that those of the young man land, after a short detour, at sexuality, at the wish to sleep with that pretty girl. It is unlikely that the thoughts of the young woman meeting the couple would go immediately to this same wish or phantasy except in an extraordinary case of a mental short cut. It may happen that also the thoughts of the woman arrive finally at sexual feelings.

I can quote at least one instance from analytical experience where the thoughts of a young girl in a situation of this type approached this aim. During the war she had encountered on the street a woman accompanied by an officer and had glanced at both. She described in her analytical session the woman, whom she called a "slut." She then went on to say: "He was British, you know, and he looked it. His lips were so defiant, like a boy's, but he was a man all right. I had to think what it would be like to be kissed by him." She got thus far in her thoughts, but no farther.

Let us confess that the nonsexual thoughts of the two people would interest us more, if we could guess what they were. We are especially interested in the divergence we see here: the man's attention is directly concentrated on the girl while the woman's, strangely enough, is concentrated on the girl almost as much as upon the man. Since the girl's companion does not have a place in the thoughts of the young man who passes the couple, we need not wonder what place he plays in the thought associations, although that dismissal itself is worthy of our interest. It is noteworthy that he was scarcely observed; he remained at the fringes of the young man's attention. If the subject of our observation should be homosexual, the girl would remain outside the sphere of his attention, which would be directed only toward the other young man.

We watched the young woman meeting the couple and saw that she looked at the man, that her glance rested on the girl and then returned to the man. Suppose we try to guess her thoughts. "He is tall and handsome. She is pretty and she knows it too; she has nice eyes but I have a better figure. She must be about twenty-one." Now perhaps thoughts whose specific content no man can conjecture come through her mind, such as: "I wonder if she bought that dress at Lord and Taylor's, I saw a dress like that at Altman's for seventy-nine ninety-five. They are wearing hats like that now—I saw one. Where was it? Oh yes, at that shop on Madison Avenue. I can't see if she is wearing a wedding ring; maybe they are having an affair. What has she got that I don't have?"

The main point in the difference in the attitude of the man and the woman is, of course, that the woman relates to the other woman, is interested in her, while the man pays scarcely any attention to the other man. Since in these introductory remarks we are more interested in the phenomenology of the difference than in psychological analysis, we choose another situation for comparison. This time it will be a social gathering—the latter part of a cocktail or dinner party. Here is a young man, at the moment without a partner in conversation, comfortably sitting in the corner of a beautifully furnished room. Across from him, not too near but near enough to be observed, is another young man with a pretty young girl. The other young man is courting her, holding her hand and complimenting her. Our subject of experiment has no special interest in the girl. She and the man are strangers to him. Is he interested in their flirtation? He has seen them and after a few seconds he turns his attention to other people. He would be bored should he continue to observe them.

We now change the person: here is a young woman in the same situation. She has no interest in the young man. She knows neither the young girl nor him. Is she interested in their flirtation? Very much so. Although the two young people are strangers to her she watches them like a hawk, though she carefully hides her interest. She is fascinated by the means and ways the other woman uses to attract the man. She is eager to observe whether the girl plays coy or hard to get, whether she encourages him, and how. She has not a personal but a "professional" or "technical" interest comparable to the one a pianist has in watching the hands of another artist playing a Mozart sonata.

The sphere of observation in the two cases mentioned is that of erotic interests of the two sexes and thus of a restricted field. Here is another corner removed from that of sexual interest. It is really an instance of a psychological experiment. Well, there is, of course, no scarcity of data from experiments in clinical psychology. On the contrary there is an abundance; but here is an instance of an experiment in psychology of another kind. You often hear the argument that psychology is not a science in the strictest sense because human behavior cannot be predicted in every case. It is very doubtful that predictability is one of the immanent qualities of a science but at the moment I do not wish to enter this discussion. I would rather report an experiment in which the behavior was correctly predicted.

We arrived in the United States as refugees from Nazi Germany in June 1938. We had been relatively well off in Europe but had lost all I had earned in thirty years of analytic practice when Hitler took possession of Austria. We had brought only a little money with us and were happy to have escaped death and torture.

Shortly after our arrival we were invited to a big dinner party given by a European analyst and his wife who had been in New York many years. It was given for New York colleagues and was a splendid affair where we met many people, some of whom we had known in Vienna and had not seen for years. We enjoyed, as did the other guests, the hospitality of our host, the stimulating conversation and the rich and varied choice of tasty dishes and drinks served at the buffet dinner.

Later my wife and I walked down Park Avenue in order to catch the cross-town bus at a corner a few blocks away. When we came to a lamppost I asked my wife to wait a few seconds because I wanted to make a note on a piece of paper. I took the old envelope of a letter from my pocket and wrote under the lamppost: "But if you would give" . . . and "criticism of arrangement. . . ."

Joining my wife I casually asked, "Well, what do you say about Mrs. White's dinner party? She really arranged everything wonderfully. Did you see how many different things there were at the table on the left? Tongue, roast beef, squab, eggs, salads. . . ." My wife also praised our hostess who had taken considerable trouble in the preparation of the successful party, but she added: "But if you would give me that much money, I would show you that it can be done much better." There followed some remarks about the arrangement of the silver that she felt should have been different—there had not been enough cups for the coffee and many other things, it seemed, could have been differently done.

It could now be argued that this was not a valid experiment concerning psychological predictability because I had, of course, known my wife a long time and would very likely be able to foresee the kind of reaction she would have to my questions. However, I am asserting that the majority of women in the same situation (refugees after a dinner party of this kind) would have had, if not the same reactions, similar ones, whether they verbalized them in similar fashion or not. They would praise the hostess and then add that they could have done better. The specific criticisms would, of course, be different according to the individuals and the circumstances. Let me add that hardly any man would think in this manner, or even anything approaching it.

The preceding comparative observations are elementary, as they are supposed to be in this introduction to our subject. They are simple little pieces of psychological field work that have to precede any interpretation of the material. The justification for taking notes on such instances of different behavior patterns of the two sexes is the fact that not even their phenomenology is well known. They are generally neglected by the psychologists who very conscientiously register in statistics and graphs the minute differences in color perception of little girls and boys.

Jacques Loeb, one of the most prominent American medical scientists, once stated, "Physiologically men and women are different species." The following chapters want to contribute to the recognition that men and women are also emotionally as different as if they belonged to two different species.

2. EMOTIONAL DIFFERENCES OF THE SEXES

In order to see an object you have to keep it at a certain distance. When you hold it too close to your eyes you will not recognize its nature. Nor will you see it when you are too far from it. While psychology acknowledges the fact that men and women react differently to experiences, behave differently in the same situations and show a decided divergence of feeling and thinking, the more you look at the two sexes as essentially similar forms of the species man the more these divergences seem to shrink. The differences are not fundamental any more when you look at them from a bird's-eye view. The question, thus considered, reminds one of the difficulties of the Indian situation in prewar British diplomacy, of which Lord Halifax once remarked: "The charm of the problem is that the farther you get away from it the easier it seems." But when you come nearer to it the differences increase. The answer to the problem of India may seem quite simple to the gentleman who reads an article in the *Times* about it in his London club but becomes rather complicated and complex after he has spent a few years in India in government service. To the psychologist the emotional differences between the sexes appear small in a laboratory but enormous during a quarrel with his wife. Everyday life has the quality of elucidating the scope of the problem. To quote Lord Halifax, who was the British ambassador to this country not so many years ago, again: his wife once visited the Zoo in New York and some reporters photographed her while she held a little monkey in her arms. When the photograph was published in the New York papers Lord Halifax was asked what people in London would think if they saw the picture. He answered: "The women would be envious of Milady and the men of the monkey." You have here certainly an example of the different emotional attitude of the sexes.

The Holy Scripture does not explicitly say that Adam wondered about Eve's behavior, but everybody who can read between the lines of the sacred text realizes that he did. Such astonishment was continued in his descendants, who have never ceased to wonder about the daughters of Eve. In the stone tablets of Babylon, in the hieroglyphic inscriptions of Egypt and in the parchments of ancient Greece you will find that the ways of the ladies were almost as puzzling to our male ancestors as they are to the man of New York, three thousand years later. The difference is that the ancient people expressed their interest in the problem in myths, tales and proverbs rather than in discussions about the second sex, the superior sex, the lost sex and so on.

The emotional differences between the sexes were so conspicuous and numerous that scientific psychology had, at last, to occupy itself with them, but, strangely enough, the more attention it paid to the differences, the more doubtful it became that herein was a problem of psychology at all. Are those emotional differences of male and female behavior patterns not the result of the biologically given duality of the sexes? The psychologist was warned not to transgress the territory of foreign sciences. Here was a strong "stop" sign. He was fenced in by boards on which he could read "Endocrinology" and "Genetics," denoting the domain of these disciplines. When he then turned to the other side he perceived other boards on which the words "Sociology" and "Anthropology" were written. A numerous group of scientists deny that there are basic and well definable important differences between the sexes. In their concept what we consider as such are results of the culture patterns in which the individual is born and bred. Margaret Mead asserts, for instance, that the qualities considered feminine and masculine are no more inheritedly linked with the sexes of men and women "than are their hats or clothes styles." She is of the opinion that "human nature is almost unbelievably malleable."

We have rather the impression that human nature has a restricted malleability and that certain characteristic emotional features of the two sexes reveal themselves everywhere and under the most variable culture patterns. We recognize, of course, the great importance that external and cultural factors have for the behavior differences between men and women, but we doubt that those divergences are only a result of cultural variations. Such a determinedly skeptical attitude does not need to diminish the value of Dr. Mead's contributions. It is likely that her observations are very correct, but that her interpretation is mistaken.

We agree with Anatole France that science is infallible, but that the scientists err all the time.

Restricted by biology on one side, by sociology and anthropology on the other, the area of psychological research into the emotional differences of the sexes shrinks more and more, since psychologists apparently accept the verdict of these other sciences. The current psychological literature is filled with reports on the differences of the efficiency of male and female typewriting and of the reaction time of 500 boys and girls of the III A grade to certain sounds. Carefully prepared experiments prove that girls of the age 7 to 17 are superior in copying a bead chain from memory while boys of the same age are better in block counting. It seems that it is expected that a report on the perception of certain colors by men and women and a comparative test of male and female automobile driving will throw a decisive light on the psychological basic differences of the sexes. No doubt much of such research, with its abundance of scores and statistic data, can prove a point but it is questionable why the point should be proven. We believe that comparative mechanical or clerical tests could lead to the core of the problem, if continued to infinity, but life is short and a better approach to the problem should be found. Here is a question of mental economy, of intellectual expediency. "Thrift, Horatio!" one would like to say to one's fellow psychologists.

In one of his last unfinished papers, not translated into English, Freud states that "the biological fact of the duality of the sexes emerges before us as a great enigma, something lost to our knowledge, defying any attempt of tracing it back to something else. Psychoanalysis did not contribute anything to the clarification of this problem. It belongs obviously as a whole to biology." In his view only reflections of that great contrast in psychical life are to be discovered. These sentences were written in October 1938. We have to confess that not many of those reflections have been discovered in the nineteen years since.

In a search for a fresh approach to the problem I found a new point of departure and arrived at some yet vague conjectures on

where the road will lead. The point of departure is a preconceived idea. I know that an explorer should blush for shame at
such a confession, but let me add that scientists also have such
hunches. (There is, however, a difference. The preconceived ideas
of scholars are not flights of fancy. They are, so to speak, scientifically preconceived ideas and have to be reached on a long
detour of strict, careful deduction and logical examination.) Such
hunches can be useful in research if they meet two requirements.
They should not be confused with well considered arguments
and they must not be evaluated and used as evidence. They have
to be freely and clearly identified as hunches or prejudices.

The preconceived idea is that the fundamental psychological
differences between men and women can be clearly demonstrated
when one considers that they are originated in their different
sexual functions. In other words, we attribute a pattern-forming
importance to the difference of men and women in sexuality. To
use a very simple simile, when you want to figure out what is
the basic difference between a male and female fixture, you will
compare their functions and essential purposes. If I thus claim
that the clue of the difference in the behavior patterns of men and
women is to be searched for in their sexuality, I have continued
Freud's concept that the sexuality of a person is pattern-forming
for his or her behavior also in other nonsexual directions. But I
have at the same time confessed to a second preconceived idea,
namely, that sexuality has a different meaning for the sexes. That
means that it does not have the same place in their life and not
an identical significance. Otherwise put, when two do the same
thing, it is not the same, even when they do it together. I am
inclined to think that this key will open the door to many rooms.
What can be determined as the basic emotional difference in the
sexuality of men and women will reflect itself in other spheres of
behavior, in attitudes and reactions that are not of a sexual
character any more.

I would like to present here only tiny samples of such conclusions, little pieces of trimmings of the problem. The samples are
at the same time examples of those reflections to which Freud

alluded. They contrast the behavior of women and men in their relations to each other, but also their general behavior patterns and attitudes. Let me immediately declare that I am here concerned only with the average man and woman of our Western civilization, that I do not consider other cultures and that I am very ready to admit that there are many exceptions determined by extraordinary or pathological circumstances. (It seems it is, nowadays, almost necessary to emphasize that there are no exceptions without a rule.) Let me further add that there are always manifestations of rudimentary behavior patterns of the other sex in men and women, that many overlappings occur so that one can speak only of the predominance of certain characteristic features in the general psychology of women and men. There are always cases, and one of them became widely known lately, where an individual desires to change his sex and its secondary and tertiary characteristics and is, to a modest degree, successful. Nature itself has provided some possibilities of this kind in which an animal, during its life history, changes its sex. What takes place there should not happen to a dog and it does not, but it can happen to a rooster or a hen and to other animals of a lower group. In spite of all masculinity factors in women and of feminine traits in men the last impression is that of an unchangeable biological fact expressed in that sentence of Freud, "Anatomy is destiny."

As emotional reflections of that biological determination we recognize many significant and contrasting traits in the relationship of the sexes. Even in the phase of courtship a characteristic divergency appears that has not yet been psychologically evaluated. A young man in love might often, during his day, experience violent attacks of longings or desire for a girl. But those often very intense trends are periodical and not all pervasive, while they, as time goes on, seem to accompany in a milder, more diluted form, the whole day of the girl who is in love. The man often feels, "I wish I were with her now," and this wish can disturb and interrupt his activity while the girl rather feels: "I want to be always around him." The longing of the one sex has the character of short and violent thrusts, forceful pushes, the desire of the woman that of a long, spread out and lingering longing. She would like, not only as he, to spend many hours with the love-object, but to be with him the whole time. Her phantasy accompanies him everywhere, when he plays bridge or when he has a conference with clients while the man's imagination calls up the image of the girl only in certain situations. Even the disappointments, caused by the necessary incongruity of that imagined picture of the partner with his actual self, are different in character with the two sexes. The disappointment of the man is violent and has the nature of a strong disillusionment; that of the woman is slow in its realization and has all the characteristics of painful astonishment. A man said the other day to a girl: "I was mistaken when I fell in love with you," as if she had betrayed the ideal image he had made of her in his imagination. But a girl, puzzled at herself, said to the loved man the wonderful sentence: "I miss you so much when I am together with you." Which poet of our time could write such a superb line, brought up from the depth of feeling?

It seems to me that these characteristic traits reflect the male and female characteristic attitudes in sex life. Their contrast is modeled on the difference of the behavior in sexual intercourse. The thrustlike desires of the man, quick ascending and rapidly decreasing, and the slower excitement of the woman with its crescendo and diminuendo. The contrast of the localized and of the pervasive longing corresponds to that of the sexual sensations during the act. A girl in one of the novels by O'Hara says to the man during sexual intercourse: "I am all around you." Her preoccupation in thoughts and imagination surrounds likewise the person and the life of the man while his thoughts concerning her have more the character of sudden intrusions and concentrated attacks.

There is, in the love life of the two sexes, another contrast reflecting their different roles. Every analyst who has treated many women will have observed that most of them are often and for longer time assaulted by the conscious and often preconscious

fear that their lover or husband will desert them, will not stay
with them, but forsake them at a certain time. A fear, comparable with that lingering thought, that is very rare with men. It
is easy enough to dismiss the impression that this almost universal fear makes upon the observer with the reference to the
reality situation. Does it not happen often enough that this fear
is realized, that husbands and lovers leave their spouses for another girl or many girls, for this reason and another or for no
reason whatsoever? And is the lot of the deserted wife not financially endangered, her social position weakened and she often
disgraced? And is the deserted girl not thrown back into her insecurity and deeply shaken in her self-confidence? All these considerations are justified and the reality has certainly given women
enough reason for these fears and doubts and a women's tradition, transferred from one generation to another, has confirmed
them. Nevertheless, the reality alone does not justify the intensity and universality of that fear. Why do men so rarely feel that
fear? And why do women feel it even if they have not the slightest objective reason for such a thought? And why do they often
consider it as foreordained, as something bound to happen? That
goes so far that a young girl about to be married to a man who
was very much in love with her, said: "I can count on a few
happy years, then he will leave me." It is not enough to make
the reality factors responsible for such a contrast in the attitude
of the sexes. It really seems as if the masculine saying, "Love
them and leave them" has a pendant, a counterpart in a feminine
warning: "Don't love them or they will leave you." There is at
the beginning of courtship a distinct reluctance of the woman
to surrender to her own affection, not any more explainable by
conscious and well considered reasons, but rather in the nature
of a danger signal of that described kind. Nothing of this kind
exists on the male side.

I daresay that there is a pattern for this contrast of the two
sexes in the psychology of the sexual act. The male who has
shown such an immediacy, urgency and intensity of sexual desire
has very soon after the emission the wish to leave the body of the

woman. The woman who has hesitatingly and much more slowly yielded to his and her own desires feels the wish that the man's genitals should stay within her. She now experiences a heightened affection for him and something akin to gratitude. I still remember some line from a book of poems by the Austrian writer, Hugo Salus, which described the astonishment of the man at this typical feminine attitude. The man, on his honeymoon, is surprised at his young wife who "thanks me for gifts I am receiving." Such a wish of the woman that the man should not leave her body after ejaculation is, characteristically enough, only felt when the intercourse was successful; that means, when the woman was sexually and emotionally satisfied. It is even often expressed in words like, "Don't go!" or, "Stay with me!"

What can be the reasons for such a divergency of attitude of the sexes? It cannot be a purely sexual sensation since the orgasm has satisfied the sexual needs of the woman. Even if we admit that the afterglow in her case lasts longer, that she is blessed or cursed with continuity of feelings and that she experiences a more gliding transition from one emotional phase to the other than the man, her increased affection and that feeling of gratitude remain unexplained. Also, the reference to the unconscious penis wish of the woman is not sufficient to explain the psychological problem here emerging. If it were, how could we understand that the wish that the man should stay within her occurs only after a successful sexual union and only after the orgasm? Why should it not also be present at every sexual intercourse in which the woman feels the penis inside of her and becomes, so to speak, its vicarious possessor? If that wish were only determined by the penis envy, how do we explain that the woman, when she is unwilling to have intercourse or if she does not reach an orgasm during it, wants the man to leave her body as soon as possible? There is no doubt in our mind that in her wish to feel his body inside her long after ejaculation, she identifies his genitals with him, with his person, as if it were not only part of him, but he, himself. Does she identify his genitals only with him or is there a yet undiscovered dynamic factor operating?

Whatever the reason, we recognize in this trifle of behavior difference a decided and decisive divergence of the emotional attitude of the sexes. Accustomed by the analytic method to evaluate such little traits psychologically very highly, we arrive at a conclusion of great importance, namely, that sexual intercourse has a different emotional meaning for women and men. Psychoanalytically considered, that contrast of seemingly unimportant small features reflects the difference of the meaning that sexuality has for women and for men. The male is eager to leave the woman's body, which he so violently intruded, after emission. ("In like a lion, out like a lamb.") His urge is satisfied and his tension has disappeared. But for the woman the reaching of the orgasm and the removal of the tension does not signify the end of the sexual process but only a station on the journey. It is as if, in that contrast, a biological as well as a psychological difference manifests itself. The biological is characterized by the fact that, for the male, the emission of semen marks the act as finished. But for the female the receiving of the spermatozoa signifies the beginning of fertilization. It is as if, for the human female, intercourse has still the unconscious meaning of impregnation as a biological potentiality, an echo of the evolutional past of animals with which the act meant reproduction in reality. The psychological difference becomes clear when one considers that the wish of the woman to feel that the man is staying inside her is, beside other sensations, an emotional expression in which the male genital is identified with the baby; as if the man were himself and his child, the continuation of himself. In the affection and tenderness for him after sexual intercourse, the maternal love for the baby dawns as an anticipated fulfillment of wishes that need not be conscious to the woman. If, thus, actual sexual intercourse ends for the male and the female at a different time, for him with the emission and for her with the premature, regretfully felt withdrawal of the man—for him with a bang and for her with a whimper—is the divergency of the finale not proof enough for the statement that the act has a different meaning for the sexes? And is there not in that difference of behavior, in the haste of the male to leave and in the regret of the woman, a biological-psychologic representative expression of the opposite tendencies in the sexes which explains the fears of so many women that the man will desert them and of their wish to tie him closer to themselves?

Let me insert here that even the castration fear of the male has a biologic pattern in the evolution of sexuality. There are certain species of animals in whose sexual intercourse the male genital remains within the female, is really lost in her. There are other species in which the whole male slips into her body and becomes a permanent parasite within her. In the castration fear of the male lives, thus, a late reflection of a phylogenetically well-founded worry although, at that phase of the evolution, the remaining within the female body has perhaps the character of a wish whose nature was later, on the human level, reversed, equipped with a negative sign.

Let me continue the line of contrasting pictures by some sketches in which not only the biological but also cultural factors manifest themselves as operating powers. We assume that in our culture pattern the man impresses us more by his accomplishments, the woman more by her personality, by which term I mean a combination of beauty or charm, gentleness and other easily definable personal qualities. The plus and minus of those features in this comparison is certainly important, because we know that men also can have charm and women can achieve many remarkable things. Nevertheless, basically, the man impresses us more by what he does, the woman by what she is. We consider a man who is only charming as feminine and a woman who neglects her appearance and attributes more importance to her achievements as masculine. If in this contrast the predominant active nature of the male and the more prevalent passivity of the female is reflected is there not also a reflection of a different kind, of the sexual behavior patterns of the sexes? Is the attraction that the female exercises on the male not also in the area of animals more of a rather passive kind, subtle in nature, effective by smell for instance, while the male in his courtship dances, sings, gives presents and woos the female in all imaginable ways? In the last analysis, the sperm cell, in its restless, highly mobile nature, is here contrasted with the passive and waiting egg cell. It is as if the individual man and woman in their behavior are enlargements of those primal biological opposites.

I would like to insert here a hypothesis, or rather a speculative kind of a hunch. To me the more urgent and, in its manifestations, immediate sexual drive of the male is perhaps an expression of his weaker biological nature, of his *Lebenshunger,* which would explain his restlessness. It seems to me that a long and sometimes invisible line leads from this contrast of the more self-satisfied and passive nature of the female with the restless and dissatisfied character of the male to the cultural fact that the artistic and scientific urge, the adventurous and exploring spirit, in short the tendency to achieve is so much stronger in men than in women. Men are trail blazers of culture, women its preservers. The continuation of that line to the other side is determined by individual experiences and cultural factors and seems to lead to another contrast. For the man in our culture pattern every sexual intercourse has the character of a test, a potency test. It is obvious that this now biologically unnecessary character is acquired by the emotional reactions to infantile experiences, especially to the castration fear. This character of the sexual act, namely, that something has to be proven by it, that of a virility test is, of course, absent with women, who do not have castration fear. If sexual intercourse sometimes acquires also for them (on a minor, if not minute, scale) the nature of a test, it can only originate in the doubt whether their attractiveness is strong enough to raise the male to potency. There is no doubt that also that added character of potency test must have a pattern-forming influence on the behavior and attitudes of many men in nonsexual directions, namely, that tendency to prove to themselves that they are masculine enough expresses itself also in the zeal and energy which they show in their accomplishments. Let me hasten to add that virility is proven not only in bed.

With this remark I arrive at the last point of my comparison of the emotional attitudes of the sexes; a difference that seems to be founded almost entirely on cultural factors. I am sure that every analyst who has observed women and men in many years of practice will arrive at a decided impression of the contrast which pervades our social world and to which I want to give a precise psychologic formulation in one sentence. Here it is: *In our civilization, men are afraid that they will not be men enough and women are afraid that they might be considered only women.* This sentence that contrasts the social and emotional insecurities of the two sexes in our culture is not a theoretical and intellectually figured out concept but the result of more than forty years of psychoanalytic observation, the summary of a careful survey. That difference reflects the social evaluation men and women have of themselves and of their own sex. It is clear that the tendency of the man to prove his masculinity ("What a big boy am I") is an echo of an infantile attitude at whose core is the high appreciation of the penis by the male child. (A patient cherished, many years after he had been in France, the memory of the admiration a Parisian woman had expressed for his erected penis in the exclamation *"Comme sculpturesque!"*) The boy's intense reaction to the castration threat and the overstrong reaction to unconscious feminine passive tendencies reflect themselves clearly in that fear of most men that they would not appear masculine enough. The condescending attitude of the male who underevaluates women because they have no penis, an attitude which women often unconsciously accept for themselves, explains why women feel that they could be evaluated only as females, not as persons, not as individual personalities.

Every psychoanalyst knows how many emotional difficulties are due to those fears and insecurities of neurotic men who are unconsciously doubting their masculinity and to the feelings of women who are unwilling to accept their femininity and the feminine role.

Those emotional differences between the sexes that are the results of sociological and cultural factors also have their deepest roots in the biological divergency. The clue for the understanding of the different behavior patterns of the sexes is to be searched for in the area of their sexuality and especially in that most intimate situation: "when a body meets a body."

3. A SINGLE SEXUAL STANDARD?

The crusaders for a single standard for both sexes usually stop in the discussion of their cause when they approach the question of sexuality. It is as though something intangible prevented them from demanding the same sexual freedom for men and women with the same unconditional and unquestioning energy with which they had demanded their civil rights or equal wages. What are the reasons for such hesitancy? Why should women not have the same rights to a free sexual life as men? Why should a single girl not be entitled to have as many affairs as the bachelor?

It is not debatable whether she should have the same rights also in sexual matters or not, but whether she wants to live in the same manner as the bachelor. And with this change in the formulation of the question we are in the center of a discussion about the difference of women and men with regard to their sex life.

Let us start from the viewpoint of social evaluation: a young man who has many sexual affairs is, in our culture pattern, envied by other men and, admittedly or not, by women. The fact that he can be called promiscuous does not damage his social reputation if he is discreet and behaves decently in all other directions. A young girl who is promiscuous decidedly loses face in our society. But she loses much more in her own evaluation. She makes herself "cheap." She degrades or humiliates herself. Society has the concept—some people would call it prejudice— that women who are promiscuous have a low opinion of their own worth and that they are justified in their self-evaluation. Also in places, and on social levels, where sexual morals are generally loosened women who behave sexually in the same manner as men are looked upon differently. They are thought of and spoken of as though there were a remnant of the old conventional and contemptuously dismissed concept. On the other hand, no society of our western civilization—except perhaps that of religious believers—will look down upon men or subject them to serious reproach because they have many love affairs.

The different social evaluation of a free or promiscuous sex life belongs certainly to a progressed phase of civilization, but it must have its roots in decisive biological and psychological divergencies of the two sexes. No "movement" will succeed in erasing these differences that originate in the biological character of the sexes.

Readers whose memory reaches back to the early years of the *New Yorker* will remember the cartoons Otto Soglow made for that magazine. One of his most popular figures was the "Little King."* The royal rank and dignity of that small man is not more than a picturesque costume. When you remove the crown and ermine cloak a little boy is revealed; a sometimes naughty, saucy, insolent or whimsical child who likes to make fun of the world of adults. In one of those cartoons—one of a series of drawings—we accompany the little king on a trip overseas to visit an African queen. We see him landing in the other continent, where he is received with great honors by high officials of the queen's government. We follow him riding on camels through the desert to the palace of the queen, who graciously welcomes him. She makes the rounds of the castle with him, shows him the throne room and her other luxurious apartments. Finally the queen takes him along a corridor to a room before whose door a Negro slave with unsheathed sword is on guard. When the door is opened, the little king sees many men resting or leisurely occupied, playing chess, smoking or chatting. The queen, who shows the royal visitor the room and its occupants, seems to explain: it is her harem.

In the imagined transference of an oriental custom to the female world the artist has expressed the grotesque absurdity of the idea of a single sexual standard for men and women.

* Collected in a book of this title, New York, 1933.

4. PHANTASIES DURING SEXUAL INTERCOURSE

In one of Arthur Schnitzler's plays, *Zwischenspiel* (Interlude), two friends, a conductor and a writer, have a conversation which drifts little by little from the discussion of everyday things into deeper waters. Both men are middle-aged, and married. The writer subtly warns his friend not to take the attraction he feels for a beautiful singer too seriously. During this discussion he denies that adventures have to be experienced. It should be possible for a man who is beyond the foolishness of youth to experience all the affairs he covets in the peace and quiet of his own home. "If he has imagination his wife, without knowing it, brings only illegitimate children into the world." In a later scene this writer teases his wife, who has fallen in love with the figure of a young aristocrat, a character who has a small role as follower of the king in one of his plays. "Previously," he says, "she became infatuated at least with the heroes of my plays. Now already the episodic figures become dangerous to her." ·

In this and other passages of Schnitzler's dialogues the theme of infidelity in imagination is alluded to. There is, for instance, the scene in *Reigen* in which a man asks his mistress in the middle of sexual intercourse: "With whom do you deceive me now?"

It is not accidental that the conversation, dealing with that subject seriously and playfully, takes place between two artists and that the advice of the writer is tinged with the Viennese variety of *esprit*.

Psychoanalysts know from their therapeutic practice that phantasies during sexual intercourse are much more frequent in women than in men, with the exception of perverted men, in whom they often occur before the sexual act. It is not unusual for a man to call up the phantasy of a certain situation in order to become excited when he is with a partner who is not too attractive or who does not inspire him sufficiently. Yet in most cases he is content with the more or less charming reality. Even in cases of minor attractiveness it will often suffice that the room be dark. The Viennese writer Karl Kraus once remarked: "In the night all cows are black, also the blond ones."

Women more frequently than men call up the image of another partner in their phantasy to reach an orgasm. A woman can imagine, for instance that she has a more aggressive or potent sexual partner. In other cases in which she is dissatisfied with the purely mechanical approach of the man she can replace reality by the phantasy of a prolonged tender foreplay. In one of my cases the wife had an almost delusional phantasy in which she imagined what her husband would say to her. She would imagine him using sweet or endearing names and how he would caress her and at which preferred spots (erogenous zones) of her body. The real situation had a much more direct and mechanical character.

In some of those phantasies it is a "man without a face" who appears in place of the actual partner, in others it is a ghost lover endowed with certain qualities missed by the woman in reality. Sometimes a real person is imagined on the stage managed by the phantasy. The obstetrician, the analyst and sometimes even a certain movie actor take the place of the real partner. Thus it happens that a man without knowing it becomes the father of illegitimate children from an imagined infidelity on the part of his wife.

There is no doubt about the fact that phantasies of this kind, if continued consistently through the years, are harmful to the emotional health of a person. They presuppose a splitting up of internal attention, and human nature cannot tolerate this mental division for long duration. I observed a case in which a woman always had the phantasy that she was embraced by the lover she once had instead of her husband in sexual intercourse. Apparently the psychic effort in imagining the other man's face, words and gestures had not much damaging effect upon her. Yet it was a symptomatic expression of a more serious disturbance that resulted in a nervous breakdown. As I have said, it seems that such cases of continued replacement in phantasies or accompaniment of sexual intercourse with images is much more rare in men, who have less difficulty in finding an appropriate object in material reality. The flight into psychical reality is much more often undertaken by women who can also conceal their phantasies much better than men.

In my experience as psychoanalyst I have encountered only very few cases in which men before or during intercourse imagined that they were someone else, not themselves. I found phantasies of this kind much more often in women, who would imagine they were very beautiful and desirable to the man. The thought: "How passionately he desires me!" or "How desirable I am to him!" often accompanies the preliminaries of sexual intercourse for women and can even herald the supreme moment. The role-taking in which the woman phantasies that she is much more attractive than she is in reality can have a sexually exciting effect upon her. On the other hand the realization that she is not very attractive to herself or that something in her presence— for instance an odor, perceived only by herself—or a physical handicap of which the man remains entirely unaware can have a sobering effect upon the woman even to such an extent that it prevents her from feeling any sexual excitement. In *Liebesfreud* and *Liebesleid* women are much more self-aware than men.

One of my cases showed an unusual phantasy of that kind in which a woman imagined, in sexual intercourse, that she was another person. The patient was a middle-aged widow, but still attractive, who had married a much younger man. She had brought an adolescent daughter from her first marriage into the new one. Once during dinner when the daughter, who was of high school age, left the table, the patient caught the admiring glance her husband gave the young girl as she walked to the door. The memory of that glance occurred to the patient during sexual intercourse on the following night and she found herself, in contrast with all other occasions, entirely disinterested. A block of wood would have been, compared to her, a model of animation as she lay in her husband's arms.

During the following days she often was surprised to find herself looking at herself in the mirror before retiring. She noticed the wrinkles on her face and the deep lines on her neck. She remained frigid in the following weeks until a phantasy appeared when her husband approached her sexually. She imagined that she was actually not the woman her husband embraced but rather herself as her daughter. In other words she became in her imagination her own daughter and phantasied how desirable she would be to her husband in this rejuvenated form. With this phantasy she again experienced full sexual enjoyment and orgasm.

Psychoanalysis succeeded, in this case, in helping the patient to regain her self-confidence as a woman and a wife. This could not be done without acquiring a certain tolerance for the concealed attraction her husband experienced for the young girl. The patient learned to look at him with some maternal feeling that did not contradict the possibility of sexual excitement when he desired her. Instead of imagining herself in the part of her young daughter she had now the new thought that her husband was the substitute for a son, and her lover at the same time.

The outcome of analytic treatment in the case of this woman was, in contrast with the case previously mentioned, favorable. The development of a maternal attitude toward the husband was certainly a helpful factor in the result obtained. The case has, of course, its peculiar features, but besides and beyond those, its analysis deepens our insights into the general dynamics of a woman's love life.

I once heard Freud, discussing cases of female patients, say that the maintenance of a marriage cannot be considered secured as long as the woman does not develop some maternal attitude toward her husband.

5. Guilt Feeling About Impotence

Here is the interesting and significant dream of a woman who was my patient, and its interpretation: *"I am walking with a preacher through the corridors of a hotel. He wants to go down-stairs to the men's room. I trip him and he falls down."* The ma-terial from which the dream was constructed, the day remnants that were used as bricks in its formation, are as follows: the dreamer had gone alone through the corridors of a hotel on the day before the dream. There she had seen a sign with the inscrip-tion "Gentlemen" pointing downstairs. On the same evening she had met her lover, who had made some critical remarks about her behavior on a certain occasion. He had "lectured" to her, as she said, and he was the "preacher" in the sarcastic expression of the dream. His criticism had hurt her feelings. These were the day remnants that became conscious in the thought associations brought out in the analytic session.

The dream anticipates a future situation: the man wants to go downstairs to the men's room. In using the inscription seen the day before a double meaning is introduced into the dream. The "men's room" symbolizes, of course, her genitals. The double meaning in calling the vagina the men's room reminds us of the affinity of dream and wit production, discussed by Freud. She trips him, does something to make him fail and he "falls down." In this sentence the expression does not mean simply the man but his penis, an identification that is often present in unconscious thought processes, of the person with the genitals. The dreamer takes her revenge for the hurt inflicted on her. In the dream she makes the man lose his erection: he "falls down."

A dream of this kind reflects a certain mood or attitude in which women sometimes make a man fail in sexual performance. This mood is often unconscious. It expresses itself not only in lack of sexual response but in some inappropriate behavior during sexual intercourse. In a case known to me the woman laughingly said to her husband near the climax: "You looked so funny just now!" The sobering effect of this remark can well be imagined.

It is remarkable how rarely a woman feels guilty about such cruelly frustrating behavior. But this is a special problem to be discussed elsewhere. We will approach the more general question of the attitude the average woman has in regard to her own frigidity or lack of sexual response compared to the emotions of the male who is occasionally or permanently impotent. Most women take their frigidity, which amounts to the counterpart of man's impotence, quite casually. In contrast to the man, who feels deeply depressed or even desperate about his failure, women rarely complain about their frigidity. They only regret it when they cannot give their mate the full satisfaction he needs. It happens, but not frequently, that a woman does feel guilty about her frigidity.

It is easy enough to discuss the question of the difference in attitude by pointing out that the male has the active part in sexuality, that he takes the initiative and is mainly responsible for success or failure. With the exception of cases such as the one shown in the dream just discussed, it is thus the woman who appears to be frustrated. In the last years, under the influence of psychological knowledge acquired through reading books and articles or listening to lectures, modern woman sometimes feels that her cooperation in sex is necessary and that she does not fulfill her part by acting the "victim" of the sexually excited man. A courageous woman called her recent book *The Sexual Responsibility of Women*. There is thus a slow change in woman's attitude toward the question, and we now sometimes see women who feel that they too are responsible for success or failure in sexual relations. But on the whole women do not experience guilt feelings when they are frigid or lacking in sexual response. The reaching of their own orgasm has for them not, as for men, the character of an accomplishment, of a task performed or of a "job well done."

The man who fails in sexual performance or who realizes that the erection of the penis is not reached or fades feels ashamed. Such shame is quite conceivable because his failure is considered by him as lack of virility. Yes, in certain cases it has for the man the character of a disgrace. But why the guilt feeling? Is it not paradoxical that the man should experience such a painful emotion? It will be advantageous to differentiate in this situation, between shame or regret and guilt feeling. The feeling of shame is the man's reaction to his failure, or to put it more strongly, to his disgrace. But how strange a reaction is that of guilt feeling over a sexual act inadequately performed or not performed at all!

When analysts speak of guilt feelings connected with sexuality they mean, of course, that the person feels guilty because the sexual act is considered sinful or forbidden. Yet here is just the opposite case: the sexual act was frustrated or prevented by the weakness or some other shortcoming of the male. Yet he feels guilty about it. Does this mean that he feels guilty because he has not "sinned," theologically speaking? We analysts are accustomed to trace the actual behavior patterns of adults back to childhood. Does a little boy feel guilty because he was not naughty?

It is at this point that we had better recognize and appreciate the new developments and changes of analytic theory as they were presented by Freud in the last years of his life, especially in *Civilization and Its Discontent,* published in 1930. These later insights, founded upon finer analytic observation, led to the theory that guilt feeling is always connected with unconscious aggression. Not the sexual drives but the unfulfilled or repressed aggressive trends of man awaken that dark sense of guilt—also in those cases in which unsatisfied sexual desires appear in the foreground. If we accept this theoretical postulate, against whom can the aggression be directed?

We will perhaps obtain some insight from the kind of reaction a man's impotence produces in women. Experienced physicians will tell us that a surprising number of women do not show any special reaction to this occurrence, especially women who had never experienced an orgasm before. They do not know what they have missed. Faithful wives, married to a weakly or capriciously potent man, can spend their lives without any strong feeling about the repeated failure of the husband simply because they have no possibility of comparing their sexual experience with other, more fulfilling experiences of the kind.

The majority of women show, however, some definite reaction: they either try to console their mate about the mishap or they get angry with him. (We are speaking here only of their reactions toward the man.) In the first case they belittle the significance of the failure, as though it were a minor traffic accident that could happen to anyone. This is the case especially when the man is depressed or apologetic about it. "But, dear, it really isn't so important. You were probably tired or worried about business. Believe me, next time you will succeed," and so on. In other words this woman would treat her mate's impotence as a bagatelle without any great importance.

The other reaction is rage or anger, as though the "misfire" were a personal insult to the woman. This resentment can express itself both in subtle reproaches and in accusations that are not so subtle. In an example of the first kind a patient said to her lover: "It is a long time since you pleased me." If the failure is repeated, it can happen that the woman becomes afraid of sexual intercourse and shows an aversion toward it because she anticipates that she will become sexually excited without release. A woman expressed her feelings about her unsatisfactory sexual relations with her husband in the drastic sentence: "I would prefer to have a tooth pulled." The resentment is sometimes intensified when the woman suspects that the man failed because he does not consider her desirable. A patient, full of indignation, once compared the lack of enthusiasm of her lover, revealed in the fading of his erection, with a ceremonial at the British royal court: "When the queen arrives in her car at Buckingham Palace the sentinel has to present his gun."

Sexual intercourse is a social act and the described reactions of women to a man's failure in it have to be psychologically evaluated because they reveal the unconscious meaning of the failure as faithfully as an echo reveals the words reflected in it. In the positive, consoling or encouraging reaction as well as in the negative form of resentment or anger the psychic impotence of the male is treated as an offense or aggression against the woman; that means a symptomatic manifestation of his hostility toward her. The anger or annoyance of the woman as an answering or corresponding reaction is too obvious to be discussed. But also the casual or consoling attitude certainly corresponds to the unconscious hostility of the man. It simply pardons it while the other condemns it; it reacts forgivingly or maternally where the other is accusing or reproachful.

It would be a serious mistake to trace the guilt feeling of the male following an unsuccessful sexual performance back to the woman only or even to all women. The more concealed part of that unconscious aggression is directed against the authorities that once prevented or condemned sexual activity, against the father and father-representative figures. The failure in sex amounts to yielding to an unconscious forbidding from this side. It is in itself the punishment for the emergence of banned sexual desires. Their repression has perpetuated the temptation to attack those authoritative figures. The guilt feeling of the man reacts to this temptation to release the pent-up aggression. We have not forgotten that in the invisible background of the sexual taboo is the desire for mother or sister who represent incestuous objects. There is a little of mother and sister in every woman.

Why is it that women do not feel guilty when they fail in sexual relations? Why is there so rarely a sense of guilt about frigidity? It is obvious that the passive part in the sexual performance will be considered important when you explore that divergence of the emotional reactions of the sexes. It is also correct that to reach an orgasm is not conceived for a woman as a task or accomplishment, as it is for a man. (It would perhaps be better to say "it was not conceived as such until recently.") But, besides and beyond those elements, there must be a biological or constitutional factor operating. It seems that the aggressiveness of the woman is not as intense nor as fully developed as that of the man. It is probable that the relatively smaller share of aggressive energy in her nature is the decisive factor in her lack of guilt feeling in sexual matters because guilt feeling is temptation-anxiety reacting on the re-emergence of hostile and aggressive tendencies.

Women also connect sexual activities with guilt feelings because they have aggressive and hostile tendencies as well as men, although to a minor degree. There is sometimes in women a sense of guilt that is alien to the man. It has not frigidity but sterility as its cause. In the unconscious concept of woman sexual intercourse is still tied to impregnation. In analysis of cases where sterility is founded upon emotional factors, such guilt feeling can even become conscious. Some women cannot tolerate contraceptives or cannot enjoy sexual intercourse on account of the circumvention of pregnancy. There are enough men whose sexual pleasure is impaired by the use of contraceptives, but the average man will certainly not feel guilty if he has not impregnated the woman during satisfactory sexual intercourse.

There is another sense of guilt that is felt much more often by women than by men: an orgasm in sexual intercourse where the man has had no ejaculation unconsciously represents for many women a failure. A patient once said that such a situation was, for her, "as lonely as masturbation." She also asserted that when she alone reached an orgasm in intercourse she felt even more frustrated than when she was left stranded before an orgasm.

The difference in the content of the sense of guilt points to the different character the sexual act has for man and for woman. I do not pretend that the preceding considerations and reflections solve the problem of the emotional disparity of the male and the female in their attitude toward sexual failure. Preliminary remarks of this kind can, however, turn our attention to the often neglected fact that there is much in sexual intercourse that is not only sexual.

6. INFIDELITY OF THE WIFE

Kinsey's report and Hamilton's research* gave us a good notion of the increase of marital infidelity in America. The explorations of Frank Capri** and other psychiatrists completed the

* G. V. Hamilton, *A Research into Marriage,* New York, 1939.
** *Marital Infidelity,* New York, 1953.

picture, adding the psychopathological aspects of promiscuity of married men and women.

It seems to me that the authors dealing with this subject neglect the psychological difference of meaning in infidelity of men and women. The factor of unfulfilled sexual urges is certainly one of the main causes of unfaithfulness in both sexes. Yet, with the exception of pathological cases, it plays a more minor role as emotional determinant with women than with men. The desire for new conquests and the need for variety in sexual experiences is more strongly developed in men than in women.

We have no means of measuring the intensity and urgency of the sexual desire of the two sexes and to compare them, but the idea that the sexual drive of the woman is generally weaker than that of the man corresponds perhaps to the real emotional and biological state. Freud's sentence, to be found in his posthumous papers, that sexuality is masculine also in women, presents the core of the problem. We know, at all events, that sexuality can mean both less and more to the woman than to the man. It means less when she is only taken. It means more when she gives herself.

The difference in the attitude of the human male and female becomes clearer when we consider that women rarely become unfaithful for purely sexual reasons or because they are sexually starved. A patient of mine asserted that she could not identify with the leading character of D. H. Lawrence's novel, *Lady Chatterley's Lover,* because a woman who feels loved by her husband and loves him will not easily be available to a man who arouses her only sexually.

On the other hand a woman is much more susceptible to the courtship of another man when she feels humiliated and despised by her husband. When she feels unwanted and has the impression that she is no longer desirable to him her wounded self-esteem is a powerful motive among the causes of her infidelity.

A patient declared that there is a difference of paramount

importance in the basic situation which leads married men and women to adultery. Having read Dr. Capri's book she critically remarked that the psychiatrist treats the infidelity of the man and the woman as though they were the same thing. She meant that the basic divergency in the situation is that the woman is sexually dependent upon the desire of the man. In her passive role she rarely refuses her husband when he desires sexual satisfaction, while he may approach or neglect her. He can easily find occasion to obtain sexual gratification elsewhere, while she generally remains attached much longer to him, even if she is not sexually satisfied.

Other patients have pointed out that infidelity of men and women has a different psychological significance in two other directions. In most cases, adultery in women is connected with the hope that they will find with a lover the consideration, appreciation and protection their husbands failed to grant them. This hope or wish is rarely a strong incentive in the infidelity of men. It is more apt to be curiosity or the need for variety of sexual experiences that propel him when he searches for adventures. Very often he only wants a "roll in the hay" and is satisfied with it.

The other difference is that repeated infidelity or promiscuity in women means, in most cases, an expression of psychic masochism. The feeling connected with unfaithfulness is, in general, that of self-degradation, of lowering of self-esteem, even when the thirst for revenge on the unfaithful husband gives the woman the illusion of justification. In an extramarital affair, and especially in several, a woman has more to lose than to gain. Nothing of such a negative effect upon the self-evaluation of a man is connected with the fact that he has committed adultery. Some men even feel that many affairs outside their marriage bolster their ego and raise their self-respect.

It has to be finally emphasized that the greater faithfulness of the married woman has also biological causes. It is the continuation of the instinctive attitude of the female animal that rejects all other males as soon as she is impregnated. A remnant of that fundamental attitude is perhaps preserved in women in their loyalty to their husbands, even when they are not pregnant. It does not, of course, always prevent them from becoming unfaithful, but it perhaps explains their longer hesitancy and reluctance when they are tempted by other men.

The moralists dealing with the problem of infidelity have to take into account those psychological circumstances that are extenuating for the unfaithful wife. The last word about the infidelity of wives cannot be spoken by moral passion but by compassion. Their need to be needed, their desire to be loved, has certainly a greater role in the psychology of women's infidelity than in that of men. Although He was not speaking of an adultress, but simply of a promiscuous woman, Jesus Christ said that much will be forgiven her because she loved much.

7. HIS JEALOUSY AND HERS

There is an abundance of descriptive and interpretive material on jealousy in the psychological and psychiatric literature. Freud and his followers have made valuable contributions to the understanding of pathological jealousy, which is only a magnified caricature of normal jealousy experiences. A survey of the scientific material gives the astonishing impression that certain aspects of the problem are almost entirely neglected. There is, for instance, the fact that the painful emotions of jealousy have another character and content when experienced by a man and a woman. It seems that the psychiatrists and psychologists consider the phenomenon of jealousy as a unity and are not concerned with the subtle differences of how it is felt by men and women. Yet the divergence is not only remarkable but also of considerable psychological interest.

The emotional character of jealousy can perhaps be generally best described as a mixture of depression, aggressiveness and envy. While rage is prevalent in this mixture in the jealous man, envy is the dominant component with the jealous woman. Superficial observation might lead to the impression that the man feels that he is deprived of his possession by his rival, that the other man infringes upon his privilege. It is in reality the woman in whose jealousy possessiveness has the greatest part. For the man, jealousy is like an illness, a weakness that makes him unsure of the world. He fights with all his power against the intruder like an organism that wards off the destructive bacilli. For the woman, jealousy is a stimulus that gives her strength, is an incentive to fight the rival with all means at her disposal. And those means are various and very impressive; the ends being pursued with a tenacity of which the man would be incapable.

But what is its aim? In most cases of jealous women, I could observe, the goal is to defeat the schemes of the rival and to win the loved man back. In this battle everything is considered fair, no means are too contemptuous. In spite of all anger against the unfaithful husband or lover the jealous woman is rarely swept by her emotions to violence and crime. A female Othello would not feel, "It is the cause, it is the cause, my soul." Is a female Othello imaginable? Is what the jealous woman feels comparable with what the man in the whirlwind of his emotions experiences? Has she that permanent kaleidoscope of hateful pictures? Is she too the helpless victim of a frenzy, tortured by an imagination without boundaries, stirred up by incessant inner voices, torn by a pain reaching to the guts? Very rarely. Only the most masculine women experience something distantly akin to the feelings of the jealous man. Where is the woman who stands before the body of her unfaithful lover whom she has killed and would feel what men in the same situation so often exclaim: "Better thus, no one else will possess her whom I loved."

No, there can be no female Othello because woman's imagination does not run amok in jealousy. Her phantasy does not go so far and it does not go into the same direction. In the foreground of her imagination, unlike that of the man, is not the visual picture of sexual intercourse of her man with the other woman but visions of the affection he wastes on the rival, presentiments of her being deserted, of the loss of his love and of her emotional

—often enough of her finanical—security. Woman is much more realistic than man and her imagination has narrower limitations even in pathological manifestations. A female Othello is unimaginable for the same reasons that we cannot think of a female Don Quixote. Women can be foolish enough, but they are rarely fools.

Other psychological divergences in the jealousy of men and women result from the different place sex has in their emotional lives. A woman I know went to a movie theater with her husband. The man was enthusiastic about Rita Hayworth and imprudent enough to express his admiration of her feminine charms as they went home. His wife resented his momentary infatuation. Her critical remarks about the other woman were followed by sharp attacks on the husband himself, directed not only at his sexual taste but at his character, his life, his relatives and friends. At the end of the argument he appeared in her sight as the vilest scoundrel. At home she made a bed for herself on the couch of the living room. And all that out of jealousy for a woman the man did not know and had seen only on a screen! Let us reverse the situation and assume that the wife, returning with her husband from the pictures, speaks with admiration and tenderness of a male star whose masculinity and strength of character she praises. Would the husband react in a similar manner? It is most unlikely. He might perhaps grunt some derogatory things about that chap, but he would certainly not feel as resentful as she or, above all, he would not feel like removing himself from the marital bedroom. He can be jealous of the man physically near to his wife, but he cannot be jealous of a shadow on a screen.

But does not this contrast show that the jealous woman is as imaginative as the jealous man, or even more so? By no means; it only shows that her imagination goes in another direction or that she is jealous of other things. In this case the woman is afraid of other dangers than the jealous man. The emotional involvement of the husband is more important to her than the sexual or rather the sensual one. Love at a distance rarely makes man jealous. The double standard that governs our mores reflects itself also in the different character of feminine and masculine jealousy. A woman learns, for instance, that her husband or lover had been unfaithful to her on a certain occasion—say, on a business trip. Her momentary grief or jealousy cannot be denied, but it is superficial and short-lived, as if that experience was just a physical release, *"une affaire de canapé,"* as Napoleon once said. What she is afraid of is that it could have been more than that or could become more, that the husband or lover could become emotionally involved or that the object of that sexual adventure could also become the object of his love. For her it is preferable that he is occupied with sex and not preoccupied with a sexual object.

The man, on the other hand, would not rage when he learns that his wife or sweetheart has a deep emotional interest in another man she has never seen. Who has even heard of a man who has only casual feelings about an occasional roll in the hay on the part of his beloved? Such a man is either a pervert or an emotional freak. Where is a man who can speak of his wife and her lover in the manner a woman spoke the other day of her husband and his mistress? She said: "He can sleep with her, but he can talk only with me." And this was said neither in bitterness nor in resignation but with the feelings of triumphant superiority, almost proudly.

It would, however, be a serious error to attribute that difference in the attitude of the two sexes to cultural factors alone and not to search deeper in the subsoil of the different significance sexuality has for the two sexes. This difference reaches to the roots of the problem, explains what a woman is jealous of and what a man. The man vaguely knows and often only unconsciously understands that sexual intercourse with another man means to the woman in general more than the touch of two skins, that a woman would only rarely sleep with a man without being emotionally involved. The woman is, on the other hand, well aware of the fact that sexual intercourse might not mean much to a man.

One scarcely runs across a discussion of still another difference in the jealousy of the sexes in psychiatric and psychoanalytic literature. I mean the different part which self-esteem and narcissistic need have in the character of masculine and feminine jealousy. In the normal as well as in the paranoiac forms of the emotion, impulses toward unfaithfulness and homosexual tendencies are warded off as analysts have often demonstrated in the presentation of clinical cases. This is valid for both cases, but it is very characteristic that a man can be furiously jealous of a rival without personally being interested in him. That does not mean, of course, that it is a matter of indifference to him who the other man is. But what he is like, whether he is married or single, what he looks like is only of small interest to him.

We cannot think of many women who, if jealous, would not take an intense interest in the other woman; that is to say, in her appearance, age, particular attractions. It is easy enough to explain that with the old refrain: "What has she got that I haven't?" but this attempt at elucidation is certainly too simplified. That interest has decidedly a much more personal feature. When you listen to a woman who wants to get detailed information about her rival the impression is almost that she wants to know all about her, wants to see and hear her, to compare herself with the other woman. No man—if he deserves the name —shows a clear interest of this kind.

I assert that even the phenomenology of this difference has been utterly neglected. At the moment I would be unable to name a single analytic book in which this issue is fully described or psychologically explained. I call as witness for the significance of this difference an outstanding authority in psychological observation and one of the greatest psychologists outside of the circle of professional men: William Shakespeare. Here are two representative instances: Julia looking at her rival's picture, in *The Two Gentlemen of Verona,*

> . . . let me see; I think,
> If I had such a tire, this face of mine
> Were full as lovely as is this of hers:

And yet the painter flatter'd her a little,
Unless I flatter with myself too much.
Her hair is auburn, mine is perfect yellow:
If that be all the difference in his love
I'll get me such a colour'd periwig.
Her eyes are grey as glass; and so are mine:
Ay, but her forehead's low, and mine's as high.
What could it be that he respects in her,
But I can make respective in myself,
If this fond Love were not a blinded god?
Come, shadow, come, and take this shadow up,
For 'tis thy rival. O thou senseless form,
Thou shalt be worshipp'd, kiss'd, lov'd and adored!
And, were there sense in his idolatry,
My substance should be statue in thy stead.
I'll use thee kindly for thy mistress' sake,
That used me so; or else, by Jove I vow,
I should have scratch'd out your unseeing eyes,
To make my master out of love with thee! (IV, iv.)

Here is a masterpiece of observation of the feminine way of
thinking and feeling, especially in the comparison of oneself
with the other woman. There is perhaps, a single characteristic
feature missing that appears in so many situations. It is significant that so many women in observing others and comparing
themselves with them often think in terms of compensation; for
instance: "She has beautiful hair, but I have a better figure," or
"She has nice legs, but I have the more beautiful eyes," or "I am
a better conversationalist."

It is certainly exaggerated to say as Anatole France does in
The Red Lily that for a woman jealousy is merely "the wound-
ing of her self-love." But this factor is certainly more emphasized
than it is in man's jealousy, which is—again, in the words of
Anatole France—"an agony with the acuteness of mental suffering and all the persistence of physical pain." The passionate
character of the emotion is assuredly present also in the jealous
woman but it has another feeling. If jealousy is, as one psycholo-

gist states,* "an enigma, the least known of all emotions, the
least spoken of human reactions," this difference will have to be
considered. Here, we may listen to jealous Cleopatra who has
heard of Octavia:

> Go to the fellow, good Alexas; bid him
> Report the feature of Octavia, her years,
> Her inclination, let him not leave out
> The colour of her hair:—bring me word quickly.
>
>   . . . Bid you Alexas
>
> Bring me word how tall she is. (II, v.)

Then the scene in Cleopatra's palace:

> Didst thou behold Octavia?
>
> Is she as tall as me?
>
> Didst hear her speak? is she shrill-tongued or low?

When the messenger says Octavia is low-voiced, Cleopatra medi-
tates:

> That's not so good:—he cannot like her long.

Again she questions:

> What majesty is in her gait? Remember,
> If e'er thou look'dst on majesty.
>
> Guess at her years, I prithee.
>
> Bear'st thou her face in mind? is't long or round?

Now a critical thought about round-faced Octavia:

> For the most part, too, they are foolish that are so.—
> Her hair, what colour?

* Boris Sokoloff, *Jealousy*, New York, 1947, p. 14.

After the messenger has come, Cleopatra has one more thing to ask him. In reality her curiosity, her eagerness to know everything about the other woman is insatiable. Even in her decision to die, the possibility of being humiliated by the victorious rival has its part:

> . . . Know, sir, that I
> Wilt not wait pinion'd at your master's court;
> Nor once be chastis'd with the sober eye
> Of dull Octavia.

In this direction one woman feels like the other. Is it the proud empress of Egypt who speaks thus?

> No more, but e'en a woman and commanded
> By such poor passion as the maid that milks
> And does the meanest chares.

8. ON SEXUAL EDUCATION

Education can fail in two ways: it may remain far below its goal or it may overshoot the mark. These are, of course, also the dangers of sexual education. Freud has shown us that there is a type of man who can reach his potency only with women he despises or looks down upon. He is impotent with women whom he considers consciously or unconsciously as belonging to the mother or sister group. Freud traces this often unconscious attitude back to the division of the primal mother figure toward whom the affectionate as well as the first sexual drives were directed. The barrier against the temptation of incest made these figures or persons representing them taboo, untouchable in a sexual sense. We have all neglected to take into account how much the later education of the boy contributes to the result which divides the female sex into "nice" and "bad" women. Many patients remember from their boyhood how their mothers and fathers admonished them to treat decent girls as though they were their sisters, which meant to avoid any approach that could be interpreted in the slightest manner as sexual. An unconscious inhibition was thus aggravated because at the most harmless caress the image of their sister reoccurred in the man. In the displacement and generalization of this unconscious taboo a considerable part of the "nice" girls, later married to those boys who have become men, will feel the ill effects of those early admonitions. Or rather, they will feel nothing in sexual intercourse. Also in the sex act:

> ". . . the native hue of resolution
> Is sicklied o'er with the pale cast of thought
> And enterprise of great pitch and moment
> With this regard their currents turn awry
> And lose the name of action."

Every psychoanalyst knows cases in which too great respect and consideration for girls is indirectly responsible for impotence or for a capricious potency. In the end this failure can be generalized, can concern all women because there is something of mother or sister in every girl. It is an odd thought that too great respect for a woman could be responsible for that lamentable and harmful result of leaving her "high and dry."

In several of my cases the initial sexual excitement of the woman evaporated because she foresaw the failure of her husband or lover. Sometimes she avoids becoming excited and learns to hate the sexual intercourse which left her unfulfilled. A woman married to a man of such very unstable character described to me that she was full of apprehension as soon as her husband approached her sexually. She turned from intercourse as one would turn from something painful and frightening. Another woman explained to me that she usually resorts to planning tomorrow's menu while in her husband's feeble embrace. At the same time she was able to go through the gestures that would indicate sexual enjoyment—a quite remarkable accomplishment.

Speaking of the failure of the sexual education of the male: the breakthrough of the forbidding does not always take the form of sexual gratification with prostitutes or promiscuous women. I know a case in which the husband could be potent only when he abused his wife, using the most vulgar four-letter words in the prelude. In addressing his wife during the foreplay in the manner he imagined one would speak to a streetwalker, he unconsciously turned his wife into the type of woman who could be approached sexually. Otherwise he considered her much too "highly" to dare to approach her sexually. He had to degrade her verbally to make her an appropriate object for sex. His wife, by the way, did not dislike those verbal preliminaries.

Here is the female counterpart: a woman married to a man who was sexually rather timid could reach an orgasm when she imagined that another unknown man who was very active and aggressive embraced her. She slept thus with another man while she remained faithful to her husband. In another case the husband behaved so prudishly that he made his wife self-conscious and ashamed of sex or of showing sexual excitement. She was finally so inhibited that she considered sexual intercourse with her husband a kind of disgrace. Whenever her husband was away on trips she let herself be picked up by all kinds of men in bars and so on and enjoyed sexual intercourse with these almost unknown men whom she despised. She could not speak in the same sentence of her husband whom she respected and consciously loved and of those despicable characters whom she never saw again after having spent an orgiastic night with them.

Returning for a moment to the husband who had to humiliate his wife to make her possible as a sexual partner, I remember an instance which proved the too high respect for women as inhibiting in a quite unexpected direction. Many years ago, I had spent the summer months at Asheville, North Carolina, where I was psychoanalytic consultant in the psychiatric Highland Hospital. Once the woman psychiatrist in that hospital asked me to interview a young sailor whom she had treated for several months without much success. The physician expressed the hope that I would perhaps discover some secrets the young man had not told her. I had a long interview with the sailor, who had been dismissed by the navy on account of his emotional disturbances. During our conversation we discussed, of course, also the man's love life. He was about twenty-eight years old. At a certain point he told me the following: "I often said to Doctor Brown (the woman psychiatrist who had referred him to me) that, whenever I had intimate union with a girl I . . ." "What did you say?" I interrupted. "Intimate union? I never heard a sailor call it that!" "But Doctor Brown is a *lady!*" said the sailor reproachfully. The respect young men have for ladies, especially in the South, had prevented him from calling a spade a spade and from speaking of sexual activities and functions in the terms used in the vernacular of the American navy. I urgently advised Doctor Brown to transfer the patient to a male psychiatrist in the Highland Hospital. I would like to repeat here that in boys as well as in girls sexual education can fail or can be too successful—which also amounts to failure.

9. PERIODICITY

Evolution emancipates man in general more and more from the periodicity of instincts, but it sets woman less and more hesitantly free from the rhythm of change than man. Men can be violent and become murderers any day. Some recent studies indicate that from seventy to eighty per cent of women's crimes of violence are committed during their premenstrual and early menstrual periods.* While men show in their sexual impulses traces of the biological rhythm, woman's sexuality is very clearly governed by the periodic laws of nature. Most women are most

* Maxine Davis, *The Sexual Responsibility of Woman*, New York, 1956, p. 245.

easily aroused a few days before, during and after their menstrual period.

Since at this time conception is not likely it seems that there
is a contrast between fertility and sexual desire. It seems that
nature had once made an attempt to evolve woman to a condition closer to that of the male, and those days are, so to speak,
a reminiscence of that frustrated attempt. This is, of course, a
biological speculation, but one cannot get rid of the impression
that psychological changes have to be traced back to biological
factors in the phases of a woman's life. The premenstrual tension, which is justifiably held responsible for so much fighting
and unhappiness in the relationship of the sexes has often been
explained as the symptomatic expression of a frustration that
could be expressed by the following sentence: "I have neither
a penis nor a child." Yet the character of irritability and belligerence directed against the man seems rather to indicate a kind
of resentment as though he were responsible for her frustration.
I have often wondered why psychoanalysts never point to the
premenstrual tension as a symptomatic expression of the unconscious penis envy of the woman. Karl Kraus once complained
that men were punished for the lack the Creator has left in
women: "Because they are reminded every month of their incompleteness, have we therefore to bleed to death?"*

It is true that men often desire "just a woman"—not this or
that woman. That means that when they are sexually starved
they want a female, and the personal object-choice recedes in its
importance before the biological urge. It is true that for women
in general sexual desire is much more dependent upon the personal relation to this or that man. But in those days in which
woman's sexual desire approaches the character of male sexuality
that personal factor of their object-choice becomes psychologically almost insignificant. If women were fully sincere they would
confess that in those short phases of every month any man would
be welcome to them. They would then be susceptible even to
the man in the moon.

* *Beim Worte Genommen*, München, 1955, p. 37.

10. WHAT DOES A WOMAN WANT?

Ernest Jones remarks that Freud found the psychology of women more enigmatic than that of men. He quotes a remark Freud once made to Marie Bonaparte: "The great question that has never been answered and which I have not yet been able to answer, despite my thirty years of research into the feminine soul, is 'What does a woman want?' "* The formulation of the question in German (*"Was will das Weib?"*) leaves no doubt about its general character. Freud does not consider this or that type of woman, but all women and their goal in life. It does not need great acumen to guess that the question is directed to the aims of women in contrast to those of men. We can guess, further-more, that the goals of life considered in Freud's query are not the narrower, more limited aims but the most essential goals toward which women strive consciously and unconsciously.

It cannot be accidental that the question was put to a woman, a woman of exceptional psychological perceptiveness and under-standing. In Paris and Vienna, where I had the pleasure of knowing Marie Bonaparte, I always admired her penetrating analytic grasp and straightforwardness in discussions about the psychological problems of women. The books she wrote later on prove that she had the talent to present those problems in a very clear and often beautiful literary form. Freud considered Marie Bonaparte as one of his most promising students. We regret that Jones did not tell us what reply the princess gave in that con-versation with her teacher and friend.

The question itself is remarkable, especially coming from one of the greatest psychologists of all time: a psychoanalyst who had studied hundreds of women as patients, a man surrounded by the women of his family, women students and admirers, doctors and psychologists. The search and research does not direct itself toward the eternal feminine but toward the eternal womanly, toward woman's aim, beyond all boundaries of class, creed or

* *The Life and Work of Sigmund Freud*, New York, 1955, Vol. II, p. 421.

nationality. The question asks what they now strive for and what they have been striving for since primordial times.

Freud asks that question but he does not answer it. Such an answer would have to encompass the goals, conscious and unconscious, of all women. Possibly there is no reply to such a general query that would take into account all the biological and psychological needs of women.

If there is such an answer Nietzsche, who was in so many ways a forerunner of Freud and had, among other things, arrived at some psychological insights into ego psychology not yet reached by psychoanalysis, has perhaps given it. Zarathustra, who prowls about shyly and cautiously in the dawn, conceals this "small truth" under his mantle: "All in woman is an enigma, and all in woman has a single solution. It is called pregnancy."

11. THE WOMANLY AND THE FEMININE

In the preceding chapter a contrast between "the eternal feminine" and the "eternal womanly" was mentioned. When I wrote those lines I was not aware that they were influenced by some remarks a lady once made to me. She had read parts of the first draft of this book and had said: "Your comments in this chapter concern the feminine but not the womanly." Astonished at the differentiation she made, I asked her to explain what she meant. She told me then that she had made that difference in her thoughts for a long time. The feminine meant to her all that was attracting and alluring, all that said, as only a woman can say: "Go away nearer!"—with the aim of tempting and enticing the male; all the tricks, wiles and ruses of the female. The womanly has, for her, the connotation of giving: the need to care for others, the instinctively affectionate or motherly. It seems that we all make this distinction without being aware of it, although we do not differentiate between the two in our loose everyday language.

It is obvious that the two qualities are often united in one

woman, representing two facets of her nature. Yet it is significant that when one of them manifests itself the other recedes.
Nature can use the arsenal of the feminine to the secret aim of
developing the womanly. On the other hand, the womanly can
suddenly break through in the middle of very feminine behavior.

We can often see the womanly as well as the feminine appearing very early in the little girl. When my daughter, Miriam, was
five years old she already knew how to be coy and how to ingratiate herself with the grownups—women as well as men. She
even knew how to play little tricks in a very feminine way to get
what she wanted. But, from this same period, I remember the
following incident. We were spending our summer vacation on
a farm in Canada. Miriam and I went into a barn to look
around. She saw, way up on a beam, a swallow's nest where the
mother swallow was raising her fledglings in safety. We could
hear the baby birds chirping. Soon we left the barn and walked
on. Suddenly Miriam dropped my hand and dashed back to
close the barn door which we had inadvertently left open. She
had seen a cat on the road and, as little as she was, had feared
it might kill the fledglings. Already the womanly was manifesting itself in the little girl.

A patient of mine remembered that, at about the same age,
she had been given a pair of guinea pigs. They had raised, to
her delight, a family that she watched over like a hawk. One day
a friend of her parents came to call with a bulldog. While no
one watched him the dog pounced upon the little animals and
killed them. The child was hysterical and her screams brought
the grownups running. The owner of the dog—a young woman—
was brokenhearted and began to cry. Suddenly the little girl ran
to her saying, "Don't cry! It wasn't your fault!" The patient had
manifested as a little girl delicacy of feeling but also motherli-
ness, the womanly.

The maternal in the quality we call womanly is its most important ingredient and is independent of the physical fact of
whether the woman is actually a mother or not. I remember that
I read, when a little boy, a short story by an early Austrian

woman writer—was it Marie Ebner-Echenbach?—which gave me
food for some very strange thoughts and made me look at my
teacher in elementary school with new eyes. If I remember correctly the story tells about a young woman, a teacher, who has
a romantic experience with a young man during a summer
vacation. Disappointed in her love the girl, who had daydreamed
of married life, of a husband, a child and a home, comes home
in the fall. Deeply depressed, she returns to her school. Feeling
herself surrounded by the many children in her class, her grief
and despair slowly evaporate on that first day. The story closes
with a sentence that has remained with me for sixty years: "The
childless woman can have the most children." It is in this best
sense that we could apply the term womanly here.

It is strange that in the childhood memories of men the feminine in their mother plays such a minor role while the womanly
continues to live in their memory. There is also a difference in
the emotional aspects of the memories in men and in women
regarding their mother in their childhood. In women's memories
mostly the feminine character of their mother is preserved. A
patient remembered that she became aware in her early childhood that mother had a "telephone voice."

The repressive effects of the incestuous taboo have certainly the
main share in the avoidance of this part of childhood memories
in men. It is noteworthy that the idealization of mother is so
intimately connected with the memory of her womanly character.
It is clear that this side of her nature is of importance also from
the point of view of the little boy's ego development.

Here is a little memory that seems to confirm this analytic
conclusion: many signs seem to speak for the fact that I must
have been a dreamy, almost indolent little boy. None of the
"bright sayings" proud mother's tell of their children have been
preserved from my childhood. The only sentence that my mother
used to quote with a smile was anything but "clever" or "intelligent." Whenever she would go out to shop or pay a visit I
would begin to cry and then complain, sobbing: "Who will pick
me up when I fall down?" It must have been at the age when

I had not yet succeeded in walking well. My sorrowful question
does not only show the crass selfishness of the little boy, but
also his utter lack of imagination. It seems as though I were
unable to think that someone else could pick me up if I were to
fall. But the restriction of this function to mother was perhaps
not the result of my stupidity but the expression of my wish to
be picked up only by her.

So tenacious was that belief in the omnipotence of the
"womanly" that it has remained somewhere in me, unaffected
by the disappointments and disillusions life brings to every man.
I still remember the echo of this childhood conviction. It sounded
in me in high school when I first read those wonderful verses
with which Goethe brings his *Faust* to its close:

> *Das Unbeschreibliche*
> *Hier ist es getan*
> *Das Ewig-Weibliche*
> *Zieht uns hinan.*

> Here the ineffable
> Wrought it with love
> The Eternal-Womanly
> Draws us above.

What I had felt as a little boy had here reappeared in its most
sublimated and mystic form.

Can we imagine that in those solemn verses the "eternal feminine" could replace the "eternal womanly?" Certainly not. The
uplifting function of the "eternal feminine" is confined to the
penis. In the beginning, it is true, mother is the object of the sensual as well as the tender longings of the little boy, but the
incest frontier is soon erected. The sexual drives soon search for
another object and mother remains the object of only tender
feelings.

The feminine is certainly old, but it is just as certainly not
eternal. It cannot be imagined that the feminine was very apparent in the women of the old stone age. It is perhaps not much

older than the neolithic age in which human culture started. The
wife and daughter of early man had certainly very few feminine
characteristics. Yet it is almost certain that they already had some
womanly qualities.

No, there is no "eternal feminine" because the feminine character features appear also in the little girl only at a certain, although early, phase of her development. Strictly speaking, there
is also no "eternal womanly" since it can, at best, be traced back
no farther than the beginning of sexual differentiation. There
were eons in which evolution did not yet differentiate males or
females and many species of protozoa still live in blissful ignorance of that important difference. But as soon as human females
first appeared on this small planet there were traces of the womanly, while the feminine entered the world only when it awakened from its long sleep. In this sense which unites the biological
and the psychological origins, you can well speak of the womanly
as the beginning and the final goal of the female, whose femininity is a transitory phenomenon. The womanly in woman is
the permanent, while her femininity is, in Charles Darwin's
words, her "evanescent" attraction.

In the best moments, the most feminine creature becomes also
aware of the womanly within herself. This essential part remains
outside the competition with man. It has an elevated place, removed from the battle of the sexes, *"hors de la mêlée."* It is the
element that is woman's power and glory. It is not affected by
the lust for power nor by the fight for woman's independence.
Anatole France thought of this eternal womanly when he once
remarked that a woman who insists on equality renounces her
superiority.

12. MEN, WOMEN AND DRESSES

A systematic and complete reconstruction of the development
of mental phenomena in the sense of genetic psychology does not
belong to the aims of psychoanalysis. But understanding of a

certain emotional process or mental state means also, to the analyst, to comprehend its origin and evolution. His method allows
him a penetration into deep levels that are not accessible to the
historic method of genetic psychology. It enables him to discover
traces of a long forgotten past in the latest phases of development. Early repressed impressions leave indelible traces in the
individual life. It is often difficult to recognize them in their
late manifestations. They are protected by a kind of mental
mimicry. They take on a protective appearance similar to that of
their surroundings, such as the circumstances of a later situation
in the individual's life. Other traces become unrecognizable by
displacement or different means of distortion and appear in the
forms of rationalization. Some early traces can, however, be discovered intact, undistorted except by their adjustment to a new
situation. They are unsuspected and remain unrecognized as
psychological signs of that original phase because they can well
pass as natural and appropriate expressions of recent phases.
Their surface resemblance with neighboring phenomena is a defensive cover and prevents the investigator from identifying them.
They are taken as contemporary expressions since they appear
among other similar ones in the middle of adult behavior patterns. It is as if you discover in the change you just got in a store
an ancient coin, for instance a drachma from the time of Alex-
ander the Great. The coin has perhaps passed through many
hands and was mistaken for a quarter of our American money,
which it resembles. Its value for the collector and connoisseur is,
of course, many times higher and you wonder how it could have
remained unidentified for so long.

In the following paragraphs two instances of such inconspicuous and not yet recognized residues are presented in the form
of two everyday sentences one hears without giving them much
thought.

The Viennese actress Adele S. visited her niece in the maternity
ward where the young woman had just given birth to a child.
When the baby was shown to her, the old actress said, "If memory does not fail me, it is a boy."

The remark concerns, of course, memories of the numerous affairs the actress had had in her youth, but she could have referred to much earlier memories. The little girl discovers early that the body of a boy is shaped differently than her own. Interested in the urinary functions, as all children are, she becomes aware that the boy has certain advantages. A little girl, seeing a boy urinating while standing at a tree observed, "How convenient!" The male organ is, however, considered not only as useful but also as ornamental by the female child. The well known pediatrician, Dr. Benjamin Spock, reported that a little girl who had observed a boy nude complained to her mother, "But he's so fancy and I am so plain."

We will not follow here the direction of the emergence of the typical penis envy and its later reactions. It is well known that the female child soon feels handicapped and that the physical difference between the sexes is transformed into an inferiority in her eyes. Psychoanalysis has made it clear in which way this early handicap is, at least to a great extent, emotionally conquered. The girl becomes proud of her figure and of the other physical gifts nature has bestowed upon her. Freud showed us, however, that feminine vanity is still a reaction to the unconscious feeling of being put at a disadvantage. The woman conceives of her physical charms as a late compensation for the original sexual inferiority feeling. She has to appreciate those physical gifts the higher, the deeper she once felt handicapped on account of her penislessness.

All this is known, but what is perhaps not yet analytically appreciated are the effects of the displacement of this compensation from the female body to the dress, to the adornment, to the attractive curtain covering the picture. It is obvious how much of the attention originally paid to the body itself is displaced to the gown. The enjoyment of the material, of its smoothness, the quality and firmness of texture, so typically feminine, is certainly to be understood as such transference of interest from the delicate female body to the garment. A deeper analytical investigation could explain why every woman wants to dress differently

from other women, yet to remain obedient to the trend of fashion. It could also explain the petty rivalry and jealousy among
women with regard to their wardrobe and the fact that woman
appears to herself as a new personality when she puts on a new
dress. Pride and shame with regard to dresses must have their
unconscious roots in the attempt at consolation and compensation by the displacement from the body to the dress.

To control the temptation of following these interesting threads
through the psychology of womanhood is easy because we discovered at least one small and inconspicuous trace in which the repressed complaint about the anatomical handicap surprisingly
re-emerges in a substitute displacement to the dress. It seems that
the feeling of being at a disadvantage which the little girl once
felt is successfully compensated for when the mature woman has
acknowledged her loss and when her vanity is satisfied by the
development of her body to beauty. Also her dress that shows it
to best advantage has helped her to forget and forgive that early
feeling of personal handicap.

There is, however, at least one typical feature of adult women
in which that old complaint, unrecognized, survives even in its
late displacement to dresses; a complaint that is almost universal
and in which that feeling of sexual imperfection is preserved
through all classes and ages. It is the complaint, "I haven't a
thing to wear." This sentence is spoken, this thought is thought,
regardless of whether the woman has really too few dresses or
whether she has double or triple the wardrobe necessary for every
social occasion. It is an idea that expresses the solidarity of all
women. A lady, who is considered one of the best dressed women
of this country, confided to me that she caught herself with that
same thought, although she knows that she has plenty of dresses,
gowns, costumes and so on for every occasion. It seems that that
idea is almost an automatic reaction, a kind of mental reflex in
every woman. We conjecture that it must have an unconscious
motivation which enables the woman to disregard the reality.

"I have nothing to wear" is, it seems to me, the old, forgotten
complaint, in a new form, dressed up as a grievance on account

of not having enough dresses. The old complaint of the little girl about the lack of a penis has followed the life of the mature woman and becomes articulate in this typical feminine sentence. It resounds in the late development which displaced the complaint from the body to the dress. Unrecognized by the woman herself, that complaint about her defectiveness has become immortal and proclaims in a new form the sentence, "Frailty, thy name is woman."

Women sometimes say that they dress for men, but most certainly not for men alone. They dress also for other women and, above all, for themselves. In fairness to their opinion one has to admit that this concept of their motives is correct. It seems that they have to like what they see in the mirror before they can hope to be attractive to others. The impression they have of their own appearance is certainly one of the most decisive factors in the anticipation of the impression they hope to make on others. The woman who looks into the mirror sees herself with the eyes of others, sometimes only with the eyes of a single person. It cannot be denied that the impression at this "dress rehearsal" is of greatest importance in deciding whether or not she will appear attractive to others later on. If she is well satisfied with her appearance it will strengthen her self-confidence and she will bloom in her beauty. A woman who wants to be attractive to others has first to appear attractive to herself. The sentence which a young patient of mine once expressed in a psychoanalytic session, "When I am shabbily dressed I hate everybody," should be posted in every dress store. It contains one of those basic psychologic truths so generally neglected. If not for esthetic reasons, the conclusion expressed in that sentence should be considered in the name of love of mankind. A woman who knows she is well dressed will, in general, be amiable and will need no effort to reach her aim to please.

No sensible woman will deny that she also dresses for men, that is, to be attractive to men. It need not be her husband; indeed, in some cases it is for all men but the husband. In one of the stories by Dorothy Parker (*The Lovely Leave*) a young wife

awaits the arrival of her husband, who comes home on leave. She
has made herself beautiful and has bought herself one of those
black, simple dresses that are so expensive because she knew he
liked black and simple dresses. She asks him whether he really
likes it:

"Oh, yes," he said, "I always liked that dress on you." It was
as if she turned to wood. "This dress," she said, enunciating with
insulting directness, "is brand new. I had never had it on before
in my life. In case you are interested, I bought it particularly for
this occasion."

"I'm sorry, honey," he said. "Oh, sure, now I see it's not the
other one at all. I think it's great. I like you in black."

"At moments like this," she replied, "I almost wish I were in
it for another reason."

The grim wish to become a widow because her young husband
did not appreciate her dress is to us men psychologically not
very understandable, but we realize that the feeling of being so
deeply hurt cannot concern this special dress alone. The woman's
emotions have their roots in the awareness that the man does not
appreciate her physical beauty and the body beneath the dress.
The old, forgotten feeling of being handicapped, a feeling from
which the little girl suffered on account of her penislessness, intensified the sensitiveness of the woman for the lack of attention
her husband showed with regard to her dress. She feels that lack
the more because she made herself attractive for him. She might
also feel hurt if she had prepared an excellent dinner for him
which he does not appreciate and eats without paying attention
to her endeavors. But the injury to her pride in the case of the
new dress has a different character because it gets its resonance
in the unconscious renewal of the infantile feeling that the boy
does not admire the body of the little girl, or rather that she felt
inadequate with regard to her own body compared with that of
the male. In the scene Dorothy Parker describes a mature man
and woman speak about a new dress, but their conversation has
undertones in which the voices of a little girl and a little boy
become audible. In the disappointment of the young wife the

disillusionment of the female child re-emerges in the displacement to the substitute of the dress.

It seems that the hope that the man will appreciate the beauty of her body also in its cover of a dress remains indelible in women. The death wish of the young wife against her husband who spoke perfunctorily of her new dress reminds us of an old French song in which a young widow is consoled: "Don't cry; the black is so becoming to you!" (*Ne pleure pas: le noir te va si bien.*)

But let us turn from the eternal and always actual theme of feminine vanity to the psychology of the man. Why does the young husband pay so little attention to the new dress his wife has bought to please him? Should we agree with her that he is thoughtless and inconsiderate, a kind of unfeeling brute? But, come to think of it, each of us has occasionally been as thoughtless and inattentive with regard to a new dress of a wife or sweetheart. Since his lack of attention or interest in this direction is typical of most men, are we males not all monsters when we appear indifferent to a new or altered dress, or when we are not aware of a new hat or a changed hair-do? Women take it for granted that we do not know much about the cuts and styles of dresses and that we do not properly evaluate the color and material combinations of what they wear, but what makes it necessary for them to turn our attention to the fact that they have a new blouse or that their dress has a new collar? They expect us to realize those facts ourselves and are disappointed when we don't. Our lack of interest or attention goes so far that we often do not even know the names of different materials and styles and sometimes have difficulty in recognizing what they mean when they discuss parts of feminine apparel.

We remember that there are certain groups of men who differ from the average male in this direction. They have an excellent knowledge of those things and show a great interest in them. They are able and willing to appreciate the specific qualities of feminine clothes. We mean a certain type of homosexual men. I heard the other day that many ladies like to show their new dresses to homosexual men who have taste and interest to such a degree that they are to be considered experts who can evaluate the special qualities and criticize the shortcomings of the dresses. It is not astonishing that a major number of male dress designers, fashion experts and dress salesmen belong to this group or have, at least, intense latent homosexual tendencies.

If the dress is, psychologically considered, an extension of a woman's body, how can it be explained that this type of homosexual men pays so much attention to feminine clothes and shows so much taste and fine appreciation for them? These homosexual men do not desire women sexually and have made them superfluous as love-objects. They identify themselves unconsciously with the woman who wears the dress, see themselves in the dress and arrive thus at a vicarious image of themselves wearing it. They are interested in women's clothes by means of this concealed detour of their feminine identification.

There is another group of males who pay special attention to feminine apparel, though rarely to dresses. Their interest is of a particular kind: it seems to be exaggerated, yes, to amount to a kind of worship for certain parts of women's wear, such as panties, brassières, stockings or shoes. We mean the group of male fetishists. (Fetishism in women is very rare.) We would expect that these men who manifest such a passionate interest and an almost religious adoration for feminine apparel would love the woman's body. But the truth is that their idolatry concerns, in most cases, the fetishistic object apart from the body. It is isolated and impersonal. A foot-fetishist does not get sexually excited by the shoes a certain woman wears but by shoes without the woman. His passion for the object is not concerned with the woman clothed with it but for the fetish separated from the woman.

Psychoanalysis leaves no doubt that the perversion of fetishism does not amount to a worship of the female body in its beauty but to an imaginary denial of its real nature. The fetish is the symbol and the substitute of the penis this body does not possess; it is unconsciously conceived as a male genital. The repressed meaning of almost all cases of fetishism reveals itself in psychoanalysis as the most energetic denial and repudiation of the fact that the woman is penisless. In the displacement to the fetish as a substitute, those men express the unconscious thought that a woman *does* have a penis. The most important motive for such an astounding belief is the warding off of the unconscious castration fear of the man. It is as if he tenaciously clings to the infantile belief that all women must also have a penis because he does not want to acknowledge the fact that there are penisless human beings, ones who *are* "castrated." If castration were possible the potential danger of castration threatens also himself.

We arrive at the astonishing result that the two types of men who show a great interest for feminine attire, the homosexual and the fetishists, do not consider the body of the woman very attractive and desirable. There sexual interests go in other directions: the homosexual's in that of other men and the fetishist's in that of inanimate objects. The average man who feels attracted to women shows remarkable lack of attention and interest for the special styles of feminine fashion and for the different parts of women's wear. He is usually bored when ladies discuss clothes in detail and he considers a visit at the dressmaker who fits a dress or the accompanying of his wife who wants to buy a new outfit at Lord and Taylor's as a minor endurance test. It can happen that a man whose wife scolded him for confusing the material of her fur arrives at a point of fatalistic resignation or supreme indifference with regard to such reprimands. He thinks that you might as well be hung for a sheep as for a lamb or a mink.

But is it really true that the average man does not pay much attention to women's wear? A man who calls to mind the figure of a woman he has admired very much at a dinner party remembers, of course, also her dress. He sees in his imagination the way she walked in beauty into the room and that she was dressed in exquisite taste. Asked what she had been wearing he might even say, "A black evening gown," and recall that she had a full skirt gliding in soft folds. Further interviewed about the material and the cut of that dress, he will be unable to give any information or answer in vague words that reveal his ignorance or his lack of attention. Yet that man is a person with a remarkable gift of observation and there cannot be any doubt that he feels very attracted to this lady. It cannot be asserted that he was unaware of the dress she had on but his interest did not concern itself with what she was wearing but with the wearer herself. The dress is, for him, comparable to the very appropriate and becoming frame of the picture that he admired. A full lack of attention for women's apparel cannot be asserted because such an assumption is contradicted by several facts. In the case of this particular man it can, for instance, be mentioned that the attractive impression a young lady had made upon him at a certain social occasion was somewhere disturbed by an observation that the seams of her nylon stockings were crooked. On the other hand his memory has kept the figure of the young girl who had been his sweetheart when he was in his late teens to such an extent that he can recall the dress she wore on their first date. He can call up the picture of how he first saw her in a wide circular blue skirt and that he composed then a poem in which he compared the girl's appearance with a bluebell. We can thus assume that the interest and attention of this man—and most men—for women's wear is of a special kind and so is his lack of interest and attention. It seems that dresses and feminine accessories make an impression upon him or intensify the impression their graceful wearer made upon him, but they affect him in their entirety, not as individual and separate objects. This impression is that of a general effect. It is that of an ensemble, of all parts seen together. The reverse side of this kind of attention is that the parts of feminine apparel remain at the fringes of observation, are either not seen or appear blurred, are seen dimly or indistinctly.

We are far from being content with the preceding general characterization of man's mental attitude to women's clothes. There must be certain aspects of this attitude which are not even mentioned in this sketchy survey. The other day the owner of one of our most elegant dress stores stated that a dress is successful when it awakens in the man who looks at the woman the wish to take it off, to undress her. This sexual side of man's attitude toward women's clothes was not considered in our survey; yet it cannot be unimportant. Women's wear as a means of attracting men's attention and interest, the dress that follows the lines of the female body, the outfit that reveals and conceals those lines as lure—how could we have left this most essential part of the problem outside our psychological consideration? The only excuse we can offer is that this subject goes beyond the narrow limitations set to us, but we are aware of how meaningful this aspect is for the evaluation of men's psychological attitude toward women's clothes. It must have a bearing on the theme of the general attention men pay to women and of the lack of attention they show, of that mixture of being interested and unobserving at the same time. Everyday experience leaves no doubt that this paradoxical attitude, contradictory in itself, is the typical attitude of the average male toward women's clothes. We guess that there are some unconscious motives operating in the genesis of this attitude besides the conscious and natural lack of knowledge. We take it for granted that women know more about their apparel, have more interest and develop a better taste for it than men, but the typical masculine attitude is too complex and conspicuous in its manifestations to be explained by these superficial factors.

Where can we find the unconscious agents determinating that attitude of the average man? A direct inquiry does not promise much hope of sufficient information. Only psychoanalysis could perhaps explore that unmapped area. Inquiry into the psychological peculiarities of homosexual and fetishistic perverts has cast an interesting sidelight on the problem, or rather at its marginal areas. But the insights we owe to the analytic exploration of those perverted men were of a negative kind. They convinced us that the men who show an intense interest for women's wear are not sure of their masculinity. The homosexuals unconsciously wish to be women themselves and the fetishists search for the penis on woman's body and are unconsciously afraid of the menace of castration. No, these men are, in their attitude toward dresses, too different from us. Their strong interest for feminine apparel is not only atypical, it is pathological. We have to search for analytical insight into the psychology of men who behave normally or at least not pathologically in this direction. The analytic practice gives us ample occasion to observe such men.

An astonishingly great number of men are of the opinion that women are more attractive partly dressed or *en déshabillé* than nude. They prefer to see women partially disrobed to the sight of complete nakedness. In many cases the development of sexual excitement is retarded or weakened by the nude body while the sight of the partly unclothed female body effects these men as exciting. Each analyst knows cases in which men reach their full sexual potency only when the woman remains at least partly dressed. When their sexual partners are entirely nude, this type of men become impotent or are only capriciously potent. Because they feel less attracted by the nude figure these men insist that the women keep their brassière, their shoes or stockings on before and during sexual intercourse. The etchings of the famous Flemish painter Felicien Rops (1833-1898) indicate that the artist belonged to this type of men for whom the partly uncovered female body is more attractive than the naked. His beautiful female nudes invariably wear either a hat or stockings and shoes.

It is obvious that denudation is, for this type of men, preferable to nudity because it meets certain requirements of sexual excitability and that this condition of their sexuality is determined by several factors, for example by unconscious memories of sexual observation in childhood. The psychological evaluation of these stimulating factors does not exclude that another essential moment has to be considered. In those cases in which the sight of the nude female body is inhibiting or disturbing to the sexual potency of the man, psychoanalysis could prove that the uncovered vagina reminded the man unconsciously of the infantile concept of the female organ as a wound and awakened his own dormant castration fear. In most cases the nudity of the female figure has to be covered at least at one place or the other to counterbalance this old impression. The brassière or the shoes provide the illusion that the woman is, so to speak, "intact." This compensatory moment will alone or in combination with old trends of voyeurism transform the pleasure at the sight of nakedness into that of denudation. Women have often sensed those special conditions of masculine sexuality and reacted to them with their fine sexual instincts in acceptance or rejection. A typical feminine reaction of this kind is to be found in a love scene between a woman and a man in the novel *Monsieur Bergeret à Paris* by Anatole France: "He came again to her, took her in his arms and overwhelmed her with caresses. In a short time she saw her underwear in such disorder that—not to mention other feelings—shame itself would have demanded to take them off."

The analytic exploration of the masculine attitude that prefers the denuded to the nude female figure suggests a psychological kinship of this type of men with the fetishists, in spite of all obvious differences. But these men behave otherwise normally in their sexual life: they do not differ from other men in the choice of their objects nor in the aims of their sexuality. Superficially considered, that preference appears as a matter of taste, but we have to conceive of it as an unconscious remnant of a reluctance to see the female body entirely naked. In analytic investigation that piece of garment the woman should keep on has its secret function: to help the man to overcome the old castration fear, to deny the infantile concept that women are castrated. That bit of feminine cloth unconsciously reassures the man that he is not threatened with castration. "It cannot happen here." In the disguise of esthetic evaluation or intensified sexual stimulation that trifling preference serves to alleviate or remove an old fear of the little boy, an obsolete childhood impression that had been buried so long ago that not even the place where it was put to rest is remembered any more. Yet we discovered that it had been unconsciously displaced from the sight of the female body to that of its cover, from the figure of the woman to her garment.

We have presented the thesis that a decisive factor in the

greater interest and attention women show for dresses is that
these dresses are unconsciously considered substitutes and com-
pensations for the lack of a penis. Psychological necessity would
make us assume that there must be an unconscious companion
picture on the side of the men, a masculine counterpart of this
attitude. That means that certain emotional or mental reactions
of men must reveal that they too are unconsciously aware of
that secret meaning of women's wear. The psychology of the
fetishist seems to confirm such a supposition, but we cannot use
that evidence because it concerns a pathological type, belongs
to the symptomatology of sexual perversion. That preference of
the partly unclothed female body to the nude is, it is true, within
the bounds of normal sexuality of the human male, but the
phenomenon can, in spite of its frequency, not be used as psychological circumstantial evidence because so many men do not
share this preference.

There is not the slightest trace in the conscious thoughts of the
average man that connects dresses in his associations intimately
with the female genitals. Yet there we have the still unexplained
lack of attention and interest of the average man for the details
of feminine apparel. Many impressions gained from years of analytic observation suggested that unconscious factors are operating
in this lack of masculine attention which is often replaced by
doubts or uncertainties about the forms, functions and materials
of feminine garments. The casualness with which the average
man glances at the gown of a woman seems to indicate that, besides and beyond the obvious and conscious moments, an unknown emotional agent is responsible for this typical masculine
attitude. Fine observation shows that the description of this attitude as lack of attention and interest is oversimplified. It is
rather a strange mixture of these traits with a kind of reluctance,
as if the man does not want to pay much attention to women's
apparel, together with some curiosity, a shy combination of
wanting to know and not wanting to know. It would, of course,
be unseemly if a man would stare at a woman's dress or even
look at it with the same scrutiny with which some women ex-

amine the clothes of other women. ("I looked her over, but good.") But that casual glance of the average man at women's wear has a peculiar character; it combines a looking at it and looking away.

When impressions that are distinct yet unable to become verbalized are accumulated, often a casual sentence spoken by another person provides a sudden clarity. Such a casual remark which a patient dropped opened the avenue to the analytic understanding of the typical masculine attitude characterized above.

I still remember this sentence, although it was said almost twenty-five years ago, because it was put in a funny way. I was practicing at that time in Berlin and many of the Berlin colloquialisms were unknown to me, who was born and bred in Vienna. The patient had spoken of his wife, who had talked at length of a dress she wanted to buy and which she described fully and in detail to him. He spoke of his growing impatience and added to his report one of those Berlin colloquialisms: *"So jenau woll'n wir das gar nicht wete,"* which is perhaps best translatable with: "We don't even care to know that so precisely." This colloquialism is often used at occasions in which people refuse to acknowledge certain unpleasant parts of reality. I heard this expression used about a documentary film in which the process of digestion was presented. The man who said then, "We don't relish to know that so accurately," expressed his displeasure at the unappetizing picture in that sentence. Its meaning is clear. It is similar to the advice of a French proverb not to look too close at life if you want to enjoy it. (*"Pour rendre agréable la vie, n'y regardons pas de trop près."*)

The patient who used that colloquialism with regard to the copious description of his wife's dress uttered the typical masculine lack of interest in a drastic form. He expressed his impatience with the attention his wife paid to the details of her garment. But I heard something else in his sentence. Its casualness could not conceal its psychological importance. It contained the key word for which I had searched so long. It is *not* simply lack of interest or attention that determined the typical male attitude to feminine garment. It is rather an unwillingness or reluctance to know all the details. What can be the reason for such an "unreasonable" attitude?

We need only to pick up the thread we dropped before, namely, the assumption that there must be an unconscious counterpart of the feminine attitude to dresses on the side of men. The factor we found is of a negative character: the masculine refusal to know "that" so precisely. The sentence of the patient could be characterized as the expression of a denial, a mechanism that tries to keep unpleasant facts from acknowledgment by the person. In the negation of such an unpleasant fact a compromise is reached between the acceptance of a truth and its rejection.

If the dress is an extension of the female body the unconscious denial of some knowledge concerned originally the woman's figure. There was in the boy who became aware of the existence of the vagina an unconscious tendency to disavow what he had observed, namely, that women have no penis. This tendency had to fight with impulses from the area of sexuality. The result of this fight is that the truth is accepted and acknowledged by reason and by the conscious part of the ego while it is denied in phantasies and in unconscious thoughts. That unconscious denial is displaced from the female body to the dress that reveals it and expresses itself in that conspicuous lack of attention paid to gowns and dresses. That infantile pattern of wanting to find out what the female body is like and the opposite tendency ("We don't care to know that so precisely.") followed the boy into later years and were displaced onto the feminine garment that covers the naked body of the woman. In partial denial, the man refuses to know all details of the garment that is a displaced substitute of the feminine figure, as if such knowledge and interest would lead to the old unpleasant and unconsciously frightening discovery of woman's penislessness.

This denial certainly does not go to the fantastic lengths the cases of fetishists show. It is rather a small, isolated remnant of the boy's attempt to disavow the fact that women have no penis and it is restricted to the withdrawal of attention and interest for feminine garments. It forms part of the masculine attitude toward dresses which is a compromise expression between the curious and the denying tendencies and leads to the casual glance at a gown which we so often observe in men. There is a trace of the disavowal in the ensemble effect of a dress on a man because the tendency goes in the direction of having a superficial picture without accurate consideration of the details.

The flippant colloquialism revealed to us a last residue of the original attitude of the man in the substitution of his old concept of the woman's body. In this detail, as in similar ones (a patient felt unpleasant sensations when the "cut" of a dress was mentioned), a very remote trace of an old fear is followed up to the mature age of manhood. The trace was not easy to pursue because it disguised itself as natural and rational social expression of the average man and it was very remote from the place where it originally showed itself. It was almost imperceptible because it seemed to form part and parcel of the usual masculine behavior pattern and we did not suspect unconscious emotional factors operating behind this screen.

Looking back at this survey of the psychological differences between the sexes as they manifest themselves in their attitude to dresses, we are astonished to recognize that decisive misconceptions on both sides do not exclude an unconscious communication. In spite of so many misgivings and mistakes there is also here a give and take between men and women.

13. SEXUALIZATION OF CLOTHES
(Counterpoint)

Are there women fetishists—women who show an abnormal attachment of an erotic nature projected onto some inanimate object? If there are, they are few and far between and the psychiatrists and psychoanalysts do not encounter many of them in their consultations. As a matter of fact an erotic or sexual overappreciation of a man's shoe or jacket can only very rarely be found in women. Why should this be so? We want to approach that question from an unusual angle.

Once a woman student in a seminar asserted quite seriously that women would not pay so much attention to clothes if men were less concerned with what women wear. That sounds paradoxical since, according to common experience, men are not too interested in the clothes women wear, excepting dress designers and people in the garment industry. Nevertheless the student's assertion makes sense; not in the primitive form of whether or not it is important to men that women be dressed or nude but in the sense that men are unconsciously fascinated by the feminine garment. I do not mean fetishists and male transvestites, but normal, average men. This special kind of interest can, in contrast to fetishism, be best described as a sexualization of clothes. This means that the sight and sometimes even the visual phantasy of a woman's clothes awakens in a man the image of her body much more often than the sight of a man's clothes awakens the image of his body in a woman.

Yes, in general women's clothes belong to the "body image" man has of the other sex. In New York slang often used in Damon Runyon's stories a "skirt" means a woman. For many men a skirt is not a garment covering the lower part of a woman's body but rather the lower part of a woman's body transformed into a garment. The sexual curiosity of the man is certainly a determining factor in this unconscious concept. August Strindberg, that monomaniac about women in attraction and hate, searched again and again for a mate and was again and again disappointed and disillusioned. (At the turn of the century they told in Vienna the anecdote that a man who was introduced to a woman at a dinner party asked her: "You are Swedish, madame? When were you married to Strindberg?") A friend of the unhappy or pathetic writer reported that he often heard him moan: "The skirts! . . . the skirts!" Those garments seem really to conceal, for many men, a secret along with the challenge to discover it.

Why are women not possessed with a similar curiosity about that concealed part of a man's body? The next, and most convenient, answer would be that the localization of the female genitals and the fact that they are hidden or concealed is responsible for the masculine search. Psychoanalytic exploration does not deny this factor but analytic penetration into the childhood memories of adults as direct observation of boys leads to much deeper insights. The little boy assumes at first that girls are formed as he is (originally he thinks that also inanimate objects—for instance a table—have a penis). When he discovers —let us say by accidental observation—the truth, he still clings tenaciously to this infantile concept. He disavows what he has seen. This seems to be odd, but not more so than the behavior of many scholars or scientists who disavow their perception because it contradicts a preconceived idea. Seeing is not believing in the case of the little boy who has observed a woman's nude body. But why this disavowal? It cannot be, as with the scientists, purely theoretical reasons operating in the little boy's clinging to his original theory that women have a penis like himself. Among the secret reasons for the tenacity of this assumption the castration fear is most important. This fear suggests that he could be deprived of his own penis if women do not possess that very valuable part. He could become like them. Unaffected by later and better knowledge, that old infantile fear continues to live unconsciously in the man.

The intimate, subterranean connections which exist between that castration fear and the attitude men have toward women's clothes were explored and presented by J. C. Flugel in an interesting and amusing book.* Also other psychoanalysts have dealt with this complicated problem. It seems to me that one of its aspects has been entirely neglected by research and I will approach the question from this angle.

It seems to me that psychoanalysts have almost never inquired into the extent to which a certain degree of fetishism belongs to

* *The Psychology of Clothes,* The Hogarth Press, London, 1930.

the sphere of sexual attraction. According to Freud* such a normal "fetishism" can be observed in a man's love life, especially in the phases in which the sexual aim is unattainable and its realization impossible at the time. Psychoanalysis, which restricts its research area more and more to the pathological, has not considered, for instance, the characteristic displacements of that normal fetishism. Why is it, for example, that a high-heeled shoe is so much more attractive on a woman than a low-heeled one? A skeptical philosopher in the salons of Paris wonders, in one of Anatole France's stories, at the fact that the attractiveness of a woman should depend upon the angle formed by the sole of her shoe and the ground upon which she treads. Well, it is of course exaggerated to assume that a woman's lure depends upon that factor, but it does form one of the tiny elements within it.

If Byron had lived in London, New York or Paris today, he would perhaps not have said of a certain beautiful woman that "she walks in beauty" had he seen her strolling along in low-heeled shoes. Pascal remarked that the history of the world would have taken another turn if Cleopatra's nose had been shaped a little differently. Is it altogether unimaginable that some national, or even international, developments could be determined, even today, by the fact that a certain lady wore high heels or sheer nylon stockings? The sexualization of women's clothes is, in general, an unconscious process in men: it takes place on a preconscious level. A new approach to the problem involves new insights into those subterranean processes by finding novel, surprising factors. Women's clothes awaken preconsciously in the male observer the woman's "body image." In covering the body they reveal its form. One of the prominent French dress designers went so far as to say that a good dress is one that awakens in the man a wish to see the woman wearing it disrobed. He certainly did not mean that the dress should be of a very low cut or otherwise "sexy." One might almost say the

* *Gesammelte Schriften,* Vol. V, p. 27.

contrary: a dress that is in excellent taste, conservative and lady-like can often awaken such a wish while a very daring costume can at times almost fulfill and thereby make it superfluous. A Viennese writer once remarked that a certain lady was daringly but disappointingly décolleté.

Disturbances in the sexualization of women's clothes (that means in the normal unconscious body image of the clothed woman) are by no means restricted to the dress alone. They can be brought about by circumstances that impair the favorable impression a dress would otherwise create. Here is an example of this kind: a young woman, before going to bed, followed a sudden impulse to show her husband the new dress she had bought. She put it on quickly and went to the drawing room where he sat. He said, "How can I say anything about the dress when I see you wearing it with your hair uncombed and your stockings hanging down?" Another man scolded his wife, who had put her bra, panties and stockings carelessly on a chair in the bedroom. "If the things were at least pretty!" he indignantly added. How far can such a saying be tied in with the alleged lack of interest men have in women's clothes?

But back to our subject! A run in a woman's stockings, or even a conspicuous wrinkle, can disturb the sexualization of clothes. A skirt that does not hang just right can equally impair the delusion. What delusion? The infantile negative delusion that there is no vagina, the unconscious denial of the little boy that women's genital organs differ from his. It is as though an overemphasis on perfection in women's clothes were a reaction formation to a deeper sense of her imperfection, and in this perfection man finds a certain reassurance.

The difficulty in recognizing the part normal fetishism plays in the love life of a man is explained by the fact that we do not pay enough attention to the displacement of interest from parts of the body to its covering, to feminine attire. Karl Kraus once wrote: "I would rather forgive an ugly foot than an ugly stocking."

Why are there so few cases of fetishism in women? There are

different reasons, the first of which is that a woman's way to sexual excitement is generally not as direct as that of a man. Also her curiosity is less aroused by the genitals of a man, which are not secret or hidden. The little girl is early aware of the morphological difference between herself and the little boy. And, above all, she is rarely frightened by it. She is free of the castration fear that haunts the male in various shapes all his life. She too has many worries but this one is not among them.

14. Men, Women and Homes

It is scarcely one hundred and sixty years since Friedrich Schiller wrote that famous poem *The Lay of the Bell* in which he presented a beautiful word picture of human life. Today the roles of the two sexes are not as distinct and sharply contrasted in their social function as they appeared in Schiller's vision:

> The husband must enter
> The hostile life
> With struggle and strife
> To plant and to watch
> To snare or to snatch. . . .

But in the house

> . . . sits another
> The thrifty housewife
> The mild one, the mother,
> Her home is her life.
> In its circle she rules
> And the daughter she schools . . .

The contrast of "the hostile life" for the man with the home as the center of the world for the woman is not as pronounced today as it was in the days when our grandparents were young. Under the influence of the industrialization and mechanization of modern life the home has lost many of its old functions for men and women. It is no longer refuge, retreat and shelter from outside dangers. Man no longer feels that his house is his castle, nor does woman consider herself queen in her home. Yet some of its functions have been preserved and have withstood all social and psychological changes. Although the home has been stripped of many functions, it has kept its unconscious meaning as the continuation of man's first domicile, which was the womb. In our dreams the house or the room has still the symbolic significance of woman's body. This kind of symbolic representation was not discovered by psychoanalysis. It was already known to the ancient people, to the Egyptians, the Hebrews and the Greeks.

There is a danger that we treat this symbolic expression as a piece of esoteric insight, a knowledge reserved only for the understanding of dreams and myths. Yet that unconscious representation is not an isolated and disconnected expression of the dream state or of folktales. It is always actual and forms part of our everyday life. The room or the house is still unconsciously felt by every woman as the extension of her own body. This representative value has its most valid reasons in the structure and the function of her body. Social changes do not affect that significance as long as women's bodies carry and bear children. Her home, the room in which she lives, is for a woman the continuation of her body; it is her true self, that which she is, physically extended. Women have therefore great interest that their home should be not only comfortable but also look beautiful. The four walls represent herself in projection. The person who enters her room is in her presence, whether she is physically there or not.

The psychoanalyst who has recognized that the home has in woman's unconscious thoughts more than a vicarious significance, that it is conceived as almost identical with herself, will understand peculiarities and ways of feminine thinking which are

alien to men. This is valid for normal as well as for pathological
phenomena, concerns everyday considerations of average women
as well as symptomatical expressions of neurotic and psychotic
personalities. Here are a few instances of such expressions whose
understanding is impossible without recognition of that unconscious significance.

In spite of all conscious efforts a patient cannot achieve the
order and tidiness her husband demands in the apartment. There
is always some disorder, toys or tools on chairs and carpets, some
garment or some package that has been delivered and left in the
hall. It is not my intention to enter into a psychoanalytic discussion of this case or of the unconscious motivations and instinctual roots of this trait. On the more superficial level to
which this discussion is restricted, and which allows some descent
into deeper strata, insights into the patient's attitude were
reached which were surprising enough. Psychoanalytic exploration revealed that her negligence and carelessness had an unconscious purpose and were intended to ward off certain fears she
did not admit even to herself. Some of them concerned, obviously, the possibility of early death, because the patient, who
was brought up by nuns and had diligently read the Holy Scripture as a child, often thought with panic of the Biblical phrase
"to set thine house in order," so often used for an activity preparing for the final departure. (Compare the bass aria in Kantate
No. 106 by Bach: *"Bestelle dein Haus! Denn du wirst sterben
. . ."*) To put the apartment in order meant unconsciously to
the patient to make oneself ready to die. Her carelessness was
also therefore intended to avoid the emergence of that anxiety.

The unconscious identification of her body and of the house
also became apparent in another train of thought. She once had
felt very hurt when her husband had reproached her because she
left their son's little trumpet on the carpet instead of putting it
away. In thinking of that incident she became aware that she
experienced a strong reluctance to remove the tiny toy. Her
thoughts led her to the conclusion that she wished to retain this
slight disorderliness because it indicated that the child was still

small and was still at home. She was thinking with apprehension of the future in which the children would be grown up and would leave the house in which there would then be implacable order and perfect tidiness. The continuation of these reflections led, of course, to unwelcome thoughts of the menopause and of the age at which women cannot have children any more. The female body image extended to the dwelling place appears in this train of thought clearly enough.

Another manifestation of the same unconscious identification reveals itself in the symptomatology of the so-called *"Hausfrauen-neurosis,"* that incessant fury of cleaning, passionate dusting and polishing that many women do.

The apartment or the house that needs such a permanent purification is not so much a substitute for the body of the woman as its continuation. It is, to use an expression Daphne du Maurier used for her place, *La belle maison sans merci,* and demands to be tidied up, washed, cleaned and cleansed. Psychoanalysts recognize that that compulsion originally concerns the body of the woman and has the character of purification and atonement for masturbatory and anal activities, later on displaced to her home.

Some traits met with in many women belong to the psychological area of the unconscious identity of body and apartment. The first, rarely missing in women, is preoccupation with thoughts of their place, a visualization of their rooms, of the furniture, of the curtains and drapes, etc. A young girl who suffered from psoriasis and considered herself very unattractive had, at least consciously, given up the possibility that men could find anything beautiful in her appearance. She believed that she was disfigured by the skin disease and she lacked feminine vanity with regard to dresses and accessories. But she spent many hours in daydreaming about how beautifully and elegantly she would furnish her apartment, how carefully she would choose every single piece and visualized every detail of the arrangement of each room. She put all her esthetic sense, all her exquisite taste and artistic abilities into the service of the imagined decor, which she carefully planned for the phantasied case that she would become a millionairess. Psy-

choanalysis of this case would convince every unprejudiced observer that the girl had displaced her desire of being physically
attractive to the apartment. This desire is in reality indestructible in women as long as they are young, and even after they
are not young any more.

A second feminine trait is the wish to enhance the appearance
of the apartment. Comparison of the masculine and of the feminine attitude toward the rooms people live in shows that men
think that furniture should be appropriate and comfortable and
fulfill its function, should be in the proper place and within
easy reach. For women the room should first of all look beautiful.
Purposeful furniture arrangement is certainly not alien to
women, but the decorative element is of primary importance.
The two points of view of the useful and of the beautiful can
well coexist, but if they come into competition it is more frequently the woman who insists on appearance and the man who
wants the advantageous and serviceable in furniture arrangement. This psychologically significant contrast of the functional
and of the decorative will often lead to friction in the life of
young and not-so-young couples.

Here is a representative case of this kind reported by a patient
who is a musician. Beside his piano is a music cabinet with sheet-
music and a recording machine. His wife does not like that ugly
machine there—it does not look nice in the room—and wants it
removed. She wishes also to put the piano at another angle and
place the bookcase behind it. The result of these "moves" would
be that the recording machine would be at a distance so that the
husband would have to go to another room in order to use it,
the piano would not have as good a light and the bookcase would
be difficult to reach because the piano stood before it. "For
Christ's sake," shouted the husband during his psychoanalytic
session, "my wife ought to know by now that she is married to a
musician. What's the use of a recording machine away from the
piano at which I play and of books I cannot reach?" You have
here a drastic illustration of the contrast of the masculine and
feminine point of view. The poor man has really not much un-

derstanding and tolerance toward his wife's attitude. He does not look at the room with her eyes; although he sees the same things, he sees them from a different "view" point; that means with another view.

Here is another instance of the clash of views with some psychological side lights. The man had in his bachelor days a hat tree in the hall of his apartment and wished to have it again in the hall when he married. Is not a home conceived as a place where you can hang your hat? His wife did not like the hat tree. She wished to have a mirror on the wall across the entrance door so that ladies who came to visit could look at themselves before leaving. Was her wish not understandable? The remarkable thing is only that that mirror, so urgently needed, is now, six months later, still to be found face down on the sewing machine. Let us imagine that we could ask the lady about it and argue the case with her. She would perhaps say, "Sure, I wanted to hang the mirror, but I had an over-all picture in my mind of a mirror with two crystal side lights, which I cannot afford at present. I prefer to wait until I can have all these things together." Such an argument is very feminine. She would use a similar one for not buying a dress for which she cannot buy the appropriate accessories. But why does she not hang the mirror anyway in the meantime? Her answer would perhaps be that this would amount to giving up the hope of ever buying the crystal side lights. She would say, that she would perhaps get used to the mirror without them, and she prefers therefore to leave it unhung and to wait. When she sees it daily on the sewing machine she is reminded of what she really wishes and hopes to afford in the not too distant future. Such quibbling could perhaps drive a man to drink but is sound from the feminine point of view. And the hat tree? If we could interview her she would perhaps say, "Hat trees are for saloons and public places. I want a closet in the hall, but I don't dare ask my husband for it because he cannot spare the money at this time. But no woman wants a hat tree in her entrance hall."

Such domestic scenes cannot be psychologically understood

without insight into the very intimate relation of the apartment and the woman. Without such comprehension the average man stands helpless before certain phenomena of feminine behavior immediately understandable to all women. There is for instance the wish to change the furniture at periodical intervals, to throw old pieces out and buy new ones, to renew surroundings, to have rooms painted a new color or to "dress up" the apartment at Easter. It is obvious that here are unconscious attempts to change something in the woman's own appearance. A similar character has to be attributed to women's habit of rearranging their rooms, of shifting pieces of furniture around because they look better another way. These improvements are rarely permanent nor are they ever restricted to a single piece. The piano is, for instance, moved to another side to make the room look nicer, but that means that the couch has to be put at a new angle, the table and chairs to be pushed around and several pictures hung somewhere else. These feminine experiments are cosmetic procedures to improve one's appearance because the woman is not satisfied with her looks, in substitute—displacement to her apartment.

A very amusing short story by Nunnally Johnson, *There Ought to Be a Law*, published in 1930, presents a vivid report of such trials in rearrangement of furniture. A man discovers soon after his wedding that his wife is driven by the mysterious urge to shift pieces of furniture, so that they are in one place when he leaves in the morning, and in quite another spot when he comes home from his office. Such a passion upsets a young man, and when the merry-go-round of pieces continues, he finally decides to ask an elderly uncle for advice. But when he casually remarks that his wife "moves furniture" his relative misunderstands him and asks: "For a living?" The husband finds out, however, that he has many fellow sufferers; for instance, another man whose wife sees a modern furniture exhibition and buys there an iron easy chair, replacing his old one with this very uncomfortable piece. The domestic developments from this peculiarity of keeping all furniture on the go are funny and pathetic—especially when one considers that the young wife is propelled by the wish to make a cozy home for her husband. Is it her fault that he looks with misgiving at the spectacle of furniture spinning round, or that he hurts himself when, returning from the office late in the night, he lets himself fall in the darkness on the place where the bed used to stand?

In contrast to such experiments at unconscious improvement of one's looks are other cases in which a wife utterly neglects her apartment. I know a case in which a young wife succeeded in not furnishing the rooms, except with the most necessary pieces, although sufficient money was at her disposal, and her husband insisted on her buying furniture. The husband did not feel at home in the house. She unconsciously refused to furnish the apartment because she subterraneously knew that her marriage was not destined to last.

The unconscious equation of apartment and the woman herself comes in these symptomatic manifestations to clear expression. The biological and psychological roots of the unconscious identification make it understandable why the womanly touch can change the character and the atmosphere as well as the appearance of the places in which we live. By her unconscious extension to the apartment, a woman succeeds in transforming a house into a home.

In more than four decades of psychoanalytic practice I have encountered only a few cases of claustrophobia in women. It is perhaps accidental that most cases of this pathological fear of enclosed spaces met with in my practice concerned men. But inquiries of other analysts seem to confirm that claustrophobia is more frequent with men than with women. This would be analytically understandable if we accept the theory that claustrophobic sensations develop as reaction to phantasies of being in the mother's womb. This phantasy of returning to the womb is, in men's thoughts, often replaced or accompanied by the idea of being caught or trapped in the vagina, a special type of castration fear. There is, of course, nothing comparable in the psychology of women. The phantasy of the return to the mother's womb has for women rather a cozy character and is often con-

tinued by an imagined identification with the mother; otherwise put, by the idea of having a baby in their own womb.

The room in which they are does not often fill women with
that paniclike impression of terrifying narrowness, with the fear
that the walls are coming nearer to them, are closing them in
without a possibility of escape. The fact that they unconsciously
identify their own body with the room explains why they have
another attitude than the man, to whom such an equation is
alien. Women feel "at home" in their home, as in their body,
which has nothing terrifying for them because they are not
threatened by the menace of castration.

The last case of a woman patient who could be diagnosed as
claustrophobic—it was at the Highland Hospital at Asheville—
revealed itself on closer observation as a case of anxiety hysteria.
It was a farmer's wife who had symptoms of accelerated heart
beating, breathlessness and paniclike sensations when she was
alone at home. These painful reactions were absent when someone, for instance her three-year-old daughter, was in the room. It
became clear in analytic exploration that the feared situation of
being alone in the house had a sexualized character. It offered,
namely, a temptation to masturbation. The woman, who was
sexually unsatisfied because her husband was not very potent,
unconsciously experienced that temptation, to which she had
yielded in younger years and which was forbidden by her religious upbringing.

The same patient had also distinct symptoms of agoraphobia.
Her fear of open spaces concerned originally only a certain beach
near the city in which she had lived as a young girl. Later on it
was displaced to the streets of this city, to which she had often
to go to shop and visit relatives. Analysis soon discovered that
her phobic fear of that beach, which she had to pass when she
drove her car to the city, was connected with the memory of an
experience during puberty. She had spent an afternoon and
evening on the beach with a boy with whom she was in love and
of whom she daydreamed as her future husband. During the

"heavy petting" in which the two adolescents indulged the girl experienced her first orgasm. The boy later married another girl and my patient took her present husband, but she never forgot that scene on the beach and often regretted that she had not gone "the limit." The first attack of anxiety she experienced some years later when, after an unsatisfactory sexual intercourse with her husband, she drove to her native town and passed the beach. She must have unconsciously thought of that evening with the boy and must have felt sexual desire for him. In her anxiety she warded off those wishes, which she considered forbidden and sinful. The phobic reactions she developed later on went, in their scope, beyond such quickly passing anxieties. They occurred when she was shopping or visiting in her native town and crossed a street or a square. Her analysis made it clear that her agoraphobia started when she thought that there was a possibility of running into her old love-object who, she had heard, had returned home. The continuation of her thought is easily guessed. There must have been phantasies of meeting the sweetheart of her young years again and of having full sexual satisfaction with him. She reacted with a heavy attack to the unconscious temptation, which was originally connected with a certain street of the city but was later displaced to all streets and places. After she experienced these painful sensations several times when she had to cross a street in the city, she refused to go there alone. A relative or a neighbor had to accompany her. Only when she was with another person did she feel safe enough to cross streets. She was then protected against the temptation that was awakened in her imagination, the temptation to have a sexual adventure with the man whom she still desired, and to be unfaithful to her husband.

This case, which was successfully treated, brings a memory of Freud to mind, a memory which proves how early one of the most decisive factors in the psychological genesis of agoraphobia was recognized by him. Besides its scientific value the anecdote will be welcome as a contribution to the biography of the great man, who was at that time in a cynical mood. If I remember correctly it was in 1912 that Freud told the story, I do not know any more whether to me alone or in the presence of other students of his. During his stay in New York in 1909 he declined to see and treat patients, whom he referred to Dr. Brill and other American psychoanalysts. A gentleman whose wife suffered from agoraphobia pleaded several times with Freud to see his wife in consultation. Freud refused, but the man pestered the famous analyst and urgently asked for advice about what could be done to prevent the occurrence of her attacks. Freud, impatient with the man, who insisted on finding a quick cure for his wife's agoraphobic fears, said he felt like advising him: "Let your wife go out only with dirty underwear."

It would oversimplify the genesis of agoraphobic attacks of women if they were to be traced back only to reactions to unconscious phantasies of sexual temptation. Yet there can be no doubt that such reactions are at least one of the decisive unconscious factors.

We arrive thus again at our original question, why in women agoraphobia is much more frequent than claustrophobia. The question can also be put in terms of the contrast of home and street. Women feel much more protected from sexual temptations at home than on the street, where they can be approached by men.*

We do not forget that the contrast of at-home and on-the-street appears also in our everyday language as significant for certain types of women. The virtuous housewife, and the "nice" girl, is often characterized as "homebody," while people say of other women, whom they suspect in a sexual direction, that they have "been around," or that they are "fast." Do we not call a low class of prostitutes "streetwalkers"?

---

* Since this paper was written Freud's letters to Wilhelm Fliess were published (*Aus den Anfaengen der Psychoanalyse*, London, 1950). Freud wrote to his friend on December 17, 1896, that his conjecture on the mechanism of agoraphobia was confirmed. In this fear the woman's wish to give herself to the first man she may chance to meet is repressed.

A beautiful collection of artistic photographs, *The Decisive Moment*, by Henri Cartier-Bresson, contains a few pictures of prostitutes at their windows in Mexico City. The vulgar demonstration of their charms brought to my mind that the French know the phrase *"faire la fenêtre"* in the sense of prostitution. A whimsical short story of Guy de Maupassant deals with the subject. By contrast, typical scenes from novels of the Victorian era occurred to me. It is there often described that a girl stands behind a curtain, hidden from view, and follows an admired man with her glances. A scarcely perceptible movement of the ruffled material sometimes gives the presence of the coy girl away. The contrast between the behavior of the prostitutes, who display their sexual attractions in the window, and the concealment of the "nice" girl, a contrast between uninhibited exhibition and modest hiding of the two types of women, is symbolized by the absence or presence of window curtains.

The continuation of this thought led to the analytical understanding of the psychological difference between the attitudes of the average man and woman toward curtains. It brought to mind a scene a patient had reported to me in his analytic session the day before. He had married a few weeks ago and the young couple, who had not much money, were busy furnishing their modest apartment. The husband was surprised when his young wife insisted that one of the first things to be bought were window curtains. In his view there were pieces of furniture, like some more chairs and chests, that were much more needed. The disagreement led to the first tiff in the married life of the couple; the young wife cried because the husband showed so little understanding of her view. But he could not see why she wanted to spend money needed for more urgent things on ruffled curtains. She seemed to be unduly excited about his suggestion to postpone their purchase. He could not understand why she considered it shameful to leave the dining room a few weeks longer without curtains.

The unconscious undertones in that divergence of opinion about the importance and function of curtains became audible in the analytic session. It was obvious that window curtains had a different place in the thoughts of the husband and his young wife. For him curtains were just a piece of material to cover windows and nothing more. For women as for men windows are openings to let in air and light, but for women they mean not only that. The house or the apartment is for a woman an unconscious extension of herself, the room, a continuation of her own body. (The old German language has the expression *Frauenzimmer,* meaning women's room, which was later—even by Goethe—used for the woman herself, as if woman and room were identical.) In the symbolical language of the dream, house or room has the unconscious meaning of woman. Windows often have in this language the significance of an opening in the body, of the vulva of the woman.

The curtains on the window take the place of the underwear covering and hiding female genitals. This unconscious significance of curtains for women explains not only the special attention paid to them in their thoughts, to their style and fabric, their color and material, but also the importance curtains have for women with regard to the ensemble of the room. Besides decorative and practical considerations this unconscious role makes questions as to whether the curtains should be ruffled or plain, whether they should be made of organdy or nylon, whether there should be under curtains or not, appear very important to the feminine mind. Above all, the necessity of curtains at the windows finds its secret justification in that concealed emotional factor which is akin psychologically to modesty. We understand better now why the young wife in her argument could speak of shamefulness in alluding to the absence of curtains in the dining room.

With the exception of interior decorators who are interested in window treatment, men are incapable of comprehending the great importance women attribute to curtains in the room. The psychological difference between the feminine and masculine attitude with regard to the role of curtains is beautifully reflected in a scene from *Cannery Row,* by John Steinbeck: Mr. and Mrs.

Malloy are so poor that they have to move to an old boiler that is not used any more. They are happy to have this miserable dwelling place that is dry and safe. Mrs. Malloy sees later "real lace curtains and edges of blue and pink—$1.98 a set with curtain rods thrown in." Mr. Malloy sits up on his mattress and asks: "What in God's name do you want curtains for?" Mrs. Malloy, whose lower lip begins to tremble, says that she always liked to have things nice for him. She accuses him of begrudging her the money, but he assures her that this is not so: "But, darling," he says, "for Christ's sake what are we going to do with curtains? We got no windows." But Mrs. Malloy cries and cries and asserts, "Men just don't understand how a woman feels." Sam tries in vain to comfort her. She sobs, "Men just never try to put themselves in a woman's place."

We return to the contrast of the two behavior patterns which was our point of departure. Did we not contrast the pictures of prostitutes leaning on their window sills and shamelessly exposing themselves with the memory of Victorian women hiding behind the window curtains and shyly glancing through the crisped white material at the street? The contrast of the curtain-less window show with the self-concealment behind the curtains becomes more meaningful now that the sexual symbolism of curtains is understood and psychologically evaluated.

As coda to this domestic suite, here is a memory dating back almost forty years that tallies with the other instances of symbolical character mentioned. The misunderstanding of its significance appears to me almost comical now, but it puzzled me then. At that time I was a young analyst too eager to understand the unconscious meaning of neurotic symptoms as quickly as possible. Freud had referred to me a young girl as patient for analytic treatment. She came from Bucharest and spoke German very badly. She had been educated in a French private school and her analysis had to be performed to a great extent in French, which I then spoke rather well.

The patient had all the symptoms of a compulsion neurosis. Besides washing compulsions, a great number of ceremonials and

seemingly absurd little actions filled most of her day. An instance
of the many symptoms of this kind, a compulsion to turn the
water faucet on and off innumerable times, was described early in
her analytic sessions. She complained that she had to convince
herself again and again that the faucet in the bathroom was
turned off. In order to do that she often had to turn it on first,
because she wanted to be sure that she had turned it off very
tightly. It dawned on me what the secret significance of that
compulsion was when, some weeks later, she spoke of the sexual
intimacies in which she and her fiancé indulged. The two young
people had long petting sessions in which they did everything,
"tout except ça" (all but that), as the patient put it. The man
rubbed his penis outside the vagina until he reached an orgasm.
It was easy to guess that the patient was often worried that some
of the man's semen would penetrate her and make her pregnant.
Her compulsion had thus the unconscious significance of convincing herself that the man had not ejaculated into her. Through
the substitute displacement to the faucet she wanted to make sure
that no drop of semen had found its way into her vagina. The
countercompulsion reveals, of course, her unconscious wish to
feel the man's semen in herself.

In an analytic session in which she had again talked of her
tedious and tiring compulsion to turn the water faucet on and
off, she mentioned that she frequently had to touch the electric
button after her fiancé had left her, and that the touch always
gave her a shock. I assumed, of course, that here was another
compulsion reported in the context of her neurotic symptoms, a
ceremonial similar to so many she had reported. I thought that
she had perhaps to push the button as if she wanted to call the
maid, who slept in a room beneath her own. Her next sentences,
however, made it clear that I was mistaken. The *"bouton électrique"* about which she spoke was her expression for clitoris, not
an electric device. The girl often masturbated after her fiancé
left her because she felt sexually excited but not satisfied.

The lesson to learn from this misunderstanding is, of course,
that we have to be aware of a tendency to think too logically, and

to make a synthesis of all that we hear our patients report in analytic sessions. At first I blamed the linguistic difficulty for it, that I misunderstood the patient's expression *le bouton électrique,* but I had finally to admit to myself that I had overlooked the intimate, unconscious connection of the room and the objects in it with the body of the woman in her thoughts.

15. An Exception

The following pages present a deviation from the pattern of this book in two directions. In most of the preceding sections pictures of characteristic feminine and masculine behavior were put side by side and contrasted. The center of this paper is the discussion of some typical feminine feature observed in a man and an inquiry into the determining factors of this psychological anomaly. While in previous chapters the course of exploration is the usual one followed in scientific contributions, the following paragraphs take another direction. Their point of departure is a train of the psychoanalyst's own thoughts pursued until they reach a certain problem and its possible solution. This different manner of presentation is exceptional within the frame of this book but not in other works of this writer. In several previous books this same method was applied.*

The train of thought described here took its point of departure from an everyday, commonplace and insignificant event: my sister Margaret had served me a cup of coffee. I had put the tray carelessly on a table near my desk, accidentally scraping some paint from it in the procedure. My sister hurriedly busied herself repairing the small damage. While occupied with this thankless task she scolded me for my negligence and thoughtlessness. I felt slightly annoyed by her nagging.

I shall now try to reproduce my train of thought as I listened to her: "Strange what a fuss she makes about a trifling thing

* *Listening with the Third Ear, The Secret Self, The Haunting Melody.*

like that. . . ! That table is valueless. . . . What difference does it make whether there is a scratch on it or not? What is so important about it? Even were I to make a hundred scratches on it, what could it possibly matter? Women are strange creatures. . . . Their hearts hang upon such material things. . . . They are pained by even the slightest damage to them—even if the objects are not their own. . . ."

The next associations are determined by the fact that I happened to glance just then at a picture which hung on the wall across from my desk. It presents this scene: a woodcutter has raised his ax to fell a tree in the forest. The beautiful body of a nymph emerges from the trunk of the tree whose branches are formed by her outstretched arms. Her face has a sorrowful or sad expression. This picture had been the farewell gift of a Dutch patient who was a successful artist. In this work the girl had shaped some phantasies which she had often described in her analytic sessions. Those phantasies circled around the process of deflowering on the wedding night. The girl's mother had died early, but she had often spoken of the brutality of men and advised the child not to marry. The patient, later on, had many masochistic phantasies in which the scene of deflowering by a cruel and brutal man emerged again and again. Her picture presents that scene in mythological garb. In the gift of her picture the patient had expressed her gratitude to psychoanalysis which had succeeded in conquering her fear of sexual intercourse.

The glance at the picture awakened a fleeting memory of my expatient's face, clearly recognizable in the features of the nymph emerging from the tree. From here my thoughts, logically enough, led to a paper by Freud dealing with the mysterious phenomenon of the taboo of virginity found in the customs of savage and half-civilized people.* One of the most important reasons for that taboo, in Freud's view, is that woman is inclined to take revenge on the man who has deflowered her and violated her corporal integrity. She has unconscious bitter and resentful feelings to-

* Contributions to the Psychology of Love, Collected Papers, Volume IV.

ward the man, as though he had damaged her body. These hostile reactions can be traced back to older and more primitive impulses of the little girl who envies the boy for his penis and feels handicapped in comparison with him on account of her anatomical incompleteness.

The thoughts on Freud's paper were immediately replaced by others that concern a patient who had been in analysis with me a few years ago. She was a fifteen-year-old girl in whose treatment many and complex masochistic-sadistic phantasies emerged. The most significant among them had the scene of the wedding night as central theme. The mother of the patient had, according to modern principles, told her the facts of life. Already as a child the patient knew how babies were born and how they got into mother's body. The girl, who pretended to be sophisticated and to know all about sexuality, arrived at fantastic notions about the first sexual intercourse. Those grotesque ideas came to the conscious surface under intense reluctance during later analytic sessions. The procedure on the wedding night was, in her mind, the following: the husband kneels before his bride and deflowers her with his hand. He stanches the heavy flow of blood and washes her. He then washes his own hands in two pots of water, standing on both sides of the bed, and dries himself and his wife carefully with prepared towels. Then sexual intercourse follows. It was easy to guess that the first part of these phantasies was influenced by the aftereffects of early masturbation on the part of the girl.

My thoughts returned to the picture. I remembered that I had had the vague feeling that the scene presented there was already familiar to me when I received the gift from my Dutch patient. The impression was that I had seen that scene or a similar one in another picture, but could not recall where. It came back to me: I had, as a boy, an illustrated book dealing with sagas and legends—especially with the deeds of medieval knights. In this book was a picture showing a knight hitting a tree with his sword. The tree nymph appears from the trunk accusing him of inflicting a mortal wound upon her.

Many years later, during an intense study of Goethe's tragedy *Torquato Tasso,* I remembered that picture in my boyhood book because it presents a scene from this poet's epic *Gerusaleme Liberata* (published in 1581). The thirteenth canto depicts the knight Tancred who has entered an enchanted wood and sees a cypress in whose bark symbols are engraved. They warn the intruder not to disquiet the sacred trees. He draws his sword and strikes the tree with full force. From its trunk bursts a fountain, "gushed forth blood and crimson'd all the ground." Tancred hears a deep moaning and the spirit of the tree speaks:

> "Too much already, Tancred, has thy blade
> Wronged me," the sad voice made exclaim;
> "My late so happy home didst thou invade,
> And rudely drive my spirit from the frame,
> In and through which it lived: why wilt thou maim
> Still the poor trunk to which my dream unblest
> Binds me?"

The nymph tells him she was Clorinda and asks him to desist from murdering her.

The remembered picture of the knight and the sylvan spirit was replaced by some etymological associations of thought: wood . . . matter . . . material . . . the word comes from *mater,* Latin for mother . . . the fundamental feminine nature of material. Have we here a psychological tie to the carefulness and preservative attention which the average woman feels toward material things? Is this significant feature rooted in woman's castration complex and does it represent her late and displaced reaction to the early impression of the little girl that she is congenitally and genitally handicapped?

While I still ponder on this theory, puzzlingly enough my thoughts turn to Mr. L. and to the dinner which I had attended at his house a few days before. Mr. L. is a middle-aged, successful manufacturer of some renown whom I had often seen socially. My impression was that he and his family lived luxuriously and beyond his income in the sense of Veblen's "conspicuous consumption." He could be very amiable but often behaved rather haughtily and was secretive and suspicious. I had had occasion to observe the man, and certain features of his behavior had puzzled me because they seemed to contradict others that were apparently dominant in his character. A vivid interest in several kinds of sport and a somewhat emphasized virility did not, for instance, tally with his mimosalike sensitiveness and sentimentality.

There was one trait that was conspicuous in its manifestations: it was the special attention paid to the slightest damage done to his furniture or to other objects in his home. He was enraged when, for instance, a chair or a table showed the smallest scratch, or when there was a tiny spot on the carpet. This intense concern with materials was not restricted to valuable objects nor to furniture; it was extended to clothes, towels, etc. He became very indignant if his wife put a dress of hers carelessly on a chair, and discussed at length the damage that could be done to the material by such treatment, how quickly it could thus be ruined and so on. He had occasional outbursts of rage at his wife and children in which he would vehemently accuse them of criminal carelessness to their things—and to his own. At the slightest negligence he called the apartment a "pigsty" and reproached his family for their uncivilized or barbarous way of living. A spilling of water and other catastrophic events of this kind brought him to a state of despair surpassing Lady Macbeth's passionate exclamation: "Out, damned spot!"

This acquaintance occurred to me at the indicated point of my thought associations. At the dinner he had sarcastically pointed out to me that his wife had put a wine glass on the table without securing a coaster for it. The glass had formed a wet ring on the table and this fact had infuriated him. The scene was all the more embarrassing since it took place in the presence of his wife and guests. The slight damage produced annoyed him to such an extent that he forgot all tact and consideration.

What possible connection was there between my previous thought associations, leading to a tentative theory about women,

and the intercurring memory of that evening spent at the manufacturer's house? There seems to be no bridge. Yet an attentive
pursuit of the thought threads leads to the following reconstruction: the point of departure is the scolding of my sister for my
negligence. Thoughts starting from here led to the onset of a
tentative theory on the origin of the carefulness of women toward
material things. Their attitude is determined by a reaction to the
little girl's view that she is physically damaged. The trend to
preserve material things and the attention and care for them
would thus be a late and displaced attempt at restitution. The
material things have unconsciously taken the place of the damaged female body.

There is another possibility of explaining the greater care
women have, in general, for material things. This trend could
also be determined by biological factors and be rooted in constitutional trends, in the same tendencies that make women take
care of the embryo and the baby. The two hypotheses rather
complement than contradict each other, since the one could concern the biological foundation upon which psychological motives
are superimposed.

My train of thought reflects the attempt to find confirmation
in the analytic material of two cases and a theoretical support
in Freud's paper on the taboo of virginity. The memory of Tancred's adventure in the enchanted wood seems to confirm it from
another side, presenting the masculine collateral attitude.

So far my train of thought follows logical lines, but in the
sudden emergence of the memory of that dinner, my associations
seem to go off at a tangent. But this appearance is deceptive.
There is a common denominator to the preceding and the new
train of thought: the exaggerated worry about possible damage
to furniture. Could there be any other connective links?

I had arrived at a tentative theory on the genesis of the greater
attentiveness and carefulness of women for furniture: they unconsciously feel damaged or handicapped and develop a late reaction to the imaginary harm done to them in the substitutional
displacement to furniture and other material objects that are
conceived as extensions of their own body. When, at this critical

point of my burgeoning theory, the thought of my acquaintance emerges, it can have only one meaning: it is an objection raised to my theory. The character of the argument is clear: here is a man who undoubtedly behaves like a woman toward furniture —shows the same sensitiveness and overmeticulous attitude toward material objects.

But together with the contradictory argument an attempt at a solution emerges. It is already preconsciously contained in the formulation of that sentence: "He behaves like a woman." That means, of course, "as if he were a woman," or that he fulfills the psychological conditions conceived as unconscious premise of that particular feminine attitude. He behaves as if he were physically damaged or castrated. It is clear that that "as if" has to be understood in a psychological sense as a repressed reality which can well be contrasted with contradictory conscious trends. His intense interest in sport and his condescending attitude toward men who do not share it amounts to an overcompensation of the unconscious self-concept—to an attempt at correcting it. Yet, in his special sensitiveness to the slightest damage to a piece of furniture, the disavowed feminine attitude appears on the surface. Let me add that my impression of the emphasized feminine character of my acquaintance was confirmed later on by added observations.

Every theoretical attempt of the described kind has to be verified again and again by the living clinical material, by experiences in the analytic penetration of people. Until now I have found no basic facts contradicting my concept that the particular carefulness and solicitousness of women for furniture has the unconscious origin explained in the preceding pages. Yet my tentative theory has to wait for confirmation and verification by other observers. The recommendation contained in Longfellow's lines is also valid for the analyst:

> Let us, then, be up and doing
> With a heart for any fate
> Still achieving, still pursuing,
> Learn to labour and to wait.

16. THE APARTMENT OF THE OTHER WOMAN

In thousands of instances we are shown by everyday experience that women react differently in the same situations than men. When we do not realize that divergence clearly it is because we do not stop to think about it and become aware of the basic emotional patterns. Here is a test case, one of the innumerable situations in which that difference becomes clear to us. The husband of a patient had fallen in love with another woman. After a long fight he had obtained a divorce from his wife. In the settlement it was stipulated that the wife would leave the beautifully furnished apartment to the husband and take only her personal belongings. The patient reported in her analytic sessions that her rival, upon returning from the wedding trip, would move immediately into the apartment with her husband. The thought that this other woman would take possession of the kitchen and bedroom, use her linens and utensils, was very painful to my patient. While I understood all this very well, I was puzzled by the conclusion she drew from the unscrupulous manner in which the new wife took possession of the apartment. Her first comment was: "Only a Broadway whore could do that!" The second was: "She cannot love him" (meaning her husband).

I failed to see how the immediate possession of the vacated apartment could put the young woman into the group of streetwalkers. She could, in my opinion, have moved into that apartment even if she had been as blameless as Caesar's wife. Also the meaning of the other conclusion, that the new wife did not love her husband, escaped me. It was, in my thinking, one of those innumerable cases of non sequitur which are so baffling to us (men) when we hear them from women's lips. My patient did not explain what she meant, but it was implied and could be understood in the following thought associations: any decent woman in the situation of the second wife would insist on new things in the apartment and would be reluctant to live among things that reflected the personal taste of the first wife. She would be highly unwilling to use the same linen and plates. It would remind the new wife most unpleasantly of her predecessor, especially when the objects used were of an intimate nature. How could a woman with even a minimum of self-esteem use the towels that had the initial of the previous mistress of the house embroidered on them?

I understood, of course, what my patient had felt once she had expressed it in her vivid terms—revealing her disgust at the behavior of her victorious rival. The meaning of her second statement was also clear to me when she explained that only a woman who does not love her husband would tolerate that there should be a "third presence" in her new home. She meant the memories of the previous wife who had used all the household things. Only a woman who is governed by financial or material considerations would fail to consider those memories unavoidably awakened in her husband when he is surrounded by things connected with his previous marriage.

I have asked myself since if a man would feel similarly in the same situation and the candid answer is no. His thoughts are not as intimately tied to the material objects of the apartment and of the household. Let us assume that a man might move into the apartment in which his wife had lived for a long time with her first husband, from whom she is divorced. It is very doubtful that he would be reminded by the things of everyday life of the previous marriage of his wife—and, were he to be reminded, he would not be depressed or grieved. It might disturb him if he were to see the slippers or the pipes of the first husband, but it would amount to no more than a fleeting feeling of discomfort.

The main difference in the emotional reactions of the woman originates in the fact that the apartment and all the objects in it are much more intimately connected with the body of the woman than with that of the man. The apartment as we have seen is the unconscious extension of the woman's body, of herself. The other woman in taking it over, with even her personal things, had in more ways than one, "hit her where she lives."

17. Is All Fair?

A patient told me about the behavior of another woman who tried to win her husband away. She knew her husband had been having an affair with the woman for several months. She clearly recognized that he wanted to get a divorce and that her rival used all the feminine devices to draw the man to her. She minded that, of course, very much. But what aroused her anger was not so much the means her rival used to win her husband away but all she surmised that her rival said—or inferred—about her in a derogatory way. My patient very acutely heard the other woman's voice in some remarks her husband made. She also sensed the criticism to which she was subjected in conversations whose content she could only guess.

While the decision of the husband was still doubtful, the other woman seemed to increase and refine all the means at her disposal to interfere in the marital life of the couple. She called the man on the telephone while he was having dinner with his wife, left messages of a mysterious character for him with the maid, in short tried to humiliate the desperate woman both in subtle and not so subtle ways. On a certain occasion she knew the couple planned to go to the theater. The car of the husband was parked in front of the apartment house. When the husband and the wife entered the car they saw, inscribed on the windshield in lipstick, "I love you. Jane." The attack of rage the patient had at this sight is difficult to describe. She felt deeply humiliated by the other woman who used such devious means to show her contempt and defiance.

We shall not even discuss the question of whether such tactics against a rival are imaginable among men. We all know men would not use such means but perhaps more open, brutal or violent methods to challenge each other. There is a proverb saying that all is fair in love and war. It seems that the saying has to be divided into two parts: all is fair in war—applying to men, and all is fair in love—where women are concerned. But even the validity of this saying is limited. Is there not the Geneva convention protecting the rights of noncombatants, of the wounded and the physicians? It seems that there is no corresponding convention or regulation in the war waged between women about a man. The term fair is not applicable here. All means may be used. The Geneva convention has the task of preventing unnecessary cruelties and making sure that warfare is carried on in a fair way and victory won by the superior army and navy. In the competition between two women who fight over a man the feminine arsenal is often used without regard for the feeling of the other woman. There is an invisible armament race going on where one woman must show she has something that the other woman does not have.

18. Projection in Homosexuality

In an early book, *Psychology of Sex Relations*,* I pointed out that many homosexual men are not entirely blind and deaf to the lure of women but deflect its initial effects. They are not insensitive to feminine charms but they unconsciously steel themselves against them. There are symptomatological signs proving that amorous stimulation can set in to be transferred immediately to a person of the same sex. I pointed out that this shifting of attention and attraction has the function of a mechanism of defense.

In presenting several cases of this kind I failed to give consideration to another mechanism of defense whose operation became obvious in other cases. I mean the mechanism of projection by which the individual attempts to deny emotions that were experienced as unpleasant or unwelcome.

Projection is perhaps the oldest psychical mechanism. It is already efficient in the baby, who puts unpleasant sensations into the external world. The tendency to project is, from an early age on, apparent in attempting to relieve guilt. Later on many

* New York, 1945.

excitations are warded off by seeing them as being outside the ego. The person gets rid of unwelcome impulses and sensations by putting them into the outside world in a manner similar to that by which a picture is thrown on a screen in our movie theaters. Projection is not only an archaic mechanism, it accompanies the development of the individual to the age of maturity. The primitive concept of the world by which we project our feelings onto nature around us continues to live in the animistic phase of early religion and still appears in the metaphors of our poets.

In the analytic treatment of several homosexuals I observed a phenomenon that puzzled me at first. While these men often emphasized their antagonism or indifference toward women, and were horrified at the thought of sexual intercourse, they frequently stated that many women had sexual designs on them. In some cases that statement sounded quite incredible—especially when a patient declared that different women tried to "make" him. The line of these alleged pursuers of his virtue reached from some high school girls to his seventy-year-old landlady. He readily described that these women used subtle and not so subtle means to attract him.

The analytic understanding of this complaint was rendered difficult by the fact that the patient courted several girls in order to appear socially or sexually above suspicion. In one case where the chances of his courtship were, in his opinion, very poor, he even propositioned a young girl. By one of those accidents that sometimes occur in analytic practice, the young lady appeared as a patient in my office. During her treatment she also mentioned that young man and the fact that he had propositioned her. She was well aware that it was not meant seriously. She said: "The poor boy! He would faint if I said yes!"

While the character of his assumption that many women wanted to "lay" him was not doubtful as projection, the dynamics of this defense became not clear. They were transparent in another case: an artist in his early thirties consulted me because he felt his work was handicapped by the diversion of his attention from it, caused by other men who were bothering him with many signs of their love. He complained that wherever he went— even when he remained at home—many men obtruded themselves on him by manifesting their unwelcome affection. To prove his point he took me to the window of my consultation room, on the fifth floor, and pointed to passers-by on the street. He said: "Do you see that man across the street? The one straightening his tie. He knows I am looking at him and he wants to make himself attractive to me. See the young man over there? Look! He is moving his hand in greeting to me." After a few seconds he exclaimed: "Now there is another man, looking straight up at the window! He is flirting with me quite unashamedly!"

Delusions of this kind, in which gestures are interpreted as relating to the patient, belong to the category of erotomania. In this form of paranoia the patients feel that they are persecuted by love. In their delusional trends they are rejecting *through projection* the temptations they feel toward other persons. It was obvious that the patient tried to ward off his own unconscious tendencies by suspecting all men of having sexual designs on him. This type of erotomanic delusion is, of course, more common among women than men, and can exist alongside a behavior that is relatively normal in other directions.

It is easy to guess that the same mechanism of projection that was used here as defense against repressed homosexual trends of the patient can also be applied to ward off the residual attraction men who are homosexual experience toward women. This type project their own unconscious heterosexual wishes, that have somewhere remained alive beside their interest for the same sex, onto men, sometimes indiscriminately. In their delusions in which they assert that all women are after them they reveal—or rather confess—that they themselves feel in various degrees the lure of all women. This is the more interesting since they consciously deny that they are in any form attracted by the other sex and assert that their love life is concentrated on men.

A side glance shows us that an erotomanic delusion of this kind with women is much more difficult to discover because it can appear for some time as an exaggeration of what is only wishful thinking of the woman who imagines herself to be the object of the amorous desires of all men. Delusions of the paranoic kind in which women are convinced that every man they see persecutes them with love have often the function of warding off unconscious homosexual trends. The importance of the psychological difference between the sexes is, however, diminished by the analytic insight that in many cases where men are frantically infatuated with a certain woman they often use the unconscious mechanism of defense against their temptation to love a man.

19. Mixed Feelings Toward Homosexual Men

A man who takes out a woman he knows to be homosexual will, of course, treat her with the consideration due to her sex. He will not attempt to approach her by way of courtship and he will carefully avoid even an allusion to her sexual taste. The phenomenon of Lesbianism holds nothing fascinating for the average man. It has perhaps a slight touch of the uncanny for him. He remains, however, aware of the feminine even in the masculine character of that woman. She can be in his eyes a perfect lady and he will think or speak of her sexual deviation with the tolerance we have toward women to whom we are indifferent: *"Tous les goûts sont dans la nature."*

Women seem, from what I have heard them say, to have mixed feelings when they are taken out by a man they know to be homosexual. Some can be quite interested in what he confides to them. We all know that such men have close friends and good acquaintances among women to whom they tell "all"—or almost all. With a characteristic mixture of pity and contempt these women play the part of the good Samaritan in being consulted about the love affairs and troubles of these men. But are these men really men in her eyes? Perhaps only in a strictly anatomical sense. Most women do not feel the desire to tempt them even to the extent of making themselves attractive and desirable.

Yet I have heard other women say just the opposite. One patient said she was always rather afraid of homosexual men because, with the subtle cattiness generally found only in women, they can hit a woman's weak points and find her flaws. In a sense they compete with women like other women; only their attack has a surprise value—they did not expect it from a "man." This same woman said she was very careful of her appearance with these men, just as she would be with other women. She also sensed their unconscious envy of her femininity and it aroused her to "compete" and be at her best when with them.

Another young woman had a different attitude; she said: "I always wonder why he has such poor taste. Surely we are more attractive. I think maybe with me he will feel differently." She said she was tempted to flirt with him, hoping he would change. Yet the attitude of the average woman seems to be: "Why make an effort that is destined to remain unsuccessful?" It is psychologically well worth while to observe the difference in the behavior of a woman who is taken out by a man considered as a possibility and by another who is homosexual and thus "impossible." On the surface everything is, of course, the same. Yes, the woman can even, in a certain sense, feel much more at ease with the homosexual man; she may be less on guard. Her skirt may climb up a little too high and it will not worry her. She may be more careless in her movements and less self-aware in the presence of this man. Subjectively she may feel no tension in his company. She is maybe even relaxed. It is as though she were in the company of another woman. It is comfortable to have a male escort when you enter a restaurant or a night club. This works both ways as it is often impossible for a woman to go certain places unescorted and it is also sometimes a convenient camouflage for the man who may not want anyone to suspect his sexual preference. To the woman he is a man, after all, only not a possible love or sex partner.

But just this lack of self-awareness, this absence of the slightest tension in the company of the man and the relaxation that can be enjoyed—all these take away a considerable part of the pleas-

ure experienced in other company. The excitement of the chase
disguised as being chased is absent. It is a pause in the battle of
the sexes—not an armistice, but peace; and a kind of peace not
even enjoyed in the company of other women, but something
more like a retreat. The woman feels safe with the homosexual
—safe from him, but especially safe from herself. It is no compliment for a man when a woman feels so utterly safe in his company.

A woman who returns from a social evening with a homosexual man might, when asked by her women friends about it,
say: "He was, of course, a perfect gentleman." This same sentence, said upon other occasions sounds differently and is not
similar in meaning. It will be the same statement, but the fundamental note in it is heard differently. In one case it might be
accompanied by an undertone of regret or astonishment—or even
disappointment that her escort was a "perfect gentleman." But
returning from the evening spent with the man she sensed to be
homosexual, it is a simple statement of fact—not even of a re-
grettable fact, but of a simple reality. She knew what she was
in for when she went out with him. He was a perfect gentleman:
he could not be anything else if he tried.

20. The Homosexuals and the Other Sex

It is well known that there is a conspicuous difference in the
attitude of society toward male and female homosexuality. The
difference reflects itself not only in our criminal law, but also in
the evaluation of those deviant appetites by society. Even in
tolerant France, the man of whom it is said, *"il n'est pas ortho-
doxe,"* is the object of some badly concealed contempt. On the
stage of our night club shows male homosexuality is openly
ridiculed and derided. Lesbianism is rarely treated in a similar
fashion.

That characteristic divergency of attitude shows itself also
clearly in the opinions you hear about members of the same sex

who search for love partners. These reactions are, of course, various and reach from pity to disgust, but it is significant that women as well as men judge female homosexuality in a milder way than the male perversion. Men, looking at manifest Lesbians, experience wonder as their prevalent emotional reaction. There is compassion rather than scorn in the attitude average men have toward women who prefer other women as sexual objects. Women in general seem to share such feelings toward those fugitives from their own sex. There is perhaps a sharper or a more critical note in their judgment, but they too feel sorry for those women as though they had renounced all competition and the emotional rewards of being loved by men.

Men in general look down upon male homosexuals as though they were freaks or eunuchs. Homosexuals have, in our often unconscious opinion, renounced the privileges of their masculinity and virility. They are seen as though they were emasculated. All masculine defiance and belligerence will usually be mobilized against homosexuals who make a pass at another "normal" man. The clearer the character of this courtship becomes to a man, the more intensely it is felt as an offense and a challenge to his own virility. No average man can tolerate the thought of submitting in a feminine way to another man.

The homosexual male is the object of the contempt not only of men but also of women. Women are, of course, too courteous or too diplomatic to show those feelings, but whenever they are among themselves or in analytic sessions, they chuckle or giggle at the alleged femininity of homosexual men. When they mimic him, imitating his unnatural way of speaking, they behave as though master actors were deriding hams who attempt to play the part of Hamlet or Faust—only with the difference that it is in this case the part of Ophelia or of Gretchen those amateurs would attempt to act.

Men sometimes assume that some women can feel, speak and act in a masculine manner, but women will never admit that any man can really feel, speak or act as women do. He has not got what it takes to be a woman. There are some confusing situations which become possible in our cultural state. During a consultation, a woman who was a successful theatrical producer complained about the behavior of an actor who created a lot of difficulties on and off stage. The lady described vividly to me an argument she had had with the actor, moving her hands in imitation of his gestures: "And then he went womanly on me. . . !" she cried. For a moment I felt confused. Imagine a woman who says about a man that he behaved femininely toward her!

I had the occasion to observe the reaction of a woman to a male homosexual who was courting her. She used to say she was tempted to say "yes" to see him run—the other way. She said he reminded her of a little pup she had had when she was a child. Her father used to scold the young dog when he chased motorcycles saying: "Little doggie, what would you do with it if you caught it?"

These few remarks will perhaps help to make us aware of the different attitude men and women have toward their own unconscious homosexual trends. The divergency confirms the impression that homosexuality is much more energetically repressed in men than in women.

21. Men, Women and the Unborn Child

It seems to me that we still make too little use of those very telling errors, of slips of the tongue and other symptomatic small actions of everyday life. We conceive of them as expressions of opposing and conflicting inner forces, but we do not strongly emphasize that they present a breakthrough of repressed or disavowed trends. In a book published more than twenty-five years ago* I tried to show that most of those symptomatic errors have another function until then not discussed: they are dictated by an unconscious compulsion to confess, an urge manifesting itself also in many other normal and pathological phenomena.

* *Geständniszwang und Strafbedürfnis,* Vienna, 1925. (Not translated into English.)

How else but by the concealed operating of this tendency could you, for instance, explain the revealing orthographic slip that occurred to a man the other day? He enthusiastically wrote his wife from an extended business trip to California that he was having a wonderful time and wished "you were her." That compulsion of confessing proved its unconscious efficiency more seriously in the letter of a patient. He had separated from his wife when it became obvious that they were incompatible on account of deep character differences. The patient, who never tired of attributing the guilt for the conflict to his wife, wrote her a letter in which he made a meaningful mistake. He wrote: "If you return, I am afraid it will *me* the same again." He wanted, of course, to write: "It will be the same again." Did he not confess in that mistake that he is also responsible for the failure of their marriage? Did he not say: we cannot live together; I am afraid I will be the same again?

Our literature presents only a few analyzed instances of another kind of the small psychopathology of everyday life, namely of unconscious hearing wrongly, of misunderstanding of what the partner in conversation had said. But those errors are in psychologic analysis just as telling as slips of the tongue or of the pen.

The instance reported in the following paragraphs is remarkable only because the differences of the emotional attitude of men and women toward an important problem are clearly reflected in the psychoanalysis of that mistake. I owe the communication of this significant instance of mishearing to a student, a young psychiatrist who used to discuss with me in so called "control-analysis" cases of neurosis he treated. He has permitted me to use his communication provided that his identity and that of his patient is concealed.

The patient of the psychiatrist, a young woman, spoke in her psychoanalytic session of a cousin of hers who had become pregnant and had then married the man who was the father of the expected child. That young man had for a long time resisted the wish of his sweetheart to get married and yielded to her suggestion only when she became pregnant by him. The patient who spoke of the recent wedding of the cousin expressed the opinion that a girl in such a situation is likely to feel resentment against the man who can be brought to marry her only under the pressure of moral obligation. The psychiatrist who listened to her significantly misunderstood what the patient had said. Instead of hearing her say "Resentment of the girl" he understood "resentment against the girl." He became aware of his mishearing during the following sentences spoken by the patient. They left no doubt about her view that girls in such cases are justifiable in feeling resentful against the recalcitrant man.

In order to understand the unconscious motives of this mishearing, we have to sketch a part of the life history both of the patient and her psychotherapist. In other words: we have to deal with the emotional situation of the person who spoke those sentences and of the other to whom they were said, of the speaker and of the listener.

As the psychiatrist knew from many months of her analytic treatment, the patient herself had some weeks before that time broken with her lover after a long affair. That man had proposed to her several times, but she had always refused to marry him. A year before the break she had become pregnant by him and had undergone an abortion because he could not marry her then. Her relationship with him had since that time decidedly changed its character. Tensions and arguments were now frequent and became finally more and more serious until she broke up the relationship. It was easy to guess that one of the most determining unconscious factors in the estrangement was the deeply felt disappointment or bitterness of the patient who had to renounce the baby she wished. This sketch of the emotional premises will be sufficient to let us psychologically understand why the patient spoke of the "resentment of the girl" in cases whose character was similar to her own.

But why did the psychoanalyst misunderstand his patient? When he first told me about his mistake, he added that it was "funny." But he became thoughtful when I pointed out to him that he must have unconsciously heard what the patient had said because he admitted that she had spoken distinctly enough. Is it imaginable that he unconsciously rejected the patient's view that girls in those situations feel resentment against a man? In this case his misunderstanding would amount to a denial of the view that women are justified in feeling this way. Such a concealed tendency to the effect of a denial is certainly not to be excluded, but in this case a more personal factor was more important than a general masculine trend.

The young psychiatrist confided to me that he had himself many years before married a woman who had become pregnant by him after a long love affair during which he often felt the wish to leave her. His marriage was successful as marriages go, but the psychiatrist must have still felt trends of unconscious hostility against the girl whom he had married not because he loved her but because he was in honor bound to do so. It is analytically easy to understand which tendency, concealed to himself, made him misunderstand the patient's words "resentment of the girl" as if she had said "resentment against the girl." In other words: he misheard the sentence of the patient under the influence of thoughts referring to what had once happened to himself. It is very likely that he acoustically heard well what the patient had said, but simultaneously misunderstood in the sense or in the direction of those hidden trends. In other words: he misunderstood her with unconscious purpose.

It was as if he refused to acknowledge that girls in such circumstances feel resentment against the man. In replacing that phrase by "resentment against the girl" he expressed his unconscious opposition: not the woman is entitled to feel resentful against the man, but rather he to feel antagonistic against her. The reference to his own history and the unconscious bitterness against his wife whom he had to marry because he had made her pregnant let him replace the phrase, correctly perceived, by another misheard one, that means by one heard only within himself.

We avoid the temptation to discuss the psychodynamics of such symptomatical slips of the analyst. They prove only that repressed and disavowed tendencies operate also in the analyst during his therapeutic work. We restrict ourselves to the remark that the analytic exploration of such psychodynamics promises to be very informative in an area which seems to be very remote: of the distortions and transformations of words and whole sentences to be observed in the psychopathology of paranoics. Mishearing and misunderstanding of pieces of conversation are put into the service of unconscious tendencies. Sentences, purposefully misheard, are repeated in the thoughts of paranoic patients, nourish his suspicions, and confirm his ideas of references. Words, tendenciously misheard, are interpreted as proof of the hostile or malicious plans of the imaginary antagonists of the patient in the same sense as harmless gestures are interpreted as signs of their evil designs. Pathologically magnified and distorted, the same small errors of everyday life appear in ideas of reference as circumstantial evidence. The patients retell themselves the same story, in their thoughts making use of misunderstood phrases or single words they have heard. The area of the pathological mishearing in paranoia is still unexplored, but we are at present more interested in another aspect of the problem introduced by the analysis of that case of misunderstanding.

We all know that the unborn child has a different meaning to women and men. It is almost always a certain proof of her love or great admiration for a man when a woman likes to think of him as a prospective father of her child. Men very rarely think of a woman in an analogous way: the thought that she will be the mother of his children is conspicuous by its absence when the man is much in love with a woman. While the wish to have children might well occur especially when the man approaches middle age, the phantasy of fatherhood as a very intensive wish represents a feminine character in a man. It is not unusual that young people discussing their future marriage mention children, but it is almost always the man who first speaks of this possibility as if it were the continuation of his courtship although he does not feel any strong desire to become a father. The girl, generally more interested in the subject, is in this situation supposed to blush and to act coy not on account of the possibility of motherhood but thinking of its necessary precondition. But she has almost certainly thought and daydreamed of having a child with this man long before the thought occurred to him.

It is characteristic that the phantasies of the two sexes about the condition of the embryo are very divergent. While the pregnant woman thinks of the state of the embryo realistically and daydreams of the arrival, the appearance and behavior of the baby embroidering the picture with glamor, the prospective father is often beset by disastrous or threatening images. One of my patients saw in his phantasies the embryo in a dark cave, crossing mysterious, water-filled tunnels at whose exit the danger of death waited. Here is, of course, a renewal of infantile theories about the prenatal situation, but the phantasies reveal also reactions to unconscious death wishes directed against the unborn child. The frequent anxiety of the father during the delivery points in the same direction. That humorous telegram, "Mother and baby in excellent state, father fair," reflects the after-effect of the paniclike mood of those hours of waiting.

Although men are aware of the important part they play in the process of fertilization, they make the woman unconsciously responsible for becoming pregnant when the child is unwanted. It is as if they attribute to the woman the role of destiny: she should have prevented the pregnancy by some magical or mechanical means. They treat the woman as if it was her wish that was realized in her becoming pregnant quite in accordance with that French proverb proclaiming that what woman wants, God does ("*Ce que veut la femme, Dieu le veut*"). The other day a young man who has two children was told by his wife that she had become pregnant again. The man was preparing to send a pair of shoes to repair and used this occasion to tease his wife by a variation of that old nursery rhyme:

"There was an old woman
Who lived in a shoe;
She has so many children
Because she did not know what to do."

On this detour we come back to the problem of the unborn child and to the emotional meaning abortion has for the two sexes. Analytic experience shows that a love relationship is often decaying when the woman has to undergo an abortion. It is as if the frustration of her wish to have a baby from the beloved man has a deep and lasting effect on her, as if that failure becomes a decisive factor in the deterioration of the relationship. Here is perhaps the psychological core of that theological belief that God "blesses" the couple with a child. The baby is, so to speak, the sanction to the young love by destiny.

To the average man who has impregnated a woman he cannot or does not want to marry, abortion means an operation that will free him from responsibilities and unwelcome worries. The embryo has almost no emotional meaning to him. For the woman who loved the man the unborn child is more than his product. It is his reproduction, he himself within her, to be reborn by her. She sees in her imagination the man in his child as she sees his child in the man. In the thoughts of a girl who had become pregnant by a sailor who had to leave for the Far East during the war, the unborn baby took the place of the absent lover. Waiting for the birth meant almost waiting for his return. The man, who wanted an abortion, looked forward to the time when he need not be worried any more about the girl. It dawned upon him that the abortion was not unwelcome because with it a future announced itself when he need not think of the girl any more at all.

The operation itself appears to the man often enough as the only way out from an oppressing situation for the woman and himself. But for her it has an unconscious meaning that is best comparable to that of castration for the man. Although the woman might consciously very well understand the rational necessity of the abortion, she feels unconsciously embittered against the man as if he were responsible for this necessity. He, on the other hand, feels unconsciously resentful against the woman, as if it had been in her power to prevent the emergency situation in which they both find themselves.

On the detour we return to the contrast of feminine and masculine attitudes toward the question of the illegitimate child and of the abortion as they were reflected in the analysis of that case of misunderstanding.

Instead of going into the discussion of the important psychological problem of why pregnancy means so much more to the woman than the act of impregnation to the man, I would like to quote a passage from an almost forgotten play, *The Lonely Road,* by Arthur Schnitzler in which that contrast is poignantly presented. In an episodic side plot of this play a middle-aged actress, Irene Harms, now long retired, meets the artist Julian Fichner, who had been her lover many years before. Their conversation, first very casual, glides into the deeper water of remembering things past. Irene recalls that she wanted to commit suicide then, twenty-four years ago, when her lover chased her away because he had discovered that she had been unfaithful to him while on the road. Now all that belongs to the past also emotionally, but Irene now asks the man: "What do you think? Would that have happened if we then had the child?" She means that she would not have become unfaithful to him if she had not been compelled to get rid of their baby. She casually remarks that she had once had a kind of vision some time ago when she wandered across a meadow. She imagined for a split second that she had the child, their child, by the hand. But then she remembered that the "child" would be twenty-three years old by now and would perhaps have become a vagabond or a prostitute. Thinking aloud she says to the man that a woman who never had a child is perhaps never entirely a woman, "but a woman who wanted a baby and could not have it . . ." She leaves the sentence unfinished: "But no man can understand that," and then she adds the telling words: "The best of you is in those things still a kind of a scoundrel."

22. REPLICAS

Freud called the dream the Via Regia to the understanding of unconscious processes. However, even a royal road may sometimes be blocked. Not all dreams reported in analytic treatment can be interpreted. The effect of intensive resistances often prevents us from penetrating the unconscious thoughts leading to the dream production. In some cases we have to be content to lift merely a corner of the veil which hides the impulses and ideas behind the dream. Sometimes all the experience acquired in many years of analytic practice seems to be of no avail.

Take the following fragment of a dream whose meaning eluded me for a considerable time because I did not take into account a state of mind typically feminine. The patient, a middle-aged divorcee, dreamed: "I have a large picture frame into which I put pictures by unknown artists." There were no thought associations to the dream except the explanation that the frame was of a kind used for mounting photographs side by side. The patient is interested in art and collects good reproductions from art journals and other sources. The dream would seem to reflect these activities. During the course of this analytic session she told me that she had thought with great bitterness of her divorced husband, who now lives with another woman. The next thought led to her children, who are grown and at whose photographs she had looked. The approach to the interpretation of the dream fragment is paved by these day-remnants. The hidden meaning of the dream can be found when you close the gaps between them and guess the emotions they aroused in the dreamer.

At first I could not understand the dream fragment because I failed to recognize the symbolical significance of the word "picture." The train of thoughts that led to the dream production had its point of departure in the patient's glance at her children's photographs. The children are replicas of their father. Do we not say of a child, "the very picture of his father" when we want to point out a strong resemblance between the two? The bitter and resentful remembrances of her unfaithful husband led to the unconscious impulses which are realized in her dream. Translated from the unconscious into the language of conscious thinking the dream shows a thought possibility as reality. The revengeful idea expressed in the form of a wish was: "I would like to have children from many men and never know who fathered what children!" The symbolical meaning of the expression "picture" has a secondary meaning. The frame is, of course, the woman's body. The artist is the child's father.

It is not unimportant in this connection that the doubt expressed in the dream had also the character of an inhibition or scruple. The dream comparing a child's father with an artist shows what great part fatherhood plays in the thoughts of women. It is a feminine trait in contrast to the attitude of average men, who very rarely consider what it would be like to have a child with a particular woman. It may be said that a woman is not really in love with a man if she does not daydream about having a child with him.

Another difference in the attitudes of the mother-to-be and the father-to-be can be observed in regard to certain fears during the pregnancy and even before it. In this time very few women are free from fears about how the baby will turn out. The prospective father, on the other hand, is seldom worried or concerned that the child might be abnormal or deformed. It happens frequently that women renounce motherhood because they are afraid that the child might have a bad constitutional inheritance or illness. The sense of responsibility of the man does not often reach as far as that. The different roles that the two sexes play in the creation of the child reflect themselves in the divergence of these attitudes. The mother hopes that in her daughter or, vicariously, in her son will be a fulfillment of all the ambitions she had once nourished for herself. These hopes are not absent in the average father, but they have not the same intensity nor the same permanence as in the mother.

The moment of impregnating is contrasted with the long period of pregnancy. After the birth of the baby the mother never tires of observing it, of comparing it with others. The ecstatic enjoyment of the newborn shows that the woman now thinks of the child as part of "her guts," as a patient once explained.

In one of my cases that feeling of woman's pride in her

children came in distinct conflict with the father's attitude. This man had a serious affair with another woman. He wished on some occasion to show his mistress his children. His wife violently opposed any such idea and forbade him to take the children with him. She justifiably reacted to a feminine attitude in her husband's wish. In the ensuing argument with him she said the following beautiful sentence: "It was not a man who said, 'These are my jewels.'" In remembering the words of Cornelia, mother of the Gracchi, she insisted not only on a womanly tradition but also on woman's indestructible rights.

23. THE NONSEXUAL ELEMENT IN THE WISH FOR A CHILD

One sometimes wishes, when reading some of the new literature, that those critical psychologists and psychiatrists who accuse Freud of pansexualism had been present upon certain occasions when Freud discussed some cases of neurosis at a meeting of the Vienna Psychoanalytic Association, in the years between 1913 and 1920. I remember vividly such an occasion where Freud discussed a phantasy a patient had while she was still in her early teens. The girl had never experienced intercourse, but her phantasy had an obvious sexual character. More than this it was undoubtedly of a lascivious or perverted nature. The daydream that recurred was the following: the young girl imagined herself sucking the penis of an unknown man.

Freud explained to us that he had encountered similar phantasies several times in very young girls. Such phantasies with the ostensibly sexual content have, Freud explained, a very harmless meaning. They express the girls' unconscious wish to have a baby. The girl, in this phantasy, takes the place of the baby who sucks the breast; the penis of the man replaces in the phantasy the nipple. The daydreamer thus acts two parts: the mother who feeds the baby and the child who is fed. It is the same double role the mother has when she speaks "baby talk" with her child. But what about the penis in the phantasy? It is obvious how the male genitals come into the picture. The young girl knows that babies are produced by the male genitals. The condensation of the two thoughts: "I want to feel a baby sucking at my breasts" and "A baby can be given me through the penis" results in that image that appears almost grotesque if you do not consider its full sexual interpretation.

Deeper psychological consideration would very likely arrive at primal biological layers of this typical phantasy; at a strata where fertilization and eating were almost identical, at a phase of evolution where impregnation was still close to incorporation of another protozoan. Here is thus a phantasy of having a baby, and this wish is expressed in a manifestly sexual and perverted image. Yet this phantasy of prepuberty allows a harmless interpretation in accordance with an infantile concept.

The intimate thought connection we make between having a baby and sexual intercourse is, by no means, always present and is sometimes unconscious even in women thinking of a child. The narcissistic and ego-gains are often in the foreground of women's daydreams. But everywhere the baby in women's thoughts is connected with its producer; the sexual factor is very often in the background and affection or admiration for the man is the strong motive for the wish for a child. It happens only rarely that a man looks at a woman and thinks: "I wish to have a child from her." Such a wish can, of course, occur to him, but in most cases it is an afterthought following sexual desire. In a woman a wish to have a baby from a certain man can occur independently from sensual trends. The false analogy drawn by men regarding the thought processes of women in this area contribute to the misunderstanding between the sexes. But so does the assumption of the woman who projects her own way of thinking upon the man.

Here is an instance of this kind from my own experience: a few days after the opening night of *The Rosencavalier* at the Vienna opera, I spoke with Ella—the young girl to whom I was secretly engaged and who became my wife three years later—about Richard Strauss. Ella admired the genius of the composer very much. She thoughtfully remarked: "I would like to have a child by him." I was taken aback thinking, of course, of the sexual connotation of this statement. She was very astonished when I expressed my indignation about what she had just said. Virginal in her attitude, she energetically denied that her wish had anything to do with a sexual desire for the composer whom she did not know personally. She insisted that it was only the expression of her admiration. She said also that it was inspired by the thought that she would like a child of hers to have a musical genius such as that of the composer. There is no doubt that the unconscious continuation of those feelings of admiration and high appreciation of the composer would finally have led to the area of sexual wishes; but, for a woman, this trail can be a long and devious one.

Analysts encounter such phantasies frequently enough in the phantasies of their female patients. No experienced analyst will be foolish enough to assume that such a wish has a personal meaning. It is simply the expression of admiration or devotion originated in transference love. This inclination should, if the analysis is successful, be transferred eventually to a man who will take the place of the analyst in the affection of the patient. While this is the ideal and desirable case, our experience shows that the wish to have a baby by the analyst can survive the treatment phase and even reappear in the choice of the name an expatient gives her baby, even several years after having terminated her analysis. In a certain case in which the analysis had to be broken off due to external reasons, that wish as symptom of unsolved transference love surprisingly reappeared at the end of the patient's last analytic session. She was a young woman about half my age who came into analysis because of several emotional disturbances; among them was a psychically determined inability to conceive. We had often discussed my role as father-representative during the analytic treatment. When analysis was prematurely terminated I wished my patient good luck and expressed the hope that I would soon hear from her that she had made me a grandfather. "I would have preferred to make you a father," she said, without the trace of a smile, as she left.

24. "WHAT IS COOKING?"

The question of whether cooking, in a sociological and psychological sense, is purely a feminine occupation, is now occasionally discussed again. In our Western civilization it is generally still the man who brings home the bacon, and the woman who prepares and serves it. But students of human evolution point out that prehistoric hunters, having killed the animals, also cooked them. Anthropologists have shown us that with quite a few prehistoric tribes cooking is done by the males. (Dr. Murdock's computation, quoted in Amram Scheinfeld's book,* proves, however, that to one tribe in which the men are cooks, there are thirty in which women prepare the meals.) Also the old argument that the best cooks are men—the famous chefs and masters of *l'haute cuisine*—is sometimes brought to the fore.

Without taking part in the discussion, the psychoanalyst can perhaps add to the understanding of some factors within the question. He will, for instance, point out that the fact that prehistoric men cooked the animals they had killed has a religious significance. The dead beast was still treated as the totemistic ancestor of the tribesmen. Boiling it was part of the sacred act of the totem meal. With the slow decrease of totemism the function of cooking lost its sacred or sacrificial character. Only remnants, such as the privilege of the man to cut and distribute meat, and certain other rituals, remind the table companions of the religious nature of the primitive meal. It is likely that memory traces of this kind survive in those tribes in which men do the cooking. It is perhaps not accidental that often men function as cooks at barbecues or feasts at which the whole animal is roasted.

Psychoanalysis can make a more important contribution to the solution of the problem by introducing some internal evidence. By this I mean expressions in that form of language which is an inherited possession of mankind and of whose origin we are rarely aware: the language of symbolism. In this forgotten lan-

* *Women and Men*, New York, 1943.

guage in which the unconscious obtains a voice, things appear in their primal significance. In most dreams, the kitchen has the unconscious meaning of a woman's body. In many productions in which the unconscious has a predominant part, cooking—the art of preparing food of all sorts for human consumption—is compared with the cyclical changes of the female organism, and is brought into relation with the productivity and activity of the sexual glands. The task women perform in the kitchen in preparing meals is compared to this other, more vital, function of women.

It will not surprise us that metaphorical language extends this comparison even to pregnancy and delivery. A patient who had an operation for a tumor of the womb reported that the gynecologist, who visited her daily in the hospital, used to ask her during her convalescence: "What is cooking in the oven?" The significance of the "oven" as a symbol of the womb and of the productivity of the sexual glands is immediately obvious, and needs no analytic interpretation.

By the same token, we immediately understand the concealed sexual meaning of certain comparisons. The people in Lower Austria had a proverbial expression: "the oven collapsed," denoting that a woman had ended her pregnancy and had delivered a child. I am grateful to Mrs. Ruth Wolfson for a communication which casts some light upon the origin of that connection in the thinking of a four-year-old child. Mrs. Wolfson chatted with the little boy of a neighbor, and told him that she expected the arrival of her grandson, who would play with him. The child asked her: "Do you cook children?" When she said "No," he said "My mother does." The continuation of the conversation made it obvious that the little boy thought that mothers cook children, produce them inside themselves as women produce meals.

Such infantile conceptions form an appropriate bridge to the unconscious idea that cooking has a magical significance. A perceptive woman has sketched this magical function of preparing the meal in her book,* where she says: "With fire going woman becomes a sorceress, by a simple movement, as in beating eggs, or through the magic of fire, she effects the transmutation of substances; matter becomes food." Culinary alchemy pursues its course, food becomes chyle and blood. The cooking woman appears as the sorceress who can provide eternal youth to man and who can bring about his rebirth. The witch in Goethe's *Faust* can restore youth to the aging man. The strange brew the witch serves to Faust is the product of her patient domestic work:

> "The devil taught her how, 'tis true,
>   Yet the devil cannot make the stuff."

The potion which the witch serves to Faust would kill, if he were not properly prepared. The cooking woman can use black magic as well as white. The sorceress Medea of Greek mythology can heal wounds with her knowledge of herbs, but she can also poison those she hates. The successor of the mythological sorceress continues to live in the witch of our fairy tales. She represents the mother in her dreaded, hated form as the witch in Hansel and Gretel, who wants to cook and eat the children.

We immediately understand when the expression "cooking" is used in everyday language in a sexual sense. A patient spoke of a young woman who was, it seemed, more successful than she in attracting a certain young man. The patient asked herself the old question, "What has she got that I haven't?" without finding a satisfactory answer as to why the other woman had so much more sex appeal. She consoled herself with a Viennese colloquialism, known to her since childhood: *"Sie kocht auch nur mit Wasser."* (She too cooks only with water.) This comparison, transferred from the kitchen atmosphere to the area of sexual attractiveness, means, of course, that the other woman uses also only the general feminine means of attracting men and has no extraordinary abilities that would explain her sex appeal.

* Simone de Beauvoir, *The Second Sex*, New York, 1950, p. 453.

To these instances, taken from everyday language, infantile thinking, mythology and folklore, a representative expression of the same symbolic significance in poetry should be added.

In Richard Beer Hofmann's beautiful verse drama, *Der Graf von Charolais,* the leading character has discovered that his young wife has committed adultery. The count thinks of their little son and swears that he will bring up the boy never to trust women. When the child is grown, he will be told to be as little ashamed of his sexual drive as of hunger. He may use women as he wishes, but when he gets up from bed:

"You get up from a meal—it must not mean more to you—
Don't search in them dark dreams' solution,
Nor rest of eternal desire—not in them.
Whatever they will serve you with words and glances
It is the same dish, brewed down below there
In their dark kitchen, wherein
At day and night their fire does not die."*

All these examples in which cooking has the same symbolic significance as in the language of the dream, remind us that woman's womb is not only man's first domicile but also his first kitchen.

25. PRIORITY

The thinker who is accustomed to looking beneath the surface of things will not doubt that the priority which children hold in the thoughts of women corresponds to the precedence existing in a man's mind for his work. There is no man who has not thought, at a certain point, that woman is a "sometime thing" and that the most vital goal in his life is his work. A man whose thoughts circle about women all the time is not much of a man. A child delivered, well formed and healthy, has its counterpart in the

* My translation.

job well done for a man. It is perhaps correct, as many psychoanalysts assume, that the penis envy which little girls experience
is paralleled by a secret envy in the boy toward women who can
bring children into the world.

It is true that there are women who neglect their children,
whose interests often reach out in other directions even while
the children are small and very dependent upon their care. There
are mothers who have very little affection for their children and
to whom they appear as burdensome and a nuisance. But this is
not the rule; it is the exception. Even bad mothers take care of
their youngsters when there is an emergency. There are also men
who dislike and neglect their work, who daydream about being
away from it all or even wish nothing more than to live an idle
life. But when the call comes, they have to be on the spot.

The biological solution of a woman's life, it seems to me, is
not the man but the child. The biological goal of the man is not
the woman but the work. It is not important what work: the
presidency of the United States or the work of a carpenter. Man's
conscience demands that the work should be done as well as
possible, whether it is the agreement with another nation or the
work involved in fashioning a table.

The sexes would understand each other much better if they
would recognize that deep-rooted biological and psychological
priority in the goals of their life. Many of their misunderstandings are founded upon mutual misconceptions of those primary
functions. A man will never really and deeply understand that
the woman sees an image of him in the child she gives him, and
not only of him, but of all men. The other day a woman complained to another woman about the naughtiness of her little
boy, adding: "All the qualities we admire in men—their energy,
singleness of purpose, their drive, zest and ferocious will-power—
what a nuisance they are when you have to educate a little boy!"
Only intellectually, not emotionally, will a man understand
what a consolation it is for a woman whose husband has to go
overseas during the war to become pregnant with his child. The
child she will bear is psychologically not merely a replacement

for him, but the man himself. As a patient said: "A pocket edition of him."

There is a kind of instinctive admiration for the function of the other sex. A woman who does not have even a clear idea of the work her husband does in the office, will look at him with some feeling of awe when he leaves for work punctually and returns home tired. A wife who has just given birth to a child is looked upon with a certain admiration and wonder by her husband, as though she had accomplished something extraordinary and wonderful. Women do not experience the same feeling toward other women after delivery. My mother used to say: "Every cow can become a mother."

The priority of the child in a woman's life and of work in the man's gives occasion to feelings of wonder; but this divergence in goals is sometimes not understood, and often not appreciated by the other sex. A patient, full of indignation, told me the following incident: her lover had given her the first draft of a novel he had just completed and asked her to look through it for corrections. On the way home she became suddenly very ill, fainted and was almost run over by a car. A policeman brought her to a doctor who treated her and sent her home. A friend of hers reported the accident shortly afterward to her lover. He turned pale, and for a moment was almost unable to speak. His first question was, however: "What happened . . . to my manuscript?"

26. EARLY IDEAS ON MARRIAGE

There is an astonishing abundance of data on the sexual life of children and on the infantile theories they build, in the psychoanalytic literature of the day. The importance of those early notions, which are often grotesque mixtures of fact and fancy, is not doubtful. I would like to add, however, some of the notions children have about marriage and married life. We hold the impression that those ideas in children leave deep traces in later emotional life.

Someone said that girls are always worried until they marry and that boys are never worried until after that. To what early age can we trace this different attitude? Perhaps to the early phase where boys play war and little girls play house. A patient remembered in analysis that he wanted to play Indians and trappers with his sister and her friends but they wouldn't and he was compelled to act the part of the husband who returns home from the office. In his analysis he smilingly remarked that this situation of early childhood was a model for the role into which he was pressed later as a man. When he began to have dates much later, he experienced great satisfaction when his mother said to a lady friend, who had spoken of the boy's going out with different girls: "Why should I worry about my sons? Let those mothers worry about their daughters." It made an impression, however, on him that his mother sometimes worried about his sister, who had only a few admirers, while mother never wasted time or thought about his future marriage.

The rule which says that boys are never worried until they are married has quite a few exceptions. I know a little boy who proclaimed at first that he would marry his mommy and his sister and occasionally the cook. Later on, he became worried about this, and at the mature age of seven, he recognized other facts of life concerning marriage. He asked his mother what she would do when he married and felt uneasy when she answered that she would move into his home. He expressed his doubt as to whether or not his wife would object to that, but decided he would give his old mother a little room below the stairs where she could live. The only difficulty was that there was no toilet for her. A few days later he felt anxious about the taxes he would have to pay for such a big house—so vivid is the impression made by talk on radio and television upon children. In general, boys aren't much concerned about future marriage. They will think about that bridge when they get there . . . and they are in no hurry to. Little boys, much more than girls, connect thoughts about marriage with sex. And not only little boys but big ones too. Three hundred years ago the famous poet, Jean de La Fontaine, then an old man, was asked if he had never thought of marrying: "Sometimes," he replied, "in the morning."

In contrast with the carefree attitude of boys, little girls think about marriage and married life early. A patient recalled an argument she had had when she was eleven years old, with her mother. The girl was to play a little piece at a performance her piano teacher gave with her pupils. The child insisted that she should wear a long dress at this, her first, public appearance. Her mother remained adamant in spite of her pleading. Sobbing, the child shouted: "You just want me to become an old maid!" The mother answered serenely, "I'll take that risk."

27. GIFTS

A lady I know, once asserted that her husband had not given her any presents in the last few years. I reminded her that he had given her a valuable pin, some earrings, a bracelet and a necklace on different occasions. To my astonishment she repeated her statement, and declared—when I protested—that she had asked him to buy the pin for her birthday, had expressed the wish to have the necklace and wanted the bracelet on the occasion of their wedding anniversary. She did not consider those objects as gifts because she had asked her husband to buy them for her. Her assertion was, thus, not the result of a failing memory, but stemmed from a denial.

I doubt whether all women would freely express such a view, but I do not doubt that most women would feel similarly. Gifts from their husbands are things given to them unasked. Not things they tell him they would like to have, but things he would like them to have. Objects for which they must ask do not deserve the name of gifts. Such a view is certainly feminine.

Only in the minds of grownups are gifts things you buy. For small children gifts are parts of your body. This infantile concept is originated in the attitude the child has toward the only gifts he can give to his parents or to the nurse: feces and urine. These evacuations are highly appreciated because they are parts of the child's body. Psychoanalytic observations confirm the theory that deliverance of the feces is, so to speak, the earliest prototype of what we call giving a present. Even the baby soils preferably those persons he likes most. Infants who are cross with their mother or nurse, often sit for a long time on the pot without "delivering"—in the analytic theory, an expression of infantile defiance or stubbornness. Many parents know that children often bring their full pots to them as a kind of proof of their love, and in the expectancy of being praised.

It seems that this basic infantile concept of the gift is unconsciously maintained more faithfully and longer by women than by men. That unconscious character of presents is transferred from the sphere of evacuation to that of sexual life. In the emotions and thoughts of women, the gift has been much more closely connected with the body of the giver and thus retains the "personal" character. Woman "gives" herself in sexual intercourse, surrenders her body and, first and last, "gives" a child to the man.

A woman unconsciously assumes that, for a man, a gift has the same personal character that she attributes to it in her feelings. She does not accept gifts from the man as ornamental or useful objects per se but as a tribute paid to her charm or beauty, as expressions of love or affection. Gifts have thus for women, besides and often beyond the objective value, a great subjective significance: they are love tokens, symbols of giving oneself. Therefore Ophelia can say, "To the nobler mind, rich gifts wax poor when givers prove unkind."

In a woman's mind the fact that a man gives her a substantial gift implies the willingness to take on some form of responsibility. When a woman gives a man a substantial gift, it means that she would be happy to be his responsibility.

Psychologists have not yet pointed out that gifts have, thus, a different unconscious significance for women and for men. Yet everyday experience could teach them that a girl who shows a ring, given her by a man, to her friends has an emotional experience that is almost alien to a man. The personal concept of the gift in women goes sometimes so far that the presents themselves are personified, as though they were living and not inanimate objects. ("Diamonds are a girl's best friend.")

Women are almost never embarrassed or annoyed at getting gifts from men, only pleased or flattered. Men are often embarrassed. They are bad receivers of gifts because they consider the objects as such, and not the giver and the spirit in which the objects were given. In one of Helen Hokinson's cartoons in the *New Yorker,* an elderly woman asks of the prissy male clerk: "What can you suggest for an old gentleman who doesn't like anything?" It is scarcely possible to range an old lady in such a category.

28. The Two Types

There is an amusing motion picture called *"Captain's Paradise,"* with Alec Guinness in the title role. This poker-faced actor plays the part of the captain of a ship which goes from Gibraltar to North Africa on a regular schedule. The captain has a wife at home who takes very good care of him. She is pedestrian, wifely and "housewifely." She is the model of a woman whose interest is concentrated upon her home and husband. She knows no other life outside of them.

At a port in North Africa the captain has a mistress who is in every way the opposite type. She likes to dance, to flirt and make the rounds of the night clubs. In other words, she is a glorified barfly. The captain oscillates between the two women very satisfactorily, in a regular rhythm controlled by the ship's schedule. In his cabin there is the photograph of his wife which can be replaced by the picture of his mistress at a minute's notice as the ship approaches the other side of the Mediterranean. As soon as Gibraltar is in sight, the photograph of the wife takes its place. Thus the captain leads a double and happy life, envied by every male in the audience.

He is envied because all men wish to have both types of women at their disposal, simultaneously or in succession, regulated by a certain rhythm. Alas, the captain is expelled from his veritable paradise on two shores. Like Adam, he becomes the victim of Eve, who is unpredictable. To his horror he finds that, at a certain point, his dutiful wife has become a siren—dancing, going to night clubs and leaving her home and the care of her husband to an old housekeeper. At the North African port his mistress has undergone a metamorphosis that is just as radical. She now dislikes dancing and the gay life. She only wishes to be to be a homebody, to cook for him, have the apartment clean and orderly and to care for him in the manner of an excellent house-wife. To see Alec Guinness' face when he is surprised by the char-acter transformations of the two women is worth the price of admission by itself.

A short time after having seen *Captain's Paradise* I met Dr. Stauber at a dinner party, a gentleman who had the reputation of being one of the best gynecologists in pre-Hitler Vienna. He is now well in his seventies, but still vigorous and is still practicing. While the young people around us amused themselves, we old boys sat in a corner and exchanged memories, in good Viennese dialect, of people and places in that lovely city that had once been our home. I don't remember any longer how the conversa-tion turned to women. It was perhaps through discussing the *"suesse Maedel,"* Schnitzler's typical Viennese girl-figure. I pre-sented to the doctor a bit of my psychological theories on women. The old man listened patiently but perhaps not too sympa-thetically to my rambling. Then he said, in a somewhat tired voice: "I'll tell you something. I have observed thousands of women. There are only two types: those that are boring and the crazy ones." (He used the jargon word, the *"meschugenen."*)

Perhaps I was mistaken, but he seemed to let his eyes wander from one of the women present to the next as if attempting to place them in his two categories. It occurred to me later that he included in the second group all kinds of emotional disturbances, not only psychoses and neuroses but also the nervous irritabilities, the passing mood swings and inconsistencies of women.

I compared his sentence with the assertion of George Meredith that women will be the last thing civilized by man, also one of those ambiguous statements born of misogyny. You can just as well say that man is the last thing civilized by woman. Are not women the educators of us all? Do they not teach men, who are brutes and unmannered, how to behave in a civilized society? But Meredith meant "civilization" in a specific British sense, and Dr. Stauber meant behavior in a purely rational sense, rational at least in the eyes of us men. The hidden potentialities of the opposite character types are in every woman, and it often depends only upon external factors or circumstances (or the age at which the events occur) whether a transformation of this kind takes place or not.

It is strange, I mused on my way home from the party, that there is no trace of such a clear distinction in the majority of average men, no such clear-cut group division. I thought of friends, colleagues and acquaintances, men in different walks of life. No, one cannot make such a bold differentiation among them. Several men came to my mind as I thought of all this: a few were boring and crazy at the same time, others were as mad as hatters and bores too. Women who are insane or neurotic are at least interesting. Those who are not might be dull, plodding and boring but at least they are reasonable . . . as women go.

29. Boys Will Be Boys

The couple whose argument I will relate were invited to the birthday party of the five-year-old child of friends. On their way to the party they decided to buy a small electric train as a birthday gift for the little boy. The child was delighted with the toy, which he took to his room. Soon afterward he appeared again and asked the guest to come with him and show him how the train functioned. The visitor stayed a long time in the child's room; when he did not return, his wife and the hostess entered the nursery. The little boy had lost interest in the train by then, and was playing with another toy. The visitor was lying on the floor, busy with the train which he tried to put in motion. "Look!" exclaimed his wife, "It is not the child who is playing with it! It's the big boy. I don't believe that fathers ever bring gifts to their sons; they buy them for themselves! Boys will be boys."

The patient who reported this little episode protested emphatically against what his wife had said and the derogatory meaning he had felt behind it. He asserted that it is the most valuable thing to a man that he can become, at times, a boy again. Well, we shall not discuss his evaluation of such a regression, or return to childhood here. We agree, however, with him that there is a possibility of a return of this kind in most men, whatever they are: merchant, lawyer or banker. It is a short-lived reappearance of the boy in the man, or a fleeting return to the playing child.

Here is, however, a difference between men and women. Men relapse, in those abrupt pauses, into boyhood. The toy train, in our case, formed a bridge into a remote past in which the man played with trains or wished to become an engineer. Here is an episode in the life of a grown-up man.

Women remain basically in a phase much nearer to the child. No transformation is necessary—only the lifting of a veil: in a woman's face the child is preserved. Listen to a woman speaking to her baby while she feeds it or plays with it. Baby talk comes naturally to her when she speaks—she "speaks to herself" as she was. Then listen to a man using baby talk with an infant. It is utterly funny, if not ridiculous. It is true: "Boys will be boys,"—but women never stopped being little girls.

30. IN DEFENSE OF WOMEN

The interpretation of the dream of a young housewife gives me an occasion to make some remarks on the theme: "Women's work is never done." The dream content is a single picture. The young woman sees her husband, with chains on his arms and legs, sitting in prison. He holds the baby in his arms.

Here are the day remnants, or the situation from which the dream arose: the patient's husband returned from his office in a "foul" mood. His wife asked him, after dinner, to help her with some household chores. He obliged, but complained later that he felt very tired, that the day at the office had been trying and overburdened with work. He compared his exhausting work with that of women in general: they "have it good." They can stay at home the whole day and do their work which is, after all, not much and can be done leisurely—a little cooking, washing, taking care of the baby. What does it all amount to, anyway? Men work like coolies.

The dream is obviously the wife's reaction to his remarks which she took silently. It expresses the wish: "I would like to see you once in my situation every day!" It shows this wish realized in the visual picture of the dream.

Here is another case of a husband complaining about his wife. He had also come home tired from his office. After dinner his wife expressed the wish to go to a movie, while he was just about to settle down quietly to read a magazine. He complained that it was the same story almost every evening: he wanted to sit down at home after work and enjoy his leisure while his wife—who is much younger—would like to go to a show, visit friends or entertain some acquaintances. Yesterday evening, he said, a short argument had developed from these contrasting attitudes. During the tiff his wife had accused him of being responsible for the fact that she was becoming fat. The reproach is easy to explain: if he does not go out with her, she is tempted to eat candy or to pamper herself with things taken from the refrigerator.

There is certainly nothing unusual in this situation. It is not uninteresting that the impression it created in me expressed itself in my thoughts by a musical association. While I listened to my patient's complaints, I heard inside me a little tune long-forgotten. The words to it came to mind almost immediately: *"Bei*

Tage bin ich hektisch, bei Nacht bin ich elektrisch. . . ." (During the day I am hectic, at night I become electric.) The song must be from an old Viennese operetta that I have never seen, but I had heard my father hum or quote it when I was a little boy. I knew the tune was meant to tease mother who, at this time, expressed the wish to go out after dinner with him. The musical association says, of course: "That's an old tune of women."

Psychologically that wish of women is easy to understand. Many women have to do rather monotonous housework during the day and they are often alone with no one to talk to. They wait for their husbands to come home from the office and hope he will bring news and interesting material for conversation. They would like to tell him all they have thought and experienced during the day. Many of them are disappointed, day after day, in this expectation. The husband returns home tired or ill-humored and wants to rest reading the evening paper. (Do you remember the cartoon in the *New Yorker* showing a widow at dinner across from the empty chair on which her husband used to sit? On the wall is his picture, nicely framed—or rather, the picture she remembers as the usual one in this situation: you see just the top of his head—the rest of his body is covered by the newspaper he is reading.)

It is clear why the wife of my patient accuses him of making her eat candy. She is frustrated because he scarcely talks with her after dinner, nor does he want to go to a movie or to see friends. The young woman, thus frustrated, is tempted to regress to the earliest kind of satisfaction: eating, and is afraid of its disastrous effects upon her figure.

31. FEMININE VULNERABILITY

Men in general admit much more readily than women that they have shortcomings and faults—or have made a mistake. That difference might not be considered by comparative psychology, but everyday experiences teach us here more than scholarliness.

That unwillingness of the average woman reaches from the denial that she has made a wrong turn in driving to the inability to admit that she has a nasty temper. It would be especially difficult for a woman to admit such things to a man, especially to a man with whom she is closely associated. Men are, by God, bull-headed, pugnacious and stubborn enough, but they are, in general, not as vulnerable to criticism as women.

Why should this be? One is tempted to explain the divergence by the greater sensitiveness of women. The higher degree of narcissism in them also has to be considered. Yet these two reasons are insufficient. The second one cannot be brought into the discussion—at least not in the sense in which we understand primary narcissism as self-love. Such an attitude would be rather an excellent protection against feeling hurt by criticism. Truly narcissistic types are not touched by faultfinding and negative comments.

Deeper observation leads to a different result: listen to a discussion between a man and woman in which the man does not even make a critical remark but says something that could lead to it. If the woman does not prefer to be silent, she will immediately be on the defensive and very often take the offensive. She will undertake a counterattack even when she knows she has made a mistake. In spite of the fact that the evidence cannot be refuted, she will project everything she senses she could be accused of onto her partner. At the slightest sign that she could be blamed, even before the argument develops, she will attack him. She will blame him to protect herself in advance, and this while the discussion is seemingly still friendly. It is as though, seeing clouds in the sky that could mean an approaching storm, she hurriedly puts up her umbrella. The counterattack may perhaps prevent the aggression that was anticipated.

Such precipitated reaction and often superfluous self-protection has sometimes the character of a feminine maneuver, but one of its most important motives is fear. What fear? The general answer is: fear of "losing face" in the eyes of the man. But such a reaction is the opposite of the one we would expect from persons with strong self-confidence. The greater sensitiveness of woman toward criticism, her vulnerability, is thus the result of a lack of self-esteem or self-confidence. He who feels strong can afford to admit mistakes, can acknowledge weaknesses and short-comings because he knows that he has qualities that compensate for them. To be unwilling to admit slight mistakes and weak-nesses means that one has little self-confidence. Such intense vulnerability shows how much has to be protected, and is con-sidered endangered. Being on guard in such an exaggerated manner against possible or actual criticism betrays doubt and uncertainty about one's qualities.

The brittleness and fragility of feminine self-confidence is at the root of woman's oversensitivity regarding criticism from men. The concealed and disavowed feeling of inadequacy often make distortions, pretexts, denials and even lies necessary. The defense and concealment can, in certain cases, obtain an almost auto-matic character. Many men are accustomed to this. The other day a patient started his analytic session with the following re-port: "I know it is foolish to expect fair play from women. They were not taught to be fair. But how do you explain this? Yesterday Anne called me and said 'Lunch is ready.' I came into the kitchen where she had just finished frying hamburgers, and sat down quietly and ate. I said then 'By the way, in the future, dear, would you boil my hamburgers rather than fry them?' It was just a remark. I remembered that the doctor had warned me not to eat greasy things. I just said that to remind her of it, but did not mention it, of course. You should have seen how she carried on and heard how she yelled at me! Where, I would like to know, was the offense in a quiet harmless remark like that? You tell me!"

Perhaps his wife considered him a hypochondriac or did not believe in the doctor's orders. Perhaps she took his quiet remark as reproach and accusation, as unjustified criticism of her and of her cooking. She got mad at him, but she also got mad at herself, and then again at him.

An old lady once said: "To the average male an honest woman

is more suspect than a gypsy fortuneteller." Women's consequently sustained defense attitude can lead to a veritable subjective denial of the fact that women possess any faults whatsoever. I saw somewhere a cartoon where a woman is complaining
bitterly that her husband is so obstinate. "It is the hardest thing
in the world," she says, "to convince him that I am always right."

There are good psychological reasons why women are thus
permanently on the defensive at the slightest criticism. They
tread warily here and are suspicious and cautious because they
have realized the intense need of man to idealize them—especially of the man who is in love with them. Ideals cannot afford
to have faults or blemishes: they would cease to be ideals. What
is divine cannot, at least in the eyes of modern man, have faults.
It has to be perfect. A woman can very clearly recognize the faults
and weaknesses of a man and continue to love him. But she fears
that, should he discover her faults and inadequacies, he would
no longer love her. Her desire is that, at least "until death do us
part" he remain convinced that he "married an angel."

When it comes to perfection, a woman's attitude resembles
that of the Catholic Church. The Church decrees that the Holy
Scripture is infallible. If there could be the slightest error in the
Bible, even in regard to dating an event, it would not be divinely
inspired. It would be human work.

One assumes that a woman's claim to flawlessness or infalli-
bility has its roots in the awareness of a hidden incompleteness
of the body, and was later displaced from it and generalized.
Which man, born of woman, would dare to say to his sweetheart:
"Darling, you are beautiful, but you have ugly elbows"?

32. AMBITION AND VANITY

The experiences of many years of analytic observation and
practice seem to push us to the conclusion that certain emotions
are incompatible with each other. It appears that they cannot
coexist in the psychical orbit. But this impression is not alto-

gether correct. It does not consider the spaciousness and depth of our emotional world.

It is, however, justifiable to assume that the one emotion has to recede or become repressed when the other prevails. Let me mention instances of such rivaling emotions which are often akin, in which case their fight for hegemony resembles that of two nations that are related. Depression and rage are almost incompatible within the same emotional household. A person who was deeply depressed has an attack of violent anger: at that moment the depression has disappeared. The replacement of the one by the other is made possible by the fact that depression is often the result of aggressiveness turned against oneself. A need for self-punishment and a conscious guilt feeling are rarely to be found side by side. It is as though to feel consciously very guilty makes an unconscious urge for self-punishment superfluous. Sincere mourning, for instance after the death of a person near and dear to us, seems to exclude sexual desire. If sexuality raises its head mourning, for the time being, has to yield. There is a good old Jewish anecdote which apparently contradicts this assertion but, if looked at properly, actually confirms it by its skeptic exposure: the husband of a woman who is going to be buried is nowhere to be found when the funeral procession begins. Finally his brother-in-law finds him in bed with the maid of the house. Full of indignation he shouts: "You rascal! At the very moment when your wife is being buried you are sleeping with a woman!" The bewildered husband replies: "How do I know what I do in my grief?" (*Weis ich was ich tu in mein Schmerz?*")

Many observations have made us come to the conclusion that strong ambition and physical vanity cannot be equally developed in one person. As I have said before, that does not mean that a person who is very ambitious and passionately wishes to be famous or socially recognized cannot be vain with regard to his appearance. It means, however, that one feeling or the other will gain priority. This is the more astonishing because ambitiousness and vanity cannot deny their emotional kinship. It is as though the two trends present two sides of a single unity, are, so to speak, branches of the same tree growing in opposite directions.

Applied to the two sexes this contradistinction takes on a definite psychological significance. The general impression is that men are more ambitious than women and that women are more vain in a physical sense than men. Traced back to the emotional sources, this divergency would mean that men in general try to overcome feelings of insecurity or inadequacy by accomplishments while women attempt to master the initial feeling of inadequacy of earliest girlhood by making themselves as attractive as possible. In terms of the psychoanalytic theory: the boy wants to accomplish something remarkable and to prove to himself that the castration dread is invalidated. The girl, who has accepted the handicap by which, in her thoughts, nature has put her at a disadvantage, wants to show that she is very attractive. She makes a virtue of anatomical necessity.

If our impression is psychologically correct, a man who is very preoccupied with his looks and highly appreciates the impression his appearance makes upon others—trying to improve it by every means—will not be very ambitious, will not strive for fame and will not concentrate his energy on accomplishing something valuable.

On the other hand, a woman who has an extraordinary thirst for fame and a desire to accomplish something—a writer or a painter for example—will not be equally interested in her looks. She will not spend too much time and attention on it nor put too much importance on dresses, jewels, caring for her complexion and so on. It is as though the interest in the one thing increases at the expense of the other, as though the two stand in the position of inverted functions.

At first blush it might appear as though we had here a special case of a psychological law to the effect that, where an intensive emotion prevails, all others have to stand back. To mention an instance from a neighboring area: a Viennese writer once asserted that a woman who is very desperate cannot be well-dressed, and a woman who is well-dressed cannot be very desperate. We shall not try to argue with that epigram which does not take feminine camouflage into consideration. We will rather return to our impression that a highly developed feeling of vanity is in most cases incompatible with an urge for accomplishment. Beauty and charm are considered as accomplishments in themselves by women. The aim that all should be pleased with them is considered higher than the transitory goal of being famous. It is not renunciation that makes them desist from striving for it. Most of them are vain but few are vainglorious.

Quite a few women develop a kind of vicarious ambitiousness: they want their husband or lover to accomplish something remarkable. They are proud of him and feel they are worthy of admiration because he loves them. His achievement heightens, so to speak, their value, as though they were extensions of his personality. Even women who obtain fame and high social recognition prefer to point to their husbands or lovers as being more deserving than they are. Observers of Madame Curie, who was one of the few women geniuses in science, reported that this woman, who was celebrated in the salons of Paris like a goddess, tried, after the Nobel Prize, to deflect the fame to her husband, the physicist with whom she had worked (*"Pas moi! C'est Pierre . . ."*). Women in general are not proud of what they achieve but of what they are. Ambition is alien to their deepest nature. It is not that sin by which those angels fall. They can be ambitious for their husbands or more so for their children but they rarely aspire to higher aims themselves. "We have better things to do," said one of them in a discussion. "We have to take care of the preservation of mankind."

In the ambitiousness of man unconscious emulation of other admired men has a great, often unconscious, part. Competition, comparing one's accomplishments with those of other men, is almost always discernible as an unconscious companion to ambitiousness. Comparing the sales graphs, the number and social importance of clients, one's own material or spiritual successes with those of other men is a touchstone on which the achievements of a man are unconsciously tested. In the vanity women develop, another related form of competition is almost always present. Mirrors are used not only for self-admiration. Women ask: "Mirror, mirror on the wall, who is the fairest of us all?"

33. Self-Awareness in Both Sexes

The phenomenon of self-awareness as such has, as far as I know, found no independent treatment in psychological literature. It is often mentioned in connection with subjects like social security, vanity, lack of spontaneity and similar topics. The initial difficulty in the discussion of the subject is the necessity to differentiate between self-awareness and self-consciousness. To be self-aware simply means to be aware of oneself; whereas to be self-conscious, although it has the same basic meaning, has come more and more to denote in colloquial English, consciousness of oneself with an undertone of self-criticism—of one's awkwardness, failure and mistakes in social relations. A person can be self-aware without being self-critical. Young women rarely fail to be self-aware, but are not always self-conscious.

The phenomenon of self-awareness becomes conspicuous as a symptomatic manifestation in the psychological treatment of timid or withdrawn neurotic personalities. In pathological exaggeration, it appears in the symptoms of ideas of reference in the psychopathology of paranoia and in states of depersonalization which are often recognized as the initial symptoms of psychotic disturbances. One is tempted to consider these symptoms as expressions of heightened self-awareness. In paranoia, a self-critical view, or awareness of the criticism of others (persecution ideas) and a feeling of one's own importance, or an exaggeration of one's prominent qualities (ideas of grandeur), gives a definite character to self-awareness. In states of depersonalization, nothing of such an inflation of the ego is discernible. In its place the self-awareness has the character of an oversharp observation of oneself, one's actions, speech and general behavior. No critical undertone accompanies this self-awareness in depersonalization. A student of mine, Mrs. Marion Lynton, who is gracious enough to acknowledge that I stimulated the research project, is working on a thesis dealing with the differences in self-awareness in men and women. She arrived at the following hypotheses:

1. The self-awareness of women is comparatively higher than that of men.
2. This difference is conditioned by the difference in upbringing and education of boys and girls.
3. This education favors the self-concept of a girl as weaker, more dependent and handicapped as compared with boys.
4. The comparatively higher degree of self-awareness in a girl is also determined by the fact that she considers her personal appearance and personality more as the object of critical attention from surrounding people than does the boy.
5. This greater degree of self-awareness is the result of culture and has scarcely any biological foundation.

Mrs. Lynton, who has allowed me to make excerpts from the outline of her research project points out the following: that self-awareness is originally the awareness of being the center of attention or becoming conscious of the reactions of others to oneself; whether this attention is positive or negative is at first unimportant.

It is paradoxical that the psychology of self-awareness means being aware of other people's reactions to oneself—seeing, hearing and even smelling oneself as one might be seen, heard or smelled by others. Very often the content of this attention concentrated on oneself is not sharply perceived. There is only the awareness of the attention of others without sharp definition of its character. It does not matter whether a situation of the kind described actually exists or whether it lives only in the person's phantasy. Thus it is possible that a person may become self-aware when alone. The psychological premise for the emergence of this feeling is the presence of others, either real or imaginary. In situations where self-awareness emerges in isolation, the imagined presence of at least two people forms its unconscious origin. The state of self-awareness originally has in its concept no self-critical note, but it emerges generally as awareness of one's peculiarities, shortcomings, weaknesses or physical defects. A person can become self-aware by thinking of his short stature, his excessive height, a red nose or a slight speech defect.

The behavior patterns resulting from self-awareness go in two sharply defined directions: one tendency can be characterized as an effort to conceal, or at least diminish, the shortcoming or personal peculiarity which attracts attention—be it in reality or only in the person's imagination. This tendency to conceal contrasts with another tendency which emphasizes certain superior qualities, bringing the stronger points of the person to the foreground and to the attention of others—"putting one's best foot forward." The coexistence and contrast of these two opposite tendencies and their compromise formations determine the resulting social behavior of the person, which might be either shy or demonstrative or even a blending of both attitudes in a rather shy demonstrativeness or demonstrative shyness.

The basic hypothesis Mrs. Lynton wants to test is that the self-awareness of women is greater in general than the self-awareness of men. In the sense of her characterization of this emotion, the statement would amount to the fact that women consider themselves more the object of social attention than men in certain situations. If this is correct we would expect that the two tendencies which we conceived as reactions to self-awareness would be more pronounced in women than in men. This is actually the case. Even superficial observation will show that women make greater effort than men to conceal certain minor physical imperfections or handicaps. It is rare that women who have a physical blemish do not attempt to hide it even if it is not conspicuous. On the other hand, everybody knows that women develop more skill and talent, spend more time and money on improving their appearance and making their physical attributes not only apparent but conspicuous. Yes, in certain cases they understand how to make a virtue of necessity, and are able to decorate or beautify a minor flaw so that it is transformed into something especially attractive.

The difference in the degree of self-awareness is not only subjectively experienced, but it is obvious in behavior patterns. If one were to compare a situation in which a young man and a young woman enter a room where many people are gathered—a party, ballroom or concert hall—the lesser degree of self-awareness in the young man is determined by the fact that he generally does not feel that the attention of everyone is focused on him. The greater degree of self-awareness in the girl is founded on the fact, real or imaginary, that she is observed by everyone. In the ensuing conversation the young man will be less self-aware than the girl. She will be more self-aware than he, even if she knows that she is attractive both in her appearance and personality.

With regard to the origin of this difference in self-awareness, it is difficult to imagine that it is biologically determined. Observation of male and female babies does not lead to the conclusion that a little girl develops a higher degree of self-awareness if she is not exposed to the educational influences of her mother or nurses and governesses. These factors of education and upbringing, whose onset varies according to cultural patterns and social layers, mold the personality of the little girl as well as that of the little boy, and decidedly favor a higher degree of self-awareness in the infant girl than in the boy. Among these educational influences we emphasize the development of an earlier and more intensified sense of shame in the little girl.

Education to shame concerns the organs and functions of evacuation and later those of sex more energetically in the little girl than in the little boy. In early childhood this sense of self-awareness with regard to the organs and functions of evacuation and sex leads to a greater degree of concealment and secrecy in girls. We observe that this self-awareness is less developed and

even absent in the boy who shows a tendency toward exhibitionism.

The educational factor is also easily observable in the development of the other tendency, the endeavor to appear beautiful or
attractive, which is not a demand in the upbringing of boys.

As the last and most determining factor causing heightened
self-awareness in girls, we recognize the cultural concept that
women are physically handicapped in comparison to men. This
means that mothers as well as mother representative figures give
the little girl the impression that her genitals are inferior to
those of boys. The unconscious continuation of this concept
leads the girl to the conviction that she is physically handicapped
compared to the boy. We deduct that the overawareness of
women as compared to men originates in what analysis calls the
castration complex. It is not inborn (with the potential exception
of an archaic inheritance) and is the outcome of culture. Education by the mother and by mother representative figures takes
over also the other task which can be conceived as consolation
for that real or imagined handicap—the endeavor to make the
appearance of the girl very attractive. We know from clinical
analysis that the little girl who has the self-concept of being
handicapped finds compensatory consolation in the fact that her
body develops in physical beauty and attractiveness. Finally the
last consolation for not being as privileged as man is found in
the creative act of bearing a child. There lies her greatest compensation and reward.

Certain forms of behavior such as straightforwardness, daring,
aggressiveness and sexual initiative are energetically suppressed
in the education of girls. Any transgression is frowned upon socially and punished. Obedience to these social rules and striving
for conformity of behavior also foster a heightened self-awareness. It is as though women were compelled to be on their guard
against the temptation to transgress and must be on a continual
qui vive in regard to their own behavior.

Mrs. Lynton tries to verify her statements by experimentation and questionnaires in the classical manner of clinical psychology. With the help of these methods the fact that self-awareness in girls generally increases at the critical time of puberty can be verified. The questionnaires seem to confirm indirectly the statement that the origin of a girl's intensified self-awareness is found in the genital differentiation and the emotional reaction to it.

Another significant factor in the comparative discussion is that women are not only more self-aware with men, but they are also more self-aware in the presence of other women than men are in the presence of other men. The questionnaires, obtained from different age groups, give interesting information about the difference in the self-awareness of men and women as they advance in age. While a comparison shows that the self-awareness of women of sixty is still noticeably higher than that of the corresponding male group, the distance decreases so that the female attitude approaches that of the male after reaching a certain progressed age.

It is noticeable that the homosexual man shows, compared to the heterosexual male, a heightened self-awareness which resembles that of the average woman. On the other hand, a relative decrease of self-awareness in female homosexuals of a certain type can be observed.

These interesting comparisons, if followed up and systematically verified, will certainly cast a light on the psychological differences of the sexes. The phenomenon of self-awareness is one of the few characteristics of women which can be unambiguously traced to social influences and factors of education and tradition.

Psychological research begins to deal with a subject that has only occasionally been discussed in novels and plays. Yet those casual observations and remarks of perceptive writers, predecessors of psychologists, should not be lost. Kitty Foyle in Christopher Morley's novel* protests about the unfairness of men who have so much more time for thinking. They have sort of "times

* New York, 1939, p. 178.

between times" that a woman never has. Men "don't have to tuck
a dress under their knees every time they sit down in a windy
subway. . . ." Kitty justly observes that a man "has more chance
to get away from being a man."

It is obvious that the heightened self-awareness of the woman
influences and colors her behavior, even when she is alone. Karl
Kraus playfully doubts that there is such a thing as a woman
alone, that means a woman unobserved by herself. Sudden self-
awareness interferes, of course, with the spontaneity and naturalness of the person. Anatole France mentions, in *Le Jardin d'Epi-
cure,* the story of the abbess of *Vermont* who was considered a
saint when she died. The nuns, who had shared in her pious
works, believed that she was in heaven and prayed for her inter-
cession. Once she appeared to them—pale, her robe blazing with
flames. "Pray for me!" she implored. "While I was still alive and
folded my hands in prayer, I once looked at them and thought
them beautiful; today I am atoning for that sinful thought in
the torments of hell-fire!"

If it is desirable to look at ourselves as others see us, women
reach this goal more often than men, at least when they stand
before a mirror.

34. DIFFERENCES IN SUPEREGO FORMATION

When we read something that has put vague thoughts and
feelings we ourselves have been unable to express into words, we
experience a particular satisfaction, sometimes even astonishment. Why had we not been able to express that idea although it
had been so near the threshold of conscious thinking without being able to pass it? It is indifferent whether it is an insight into
a psychological connection or a general observation, whether the
conclusion reached by the writer is founded on clinical material
or is the result of experience of many observations coalesced at

last in a single sentence of poignant interest. The feeling of hearing or reading such an idea is: "I had somewhere known that all the time, but why could I not say it in such a clear and original formulation?" Such was the case when Freud expressed the view* that certain character traits for which women have always been criticized and reproached, namely, "that they have less sense of justice than men, less tendency to submit themselves to the great necessities of life and frequently permit themselves to be guided in their decisions by their affections or enmities," are due in large part to a difference in their superego formation.

The same feeling of familiarity was experienced in reading Hanns Sachs' conclusion that the superego does not develop the same severity and is not as exacting in woman as in man. It is more lenient and does not put such high demands upon her. The flexibility and tolerance of woman's conscience contrasts with the rigidity and cruelty of man's. I had often wondered about that without connecting the difference with biological and psychological divergences. Yes, even without giving it a second—and that means here a psychoanalytical—thought, I had been aware even of those differences in their external manifestations. For a man a policeman is unconsciously the personification of the law —even for the gangster who shoots him. For the average woman a policeman is a man in uniform, and nothing else.

Penetrating and surprising psychological insight is to be found in the writing of many authors whose purpose is very far from scientific research in psychological problems. The other day I ran across the quotation of a casual sentence that Joseph Joubert once wrote. It was again one of those psychological observations that can be made in everyday life and are passed over by students of comparative psychology. The French writer states that women believe that everything they dare to do is innocent. (*"Les femmes croient innocent tout ce qu'elles osent."*) In other and too many words, women in general are cautious, afraid and doubtful when

---

* *Einige psychische Folgen des anatomischen Geschlechtsunterschieds*, Gesammelte Schriften, Vol. IX, p. 18.

they would like to do something against the mores, but if they have overcome those fears or scruples and have done what they feared, they feel that they have been justified—that they are innocent. They rarely feel guilty afterward. The time of doubt and scruples was before the deed.

(In one of Anatole France's novels, *La Revolte des Anges*, a young aristocrat surprises his mistress in bed with his best friend. She regains her poise and looks at her previous sweetheart with a look of offended virtue. When he heaps abuse on her for her infidelity, she becomes very angry and accuses him of having driven her into the other man's arms. She demands that a car be brought for her and, taking her leave, she looks at Maurice (her official lover) with that glance of contempt due to the man a woman has just deceived.)

We shall immediately discuss how many exceptions seem to contradict this general statement. These restrictions do not invalidate its correctness. But does that mean that women in general feel guiltless after having conquered those doubts and fears preceding the deed, while men do not go through such a phase before committing the act and only feel these emotions later? Do men rush in where those angels fear to tread? That seems indeed the implied meaning of Joubert's sentence. There is thus the picture of two distinct behavior patterns of the sexes: men go forward and often unhesitatingly do things of which they later repent and about which they feel guilty. Women wait and postpone the deed, but after they have done it, they are convinced that they were entitled to do it, that they are innocent even if it is a crime they have committed.

Those two different reactions after the deed are often observable, for instance, in a man's guilt or remorse after having committed a crime and the defiance and stubbornness of a woman under the same conditions. In the case of female patients the analyst is often surprised to find that women who have done something very unconventional, or something that was in full contrast to their upbringing or previous behavior, obstinately assert that they were right, and remain headstrong and closed to every opposite feeling or argument.

The two behavior patterns exhaust together the possibilities of reaction to something originally rejected, to a deed considered immoral or criminal: defiance against society and then collapse under the burden of guilt feeling on the one side, and obstinacy and defiance after the deed on the other.

The reader will immediately remember several instances in which men and women behaved quite differently, did not follow the course of the typical reactions described. The biographies of many historical figures and the life stories of contemporary men and women present enough instances in which men were first hesitant and fearful, then, after the deed, defiant; and women who plunge into a situation and then feel very guilty afterward. Those cases are, of course, not restricted to neurotic characters. They belong to the area of normal people. Yet that behavior is so atypical that it often becomes the subject of special attention or interest, of admiration or criticism. The doubt and hesitancies of Hamlet and the determination of Lady Macbeth are perfect examples from literature, but there are many other historical characters who could be brought into the discussion. The Roman consul Quintus Fabius Verrucosus Cunctator who died in 203 B.C. got his byname Cunctator ("the hesitator") because he always avoided open battle against Hannibal. Yet once he had decided on a plan he carried it to its end vigorously and successfully. George Sand and other women belong to the opposite type who go directly and unhesitantly to their goal pushing aside all conventional considerations.

The next point tells us that psychological generalizations like the one in Joubert's sentence are not diminished in their validity and significance by such contradictory examples. The clean cut division into men and women does not take into account psychological characteristics of the individual and is not appropriate to their behavior traits. There is much of the feminine in men and much of the masculine in women. Besides and beyond the factor

of bisexuality in general, there is no doubt that individual men
show a constitutional or acquired higher degree of femininity
and its psychological collaterates than others, and some women
the corresponding masculine traits.

It is tempting to put that statement to the test by citing literary examples that clearly contradict it in contrasting the behavior
of a man and of a woman in a situation of crime. Of all Shakespeare's tragedies, *Macbeth* is the swiftest and the plot follows
the simplest outlines. Radical changes in the characters of Macbeth and of the lady take place in about a week or ten days' time.
When we meet Lady Macbeth, she is determined, and striving
toward her aim with undivided energy, a woman ready to sacrifice even her womanliness to her plan of murder. She asks the
spirits to "stop up the access and passage to remorse . . ."

> "Come to my woman's breasts,
> And take my milk for gall . . ."

She is contrasted with her husband who is ambitious, but has
milder feelings and hesitates. He is, the lady fears "too full o' th'
milk of human kindness." If the couple had lived in New York
today, the wife would have perhaps called him sarcastically
"Casper Macbeth Milquetoast." Up to the time of the deed it is
she who encourages him and remains steeled. A psychiatrist said
the other day about the mother of a patient: "But that is not a
woman, that is a steamroller." Such is Lady Macbeth until she
collapses in that grandiose scene in which we see her trying to
wash her bloody hands.

Macbeth, who had been doubtful, hesitant, "not without ambition, but without the illness should attend it . . ." (Act 1,
Scene 5) becomes, after the deed, pitiless. More than this, he is
ruthless, reckless and remorseless. He hears that the queen is
dead and reacts to the news with the casual sentence:

> "She should have died hereafter.
> There would have been a time for such a word."

He who had been mild says: "I have almost forgot the taste of fears." Casper Milquetoast is transformed into a monster.

Freud has attempted to explain the change of the two main characters of the tragedy using analytic insights acquired during the analysis of similar character types.* He believes that the key to the transformation is contained in that condensed sentence of Macduff: "He has no children." Yet he guesses that the problem of Macbeth and of the lady has to be solved by understanding the technique that Shakespeare sometimes uses. Ludwig Jekels had remarked that the poet often divides a character into two figures, attributes features originally to be found in one person to two characters of a play. It is perhaps thus with Macbeth and Lady Macbeth too. She became repentant after the deed; he became defiant. Together they exhaust the potentialities of re-action to the crime. Freud did not follow up this track, but considered its pursuit promising. We will venture here only a few steps beyond the point reached by him.

Even if we accept the concept of Freud or of Jekels, some psychological interest remains concentrated upon why Shakespeare attributed the scruples and recklessness, followed by neurotic breakdown after the deed, to the woman figure while he allotted the opposite emotional sequence to the man. Shakespeare's sources, especially Holinshed's chronicles, contains almost nothing pointing in the direction of such a development of two figures. It seems to me that there are two possibilities that could explain the attribution of such an atypical attitude to Lady Macbeth. Shakespeare thought, perhaps, of real contemporary women who could not have children and showed an unusual share of masculine character features. In this case the impenetrable determination and ruthlessness of Lady Macbeth had its prototype in life in a woman figure at the time of Shakespeare; the virginal Queen Elizabeth herself was perhaps the model for Lady Macbeth. But also a second possibility as to why the poet

* *Einige Character typen in der analytischen Arbeit,* Gesammelte Schriften, Vol. X.

attributed the typical masculine reaction to a woman has to be considered. The reversal of the roles could be the result of the playwright's homosexual tendencies, or of a hostile attitude toward woman expressed in having her appear as a seductress, causing the fall of man as in the biblical story of Eve.

Life confirms what Friedrich Schiller expressed in the sentence that a deed has a different face before and after it is committed. Joubert's luminous saying concerned these two faces the deed shows to the average woman, and we completed his statement adding the contrasting picture of the man. In spite of the many social and economic changes that have taken place in the hundred and twenty years since that sentence was written by the French moralist, women still react generally in the same manner. They still feel innocent of all they dare to do, and still feel justified after they have mastered their initial doubts and fears. Often, after the deed has been committed, they refuse obstinately to listen to any argument showing that they had been wrong in what they had done.

It cannot be only defiance, stubbornness or pride that determine such a typical feminine attitude. It is as though their belief of having done the right thing and their conviction that they were justified or entitled to do something generally considered wrong —or bad—is fed by some hidden source. Persons impaired by nature in their physical component often behave as if the world owes them compensation or exemption. They feel they can expect some exceptional treatment. They stubbornly refuse to be corrected or set right. Is there such an analogous subjective and unshakable subterranean foundation for the conviction of women that they are right? Yes, they unconsciously believe that nature has handicapped them in making them women, in depriving them of the envied male genitals. To them, in their unconscious thoughts, the world is divided into two parts: the "haves" and the "have nots."

35. On the Sphere of Interest

The basic technique of this study is the presentation of the contrasting pictures which the behavior patterns of men and women show. Not all the pictures are equally developed. Some are carefully selected and others are, so to speak, catching the object in certain situations and under peculiar circumstances. The general trend moves, however, in the direction of the typical in the different spheres of thoughts and emotions of the sexes. There is enough space for individual divergences and deviations within this frame. The comparison of the pictures, taken under changing conditions, forms distinct impressions of the family of man comprising males and females. Cultural differences are, of course, to be considered. The varieties of the different culture patterns will influence the morals, the education and finally, the behavior, but only to a certain degree. The basic design remains unaffected by those inferences. *"Plus que ça change, plus c'est la même chose."* Also in the decisive attitude of men and women.

Take the following instance: a young patient reported that she had an amusing evening the day before at a party given by her sister-in-law. That woman happened to be interested in a young artist whom the patient had also met several times before at social occasions. The patient had been well aware of her sister-in-law's interest and, since she herself is engaged, feels sympathetic toward her friend. An hour before the party the two women dressed together and chatted. My patient told her sister-in-law about some remarks that the young artist had made to a friend. Those remarks concerned the sister-in-law of whose feelings he had remained unaware. He had said that she seemed to be a rigid personality, was politically rather reactionary and that he had little sympathy for her attitude. My young patient described, in her analytic session, the effect these comments made upon her friend and the distinct change in her sister-in-law's behavior before and during the party.

She immediately changed clothes and chose a rather loud dress instead and brought her careful hairdress into disorder. Shaken by laughter, my patient described the radical transformation of her friend's behavior, who really has a rigid character and is conventionally brought up in a very rich family. The young lady now crossed her legs during the party, in a rather conspicuous manner, spoke in a loud voice and made very vivid gestures. She behaved contrary to all her usual habits in a way which she considered bohemian. During the conversation she almost passionately accused the privileged classes of neglecting the poor people and pleaded for social justice, all that to attract the artist. The patient who watched her friend in fascination, mimicked her transformed sister-in-law and said, "I almost died of laughter." Such a watchful and intensely interested attitude would certainly be alien to the average young man, not to mention that a transformation such as was described by my patient would scarcely be possible to him.

The vicarious interest a woman takes in other women will, of course, change its character with age, but it will still be centered around other women's relations with men and her immediate family. A man can frequently speak with other men without knowing—more than that, without being interested in—whether that man is married or single, if he has any children and so on. A woman who sees another woman many times will most likely know whether the new acquaintance is married, will know the number, ages and names of her children and so on.

Men who get old lose more and more their interest in the personal affairs of other men—if it ever was there to a great degree. They become more and more rigid in the sphere of their interest, almost jaded within the narrow realm of their professions, properties, politics. Women will always remain more interested in human concerns. It would be superfluous to tell woman that the proper study of man is man. She will never be deeply interested in anything else.

36. ABSTRACT AND CONCRETE

Women are quite capable of abstract thinking, but it does not come easily to them and they do not like it. They are not deeply interested in remote areas. The phases of the moon certainly concern their biological functions, but its landscape and the possibility of reaching it are not the objects of their thoughts.

Their daydreams have various contents, but they rarely concern the prehistory of mankind nor its remote future. I am suspicious that they pay only lip service to the Christian belief in the hereafter as a part of religious doctrine. In reality they are creatures of the present. Their kingdom is of this world.

In a certain sense the eons of prehistory before man became homo sapiens, and the distant future which we cannot foresee and in which man will probably become something else, belong also to the area of the abstract. In the thoughts of woman, that past beyond all human memory does not become alive. A future into which we cannot look is not quite imaginable to her. Few women are passionately interested in the mysteries of the paleolithic past and fewer are building utopian phantasies of the millennium in which the grandchildren of their grandchildren might live.

In *Civilization and Its Discontents* Freud points out that human sexuality will slowly decrease and finally disappear because man—in the struggle of life, in his cultural tasks that take his interest away from the family—will experience less and less sexual desire. Such a prediction will perhaps arouse dark anxieties in women for a moment, but the next time they discuss it they will be thoroughly convinced that sex is here to stay. Certainly Freud's speculation does not concern the foreseeable future. The situation sketched by him reminds me of a little story I once heard in Paris. A prominent French writer visited the Observatoire. There an astronomer who was a friend of his explained the wonders of the starry world above to him. The scholar mentioned also that in a million years the warmth of the sun would decrease and all life on earth would perish. While he listened to this prediction attentively, the writer became very gloomy. His friend, accompanying him to the door of the Observatoire, noted his mood and said: "In the meantime, you had better be careful when you cross the Place de la Concorde. You might get hit by a car!" Such an admonition or warning would be superfluous in the case of a woman were she to visit the observatory. First of all, she would not believe the astronomer. Her instinct of self-preservation is stronger than that of man because it includes the preservation of the species.

Women, who were there before the male, and will perhaps survive his sex, need not be theoretically concerned with the remote past and the distant future of mankind. Many men of science turn their interest backward and forward into the dark past and into the unforeseeable future of mankind. Quite a few scholars and writers, approaching or having passed their seventies, turn their attention to the future and love to daydream of the world to come. It is strange that this lively interest in the future is especially felt by men whose thoughts were once preoccupied with the remote past—yes, even with prehistory. Ernest Renan, whose research led him to the age of the Phoenicians and of ancient Israel, sought to forecast man's future. H. G. Wells, who wrote a history of mankind, projected visions of the shape of things to come. Freud, who reconstructed in *Totem and Taboo* the primal origins of religion and social organization, turned his gaze upon the future of mankind in the final phase of his writings (*The Future of an Illusion* and *Civilization and Its Discontents*). Anatole France, who chose ancient Greece and Rome as backgrounds for many of his novels, portrayed the prospect of the annihilation of the present civilization and of a new mankind in *L'Ile des Pingouins*.

Not even the dresses and costumes worn by women in the remote past are of special interest to the ladies of our time. Beyond the period of their grandmothers they are not intrigued by past fashions. Anatole France once confessed to his young Provençal secretary, J. J. Brousson, that he was more curious about what the ladies would wear in very distant times than about the novels the writers would then produce. Looking back into his youth, the eighty-year-old sage of the Villa Saïd told his friend, Michel Corday, that thirty years ago fashions were very cruel toward lovers. Dresses had, then, eighty buttons.* *("Il y a trente ans, les modes feminines etaient bien cruelles pour les amants. Les robes avaient quatre-vingt boutons.")*

37. MACHINES

It has now happened several times that, after having looked up the scientific literature on a certain problem without finding any essential help, I picked up an issue of the *New Yorker* to forget all about it and I have been stimulated by a cartoon or a short story that has set my thoughts going back to the problem, but in another direction. It would be of psychological interest to know if the accidental glance at a cartoon or the reading of a short story had awakened some dormant thoughts which were close to the threshold of consciousness. In some cases the subject of the cartoon or the theme of the story touched the fringes of the problem, but in others no such connecting link could be found. I hasten to add that there was in the majority of those cases a time interval between the perception and the new idea, or rather that there was no immediate thought contact. The cartoon or the short story came to mind on my way to some new insights. To use some half-psychological terms: it was not an "Aha!" experience, no sudden clarity or elucidation, but rather a dubious memory: "Was there not a cartoon in the New Yorker. . . ?" or some such thought.

Here are two examples of this kind: I had gone out of my

* Michel Corday, *Anatole France d'après ses Confidences et ses Souvenirs,* Paris, 1927, p. 223.

way to look up what the newer psychologic and psychoanalytic
literature had to say about the origin and character of intuition.
I was especially interested in the question of why we attribute
that problematical faculty to women so much more than to men
—a question upon which I had gathered quite a lot of material
in my analytic practice. The best, or most general characterization of intuition was "knowledge or insight whose sources remained unconscious." That was, after all, almost what the dictionary said: perception of truth or facts without reasoning. In
the pertinent literature I encountered quite a few illuminating
instances of the intuitive process and some very fitting remarks
upon why women are supposed to be much more intuitive than
men. The material on the question was certainly informative,
but I was unsatisfied. Something—and it was something essential
—was lacking in the different excellent descriptions and characterizations of the intuitive process by psychologists. Something
was missing, but I did not know what it was.

It happened then that I remembered a cartoon seen in the
New Yorker several months ago. There is a courtroom scene and
a lady, member of the jury, says to her friend: "I never listen
to evidence." That is no doubt funny, but what does it have to
do with the problem of feminine intuition? The cartoon makes
fun of a particular type of woman in a certain situation. It says,
not in so many words—really only in five words—that women
judge not by rational and logical reasons but by paying attention
to their emotions. If you exaggerate the meaning of the cartoon
it could lead to a frightening conclusion: that woman-representa-
tive of the jury would, if she felt so inclined, declare a murderer
innocent, even if he were caught in the act. Or she might condemn an innocent man to the most severe sentence if she felt
him to be guilty, even if the evidence were to prove that he
were not. The neglect of factual evidence and proof in favor of
a decision based upon emotions would be especially disastrous
in the sphere which the cartoon depicts: in the courtroom. Here,
if anywhere, the evidence is of utmost importance. All emotional

elements, all bias and preconceived ideas, should be banned and only rational considerations should be heard. Don't we say "sober as a judge"? And the jury is, so to speak, his assistant, helping him in his difficult task. A verdict that has not considered the evidence is not justifiable.

The woman in the cartoon arrives at her decision in the courtroom by way of intuitive thinking. Here we are back at our problem: the character of feminine intuition. She pays no heed to evidence and the deductions stemming from it. The contribution to the characterization of intuition provided by the cartoon is thus the following: an essential precondition of intuitive thinking is the exclusion of rational and factual considerations. Here, then, is a negative factor operating in the origin of intuition. The inattention to, or neglect of, the rational, logical processes is the preliminary condition without which intuition is impossible. I do not believe that this unconscious exclusion or suppression of what is popularly called reason was sufficiently stressed in the psychological descriptions of the intuitive process I had found in the scientific literature.

It would be tempting to imagine a "countercartoon" poking fun at men, especially in situations in which they exclude the slightest interference with their rational way of thinking, from the emotional or unconscious side. We might imagine, for instance, a psychoanalyst who works only with facts and figures and considers only the external evidence in the conflicts of his patients. Or we could consider a writer who composes a novel only according to an intellectual, rational plan without listening to a voice within himself. Yet there have been cases in the courtroom where the evidence was listened to attentively and where miscarriages of justice were performed in the name of pure reason. In those cases, hunches and warnings, unconscious messages emerging from the native land of intuition, were neglected, and the result was often a terrible mistake founded upon deceptive circumstantial evidence.

A short story in the *New Yorker* helped me in the elucidation of another problem of comparative psychology. The problem was brought to my attention during a visit to friends who had a little son. Later, as that problem presented itself, the short story in the *New Yorker* returned to my mind. I had joked with the little boy who had shown me, with great pride, a toy watch that had been given to him. I playfully told him that all watches attend in the night a "watch-school" where a teacher shows them how they should move their hands to indicate the time. At half past eight in the evening a school bus picks all the little watches up, takes them to this school and so on. The little boy was rather skeptical, and soon I saw him taking his watch apart to find out what made it tick.

His mother later on told me that he was very mechanically minded and that his interest reached from his toy automobile to the electric dishwasher. When I remarked that his sister, a few years older than he, never showed any interest in machines, she explained that this interest is induced or encouraged in boys while girls are educated to turn their attention to dolls and so on.

This special problem of the difference of interests recurred during my comparative study of the sexes, especially the question of why boys in general are so much more interested in machines than girls. Together with the memory of that little scene, examples from psychoanalytic practice seemed to lead to a preliminary theory whose outline appeared first in a vague form.

At a certain point of my thought associations I remembered the short story previously mentioned: "Less Said," by Louise Field Cooper. I had read it a few weeks before in the *New Yorker* (March 9, 1957). A couple has moved from the upstairs bedroom of their home to the downstairs guest room. Nearby is the artesian well with its electric pump whose interminable noise disturbs them. The wife is not concerned with what goes on among the pipes and valves of the water system and in the mysterious fuse boxes. She is only enraged and frustrated because her husband insists upon explaining plumbing and electricity to her while he lies there sleepless, listening to the noise of the pump. Some evenings he turns the pump off before going to bed and then turns it on again, awakened by the alarm clock at three A.M. The broken nights disturb the wife who asks her husband why he has to take such care of the pump. He replies very grimly, "Because it has a high head and a small bore." In order to spare the leathers which are wearing, he thinks of giving up the dishwasher and of restricting the amount of water for baths. He telephones the plumber. The writer amusingly describes that two or three workers arrive, lay their greasy tools down on the white rug, flick cigarette ashes all over, check everything and look solemnly into the dark mouths of the pipes, as though they were mysterious oracles and call to her: "See! you can see how she keeps leaking and leaking." ("She!" thinks the woman.)

Finally they conclude that graphiting will be necessary. Before that decision, they point out to the lady that "the female joint is stripped" so they will have to use a threader, but they cannot do it now because they have to go back to town to get one. The lady comes to the conclusion that no woman born of woman wants to know about valves and traps and elbow joints . . . and the seat of all that trouble. She feels it to be most unfair. When has she ever forced an electrician or her husband to come close to her sewing basket and then said to him, "You see, before I can sew a button on this shirt, I have to do this to the thread," and made him attend the performance that results in a knot at the thread's end? She never tipped the mingled content of her basket all over the floor, remarking that she must leave it there while she goes to town to get a button because this button doesn't fit the buttonhole. The lady ruminates, "High head and small bore indeed! High head and a big bore, more likely."

The charming sketch whimsically contrasts the masculine preoccupation with machines with the feminine indifference to the subject. But it does more than that: it shows, without being aware of the fact, the psychological reasons for this divergence of attitudes.

I would take an oath on a stack of bibles that the writer did not have an inkling of a notion that her sketch had a secret compartment, a concealed meaning. But everyone who has learned to listen with the third ear and to understand the forgotten language of symbolism, will be able to discover the hidden significance in the events just described. One need only translate the story from the sphere of the unconscious repressed from the world of infantile thoughts into the expressions of every day to reconstruct that second meaning. With the change of bedroom the trouble begins. The husband starts to be worried about the subterranean pump. If we transpose the whole scene from the life of grownups onto the level of a boy's thoughts, the idea is the following: a boy is preoccupied with the mystery of sexual intercourse and with the enigmatic form and function of the female genitals. The unconscious worries of the man, displaced to the subterranean pump, become analytically transparent. Traced back to the boy's sexual curiosity, his thought about the "high head and the small bore" makes good sense. Behind those technical terms for the pump, sexual expressions are, of course, concealed. They concern the erect penis and the small female opening. It is not accidental that the lady wonders why the plumbers speak of a "female joint" and call the pump "she." The woman is not concerned. She justly remarks that no woman wants to know about the intricacies of machinery; she is not worried about "her" functioning. She takes it for granted, and she feels no need to explain to men, how she threads a needle and sews a button—again an unconscious allusion to the sexual performance. There is no mystery for her in introducing the penis into the vagina; she is not worried that the button will not fit. She wonders about the typical male's preoccupation with the problem of a "high head and a small bore" which does not appear as a problem to her. The last line of the amusing sketch—

its "point" so to speak—is a pun: "High head and a big bore, more likely."

The lady's disgust and rage at the hypertrophic and superfluous male interest in machinery comes here to a lively expression. But is there not another meaning to that pun? The word bore is here used by the woman in the sense of a dull and tiresome person. But there is another pun hidden here, and we will not hesitate to disclose it. What is good for the goose is good for the gander. Does "high head, big bore" not also mean: "You stupid men! You need not worry, the 'high' (erect) penis can be fitted into the bore. The bore is not as small as you think. It is, as a matter of fact, big"? If the writer had been aware of that unconscious undercurrent and of the second meaning of her sketch, she might perhaps not have written it, and we would have been deprived of a little literary gem.

We wondered why men are so much more interested in machinery than women. This sketch in the *New Yorker* presents, without intending to, a psychological contribution to the solution of the problem. Its value stems mostly from the fact that the writer is unaware of her unconscious knowledge. It is true that she does not give us the whole answer, but what she presents is still better than the shallow answers we could find in many textbooks of comparative psychology.

38. MAN AND MONEY

The unconscious connections between the concepts of love and of money are well known to the analyst. He has seen many cases in which the fear of being impoverished is a manifestation of the unconscious perception of the dwindling ability to love. Also other cases in which that fear was traced back to doubts about a man's potency are frequently met with in psychiatric consultation rooms. The complexity and multiplicity of the connections between the two ideas of love and money justify the following remarks, which isolate a single thread and follow it a short distance. Let us discuss the unconscious significance of the resentment many men experience when they think of the money their wives spend. It is, of course, difficult to decide whether the reproach that the wives are extravagant is justified or not, and we are not concerned with the conscious and objective factors in the individual situation.

In the analysis of several cases in which that reproach recurred in a compulsive manner, it became transparent that the accusation was only a screen behind which another reproach was hiding itself. The continued resentment against the wife and her spending too much money was motivated in unconscious reality by the impression that the woman deprives the man of power—especially of sexual potency. In other words, the unconscious content of the accusation is that the wife is emasculating her husband. It is a symptomatic expression of castration fear displaced to a material substitute for love or for its representative in the form of sexual power. The unconscious content of the reproach is: she, the wife, deprives me of sexual vigor, castrates me. The resistance against the spendthrift wife is intensified by the influx of unconscious trends that originate in the castration fear of the male. The unconscious significance of money as replacement or substitute for love provides the psychological explanation for the transition from one sphere to the other and shows us how this shift became possible. Many men give their wives money instead of love, and many others resent giving even this substitute for affection.

The ways of the unconscious are as dark as those of the Lord, but their results are clearly recognizable. The communication between the unconscious of two persons can be understood also in the field of their money interests. A great number of wives behave as though—and in this "as though" is the unconscious meaning contained—the fears of their husband concerning money spending were psychologically well founded on reality. These women unconsciously conceive of money as a substitute for love. They squander money, spending it foolishly and in this fashion get even with their husbands who are withholding love from them. They unconsciously castrate them in spending their money, depriving them of the material power which, for so many men, is unconsciously conceived as equivalent to sexual potency.

Following their way of reasoning, women feel that a man who spends money on them instead of giving them his love is offering them only a second best. But that appears to them as a poor substitute and not good enough—or only good enough to be carelessly spent.

39. ENEMIES

We hear or read in the eulogies of many men that they had no enemies; we assume then that they got along with people and were generally liked. The biographer who would say this in praise of a man would perhaps also have but little to say about his accomplishments and achievement. There is hardly a great man or benefactor of mankind in any field who had no enemies. The Germans have a proverb, *"Viel Feind, viel Ehr."* (Many enemies, much honor or appreciation.)

Does the same apply to women? It seems that we think well of women who are liked by both men and women. We have an unconscious preconceived idea that women should have no enemies. It even awakens a prejudice in men against a woman when they hear that she is disliked by many other women.

Here is a contrast in our attitude on the surface easily explained. Men stand in the whirlwind of professional life, have to compete with each other, to a certain extent fight with each other, in order to make a place for themselves in the world of men. A man has to stand his ground against others and conquer them. The competition among women does not have that aggressive and emotionally charged character. Especially not after marriage, after a woman has a husband, a home and children. Thus a great stumbling block on a woman's road through life is removed. The different position of women and men in social life is certainly one of the decisive factors in the fact that women make fewer enemies. The psychological difference results thus from a sociological divergency. Other determining factors are to be found in the realm of the constitutionally smaller degree of aggressiveness of the female. Even this minor component is energetically suppressed by education of the little girl. This, as well as the organic changes of puberty development favor the greater sociability of women. These factors will mitigate and soften the hostile, envious and competitive feelings, or at least their expressions. The combination of external influences and inner transformations will support the unfolding of social graces.

To speak of a side issue in that area: there is no doubt that the particular quality or the power of delighting people which we call charm is developed in women under the influences we have mentioned. Is charm a specific feminine feature? I think so. To test the validity of that impression, a simple experiment in thought is recommended. When we say a certain woman has much charm, it is certainly praise. When the same is said about a man, it is not always complimentary. It might mean that he has nothing but charm, or even that he has a certain feminine quality. (To register a contradictory voice: a woman asserted the other day that there is a feminine and a masculine kind of charm; but she corrected herself adding: "One should really call it 'magnetism' in men.") The last king of Great Britain said of his daughter, Margaret, that she could charm the pearl out of an oyster. That was, no doubt a tribute to the femininity of the princess.

All that was said here in regard to enemies among the same sex is more or less known. A factor that was almost neglected in the evaluation of the divergency of women and men in this direction is the greater tolerance with which society treats the manifestation of sublimated homosexuality in women. When we see women kiss each other as they meet, we take this expression of affection for granted. We would, however, be slightly astonished if we were to see two men greet each other with a kiss—except in France, of course. This greater social tolerance toward female homosexuality in its sublimated form reflects, of course, the attitude individual women have toward the members of their own sex. It is easy enough to explain that difference by pointing to the greater sociability of women, to the easygoing familiarity they show in social intercourse. But this explanation simplifies the psychological situation. It begs the question.

Let us imagine two women sitting idly on a bench in Central Park on a summer afternoon. It will not be long before we see them in conversation. It scarcely matters that their ages or social position is different. Two men in the same situation will have greater difficulty in entering into conversation. They may prefer to refrain from it altogether. Two Englishmen could wait indefinitely, or at least until the second coming of Christ, before they would speak to each other.

I am inclined to make a negative psychological factor responsible for this greater reticence of the man as compared with the social flexibility of the woman. Homosexuality, even in its sublimated forms, meets stronger obstacles in men than in women because it threatens the man with loss or decrease of his masculinity, of which he is proud. It means submission to another man, and with it the adoption of a certain feminine attitude toward men. The rigidity of this position of the male in society is explained to a great extent by the intense resistance such an alleged submissive or feminine attitude awakens in the man. Yet without a certain pliability or tractableness among men no society can exist. It would perish by the fight of all against all.

Every adult male is on his guard against the possibility of being pressed into the submissive role. We learned from the study of the neuroses and psychoses that an especially intense resistance against the same sex in forms of querulous or belligerent behavior is often a reaction to homosexuality that is too energetically repressed. In the symptomatology of paranoia the rejection of unconscious homosexual tendencies appears as extreme suspiciousness toward and as ideas of persecution from a man or a group of men.

No such intense reaction against the unconscious possibility of homosexuality can, in general, be observed in women. (Wherever it appears, we can be sure that the sex appeal of other women is especially strong.) There are certainly several reasons for this difference in attitude. The decisive factor is that the resistance against homosexuality in women is not developed as much as in men because it does not threaten their ego feelings, does not menace them with the loss of all they feel are the best qualities of their sex. A woman can well imagine being the love-object of another woman and still feel womanly. The average man would be repelled by the phantasy of being sexually loved and possessed by another man because that would mean renunciation of his virility. We recognize again in the analytic exploration of this difference in the sexual attitude the importance of the role of concealed ego interests within the sexual imagery and reality.

Male homosexuality is, in its passive form, unconsciously connected with the loss of that "little gadget" (to use a term employed by one of my patients not long ago when expressing her anger at the superiority of the male sex) of which the boy is so proud. The girl has nothing to fear in this direction. Her fears are quite different. The analyst, who has occasion to observe again and again the effects of that emotional difference, will nevertheless wonder to what exaggerated conclusions both sexes are led by a slight anatomical divergency.

Oh, the little more and how much it is
And the little less, and what worlds away!

40. TRANSFERENCE DIFFICULTIES

In some phases psychoanalysis resembles a machine which functions only after having conquered certain resistances. Of those counteracting forces, transference is the most significant—the repetition of emotional attitudes acquired early in life and transferred to the analyst. To recognize the expressions of transference in psychoanalysis is relatively easy. To handle the various problems emerging as transference resistance is often a very difficult task. It is, of course, excluded that the analyst may react to those manifestations with expressions of countertransference, that means of affection or hostility, loving or resentful feelings. He has to conceive of the patient's attitudes as revivals and repetitions of unconscious impulses, and must interpret them as such. The handling of the transference difficulties in psychotherapy, in borderline and prepsychotic cases, is different from that in psychoanalysis.

Although transference as resistance occurs in the analytic treatment of both sexes, its symptoms are not the same. Here are two instances of dealing with transference—difficulties in an analytically unorthodox manner. Both cases were treated many years ago, when I was psychoanalytic consultant at the Highland Hospital in Asheville, North Carolina. Both cases were outpatients of the hospital, in analytic psychotherapy. The first patient was suspicious and suffered under decided inferiority feelings, especially because she had often been told that she was not attractive. Once she had to wait five minutes while I was in an analytic session with another patient. Her predecessor was a very pretty blond woman. My apology for the delay was of no avail. The patient began her session with violent accusations because I preferred, in her opinion, the other woman to her. The therapeutic hour was filled with a torrent of reproaches and abuses. This crescendo of criticism did not only attack my "unprofessional behavior" and my therapeutic abilities, but also my character, expressing serious doubts about my functions as man and husband, to say nothing of my doubtful human ancestry. She was convinced that I was interested in "that blond floozie" much more than in her. I had remained silent during the session, but when she got up from the couch I said: "It is not always

pleasant to listen to you, but always pleasant to look at you."
As she stood there, smiling through the tears that ran down
her cheeks, she was really attractive. She said: "That is very
sweet of you." Such compliments are not inappropriate in a
case of short-time psychotherapy.

The character of transference resistance cannot always be conjectured as easily as in this case. Another patient showed a feature of behavior that baffled me for a time. When the session
approached its end, she became restless, as if she had an invisible
watch. Occasionally she asked, "What is the time?" She could
not see the clock on the wall behind her. I thought at first that
she wished to lengthen the session or was afraid there would
not be enough time left to tell me certain things. But this impression had to be corrected because her question, "What is the
time?" soon became a regular habit when the session was near
its close. When she did not ask it, she sometimes got up from
the couch a few minutes earlier and said good-by. I understood
then that the proud girl could not tolerate being told that it
was time for her to leave—or to be, so to speak, dismissed. She
preferred, therefore, to end the session herself. When she once
again asked what the time was, I said: "There is a difference
between you and the watch. The watch reminds me of the
time, and you make me forget it." By the way, this complimentary remark did not change her habit of ending the session herself, but I do not doubt that it had some more important emotional effect.

Dealing with the transference resistance belongs to the most
delicate operation of psychoanalytic technique. It is obvious that
the analyst is here faced with a very unconventional situation.
Let us assume that the transference love of a woman has become
a serious resistance in her treatment, blocks her way to free
associations and leads to long silences. The analyst has to interpret that mysterious resistance. He has to tell the woman that
what hinders the common work is the fact that she has fallen in
love with him. Imagine a dentist who has a girl as technician

who was very efficient but suddenly is no longer satisfactory in her work. The dentist has to tell her that he believes the sudden change in her work must stem from the fact that she is in love with him. This would be impossible from a social point of view and he would show no tact if he acted this way. If such a situation were imaginable it would become even more impossible if the following effect were desired: that the insight into the girl's feelings should help her to conquer them, and that the revelation should not hurt her pride and should improve her efficiency as a technician. Yet the analyst is faced with that very task. He must make such an impossible situation possible. It does not help him much to explain to the patient that her feeling is not real love but a feeling she once had for her father or brother and that is now transferred to him from these figures in her childhood.

The timing of such an explanation or interpretation is certainly important, but the approach to this operation is itself a great problem. There is scarcely a possibility of circumscription. You have to call a spade a spade but the sentence in which this idea is used can be differently formulated. It is preferable, for instance, to use the phrase: "You are fighting against falling in love with me," rather than: "You have fallen in love with me." This not only because it spares the woman's pride but also because it is more psychologically correct—otherwise, why would the transference take the form of resistance?

I said before that in dealing with the transference resistance the direct method of interpretation is the best. There are, however, exceptions. Certain delicate situations and characteristics of the patient, certain features in the course of the analytic treatment, and even phases of the analyst's countertransference, not clearly mastered, will favor a more subtle or indirect approach.

Here is an instance of such an exceptional technique, determined, certainly, by personal factors within the analyst. Many years ago I treated a young girl whose emotional problems threatened to ruin her social life. During the first weeks the analytical sessions were peaceful. The patient relived in vivid memories her childhood experiences and her life in her early teens. She showed herself intelligent and cooperative. At a certain point her behavior underwent a radical change. She became sarcastic toward me, criticized sharply everything I had said, mocked my manner of speech and way of moving and so on. The analytic work seemed to be interrupted. Her whole interest was directed toward devaluating and humiliating me. The analytic sessions were governed by the spirit of merciless mockery. (As a sample: "Your brain must look quite new. You never use it.")

I was puzzled by this change in the behavior of the girl who had been trusting and willing to work with me. Nothing in the material she had reported to me until then, and nothing in the few interpretations given by me, could have caused that change. The patient's attitude was conspicuous during several analytic sessions without my being able to explain it to myself. I remained, thus, mostly silent.

It would be tempting to discuss here the unconscious ways in which I arrived at the understanding of what that change in my patient's behavior meant. But such a discussion belongs to the problem sphere of the unconscious determinants of analytic technique and would lead us too far away from the specific question. While I listened to the patient, who again took me through the wringer of her criticism, the name "Booth Tarkington" occurred to me, together with the visual picture of a book by this American writer. At first I could not remember the title of the book. (It was certainly not accidental that I forgot it: the title is *The Fascinating Stranger*.)

Instead of following the path of self-analysis, I shall report what I said to the patient, interrupting the uncomfortable silence that had followed her last critical remark. What I said seemed to have no connection with her criticism and was spoken in a casual manner, as though I were telling a story: "When I was a young man, I had no idea that there was something like contemporary American literature. Once I accidentally picked up

a book by Booth Tarkington in a second-hand bookstore in
Vienna. It was a collection of short stories. I still remember that
I had some difficulty in understanding quite a few slang expressions. I especially liked one of the stories. It was called 'Ladies'
Ways.' The plot is very simple: there are two young people just
out of college who live across from each other in a Middle Western town. The young man courts the girl in a clumsy and shy
manner. She tells him how she hates their home town, which she
considers 'a cultural desert, utterly savorless.' She feels the whole
atmosphere of the place is Victorian, and so are all the people
living there, the young man included. She states that she has
nothing in common with a single soul in the place, does not
think in the same manner and does not even speak the same language. She reacts to his shy courtship sarcastically and scolds him
because he does not do anything worthwhile with his mind.
Later on the young man sadly walks over to his own yard where
he sits down on a wicker chair, under a walnut tree, very depressed by the rejection. There are half a dozen very lively
children in the yard, among them Daisy, the young man's little
sister. The eight- and nine-year-old boys and girls play rough
and noisy games. A dainty little girl, Elsie, is chosen as umpire.
This child is especially severe toward a boy whom she condemns
to be spanked by all the other children. The overactive and
shrill little mob arouses the young man from his daydreams
when master Lawrence appeals to little Elsie, who remains aloof.
He had let her choose the game to be played and his speech and
gestures show plainly his admiration for her. The children get
into a melee. Their sharp and shrill voices interrupt the young
man's thoughts that circle around that young girl.

"After the other children have left, he turns to his little sister,
who is chewing a dandelion. He hopes that she can shed some
light on something that had puzzled him as he watched the
children playing. Why was Elsie so mean to poor little Lawrence
who was so nice to her and admired her? Why did she take the
first chance to set the whole pack of children on him? 'Oh well,'

said Daisy casually, 'she likes him the best of all the boys in town.' Then, swallowing some petals of the dandelion, she adds, 'She treats him awful.' The young man looks thoughtfully at his little sister and then his wandering eyes move slowly upward to the window in the house where that girl Muriel lives. 'So she does,' he says."

I am now very critical toward this kind of indirect interpretation which betrayed my countertransference, but that is not the point of this context. My patient was silent a few moments, but she smiled. Then she said something to the effect that Booth Tarkington was very dated and that my literary taste was lamentable. The session ended on this note, but her comments obviously had the character of a rear-guard action. When she came for her next visit she again had become a "good patient," friendly in her manner and cooperative. For the time being her transference resistance seemed to be overcome. It returned much later but was "worked through," and her analysis could be brought to a very satisfactory close. The communication of the story had been effective and had the advantage of time-gaining in an early phase of analysis.

The foregoing discussion was part of a seminar in which my students reviewed with me the techniques of dealing with transference and resistance. The introduction of these technical problems here can perhaps be justified by the question a student raised in that seminar. He asked if such a technique as I had sketched in these cases could be applied in the analysis of male patients. No man, he said, would be as easily reconciled as that girl at Asheville by a complimentary remark—and no man would appreciate the allusion in my story. That may be as it is, but it is certain that the technique of transference resistance treatment has to be different in the case of men and women. It has, however, to be flexible with both sexes, without abandoning its basic principle.

41. THEIR RELIGIONS

Reflection as well as observation come to the conclusion that the attitude of men and women toward God is very different. As I have indicated before, I do not believe that the idea of immortality was conceived by woman. She does not need that concept because she continues her existence in her children. The idea of a "beyond" is unnecessary to her way of thinking. Woman's paradise and hell are of this world. Only men could have been imaginative, or rather, unrealistic or fantastic enough to think of angels who have no body. The idea is a contradiction in itself to women to whom a being without a body could not be an angel. To her, very real creatures of flesh and blood take the place of this imaginative concept of men. Women accepted and acknowledged, of course, the religious beliefs of their men and the traditions their mothers transmitted to them. They became, later on, even more faithful followers and religious believers than men. Yet with that instinctual certainty belonging to them, they know deep within themselves that the only form of continued life granted to mortals is in their descendants.

The different quality of religious belief and devotion in men and women can be observed in their relation to God, to Christ and the Holy Virgin. Women have perfect trust in the mother of Jesus; she is a woman and she understands what women feel. She would grant prayers of a kind that would not be comprehended by men. Christ is the divine son and, in the phantasies of the nuns, they even see themselves as Christ's brides. Their habit can appear to them, in their daydreams, as a wedding dress. Their relation to God the Father is modeled after the pattern of the emotional attitude to their father whose elevated and sublimated image continues to live in the figure of God. It is obvious that this image is different for girls and for boys. In the development of girls, the phase of rebellious and fierce defiance against their fathers is absent or of a very short duration.

The reactions of intense guilt feelings and the urgent need for atonement are not as developed in women as in men. There are fewer women martyrs, and the self-torture of the religious mind is almost alien to women. On the other hand women are not given so much to blasphemy, to verbal or mental forms of rebellion against God and His commandments. Luther threw his ink bottle at the devil who tempted him. Saint Teresa, to whom the evil one appeared about four hundred years ago, reports in her autobiography that she put her right thumb between the next two fingers to indicate what Satan should do to himself. It was certainly not meant as a vulgarity. The saint followed the customs of her time, and the gesture had, in her conscious thoughts, perhaps not even a sexual connotation. It is doubtful that the Spanish saint was aware of the sensual character of her religiosity which, according to William James, "seems to have been that of an endless amatory flirtation—if one may say so without irreverence—between the devotee and the deity."

The maintenance of religious ceremonials is natural to women as expression of the conservative tendency of her mind. The same trend operates in the fact that women are much more inclined to keep superstitious beliefs alive along with their religion—yes, even to combine both as if the prephases of religion were entitled to exist side by side with more progressed forms of belief. It is difficult for a woman to throw away things that might come in handy in an emergency.

Churchgoing is for women more than for men an inner obligation—not only a religious but also a social need. God sees what is in their heart, but it is also important to be seen by Him when one is well-dressed. To attend the service is necessary for one's peace of mind. This goal does not exclude the by-product that one's entrance could, and should, disturb the peace of mind of others, awaken the envy of women and the desire of men. Young, pretty Clarence, in Anatole France's novel *L'Ile des Pingouins* attends the church service with her mother, and remains a long time kneeling because "the attitude of prayer is natural to virgins and advantageously displays the curves of the body."

But back to the different attitude women have toward God, whose image is unconsciously conceived as that of a supreme father-representative figure. The invisible monument of the parents which we all erect in ourselves without knowing it does not tower as high and as menacingly over the everyday life of women as it does for men. The face of those figures has not such an intimidating and terrifying expression as it has in the imagination of men. The girl is less afraid of her father than the boy. She is also less driven to fight his authority, and she learns early to get her way by other means than by open defiance and disobedience. As a residue of that attitude and of the possibility of having her way by getting around her father, she remains convinced that God also will be more lenient and indulgent toward her than toward men. She becomes aware early of the power her charm has over her father. As an adult woman, she hopes that some of that magic will soften or bend the will of the Almighty. And, as though miracles were never to cease, her prayers are often fulfilled. It must be this concealed belief in women that has impressed itself also upon men and made them coin the saying that "what a woman wants God also wants." (*"Ce que veut la femme, Dieu le veut."*)

42. ARE WOMEN WITTY?

I cannot recall any longer how we, a group of sociologists, psychiatrists, and psychologists, drifted into a discussion as to whether or not women are witty. A chance remark of one of us led to this digression, which now became the center of our conversation. There was a lot of confusion in our discussion until we decided that we must differentiate between wit and humor as Freud has done in his book on wit. After this was settled, examples of witty females were quoted to prove that woman's wit is equal to man's.

One of the ladies present reminded us of many women-figures in Shakespeare's comedies who are past masters of quick repartee. Dorothy Parker, Tess Schlesinger, and a few others were mentioned. The ladies at the court of Louis XV were mentioned as famous for their witty remarks. A Viennese psychologist remembered a scene from a play by Schnitzler, *The Wide Country*, in which a woman is accusing her lover of flirting shamelessly with a very young girl. He protests that such a suspicion is ridiculous: "A girl whom I have dandled on my knees." "That doesn't prove anything," is the answer. "In that position, you get with women of all ages." Someone else reported that when he and his wife arrived too early at a dinner party the other day, they found their hostess not yet at home. She came in a few minutes later, apologized, rushed out to bring in the cocktails and served them to her guests. A little while later one of her lady-friends said: "It is warm here and we have had sufficient opportunity, Mildred, to admire your new fur coat. You may take it off now." We agreed that this and some other remarks which were quoted were catty rather than witty. We had, however, to concede the quality of wit in the following instance concerning a young, handsome lawyer, who was the center of parties and activities at a summer resort. He used to drive once a week to New York, ostensibly to see his wife, who had to stay in the city for some reason or other. One day one of the young ladies asked him with a most innocent face: "Tell me, Mr. Harding, is your wife married?" We laughed a good deal about the witty form in which she expressed her justified doubt. Also quoted was this instance of female wit: a lady said about another woman that she "moved in the best circles." The rejoinder was: "That is a mistake in geometry, you mean in the best triangles." We all agreed that women can be quite as witty as men, but prefer, for some mysterious motives of their own, not to be. Dorothy Parker and the other authors quoted were considered to be exceptions that confirmed the rule.

What are the motives which prevent women from being witty? In trying to answer this question, I remembered two instances in which women were witty without being aware of it. Both are taken from my psychoanalytic practice. One concerns a young girl, who spoke about her aunt, characterizing her with these words: "She is a real lady. She never said an honest word in her life." This was said quite spontaneously without any intention of being funny, but the remark does sound as if it had been made by Oscar Wilde. Another young girl discussed her friends, whom she was criticizing: Mary was gossipy, Jane was showing off, Ann had too many dates and Dorothy was mean and envious. She finished her survey with this statement: "I don't like any of my best friends." In both cases the speaker was quite unaware of the witty character of what she had said and was most surprised to hear me laugh.

It is just such examples which give an excellent insight into the psychology of wit because they reveal the unconscious motives which lead to the production of involuntary wit. The atmosphere of free and uninhibited speech during psychoanalytical sessions favors and facilitates such productions.

Psychoanalysis asserts that our pleasure in wit is twofold: the enjoyment of the verbal form and of the concealed meaning of the wit which we suddenly realize. The witty form functions as a premium, as bait or lure which makes us accept and even welcome statements which we would not accept otherwise. Wit is a concealed attack either upon persons or upon social institutions such as marriage or religion and so on. If such attacks were expressed in a serious unwitty form we wouldn't like them: we would perhaps even feel repelled by them. They would arouse contradiction in us or make us feel that we ought to protest against the brutality or viciousness of the criticism expressed. Weaknesses of persons whom we respect, faults and failings of social institutions which we consider valid otherwise are mercilessly exposed in wit. For a moment, the burden of inhibition is lifted and feelings of awe, pity or respect are done away with.

The special pleasure in wit results from a sudden breaking through of inhibitions which we had held in great esteem. Wit reveals the hidden foibles and failures of men and women, the failings of mankind and the shortcomings of social institutions. Wit bribes us by its form to laugh at attacks on them, to approve of such attacks which we would not do otherwise. Another group of wit is a more or less concealed expression of sexual tendencies, a verbal attack against social convention or morals and an exposure of social hypocrisies and lies.

Such insights into the unconscious premises of wit production makes it easier to understand why the average woman is rarely witty. Tradition as well as education have taught her to check expressions of aggressive and hostile tendencies. Tact and taste prevent her from attacking persons and acknowledged social institutions. Women are discouraged from expressions of aggressiveness by the patterns of behavior which our society dictates to them. While destructive and aggressive tendencies are not lacking in the woman's makeup, they do not reach the intensity they have in man. It is not to be doubted that the production of wit, which reveals and exposes the hidden weaknesses of others, is apt to bring women into conflict with their social task, with their aim to please. To be witty means to make enemies.

It is obvious why women will not indulge in dirty stories and obscene wit, which would tend to reveal their own sexual interest and expose other persons sexually. A woman who fancies herself a wit in a coarse way and who makes dirty cracks will not appear attractive to men. Laughter and levity in sexual matters disturb the man's desire to see the women in a romantic light. Men might enjoy a certain amount of drawing room wit in women, but they do not like it when it approaches the spheres of bedroom and toilet. A young man who had felt attracted to a girl took her once to a party where she drank a little more than was good for her. He told me in the psychoanalytical session of the following day that she had laughed loudly at some risqué stories which had puzzled him, and he was quite taken aback by this reaction. "Does she really like this sort of thing?" Later on, when she herself told a story which was slightly off color he felt disgust for her, as if she had undressed in public. The other day a New York society woman expressed her enjoyment of a party at a night club in the words: "It is the greatest fun I ever had with my hat on." The men present laughed, but it is doubtful if the sexual allusion heightened their respect for the witty lady.

It seems that even in these days such bravado has a sobering effect on men since it conflicts with their ideas about the social graces they expect from women. It is significant that men sense as "shameless" even a certain quality of laughter from a woman when a risqué joke is told. We are well able to understand this reaction: obscene jokes told in the presence of women are a substitute for sexual attack, are verbal aggressions of a crude sexual nature. The woman who laughs loudly at them thereby appears to approve of them and enjoy the exposure.

There is another factor which discourages the production of wit by women, namely the social reaction. Men do not consider witty women as attractive even though they may enjoy their swift repartees and quick rejoinders. They do not find women of sharp wit desirable because they do not like aggressiveness in women. It would seem that nature and society alike exert pressure on women to make them cede the realms of wit, satire and sarcasm to men only. And women themselves? They regard other women who are in the habit of telling dirty stories as vulgar, and they avoid too those women whose criticisms of others are characterized by the incisiveness of their wit, almost as if they were afraid of their attacks. They look upon females who indulge in this particular species of wit as another breed of cat altogether.

43. CATTY

There are preconceived ideas which all men have about women; they are natural assumptions. When a singular case

contradicts them, everything suddenly seems to be out of joint.
We assume thus, or we take for granted, that every woman can
sew or cook. That does not mean that we expect her to do it
every day—or even occasionally; but it means that we expect her
to be able to do it if necessary. Although nothing in experience
really proves that the faculty of either sewing or cooking is a
tertiary sexual characteristic, we still expect a woman to be able
to sew on a button or cook eggs. If she were to confess her inability to do these things, we would look at her as though she
were to say she had not the slightest trace of a breast—almost as
if she were a freak.

To those self-evident assumptions belongs the belief that
women can be catty. Not that every woman is always catty, but
that she can be if necessary. The majority of women known to
me are gentle and mild creatures, but I know intuitively that
each of them can be catty in an emotional emergency. There is
something odd or unnatural about women who cannot be catty,
even in their thoughts.

It seems to contradict our basic teleological concept of nature.
It is almost as though some one were to assert that certain cats
have claws, but cannot scratch anyone. I have come across some
women in analytical practice who lacked the faculty of being
catty. They were either emotionally perverted, masochistic,
homosexual or neurotic and even prepsychotic. A young woman
I observed while in analysis showed a conspicuous inability to
be, even in the slightest way, catty. The patient had another
emotional feature which I did not, at first, connect with this
trait: she cried at the slightest bit of unhappiness or misery that
she saw or of which she had only heard. She cried about the
neighbor's child, who had fallen and bruised his knee, and she
cried when she read about a famine in a certain province of
China. I was not astonished when she remembered, in later
analytic sessions, that she and another young girl—in their early
teens—had indulged in daydreams of unheard-of cruelty. The
two young girls did not tire of imagining the most atrocious and

refined tortures to which they subjected their relatives and friends in their common phantasies. Her extreme pity and compassion for all suffering creatures had all the characteristics of an emotional reaction-formation to intensely cruel impulses.

Women can be catty to each other when a man is present who may be entirely unaware of it. He hears what one woman says to the other, he understands the words that have been said, but he does not catch their second meaning. Yet it was not a secret language. The words used were those of everyday, ordinary conversation. A concealed meaning was there and understood by the other women as in the best of spy thrillers. When this is explained to a man later on, he is astonished. A husband was present at a dinner party when one of his wife's friends said to her: "You know, Anne, I always admire you in that dress." He had not even the inkling of a notion that the compliment contained a criticism; nor would he, at first, believe his wife, who took this little incident as opportunity to reproach him for not wanting to buy her a new dress for the occasion.

One could wonder why women do not discuss, and quote more often, the catty remarks of others—and also their own. It is perhaps to be explained by the fact that they are not unusual between women when they speak to one another, but are part of their everyday conversation.

Men react to these catty remarks in different ways: they are either bored or annoyed, astonished or delighted by them. Yet men should study those instances of actual and potential (in thoughts) cattiness because they belong to women's tertiary sexual characteristics.

Women do not only understand catty remarks as soon as they are expressed but can almost always retort appropriately in kind. There are, of course, exceptions. Here is one: some time ago, I was seated at a dinner party next to a young woman. An older lady passed our table and said, with a kind smile: "You look so pretty tonight, Muriel, I scarcely recognized you." My neighbor was pretty, but at this moment (I glanced at her) her face had almost a stonelike expression. There was no reply. I have, since, asked many women what would have been the appropriate answer to this remark. No one has been able to think of one that would be witty or subtle.

The faculty of being catty is, no doubt, an acquired one. It became a necessity in the struggle for feminine existence. But this acquisition is perhaps connected with some constitutional factors of feminity.

There is no doubt that not only temperamental but also educational differences are expressed in the individual manifestations of cattiness. It is aggression to which strings of feminine behavior have become attached.

Here is my question: can men become catty? Certainly men could be taught to crochet and to wear skirts. Yet this would not come naturally to them. Take a test case: in a cafeteria near Columbia University the following fragment of a dialogue between two college girls was overheard:

First girl: "Tell me, what do you think of Jane?"
Second girl: "Well, Jane is a very nice girl."
First girl: "Oh, I am so glad you do not like her either!"

My question still is: is it imaginable that a man could speak this way—or, what is more important, think this way? Not by a stretch of Shakespearean phantasy! Should men even be trained to do it, they would flabbergast us as would monkeys playing the violin.

I feel that the phenomenology of cattiness is not properly studied even by psychology. Certain professions and trades have a language all their own, a jargon or "lingo" not easily understood by people outside their circle. The linguists and psychologists have studied these terminologies. Why has no one yet studied the dialect that women still use in speaking to each other? A collection of "cattinesses" would be not only very amusing but very educational to men. Yes, there is an urgent need to collect as many remarks of this kind as possible for the students of psychology. Even an elementary dictionary of catty expressions would be welcome as an introduction.

We often say that we do not know how the other half of the world lives. We do not even know how they communicate with each other. The study of cattiness is only a small part of feminine mass communication. In attempting to understand these areas of a woman's world, a man is as lost as a sailor marooned on an unknown continent.

44. MEN AND WOMEN SPEAK DIFFERENT LANGUAGES

John P. Marquand is certainly neither a great writer nor a penetrating psychological observer. Yet, gifted with a good ear for the dialogue of a certain social class and with perceptiveness for its mores, he can well be quoted as a representative writer who depicts certain phases of American life. In a flashback of one of his novels,* he depicts two young people who have grown up as neighbors and meet again after several years. Bob Tasmin, who is employed by a law firm, remarks that Polly has become a big girl. She says: "Yes, I am . . . I'm getting too big for my pants, I guess." Bob's answer indicates that it is a problem. "It's a coarse expression, isn't it?" Polly says. "Excuse me. Girls get to use most awful words in college."

This bit of dialogue which takes place about twenty years ago reminds us that girls who now leave college would scarcely excuse themselves nor consider that expression coarse. They use many more "awful words" nowadays. Yet there are men and women living who still remember that pants were called "unmentionables" by women. Polly Fulton in Marquand's story unhesitatingly uses that colloquialism, but then becomes aware of its coarse character. There is no avoidance of the expression, but there is a remnant of consciousness that it should be avoided in conversation with a young man. Listening to well-bred young

* *B. F.'s Daughter.*

girls and young men speaking in this progressed age one might
wonder whether feelings of this kind have been entirely lost or
whether vestiges of such an awareness have remained, well disguised and consciously disavowed by the present generation. A
young girl, home from college, was frequently admonished by
her father not to use four-letter words. When, once again, she
said "shit," she apologized: "I'm sorry. I thought I was talking
to the girls."

Polly Fulton used a colloquialism you frequently hear men
saying. There is certainly nothing indecent or frivolous in their
statement that one is getting too big for one's pants. Why the
excuse? Why does Polly consider the expression coarse? It cannot
be that the word pants, pronounced by a woman, obtains this
character. Everyday experience shows that there is not a trace of
self-consciousness in women in uttering that word. Could it be
that the character of coarseness hangs on the fact that a girl uses
the expression about herself? Decidedly not. Let us assume that
a girl who has, for instance, the part of Portia in a theatrical
performance would say that she is getting too big for the pants
which she has to wear in her disguise as learned lawyer in the
courtroom scene. Nothing coarse about it. Nor would we consider it coarse when a woman remarks about another that she
wears the pants in the family.

Let us try an experiment in thought and imagine that Polly
would have said: "I'm getting too big for my panties, I guess."
Such a statement would, strangely enough, sound even more
coarse or would even sound lascivious. The character Polly attributed to her statement hangs on the fact that that colloquialism, generally used by men, is here said by a girl in conversation
with a young man.

The bearing of this fact becomes immediately clear when we
continue our semantic experiment and imagine the situation in
reverse. Polly, who has not seen Tom for a considerable time,
expresses her astonishment about how tall the young man is and
he says: "I'm getting too big for my pants, I guess." Or another

situation: Tom tells his playmate of old days that he, after his graduation from law school, has entered the firm of Barstow, Barstow and Bryce and hopes to become a junior partner some day. Then he uses that colloquialism. Nobody will consider it coarse whether it is used in speaking to a girl or a man. The meaning of that sentence is not ambiguous.

We become, at this point, aware that the statement made by Tom about himself, and the same made by Polly about herself, do not say the same thing. Spoken by Tom, it indicates that he is becoming conceited or too ambitious, pretends more than he can be or achieve. But this same sentence, uttered by Polly, can awake associations of a very different kind in the young man with whom she speaks. It can make him think of the lower part of the girl's body covered with pants. It has, said by her, nothing more to do with pretense, make-believe and too high ambitions, but can awaken a sexual image in Tom's mind. It has obtained a sensual or lascivious character. The same words, pronounced by the young man and the young woman, have thus a different meaning in the thoughts of the partner of the conversation. They have different connotations for the two sexes on account of the divergence of the mental image awakened by the listener. The same sentence denotes different things when Polly Fulton says it to Bob Tasmin and when Bob Tasmin says it to Polly Fulton.

Reading that passage in Marquand reminded me of a certain incident in a case of my analytic practice in which the use of a similar phrase had almost disastrous effects and became the source of a serious disturbance in the married life of a couple. My patient was a still attractive widow in her late forties who had married a much younger, handsome man. Soon after the honeymoon, Ethel experienced the first intense feelings of jealousy and the first doubts concerning the faithfulness of her husband. Without any tangible cause she suspected that the man violently flirted with several women and in a short time became convinced that he had secret love affairs with some wives of his friends. She made furious scenes at home in which she accused her husband, who was innocent, of repeated infidelity and the young marriage seemed to go on the rocks. In her psychoanalytic treatment it soon became obvious that the pathological jealousy under whose tortures she suffered was not restricted to younger or more attractive women but sometimes concerned older and unattractive members of her sex. The paranoid character of her attitude showed itself in different ideas of reference, in many misinterpretations and distortions of small features of the behavior of her husband and his imaginary mistress. In her jealousy she used her gift of sharp observation to draw logical conclusions from harmless words and gestures which she used as psychological circumstantial evidence for her suspicion that her husband had sex relations with this or the other woman. The arguments she introduced into her brooding and into the turbulent scenes with her husband were often of that great ingenuity and accuracy so often met with in paranoic system-formations. Her highly perceptive observation as well as her intelligence made it very difficult to refute the logic of the arguments she set forth and to prove to her that the conclusions she drew were wrong. All protests and denials of the husband were helpless to weaken the dynamic power of the unconscious projections by which she transferred her own secret homosexual tendencies to him.

Here is an instance of such an argument based on a sequence of events at the time of her psychoanalytic treatment. She and her husband had been invited to the home of a couple whom they had known for some time. Before, during and after dinner the four people drank a considerable amount of liquor and while Ethel remained mildly stimulated, the hostess, a young and beautiful woman, got high, became exuberant and talkative and finally passed out. Her husband and Ethel's husband carried the unconscious woman to her bedroom and put her, fully dressed, on the bed. The two men returned together to the dining room after a few minutes. Several days after this scene Ethel and her husband were at a fashionable restaurant when the other couple unexpectedly appeared. They passed the table at which Ethel and her husband sat, saw and greeted them, exchanged a few remarks and joined another group of people. During the hour following her return home, Ethel threw one of her most furious scenes in which she attacked her husband not only verbally, but also physically. The cause of her outbreak was, of course, her jealousy which had already been aroused at that party a few days before and had been intensified by a casual remark the hostess of that evening had made while she spoke with Ethel's husband in the restaurant. Alluding to the finale of that drinking bout and of her passing out on this occasion, the young woman had flippantly said: "Well, the other day you caught me with my pants down."

This remark became the center of the furious argument in which Ethel quoted it using the very wording of the sentence as irrefutable proof that sexual relations existed between her husband and that woman. Ethel asserted that her rival would not have used those words if her husband had not seen her in the nude. The patient knew, of course, that the other woman had been fully dressed when the two men had carried her to her bed. Ethel nevertheless insisted that that woman had shown herself naked to her lover, if only for a minute or two. How could she otherwise have said that he had caught her with her pants down? The patient thus took the phrase literally bringing it forth as clear evidence for the existence of sexual relations between her unfaithful husband and that woman.

In a later phase of her psychotherapeutic treatment, Ethel was ready to yield on this point and to admit that that expression used by her rival did not prove that she had been nude on that occasion. But the very fact that she, a well-bred woman, had used that colloquialism at all was now evaluated as evidence that sexual relations had existed between her and Ethel's husband before the party. The patient thus changed her suspicious train of thought only on the surface, replacing a factual proof by a psy-

chological one. She emphasized now that the other woman had
perhaps not shown herself naked at that party, but on previous
occasions; otherwise she would never have used that vulgar expression.

Considered purely psychologically the fact that the colloquialism was used, is, of course, not only inappropriate as psychological evidence, but could almost serve as counterevidence. If
a sexual affair had existed between the woman and Ethel's husband she would certainly have not used that expression, especially not in the presence of her lover's wife. The flippant
sentence points rather in the opposite direction: in that of an
embarrassment when meeting the man again who had seen her
in the degrading situation of being drunk and of an antagonism
against the man because he had seen her in humiliating circumstances. Using that typically masculine expression flippantly not
only conceals the woman's feeling of discomfort and shame but
reminds the witness of her weak moments that men have faults
and foibles too. It amounts to a concealed attack against the
male, who generally drinks much more than women.

But should a woman not say, "You caught me with my pants
down"? And why should we—and perhaps she herself—conceive
of this expression as flippant, coarse and vulgar while it has no
such connotation when used by a man? Because it has two meanings when uttered by a man and a woman. In the mouth of a
man it denotes only that he was unpleasantly and unpreparedly
surprised, was in a state of defenselessness and helplessness. When
used by a woman, the same expression brings to mind the image
of the lower part of her body. The same situation, described by
that expression, awakens in the listener different pictures. A
well-bred woman will avoid that colloquialism because it can
awaken in the listener the image of her denuded body. She
would verbally conjure up a situation of which she would be
ashamed in material reality. We have to admit that there is a
grain of truth in Ethel's statement that that woman had shown
herself nude to her husband, if only in words.

The two instances here described, that of Polly and that of Ethel, the normal and the pathological case, have in common that a woman uses an expression that is usually spoken by men, and it obtains, pronounced by her, a significance it does not have when uttered by the male. The two instances seem to indicate that when the two sexes say the same, it is not the same any more. Otherwise put: the two sexes speak different languages.

When somebody says that men and women speak different languages he does not mean that literally. He thinks of the different interpretation they connect with the same word; for instance with the expression, love. But there are many societies in which men and women use really different words when they speak of things belonging to men and women, use different pronouns and verbs according to the sex. There are languages in which there is really a man's "talk" and a woman's "talk."

More than thirty years ago I encouraged a student of mine in Vienna, Mrs. Flora Kraus, to make an analytic study of the puzzling phenomenon of the different women's languages among many primitive tribes of Africa, America and Australia. Since her paper, published in 1924,* is not translated, the following will present excerpts of the rich material, to which I have added some comments of my own.

With the Cakchipeles tribe in Guatemala, a man calls his son-in-law *ali,* his father-in-law *himmu,* his mother-in-law *hi-te,* while a woman names those relatives *ali, alumum* and *alite.* Women have a great number of expressions never used by men, who have their own words for the same objects. Among the Caraja Indians on the Rio Araguya in Brazil and the tribes of the Quaicurus and Chiquintanos men and women speak differently. Only a few words are entirely different, it is true, but most words are modified in the language of the second sex. When for instance in the language of men two vowels follow each other, the women's dialect puts a *k* between them. Men call a Negro *bi-u,*

* Flora Kraus, *Die Frauensprache bei den primitiven Völkern.* Imago X, Heft 215, 1924.

women *biku*. A German explorer, Paul Ehrenreich, published a vocabulary of fourteen pages of expressions of women's language in which especially parts of the body like lungs, hair, back and so on are often very different from the words men use. Traces of a divergent women's language are to be found in most American tribes. The Chiglit Eskimo women have expressions never uttered by men. The Choctaw Indians have words like *ehwak* (fie!) never spoken by men. The Chiquitos men and women speak the same language, but many words, used by women, have changed final syllables. The significance of various words is divergent, but sometimes the words themselves are different, when pronounced by a Ubaya man and woman. Dobritzhoffer reports in 1783 about the now extinct Abipones natives that the old women of the tribe had the task of inventing new expressions for a special women's language which the men could not understand. A Kaffir woman is not supposed to pronounce a word connected with the name of any man related to her by marriage. A Zulu daughter-in-law must not voice the name of her father-in-law or of his brothers. If in a conversation a similar word or even a syllable to be found in the forbidden name occurs, the Zulu woman has to invent another name. For instance a woman whose brother-in-law has a name ending in *ja* will never pronounce the word *kenja* (bachelor) because the syllable *ja* appears in it, but will say *kekipi* instead, a word otherwise used for wood. Missionaries report that a Zulu woman had in such a case to say "that of the tail" instead of sheep because in the word for sheep the tabooed syllable appeared. Such circumlocutions for forbidden names are sometimes very poetical, for instance the sun is called "that which shines," the road "that which is trod on." To show how widespread those speech avoidances are: the Kirghizes in Central Asia, so remote from the African Negroes, consider it indecent for women to pronounce the name of a male member of the household. To the women of the Warramumgo tribe in Central Australia it is not permitted to utter a man's ordinary name though she knows it. The

Suahli women have a symbolic language denoting intimate parts of the body. The vagina is, for example, called yard, shell or woman in woman's language. Special vocabularies of this kind are widespread: in Samoa young girls have a euphemistic name for penis, the word *analuma,* which is not in common use. In Northwest Central Queensland there is both a decent and indecent vocabulary for the genital parts and the women use only expressions of the first kind. The Island Carabians have two vocabularies: the one is used by men and women speaking to men, the other by women talking together or by men when they quote the conversation of women. There is even a different syntax for men and women in Japan: the Japanese alphabet knows two kinds of written signs used by the two sexes.

The impression we receive from this abundant material is two-fold: all those customs of primitive and half-primitive tribes of America, Australia and Africa appear odd and strange to us. Yet some of the features reported strike us as if they resemble familiar traits in our own civilization. Those two impressions concern both the word taboos themselves as well as the forms of avoidances, circumlocutions, distortions and mutilations of expressions. What is the opinion of the anthropologists, historians of civilization, the linguists and semanticists about that puzzling phenomenon of a separate women's language? There are historical, sociological, religious and general psychological theories of those speech conventions and customs. Flora Kraus, who presents a survey of those theories before she makes a psychoanalytic attempt at explanation, acknowledges that many factors in the theories of Frazer, Crawley and others are valid, but emphasizes that the analytic method opens a new avenue to the problem that was not accessible to those scholars. She expresses, however, a justified criticism in referring to most of the interpretations attempted until now.

In the material presented by anthropologists and missionaries different kinds of examples, belonging to various groups of speech conventions, are thrown together without discrimination.

Take examples of divergent primitive word avoidances: with the Guadays in Queensland and the Kowraregas of the Prince of Wales Island, a man carefully avoids pronouncing the name of his mother-in-law and a wife that of her father-in-law. Among many tribes of Victoria a man may not speak to his mother-in-law. When he or she speaks to some other person in presence of the relative, he or she uses a special kind of language which the British called "turned tongue." J. Dawson, who studied the Australian aborigines, remarks that it is not done with the purpose of concealing the meaning of words because this kind of language is known to everybody. The variation of common speech is in this case determined by the family relationship.

Let us first ask what might be the reason for the avoidance of pronouncing the names of relatives. When women are supposed not to pronounce the names of their father or brothers-in-law or even of their husbands' grandfathers we remember that names are much more meaningful to the primitive tribes than to us. He or she who mentions a name comes, so to speak, in magical contact with the person himself. Those avoidances of names are measures of protection against the danger of getting in touch with forbidden objects. Think of the positive counterpart of such an attitude: lovers who pronounce the names of their absent sweethearts bring them into their nearness, call them up by the magic of the dear name that is a part of them. The taboo of the name of relatives by marriage is not restricted to women; men also observe it, although women are more conscientious about it. Take a representative example an anthropologist reports from a Melanesian native: this man spoke with him of his daughter-in-law and, avoiding her name, pointed to his house because in her name the word for house appeared. When this hint was not understood he touched the roof with his hand. When even this demonstration was not understood, the native looked shyly around and whispered not the name of his daughter-in-law, but a respectful substitution for it: *amen Mulegona* (she who is with my son.)

Is there anything comparable to this avoidance of the names of relatives in our civilization? Examples of a similar kind can be observed as symptoms in our neurotic patients. Flora Kraus quotes in her paper a case of mine in which a young man avoided, in his psychoanalysis, pronouncing the name of his sister-in-law. The patient used circumlocutions like "the wife of my brother." When I finally asked him energetically to tell me the name of his sister-in-law, he refused to utter it and pleaded with me to think of the leading female character of Wagner's *Lohengrin*. The dangerous name was Elsa. But there are many traces of name avoidances also in the area of the nonpathological, in the everyday life of normal men and women—and also here women seem to be more eager to observe that custom that obtains almost the character of etiquette with a certain social class. We know many cases in which husband and wife avoid addressing each other by name. In the life of many couples it would be wise not to mention the names of relatives by marriage and it is really often strictly avoided. When in these counterparts of primitive customs unconscious hostility and antagonism are decisive factors, there is in that avoidance of names of husband and wife also a tendency to elude the awareness of intimacy. Strangely enough, this avoidance concerns only the first name. Wives of a certain social level speak of their husbands as Mr. Smith and husbands of Mrs. Smith instead of saying "Bill" or "Jane."

In the displacement and generalization of the primitive avoidances even syllables which occur in forbidden names are unmentionable. The companion picture is to be found in the forgetting of parts of words that remind the speaker of some forbidden subjects. Compare the famous example of the Latin word *aliquis* in Freud's *Psychopathology of Everyday Life.* * Robert Lasch, who studied the linguistic processes of the primitive languages and who emphasized the importance of word-

* Macmillan, New York, 1914.

transformation by inversion, insertion and gemination of consonants and syllables, compares the women's language with the secret language children invent to conceal their meaning before adults. Those distortions also have a neurotic analogy: a patient of Dr. Karl Abraham used partrerre and codolence instead of parterre and condolence in order to avoid the words pater and condom. Another patient was tempted to say angora instead of angina because the later word reminded him of vagina. Here is the analogy of the avoidance of syllables we found with the women's language.

Even the "turn tongue" has an analogy in our civilization: that affected or unnatural restrained way of speech can well be compared with conversations of relatives whose attitude toward each other is highly ambivalent and who are compelled by convention to speak to each other in the presence of strangers.

Another group of examples of women's language is formed by a great variety of words denoting parts of the body or intimate functions of the female organism. When women want to discuss sexual matters they use different expressions when speaking together and when speaking before men. Many of those expressions concern not only sexual functions but also the processes of evacuation, for instance, the circumlocution "to go to powder one's nose" for going to the toilet. Even the state of pregnancy was, and sometimes still is, not directly mentioned before men, but alluded to. The manner of circumlocution is often clever. A young lady asked her friend whom she met at a party the other day: "Any activity in this week?" She wanted to know whether her friend who was pregnant had already felt the first movements of the child. When I was a young man the Viennese girls said: "My aunt will visit me on Thursday" when they wished to indicate to other women in the presence of men that they expected their monthly period on this day. This phrase replaced another one which expressed the fear that Thursday will be bad weather. Flora Kraus cites two French-speaking patients of mine. Those young girls had developed a secret

THE EMOTIONAL DIFFERENCES OF THE SEXES

language used when they spoke with each other. The penis was called *l'affaire,* the vagina *la labyrinthe* and so on.

We psychoanalysts are often surprised and sometimes puzzled by the indirect and often too delicate way in which women patients speak of sexual matters in their analytic sessions. Here are a few samples: "they live together" instead of they sleep together, "I had a good time" for I reached an orgasm, "he made such an effort, but he did not succeed" about a man who could not keep the erection of the penis, "he has not enough consideration for me" or "he is always in such a hurry" for premature emission. The novels and plays of the twenties and thirties of this century reflecting the mores of that age contain many instances of such elusive and allusive women's talk. I just remember a scene from a French play—was it in Henri Lavedan's *Le lit?*—in which a couple is in bed after sex intercourse. The man asks the woman whether she loves him and she answers "How can you doubt that after what we have said to each other?" (. . . *"après ce que nous avons dit l'un à l'autre?"*) Even where women take the sexual initiative they know how to communicate their desire to the man in an indirect and delicate manner. A young woman asked her husband before falling asleep: "Are you tired?" When he said he was, she was silent for a few minutes, then asked hesitatingly, "Are you too tired?"

Looking back at the speech conventions of our primitive cousins in Australia and Africa, we recognize that many of their language customs have survived in our culture pattern: not only the reticence of the women's speech in sexual matters but also the taboo of certain words. Also with us, women form a "speech community" of their own. We found some concealed reason in the magical belief in the taboo of words of those primitive tribes. No doubt, there is also some magical belief in the reason we civilized people give for our speech convention. The etiquette of the Australian and African native tribes concerning the speech of women is as rigid as that of Emily Post. No doubt, too, the girls in the Australian bush are sometimes admonished, "Watch your language," because speaking means doing in words.

Anthropologists report about many primitive tribes in which the men often do not know the meaning of many expressions women use. On the other hand Rochefort says of the native of the Island Carabais that women have words men know, but don't use *"à moins que de se faire moquer."* Also men in society use certain feminine expressions when they imitate women's talking or when they are making fun of women's way of expressing themselves.

We all know that men are careful in chosing their words when in the presence of women and that the consideration they have for well-bred members of the other sex shows itself also in the avoidance of coarse or vulgar expressions.

Impressions resulting from an admittedly restricted reading of semantic literature indicate that the scholars of this young science of the meaning of words have not given enough attention to the sexual differentiation of speech conventions and customs. With the Choctaw Indians the expression *ehwak* (shame!) is used only by women in the same way as the English "shame on you," the German *pfui* and the French *fi donc* are much more often voiced by women than by men.

We all know that there is a "man talk" and a "woman talk." That means that men and women usually talk of different things, but this divergency concerns the content of the conversation. Too little attention was, I think, given to the fact that there is women speech and men speech. You hear very rarely from women's lips the words "a regular guy" or "a good Joe." The word "cute" is rarely used by men. Women do not say "paying through the nose"—perhaps because the expression is not dainty. Some adjectives, often occurring in women's conversation, are scarcely used by men. A man might call his sweetheart "darling," but he will not apply the word in the form of an adjective. ("I saw the darlingest dress today. . . .") Men will not speak of "letting their hair down" except when they are homosexuals. They will not call people or things "divine" or "sweet," will not easily consider someone or something "adorable" as women frequently do. Men will in general avoid very emotional expressions and feel some, voiced by women, very exaggerated ("I could just scream . . ." "I nearly fainted . . ." "I died laughing . . ."). Men on the other hand will not hesitate to say "hell" or "damned," will speak of "shooting the works" and of "firing away." Women will rarely say "It stinks" preferring to state that it has a bad smell. A patient of mine used the word "unswallowing" for vomiting. Men will not call each other "honey" or "dearest" and will much more rarely use diminutives and endearing terms. They will not easily say of someone he is "dreamy" nor use as often the words "I love it" when they mean that they like or cherish something much.

An attentive and perceptive semanticist could easily publish a vocabulary of the different expressions and colloquialisms men and women use in the streets of New York, Boston, San Francisco and Denver.

When we say that men and women speak different languages the word "language" is not restricted to spoken or written words. Language is here conceived of as any means of expressing thoughts or feelings. Men and women have different thoughts and feelings connected with the same words and with the ideas expressed by them. When a man and a woman speak of marriage they use, perhaps, the same word, but the emotional character, the thought of marriage is not the same. The same is true with words like love, sex, home, babies and so on.

The impact of the semantic problem reaches thus from the difference of words used by the two sexes to the divergence of the emotions and thoughts connected with the same words. Yet this side of the problem seems even more interesting and intriguing than the existence of a women's and a men's language in primitive and civilized societies. Otherwise put: it is more interesting for the psychologist to explore the idea that men and women speak different languages even when they use the

same words. The misunderstanding between men and women
is thus much less a result of linguistic or semantic differences,
but of the emotional divergencies when the two sexes use identical expressions. (It is perhaps not superfluous to remark that
a woman who listens for a longer time to the conversation of
men is perhaps puzzled and finally bored with it—although she
might understand quite well what the men mean in their words.
Likewise men who spend some hours listening to women speaking among themselves feel that old urge to get away from it all
although they understand every spoken word.)

More than two hundred fifty years ago the famous French
writer Bernard de Fontenelle confessed, looking back at his
life, that he had always loved women and music without understanding much of them. The *bon mot* of the old writer reminds
us men that it is perhaps more important to appreciate music
and women than to understand them. There remains, however,
the question: would we not appreciate and enjoy both more if
we understood them better?

45. WORDS AND GESTURES

There is a delightful little piece of writing by Franklin P.
Adams called "A Pair of Sexes" contrasting the half dozen words
necessary for a man to make a luncheon date with a male friend
and the three or more pages of monologue necessary for a woman
to accomplish the same purpose with a girl friend.* In a
kindly, if somewhat wry, fashion the writer shows that there
is no such creature as a woman of few words. We are here interested only in the question of whether or not psychology is
competent to explain the case. There seems to be no doubt that
not much difference can be observed between the sexes when
they are small children. A child under five or six gives the impression that he or she says everything he or she thinks or feels.

* In *The Column Book of F.P.A.*, New York.

At this age thinking is almost identical with speaking. A few years later the child has learned to think without the necessity to put his thoughts into words. We have all observed the intent expression on the face of a child who is thinking something over but postpones or even renounces voicing his thoughts. If asked what he is thinking about he often reacts with anger or embarrassment, sometimes even running to hide behind furniture or under a table—from these vantage points he may yell meaningless but loud sounds, "Bla, bla, bla, bla, yuk, yuk, yuk, phooey, phooey," etc. It is painfully plain that he suffers both from the wish to reveal and to conceal and is unhappy about the whole thing.

This behavior is valid for children of both sexes up to a point. However it is precisely at this point that an important difference in the way the girl may often react shows itself for the first time. Instead of being thrown off balance by any conflict in herself she, seemingly out of nowhere and at the tender age of five or six, has found the power to protect herself by the sweetest and most beguiling insincerity. "I was just thinking about my dolly" or "I was thinking how much I love you." The typical male child is unable to safeguard himself in this way. He is, in fact, destined to be the most natural victim of this feminine characteristic, since he will go through life assuming that, like himself, a woman is thinking what she says she is thinking. When he becomes a man of much sensitivity or hard experience he will know this isn't always the case with a woman. Yet he will still practically never be able to figure out what her concealed thought may be. It is absolutely impossible for a man with even a great amount of awareness to guess that feminine guile could hide the stupidest and most mundane ideas. For a man, any man, concealment means that there must be something worth the subterfuge—something to do either with sex or money or some thought directed against himself. Never does it occur to him that what he takes as smoke screen could merely be a fog of cogitation involving painting the kitchen, changing the hairdo or trying to cut down on the laundry bills.

On the other hand it is equally impossible for a woman to realize that a man doesn't know exactly what her real thought is. Women absolutely believe and are comfortable in the thought that men know exactly what they mean by their seemingly absurd or irrational remarks. This has provided a basis for a thousand well-worn jokes. For instance, a girl says to her fiancé or husband, "Oh please don't bother about my birthday, save your money, dear." She has no intention of concealing or even of being perverse. She assumes that this is clearly understood by him as code language for letting him know that she expects him to loosen up and give her a wonderful surprise, one that costs only a little more than he can afford. One could fill a book with such examples in jokes and cartoons, many of them culminating in a male standing with a befuddled expression on his face while the female, old or young, buries her face in a handkerchief and sobs, "Boo hoo! You never understand me!"

The psychologists who have observed that women speak, in general, more than men, concluded in their evaluation of this difference that language has also a function in the concealment of thoughts. But perhaps it is premature to approach the problem from the psychological view before we consider it from the biological standpoint. Little girls are usually ahead of boys in the development of the speech faculty just as their general development is in advance of that of male children of the same age. Biologists are inclined to assume that the later development of the male goes beyond the initial undifferentiated state into a new phase of evolution while the female remains biologically at the stage once reached. The collateral psychological aspect points to the idea that the human female remains, in certain ways, more childlike than the male. Some sociologists, for instance Ashley Montagu, sees in this difference a manifestation of the natural superiority of woman.

It is to be conjectured that the difference expresses itself also in the relation of thoughts and speech. This would mean that, with the exceptions mentioned before, woman still reacts much more as a child who verbalizes all that occurs to her. The connecting link between thought and speech in woman is much more intimately tied than with men. We would thus find a decisive factor responsible for the difference in the basically childlike nature of woman. I need not point out that this feature can well coexist with a greater maturity in certain directions. Women might often be more childlike where men are sometimes childish. The decisive impression is, however, that women's development remained psychologically as well as anatomically arrested at a certain phase of evolution. More than two hundred years ago Lord Chesterfield wrote in his letters: "Women are only children of a larger growth."*

It would be tempting to assume that another undeniable, even statistically proven, fact can be explained by this kind of "arrested development." Women very rarely stutter. That is, the number of women stammerers is much smaller than the male. Since we know that stammering is, in most cases, originated in the interference of suppressed thoughts and tendencies with the function of speaking, that difference between men and women leads to certain conclusions. Either those impulses whose emergence results in speech disturbance are stronger in men or they can be more easily overcome by women. In the second case the opposing, censuring, rejecting tendencies do not possess the same power as in men stammerers. Another consideration is deserving of a hearing: the age or phase of individual development. It is obvious that the age at which the suppressing forces begin to operate has also to be considered and psychologically evaluated. It is very likely that the combination of all these moments will explain why for every female stutterer there are five male stutterers. There is no doubt that women are the stronger sex at the task of overcoming the various difficulties of speaking.

But to return to the "talkativeness" of women compared with

* September, 1748.

that of men. It seems that we have neglected several factors in
our attempt at explanation: all of them mixtures of constitutional
and of cultural determinants in different ration. Purely cultural
is, for instance, the fact that Southern women talk more, usually,
than Northern women. Montagu, who wonders about that, suspects a connection between this loquacity and the "refined" form
of subjection of women in the South.* I am rather skeptical.
This sociologist is also of the opinion that women are more
talkative because they find speech the most readily satisfactory
of all tension releasers. This is, of course, true and many husbands know from arguments with their wives how satisfactory
this tension release can be. One of them stated that his wife has
the last word even with the echo. Montagu's so-called psychological explanation begs, however, the question.

If we take that general function of speech for granted and
approach the question from the angle of communication, it
would be more meaningful to state that women are on the whole
more sociable creatures than men. But you have to ask yourself
then, why is that true. The answer will first point out that the
group of mother and children form the nucleus of society and is
society *en deux*. This company she keeps makes mothers commu-
nicative because education without speaking is almost impossible.
It is easily imaginable that wife and husband go about the
business of living together without speaking much together. It is
imaginable, I said? There are examples enough proving that
the two are at certain times not on "speaking terms" and the
observer of some couples can occasionally be reminded of two
members of the Trappist order. But you cannot think of a
mother not speaking to her little son or daughter. The psychological necessity of talking in their situation satisfies an imperative need of the mother.

Two other factors favor the communication of speech in
women as compared with that of men. Words are, in a majority

* Ashley Montagu, *The Natural Superiority of Women*, New York, 1953,
p. 97.

of cases, substitutes for deeds. Speaking is a trial doing, acting in
small quantities of sound-making. Women, whose field of activity
is so much narrower than man's and who do not feel that urge
of acting as strongly and permanently as men, are easily led to
remain in that prephase of speaking. Talking becomes thus,
often enough, a substitute for doing, and the energy of the female
expresses and sometimes exhausts itself in speech, where a man
is driven to do things, to change situations and to realize his
aims. Hamlet's inhibition has the consequence, lamented by himself, that he must "like a whore unpack my heart with words."
It is in this sense that we understand statements in which actions
of the man appeared contrasted with talking of the woman.
George Herbert even arrived at the sentence: "Words are women,
deeds are men."

The inner urge of the male for immediate action, an urge very
likely necessitated by constitutional causes, makes communication by speech often superfluous. Another moment restricts it:
the higher aggressiveness of the male does not favor nor facilitate
sociability while the congenitally weaker and culturally more
suppressed aggressiveness of women does not prevent them from
easy conversation. Women are sisters under the skin, men are
hostile brothers.

There are, as I have only hinted here, a number of factors
determining why women are more talkative than men, but first
among them is the biological fact that the human female is nearer
to the child than the human male. (The anatomical corollary is
that the female skull looks more like that of an infant than does
the male skull.)

I suspect that the greater biological-psychological nearness of
woman to the child can, if not explain, provide an important
contribution to the understanding of other characteristics of her
that charm and sometimes exasperate men. To mention only an
instance of the first kind: women have more vivid gestures and
plays of facial muscles than men. I never met a poker-faced
woman.

The Italians, the Greeks and the other Mediterranean people are sometimes ridiculed because of the vivacity of their gestures and of the animated facial expressions which accompany every spoken sentence. The Jew, living among Nordic nations, is often made fun of on account of those characteristic features. There might be cultural and sociological differences in the reactions of different national groups and of individuals to such animation of speaking. But who has ever heard an objection raised to the gestures and to the pantomime, the change of facial expression accompanying the speech of women? Nobody will deny that women show a greater richness and variety of this kind of gesticulatory and facial communication.

Men, too, make gestures and show in the play of their features what they mean and feel, but to a much lesser degree and certainly not with the persuasiveness characteristic of the speaking woman. The character of the gestures of man and woman is generally different. Those of the man denote or describe objects while most gestures of woman express the emotional notes of herself or others. The comparison with the sign language of the conductor, of the artist who speaks with the hands occurs to us: man's gestures resemble those of his right hand that mark the beat. Women's gestures are more like those of the left hand that illustrates the phrase.

We men are so accustomed to woman's gesture language and of the change in her facial expressions that we are scarcely aware of that divergence of the sexes. Or, to continue the previous comparison, we are as little aware of them as the audience is of the individual signs of the conductor while we listen enchanted to a Mozart symphony. When we become attentive to woman's gestures and to expressions of her face, we enjoy them in most cases. Is it because those gestures are not only so expressive but also so gracious that we very rarely follow them with critical eyes? It must be that they preconsciously remind us of the animated signs with which children accompany the report of what they have experienced, seen or heard. We take the vivacity accompanying their words for granted, but when we pay special attention to it we like it: *"Oh wüst, ich doch den Weg Zurück den Weg in's Kinderland"* (If I but knew the way back into childhood's land) sings a Brahms song. The gestures and the play of facial expressions in women serve as one guidepost to that paradise lost.

The other day I listened in the subway to the conversation of several high school girls. I heard only snatches of what was said, but observed the movements of their hands and the changes in voice and facial features. The observation of women speaking is almost always grateful to the eyes and ears and sometimes rewarding even to the mind. Some male friends assure me that listening to women speaking while overhearing what they say has an intellectually stimulating effect. Such hearing in which many words are missed can sometimes help to bring ideas to the surface. Beethoven listening to the murmur of the Schreiberbach near Heiligenstad created that beautiful motif of the *Pastoral.* The remarks, before quoted, are of course, misogynous and vicious. We all know that the speech of women is full of common sense and wisdom and well worth listening to. But sometimes, under special circumstances, in certain moods and situations, men who are wise do well not to listen too carefully to what women say but how they say it, to observe their gestures and faces. One such picture is worth a thousand words.

46. LIES

Lies are weapons often used in the battle of the sexes; lies in their different forms of open untruth, saying things with our tongue in our cheek, distorting and evading the essential in keeping silent about certain things and so on. In some cases the meaning of the expression "lie" becomes ambiguous itself in the mind of the psychologist.

Freud once told us, on one of those Wednesday evenings at his house, about a lie a woman patient remembered when she had returned in her analytic session to childhood memories. She remembered that while she was in grammar school she had told the other children that they had at home three refrigerators. Another little girl had spoken of a refrigerator. The patient had never heard of such a thing and had no idea what the little girl meant. In contrast to the other children at school, her family was very poor. Her fear that the other children would discover their poverty prompted the story that her parents had three refrigerators in their apartment. It is obvious that here the wish is father to the thought, and that the statement is materially a lie. But the question is not one of material but of psychical reality: the girl, ashamed of the poverty at home, wished so much that it were different that she imagined it was.

Women as well as people of the Orient are more inclined to deal with material reality in a sense of sovereignty. "It could have been like that" is easily confused with or replaced by "it was like that." In the discussion of the case Freud remarked that the frontiers between lie and truth are in a psychological sense fluent. The psychologist's view, in that realm, could be compared with the view a person might have if he were to see all the great changes the earth has been submitted to in millions of years in one single glance. To such an observer who sees all geological metamorphoses in one moment, mountains and valleys, earth and sea, would pass into each other and all frontiers would become fluent.

Women lie more about facts, men more about feelings. Women take to lies as to an escape. They lie out of vanity or to cover something they are ashamed of or embarrassed about. While men are more truthful about facts, women treat them as leisurely and casually as small children who do not differentiate between reality and phantasy. After all, what are facts? Things, as they appear to us at a given moment. It is quite possible that they will look quite differently in the next moment. The main things are feelings; women lie less about their feelings than men.

Here are two instances proving that women's lies are an

amendment of unpleasant reality in the sense of wish fulfillment. Some years ago, a young woman told me in her analytic session that she had bought a new dress that she liked. She looked forward to having dinner with her fiancé that evening. When he saw her, he remarked that the dress was not very becoming and asked if it was new. "Of course not," she replied. "I had it put away in a drawer for two years and just thought I would wear it once again." Since she had bought it that very morning, this was certainly a lie. But can we consider it psychologically as a lie? The patient wished she had not bought the dress since her fiancé had not liked it. She wished that, as she had said, it had been an old dress just worn "once again."

The other instance concerns a woman who had gone to Macy's to buy slipcovers for her couch and chairs to brighten her drawing room. The saleslady recommended a certain material because it was practical—especially where there were children around. "That's true," said my patient. "My kids are always jumping around on the couch and chairs." She never had had children. Having had a hysterectomy she could not even hope for any of her own. Is what she said a lie? Certainly, but psychologically it is a pathetic attempt to improve reality. Many of the lies women tell are of this kind. They are "but the truth in masquerade" to use Byron's expression.*

In situations where they would feel exposed to shame or embarrassment, women will lie much more readily than men. The male is more truthful about facts and less so about emotions. He will not hesitate to lie about his feelings. He will swear that he loves a girl when he only desires her.

Women lie less about their emotions. At least what they say about them is genuinely felt at the time when they express it. It is the privilege of their sex to change their mood and, as we all know, they are given much more to mood swings than men. It is more difficult for them to express a feeling they do not experience. I just remembered the beautiful words a girl said

* Don Juan, c. XI.

to her sweetheart: "I cannot say 'I love you' until it says itself."
On the other hand, women are good at not saying things. As a
matter of fact they are much better at it than men.

Let us confess that the situation existing in a romance is such
that it is almost unavoidable that both sexes sometimes must
lie about the ubiquity and pervasiveness of loving feelings. An
old, now forgotten song of the Viennese characterizes the emotional state of romance in simple words:

> *A bisser'l a Lieb'*
> *Und a bisser'l a Treu*
> *Und a bisser'l a Falschheit*
> *Is' auch immer dabei.*

> A little bit of love
> And of faithfulness a bit
> And a little bit of falsehood
> Must also be in it.

47. SMILES

Why do women smile more often than men, and why do they
smile when men would not? That might be an idle question, but
answering it might contribute to the comparative psychology of
the sexes. Someone called women "sisters of the smile," and
everybody knows that they smile upon occasions which would
not bring that pleased and pleasant look to a man's face. A smile
is, for them, a salutation ("She smiled at me."—"she greeted me
with an expression of welcome and consent") or an expression
of thanks. It is for women in general a manifestation of kindliness or friendliness—much more so than for men. When we say
"fortune smiled" upon something, we are using the expression
in the sense of looking at it with favor. A woman's smile can
have many meanings and every woman can produce a smile as
puzzling as that of Mona Lisa, while we are rarely intrigued

by the smile of a man. Yet it does not happen very frequently
that a woman smiles in a sardonic or malicious manner, because
it would not be becoming to her.

Why do women smile so much more often than men? Should
we argue that they are more sociable and friendly? One would
like to think that—even in the more appropriate form that their
aggressiveness is less developed or more successfully suppressed.

It seems to me that it is more in the spirit of psychoanalytic
research to disregard such general or preconceived ideas and to
choose a more specific line to follow. Our point of departure will
be the psychology of smiles. Smiling is, really, a mild or more
moderate form of the facial expression of laughter. At this point
our exploration can join an analytic theory on humor which
I formulated in two books* not yet translated into English,
more than twenty-five years ago. I pointed out there that the
first reaction to hearing a witty remark is one of unconscious
fright. It can be conceived as a heightening of a free-floating
anxiety that lives in us in a latent state. Why is that potential
anxiety actualized and enlarged? Wit which attacks persons or
institutions awakens within the listener the temptation to do the
same—and with it comes the fear of retaliation or punishment.
But this readiness to be frightened will immediately be recognized as superfluous or as having come too late. Someone else
has attacked persons or institutions deserving of our respect instead of our doing it ourselves.

The comic effect of wit is thus, to a great extent, determined
by a sudden suspension of fright that had been unconsciously
experienced for a second, of a fear that was released. Pursuing
that theory in the direction of emotional manifestations, it becomes possible to define the origin and nature of laughter.
Laughter is the facial and vocal expression originated in a
sudden relaxation of the muscles of the face that had been tightened or strained by fear, tension or only attention. The play of

---

* *Lust und Leid im Witz*, Vienna, 1929, and *Nachdenklishe Heiterkeit*,
Vienna, 1933.

muscles can be described in the following manner: an impression that would arouse fear or mobilize the defenses is recognized as not dangerous and the relief from the superfluous emotional strain reflects itself in relaxation of the facial muscles.

Smiling is a milder form of laughter. From this characterization we could conclude that prior to the smile anxiety, fear, embarrassment or similar unpleasant emotions exist in a lesser degree. Release from greater degrees of fear would manifest itself in an explosion of laughter.

Returning to our theme, we can perhaps now venture to guess why women smile so much more than men. There must be more occasions that awaken in them fear, tension or emotions of a similar kind. The onset of these frequently occurring feelings is quickly replaced by a relaxation of the tension caused by them. The transition to the new phase is expressed in a smile. This hypothesis can be made more plausible when we add that many social occasions awaken these feelings in women while they do not awaken them in men. We have to expect that similar emotions exist in a minor key in women so that the tension aroused by them is not as intense as it is in men.

This is possibly the appropriate place to point again to the fact that women are less aggressive than men. Their emotional reaction in the form of fear of retaliation will therefore not be as intense. The combined effect of these factors is perhaps sufficient to explain why women smile more often than men. A frightened tension will be unconsciously experienced more often in women due to their social insecurity. The impression that they are observed by other women as well as by men heightens their awareness and anxiety.

Taking our psychological assumption into account, we would easily understand that smiling became a form of salute for women. Meeting someone known awakens in them a fleeting feeling of anxiety (because of the possibility of being critically observed). This faint feeling of anxiety or heightened tension is dismissed and a smile appears as the facial expression of emoional relief. The greater frequency of women's smiles would thus, in general, correspond to a greater amount of social situations awakening tension or embarrassment conquered by regaining balance. Also the phenomenon of the "frozen smile," rarely observed in men, would find its psychological explanation in the continued attempt to master fear or insecurity.

In the preceding psychological considerations we did not consider two facts granted readily by everyone: the greater warmth expressed in a woman's smile and its beautifying effect upon her. In our evaluation of this smile we perhaps experience once more, in a hidden memory, the first smile to be seen by everyone: the smile of a mother bent over a crib. This smile has left more lasting memory traces than any other expression seen by a baby. It is the model of beauty that we unconsciously place in the sight of a familiar face. It is possible that we search for our mother's smile in that of every woman. At all events, our wish is that she "keep smiling"—not only because we want to see more kindliness around us but also more beauty in the world.

48. ARE WOMEN THE BETTER PSYCHOLOGISTS?

"My dear Theodor," said my visitor, who is a lecturer of clinical psychology at a Midwestern university. In apostrophizing me like that he put his hand cordially on my shoulder, but his voice sounded condescending. He knows quite well that he is superior to me in dialectics and had remained victorious in quite a few arguments with me. "My dear Theodor, you are, no doubt, original in your thinking but occasionally you are just plain funny, to phrase it charitably. You cannot mean seriously what you said, that women are in general better psychologists. You know the history of our science perhaps better than I. Will you please name the great women in psychology for me?"

"You did not listen attentively to me, George," I answered, "therefore you create difficulties where there are none, I mean semantic difficulties. Every dictionary will tell you that psychology has two meanings in English. Psychology is the science of the mind. It explains why people act, think and feel as they do. But psychology also means the mental states and processes of a person or persons, their mental and emotional behavior. Let me see. Mrs. Jones does not know anything about experimental psychology nor would she understand, for instance, experiments investigating the functional properties of perception. But Mrs. Jones understands the moods of her husband when he returns home from the office; that means his psychology. These two sentences do not contradict each other."

"Don't be evasive," George said. "I asked you to name the prominent women psychologists of our time. You will admit that even in the lamentably narrow field of psychoanalytic research the most important contributions were made by men. You have a few women analysts who are known: Anna Freud, Marie Bonaparte, Helene Deutsch. I really do not remember any other names."

"I could argue this point," I replied, "but the question itself is not correctly phrased. You say: 'Name the women psychologists.' That's just it. There are no names. I mean all women or, if you like, the average woman, the nameless women, are better psychologists than the average man."

"For the sake of argument, let us admit that for a moment—mind you I don't, but just for the hell of it. How do you explain that so few women have made any remarkable contributions to scientific psychology?"

"With the same justification you can ask: why are so few women prominent physicists, astronomers, linguists or mathematicians? That is a wide field and the answer would have to deal with many aspects of the sexual difference of mentality, especially with the forms of creativity in men and women."

George insisted on the statement that women, who are in my opinion better psychologists, must be somehow prevented from proving it. He even tried to help me find some reasons why that might be so. We found two main differences in masculine and feminine attitudes in this area—quite apart from the general divergence of the sexes where research and scientific work are concerned. We agreed that women do not feel the need to verbalize the psychological insight they have into emotional and mental processes. Most of those insights are either preconscious or remain unconscious because only that which is transformed into word-presentation is clearly and consciously thought. Sometimes it is true that women, especially when pressed by inner necessity, verbalize the results of their intuitive recognition and we are often surprised then by their perceptiveness.

"The ladies are otherwise not at a loss for words," George commented, "how do you explain their reticence to express themselves, or is it rather a lack of terms in this direction?" I had no ready answer, or rather I had so many that I could not find the right one and we decided that this was a side issue to be discussed at another time. Whatever the sociological or psychological reasons are, women in general, we agreed, rarely express in words what they have guessed or understood about the psychology of others.

"There is another obstacle in their way to becoming psychologists in the scientific sense you mean," I remarked. "Women do not see or feel the necessity to comprehend or comprise all phenomena and to find the laws that govern emotional and mental processes. They are satisfied with conjectures and insights into individual cases. Let us say, Mrs. Brown is content with understanding what goes on in Mrs. White, and Mrs. Black in what makes Mrs. Jones tick; but psychological processes as such in their lawful course are not very interesting to them."

"That is not specific for the area of psychology," George inserted, "to return to a region that is remote from emotional or mental problems. I can well imagine that a woman is fascinated by the evening star while she has God knows what phantasies, but she will scarcely be attracted to the laws that astronomers have detected."

"Well," I said, "women are much more practical than men and decidedly more earthbound. They look in general at a starry sky and have their own thoughts about the course of the planets. It is difficult for us to guess what those thoughts are. I just remember that I once saw a modern play on Broadway in which a young couple sit on a bench one summer evening. There is some embarrassed silence, then the girl says: 'There is a full moon tonight. I must wash my hair.' "

We both smiled that superior smile older men so often have when they discuss the funny ways of women, and George, who sometimes likes to appear as a misogynist, ventures an epigram: "It seems that the cosmos of women should be called cosmetic."

I do not remember any longer how we arrived from there at the mention of special psychological understanding which women have for members of their own sex. George quoted a remark of—if memory does not fail me—Wilson Mizner, who said: "Women can instantly see through each other, and it is surprising how little they observe that is pleasant."

There were a few moments of silence as if we were both a little embarrassed because we had lowered our theoretical and academic discussion to a level of levity. George sipped his coffee and I lit a new cigarette. "You know, George," I said, "there is a psychological fact we both have overlooked. Women see through each other, but they rarely look into themselves. I mean they are not inclined to self-analysis, to search for unconscious motives and repressed tendencies within themselves. I don't believe that many of them feel as did Pascal, that the self is hateful; and no woman could have discovered the technique of self-analysis in the sense of Freud. They are not curious about what goes on in their unconscious depths. They are, perhaps, afraid or ashamed of what they could find out about themselves."

"They are perhaps not ashamed of their depths but rather of their shallowness. The sphinx has no riddle for herself." I grinned, and replied:

"I am sure that remarks like this one would endear you to the ladies. But seriously speaking, women rarely develop those self-searching and sometimes self-torturing tendencies that head toward self-analysis. They shy away from the recesses of their souls."

"You mean they have a kind of inner daintiness?"

"If you want to call it that. But more important, they do not look at their own emotions and thought processes in the spirit of objective or scientific research."

"Yet you assert that they are 'better psychologists than men.' I am curious to learn from you what would awaken psychological interest in them at all."

"I can tell you at least one decisive moment favoring that interest: they are the weaker sex insofar as they are dependent on man. But who is weaker has to be on guard against the brutality and despotism of the stronger, and has to watch and protect himself. In the case of women, they had to develop a greater sensitiveness to man's sexual desires since they have the passive role. Man had nothing to fear from woman, at least as long as he has not recognized that the female of the species is more deadly than he. A club in one's hands is a much more primitive but also more effective weapon than psychological observation. As a matter of fact, it makes psychology superfluous. The position of weakness, dependancy and insecurity favors the gift of psychological observation. Man did not need to develop it in the same degree as woman."

"Don't let us be carried away into the field of prehistory. Let's restrict ourselves to the life of the individual. You will not assert that women are constitutionally better psychologists, that they bring that talent into the world with them when they are born?"

"I really do not know anything about that although I believe that there is something like a race memory and consequently also memory traces of the past of man and woman. But quite apart from that there are phases in the life of girls in which organic and emotional changes help those psychological gifts to unfold. By the way, that brings me to a second general precondition to the development of psychological gifts, namely to the turning away from action and the turning toward introversion. When one's attention is always directed to the world around and when one's energy is spent in changing it or modeling it in the sense of one's wishes, psychological interest will not develop. Extreme activity is not compatible with great attention to one's own thoughts and feelings. Introversion emerges only after the active individual interest in what is going on around you recedes.

"Apropos, here is an instance of the psychological insight of a prominent woman analyst. Helene Deutsch has courageously analyzed the belief that boys at puberty develop great activity while girls at the same age withdraw into themselves and become passive. This has all the earmarks of a scientific superstition. Girls during those years *do* develop an intensified activity as do boys, but this activity is turned inside. It is at this age that they develop intuition, delicacy of feeling, social tact, a sense for the graces and other talents we admire and appreciate in women. This introversion favors the emergence of psychological talents also."

"I cannot let you get away with that," George interrupted, "just a few minutes ago you yourself asserted that women are disinclined to look into themselves, shy away from self-analysis, and that is to say that they don't know themselves. Now you state that they are introverted and have great interest in their own emotional processes. You cannot eat the cake of your theory and have it too."

"The contradiction can be easily solved because it is only fictitious. I only said that women in general do not like to analyze themselves or to explore their emotions analytically, but this does not exclude a special kind of familiarity with their own and others' psychological life. This knowledge or, if you like, foreknowledge may not be found in your textbooks of psychology, but it is the same that the great writers show in their novels and plays. There is an abundance of psychological insights not obtained by objective analysis but by projection of one's own emotional processes, unconsciously perceived, into other people."

"Oh, is that the kind of psychological accomplishment you mean! Well, I shall not deny that there is a certain restricted value in the insights of the great writers although I wish they had brought them in a scientific, verifiable form that is less impressionistic and personalized." He had a sardonic smile when he presented his next argument.

"If memory doesn't fail me, those great writers from Shakespeare and Goethe to the moderns who made us understand women's ways were men, not women, were they not? Touché, aren't you?"

"Only slightly, George. Those great writers who understood women so well used their femininity or their feminine talents to reach them psychologically. It will perhaps sound paradoxical to you, but I believe that writers who are strongly masculine, or, let us say, too masculine, are almost unable to portray feminine characters and show a poor understanding of women's emotions. Think, for instance, of Friedrich von Schiller."

"In other words, you mean that novelists and playwrights who show excellent insights into feminine ways of thinking or feeling are latently homosexual. What an assertion! I admire the moral courage you show in your statements."

"If you replace the expression by emphasized bisexuality, I really believe that."

"You said before that those writers are using feminine talents in their psychological understanding of women. Do you mean that they are operating with intuition, with hunches and presentiments, that they have unusual perceptions, a gift of fine hearing for unconscious processes and the denied, disavowed facts of emotional life? You will admit that this area of scientific research is very limited compared with the wide field of the tangible, observable and experimentally verifiable; or, in short, of clinical psychology."

"But women are not interested in scientific prodding. They

are pragmatic. They are perhaps not as good as practicing psychologists as men but, in general, they are much better as practical psychologists. Let me say that I cannot disagree more with your other statement about the spaciousness of the two areas. If you are so keen on comparisons, the field of clinical psychology as you define it, is like the area of the great planets, of the earth, the sun and best-known stars which we can observe with astronomical instruments. But those areas in which finer perceptiveness and intuition are needed, the region of unconscious communications between people and groups, are comparable to the galaxy of a hundred thousand million suns and stars in the universe."

Our discussion went on and on, lost itself in attempts to define what intuition and wordless communication is, and so on. I often had to surrender ground to his superior knowledge of psychology and his better endowment of didactic gifts, but I sometimes succeeded in regaining some of the lost ground. At the end I mustered up all my courage in a bold stroke:

"Tell me, George, does your wife understand other women better than you? Do you admit that she and all women understand children better than you?"

"I grant that."

"Good. Now, George, look around you. We are alone. Nobody can hear you but God. I appeal to your professional sincerity as a psychologist. Does your wife understand you better than you do her?"

He nodded almost in spite of himself, but hastened to contradict it immediately. "Look, Theodor, you can't do that; that is an argument *ad hominem*. If you want to prove that women are better psychologists than men, you have to prepare a series of careful experiments and use the scientific methods, especially those of statistics and . . ."

"Leave it to George," I said spitefully.

49. The Last Chord

To a visitor from another planet who would try to orient himself regarding the inhabitants of the earth, the differences of race, color and creed would appear infinitesimal. The most significant difference within the human species conspicuous to him would perhaps be its division into males and females. He would observe that the two sexes go differently about the business of living, that they feel, think and act differently. Yet, after having looked at life here below for some time, the extraterrestrial visitor would realize that those divergencies seem to shrink when seen from a great distance. Women and men are born and die the same way, are subjected to the same vital necessities of existence on our small and poor planet.

We have presented a view on the emotional differences between men and women. As those variations on our theme come to a close, the numerous divergencies of the sexes are dissolved in the unity of mankind. The first chapter of the Holy Scriptures reports that God created men—"male and female He created them." But before that it says: He created Man.

BY THE J. MacLEOD

to a visitor from another planet who would try to orient himself regarding the inhabitants of the earth, the differences of race, color and creed would appear unimportant. The most significant difference within the human species compliment to him would perhaps be its division into male and female. He would observe that the two sexes go sufficiently about the business of living, that they feel, think and act differently. Yet after having looked at life here below for some time, the casual observer-visitor would realize that these divergences seem to shrink when seen from a great distance. Women and men are born and die the same way, are subjected to the same vital necessities of existence on our small and poor planet.

We have presented a view on the emotional differences between men and women. As those variations on our theme come to a close, the numerous similarities of the sexes are disclosed in the unity of mankind. The first chapter of the Holy Scriptures report, that God created man—male and female He created them—But before that it says: He created Man.